TRADE AND POVERTY REDUCTION IN THE ASIA-PACIFIC REGION

This book explores the complex relationship between international trade and poverty reduction through a combination of research papers and contemporary case studies. Written mainly by developing country authors in consultation with local businesses and communities, the case studies contribute to our understanding of the ways in which low-income communities are dealing with trade as a practical challenge, especially in the Asia-Pacific region where approximately two thirds of the world's poor live. While making it clear that there is no 'one size fits all' formula, the research and stories highlight a number of necessary preconditions – such as political commitment and cooperation at all levels – if trade is to successfully reduce poverty. Openness to trade, serious commitment to domestic reform, trade-related capacity building, a robust and responsible private sector and access to the markets of developed countries are all identified as powerful tools for building trade-related sustainable development.

ANDREW L. STOLER is Executive Director, Institute for International Trade, University of Adelaide and former Deputy Director-General of the WTO.

JIM REDDEN is Director, International Programmes for China and the Pacific and Senior Lecturer at the Institute for International Trade, University of Adelaide.

LEE ANN JACKSON is Economic Affairs Officer in the WTO Agriculture and Commodities Division.

TRADE AND POVERTY REDUCTION IN THE ASIA-PACIFIC REGION

Case studies and lessons from low-income communities

Edited by

ANDREW L. STOLER, JIM REDDEN AND
LEE ANN JACKSON

WORLD TRADE ORGANIZATION
ORGANISATION MONDIALE DU COMMERCE
ORGANIZACIÓN MUNDIAL DEL COMERCIO

Australian Government
AusAID

INTERNATIONAL TRADE
INSTITUTE FOR
Incorporating the Institute for International Business, Economics & Law

CAMBRIDGE
UNIVERSITY PRESS

CAMBRIDGE UNIVERSITY PRESS

Cambridge, New York, Melbourne, Madrid, Cape Town, Singapore, São Paulo, Delhi,
Dubai, Tokyo

Cambridge University Press
The Edinburgh Building, Cambridge CB2 8RU, UK

Published in the United States of America by Cambridge University Press, New York

www.cambridge.org
Information on this title: www.cambridge.org/9780521745307

First published 2009

Printed in the United Kingdom at the University Press, Cambridge

A catalogue record for this publication is available from the British Library

ISBN 978-0-521-76836-8 Hardback
ISBN 978-0-521-74530-7 Paperback

Disclaimer

CONTENTS

List of contributors   xi

Acknowledgements   xv

List of abbreviations   xvii

Introduction   1

JIM REDDEN

Overview paper: The economic effects of trade on poverty
reduction: perspectives from the economic literature   21

EUAN MacMILLAN

PART I   **Transnational corporations, trade and
poverty reduction**

1   Transnational corporations and the global supply chain   69

ANDREW L. STOLER

Case studies

1.1   Cambodia's textile and garment industry   97

PETER VAN DIERMEN

1.2   Australia's WTO trade-policy changes and the future of a
Samoan car-parts investor   112

MARGARET B. MALUA

1.3   The textile and clothing sector in Indonesia   131

OMAS BULAN SAMOSIR

1.4   Transnational corporations and the footwear industry:
women in Jakarta   146

BETA GITAHARIE LAKSONO

vii

1.5   Pakistan: the arrival and departure of Nike   160
       SAFDAR SOHAIL

1.6   Vietnam: Intel and the electronics sector   175
       ANDREW L. STOLER AND PHAN VAN SAM

PART II   Trade in agriculture and poverty reduction

2   Agriculture and trade solutions for rural poverty   195
    LEE ANN JACKSON

    Case studies

2.1   Food aid: commitments and oversight   227
       JOHN FINN

2.2   Indigenous Nepalese and trade liberalisation   252
       PURUSHOTTAM OJHA

2.3   Samoan agricultural policy: graduating from
       least developed country status   270
       HAMISH SMITH AND LEE ANN JACKSON

2.4   Bali's ornamental fishing industry   287
       LYDIA NAPITUPULU

2.5   The rice sector in West Java   306
       MILDA IRHAMNI AND CHAIKAL NURYAKIN

2.6   Chinese agricultural policy: central and
       western province   325
       SHUNLI YAO

PART III   Trade in services and poverty reduction

3   The future of trade in services for developing countries   341
    JOY ABRENICA, CHRISTOPHER FINDLAY AND AIK HOE LIM

    Case studies

3.1   Information and communications technology services in
       Uganda   364
       SIDDHARTHA PRAKASH

3.2   Health services in Malaysia   385
      AIK HOE LIM

3.3   Trade in services liberalisation in India   405
      AJITAVA RAYCHAUDHURI AND PRABIR DE

3.4   Trade, aid and services in Tanzania   426
      AMANDA SUNASSEE LAM

3.5   Telecommunications reform in the Pacific and the case of
      Vanuatu   449
      CHAKRIYA BOWMAN

PART IV   **Migration, labour mobility and poverty
          reduction**

4   Migration, labour mobility and poverty   465
    GRAEME HUGO

Case studies

4.1   Migrant labour and remittances in Bangladesh   513
      FAHMIDA KHATUN

4.2   Migrant remittances in the state of Kerala, India   540
      SAIBAL KAR

4.3   Migrant workers and the role of remittances
      in Indonesia   556
      NUR HADI WIYONO AND DWINI HANDAYANI

4.4   Labour mobility and poverty reduction in Tonga   572
      SALOTE VAIMOANO TAUKOLO, JIM REDDEN AND
      RAELYN ESAU

PART V   **Trade and poverty reduction in small and
         vulnerable economies**

5   Trade strategies for poverty reduction in small and vulnerable
    economies   595
    JIM REDDEN AND RON DUNCAN

Case studies

5.1   Lombok pots   648
      HEATHER BAIGENT

5.2   Plantations to professors in Grenada   665
      SACHA SILVA

5.3   Fisheries subsidies and the western and central Pacific   690
      MANLEEN DUGAL

5.4   Trade and youth unemployment in Timor-Leste   707
      JOAO SALDANHA AND JIM REDDEN

5.5   Trade reform and poverty reduction in Papua New
      Guinea   731
      NOLPI KILWA

5.6   The future of the Fijian garment industry   748
      BIMAN CHAND PRASAD, YENTESHWAR RAM AND ARIEL MARR

Index   *768*

CONTRIBUTORS

Editors

ANDREW L. STOLER is Executive Director, Institute for International Trade, University of Adelaide and former WTO Deputy Director-General.

JIM REDDEN is Director, International Programmes for China and the Pacific and Senior Lecturer, Institute for International Trade, University of Adelaide.

LEE ANN JACKSON is Economic Affairs Officer, WTO Agriculture and Commodities Division.

Assistant editors

CHRISTOPHER FINDLAY is Head of School, School of Economics, University of Adelaide.

GRAEME HUGO is University Professorial Research Fellow, Professor of Geography and Director, National Centre for the Social Applications of GIS, University of Adelaide.

PATRICK LOW is Director, Economic Research Division, WTO.

Authors

JOY ABRENICA is Associate Professor, School of Economics, University of the Philippines.

HEATHER BAIGENT is an independent consultant, Auckland, New Zealand.

CHAKRIYA BOWMAN is Trade Advisor and Acting Director, Pacific Growth Section, Australian Government aid agency, AusAID.

PRABIR DE is a fellow, Research and Information System for Developing Countries (RIS), New Delhi, India.

MANLEEN DUGUL is Technical Advisor (Trade Policy) and Permanent Representative for the Pacific Island Delegation to the WTO.

RON DUNCAN is Professor Emeritus, Crawford School of Economics and Government, Australian National University.

RAELYN ESAU is Deputy Director, Policy and Planning Division, Ministry of Education, Tonga.

CHRISTOPHER FINDLAY is Head of School, School of Economics, University of Adelaide.

JOHN FINN is a counsellor, WTO Agriculture and Commodities Division.

BETA GITAHARIE LAKSONO is a senior researcher, Faculty of Economics, University of Indonesia.

DWINI HANDAYANI is a researcher, Demographic Institute, Faculty of Economics, University of Indonesia.

GRAEME HUGO is University Professorial Research Fellow, Professor of Geography and Director, National Centre for the Social Applications of GIS, University of Adelaide.

MILDA IRHAMNI is a research fellow in the Faculty of Economics, University of Indonesia.

LEE ANN JACKSON is Economic Affairs Officer, WTO Agriculture and Commodities Division.

SAIBAL KAR is a fellow in Economics, Centre for Studies in Social Sciences, Calcutta, India.

FAHMIDA KHATUN, PHD is Additional Director, Centre for Policy Dialogue (CPD), Dhaka, Bangladesh.

NOLPI KILWA is Principal Research Analyst, Policy Planning, Research and Information Division, Department of Commerce and Industry, Papua New Guinea.

AMANDA SUNASSEE LAM is an IF facilitator specialist and a consultant, Ministry of Industry and Commerce, Foreign Trade Policy Department, Lao PDR.

AIK HOE LIM is a counsellor, Trade in Services Division of the WTO Secretariat.

EUAN MacMILLAN is a consultant, WTO Economic Research Division.

MARGARET MALUA is Director, Small Business Enterprise Centre, Samoa and an Economic and Trade Consultant.

ARIEL MARR is a postgraduate student at the University of the South Pacific, Suva, Fiji Islands.

LYDIA NAPITUPULU is a research fellow, Faculty of Economics, University of Indonesia.

CHAIKAL NURYAKIN is a research fellow, Faculty of Economics, University of Indonesia.

PURUSHOTTAM OJHA is Secretary, Ministry of Industry, Commerce and Supplies, Government of Nepal.

SIDDHARTHA PRAKASH is Senior Manager, Government Regulation and Institutional Development, PricewaterhouseCoopers Pvt Ltd, India.

BIMAN CHAND PRASAD is Professor of Trade and Development and Dean of Faculty of Business and Economics, University of the South Pacific.

AJITAVA RAYCHAUDHURI is Professor and Coordinator, Centre for Advanced Studies, Department of Economics, Jadavpur University, Kolkata, India.

JIM REDDEN is Director, International Programs for China and the Pacific and Senior Lecturer, Institute for International Trade, University of Adelaide.

SOHAIL SAFDAR works with the Commerce and Trade Group, Pakistan and is former Secretary, Ministry of Women and Development.

JOAO SALDANHA is Lead Negotiator on the Millennium Challenge Account, Ministry of Finance, Timor-Leste.

OMAS BULAN SAMOSIR is a senior researcher, Faculty of Economics, University of Indonesia.

SACHA SILVA is a consultant, Caribbean Regional Negotiating Machinery, Barbados.

HAMISH SMITH is an economic affairs officer, WTO Agriculture and Commodities Division.

ANDREW L. STOLER is Executive Director, Institute for International Trade, University of Adelaide.

SALOTE VAIMOANA TAUKOLO is Deputy Director, Tonga Trade, Ministry of Labour, Commerce and Industries, Kingdom of Tonga.

PETER VAN DIERMEN is Economic Adviser, Australian Government aid agency, AusAID.

PHAN VAN SAM is Dean, Mekong University, Vietnam.

NUR HADI WIYONO is a researcher, Demographic Institute, Faculty of Economics, University of Indonesia.

SHUNLI YAO is Associate Professor, School of International Trade and Economics, University of International Business and Economics, Beijing.

ACKNOWLEDGEMENTS

We, the editors, would like to express our sincere thanks to the authors whose research papers and case studies appear here. Their insights make this book a unique contribution to our understanding of the complex links between trade and poverty reduction strategies. We are grateful for their willingness to go beyond the theoretical perspective. As a result of their consultations with government, the private sector and local communities, and as a result of their own comprehensive research, we find a variety of practical suggestions for readers generally and for trade and development policy makers in particular to consider.

This project would not have been possible were it not for the enthusiastic support and funding it received from the Australian Government's international development agency, AusAID, and from the WTO Secretariat. On the AusAID side, we are indebted to the support received from Mark McGillivray, Chakriya Bowman, Janet Donnelly, Peter Van Diermen, Steven Kaleb, Tim Murton, Anne Rigby and Lydia Bezeruk. On the WTO Secretariat side, particular thanks are due to Patrick Low, Director of Economic Research and Statistics Division, for his warm support throughout the project, and for the contributions or assistance given by Marion Jensen, Hans-Peter Werner, Peter Pedersen, John Finn and Aik Hoe Lim.

Throughout the Asia-Pacific region, and indeed globally, a number of experts were particularly helpful in offering advice or in promoting the project, including Aldo Caliari, Sophia Murphy, Hugo Cameron, Roman Grynberg, Kamal Malhotra, Liam Campling, Sara Carley, Maryann Athaide and Pierre Encontre.

At the Institute for International Trade, Graeme Hugo, Christopher Findlay, Keith Wilson and visiting WTO Fellow Victoria Donaldson contributed considerable time and effort to the editing of this volume.

Valuable comments and support were also provided by Letizia Raschella-Sergi, Peter Gallagher, Simon Molloy, John Spoehr, Mark Collett, Jameson Henderson-Redden and Ngaire Henderson. Finally, special thanks are due to IIT's Office Manager, Marie Gutsche, as well as to Maria Naso and Morgan Reid, all of whom put in many hours on this project.

ABBREVIATIONS

ACFTA	ASEAN-China Free Trade Area
ACP	Africa, Caribbean and Pacific (countries that are parties to the Cotonou Agreement between the EU and the ACP states)
ADB	Asian Development Bank
AfDB	African Development Bank
AfT	Aid for Trade
AFTA	ASEAN Free Trade Area
AGOA	Africa Growth and Opportunity Act
AIRTIA	ASEAN-India Regional Trade and Investment Area
AKFTA	ASEAN-Korea Free Trade Agreement
APEC	Asia-Pacific Economic Cooperation
ASA	Association for Social Advancement
ASCM	Agreement on Subsidies and Countervailing Measures
ASEAN	Association of Southeast Asian Nations
ATC	Agreement on Textiles and Clothing
AusAID	Australian Agency for International Development
BIMST-EC	Bengal Initiative for Multi-Sectoral Technical and Economic Cooperation
BIT	bilateral investment treaty
BMET	Bureau of Manpower Employment and Training
BOESL	Bangladesh Overseas Employment Services Limited
BOMSA	Bangladesh Women Migrants Association
BPO	business process outsourcing
BRAC	Bangladesh Rural Advancement Committee
CARICOM	Caribbean Common Market
CCN	collusion, corruption and nepotism
CEDAW	Committee on the Elimination of Discrimination Against Women
CEP	comprehensive economic partnership
CET	common external tariffs
CGE	Computational General Equilibrium
CMT	cut, make and trim
CPI	consumer price index

CSA	corporative social responsibility
CSSD	Consultative Subcommittee on Surplus Disposal
CTC/CTH	Change in Tariff Classification / Change in Tariff Heading
CTEP	comprehensive trade economic partnership
CV	coefficient of variation
DAC	Development Assistance Committee
DDA	Doha Development Agenda
DFID	Department for International Development
DTIS	Diagnostic Trade Integration Study
DTT	double taxation treaty
DWF	distant water fleets
DWFN	distant water fishing nation
EAC	East African Community
EBA	Everything But Arms
EC	European Community
EEZ	exclusive economic zone
EIAPA	Enterprises Incentives and Export Promotion Act 1992–93
EPA	economic partnership agreement
EPZ	export processing zone
ERT	European Round Table
EU	European Union
EVI	economic vulnerability index
FAC	Food Aid Convention
FAO	Food and Agriculture Organization
FDA	foreign direct assistance
FDI	foreign direct investment
FFA	Forum Fisheries Agency
FGO	focus group discussion
FIC	Forum Island country
FLA	Fair Labour Association
FSM	Federated States of Micronesia
FTA	free trade agreement
FY	financial year
GATS	General Agreement on Trade in Services
GATT	General Agreement on Tariffs and Trade
GDP	gross domestic product
GMAC	Garment Manufacturers Association of Cambodia
GSP	Generalised System of Preferences
HCR	head-count ratio
HDI	Human Development Index
HIPC	Heavily Indebted Poor Countries Initiative
IBRD	International Bank for Reconstruction and Development

ICS	Import Credit Scheme
ICT	information and communications technology
ICTSD	International Centre for Trade and Sustainable Development
IF	Integrate Framework
IFC	International Finance Corporation
IFPRI	International Food Policy Research Institute
IGC	International Grains Council
IGO	inter-governmental organisations
IJEPA	Indonesia-Japan Economic Partnership Agreement
ILO	International Labor Organization
IMAC	Independent Monitoring Association for Child Labour
IMF	International Monetary Fund
INTERFAIS	International Food Aid Information System
IOS	International Organization for Standardization
IPEC	International Program on the Elimination of Child Labour
ISIC	International Standard Industrial Classification
IT	information technology
ITC	International Trade Centre (UNCTAD/WTO)
ITES	information technology-enabled services
JITAP	Joint Integrated Technical Assistance Programme
LDC	Least Developed Country
LPC	Lombok Pottery Centre
MAC	Marine Aquarium Council
MDG	Millennium Development Goal
MFA	Multi-Fibre Arrangement
MFN	Most Favoured Nation
MIC	middle-income country
MNC	Multinational corporation
MOEWOE	Ministry of Expatriates' Welfare and Overseas Employment
MOU	Memorandum of Understanding
MRA	mutual recognition agreement
MRP	mixed recall period
MSG	Melanesian Spearhead Group
MTI	Ministry of Trade and Industry
NAFTA	North America Free Trade Agreement
NBER	National Bureau of Economic Research
NCFMEA	National Committee of Foreign Medical Education (US) and Accreditation
NGO	non-governmental organisation
NISIT	National Institute of Standards and Industrial Technology (PNG)
NRD	New Rural Development
NSDP	net state domestic product

NTB	non-tariff barrier
NTP	National Trade Policy
NZAID	New Zealand Aid
OBM	original brand name manufacturing
OCHA	Office for Coordination of Humanitarian Affairs
OCW	overseas contract worker
ODA	official development assistance
OECD	Organisation for Economic Cooperation and Development
OEM	original equipment manufacturing
PACER	Pacific Agreement on Closer Economic Relations
PACP	Pacific Africa, Caribbean and Pacific
PCI	per capita income
PCISE	per capita income from services export
PESA	Private Enterprise Support Activities
PFI	Policy Framework for Investment
PIC	Pacific Island country
PICTA	Pacific Island Countries Trade Agreement
PIFS	Pacific Islands Forum Secretariat
PNG	Papua New Guinea
PPF	production possibility frontier
PPP	purchasing power parity
PRIME	Project for Rural Initiatives in Micro-Enterprise Development
PRSP	Poverty Reduction Strategy Papers
PSD	private-sector development
R&D	research and development
RCDF	Rural Communications Development Fund
RCDP	Rural Communications Development Policy
RFMO	regional fisheries management organisation
RGDP	regional gross domestic product
RMMRU	Refugee and Migratory Movements Research Unit
ROO	rules of origin
RSE	Registered Seasonal Employer
RTA	regional trade agreement
SAFTA	South Asian Free Trade Area
SDS	Strategy for the Development of Samoa
SDT	special and differential treatment
SECO	State Secretariat for Economic Development
SES	Statement of Economy Strategy
SIDS	small island developing states
SLOM	Senior Labour Officials Meeting
SME	small and medium enterprise
SMME	small, medium and micro enterprise

SOE	state-operating enterprise
SPARTECA	South Pacific Regional Trade and Economic Cooperation Agreement
SPS	sanitary and phytosanitary
SVE	small and vulnerable economy
TBT	technical barriers to trade
TFF	Tax Free Factories
TNC	Transnational Corporation
TRAOE	Tariff Relief Assistance for a Development Economy
TRQ	tariff rate quota
TTP	textile and textile product
UCC	Uganda Communications Commission
UMR	Usual Marketing Requirements
UN	United Nations
UNCDP	United Nations Committee for Development Policy
UNCLOS	United Nations Convention on the Law of the Sea
UNCST	Uganda National Council for Science and Technology
UNCTAD	United Nations Conference on Trade and Development
UNDP	United Nations Development Programme
UNECOSOC	United Nations Economic Social Council
UNEP	United Nations Environment Programme
UNESCAP	United Nations Economic and Social Commission for Asia and the Pacific
UNIDO	United Nations Industrial Development Organization
UPTC	Uganda Post and Telecommunications Corporation
UTL	Uganda Telecom Ltd
US	United States of America
USAID	United States Agency for International Development
USDA	United States Department of Agriculture
USG	St George's University School of Medicine
USGAO	United States Government Accountability Office
UNU-WIDER	United Nations University – World Institute for Development Economic Research
VAT	value-added tax
WARBE	Welfare Association of Returnee Bangladeshi Employees
WCPO	Western and Central Pacific Ocean
WFP	World Food Programme
WHO	World Health Organization
WIBDECO	Windward Islands Banana Development and Exporting Company
WPR	worker population ratio
WTO	World Trade Organization

Introduction

JIM REDDEN[*]

Why this book?

International trade is one of the greatest sources of modern wealth. However, it can be challenging and disruptive, especially to poor people[1] who usually have very few resources and little capacity to cope with changes in the price of what they produce and consume. To share in higher global living standards, the poor must gain access to the benefits that international trade has to offer. But how?

There is a rich vein of academic analysis that deals with this question, much of it from a theoretical perspective. We wanted to contribute to an understanding of the ways in which governments and communities have dealt with trade as a practical challenge, especially in the Asia-Pacific region where approximately two thirds of the world's poor live.

Two years ago, we launched a project that has been jointly supported by the Australian Government's official aid agency, AusAID, and the World Trade Organisation (WTO) to investigate this complex trade-poverty relationship through a series of research papers and case studies. We decided to look beyond ideological debates about free or fair trade, to see what is happening on the ground in low-income communities across a range of Asia-Pacific countries. The accounts collected in this book provide the reader with a rich experience of the successes, the failures and the challenges of trade policy and its ability to contribute to sustainable development.

Although our main interest in this book is to record significant recent experiences and to allow you, the reader, to draw your own conclusions,

---

[*] Jim Redden is Director of International Programmes for China and the Pacific and Senior Lecturer at the Institute of International Trade, Adelaide.

[1] The expression 'poor people' is used in terms of those who are deprived of capital and income, for example people living on less that US$1 per day. The term does not reflect on the cultural, social or spiritual wealth of those considered 'economically poor'.

we bring a particular analytical perspective to our work. Economic growth and increased trade are necessary but not sufficient conditions to ensure sustainable development and poverty reduction. Although trade liberalisation, if appropriately harnessed, has the potential to drive wealth creation and cut poverty, many other factors such as appropriate economic policies, functional institutions, well-targeted capacity building and development aid also make an essential contribution, especially to the distribution of wealth.

More open economies and trade-led development in Asia have helped to reduce overall levels of poverty in the region, with some dramatic results. But the problem of uneven growth within and between nations remains a major contemporary issue for national and global policy makers. In 1990, one in three people in China lived on less than US$1 a day, whereas today it is just one in ten. However, even today, almost one out of every two Chinese still lives on less than US$2 a day. In India, a booming coastal belt contrasts with an impoverished rural hinterland, where the World Bank estimates that 903 million people are living in poverty.

In less than two decades, countries as diverse as South Korea, Mauritius, Chile and Vietnam have made remarkable progress in finding and developing their competitive advantage and transforming their economies through greater openness to international trade, appropriate domestic reform and capacity-building programmes. But other countries in the Asia-Pacific region, such as the Philippines or Indonesia, that have undertaken some trade liberalisation policies are struggling to achieve the same rates of growth. Most of the Pacific Islands have relatively low formal trade barriers, yet at times some seem to be on the brink of economic collapse. Does this reflect a reluctance to embrace difficult but 'pro-poor' trade reform? Is it more about the barriers they face in vital markets in developed countries, or are there other explanations?

What is certain is that these contrasting experiences call for a better explanation of the reasons for trade-related successes and failures and for differences in growth rates and levels of human development. The studies we have gathered in this book are part of our search for that explanation. Each one attempts to sketch some aspects of the complex links between growth, trade and poverty reduction strategies.

What is in this book?

Thanks to strong support received from AusAID and the WTO, we were able to work with experienced researchers, policy makers, business people and community leaders who collected data, historical records, trade policy information and primary materials in over twenty different economies and several geographical regions from East Africa to the Caribbean. They have contributed thirty-three research papers and case studies with the explicit aim of informing trade policy and trade-related capacity-building priorities of national governments and donor bodies concerned with long-term poverty reduction strategies for low-income communities.

The book opens with an overview paper summarising a wide range of economic literature on the subject of trade and poverty reduction in order to set the stage for the research papers and case studies that follow. The book then divides into five parts comprised of the following:

(1) transnational corporations, trade and poverty reduction
(2) trade in agriculture and poverty reduction
(3) trade in services and poverty reduction
(4) migration, labour mobility and poverty reduction
(5) trade and poverty reduction in small and vulnerable economies.

Each section begins with a thematic overview paper that outlines current trade policies relevant to the theme, discusses the key challenges or 'hot issues' facing policy makers and assesses policy priorities for the future. Many of these 'hot issues' then feature in the case studies in that section. Each of the thematic papers offers the perspective of a noted academic analyst or experienced policy maker on trade-related development matters.

We have gathered the case studies from around the Asia-Pacific region and elsewhere, calling on contributions from authors closely associated with the country or community that is the subject of the study. In some studies, either current trade negotiators or policy makers close to the negotiations are the principal authors, and they offer unique insight into the demanding task of aligning trade policy with economic and social development needs.

Because they are often closely connected to the communities that figure in the case studies, we asked our authors to consult with and, wherever possible, to interview members of the community that figure in their analyses. Consequently, this book features the voices of women potters from Lombok, indigenous Nepalese from the Byas Municipality and young people in Asia's newest nation, Timor-Leste, expressing their hopes, concerns and views about the future.

Although the focus of the book is on the Asia-Pacific region, we also draw specific lessons from other regions, including an intriguing study on the transformation of Grenada from an economy based mainly on its banana industry to a more robust services-based economy. In Chapter 3 (on trade in services), we highlight the success of a strategic approach to trade liberalisation that has enabled Uganda to begin developing a competitive and 'pro-poor' information and communications technology industry.

The case studies fill in details not supplied by the thematic overview papers. They frequently reflect on the impact of trade policies at the level of households and firms, with special attention in a number of studies to the impact on women. The lessons for the reader, for students of trade and for trade policy makers are diverse. Some communities experience an income boost from trade-related labour market policies, for example, while others seem trapped in industries that struggle to stay profitable in new and perilously competitive conditions.

For ease of comparison, most of the case studies and the overview papers are structured in the same way. They begin by providing a context-setting introduction, followed by a description of the key trade and development challenges facing the economy or community in question. The results of surveys or consultations are set out, and the analysis concludes with a final section articulating suggestions and recommendations as to how that region, country or community might successfully move forward to deal with the challenges it faces.

Our final request to our authors was that they should try to identify constructive proposals that arose from, or could be adopted by, the low-income communities and developing countries they studied. We have no interest in covering up or minimising the difficult challenges confronting those who, to date, have not benefited from more open trade and economic integration. But we want this book to help improve trade policies and to assist with the identification of strategies to deliver concrete poverty reduction outcomes.

The emerging themes

Many of the concerns and solutions identified are specific to the context of the individual case study, but considering the variety of countries and regions discussed in this book, that is both inevitable and desirable, according to Euan MacMillan's overview of the literature on trade and development.

MacMillan points out that the effects of trade on the poor are often highly context-specific. He acknowledges that trade influences product prices, wages, employment, government revenue and therefore inequality. But he argues that because many of these factors pertain to country-specific characteristics, disaggregated analysis of the kind provided by these case studies is the best way to ascertain the specific effects of trade liberalisation on poverty. He concludes, nevertheless, that there are a number of common approaches, such as the development of strong institutions to regulate the nature and timing of liberalisation, which can create a conducive environment for trade-related poverty reduction.

These case studies reinforce this conclusion. Obviously, context-specific conditions mean different trade strategies are required. Trade strategies for larger developing countries such as Bangladesh and Nepal will clearly differ from those that would work for Vanuatu or Grenada. But even between two island economies of similar size such as Vanuatu and Grenada, our case studies reveal that there are historical and geographical differences that require different approaches to the liberalisation and regulation of education markets or foreign investment laws.

MacMillan's second finding, that there are several common factors and approaches in cases of successful trade-related poverty reduction, is also borne out by the thematic papers and the case studies in this book. Five key elements emerge as fundamental pre-requisites for developing a positive trade and poverty reduction relationship. The book shows that:

(1) Increased openness to international trade can have a positive impact on poverty reduction. Some of the most obvious examples can be seen in the sections on services liberalisation, where countries such as Uganda and Grenada have secured a macro-level boost for the entire economy by opening up their services markets, or in the section on labour market liberalisation, where specific groups in Tonga and Indonesia have been able to successfully raise incomes at the household level and reduce poverty. These and other studies exemplify the potential for low-income economies to benefit from well-designed, more open and transparent international trade policies.

(2) Openness alone is insufficient. There must also be a strong and consistent commitment to domestic policy reform on two fronts: (i) policies to regulate and protect vulnerable groups from trade liberalisation; and (ii) policies to increase productivity and competitiveness and capture the gains of trade. The thematic chapter on small and

vulnerable economies cites economist Jeffrey Sachs, who asserts in
relation to developing nations that:

> Openness is not sufficient unto itself – much depends on the way a
> country opens up, the sequence that is followed, the speed and the
> internal capacity to manage the process. Improvements in productivity
> and competitiveness through trade liberalisation require a compre-
> hensive policy for human resource and infrastructure development,
> education, technology, a policy that includes small and medium size
> enterprises, a strategy to raise the productivity of subsistence farmers
> and other measures.[2]

Sachs' argument in favour of a strategy to raise productivity is reprised
in the chapter on trade and poverty reduction for small and vulnerable economies. Strategic liberalisation policies acknowledge the
benefits of liberalisation but seek to ease transition costs and address
inequalities. However, strategic liberalisation policies also recognise
that liberalisation is very incomplete on a global basis, and so therefore takes a pragmatic view of the need to consult, inform and involve
low-income communities in decisions about domestic trade reform
and related development priorities.

(3) The engine room of reform must be the private sector. While governments should do all they can to create the environment for increased
productivity and competitiveness, ultimately it is the private sector
that will drive economic growth. Support for the development of
small and medium enterprises is therefore seen as crucial, as is the
need for transnational companies and foreign direct investment (FDI)
to create productive employment and sustainable poverty reduction.
However, the benefits from transnational companies (TNCs) will
depend firstly on the right regulatory and legal environments being
in place, and secondly on TNCs being clearly responsible to the environment and the communities in which they operate.

(4) International trade reform must be led by Organisation for Economic
Cooperation and Development (OECD) countries, along with the
larger developing countries. Time and again, case studies refer to the
need for greater market access, 'policy space' for sequencing reform
and flexible timeframes and capacity-building support from multilateral institutions and from developed-country trading partners in
order to sustain domestic trade reform and poverty reduction. The

---

[2] Sachs, J. (2007), 'Breaking the Poverty Trap', *Scientific American* September.

future of Cambodia's textile and clothing industry depends not only on its own ability to survive in a highly competitive world, but also on its ability to meet US preferences on core labour standards, making it vulnerable to any change in the policy stance of the US on Cambodian imports. There are well-known concerns expressed by African farmers about the slow pace of reform in agricultural trade related to subsidies and other trade barriers that exist primarily in developed nations. Trade-related poverty reduction strategies therefore require commitment from developed countries to market access, flexibility in trade negotiations and agreements, support for reasonable special and differential treatment and support for the financing of technology transfer and capacity building. It is observed that some developed-country trade negotiators are consumed by a somewhat narrow version of 'the national interest' undermining the broader, global interest of a healthy multilateral trading system.

(5) Finally, we conclude that because openness and unilateral reform alone are insufficient, the deficit of political will needs to be addressed at the multilateral and regional trade levels as well as the local level. This fifth key factor in the case studies follows on from the first four. Without strong cooperation between local, national, regional and multilateral levels of government, many of the benefits of reform can be lost. Various studies highlight a deficit of 'political will'. This deficit may be due to developed country disengagement or the disengagement of elites in developing countries, or it may be due to the resistance of private-sector interests fearful of losing preferential treatment. To fully embrace and finance the support and reform needed to include the 'poor' in trade and arrest the widening global gap between rich and poor requires reform and cooperation across the board.

In summary, the case studies in this book suggest that a national and international economic environment in which trade will contribute to the reduction of poverty is most likely to be characterised by:

(1) openness and commitment to international trade
(2) a firm commitment to domestic reform
(3) the development of a robust and responsible private sector
(4) a firm commitment from developed countries to trade reform, technology transfer and capacity building in developing countries

(5) political will and strong cooperation across national, regional, local and multilateral levels.

Highlights and insights

Transnational corporations and the global supply chain

The thematic paper that opens Part I of the book asks whether the 60,000 to 80,000 TNCs that play an important role in the global economy, everywhere from Singapore to Samoa, have contributed to poverty reduction. The answer is a conditional 'yes'. The thematic paper suggests that, with the right regulatory environment and an equitable legal environment, national governments can set the stage for attracting TNC investment that will contribute to poverty reduction in a sustainable fashion.

The individual case studies shed light on a number of examples of the role of TNCs, their global supply chains and their impact on individual firms and particular communities.

Peter Van Diermen describes in his case study the struggle of the Cambodian garment industry to overcome challenges posed by impending competition from China and elsewhere. The sector employs more than 300,000 women, mostly from rural areas. These women, who earn above-average wages, remit about 60 per cent of their pay to their families in home villages, contributing directly to higher living standards and to poverty reduction. Although the Cambodian industry serves a niche market that exploits its adherence to internationally recognised core labour standards, its viability is imperilled by the coming end of safeguard measures limiting Chinese imports and by other factors that contribute to Cambodia's high cost of doing business.

In her compelling account of how the Yazaki company came to be one of the most important employers in Samoa, Margaret Malua details the successful history of this TNC's automobile electric-harness factory in the South Pacific, currently employing approximately 1,500 workers, the majority of whom are female. Over the years, the company's operations have made a substantial contribution to poverty reduction and to the employment of women, who tend to spend large amounts of their pay cheques on improving the lot of their families. Now, a change in the way Australia implements the SPARTECA (South Pacific Regional Trade and Economic Cooperation Agreement) trade scheme may call into question Yazaki's continued operation in Samoa, with serious consequences for the local community.

In a dramatic case that illustrates the importance of the textile and clothing sector for employment in developing countries, Omas Bulan Samosir surveys the views of workers in Indonesia on their working conditions, and describes the challenges facing the industry in a country where it directly and indirectly employs more than 5.5 million people. If the industry is to survive, it has to deal with problems relating to very old manufacturing equipment and tough competition from China in export markets, while trying to obtain credit from local banks that seem already to have written off the sector as a high risk 'sunset industry'.

A colleague of Omas Samosir (also at the University of Indonesia), Beta Yulianita Laksono, contributes a case study of the sports footwear sector in the country. In this most labour-intensive of manufacturing sectors, multinational companies based in China and Vietnam are increasingly investing in Indonesia to produce sports footwear under contract to Nike, Reebok and other branded shoe retailers. The sector has a big impact on poverty reduction because experienced workers are paid considerably more than local minimum wages, and a strong multiplier effect has been observed in communities where footwear production facilities are located. The author describes the challenges facing the industry where its competitive position is threatened by high transportation costs and infrastructure bottlenecks.

A case study by Safdar Sohail discusses the impact on the incomes of rural families in the region of Sialkot, Pakistan, with Nike's decision to terminate a contract with a local producer of hand-stitched footballs. Half of the football stitchers came from landless families, and a further third from small farms with less than two hectares of property. When the local producer lost the contract for failing to abide by the labour standards set by Nike, the consequences for the incomes of poor people were enormous.

The final case study in this part of the book discusses the evolution of the electronics sector in Vietnam and its role in helping to lift local people out of poverty. Andrew Stoler and Phan Van Sam show how the Vietnamese Government's acceptance of the need for a stable investment climate and good governance has encouraged Intel Corporation and others to make billions of dollars worth of investment in the country, employing thousands of people in good jobs with important side benefits for the workers and their families.

The themes that run throughout all of these real-life accounts are that foreign-owned transnational companies and the employment they provide to local, often rural, populations can be a substantial factor in achieving poverty reduction goals, but that the continuing viability of the companies' operations (or of the locally-owned firms contracting for these TNCs) often depends critically on the national and global trade-policy environment. The studies reinforce the need for a well-regulated legal environment and accountable corporate behaviour in order to maximise poverty reduction outcomes.

Trade in agriculture

Agriculture is at the forefront of the trade and development debate in the Doha Round. In her thematic paper, Lee Ann Jackson suggests that developing countries need to make strong investments in their agricultural sectors, but she expects the impact of these policy interventions on levels of poverty to vary, due to country-specific characteristics. Jackson notes that economic growth in South Asia will lead to increases of nearly 100 per cent in the output of meat, eggs and fish, while at the same time the resource base upon which agriculture is built will shrink due to resource degradation, climate change and competition from urban expansion. She argues that one policy approach will definitely not fit all countries – a view that is borne out in the case studies in this section of the book.

The study by John Finn on food aid shows the importance of international and national coordination and cooperation. The case study makes compelling reading for those interested in recent food shortages, rising food prices and the challenges of efficiently delivering food aid free of market distortions. Finn acknowledges that the formal role of the WTO in food aid is limited to trade-related issues such as commercial displacement. However, he points out that compliance with WTO rules on trade liberalisation and regulatory transparency can help ensure the delivery of aid that does not distort markets or hurt local production or prices in developing countries. He concludes with an important warning: if food aid levels continue to drop due to rising food prices and related factors, it will put a number of vulnerable communities at serious risk and will undermine stated global commitments to the Millennium Development Goals.

In the case study of Nepal's indigenous people and the impact of agricultural trade liberalisation, Purushottam Ojha relates an interesting story of cautious optimism as farmers such as Lal Bahadur Bote manage the transition from a traditional agricultural community to a more prosperous market-based community. The case study demonstrates the importance of allowing time for adjustments to take place and the crucial role of investment in the diversification of farm productivity, in off-farm production and in linking small farmers and entrepreneurs to existing and newly emerging trade opportunities.

Hamish Smith and Lee Ann Jackson's case study on agriculture in Samoa discusses the potential costs and impacts on trade and poverty reduction for a small economy graduating from least developed country (LDC) status. It concludes that the impact for Samoa should not be significant so long as such factors as concessional loan facilities and trade-related capacity-building arrangements remain in place.

Lydia Napitupulu discusses a rarely explored industry in a case study of ornamental fish farming in Bali, Indonesia. International trade in Bali's ornamental fish species is important for small-scale coastal fishermen in Indonesia, and large volumes are being harvested to meet the demand. However, harvesting methods continue to include the use of cyanide, a method that is highly destructive, leading to both overfishing and the loss of ecological conservation in the reef's ecosystem. This case study focuses on one community of fishers that has successfully made the transition to sustainable harvesting and breeding of ornamental marine species.

From sea farming we turn to land farming. The Indonesian case study on the rice sector in West Java by Milda Irhamni and Chaikal Nuryakin examines the impact of trade liberalisation on rice production and rice prices. It suggests that the impact of rice trade liberalisation might be somewhat limited, although opposition from some producers can be expected. The case study notes that the price of rice in Indonesia is rarely the main driver of farmers' decisions to sell or diversify their production and that, in fact, the lower prices that liberalisation would bring would benefit many farmers who are net consumers of rice. While liberalisation could have a negative impact on some farmers in the short term, this impact could be minimised with good support for 'behind the border' government policies.

Shunli Yao notes that trade-related poverty-alleviation policies across western and central China need to be more closely linked with horticultural development through preferential policies for foreign investment in this sector and through stricter testing and certification systems that guarantee the authenticity of organic produce for consumers in China and abroad.

Trade in services

In their thematic overview paper to Part III, Joy Abrenica, Christopher Findlay and Aik Hoe Lim argue that reform and openness to trade in services can bring new technology in a physical sense (e.g. digital technologies associated with telecommunications) to the poor in developing countries, as well as new and more efficient structures of organising businesses (as in the case of logistics). They contend that the openness of local markets increases both the potential for entry of new competitors as well as the quality of actual entry, leading to higher levels of efficiency, greater productivity and increased incentive to innovate. Better quality education and health systems that are associated with the reform of those markets can add to the rate of accumulation of human capital and thereby growth. However, their paper acknowledges that, during transition periods, there can be job losses across both high- and low-income levels – requiring governments to devote resources to training or retraining, industry restructuring and safety-net facilities.

The case studies in this part of the book are striking in their support for these findings – that is, on the potential of services liberalisation to contribute to economic growth and poverty reduction if the appropriate regulatory regimes, training and institutional capacity are put in place.

A case study from Uganda illuminates the link between the liberalisation of the ICT sector in an African country and the welfare of the poor. The study explores policy reforms implemented at the national level in the ICT sector and the subsequent growth of the Nakaseke telecentre in a remote town of Uganda. It shows that a combination of a positive regulatory-reform framework and donor support led to the growth of the telecentre, which transformed the lives of the local farmers, women and young people. Siddhartha Prakash draws many policy lessons for successful services liberalisation and related sector reforms, but also offers practical guidance on making ICT services work for the poor. He identifies the importance of rural electrification infrastructure, developing special content and applications for illiterate communities based on simple ICT applications and changing social attitudes towards the value of a knowledge-driven economy.

In his study on 'health tourism' services in Malaysia, Aik Hoe Lim reflects on the importance of strategic domestic trade reform through appropriate regulation. He examines the impact of services liberalisation in Malaysia and the rise of 'health tourism', involving patients from developed countries who seek cheaper treatment at private hospitals and clinics in developing countries. He finds that the outcomes can be ambiguous. On the one hand, exporting countries can earn more foreign exchange and generate additional revenue for investment in their public healthcare, of particular significance for the poor. On the other hand, increased commercialisation of health services without an appropriate regulatory framework or safeguards on access and equity may result in a dichotomy with a well-resourced private sector catering to foreigners and wealthy nationals and an under-resourced public sector serving those who cannot afford private care.

In their study of India, Ajitava Raychaudhuri and Prabir De examine the recent patterns of trade in services, particularly the rapid growth of exports of information technology and labour services. They also examine the associations between the growth of trade and the levels and distribution of income. They observe that whilst urban inequality may have increased, the bias towards employment of males in the services sector may have, in fact, declined. Services-sector growth, they suggest, has created employment opportunities for females. They remain concerned about the risk of rising income inequality in urban areas, and suggest a number of initiatives to create a greater demand for workers who presently have relatively low skill levels. These include access to education, the design of curricula relevant to the ICT sector and on-the-job training. The authors stress the importance of state and local government participation in the central government's intervention strategies.

Amanda Sunnasse's paper on Tanzania analyses the link between the services sector and the supply-side constraints faced by an LDC, using the Tanzanian transportation and logistics sector as a case study. The unique contribution of her case study is its special focus on the role of Aid for Trade (AfT). Sunnasse explores means of using AfT to add value, attract trade and investment – and hence jobs for low-income communities – in the services sector.

Last in this section is an important contribution from Chakriya Bowman on telecommunications reform in the Pacific, with a particular focus on Vanuatu. Connectivity within and between Pacific Island countries has always been weak, she argues, but small island states can reap the benefits of services liberalisation if they are prepared to reform poorly performing sectors. Her study relates the success story of Vanuatu, where reform of the Telecom Vanuatu Limited monopoly has resulted in increased competition in the sector, a major inflow of FDI and the delivery of telecommunications services to previously unserviced ni-Vanuatu living in remote and rural locations.

Labour mobility

Part IV of the book is devoted to the debate on the opening of labour markets to the temporary movement of both skilled and unskilled workers. Both of the thematic papers on services, which comprise the thematic

papers to Parts III and IV, show that almost every study of the temporary movement of natural persons demonstrates absolute poverty-
related gains to developing countries as a result of the liberalisation of
the movement of low and unskilled workers.[3] Greater liberalisation of
labour mobility allows developing countries the opportunity to exploit
their relative abundance in low and unskilled labour. There are, of
course, various social and political complexities that accompany trade
in skilled and unskilled labour, and these issues receive thorough treatment in Graeme Hugo's thematic paper and the case studies that follow. Hugo calls for a far more integrated approach than what exists
at present between migration and development policies, pointing to
the need for a whole-of-government approach to migration and labour
mobility.

Despite the complexities, this chapter firmly establishes the economic
benefits of remittances, which increase the per capita income of the
remittance-receiving countries and thereby can have a significant poverty-
reducing effect on the economy. Cross-country and micro-based estimates
have supported this, showing that, in general, the fraction of a population
living in poverty is reduced by about 0.4 per cent for each percentage point
increase in the share of remittances to gross domestic product (GDP).[4]
International remittances in Bangladesh, for example, have reduced the
poverty head-count ratio there by 6 percentage points according to the
first case study in this part of the book.

Fhamida Khutan shows that Bangladesh has benefited significantly
from an increase in remittances due to the movement of its human
resources. The abundance of labour supply in Bangladesh has given
it a comparative advantage over other countries in the global market.
Bangladesh earns a huge amount of foreign exchange through the remittances of its workers abroad. Khutan shows that these remittances have
not only cut the current account deficit and stabilised the balance of payments of the country for the last few years, but they have also helped
to improve the standard of living of a large section of the population
through employment of its workers. Bangladesh could have done even

---

[3] See Winters, L. A. (2002), 'The Economic implications of Liberalising Mode 4 Trade', paper
prepared for joint WTO-World Bank Symposium on Mode 4, WTO, Geneva, 11 to 12 April
2002; Winters, L. A., Walmsley, T. and Wang, Z. K. (2003), *Liberalising Labour Mobility
under the GATS*, Commonwealth Secretariat: London; Walmsley, T., Ahmed, S. A. and
Parsons, C. (2005), 'The impact of Liberalizing Labour Mobility in the Pacific Region',
GTAP Working Paper No. 1874, Centre for Global Trade Analysis, Perdue University: West
Lafayetts, IN.
[4] World Bank (2005), *Global Economic Prospect*, World Bank: Washington, WA.

better, according to Khutan, had there been a comprehensive whole-of-government policy in the country to facilitate the movement of all categories of workers from Bangladesh, with fewer barriers imposed by the importing countries.

The case study by Saibal Kar focuses on the impact of migrant remittances on the level of poverty, particularly for lower-skilled workers from the state of Kerala in India. The non-migrant members of households in Kerala enjoy better living standards, higher levels of school attendance, access to healthcare facilities and provisions for the future with the aid of such remittance receipts. Of interest to policy makers, the study highlights evidence that lower-skilled workers remit larger amounts more frequently than their higher-skilled counterparts, as their families or communities are in greater need and rely more heavily on regular remittances.

Nur Hadi Wiyono and Owini Handayani, in their case study on Indonesia, recount the interesting story of one returned migrant worker (twenty-five years old, married with one child) who used his remittance to purchase three hectares of fertile land at a price of Rp 300 million to provide him with the income to continue school and finish his university degree. He married an ex-migrant worker who had worked as a domestic worker in Saudi Arabia. He was already known as a successful person in the village because he owned a house and had a steady income from his paddy field. However, his business sense led him to open a new waste-collection business – previously unheard of – as a joint venture with other returned migrant workers. The multiplier effect not only resulted in employment and income for other villages, but has also had positive environmental consequences.

The study on Tonga by Salote Vaimoana Taukolo, Jim Redden and Raelyn Esau notes that up to 45 per cent of Tonga's GDP comes from remittances. Contrary to the view held by some that remittances will decrease over generations, the study shows the general sustainability of remittances in Tonga over the last decade. It points to a useful model for community-based temporary labour market schemes with an early evaluation of the Recognised Seasonal Employer scheme between New Zealand and Tonga. It highlights the importance of continuous training and up-skilling of low-income, low-skilled workers and the important role of remittances in savings and job creation back home. The conclusion underlines the role of temporary labour mobility and remittances as a vital 'safety valve' that can allow Tonga the time and revenue base to invest in a more sustainable economy based on the expansion of services and increased agricultural productivity.

Small and vulnerable economies

Most small and vulnerable economies (SVEs) in the Pacific, and Timor-Leste in Asia, have relatively low trade barriers according to the authors of the thematic paper to Part V, Jim Redden and Ron Duncan. They argue that the contemporary challenge for SVEs is to embed the fundamentals of future competitiveness – taking account of transition costs – while ensuring safety nets are firmly in place to allow people to adjust to, and benefit from, future trading arrangements. They contend that this transition will require clear support for flexible trade arrangements and the financing of trade-related capacity building from their major trading partners.

The case studies in this Part of the book contain two main messages. Firstly, although the trade challenges must, at times, seem daunting, there are a plethora of practical opportunities for Pacific SVEs to benefit from trade and to implement more sustainable poverty reduction processes.

The second message is that developed and larger developing countries should recognise the 'multitude of challenges' facing SVEs and intensify their own political efforts to ensure that sufficient market access, adequate time and 'policy space', technology transfer and capacity-building support is given to SVEs to assist in consolidating reform.

The study on women potters in Lombok, Indonesia, by Heather Baigent tells the story of a successful export business that needed considerable local determination and external support to overcome a range of internal obstacles and international trade regulations on health and technical standards. The lessons from this study include the value of assisting women to directly manage such projects – with technical assistance and training from abroad – and the value of marketing support in overcoming a number of trade barriers. Although the women in Lombok are now much better off than before, they remain relatively poor. Overall, the case study illustrates the ongoing need for domestic reform and capacity building that need to be supported by external assistance to small and medium enterprises in small and vulnerable communities.

Sacha Silva reveals an intriguing study of the problems faced by Grenada as it transitions from an economy facing eroding preferences for its chief agricultural export (bananas) to one that is becoming increasingly based on services, especially educational services. The study describes the vital role of education and training of human resources and the complex issue of dealing with wage expectations and differentials if the transition is to continue to be successful.

Manleen Dugal, in the study on the western and central region of the Pacific recommends a series of trade strategies on both the multilateral and domestic fronts to assist in the development of a viable fishing industry and to help lift local artisan fishers in the Pacific out of poverty. The author describes a comprehensive 'green box' of subsidies that should be allowable, and which would assist small island states in the western and central Pacific to develop their fishing capacity and fisheries sectors.

President Ramos-Horta is lauded for advocating a trade- and investment-friendly Timor-Leste in the case study by Joao Saldanha and Jim Redden on the relationship between international trade and youth unemployment. The research and consultations undertaken in Timor-Leste point to a qualified but positive relationship between well-crafted trade policies and job opportunities for young people. However, the study emphasises the importance of long-term political stability to allow government to harness oil and gas revenues for financing necessary economic reforms and for investing in infrastructure, services and the agriculture sector so as to create sufficient jobs for low-income and under-skilled young people.

The case study on Papua New Guinea by Nolpi Kilwa invites the reader to explore the important relationship between local, regional and multilateral trade initiatives. Papua New Guinea lacks a coherent trade strategy and has little experience in trade negotiations, but, according to the author, there are ample natural resources and potential competitive advantages that Papua New Guinea can pursue. However, it requires, he argues, not only domestic reform but greater support and flexibility on the part of developed nations in the Doha Round and in regional trade negotiations. The study focuses on current EU negotiations with Papua New Guinea and the Pacific region as part of the Cotonou Agreement, highlighting the need for more flexible arrangements, for example, on how rules of origin are interpreted. Papua New Guinea and other Pacific SVEs, according to the case study, sought context-specific rules appropriate to the region given the multi-country, multi-industry nature of global supply chains in goods manufacturing.

Biman Chand Prasad, Yenteshwar Ram and Ariel Marr analyse the relationship that exists between trade polices and poverty in the garment industry in Fiji. Their findings point to a number of factors that will need to be in place if the Fijian clothing and textile industry is to survive and increase its productivity. The requisites for success include the orderly exit of uncompetitive firms, strong improvements to Fiji's trade facilitation processes, accommodating outcomes in upcoming PICTA, PACER Plus and EPA regional trade negotiations, more training and wage restructuring and last, but certainly not least, the need for ongoing political stability. As with the case studies on Papua New Guinea and Timor-Leste, both of which deal with whole-of-government approaches to trade and poverty reduction, the Fiji study emphasises the importance of an approach to trade reform that results from a collaboration between the private sector and government at the national level, and one that includes support from developed nations involved in trade negotiations and agreements.

The three case studies in this part of the book on Fiji, Papua New Guinea and Timor-Leste further confirm the importance of political stability, good governance and an economy-wide perspective as key pre-requisites for the design of successful trade reform and poverty reduction.

All of the case studies in Part V note the ongoing importance of trade-related technical assistance and capacity building as essential for poorer nations seeking to engage successfully in the international trade environment while building the necessary infrastructure, institutions and human resource skills at home.

Conclusion

Anecdotally, quantitatively and qualitatively, the case studies demonstrate positive correlations between more open, competitive trade policies and sustainable poverty reduction – so long as certain pre-conditions are in place.

With respect to the five overriding policy elements referred to earlier (trade openness, domestic reform, a robust and responsible private sector, international reform and political will), it is now possible to distil a further set of more specific criteria for trade-related poverty-reduction strategies that have emerged from the context-specific case studies.

At the top of the list for many are training and education strategies that allow poorer communities greater self-reliance and that enhance their ability to participate in trade and economic growth. Literacy and vocational training find particular resonance across the studies, as does the importance of inclusive planning that allows lower-income communities to participate in and support trade-related development reforms.

Supply-side reform and removing domestic trade and economic barriers to doing business feature strongly in many of the case studies. A number suggest that supply-side reform should be led by institutional reform, which in turn can drive legislative and regulatory reform, address physical infrastructure and logistical services needs, drive sectoral-specific productivity gains and generally establish a more conducive climate for business investment and employment creation. Political stability, transparency and good governance are all seen as absolute pre-requisites to this end.

A number of case studies argue that trade reform will require domestic governments to use taxation and fiscal equalisation policy to implement more efficient wealth redistribution programmes that assist in directing income to lower-income communities, and that help to finance key rural and urban poor expenditure programmes. A number of the case studies emphasise the importance of government planning for the provision of safety nets and compensatory packages that allow time for the economy to absorb industry restructuring costs or job losses that may occur during transition periods. The authors make it clear that some economies face considerable economic 'pain' as manufacturing struggles in the face of competition from lower-cost producers in Asia, and from preference erosion globally.

Several studies identify market access, technology transfer and solid commitments to trade-related aid or capacity building as the most important means to helping poorer communities trade their way out of poverty. Labour market access is frequently cited for the direct benefits employment, training and remittances can potentially bring. The roles of developed countries and larger developing countries are seen as critical in providing the necessary market access and flexibility, whether for services exports generally or labour mobility in particular.

Finally, the concept of 'strategic liberalisation' finds favour in many of the studies. They call for the careful sequencing and timing of reform, for example the introduction of an appropriate regulatory framework and safeguards on access and equity in advance of liberalising specific trade in services. Services liberalisation is considered by several of our authors to hold the key to future poverty reduction. But they are also at pains to highlight the ongoing importance of agricultural reform and manufacturing reform aimed at productivity increases, supply-side diversification and identification of niche markets able to integrate with global supply chains. The special needs of SVEs are well noted, but most argue that support is required to sequence and accelerate reform rather than delay it.

Although the case studies focus predominantly on the Asia-Pacific region, we hope they contain useful insights that can inform government policy makers, community leaders and private-sector corporations throughout the world, all of whom can play such a vital role in expanding trade and reducing poverty in a sustainable fashion.

A full commitment to the adequate financing of reforms needed to include the 'poor' in trade and help arrest the widening global gap between rich and poor will require strong cooperation across the board. The overriding message of this book is the need for greater political commitment and cooperation at all levels – locally, domestically, regionally and internationally – in support of practical trade-related development strategies.

The economic effects of trade on poverty reduction: perspectives from the economic literature

EUAN MacMILLAN*

Introduction

Economists have championed the merits of international trade since Adam Smith. Indeed, advocacy of free trade permeates the field to such an extent that 97 per cent of economists believe that tariffs and quotas diminish welfare.[1] However, the poverty-alleviating potential of trade is not something that is necessarily realised; thus care must be taken to temper this advocacy with consideration of the transmission mechanisms between trade and the poorest members of society. Accordingly, the economic literature is replete with such considerations. The purpose of this chapter is to provide an overview of this literature in order to establish the theoretical background for the case studies that comprise this volume. One of the key outcomes is that the effects of trade on poverty are context specific. Consequently, no attempt is made here to derive a holistic or definitive description of the impact of trade liberalisation on the poor, as, in reality, there are a multiplicity of effects that vary across countries and across time. Instead, this study develops a set of factors that can potentially influence the nature and magnitude of the effects of trade on poverty alleviation. In each individual setting, a different set of factors will pertain, leading to different outcomes. Accordingly, policies should be tailored to the prevailing conditions within the country in question. Nevertheless, some generalised policy prescriptions can be derived and, as such, this chapter concludes with a discussion of how policy makers can influence the factors that mediate the effects of trade on poverty.

* The author would like to thank Patrick Low, Marian Jansen, Jim Redden and the participants of the Development Studies Association Scotland June 2007 meeting for useful comments. Responsibility for remaining errors lies entirely with the author.
[1] According to a survey reported in Ruffin and Gregory (1990).

The effects of trade on an economy can be broadly categorised as either static or dynamic in nature. The static effects of trade are those that occur in the short-run from trade liberalisation, such as changes in prices and factor rewards. The dynamic effects are those that occur across time, such as changes in the rate of economic growth. However, the extent to which these effects pertain in reality, and the extent to which they influence poverty, are dependent upon the specific nature of the economy. For example, if an economy cannot adapt to changes imposed by trade, then it will not be able to counter the negative impacts by taking advantage of the opportunities it affords. Moreover, the pass-through of the effects of trade to the poor depends upon numerous factors, such as the nature of the distribution of goods and services, the efficiency of factor markets and the behaviour of the government. Consequently, in elucidating the role of trade on the alleviation of poverty, this study adopts the following structure. The next section outlines how the nature of an economy affects the pass-through between trade and households. The paper then goes on to discuss the static effects of trade liberalisation. A discussion on the dynamic effects of trade on poverty alleviation follows. The following section highlights how wider events and the behaviour of external factors can affect poverty in countries open to trade. Throughout each of these sections, the factors determining the poverty-alleviating potential of trade are highlighted in bullet points. Box D collates these factors under the headings of the effect of trade on poverty alleviation via: prices and government spending; wages and employment; the adaptability of the economy and the efficiency of markets; and growth. After that, there is a section on the effect that policy makers can have on each of these channels. The final section summarises the key findings of this study.

The transmission mechanisms from trade to poverty alleviation

Overview

When considering poverty, the unit of analysis used here is that of the 'farm household' as utilised by Winters (2000, 2002) in earlier studies.[2] The farm household is defined as any household which makes production as well as consumption and labour-supply decisions. The welfare of such

---

[2] For the purposes of the present analysis, the principle variable of concern is that of absolute poverty, which is usually defined in economic literature by some form of income or consumption metric such as the percentage of the population living on less than US$1 a day or US$2 a day (see Ravallion (1994) for a survey of the literature regarding the measurement of poverty).

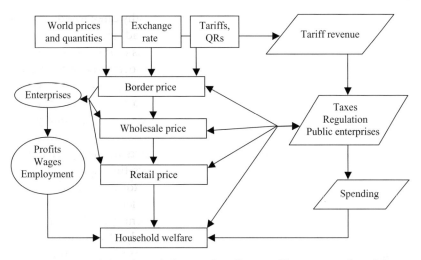

Figure A   Transmission channels from trade policy to welfare. *Source:* adapted from Winters, 2002, p. 1344.

households can therefore be regarded as depending upon the income received from the factors of production owned by the household, the prices of all goods and services that the household faces, and the value of net transfers between the household and its government. Thus, following Winters (2000, 2002), trade can be considered to interact with poverty through three main channels: (i) the distribution channel (affecting the price of imports consumed and the price received for self-produced export goods); (ii) the enterprise channel (affecting the wages received); and (iii) the government channel (affecting the taxes paid and the social spending received, as well as the policies that interact with the trade-poverty relationship). Figure A illustrates the foundations of these three channels, each of which is then discussed in turn. It is important to note that the interactions between trade and poverty through these channels are mediated by the institutions of the economy. If institutions are weak, factor markets may be inefficient and the economy may not be sufficiently flexible to take advantage of the opportunities afforded by trade. More-over, realising the benefits of trade will be further impaired if there are other impediments to market efficiency, such as imperfect competition, missing markets, poorly administered customs procedures or excessive bureaucracy. Consequently, this section concludes with a discussion of the factors governing the adaptability of the economy and the extent to which institutions and market inefficiencies affect the influence of trade on poverty.

The first three boxes of Figure A (world prices and quantities, exchange rate and tariffs, QRs (quantitative restrictions)), when taken together, determine the domestic prices faced by producers and consumers, labelled as 'border price' in the diagram.[3] The third box (tariffs, QRs) is the main determinant of the extent to which the country in question is open to trade; the more open the country, the closer the border price corresponds with the world price. The two market-driven channels (i.e. enterprises and distribution), are affected directly by the border price, whereas the third channel (government) interacts with the transmission mechanism at a number of points. First and foremost, the government controls trade policy via tariff-setting, and thereby determines the degree to which the country is open to trade.

Secondly, by setting tariffs, the government generates revenue that it can redistribute to households via spending. However, such tariff revenue is augmented by other taxes, which, in combination with regulations, can potentially influence both the distribution and enterprise channels at various stages.

The distribution channel

The distribution channel is represented by the boxes following on from the border price box. This chain of distribution between households and the border can be considered in two directions: downwards for imports and upwards for exports. For an import, the wholesale price is determined first by the trade policy-influenced border price, and then by various factors such as domestic taxes and regulations, transportation costs between the port and regional distribution centres and the possibility of compulsory government procurement, all of which can potentially raise the price. From regional distribution centres, the imported goods will be transported to local distribution centres, during which time further transportation costs will be incurred and further taxes and regulations may be imposed. At each stage, the price may also be 'marked-up' in order to generate profits for the firms involved. The resulting price is termed the retail price, and at this stage, the imported product is distributed to

---

[3] It is important to highlight that myriad external factors influence world prices. Whilst such factors are undoubtedly integral determinants of the poverty-alleviating potential of trade, they are largely immune to small country influence. Accordingly, this chapter focuses more heavily on domestic factors over which policy makers wield greater control. However, a later section provides some discussion of the impact of external factors on the trade-poverty relationship (see p. 53).

households. For an exported good produced by households, for example in situations where households are engaged in small-scale farming, the distribution mechanism is reversed. Household produce is transferred into local marketing networks and then aggregated such that it can be marketed abroad. Similar transportation costs, taxes and costs associated with regulations augment the so-called 'farm-gate' price that households receive (denoted as the retail price in Figure A) at both the regional (i.e. wholesale price) and national (i.e. the border price) level. However, it is highly likely that the country in question shall be a price-taker on international markets, especially in the case of small developing countries. Thus, the price received for the goods will depend on global demand and supply conditions, as well as any restrictions imposed upon the country's exports by trading partners.[4] The amount of the resulting profit or loss that is appropriated to the households depends upon the composition of the industry at each stage of the distribution chain. For example, if producers' marketing cooperatives operate, then these are more likely to pass profits onto households than private enterprises are.

The effect of trade on household welfare via the distribution channel thus filters through the border price, either by raising or lowering the price national marketing organisations receive for the products they export, or through raising or lowering the initial price of imports. The extent of this pass-through is in turn determined by the following factors:

- **The efficiency of customs procedures**
  Any form of protectionist intervention requires customs procedures to ensure that it is enforceable. However, if customs procedures are unnecessarily complicated and time-consuming, then deadweight losses may arise from the addition of extra costs to businesses involved in importing or exporting. Within the WTO, trade facilitation negotiations aim to harmonise and simplify customs procedures in order to reduce such costs. Indeed, in an empirical study, Wilson, Man and Otsuki (2004) find that domestic trade-facilitation efforts lead to substantial benefits in both imports and exports, and that in developing countries the rise in exports is relatively larger as improved customs procedures induce increased shipments to OECD (Organisation for Economic Cooperation and Development) countries.

---

[4] A large literature exists regarding the effects of liberalisation in countries that do have a degree of market power on world markets. Under such circumstances, increased export volumes can lower export prices and thereby transfer some of the domestic gains from trade to trading partners. For a review of the literature on this topic, see Mayer (2002).

- **The pattern of protection and the nature of trade liberalisation**
  By restricting trade, interventionist trade policy generates rents. Rents result from the difference between domestic prices and international prices. The rents from protection in the form of tariffs accrue to the government; however, protection in the form of non-tariff barriers (NTBs) may be captured by firms. If such rents accrue to the poor, then the removal of NTBs associated with liberalisation may be detrimental to poverty alleviation in the short term. Such interventionist policies need not be imposed by the domestic government. For example, the recently eradicated Multi-Fibre Arrangement (MFA) involved the extensive application of product- and country-specific quotas by major industrialised importers on exports from a number of countries. Textile firms in countries not subject to MFA restraints flourished as a result of preferential access to large countries. The end of the MFA thus engendered increases in unemployment and wage inequality in such countries because of increased competition from previously restricted economies.[5]
- **The nature of non-trade taxation and spending policies**
  Governments can mitigate the effect of trade-induced price changes utilising tax policy. By raising taxes when the price of imports falls and when the price of exports increases, governments can capture the gains from trade for themselves, thus making the direct effect of trade on household welfare neutral. Conversely, governments can lower taxes in response to opposite price shocks to insulate households.
- **Price regulations**
  The transmission of price shocks to the household level can be mitigated by regulations that fix market prices by flat or by compensatory stock-piling.
- **The quality of infrastructure**
  High transportation costs associated with poor infrastructure add further costs to both importing and exporting, and thus impede the ability of a country to capture the benefits of trade.
- **The nature of intermediate organisations in the distribution chain**
  In an imperfectly competitive setting, monopsonistic buyers of export crops will only pass a portion of price increases on to their suppliers. In contrast, in a perfectly competitive setting, or where producers' marketing cooperatives exist, it is more likely that price rises will be

---

[5] For example, Marouani (2007) finds that the end of the MFA caused increases in unemployment and wage inequality in Tunisia.

passed on to producers. Similarly, if importing firms are monopolistic, then falls in the border price may not translate into falls in the retail price. Moreover, if elements of the distribution chain are operated by the government, then there is the possibility that corruption may hamper the transmission of beneficial price changes to households.

- **The completeness of markets**
  If elements in the distribution chain are missing, then the plight of the poor may be relatively unaffected by trade. However, as noted by Winters (2000, 2002), even worse is the possibility that liberalisation may be associated with the removal of certain markets, thereby delinking the distribution chain and alienating the poor. For example, Oxfam-IDS (1999) note that remote farmers in Zambia were left without access to the distribution chain for their crops after the government privatised part of the distribution network during liberalisation.

A pertinent illustration of the importance of the distribution chain in mediating the effects of trade liberalisation is discussed in McMillan, Rodrik and Welch (2002), who study the controversial World Bank-prompted elimination of restrictions on exports of raw cashew-nuts in Mozambique. The export restrictions, imposed in the 1970s, reduced the price of raw cashew nuts and thereby stimulated the growth of the cashew-nut processing industry. Standard economic theory posits that the removal of such restrictions should have lead to a rise in the domestic price in raw cashew nuts and an associated movement of resources out of the cashew-nut processing industry and into more efficient endeavours. McMillan, Rodrik and Welch (2002) find that these twin 'textbook' gains of improved distribution and efficiency did occur post-liberalisation, but that the magnitude was small in relation to expectations. Indeed, they estimate that only 40 to 50 per cent of price rises were captured by farmers, the remainder being captured by intermediary firms in the imperfectly competitive distribution network.[6]

Second-round effects

Another important factor to consider is the effect that trade-induced shocks in one market have on prices in other markets, so-called 'second-round' effects. Authors such as Timmer (1997), Delgado, Hopkins and

---

[6] Moreover, it appears that as much as 90 per cent of workers originally employed in the cashew nut-processing industry were unemployed for several years after liberalisation because they had not yet been channelled into other sectors.

Kelly (1998) and Mellor and Gavian (1999) posit that agricultural liberal-isation and productivity growth produce significant second-round effects that substantially alleviate poverty. For example, Delgado, Hopkins and Kelly (1998) note that in South Asia during the so-called 'Green Revo-lution', in which agricultural productivity increased significantly due to global technological diffusion, farmers and labourers spent extra income on both agricultural and non-agricultural products. Moreover, as agri-cultural prices fell, land owners invested heavily in labour-intensive non-agricultural industries. The result was the rapid development of industry in tandem with agricultural growth. However, Delgado, Hopkins and Kelly (1998) point out that such success does not necessarily flow from one sector to another; linkages are dependent upon:

- **The extent to which extra income is spent on local industries**
  Beneficial second-round effects require that additional income earned from trade be spent on goods and services produced locally; otherwise, potential gains may be 'lost' to imports.

The enterprise channel

The enterprise channel, represented by the left-hand side of Figure A, influences household welfare via three variables: profits, wages and employment. Various sections throughout this chapter discuss the poten-tial effects that trade can have on these variables; however, it is first necessary to discuss how the nature of the enterprise channel determines the pass-through of these effects to the poor.

Following Winters (2000, p. 51), enterprises, in the current analytical framework, are defined as 'any unit that produces and sells output and employs labour from outside its own immediate household'. Similar to the distribution channel, the extent of competition (in this case for work-ers) determines the pass-through of shocks to households. Thus, poverty alleviation via the enterprise channel is dependent upon:

- **The nature of competition in the labour market**
  In an imperfectly competitive setting, monopsonistic employers will be less likely to pass on price rises to employees in the form of higher wages.

Moreover, as is discussed later, the nature of the supply side of the labour market further determines how the enterprise channel affects poverty alleviation.

The government channel

The effects of the government channel illustrated on the right-hand side of Figure A permeate the economy. However, for the sake of maintaining logical flow, only the connection between the government and the border and wholesale prices are discussed here; discussion of the myriad policies that governments can utilise throughout the system is left for later sections.

Firstly, the government influences the openness of the economy, and hence the extent of the divergence between domestic and world prices. However, this may not be solely decided upon by the incumbent political party; by design, WTO and regional trade agreement (RTA) commitments constrain the government's ability to erect trade barriers. A large literature exists regarding the benefit of utilising trade agreements as a commitment device to circumvent time-inconsistency problems. Such problems arise when special-interest pressure groups subvert the egalitarian efforts of the democratic system by using interventionist trade policy to redirect wealth to those who wield enough political influence to manipulate government decision making.[7] However, Winters (2000, 2002) notes that trade agreement commitments could prevent the government from engaging in pro-poor interventions, such as the application of variable levies to counteract price variability by stabilising the domestic prices of traded goods, and the granting of development-stimulating production subsidies. Thus, the effect on the border and wholesale prices of government intervention is determined by:

- **The trade policy of the government**
  The trade policy stance of the government is the most important way through which the government influences the effect of trade on poverty.
- **The nature of trade agreement commitments**
  Trade policy making is constrained by the nature of the commitments that governments and their predecessors have made in trade agreements.

Secondly, if governments rely upon trade intervention to generate revenue, then liberalisation can induce reductions in revenue, and hence spending. Winters, McCulloch and McKay (2004) note that a large literature exists which suggests that social expenditure is relatively impervious to trade policy shocks. However, this does not negate the possibility that trade-induced changes in government revenue could potentially filter into the welfare of households:

---

[7] See WTO (2007) for a discussion of this rationale for trade agreements.

- **The nature of non-trade taxation and spending policies**
  Poor households may well be more dependent upon social expenditure
  and be affected to a greater extent by the effects of taxation.

Adaptability of the economy and the strength of institutions

Integral to the determination of the magnitude of the effect of any shocks
on the economy is the extent to which agents can adjust in response to
changes in prices. If adjustment is costly and time-consuming, then negative shocks will be felt unabated and the opportunities afforded by positive
shocks will not be capitalised upon.[8] In terms of poverty alleviation, one
of the most important adjustment mechanisms is that which equilibrates
factor markets. The efficiency of the labour market is particularly relevant for poor workers outside of subsistence farming. Whilst the hardship
of temporary unemployment can be mitigated by savings and access to
credit amongst the relatively well-off, poor and unskilled workers may
not have the luxury of such resources and will therefore lack the ability to
smooth their consumption across periods of low income. Moreover, the
ability of workers to move from one job to another is constrained by their
level of generic human capital obtained from education; something that
the poor generally have in small measure. Empirical evidence on the costs
of labour-market adjustment in developing countries is scant, although,
in a survey of the literature, Matusz and Tarr (1999) conclude that adjustment costs tend to be small compared to the resulting benefits, even in
the short-run. However, a more recent study by Davidson and Matusz
(2000) suggests that such adjustment costs may be more significant than
previously thought.

  For producers, market flexibility may be just as important. If farmers
or small-scale enterprises cannot move out of declining industries and
into more lucrative endeavours, then the poverty-alleviating potential of
trade may fail to materialise. Such flexibility requires fully developed
and properly functioning factor markets, as well as adequate infrastructure. For example, the World Bank (2001) notes that, because of
a lack of sufficiently developed land and water markets in Egypt, coupled with poor transportation infrastructure, farmers could not make the
switch from traditional crops to more profitable labour-intensive export
crops like fruits and vegetables. Moreover, Corden (1997) notes that

---

[8] For a more thorough survey on the literature regarding the ability of an economy to adjust
to trade liberalisation, see Bacchetta and Jansen (2003).

under-developed, myopic and fragmented capital markets may hamper the establishment of new enterprises, particularly in developing countries. Indeed, the World Bank (1997) notes that the most significant impediment to adjustment faced by small firms following trade reform in Ghana was a lack of access to capital for new investments. Bigsten *et al.* (1999) find similar results in an econometric analysis of Cameroon, Ghana, Kenya, Zambia and Zimbabwe.

Thus, the adaptability of an economy is dependent upon:

- **The stock of human capital**
  Without sufficient generic knowledge, poor workers will not be able to move easily between jobs. Indeed, Kim and Kim (2000) argue that education was a fundamental catalyst for promoting the beneficial aspects of trade in the newly industrialised Asian countries.
- **The effectiveness of factor markets**
  The shorter the period of transitional unemployment for affected workers, the less are the adjustment costs of trade liberalisation. Moreover, the ability of enterprises to take advantage of the positive benefits of trade liberalisation requires effective land, capital and labour markets.
- **The completeness of markets**
  If markets are not complete, then the effectiveness of factor markets will be severely impaired.
- **The quality of infrastructure**
  Without transportation links to connect suppliers and purchasers, ports and markets, farm gates and ports etc., an economy cannot adapt to deal with the effects of trade liberalisation.

Market failures in the product market also impact upon the poverty-alleviating potential of trade. Incomplete markets, imperfect competition, overly complicated bureaucracy etc. can cause deadweight losses to society and can thereby impede the adaptability of the economy.

The functioning of any economy, in particular the factor markets and adjustment mechanisms therein, is mediated by the institutional arrangements and the associated level of governance inherent within the nation.[9] The precise meaning of 'institution' remains a contentious issue. However, the definitions provided by North (1991, p. 97) are suitable in the current context: 'institutions are constraints that structure political, economic

---

[9] For more in-depth surveys of the connections between trade, institutions and poverty, see Sindzingre (2007) and Francoise and Manchin (2007).

and social interactions, and consist of informal (self-enforcing) constraints . . . and formal regulations (constitutions, laws, property rights)'.
Weak institutions impede both the functioning of the economy and trade
itself. Empirical evidence from authors such as Acemoglu, Johnson and
Robinson (2001) shows that the economic performance of a nation is
significantly related to the quality of its institutions. Further evidence
appears to suggest that the primary channel for this effect is through
the impact that institutions have on investment. Indeed, de Soto (2000)
argues that poorly enforced contracts and property rights, low protection
of creditors and a lack of supervision of the financial system may hamper
the formation of financial markets. The connection between institutions
and trade has been established by authors such as Jansen and Hildegunn
(2004) and Khalid and Pierre-Guillaume (2006), who observe that indicators of good institutions are positively correlated with trade flows. Thus
the adaptability of the economy and the efficiency of its markets are highly
dependent upon:

- **The strength of institutions**
  The effectiveness of factor markets, the level of infrastructure, even the
  extent of trade, all rest upon the strength of institutions inherent within
  an economy. Institutions mediate all economic transactions, and, as
  noted by myriad authors, the lack of institutional quality in developing
  countries can be a major inhibitor to their ability to capture the benefits
  from trade.

The static effects of trade liberalisation

Overview

The above section detailed how the effects of trade filter through the
economy to the poor. The next two sections detail what those effects are.
The current section outlines the static effects of trade liberalisation. The
static effects are those that occur in the short-run and which affect the
level of total factor productivity through the redistribution of resources.
Standard economic theory posits that trade liberalisation will necessarily improve national welfare at the expense of some members of society.
Whilst, in theory, redistributive policies can compensate the injured parties, this relies upon the government having a great deal of information
and flexibility, which it is unlikely to have. In order to assess the impact
that the static effects of trade will have on poverty, it is thus necessary to consider all three channels through which the poor are affected.

Consequently, the following sections deal with the static effect that trade has on prices, the static effects on wages and the static effects on the government.

The static welfare gains from exchange and specialisation

Box A illustrates the standard economic approach to the static welfare benefits of trade liberalisation in a two-country, two-goods model. Two sources of gains from trade are identified in this approach: the gains from exchange and the gains from specialisation. The gains from exchange simply arise from the fact that when individuals or countries are endowed with different amounts of goods, have different preferences, or have different technologies, relative prices will be different between them, and they can thus benefit from trading with each other. The gains from specialisation represent the increase in total output that results from specialising in the production of goods that can be produced relatively efficiently.

Underlying this approach is the principle of comparative advantage. This states that it does not matter whether one country is more efficient in the production of every good than the other; as long as each country specialises in, and trades, goods in which they are *relatively* more productive, both will gain from trade with each other. Different (but complementary) economic models of trade posit different sources of comparative advantage:

- **The relative level of technical knowledge of the trading partners**
  The Ricardian model of trade posits that the basis for trade is a difference in technology. The wider this difference, the greater the scope for trade.
- **The relative factor abundances between the trading partners**
  The Heckscher-Ohlin trade model posits that the basis for trade is a difference in factor abundances between two countries. The greater the difference in factor abundances, the greater the scope for trade.

The above analysis demonstrates that trade benefits the economy in aggregate. However, it is important to note that the welfare of every individual does not necessarily improve following trade liberalisation; some will be made worse off through higher prices and lower wages as is discussed at p. 35, below. Theoretically, redistributive policies could lead to a Pareto improvement, i.e. a situation where at least one person is made better off without making anyone else worse off. However, this is dependent

---

BOX A   THE STATIC EFFECTS OF TRADE LIBERALISATION

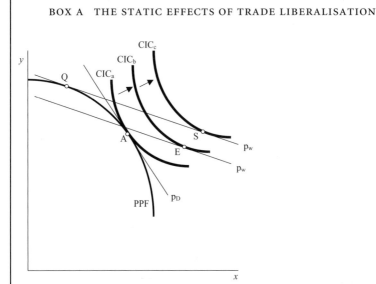

Figure B   The static effects of trade liberalisation.

Figure B shows the production possibility frontier (PPF)[10] of a country that produces and consumes only two goods, x and y, before and after trade, and which has a comparative advantage in the production of good y. Point A with relative prices p_D (where $p_D = P^x_D/P^y_D$) represents the autarkic equilibrium, i.e. the point at which the marginal rate of transformation (MRT)[11] associated with the domestic PPF is equal to the marginal rate of substitution (MRS)[12] associated with the community indifference curve (CIC).[13] However, the change in prices from p_D to p_w (where $p_w = P^x_w/P^y_w$) when trade is allowed shifts production to point Q and consumption to point S, and thereby generates total gains shown by the move from CIC_a to CIC_c. These gains can be disaggregated into the gains that accrue from exchange (the move from CIC_a to CIC_b), and those that accrue as a result of specialisation (the move from CIC_b to CIC_c).

---

[10] The PPF shows all possible combinations of goods x and y that the country can produce, given its factor endowments and technical knowledge.
[11] The MRT is the slope of the PPF, and gives the rate at which production of good y can be exchanged for production of good x.
[12] The MRS is the slope of the CIC, and gives the rate at which consumers would be willing to exchange good y for good x.
[13] The CIC shows all possible combinations of goods x and y that give (aggregated) consumers a fixed level of welfare; the further northeast the CIC, the higher the level of welfare obtained.

upon the ability of the government to enact such policies, which is in turn dependent upon the prevailing political conditions. Moreover, the above analysis only goes as far as the border; the internal conditions discussed above determine how the price changes illustrated in Box A are passed onto consumers.

The analysis summarised above pertains to the two-goods case. In reality, multiple goods will be affected. Thus, the overall effect on the poor depends upon:

- **The combined impact on the poor of the liberalisation of many different goods**
  Liberalisation usually entails removing restrictions on several goods simultaneously. Thus, the effect that this has on the poor will depend upon whether they are net producers or consumers of each product, and the extent to which each product is used as an intermediate good in the production of another good. The combined effect on the poor is thus complicated and highly context-dependent. For example, a case study of Jamaica by the Women's Edge Coalition and CAFRA (2004) finds that trade liberalisation decreased food prices to the benefit of consumers but to the detriment of producers. However, the study finds that poverty rates following liberalisation have increased due to the fact that the livelihoods of a large number of Jamaica's poor are dependent upon agriculture.

The gains from increased competition

In the absence of perfect competition, trade can add further static gains to welfare from the expansion of competition in the domestic market.[14] Two basic mechanisms are responsible for eliciting this effect: increased domestic-competition and the introduction of foreign competition. The increased domestic competition channel occurs from the extension of the domestic market to the global level, which entices more domestic firms to enter and compete away super-normal profits. This improves national welfare by expanding consumer welfare (through reducing consumer prices) more than it reduces producer welfare (through lowering revenues to firms). The foreign competition channel arises from the fact that trade invites foreign competition into the domestic market, which

---

[14] Increased competition can also add dynamic gains through increased incentives to engage in efficiency enhancing endeavours, which can feed into higher growth. This is discussed further at p. 42.

thereby increases efficiency in a similar manner. Indeed, several empirical studies have observed reductions in price-marginal cost mark-ups following increases in international trade in a number of nations, including Turkey (Levinsohn, 1993), Cote D'Ivoire (Harrison, 1994) and India (Krishna and Mitra, 1998).

Clearly, the extent to which increased competition alleviates poverty in this manner is dependent upon:

- **The level of competition in the market prior to trade liberalisation**
  If markets are already highly competitive, and if efficient market institutions are in place to facilitate competitive practices, then trade liberalisation will do little to improve efficiency by diminishing super-normal profits.

However, Winters (2000, 2002) notes that in many cases, trade liberalisation is also associated with changes in domestic marketing arrangements, such as the abolition of government-controlled purchasing monopsonies. The meaning of 'consumers' and 'producers' in this context needs some clarification. If the imperfectly competitive industry in question is that of monopsonistic purchasers of farm produce, then 'consumers' will be harmed by increased competition, in that they will have to pay producers a higher price. This is thus beneficial for poverty alleviation; farmers will receive higher prices for their produce. However, in a study by Oxfam-IDS (1999), it is clear that the effects of liberalisation in this regard are highly situation-specific. In Zimbabwe, the abolition of the official Cotton Marketing Board resulted in the emergence of three private buyers, including one owned by the farmers. This caused a rise in cotton prices and thus a rise in farm incomes. In contrast, when liberalisation was undertaken in the maize market in Zambia, two private firms emerged that abandoned purchasing in remote areas altogether, and possibly colluded to keep prices low. Accordingly, the incomes of remote farmers were significantly impaired by liberalisation. Winters (2000, 2002) suggests that two main factors are integral to whether liberalisation of this kind benefits or harms the poor:

- **The pattern of protection and the nature of trade liberalisation**
  If import restrictions and government-controlled monopsonies act to the benefit of the poor, then removing them will not alleviate poverty. Indeed, Hanson and Harrison (1999) suggest that the removal of trade barriers in Mexico in the 1980s did not alleviate poverty precisely because these restrictions had been in place to protect the poor in the first place.

It is important to stress again that the nature of institutions and the efficiency of markets are highly important factors in this context. Increased foreign competition displaces domestic firms. Standard economic theory holds that this 'iconoclasm' (i.e. creative destruction) is required to transfer resources into more efficient industries in which the country in question has a comparative advantage. However, this relies upon the proper functioning of labour and capital markets and on an adequate level of unemployment support. As argued by Stiglitz (2003), amongst others, the incipient factor markets and lack of unemployment protection that characterise developing countries means that such countries may not be able to sufficiently withstand the negative effects of trade liberalisation to ensure that the net effect is positive.

The static effects on wages

There are two differing theories relating to how trade will affect poverty via wages: the Stolper-Samuelson theorem and the Lewis model. Each of these approaches is dealt with in turn below.

The Stolper-Samuelson theorem

The Stolper-Samuelson theorem forms part of the Heckscher-Ohlin model of trade that regards relative factor abundance as the driving force behind trade, and is expressed in terms of two countries (Home and Foreign), two factors (the abundance of which differs between the countries) and two goods (each of which relies more heavily on one factor than the other in its production). The Stolper-Samuelson theorem holds that the ratio of the abundant factor-price to the scarce factor price in each country has a one-to-one relationship with the ratio of the price of the abundant factor-intensive good to the price of the scarce factor-intensive good. The Heckscher-Ohlin theorem states that countries export goods that use intensively those factors of production that are relatively abundant at home, and import goods that use intensively factors that are relatively scarce. As is illustrated in Box B, this pattern of trade will lead to a rise in the relative price paid to the abundant factor.

Wood (1997) notes that in developing countries, the relatively abundant factor is low-paid unskilled labour, whereas the relatively scarce factor is high-paid skilled labour. As such, he argues that trade, as it favours the abundant factor, will lessen the income differential across factors and thus decrease within-country inequality. However, this result has not gone

BOX B   TRADE-INDUCED FACTOR PRICE CHANGES

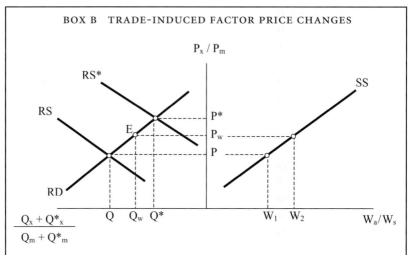

Figure C   Trade-induced factor price changes.

Shown in the left panel of Figure C is the interaction of the world-relative demand curve for the domestic export good (RD) and the domestic- and foreign-relative supply curves (RS and RS* respectively). Prior to trade, the domestic relative consumption of the export good is Q, with a corresponding relative price of P, whereas the foreign-relative consumption is Q* at a relative price of P*. Following the commencement of trade, the relative prices converge to P_w, which represents a fall in relative prices abroad but a rise at home. This domestic rise in relative prices feeds through into the right panel of the diagram, which shows the relationship between relative goods prices and relative factor prices (abundant over scarce) vis-à-vis the Stolper–Samuelson theorem (SS). It can be seen that the trade-induced rise in the relative price of the export good leads to a rise in the relative price of the abundant factor from W_1 to W_2.

unchallenged; alternative theories of trade posit that trade liberalisation will have the opposite effect in developing countries. For example, some variants of monopolistic competition theory, such as that proposed by Manasse and Turrini (2001), hold that efficient firms self-select to enter export markets and expand by doing so. Thus, given that such firms will employ skilled workers, the skills premium in terms of higher wages will increase both within and between sectors in all trading countries. Zhu and Trefler (2005) find a similar result in a model where technological catch-up causes production of the least skill-intensive northern goods to migrate south where they become the most skill-intensive southern goods. Thus, the demand for skills and hence wage inequality rise in both regions. However, given the complex nature of international trade, there is nothing to say that opposing theoretical perspectives are mutually exclusive; multiple effects could occur at the same time and may counteract each other when viewed from an economy-wide perspective. There is no prior reason to suspect that one effect will dominate the other; the relevant mix of effects that is applicable in reality is thus an empirical question.

Empirical work regarding causal links between trade and inequality has generated conflicting results. For example, Wood (1994) provides substantial empirical evidence from East Asia that confirms the predictions of traditional trade models, i.e. the gap in wages between skilled and unskilled workers narrowed in the decade following trade liberalisation. However, Latin American evidence from Wood (1994), Robbins (1996) and Slaughter (2000) suggests that trade liberalisation has coincided with an increase in both income and wage inequality. Several explanations have been posited for these opposing results. One line of argument focuses on the fact that Latin America opened its markets later than East Asian economies (Wood, 1994). As a result, the entry of China and other large low-income Asian countries into the world market for labour-intensive manufactures in the 1980s shifted the comparative advantage of middle-income Latin American countries into goods of medium skill intensity. Increased openness in middle-income countries thus reduced the relative demand for unskilled workers by causing sectors of low-skill intensity to contract. This would explain why relative wages of unskilled workers decreased. Another explanation for rising inequality in some developing countries is that liberalisation introduces new skill-intensive activities into developing countries in accordance with the Zhu and Trefler (2005) model discussed above.

Thus, the context specificity of the effects of trade on inequality is supported by both theory and evidence. The factors governing the impact on inequality appear to include:

- **The relative factor abundances between the trading partners**
  The Stolper-Samuelson theorem predicts that trade will favour the factor in relative abundance. If the abundant factor in developing countries is poor workers, then, according to this theorem, trade should alleviate poverty.

- **The relative level of technical knowledge of the trading partners**
  The transfer of technological know-how or the shifting of production
  from high-skilled to low-skilled nations can raise the skill premium in
  the recipient country and thereby exacerbate inequality.
- **The pattern of protection and the nature of trade liberalisation**
  Liberalising an industry that is heavily protected will have more of an
  impact than liberalising a less-protected industry.
- **The impact of global economic events and the timing of trade liberalisation**
  If liberalisation of an industry occurs after competitors have established
  a foot-hold in that industry in world markets, then the industry could
  suffer.

The Lewis model

Underlying the Stolper-Samuelson theorem is the assumption of full
employment. Under these conditions, the increase in labour demand
associated with the liberalisation of trade in a labour-abundant country
cannot raise employment, as the labour supply is inelastic (i.e. *unrespon-
sive* to changes in the wage rate). Thus, the increased demand directly
raises wages and thereby alleviates poverty. However, Lewis (1954) suggested an alternative scenario whereby the supply of labour is highly
elastic (i.e. *responsive* to changes in the wage rate). This can occur when
the tradable-goods sector can draw on a 'reserve army' of workers from
the informal sector, or those that are unemployed or under-employed.
In this case, wages are set by how much the workers in the tradable sector could receive elsewhere, and the increased labour demand associated
with trade leads only to a rise in employment, not a rise in wages. These
alternative scenarios are illustrated in Box C below.

Winters (2000, 2002) notes that, in itself, the Lewis (1954) scenario
will not directly alleviate poverty unless the loss of labour from the sub-
sistence/informal sector allows remaining workers to raise their wages as
labour becomes relatively scarcer. Thus, the poverty-alleviating potential
of trade further depends upon:

- **The level of unemployment prior to liberalisation**
  If increased labour demand raises employment in the tradable sector
  but not wages, then it is unlikely to have much of an impact on poverty.
  Indeed, CUTS (1999) finds that, after liberalisation in India, formal
  manufacturing-sector employment grew more rapidly, but wages grew
  less rapidly than prior to liberalisation.

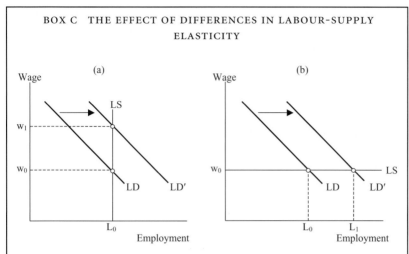

BOX C   THE EFFECT OF DIFFERENCES IN LABOUR-SUPPLY ELASTICITY

Figure D   The effect of differences in labour-supply elasticity.

The Stolper-Samuelson theorem scenario is shown in panel (a) in Figure D, in which the trade-induced rightwards shift in the labour demand curve from LD to LD′ causes a one-to-one upwards movement in wages from w_0 to w_1 because the labour supply curve, LS, is perfectly inelastic. The Lewis (1954) scenario is shown in panel (b), in which the trade-induced rightwards shift in the labour demand curve causes an increase in employment from L_0 to L_1, but leaves wages fixed at the prevailing rate of w_0.

The effect on the government

It is often thought that trade liberalisation will result in a reduction in tariff revenues; however, in reality, this is not necessarily the case. Indeed, Ebrill, Stotsky and Gropp (1999) note that a number of developing countries, such as Ghana, Kenya, Senegal and Malawi, have implemented success-ful trade reform programmes without significant loss of revenue. There are three main reasons why trade may lead to effects that offset the lost revenue associated with tariff reductions. Firstly, developing countries tend to utilise quantitative restrictions as a major trade policy instru-ment. The conversion of such restrictions to tariffs (as is required when a country accedes to the WTO) generates tariff revenue. Secondly, the reduction of high tariff rates will induce a greater quantity of imports, which will generate tariff revenue. Thirdly, the reduction in, and simpli-fication of, tariff rates can reduce the incentives for tax evasion, and can improve the efficiency of collection. Matusz and Tarr (1999) note that the net effect on government revenue of trade liberalisation is dependent upon:

- **The pattern of protection and the nature of liberalisation**
  If tariffs and quantitative restrictions are already low prior to liberalisation, then liberalisation is more likely to result in net revenue losses. Moreover, if imports are price-inelastic, then tariff reductions will not lead to offsetting increases in import volumes. As noted in a recent joint study by the Institute for International Trade and the Pacific Trade Consult (2007), small economies, such as Kiribati, are so trade dependent that liberalisation (such as that which would result from the proposed Pacific Island Countries Trade Agreement) would result in net revenue losses.

In the case where liberalisation does reduce government revenues, governments have to tread a careful path in terms of the resulting changes in taxation and spending so as not to exacerbate the plight of the poor. However, as noted in the aforementioned Institute for International Trade and the Pacific Trade Consult (2007) study, the availability of alternative sources of tax revenue is often significantly limited in small developing economies.

As was mentioned earlier, government commitments vis-à-vis trade agreements can potentially have effects on the government's ability to alleviate poverty. Thus, the impact that each agreement has on government flexibility needs to be taken into consideration.

Dynamic effects of trade on poverty alleviation

Overview

The dynamic effects of trade are those that occur in the medium to long term and which expand the production possibility frontier (PPF in Figure B), i.e. the output potential of a country, leading to a higher level of community welfare. According to studies utilising Computational General Equilibrium (CGE) models, such as that by Cline (2004), the dynamic effects of trade are substantially greater in magnitude than the static effects. Various interconnected dynamic effects are associated with trade. However, for ease of exposition, the medium- and long-term effects are dealt with in separate sections below.

Dynamic effects in the medium-term

In the medium-term following trade liberalisation, an economy converges to new 'steady-state' levels of the capital stock, and hence output. Essentially, this occurs when the increased incentives to invest brought about by trade lead to an expansion in the capital stock. In CGE models, this is usually modelled by stipulating that the capital stock expands sufficiently to bring the post-liberalisation rate of return on investment back down to the pre-liberalisation rate.

Cline (2004) notes that the feasibility of amassing sufficient capital to take advantage of the opportunities made available by trade rests upon:

- **The mobility of capital both domestically and from abroad**
  Capital markets have to be sufficiently developed so as to channel capital to where the return on investment is highest. Cline (2004) argues that, in poor countries, this requires 'trade and aid', whereas in middle-income countries, it requires capital inflows from global markets.

Dynamic effects in the long run

In the long run, there are further dynamic gains from trade that are conceptually different from 'steady state' gains. Such gains occur from an increase in total factor productivity, instead of the increases in output per worker that arise from increased capital per worker. Figure E details three interconnected channels through which trade influences poverty in the long run: growth, inequality and volatility.

This section deals with each of the three factors influencing household welfare separately.

Economic growth

The key to long-term poverty alleviation is economic growth. The contention that trade acts as a catalyst for growth is one that has a long history in economics. However, competing theoretical models have been developed, some of which posit that trade is the 'engine of growth', and others which posit that trade will have little effect on growth. The correct theoretical model to apply in reality is thus an empirical question, but the empirical literature regarding the trade-growth relationship is fraught with controversy and yields no concrete results one way or the

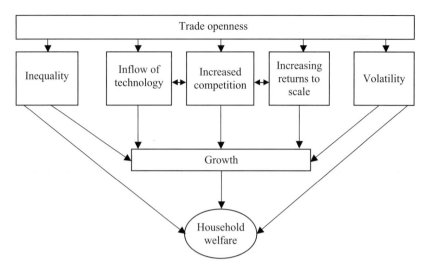

Figure E   Long-term dynamic effects of trade on poverty alleviation.

other.[15] Whilst notable cross-country studies have been conducted that find support for trade as a catalyst for growth, for example Dollar (1992), Sachs and Warner (1995) and Edwards (1998), such studies have been severely criticised by authors such as Rodriguez and Rodrik (2001) on the grounds that they rest upon weak empirical foundations. Indeed, Bhagwati and Srinivasan (2002) argue that the best evidence in support of the notion that trade promotes growth comes from the nuanced, in-depth studies of the experiences of individual countries that were conducted by the OECD, NBER (National Bureau of Economic Research) and IBRD (International Bank for Reconstruction and Development) during the 1960s and 1970s.[16]

Figure E above details five channels through which trade can potentially affect growth. Two of these channels (inequality and volatility) also affect household welfare directly, and so are tackled in separate sections. The remaining three (the inflow of technology, increased competition and increasing returns) are discussed individually below. However, the most important link for poverty alleviation is the one connecting growth with household welfare. As noted by Bhagwati and Srinivasan (2002), if technical progress passes the poor by, growth can be immiserising due to

[15] For a survey of the empirical literature regarding the connection between trade and growth, and a discussion of the controversies therein, see Baldwin (2003).

[16] As an example, see Little, Scitovsky and Scott (1970) for a survey of the OECD country surveys.

its negative effect on prices. Accordingly, the final subsection deals with the factors determining whether growth is 'pro-poor' or not.

Inflow of technology

In a wide-ranging literature survey and empirical study, Easterly and Levine (2001) argue that most cross-country variations in GDP growth cannot be attributed to differences in factor accumulation; thus technical progress is the main determinant of growth. Another empirical study by Keller (2000) finds that 20 per cent of the variation in cross-country productivity growth rates can be explained by differences in technology inflows related to the pattern of imports. Thus, the trade-facilitated transfer of technology is an important determinant of technical progress, which is an important determinant of growth. This conclusion is also supported by the theoretical literature; for example, Grossman and Helpman (1991, 1995) and Barro and Sala-i-martin (1995), amongst others, posit that knowledge spillovers associated with trade are a crucial spur to economic growth. Two primary channels facilitate the trade-induced transfer of technology across borders: imports of technologically superior goods and foreign direct-investment (FDI) inflows, which, as noted by Markusen (2000) vary positively with the degree of trade openness, provided that the countries in question are sufficiently dissimilar.[17] The first channel can be subdivided further into imports of technologically superior intermediate goods that improve productive capacity directly, and imports of goods from which developing country manufacturers can glean knowledge that they can imitate or use to improve their own processes. Keller (2000) notes that the extent to which the pattern of imports affects productivity will be large for least developed countries (LDCs), given their relative dependence on imports as a source of technological improvement. However, one important factor determines the magnitude of this effect:

- **The relative level of technical knowledge of the trading partners**
  In order to maximise technological transfer, the majority of a nation's import share should come from 'technology leaders', i.e. countries that

---

[17] FDI can take two forms: horizontal, where FDI is a substitute for trade; and vertical where production stages are disaggregated and spread around the world, in which case, FDI is a complement of trade. Vertical FDI is more likely to occur between dissimilar countries, as multinational enterprises will take advantage of differing factor costs. Thus, a higher level of trade openness on the part of a developing country will encourage developed countries to shift production there and then export the produce to their existing markets.

invest heavily in research and development (R&D), rather than from 'technology followers' such as other LDCs.

On the FDI channel, Saggi (2002) provides a survey of the literature. He notes that there are three main mechanisms through which foreign-owned firms diffuse knowledge to the rest of the economy: demonstration effects, labour turnover and vertical linkages. Demonstration effects occur when local firms adopt technologies used by foreign firms either through imitation or reverse engineering. The labour-turnover mechanism refers to knowledge transferred into the local economy by ex-employees of foreign firms who switch employers or initiate their own enterprises. Vertical linkages are those that occur when technology is transferred from foreign-owned firms to local businesses that are potential suppliers of intermediate goods or buyers of their own products. The magnitude of these effects is dependent upon myriad factors, although Saggi (2002) posits two overarching conditions that will determine whether the FDI channel will promote growth:

- **The ability of the country to attract FDI**
  Clearly, policies that impede FDI inflows will suppress this channel of technological transfer. Moreover, Saggi (2002) notes that weak intellectual property-rights protection will deter investment from more high-tech firms.
- **The ratio of vertical linkages versus displaced firms arising from FDI**
  Whilst vertical linkages between multinational and local firms may well lead to technological diffusion, the net effect upon welfare may be deleterious if too many local firms collapse under the weight of foreign competition.

Of crucial importance to the link between technology and poverty alleviation in both the trade in goods and the FDI cases is the rate at which new ideas are adopted. Numerous authors discuss the factors determining the likelihood that technology will be adopted in a developing country. The main determinants are:

- **The stock of human capital**
  Authors such as Keller (1996) and Borensztein, De Gregorio and Lee (1998) note that a threshold level of human capital is required for a country to successfully adopt new technology. This theory is supported by empirical evidence in a study by Xu (2000), who finds that FDI inflows do not contribute to productivity growth in less-developed countries for this reason.

- **The level of R&D in the host country**
  In addition to sufficient human capital, adopting new technologies requires R&D spending. With low levels of R&D activity, new technology is unlikely to be adopted.
- **The availability of capital, credit and risk-sharing**
  The adoption of a new technology may require considerable sunk investment, and may well be associated with a substantial risk of failure. Accordingly, without adequate capital, credit and risk-sharing arrangements, resource-constrained farmers could be reluctant to bear the risk of potentially lucrative new technological developments, as sunk adoption costs cannot be recouped in the event that the technology yields less profit than expected.
- **The availability of information**
  Knowledge of the likelihood of success reduces the uncertainty that impedes technological adoption. Key to the acquisition of such knowledge are the institutions in place to assist the diffusion of accurate information. Zhao (2007) notes that in poorer countries, information is disseminated as a positive externality by 'leaders' who adopt the technology first and are then followed by others if the technology proves successful.

Increasing returns

As was discussed above, trade involves specialisation, which generates static efficiency enhancements as resources move into industries in which they are relatively more productive. However, if increasing returns to scale occur, then such specialisation may also lead to dynamic benefits. Increasing returns occur when economies of scale exist, of which there are two types: internal and external. Internal economies of scale are those that occur within the individual firm as the expanding volume of production facilitates specialisation. Such economies include learning-by-doing and making use of specialised equipment, both of which improve productivity. External economies of scale are those that occur at the industry level, such as making use of specialised suppliers, labour-market pooling and knowledge spillovers.

Increased competition

The trade-induced increase in competition mitigates the distortionary effects of imperfect competition in the domestic economy. Whilst this gain is static in nature, the increased level of competition can also encourage the pursuit of efficiency-enhancing endeavours. Several authors, such as Holmes and Schmitz (2001), argue that the increased competition associated with trade liberalisation reduces incentives to engage in unproductive entrepreneurial activities (such as blocking competitors' potential innovations) and increases the incentives to invest in R&D. Empirical research supports this theoretical standpoint. For example, Tybout and Westbrook (1995), Krishna and Mitra (1998), Euysung (2000) and Fernandes (2003) have observed increases in the rate of growth of productivity in industries that experience increased competition following trade reforms.

In Figure E above, the inflow of technology, increased competition and increasing returns boxes are illustrated as interlinked. Clearly, these channels are not fully independent from each other. The incentives to engage in efficiency-enhancing expenditure are increased by both the access to foreign technology and the increased competition associated with trade liberalisation. Moreover, these channels are mutually reinforcing; foreign competitors utilising more advanced technology induce domestic firms to utilise foreign technology in order to keep up. Similarly, increasing returns can cause imperfect competition, the negative effects of which can be alleviated by increased exposure to foreign competition. Moreover, the productivity improvements induced by increased competition can, via increasing returns, lead to increased growth.

Is growth pro-poor?

The World Bank (2000/2001, p. 47) notes that household studies generally find that a 1% increase in real per-capita income reduces the incidence of poverty by 2%. However, this result is not necessarily guaranteed; if growth is sufficiently skewed in favour of the rich, it may not aid poverty alleviation; thus, growth may not be 'pro-poor'. As noted by Lopez (2005), pro-poor growth has received considerable attention amongst development practitioners over the past few years, yet a concrete definition of the term remains elusive. On the one hand, pro-poor growth can be taken to mean growth that is skewed in favour of the poor; on the other hand, it can simply be taken to mean growth that helps to alleviate poverty. Given that this paper is primarily concerned with absolute poverty, the second of these definitions applies in the current context (the relationship between trade, inequality and growth is discussed in the following section).

Lopez (2005) surveys myriad cross-country and country-specific studies and concludes that several factors influence whether growth is poverty alleviating or not:

- **The stock of human capital**
  With high levels of education throughout the workforce, the poor will be in a better position to capitalise on the opportunities offered by growth.
- **The strength of institutions**
  Without adequate institutions, growth may be appropriated by those with power at the expense of the poor.
- **The quality of infrastructure**
  Sufficient infrastructure is necessary to include the poor, especially the rural poor, in the benefits of growth.
- **The level of volatility**
  Macroeconomic instability is more likely to impede the poor from prospering than the rich.

As Lopez (2005) notes, these factors all have strong priors; thus, a substantial effort has to be made to escape from 'poverty traps'. Clearly, for poverty alleviation to be successful, policies that are inclusive of and which target the poor are required. Indeed, in a recent cross-country survey, the Institute for International Trade (2006) has examined the use of policies to tackle uneven growth in a number of Asia-Pacific Economic Cooperation (APEC) countries, including China, Indonesia and the Philippines. Whilst some of these policies have been more successful than others, the authors note that there is significant scope for well-constructed, and measured, government intervention in order to make growth more balanced.

Inequality

If openness to trade causes variations in income inequality, then it is important to analyse the effect that this will have on economic growth. Economic literature yields two opposing approaches with respect to this issue: the classical approach, associated with Kaldor (1956), and the so-called new political-economy approach, associated with authors such as Thorbecke and Charumilind (2002).[18] Kaldor (1956) argues that, due to the relatively higher marginal propensity to save amongst the rich,

[18] Nissanke and Thorbecke (2007) provide a more in-depth discussion of the globalisation-inequality-poverty relationship.

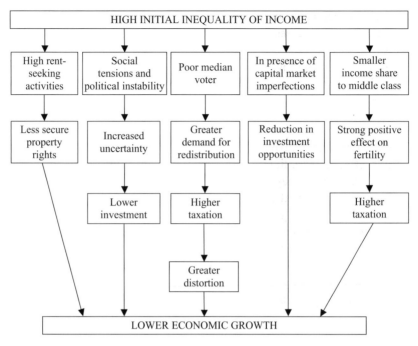

Figure F   Channels connecting inequality and growth (adapted from Nissanke and Thorbecke, 2007, p. 28).

income inequality will lead to greater savings, capital accumulation and hence growth. The contrasting approach posits that inequality has a deleterious effect on growth through multiple channels, illustrated in Figure F.

Whether inequality leads to lower growth in reality or not is an empirical question. Unfortunately, empirical evidence in this area is somewhat lacking. However, a few studies merit mention. Benjamin, Brandt and Giles (2006) analyse the effect of inequality on growth in rural China, and found robust, statistically significant evidence of a negative relationship between inequality and growth. A more complicated relationship has been identified by Cornia (2004) and Addison and Cornia (2001). These studies indicate that growth can be low at both high and low levels of inequality. Income equality can lead to disincentive effects, whereas income inequality appears to lead to low growth through the reduction in private investment engendered by social conflicts. Thus, they argue that there is an optimal range of inequality labelled the 'growth-invariant efficient inequality range'. However, given that nearly all developing countries suffer from significant levels of income inequality, it seems clear that, in most cases, equitable, pro-poor growth policies are badly needed.

Clearly, in evaluating policy options that may lead to variations in inequality, a government should take into consideration the following factors:

- **The initial level of inequality**
  At low levels of inequality, a rise in inequality may be desirable from the perspective of increasing growth. Conversely, at high levels of inequality, further inequality may hamper growth.
- **The strength of institutions**
  The ability of the government to mitigate the effects of inequality depends upon several country-specific factors. For example, rent-seeking activities are more likely to lead to less secure property rights in nations where corruption is already a problem. Moreover, investment-reducing uncertainty may be less of an issue in countries where the government enjoys considerable popular support.

Volatility

As noted by Nissanke and Thorbecke (2007), a greater degree of trade openness tends to be associated with greater volatility and economic shocks. Moreover, empirical evidence provided by Laursen and Mahajan (2005) suggests that the poor are harmed disproportionately more during periods of economic contraction.[19] In fact, the welfare implications of volatility can be so severe that Pallage and Robe (2003) conclude that in many developing countries, economic agents would strictly prefer to have macroeconomic fluctuations eliminated to receiving a permanent 1 per cent increase in annual consumption growth.

Openness to trade can induce volatility through a variety of channels. Winters (2000, 2002) notes that at a simple level, if one supposes that all countries experience independent random shocks, then the increased exposure to foreign conditions associated with trade liberalisation will cause greater volatility by increasing the importance of foreign shocks in the determination of domestic welfare. Moreover, as trade facilitates specialisation in production, it increases aggregate volatility by

---

[19] Accordingly, volatility may also exacerbate inequality.

reducing risk-spreading throughout the economy.[20] However, whilst trade can potentially reduce risk-spreading domestically, it is likely to increase it internationally, which can also lead to volatility. For example, in an autarkic situation, variations in output caused by random events (such as a bad crop harvest) lead to price changes that maintain stable producer incomes. However, opening such variable output markets to foreign competition engenders greater price stability, which increases the volatility of domestic producers' incomes.

The extent to which volatility affects household welfare is dependent upon the extent to which price shocks are transmitted to the poor via the channels discussed at p. 50, above. However, Newberry and Stiglitz (1984) noted that the impact of trade-induced volatility can also be mitigated by:

- **The availability of output and price insurance**
  Without output and insurance arrangements, producers will shift out of markets made more volatile by trade, causing a rise in the average price. Producer welfare would thus decrease with the greater risk associated with income, and consumer welfare would decrease with the price rise.

Volatility is a double-edged sword; not only can it affect the poor directly, but, as is illustrated in Figure F above, it can have second-round deleterious effects on economic growth. Empirical work by Ramey and Ramey (1995) confirms this relationship. Moreover, a number of more recent studies, such as Kose, Prasad and Terrones (2006) and Hnatkovska and Loayza (2005) find evidence that the negative link is exacerbated in developing countries due to deficits in the following factors:

- **The strength of institutions**
  Well-developed financial markets can decouple consumption from output volatility and thereby smooth the effects of economic shocks. However, de Soto (2000) argues that weak institutions, in terms of poorly enforced contracts and property rights, low protection of creditors and a lack of supervision of the financial system, may hamper the formation of financial markets.
- **The ability of the government to utilise countercyclical policies**
  As noted earlier, the ability of the government to counteract trade-induced shocks is an important factor in determining the extent to which the welfare of the poor is affected by openness to trade. Both

---

[20] Whilst this source of volatility appears theoretically sound, studies such as Lutz and Singer (1994) have struggled to find empirical support for this contention.

countercyclical fiscal spending and the use of temporary tariff measures are important tools in this regard. However, fiscal spending may well be impeded by a lack of revenue in developing countries, and WTO commitments may constrain the ability of the government to impose protectionist measures.[21]

Wider events and the behaviour of external factors

The analysis thus far has concentrated on the nature of the domestic economy and the behaviour of the domestic government; however, in reality, an important caveat must be highlighted: the effects of trade on poverty alleviation will also be highly dependent upon events outside of the country itself. Such events will, for developing countries in particular, be difficult to influence as their bargaining power vis-à-vis TNCs, inter-governmental organisations (IGOs) and foreign governments will be relatively weak and their impact upon world prices relatively limited. Moreover, the smaller the economic might of a nation, the more sensitive to world price conditions it will be.

A pertinent example is provided by the case of developed country agricultural subsidies and import barriers, which distort international prices to the detriment of many developing countries.[22] Myriad authors, such as Anderson, Martin and Van Der Mensbrugghe (2006), Tokarick (2005) and Hoekman, Ng and Ollarreaga (2004), have provided empirical estimates of the benefits to developing countries of the removal of these barriers, and have found that, in general, such liberalisation would provide net welfare gains to most developing countries.[23] Negotiation regarding these barriers takes place within the WTO; however, from the numerous deadlocks that have plagued WTO meetings throughout the Doha Development Agenda, it is clear that small countries struggle to convince larger countries to liberalise these barriers by as much as they would like.

Furthermore, as has already been mentioned, world prices can move in ways unfavourable to developing countries following liberalisation by their competitors, for example China. In the case of China, the nature of

---

[21] It is important to note, however, that WTO jurisprudence allows countries to impose temporary protectionist measures known as 'safeguard measures' to protect industries from unexpected build-ups of imports.

[22] For a comprehensive survey of the use, and effects, of subsidies, see WTO (2006).

[23] Some net-food importers would, however, suffer.

its recent liberalisation process was partly determined by the WTO accession procedure, which is again an area where the impact of developing
countries is limited by their relatively weak bargaining power. Similarly,
countries that were harmed by the end of the MFA were those that were
not subject to MFA restrictions, i.e. those that enjoyed preferential access
to developed country textile markets. As these countries were outside
of the MFA, the removal of restrictions on textile trade was also largely
outside of their control.

Policy conclusions

Box D lists the factors connecting trade with policy alleviation identified
in this paper under four headings: the effects via prices and government spending, via wages and employment, via the adaptability of the
economy and the efficiency of markets and via growth. The 'effect upon
growth' section is further divided into the effect upon growth through
technological improvements, inequality, volatility and the effect of growth
upon poverty alleviation. Given the interrelated nature of many of these
factors, some appear under several headings. For example, volatility will
affect prices, wages and growth, and so the factors underpinning volatility
appear under all three of these headings. Similarly, the effect of institutions permeates the entire economy and, as such, this factor is also listed
under every heading.

   In evaluating whether trade liberalisation will facilitate poverty alleviation in a specific context, policy makers must take consideration of all four
channels listed in Box D. In considering poverty alleviation via the effect of
trade liberalisation on prices, governments must assess the relevance of all
the factors under this heading. The majority of these are within the ambit
of government authority/control, and thus policy makers have some scope
for ex-ante improving the poverty-alleviating potential of liberalisation.
For example, by cutting red tape at customs and by investing in infrastructure, governments can reduce the costs of trade. Moreover, implementing
pro-competitive policies and reducing corruption in any remaining state
trading enterprises can help to mediate the pass-through of beneficial
price effects to households. However, post-liberalisation intervention in
the form of redistribution may still be required if trade ostracises poor
groups within the economy either through the erosion of certain markets or through the losses to import-competing industries. On the other
hand, the extent of second-round effects is something over which governments will have relatively less control. Nevertheless, policies designed to

BOX D   FACTORS DETERMINING TRADE-INDUCED EFFECTS ON
POVERTY ALLEVIATION

Via prices and government spending
- the trade policy of the government
- the nature of trade agreement commitments
- the pattern of protection and the nature of trade liberalisation
- the relative factor abundances between the trading partners
- the relative level of technical knowledge of the trading partners
- the efficiency of customs administration
- price regulations
- the quality of infrastructure
- the strength of institutions
- the nature of intermediate organisations in the distribution chain
- the completeness of markets
- the nature of non-trade taxation and spending policies
- the extent to which extra income is spent on local industries
- the combined impact on the poor of the liberalisation of many different goods
- the availability of output and price insurance
- the ability of the government to utilise countercyclical policies

Via wages and employment
- the nature of competition in the labour market
- the relative factor abundances between the trading partners
- the relative level of technical knowledge of the trading partners
- the pattern of protection and the nature of trade liberalisation
- the level of unemployment prior to liberalisation
- the efficiency of factor markets
- the strength of institutions
- the availability of output and price insurance
- the ability of the government to utilise countercyclical policies

Via the adaptability of the economy and the efficiency of markets
- the stock of human capital
- the effectiveness of factor markets
- the quality of infrastructure
- the strength of institutions
- the completeness of markets
- the mobility of capital both domestically and from abroad
- the level of volatility

Via growth: through technological improvements
- the relative level of technical knowledge of the trading partners
- the ability of the country to attract FDI

- the ratio of vertical linkages versus displaced firms arising from FDI
- the stock of human capital
- the level of R&D in the host country
- the availability of capital, credit and risk-sharing
- the availability of information
- the strength of institutions

Via growth: through inequality
- the initial level of inequality
- the strength of institutions
- the relative factor abundances between the trading partners
- the relative level of technical knowledge of the trading partners
- the pattern of protection and the nature of trade liberalisation

Via growth: through volatility
- the availability of output and price insurance
- the strength of institutions
- the ability of the government to utilise countercyclical policies

Via growth: through the effect of growth upon poverty alleviation
- the stock of human capital
- the strength of institutions
- the quality of infrastructure
- the level of volatility

encourage spending on local industries can mediate the diffusion of the benefits of trade-induced price movements throughout the wider economy. It is important to note that the combined impact on the poor of the liberalisation of many different goods will be highly complicated, and thus in-depth analysis must be undertaken in order to design an optimal liberalisation strategy. Moreover, governments must take into consideration the impact of external events and the behaviour of foreign factors. Whilst governments have little control over these factors, they can attempt to counteract any adverse effects engendered by them.

The effect upon wages and employment of trade liberalisation is ambiguous and depends upon factors that are largely immune to government intervention, at least in the short term. For example, the level of competition in the labour force is dependent upon the size of the working population, and the relative level of technical knowledge of trading partners is for the most part exogenous (especially if the country in question is a WTO member, in which case discriminating between trading partners is prohibited under the Most Favoured Nation principle). However, governments can take these factors into consideration when engaging in liberalisation, such that highly protected industries, which support poorer members of society, are given more time to accommodate the impact of reductions in trade barriers. Moreover, there is much that governments can do to prepare their economies for the impact of liberalisation, and then much that they can do in the medium to longer term to ameliorate any negative effects.

The adaptability of an economy and the efficiency of its markets are perhaps the most important elements linking trade liberalisation with poverty alleviation. Trade liberalisation does not necessarily lead to increased trade flows; a healthy environment for trade must exist for liberalisation to be effective. Moreover, if an economy does not respond to trade effectively, then the benefits of trade may not emerge. Adaptability, efficiency and stability are also necessary to foster an environment for growth, especially growth that is pro-poor. Fortunately, these are areas where policy makers have a lot of scope for making improvements. As noted earlier, institutional quality is essential for adaptability, and is highly correlated with trade. Thus, government policies to reduce corruption and promote the protection of property rights and the enforcement of contracts will tend to improve the volume of trade in a country. Furthermore, providing education and training will allow workers to shift into industries where they are needed most, and will facilitate the diffusion of technical knowledge. Similarly, providing a stable platform for forward planning vis-à-vis sound macroeconomic management not only acts as a catalyst for growth but also dampens volatility that is particularly deleterious for the poor.

Technological improvement requires more than just sufficient human capital; it requires R&D, FDI, access to resources and insurance, effective information dissemination and, in some cases, the stimulus provided by foreign competition. These are all areas where governments can play a role. For example, governments can subsidise early adopters of new technology in order to create examples that other producers can follow. They can also distribute information regarding new technology and techniques to small-scale producers who do not have access to such information themselves. They can provide insurance to protect early adopters of new technology against the risk that such technologies bring, and they can provide financial incentives for R&D to bolster the adoption of foreign technology.

The literature regarding the trade-inequality-growth relationship suggests that the effects of trade are particularly context-specific in this regard. In some situations, trade may increase inequality; in others, it may diminish it. Similarly, in some situations, increasing inequality may be a stimulus for growth; in others, it may discourage growth. Thus, governments have a role to play in assessing the extent to which inequality is or is not desirable, and should tailor liberalisation accordingly.

The effects of volatility permeate the economy. A volatile economy can act as an impediment to growth, yet increased volatility is a likely outcome from trade liberalisation. Thus, governments must decide to what extent their economies can handle volatility before engaging in liberalisation.

As was noted earlier, much evidence suggests that the key to long-run poverty alleviation is economic growth, yet growth must be pro-poor in order for this to happen. Whilst some authors find that growth in general will automatically lead to poverty alleviation, others posit that good education, infrastructure, institutions and macroeconomic stability must be in place for the poor to be able to take advantage of trade-induced growth. All of these factors can be affected by the government, and thus a poverty-minded government will have a role to play in these areas as well.

It is important to note that the implementation of the policies discussed in this section is constrained by the resources at the disposal of governments. Given that developing country governments are particularly resource-constrained, a useful endeavour for future research would be the establishment of a ranking of the importance of each of these policies.

Conclusion

The economic literature on the subject of the connections between trade and poverty alleviation is voluminous, and that which is reviewed here and the factors listed in Box D are by no means exhaustive. Moreover, there are multiple avenues for future research that will undoubtedly add to the existing stock of knowledge on this subject. Nevertheless, it is possible to draw a number of conclusions at this stage. First and foremost is the fact that the effects of trade are highly context-specific; a notion evidenced by the myriad factors documented in Box D. Trade can influence poverty through its effects upon: product prices, wages, employment, government revenues, inequality, volatility and, above all, economic growth. Underlying these channels are multiple interrelated contributory factors.

The majority of these factors pertain to country characteristics, and thus detailed micro-level analysis is necessary to ascertain the likely outcomes from trade liberalisation in each individual case.

If governments have discretion over the nature and timing of liberalisation, then by considering the unique position of their country vis-à-vis the factors documented here, they can tailor liberalisation to maximise poverty alleviation. However, numerous policies can be implemented pre- and post-liberalisation that can galvanise the pro-poor effects of trade. One of the most important objectives of such policies should be to cultivate an adaptable, efficient and stable market system capable of capturing the benefits of trade, withstanding the adjustments it necessarily involves and reacting appropriately to the external events that trade necessarily exposes a nation to. Not only does this foster an environment suitable for the shifting of resources in accordance with a nation's comparative advantage and facilitate economic growth, but it is more likely to prevent the alienation of the poor. In order to achieve this objective, governments must build strong institutions, eliminate corruption, increase competition, provide adequate infrastructure and assist markets where they fail. In addition to providing sound fundamentals, government policy can also act as a catalyst to the beneficial effects of trade. For example, governments can endeavour to attract FDI, especially FDI embodying more advanced technology than is currently available in the economy. Similarly, governments can encourage the adoption of new technology by providing financial incentives and disseminating information.

Finally, whilst the discipline of economics generally champions the merits of trade as a force for alleviating poverty, it cautions against being overzealous; trade requires adjustments that will inevitably harm some members of society. As such, governments will have a role to play in compensating those that have been hurt by trade and helping them to adapt to the post-liberalisation economy. Essentially, trade has great potential for alleviating poverty, but its beneficial effects are not guaranteed. Country-specific factors, along with international conditions, must be considered in determining appropriate policies for trade-led growth that is capable of reducing poverty.

References

Acemoglu, D., Johnson, S. and Robinson, J. (2001), 'The Colonial Origins of Comparative Development: An Empirical Investigation', *American Economic Review* 91(5): 1369–401.

Addison, T. and Cornia, G. A. (2001), 'Income Distribution Policies for Faster Poverty Reduction', UNU-WIDER Discussion Paper 2001/93.

Anderson, K., Martin, W. J. and Van Der Mensbrugghe, D. (2006), 'Would Multilateral Trade Reforms Benefit Sub-Saharan Africa?', *Journal of African Economies* 15(4): 626–70.

Bacchetta, M. and Jansen, M. (2003), *WTO Special Studies 7. Adjusting to Trade Liberalization: The Role of Policy, Institutions and WTO Disciplines*, WTO: Geneva, Switzerland.

Baldwin, R. E. (2003), 'Openness and Growth: What's the Empirical Relationship?', NBER Working Paper 9578, National Bureau of Economic Research.

Barro, R. J. and Sala-i-martin, X. (1995), *Economic Growth*, McGraw-Hill: New York, NY.

Benjamin, D., Brandt, L. and Giles, J. (2006), 'Inequality and Growth in Rural China: Does Higher Inequality Impede Growth?', *University of Toronto Working Paper*, available at: www.economics.utoronto.ca/benjamin/BBG2.pdf [last accessed 2 February 2009].

Bhagwati, J. and Srinivasan, T. N. (2002), 'Trade and Poverty in Developing Countries', *American Economic Review* 92(2): 180–3.

Bigsten, A., Collier, P., Dercon, S., Fafchamps, M., Gauthier, B., Gunning, J. W., Oduro, A., Oostendorp, R., Patillo, C., Söderbom, M., Teal, F. and Zeufack, A. (1999), 'Adjustment Costs, Irreversibility and Investment Patterns in African Manufacturing', IMF Working Paper WP/99/99, International Monetary Fund: Washington, WA.

Borensztein, E., De Gregorio, J. and Lee, J.-W. (1998), 'How Does Foreign Direct Investment Affect Economic Growth?', *Journal of International Economics* 45: 115–35.

Cline, W. R. (2004), *Trade Policy and Global Poverty*, Center for Global Development and Institute for International Economics: Washington, WA.

Corden, W. M. (1997), *Trade Policy and Economic Welfare*, Clarendon Press: Oxford.

Cornia, G. A. (ed.) (2004), *Inequality, Growth and Poverty in an Era of Liberalization and Globalization*, Oxford University Press for UNU-WIDER: Oxford.

CUTS (1999), 'Conditions Necessary for the Liberalization of Trade and Investment to Reduce Poverty', Final report to DfID. Cited in Winters (2000, 2002).

Davidson, C. and Matusz, S. J. (2000), 'Globalization and Labour Market Adjustment: How Fast and at What Cost?', *Oxford Review of Economic Policy*, 16(3): 42–56.

de Soto, H. (2000), *The Mystery of Capital: Why Capitalism Triumphs in the West and Fails Everywhere Else*, Basic Books: New York, NY.

Delgado, C., Hopkins, J. and Kelly, V. (1998), 'Agricultural Growth Linkages in Sub-Saharan Africa', Research Report No. 107, International Food Policy Research Institute: Washington, WA.

Dollar, D. (1992), 'Outward Oriented Economies Really Do Grow More Rapidly: Evidence from 95 LDCs, 1976–1985', *Economic Development and Cultural Change* 40(3): 523–44.

Easterly, W. and Levine, R. (2001), 'What Have We Learned from a Decade of Empirical Research On Growth? It's not Factor Accumulation: Stylized Facts and Growth Models', *World Bank Economic Review* 15(2): 177–219.

Ebrill, L., Stotsky, J. and Gropp, R. (1999), 'Revenue Implications of Trade Liberalization', IMF Occasional Paper 180, International Monetary Fund: Washington, WA.

Edwards, S. (1998), 'Openness, Productivity and Growth: What Do We Really Know?', *Economic Journal* 108(447): 383–98.

Euysung, K. (2000), 'Trade Liberalization and Productivity Growth in Korean Manufacturing Industries: Price Protection, Market Power and Scale Efficiency', *Journal of Development Economics* 62(1): 55–83.

Fernandes, A. M. (2003), 'Trade Policy, Trade Volumes and Plant Level Productivity in Colombian Manufacturing Industries', Policy Research Working Paper 3064, World Bank.

Francoise, J. and Manchin, M. (2007), 'Institutions, Infrastructure and Growth', CEPR Discussion Paper 6068, Centre for Economic Policy Research.

Grossman, G. M. and Helpman, E. (1991), *Innovation and Growth in the Global Economy*, MIT Press: Cambridge, MA.

(1995), 'Technology and Trade', in G. M. Grossman and E. Helpman. (eds.), *Handbook of International Economics*, vol. III, Elsevier Science: Amsterdam.

Hanson, G. H. and Harrison, A. E. (1999), 'Trade Liberalization and Wage Inequality in Mexico', *Industrial and Labour Relations Review* 52(2): 271–88.

Harrison, A. E. (1994), 'Productivity, Imperfect Competition and Trade Reform: Theory and Evidence', *Journal of International Economics* 36(1–2): 53–73.

Hnatkovska, V. and Loayza, N. (2005), 'Volatility and Growth', in J. Aizenman and B. Pinto (eds.), *Managing Economic Volatility and Crises: A Practitioner's Guide*, Cambridge University Press: New York, NY, pp. 65–100.

Hoekman, B., Ng, F. and Olarreaga, M. (2004), 'Agricultural Tariffs or Subsidies: Which are More Important for Developing Countries?', World Bank Economic Review 18(2): 175–204.

Holmes, T. J. and Schmitz Jr., J. A. (2001), 'A Gain from Trade: From Unproductive to Productive Entrepreneurship', *Journal of Monetary Economics* 47(2): 417–46.

Institute for International Trade (2006), 'Study of Uneven Growth within the APEC Economies', University of Adelaide: Adelaide.

Institute for International Trade and the Pacific Trade Consult (2007), 'The Potential Impact of PICTA on Smaller Forum Island Nations', University of Adelaide: Adelaide.

Jansen, M. and Hildegunn, N. (2004), 'Institutions, Trade Policy and Trade Flows', CEPR Discussion Paper 4418, Centre for Economic Policy Research.

Kaldor, N. (1956), 'Alternative Theories of Distribution', *Review of Economic Studies* 23(2): 83–100.

Keller, W. (1996), 'Absorptive Capacity: On the Creation and Acquisition of Technology in Development', *Journal of Development Economics* 49: 199–227.

(2000), 'Do Trade Patterns and Technology Flows Affect Productivity Growth?', *World Bank Economic Review* 14(1): 17–47.

Khalid, S. and Pierre-Guillaume, M. (2006), 'Institutional Quality and Trade: Which Institutions? Which Trade', Université Libre de Bruxelles, Department of Applied Economics (DULBEA) Working Paper 06–06.RS.

Kim, S.-J. and Kim, Y-J. (2000), 'Growth Gains from Trade and Education', *Journal of International Economics* 50: 519–45.

Kose, M. A., Prasad, E. S. and Terrones, M. E. (2006), 'How do Trade and Financial Integration Affect the Relationship between Growth and Volatility?', *Journal of International Economics* 69(1): 176–202.

Krishna, P. and Mitra, D. (1998), 'Trade Liberalization, Market Discipline And Productivity Growth: New Evidence From India', *Journal of Development Economics* 56(2): 447–62.

Laursen, T. and Mahajan, S. (2005), 'Volatility, Income Distribution, and Poverty', in J. Aizenman and B. Pinto (eds.), *Managing Economic Volatility and Crises: A Practitioner's Guide*, Cambridge University Press: New York, NY, pp. 101–37.

Levinsohn, J. (1993), 'Testing the Imports-As-Market-Discipline Hypothesis', *Journal of International Economics* 35(1–2): 1–22.

Lewis, W. A. (1954), 'Economic Development with Unlimited Supplies of Labour', Manchester School; reprinted in A. Agarwala and S. Singh (eds.) (1975), *The Economics of Underdevelopment*, Oxford University Press: Delhi.

Little, I., Scitovsky, T. and Scott, M. (1970), *Industry and Trade in Some Developing Countries: A Comparative Study*, Oxford University Press: London.

Lopez, J. H. (2005), 'Pro-poor Growth: A Review of What We Know (and What We Don't)', PREM Poverty Group Paper, World Bank, available at: http://siteresources.worldbank.org/INTPGI/Resources/15163_ppg_review .pdf [last accessed 2 February 2009].

Lutz, M. and Singer, H. W. (1994), 'The Link between Increased Trade Openness and the Terms of Trade: An Empirical Investigation', *World Development* 22: 1697–709.

Manasse, P. and Turrini, A. (2001), 'Trade, Wages, and "Superstars"', *Journal of International Economics* 54(1): 97–117.

Markusen, J. R. (2000), 'Foreign Direct Investment', CIES Working Paper 19, Centre for International Economic Studies.

Marouani, M. A. (2007), 'Is the End of the MFA a Threat to the Tunisian Economy?', DIAL Working Paper DT/2007/05.

Matusz, S. J. and Tarr, D. (1999), 'Adjusting to Trade Policy Reform', Policy Research Working Paper 2142, World Bank.

Mayer, J. (2002), 'The Fallacy of Composition: A Review of the Literature', *The World Economy* 25(6): 875–94.

McMillan, M., Rodrik, D. and Welch, K. H. (2002), 'When Economic Reform Goes Wrong: Cashews in Mozambique', NBER Working Paper 9117, National Bureau of Economic Research.

Mellor, J. W. and Gavian, S. (1999), 'The Determinants of Employment Growth in Egypt: The Dominant Role of Agriculture and the Rural Small Scale Sector', Impact Assessment Report No. 7, Abt Associates Inc.

Newberry, D. M. G. and Stiglitz, J. E. (1984), 'Pareto Inferior Trade', *Review of Economic Studies* 51: 1–12.

Nissanke, M. and Thorbecke, E. (2007), 'Channels and Policy Debate in the Globalization-Inequality-Poverty Nexus', in M. Nissanke and E. Thorbecke (eds.), *The Impact of Globalization on the World's Poor*, Palgrave MacMillan for UNU-WIDER: New York, NY, pp. 23–55.

North, D. (1991), 'Institutions', *Journal of Economic Perspectives* 5(1): 97–112.

Oxfam-IDS (1999), 'Liberalization and Poverty', Final Report to DfiD. Cited in Winters (2000, 2002).

Pallage, S. and Robe, M. A. (2003), 'On the Welfare Cost of Economic Fluctuations in Developing Countries', *International Economic Review* 44(2): 677–98.

Ramey, G. and Ramey, V. A. (1995), 'Cross-Country Evidence on the Link between Volatility and Growth', *American Economic Review* 85: 1138–51.

Ravallion, M. (1994), *Poverty Comparisons*, Harwood Academic Publishers: Chur, Switzerland.

Robbins, D. (1996), 'HOS Hits Facts: Facts Win; Evidence on Trade and Wages in the Developing World', Development Discussion Paper 557, Harvard Institute for International Development, Harvard University.

Rodriguez, F. and Rodrik, D. (2001), 'Trade Policy and Economic Growth: A Skeptic's Guide to the Cross-National Evidence', in B. S. Bernanke and K. Rogoff (eds.), *NBER Macroeconomics Annual 2000*, MIT Press: Cambridge, MA.

Ruffin, R. and Gregory, P. (1990), *Principles of Microeconomics*, 4th edition, Scott Foresman: Glenview, IL.

Sachs, J. D. and Warner, A. M. (1995), 'Economic Convergence and Economic Policies', *Brookings Papers on Economic Activity* 1: 1–95.

Saggi, K. (2002), 'Trade, Foreign Direct Investment and International Technology Transfer', *World Bank Research Observer* 17(2): 191–235.

Sindzingre, A. (2007), 'Explaining Threshold Effects of Globalization on Poverty: An Institutional Perspective', in M. Nissanke and E. Thorbecke (eds.), *The Impact of Globalization on the World's Poor*, Palgrave MacMillan for UNU-WIDER: New York, NY, pp. 271–99.

Slaughter, M. (2000), 'Trade and Labour-Market Outcomes: What About Developing Countries?', Paper prepared for NBER Inter-American Seminar on Economics, National Bureau of Economic Research.

Stiglitz, J. (2003), *Globalization and Its Discontents*, W. W. Norton & Company, Inc.: New York, NY.

Thorbecke, E. and Charumilind, C. (2002), 'Economic Inequality and its Socioeconomic Impact', *World Development*, September: 1485–98.

Timmer, P. (1997), 'How Well Do the Poor Connect to the Growth Process?', CAER Discussion Paper 17, Harvard Institute of International Development, Harvard University.

Tokarick, S. (2005), 'Who Bears the Costs of Agricultural Support in OECD Countries?', *The World Economy* 28(4): 573–93.

Tybout, J. R. and Westbrook, M. D. (1995), 'Trade Liberalization and the Dimensions of Efficiency Change in Mexican Manufacturing Industries', *Journal of International Economics* 39(1–2): 53–78.

Wilson, J. S., Mann, C. L. and Otsuki, T. (2004), 'Assessing the Benefit of Trade Facilitation: A Global Perspective', Policy Research Working Paper 3224, World Bank.

Winters, L. A. (2000), 'Trade and Poverty: Is There a Connection?', in *WTO Special Studies 5: Trade, Income Disparity and Poverty*, pp. 43–69.

 (2002), 'Trade Liberalization and Poverty: What Are the Links?', *The World Economy* 25: 1339–67.

Winters, L. A., McCulloch, N. and McKay, A. (2004), 'Trade Liberalization and Poverty: The Evidence So Far', *Journal of Economic Literature* 42: 72–115.

Women's Edge Coalition and CAFRA (2004), 'The Effects of Trade Liberalization on Jamaica's Poor', available at: www.iiav.nl/epublications//2004/EFFECTS_OF_TRADE.pdf [last accessed 2 February 2009].

Wood, A. (1994), *North-South Trade, Employment and Inequality: Changing Fortunes in a Skill-Driven World*, Clarendon Press: Oxford.

 (1997), 'Openness and Wage Inequality in Developing Countries: The Latin American Challenge to East Asian Conventional Wisdom', *World Bank Economic Review* 11(1): 33–57.

World Bank (1997), *Global Economic Prospects and the Developing Countries*, World Bank: Washington, WA.

 (2000/2001), *World Development Report 2000/2001: Attacking Poverty*, World Bank: Washington, WA.

 (2001), *Arab Republic of Egypt toward Agricultural Competitiveness in the 21st Century: An Agricultural Export-Oriented Strategy*, Report 23405-EGT, World Bank: Washington, WA.

WTO (2006), *World Trade Report 2006. Subsidies, Trade and the WTO*, World Trade Organization: Geneva, Switzerland.

(2007), *World Trade Report 2007. Sixty Years of the Multilateral Trading System: Achievements and Challenges*, World Trade Organization: Geneva, Switzerland.

Xu, B. (2000), 'Multinational Enterprises, Technology Diffusion, and Host Country Productivity Growth', *Journal of Development Economics* 62(2): 477–93.

Zhao, J. (2007), 'The Role of Information in Technology Adoption under Poverty', in M. Nissanke and E. Thorbecke (eds.), *The Impact of Globalization on the World's Poor*, Palgrave MacMillan for UNU-WIDER: New York, NY, pp. 191–203.

Zhu, S. C. and Trefler, D. (2005), 'Trade and Inequality in Developing Countries: A General Equilibrium Analysis', *Journal of International Economics* 65(1): 21–48.

I

Transnational corporations, trade and
poverty reduction

Transnational corporations and the global supply chain

ANDREW L. STOLER[*]

Introduction

Accounts differ, but it is probably right to say that there are between 63,000 and 77,000 transnational corporations (TNCs) driving today's global economy. TNCs' presence and influence are felt everywhere from New York to Bangalore to Nairobi, by people in all walks of life, by wealthy shareholders and assembly-line workers earning the minimum wage. TNCs dominate world production, foreign direct investment (FDI) and international distribution networks. Their assets and revenues are sometimes compared (usually incorrectly) with small nations' gross domestic product (GDP). Such comparisons are utterly misleading because those making them usually confuse the gross sales of the companies with countries' GDP.[1]

Transnationals are praised by those who maintain that they are efficient at creating new employment opportunities in developing countries and at serving as the link between local businesses and overseas markets that these businesses might not otherwise access, and that they are an important source of technology transfer to host countries. TNCs are also the principal targets of anti-globalisation critics. Some argue that TNCs are associated with environmental degradation, abuse of labour rights and exploitatively low wages, and that their activities are damaging to the prospects for sustainable growth in poorer regions of the world. We

[*] Andrew L. Stoler is Executive Director of the Institute for International Trade at the University of Adelaide, and former WTO Deputy Director-General. The author is deeply appreciative of the comments and drafting suggestions on this chapter provided to him by Professor Prema-Chandra Athukorala of the Australian National University.
[1] As Martin Wolf points out (Martin Wolf (2004), *Why Globalization Works*, Yale University Press: New Haven, CT, p. 222), using a value-added GDP-style approach to measuring the economic importance of companies in order to equate them with national GDP figures dramatically reduces the relative importance of corporate activity.

have all seen the sweatshop accusations by critics of TNCs. In China, TNCs have contributed to the huge FDI flows that have powered the economy at a white-hot rate of growth, but some economists argue that manufacturing in China is a modern example of immiserising growth.

This overview chapter will examine the extent to which the efforts of TNCs to spread their production-sharing arrangements have contributed positively or not to the reduction of poverty. In this chapter, we will look at TNCs and their production-sharing arrangements and some theories on why these are created and their effects. We will also canvass the role of FDI and who is investing where. The chapter will review the recent history of economic growth and poverty reduction with a focus on the Asia-Pacific region, and will consider aspects of a framework through which we might analyse the impact of TNCs on poverty. Related to that framework, the chapter will look briefly at some of the hot issues for TNCs in the area of corporate social responsibility (CSR). Before leading in to the more detailed case studies written for this section of the book, we will discuss public and private policies that seem to help harness the gains of TNC activity for the benefit of poorer and disadvantaged communities.

TNCs in the global economy: background and context

Agents of change?

Writing in *Yale Global Online*,[2] George C. Lodge and Craig Wilson argue that poverty reduction can only be achieved with the active involvement of TNCs for two reasons: (i) economic growth and poverty reduction depend on business growth, and TNCs facilitate access to those things local business needs to grow but might not otherwise be able to find – like technology, credit and access to global markets; and (ii) TNCs can be a powerful force for the systemic changes often required in developing countries before business and workers can flourish. Lodge and Wilson believe that TNCs help to bring on needed change through their contribution to local infrastructure, their leverage on local governments to lift their game and their ability to help empower youth – who often have little hope for good jobs or longer term opportunities before TNCs arrive on the scene. The contributions of the TNCs might be particularly significant in previously mismanaged and poorly governed countries. (There is considerable literature that backs the view that the prospect of good

---

[2] 'Multinational Corporations: A Key to Global Poverty Reduction – Part I' (2 January 2006).

governance/policy transparency is a key factor that determines the attractiveness to TNCs of a given country.) And official aid only rarely contributes to the creation of the kind of sustained employment that results from a TNC's investment in the country. Lodge and Wilson argue for the creation of a World Development Corporation that would have TNCs and international intergovernmental organisations like the UN work together in practical ways to marry the profit-related interests of the TNCs with the poverty reduction programmes of the organisations.

If only large TNCs have the resources, technology and reach to bring about sustainable economic growth and poverty reduction, what about the charge that they make profits through exploitation of poor workers, poorly paid in poor countries? We will address aspects of this question in a bit more depth later in this chapter. However, in its essence, it is a question that Martin Wolf addresses forthrightly in his book *Why Globalisation Works*. Wolf writes that it is important to realise that there are two answers to the question: yes and no.

> The 'yes' answer is that the business of any company is to look for opportunities to turn something cheap into something more expensive. It is, in other words, to add value. The better it is at identifying opportunities and knowing how to add value when it has identified them, the more successful a company will be. One of those opportunities is to use resources (including people) that have historically fallen outside the global economy and are, correspondingly, cheap. If it is operating in a competitive economy, however, a company will find it impossible to keep the gains to itself. It will have to share them with its suppliers, its workers and its customers. No doubt it will prefer not to do so. But if it fails to do this, its suppliers, workers and customers will go elsewhere and, in the end, it will go out of business.
>
> The 'no' answer is, however, more important than the 'yes' one. It is not true that most of the opportunities transnationals find to exploit are in poor countries. On the contrary, as we will see, they are finding too few. The difficulty facing most poor countries is that they – or, more accurately, the opportunities their poverty would appear to offer – are not being exploited enough. It is also not true that, when opportunities are exploited in poor countries, their citizens are made worse off thereby. Economic life is about beneficial mutual exploitation or, if one wishes to describe it more benignly, about playing positive sum games. It is right to say that transnational companies exploit their Chinese workers in the hope of making profits. It is equally right to say that Chinese workers are exploiting transnationals in the (almost universally fulfilled) hope of obtaining higher pay, better training and more opportunities that would otherwise be available to them.[3]

[3] Wolf, *Why Globalization Works*, p. 230.

Transnational corporations and production-sharing arrangements

Before a TNC can begin operations in a developing country, it needs to set up an affiliated company (a fully owned affiliate or a joint venture) or it needs to enter into a contract with a locally established firm that will become part of its supply chain. The decision to make an investment in new manufacturing or supplying relationships cannot be taken lightly, because the consequences of a bad decision can be extremely costly to the TNC and its shareholders. An important part of this overview is a look at why TNCs decide to make these investments in foreign manufacturing in developing countries, and why some countries are more favoured as locations than others. There are a number of questions to ask here, and many of them bear eventually on the bigger question we are addressing in this section of the book (whether and how TNC activities contribute to poverty reduction). Is a TNC investment in a poor developing country made for the purpose of serving the local market or is it primarily about dividing up production to take advantage of different locations' ability to produce components at the cheapest cost? Does it matter in which sector the TNC is operating? TNCs in mining and extractive industries seem to have the most negative reputations. Are we talking about manufacturing that involves labour-intensive assembly operations and, if so, at which price point does the relative advantage shift from one location to another? Do tax issues and/or local government incentives play a big role in the decisions of the TNCs? What about labour and environmental standards?

For the past several years, China[4] has been by far the largest recipient of FDI in the developing world, raking in US$79 billion in 2005. This level of FDI going to China is so much greater than that which has been flowing to other developing countries in the region – including India – that it is worthy of study in itself. According to World Bank researchers,[5] the number of people in China living in absolute poverty declined by 400 million in the twenty-year period to 2001. Given China's welcoming attitude toward FDI in this period, there is at least a prima facie argument here that TNCs and their investments in manufacturing have contributed positively to poverty reduction. Many operations in China are linked to supply chains that stretch often to several other countries in Southeast

---

[4] China itself is now a major provider of FDI, particularly in Africa where Chinese TNCs are active in mining and extractive industries as well as the garment sector.

[5] Shaohua Chen and Martin Ravallion (2005), *How Have the World's Poor Fared Since the Early 1980s?* Development Research Group, World Bank.

Asia, so we would expect to see a spillover effect of TNC activities into those economies as well. If there are positive impacts on poverty, are they likely to be sustainable over time?

In an article appearing in the *Economist* on 20 January 2007,[6] the author explored both the traditional explanations and theories of why TNCs move some production to offshore locations, as well as some interesting new ideas about the competitive forces that motivate the creation of international supply chains. In effect, technological developments, particularly since the late nineteenth century, have spurred changes in the way corporations have approached the production and distribution of the goods and services they sell. At first, a dramatic fall in the cost of transportation made it both feasible and profitable to produce at locations far away from where final products were destined to be consumed. In some sectors, this contributed to TNCs' decisions to move entire factories or production lines overseas, where the advantage of producing in a cheaper location outweighed the increased cost of transporting the goods to market. In the second half of the twentieth century, advances in technology (particularly in communications and information technologies) dramatically improved TNCs' ability to coordinate and track production of products over a far-flung network, obviating the need to keep different manufacturing stages in close proximity to each other. Economists refer to these technology-initiated changed ways of behaving as an 'unbundling' of the production process.

What distinguishes the modern phase of unbundling from the first phase is that what is going on now is the segregation of production by tasks. Modern TNC supply chains are based more and more on the location of tasks where they can be most efficiently performed. It might make sense for a silicon wafer to be produced in Vietnam, a motherboard in Singapore and final assembly of a product to take place in China. Among other things, this has important implications for the ability of important sectors of even a developed country economy to remain competitive. As the *Economist* article points out, because they have moved their assembly lines to China, where cheaper labour and component costs help to keep prices lower for the final product, Japanese electronics companies are able to continue to flourish in the American market. Whether it is characterised as slicing up the value chain, off-shoring, vertical specialisation or production fragmentation, today's unbundling activities – which

[6] 'Economic Focus: The Great Unbundling – Does Economics Need a New Theory of Offshoring?', *Economist*, 20 January 2007, p. 86.

increasingly are found in services as well as goods production – are changing the way TNCs make their decisions about investment and production
in the developing world.

One economist who has done a considerable amount of work on production fragmentation and its influence on trade and investment patterns
in Asia is Prema-Chandra Athukorala at the Australian National University in Canberra. Athukorala has written extensively about the reasons for
production fragmentation in East Asia and its consequences for economic
development in countries in the region. In his studies, he points out that
fragmentation-based trade is far more important and is growing more
rapidly in East Asia than elsewhere, but that because the phenomenon
is not properly understood, many people draw the wrong inferences
about regional trade, the relative importance of global markets and also
the extent to which participation in a supply-chain network necessarily
implies involvement in a sophisticated, high value-added manufacturing
process.

Earlier, international specialisation within a TNC would normally have
taken the form of a company building a facility abroad that might produce some parts to be used in its vertically integrated manufacturing
process. Trade in the essentially 'in-house' parts and components had a
direct relationship to the TNC's FDI. This pattern is changing. Instead
of producing all of what it needs for the supply chain in the local subsidiary of the TNC, the subsidiaries now often subcontract with local
host-country firms. There can be an important technology-transfer element here, as the TNC will often need to supply the local firm with some
of its production technology as well as detailed specifications in order to
obtain the quality it needs from the subcontractor. In addition, because
today many parts used in the production process have effectively become
what Athukorala calls 'standard fragments', it is often possible for TNCs
to use independent contract manufacturers in their established supply
chains. Over the past four decades, researchers have seen these TNC production networks – based on a complex trade in product fragments –
expand from their origins in the clothing and electronics industries and
spread into a wide range of industries including power and machine
tools, cameras and watches, automobiles, sport footwear, televisions and
radio receivers, office equipment, sewing machines and even printing and
publishing.

The operation of these international supply chains through trade
in product fragments has been the object of some very interesting
analysis by Athukorala. In a soon to be published chapter of a new

book,[7] he points out that the share of components in total intra-regional exports in the ASEAN Free Trade Area (AFTA)[8] countries increased from 89.1% in 1992 to 92.3% in 2004. On the import side, the increase was from 75.3% to 84.4%. The regional share of total Chinese imports of components increased over this period from 37.6% to 77.7%. Athukorala points out that the most notable development in China's import trade over this period was the rapid growth of the combined share of AFTA countries, from a mere 0.9% in 1992 to 19.3% in 2004. Are these trade patterns indicative of an increase in two-way trade of a type that supports regional economic integration theories?

Apparently not. A look at the pattern of China's export trade shows a dramatically different story:

> On the export side, China's aggregate intra-regional share has declined persistently in both total manufacturing and component exports. Overall, China's evolving export patterns exhibit a clear and increasing extra-regional bias, in contrast to greater regional integration on the import side. This difference reflects the increasingly important role for China as a final product assembler for advanced country markets using middle products procured from the region. Since about the mid-1990's, China's net imports from countries in developing East Asia have increasingly exceeded its exports to those countries. The main reason for this trade deficit has been China's increasing reliance on countries in the region for parts and components for its booming final-goods assembly activities.[9]

The author goes on to point out that one should not misinterpret China's growing exports of final products as an indication of the increasing sophistication of Chinese manufacturing. Rather, the focus of the TNC subsidiaries in China on final goods-assembly activities suggests that most TNCs have located their investments in the country to take advantage of China's low-paid assembly-line workers. If that is the case, what are the implications for China's longer term economic development, and what happens if China loses its cheap labour advantage?

Is the situation documented by Athukorala indicative of a pattern that is likely to persist into the future? Have TNCs operating in the region – both those from advanced countries and increasingly those based in developing

---

[7] Prema-Chandra Athukorala (2007), 'Multinational Production Networks and the New Geo-economic Division of Labour in Pacific Rim Countries', in Juan J. Palacios (ed.), *Multinational Corporations and the Emerging Network Economy in Asia and the Pacific*, Routledge: London, pp. 208–31.

[8] AFTA countries include Brunei, Cambodia, Indonesia, Laos, Malaysia, Myanmar, the Philippines, Singapore, Thailand and Vietnam.

[9] Athukorala, 'Multinational Production Networks'.

countries in East Asia – locked themselves into supply chains where all roads lead to China for final assembly and export to the developed world? What might be some of the implications of this for the role of TNCs in poverty reduction in East Asia?

Trade and investment policies' impact on corporate strategy: TNC contributions to growth

Economic and country risk considerations

The *Straits Times* reprinted an article from the *Economist*[10] documenting TNCs' increasing unwillingness to put too many of their 'eggs' in the China 'basket'. As a potential market for final products, China will always be an attractive location for doing business, but many of the features of doing business in China that helped boost TNC competitiveness are fast eroding. Both rising costs and a desire to diversify are cited by experts as mitigating against too much activity in the Middle Kingdom.[11]

According to the *Economist* article, for several years, pay rates for Chinese factory workers in busy coastal areas have been accelerating at double-digit rates. Factory workers in Shenzhen now get an average total monthly remuneration (including benefits) of around US$250, with labour costs US$100 per month higher still in Shanghai. This compares to monthly wages of around US$100 in Indonesia, US$150 in Thailand and US$200 in Manila. While pay scales are rising for factory workers in Indonesia and Vietnam, they are still up to 35 per cent lower than in the cities of coastal China.[12] Office rents and land values are also skyrocketing in eastern China. Moving a manufacturing investment to western China might work for some TNCs (Intel built a US$525 million plant in Chengdu in 2004) but does not work for others. Flextronics executives maintain that the lower wage costs are, for them, more than outweighed by the expense of getting products produced in western China to Europe and America. Part of the increased expense is related to the relatively less-developed infrastructure in western China.

---

[10] 'The Problem with Made in China', *Straits Times*, 27 January 2007, pp. S12 and S13.
[11] See also Geograry J. Gilboy (2004), 'The Myth behind China's Miracle', *Foreign Affairs* 83(4): 33–48.
[12] One reason for the increase in manufacturing wages in China is the prevailing internal migration policy (*Hukau* system). Migrants coming to the cities from rural areas do not have access to general welfare services, and are not permitted to send their children to government schools.

But for the TNCs building their supply chains and coordinating their fragmented production networks, labour and other costs are not the only factors that count. The *Economist* article points out that in a research report commissioned by the Japanese External Trade Organization, the authors reached a conclusion about doing business in China that should worry Beijing:

> Due to the country's increasing business risks and rising labour costs . . . Japanese firms employing a 'China-plus-one' strategy – in which they invest in China and another country, namely in ASEAN – should consider placing more emphasis on the 'plus-one' country.[13]

Not only Japanese TNCs seem to be heeding this message. Intel has recently invested over US$1 billion in Vietnam. Flextronics has made a big investment in a new factory in Malaysia producing computer printers on contract to Hewlett Packard. Yue Yuen, a Hong Kong-based footwear manufacturer, is ramping up production for its Nike and Adidas clients in factories in Vietnam and Indonesia.

Foreign direct investment, employment and poverty reduction

It stands to reason that FDI by TNCs are likely to have both direct and indirect impacts on poverty. Employment generation and wages paid by the TNC itself are direct effects, while the contribution of the TNC's local activities to economic growth through multiplier effects and the stimulation of linkages to local businesses might be seen as more indirect impacts. One approach to trying to measure the contribution of TNCs and their global supply chains to poverty reduction could involve looking at the nature of their FDIs. Where are the TNCs investing? What is the nature of the economic activity associated with the FDI? What about employment and economic development fostered by TNCs' FDI?

The latest *World Investment Report* produced by the United Nations Conference on Trade and Development (UNCTAD)[14] demonstrates how difficult it is to tackle these issues. According to UNCTAD, global inflows of FDI in 2005 reached US$916 billion, an increase of 29% over 2004 inflows, with US$542 billion (or 59%) of this total going to developed countries. In the developing world, East Asia saw US$118 billion in FDI

---

[13] See note 12, above.
[14] United Nations Conference on Trade and Development (2006), *World Investment Report 2006: FDI from Developing and Transitional Economies: Implications for Development*, United Nations: New York, NY and Geneva.

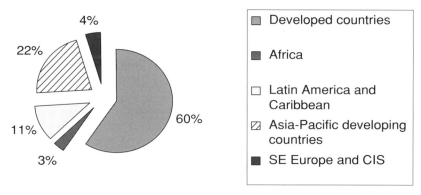

Figure 1A   Global FDI inflow shares 2005. *Source:* UNCTAD 2006 Report.

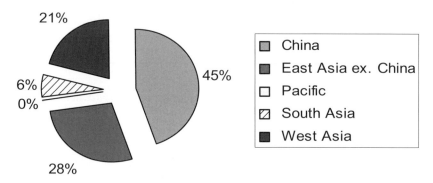

Figure 1B   Developing Asia-Pacific FDI shares 2005. *Source:* UNCTAD 2006 Report.

inflows in 2005, US$72.4 billion of which went to China. Southeast-Asian developing countries accounted for US$37.1 billion in FDI inflows. The markedly different performance of developing countries in attracting FDI is demonstrated by the fact that South Asia received just US$9.8 billion in FDI inflows, and the developing countries of the Pacific attracted just US$400 million in FDI. Figures 1A and 1B are derived from Table 1 in the UNCTAD 2006 report.

To assess the contribution of this FDI toward economic growth and poverty reduction, it might be worthwhile to consider netting-out FDI associated with cross-border mergers and acquisitions. Merger and acquisition activity was a very large portion of the 2005 investment inflow figure, calculated by UNCTAD at US$716 billion – over 78 per cent of all FDI in that year. To the extent that this merger and acquisition activity is one TNC buying another or one of the many recent mega-deals occurring in consolidating sectors, the investments might not be adding significantly to global production and employment.

That said, there can be no doubt that TNCs and their foreign affiliates are significant actors in global production and employment. The UNCTAD report states that the 770,000 foreign affiliates of TNC parent companies employed 62 million workers and exported goods and services worth more than US$4 trillion in 2005. While most of the largest TNCs still operate out of developed countries, UNCTAD notes that TNCs from developing countries employed 6 million workers and generated total sales of US$1.9 trillion in 2005. Even if there can be a huge difference today in the overall size of a developed versus developing country TNC, the latter may nevertheless be impressive in its operations. General Electric (US) ranked first with foreign assets of US$449 billion, 787 foreign affiliates and 142,000 foreign workers. Samsung Electronics (Korea) had foreign assets of US$14.6 billion, 75 foreign affiliates and employed 21,259 foreign workers.

As noted earlier, a very considerable amount of TNC FDI is directed to East Asia (mainly China) and to Southeast Asia (US$37.1 billion in 2005). Within Southeast Asia, and setting Singapore to the side, the recipients of the greatest amount of FDI by TNCs have historically been Malaysia, Thailand and Indonesia. Is there a positive relationship between these FDI flows and human welfare / poverty reduction? One objective measure could be to look at movements over time in per capita GDP (purchasing power parity (PPP) basis). In the period from 2001 to 2005, per capita GDP (PPP) has risen from US$8,912 to US$11,201 in Malaysia; from US$6,411 to US$8,368 in Thailand; and from US$3,534 to US$4,459 in Indonesia. In Laos, per capita GDP was just US$2,118 in 2005. Meanwhile, in India, which receives little by way of TNC FDI, per capita GDP stood at just US$3,320 in 2005, considerably less than in Indonesia and less than half of China's estimated per capita GDP of US$7,198.[15] In addition, FDI into East-Asian countries (where the policy regimes are distinctly outwardly focused) is mostly in labour-intensive production activities, whereas the small amount of FDI attracted to India is predominantly in domestic market-oriented (and hence capital-intensive) industries – which makes the poverty alleviation impact of FDI in India even smaller in comparison with East Asia.[16]

---

[15] Department of Foreign Affairs and Trade (Australia) website, country fact sheets, available at www.dfat.gov.au [last accessed 3 February 2009].
[16] Observation by Professor Athukorala to the author.

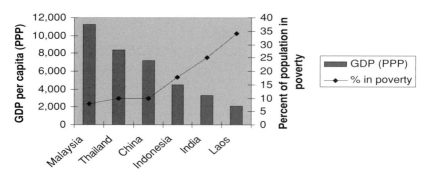

Figure 1C GDP per capita and per cent in poverty. *Source:* Chart derived from DFAT- and CIA-cited sources.

Not surprisingly, there also seems to be a relationship between investment, income and measures of wellbeing such as life expectancy and the proportion of a population living below the poverty line. In China, Malaysia and Thailand, life expectancy at birth is over 72 years, and just 10% or less of the population lives below the poverty line (see Figure 1C). In Indonesia, life expectancy is just below 70 years, with 18% of the population below the poverty line. In India, life expectancy is commensurately lower (65 years), with about a quarter of the population below the poverty line. Of this sample, Laos, again, fares worst, with life expectancy of 56 years and 34% of the population below the poverty line.[17] As a land-locked country with an economy still in the very early stages of transition to a market economy, and flanked by dynamic neighbours, Laos needs to make an extra effort to lift itself out of this unenviable situation.

Transnational-corporation forgein direct investment motivations

While the effects of TNC FDI and local manufacturing and employment are therefore likely to make an observable contribution to poverty reduction at a broad macroeconomic level, the situation is clearly very different from one particular investment to another. There are also likely to be different impacts on the local economy resulting from the establishment of a local facility of a TNC as opposed to the integration into a TNC supply chain of locally owned contractors. But the TNCs are not operating on an altruistic plane; they are motivated by a desire to make profits or realise

[17] CIA Factbook (2006), country profiles, available at www.cia.gov [last accessed 3 February 2009].

some other contribution to profits that flows from the investment. We should at least try to understand some of the reasons the TNCs decide to make their investments in one place as opposed to another.

It seems clear that many governments today realise the benefits that can flow to them from structuring a policy environment that is more likely to attract investment and TNC activity. UNCTAD's *World Investment Report* analyses national regulatory changes to identify those that are more or less favourable to FDI. In 2005, ninety-three different countries introduced some 205 regulatory changes to their investment regimes, with 164 of the changes deemed by UNCTAD as more favourable to FDI.[18] In fact, in every year since 2000, the percentage of regulatory changes more favourable to investment has been even higher than that – averaging over 90 per cent. At the same time, we have witnessed an explosion in international investment-related agreements, with 2,495 bilateral investment treaties (BITs) and 2,758 double taxation treaties (DTTs) in place at the end of 2005.[19]

Sometimes, foreign investors may be influenced by a government's extra inducements designed to attract FDI and stimulate employment and exports. There are many instances of tax holidays offered to foreign firms in a type of reverse discrimination that penalises locally owned firms. Such artificial inducements are not symptomatic of good governance, and may end up with the government in a long-term hostage situation where the beneficiary demands ongoing subsidies or threatens to take its business elsewhere. This is also a reason why well-versed negotiators always include a demand for the better of most favoured nation (MFN) or national treatment in free trade agreement (FTA) investment chapters and bilateral investment treaties.

How a change in the investment climate can influence FDI inflows is the subject of an article on Australia-Malaysia business relations that appeared in the *Australian Financial Review* on 31 January 2007.[20] For many years, Australian FDI into Malaysia suffered from the effects of near-continuous anti-Australian public positions taken by former Malaysian PM Mahathir Mohamad, with the perverse effect that Malaysian-origin FDI into Australia considerably exceeded the book value of Australian investment in Malaysia. By the end of 2005, total Australian FDI in Malaysia came to just AU$371 million. But with the anti-Australian campaign

---

[18] UNCTAD, *World Investment Report 2006*, p. 11.   [19] Ibid., p. 9.
[20] 'Foreign Investors Rediscover Malaysia', *Australian Financial Review*, 31 January 2007, pp. 52–3.

turned off by the current government in Kuala Lumpur, the situation is changing rapidly. The *Australian Finance Review* article cites a number of case studies of Australian firms that have recently made the decision to invest in Malaysia and their reasons for doing so. Neal Marston, of Grange Resources, acknowledged that his company received a tax break on its new investment in the country, but added:

> We found Malaysia had a lot of benefits going for it . . . It's a very stable country; it has a good legal system, which is enforceable and one that we're familiar with because it's based on British law. They also have a very strong focus on encouraging investment since the Asian financial crisis and with manufacturing shifting to China.

In another example of how not to attract foreign investment, the *Australian Finance Review* article cites Lynas Corporation's investment decision relative to a processing plant for rare earth metals (used in plasma screen televisions, hybrid cars, DVD drives and iPods). The firm was all set to make the investment in China when the Chinese authorities imposed export quotas on the rare earth metals that the firm would have produced at the plant. This kind of action, coupled with the other concerns about investing in China cited earlier in this chapter, have ensured that China will continue to share a sizeable portion of the FDI pie with its Southeast-Asian neighbours for the future.

Sometimes, the decision by a TNC to pursue an investment in a developing country can have as much to do with the corporate operating climate at home as it does with the investment climate in a given host country. One 1999 study of TNC FDI in Asia[21] looked at the changing reasons for FDI in other East-Asian countries by Japanese food-processing companies. Initially, the Japanese TNCs set up production facilities in developing East Asia to take advantage of wage-rate differentials and other lower costs, primarily with a view to enabling the TNC to remain competitive in the home market through the importation into Japan of certain intra-industry-traded intermediate products. International trade in these goods was complementary. However, the situation changed in the post-1985 period, in part because of changes in the domestic economics of the industry and in part because of rising standards of living in the neighbourhood. The authors cite a Ministry of International Trade and Industry report documenting emerging differences between the financial performance of Japanese domestic companies in the sector and their

---

[21] Lily Y. Kiminami and Akira Kiminami (1999), 'Intra-Asia Trade and Foreign Direct Investment', *Papers in Regional Science* 78: 229–42.

overseas subsidiaries, with the latter found to have a higher ratio of operating profit to sales. Thus, in more recent years, establishment of an overseas market base in countries with rising living standards has been a more important motivation behind Japanese food-processing FDI than the original idea of facilitating the re-import of intermediate goods into Japan from lower-cost subsidiaries.

A TNC's decision to develop a global supply chain, relying on overseas suppliers for parts and subassemblies, might also have very little to do with relative labour rates or FDI opportunities. In fact, it might be for reasons almost exactly opposite to those we have discussed so far in this chapter. In the hugely capital-intensive civil aircraft sector, Boeing and Airbus appear to be shifting ever-growing percentages of airplane production offshore as a way of gaining locked-in access to foreign capital, substantially reducing the need for the aircraft builders to self-finance new aircraft development. According to Bruce Stokes,[22] half the airframe for the A350 XWB is expected to be outsourced, and Japanese manufacturers will supply 35 per cent of the 787 airframe. Both Airbus and Boeing are increasingly requiring hardware and airframe suppliers to contribute to development costs, to finance preproduction and to test hardware and thus become partners in risk-sharing.

Transnational corporations as a positive force? The hot issues

Today's TNCs are often criticised on grounds that their global supply chains employ sweatshop workers, benefit from exploitative child labour and undermine women in the workplace. Certainly, there are always exceptions to any rule, but the overwhelming objective evidence today seems to support the contention that TNC production activities in developing countries have had positive impacts not just on the wages of local workers but also on human development.

In the broadest sense, it is easy to see that the story of TNCs and their role in the global economy is not a black or white / good or bad story. There are probably TNCs whose activities have been mostly good for local economic development, and others that have behaved very badly. But even some of the most notorious TNCs often made some contribution to poverty reduction. An interesting case in point is the United Fruit Company, which at one point in time controlled three quarters of banana production and trade in the US and Europe and which depended on

[22] Bruce Stokes, 'Economic Interests', *National Journal*, 10 February 2007, p. 59.

corrupt Central American governments to maintain its dominant position. United Fruit was said to have created and maintained the 'Banana
Republics'. The company supported dictators and even worked to topple
a democratically elected government in Guatemala. United Fruit took
advantage of government policies that dispossessed Indians of their land
and combined its banana business with a quasi-monopoly of the Central
American railroad transportation system. The company's dominance of
markets and governments begat a certain corporate arrogance that was
eventually to contribute to its demise. But even the operations of the
United Fruit Company produced some important local benefits.

In his excellent account of United Fruit's activities in Guatemala, Daniel
Litvin details two important positive impacts the TNC had in the country:

> To protect its workforce from the diseases that wiped out thousands of
> Minor Keith's[23] men, United Fruit invested in programs to eradicate
> malaria, yellow fever, hookworm and other tropical ailments. It set up
> clinics and inoculation programs, drained swamps and installed sanita-
> tion systems, and these efforts benefited not just workers and their families
> but entire communities. The results were often significant: the incidence of
> malaria among the company's workers on the Atlantic side of Guatemala,
> for example, fell from 22 per cent in 1929 to 0.3 per cent by 1955.
>
> . . .
>
> Under Samuel Zemurray, United Fruit established a tropical agricul-
> tural school in Honduras, which provided free education to poor farm
> workers from across Central America. Sam-the-banana-man also funded
> a botanical garden in Honduras, and a center for the study of Mayan art
> and Middle American research at Tulane University in the United States.
> The company's research into agricultural technology and the control of
> plant diseases was another activity which benefited the region as a whole.[24]

Labour standards

Anti-globalists have their own stories to tell, and they are usually a good
deal less than positive. Greenpeace and an Australia-based consulting
firm, ITS-Global, have been trading blasts in the press and over the internet concerned with the logging activities in Papua New Guinea of a TNC
called Rimbunan Hijau. Citing a number of reports prepared by different
groups, Greenpeace makes the case that Rimbunan Hijau pays local workers a pittance, imports large numbers of illegal foreign workers for logging

---

[23] Minor Cooper Keith founded the United Fruit Company in 1899 as a merger of a number
of his Central American-based trading, transportation and fruit-growing businesses.

[24] Daniel Litvin (2003), 'Jungle Culture', in *Empires of Profit: Commerce, Conquest and Corporate Responsibility*, Texere: New York, NY, pp. 132–3.

and that, generally, the company's treatment of its labour force reflects such an appalling lack of respect for safety, hygiene and employment conditions that it should be condemned. In its own report, commissioned by Rimbunan Hijau, ITS-Global counters that these biased findings were later overturned, with a new investigation finding that the company complied fully with all relevant labour laws.[25] When the action is taking place in a remote jungle area of a poorly developed country that is notorious for its lack of good governance, it may be practically impossible to say who is telling the truth in fights like this.

But it is not just the anti-globalists that tell negative stories about TNC abuses in developing countries, and we can be fairly certain that not all TNC investment in either developed or developing countries is benign. In an article published in *The Australian* on 12 February 2007,[26] a Chinese TNC is accused of treating its local workers like slaves and proceeding with construction without the requisite government approvals. The TNC concerned is Metallurgical Group Corp., known as MCC, and with US$15 billion in revenue in 2006, it ranks twenty-sixth among world contractors and is the thirty-ninth biggest company in China. According to the article, in MCC's early stage development of a new US$1 billion nickel project in Papua New Guinea, local employees have been poorly paid and have been made to work in abominable conditions. When, after receiving a large number of complaints about the MCC operation, Papua New Guinea Labour Secretary David Tibu flew unannounced to the construction site:

> His conclusion was that the PNG workers were being treated like slaves. They were being paid just $4 a day, with overtime compensated by tins of fish rather than kina, with canteen arrangements 'not fit for pigs' and toilet facilities so inadequate and public that employees used nearby bushes instead, out of embarrassment. He warned that if there was not a rapid improvement, he would close the site.[27]

Stories like this can help to spice up what might otherwise be a somewhat dry account of the role of TNCs and their global supply chains in international trade, economic development and poverty reduction. The modern-day situations and TNC activities addressed through this section's case studies are designed to give a real-life quality to this project,

[25] Greenpeace (2006), *Crime File – August 2006*, 'Rimbunan Hijau Can't Handle the Truth', available on the Greenpeace website: www.greenpeace.org [last accessed 3 February 2009].

[26] Rowan Callick, 'China's Neo-colonial Slavery in PNG', *The Australian*, 12 February 2007, p. 30.

[27] Ibid.

helping readers to see how – at the practical level – the stuff of economic theory and macroeconomic statistics is translated into an impact on poverty at the local level.

It has been fairly well documented[28] that global TNCs like Nike, which have been the target of anti-globalist protesters in the past and which have an over-arching interest in protecting their image and brand, have made extensive efforts to ensure that their subcontractors in developing countries adhere strictly to codes of conduct and provide workplace environments that are clean, well lit and safety conscious. As with the United Fruit operations of the last century, part of the deal in working for the TNC supply chain is often access to modern clinics and free healthcare. We also know that, in general, foreign-owned firms regularly pay considerably higher wages than locally owned firms and that, on a broader level, TNCs like Nestlé, Coca-Cola, Unilever and Intel have worked closely with enlightened local governments to change broken systems and contribute in other ways to overall human development in developing countries.

Conditions of work and respect for basic labour standards in the workplace are important aspects of CSR, particularly for those TNCs like Levi Strauss, Nike, Adidas, The Gap and others that need to project a positive image and protect their brand. But dealing effectively with these questions is often complicated by the fact that TNCs often do not own the overseas production facilities themselves, depending instead on a supply chain composed of independent subcontractors. At one time or another, abusive behaviour on the part of these subcontractors has rebounded on the TNCs, and they have generally been forced to accept responsibility for upholding labour standards throughout the supply chain.

One of the chapters in Daniel Litvin's book[29] examines these issues through Nike's corporate experience. When it became clear that charges of poor working conditions and low pay in Nike suppliers' factories were undermining the company's brand and threatening sales, the company's management undertook a number of initiatives in the later half of the 1990s that were designed to correct problems in the workplace and counter a growing negative public image. It signed up to the UN Secretary General's 'Global Compact' and joined Bill Clinton's 'Apparel Industry Partnership'. It also took on new environmental policies, making shoes from recycled materials and reducing unhealthy fumes inhaled

---

[28] See, for example, Daniel Litvin (2003), *Empires of Profit: Commerce, Conquest and Corporate Responsibility*, Texere: New York, NY, pp. 227–48.

[29] Ibid., Chapter 7: 'The Contortions of Corporate Responsibility: Nike and its Third-world Factories'.

by workers by insisting that only water-based solvents should be used in factories in its supply chain.

On the labour-standards side, the company helped to found an organisation called the 'Global Alliance' that was designed to undertake research on workers' views as a collaborative effort of TNCs, non-governmental organisations (NGOs) and intergovernmental organisations like the World Bank. And Nike introduced a code of conduct in its plants and those of subcontractors feeding its supply chain. The Nike code prohibits work by children under the age of sixteen, supports freedom of association and the right to collective bargaining and sets a maximum working week of sixty hours. To enforce its code, Nike employs more than thirty labour-compliance staff.

Other TNCs have adopted a similar approach. The Gap maintains a code of social responsibility mandating freedom from harassment in the workplace, a healthy and safe working environment, working hours, wages and overtime pay that conform to standards set in law, and legally mandated benefits. These are unquestionably admirable efforts; however, adequate enforcement will always be a daunting task. The Nike staff have to monitor 700 factories employing 500,000 people. The Gap uses ninety vendor-compliance officers. In 2003, The Gap team conducted 13,000 inspections of 3,000 factories in fifty countries and banned 120 of these factories from doing business with the company as a result of non-compliance with the social responsibility code.

Gender issues

If TNCs can somehow be important agents of change, how might their activities affect those elements in poor countries' societies that are most vulnerable? Take the case of women in the workforce. In his book, Martin Wolf takes on the question of gender impact and suggests that merely having a paying job may often be revolutionary for women in developing countries:

> Consider Bangladesh, for example. Before there was a clothing industry, local traditions forbade women from working in factories. Now 95 per cent of the 1.4 million workers in clothing manufacture are women, while 70 per cent of all the women in formal sector employment work in this industry. Bangladeshi women, as is true of other female workers in Asia and Latin America, indicate that factory work offers a measure of autonomy, status and self-respect. As female participation and female incomes rise, a higher proportion of family incomes tends to be spent on education, health

and nutrition. Working in factories postpones marriage and increases the
resources future wives bring into marriage. All these are enormous gains.
For a western visitor such jobs may seem unimaginably bad. But some
of the alternatives – total dependency as housewife or despised daughter,
prostitution, agricultural labour or begging – are worse.[30]

The contribution that factory work has made to the social transformation of women in developing countries is also treated by Litvin in his
book, where he cites a study of garment industry workers carried out
by a British academic, Naila Kabeer. Broadly speaking, Kabeer's findings
support the comments made by Wolf. In patriarchal social systems, the
autonomy gained by wages earned in factories often benefits women more
than men (who already enjoy a higher level of autonomy in local society).

Industrialisation and economic development in Europe and North
America led to an important transformation of social systems and the role
of women, so it should come as no surprise when similar societal changes
are brought about in the newly industrialising developing countries. Some
might argue that those changes would have taken place anyway through
the activities of locally owned firms as countries increasingly integrated
into the global economy, but there would seem to be little reason to doubt
that this process has been hastened by the establishment of TNC global
supply chains.

Wage rates

What about wages? By now, a considerable amount of evidence has been
collected that contradicts claims of TNCs engaging in under-paid sweatshop labour. Two economists who have done a very considerable amount
of work in this area are Robert E. Lipsey and Fredrik Sjöholm. In a May
2001 working paper,[31] they used empirical data from 19,911 plant observations in Indonesia to study wage rates paid by foreign-owned firms in
the country relative to those paid by domestic firms. From their extensive
analysis, they concluded:

> that foreign-owned plants in Indonesia pay a higher price for labour than
> domestically-owned plants. They pay higher wages for workers of a given
> educational level, by a margin of about a quarter for blue-collar workers

[30] Wolf, *Why Globalization Works*, p. 239.
[31] Robert E. Lipsey and Fredrik Sjöholm (2001), 'Foreign Direct Investment and Wages in Indonesian Manufacturing', NBER Working Paper No. 8299, National Bureau of Economic Research.

and over a half for white collar workers. Furthermore, those higher wages for workers of a given educational level do not reflect only the greater size and large inputs per worker in foreign plants, or their industry or location. Even taking account of all these factors, wages in foreign-owned plants are about 12 per cent higher than in domestic plants for blue-collar workers and by more than 20 per cent for white-collar workers.[32]

In addition, they explain that foreign ownership in an industry can also act to increase wages in domestically owned plants for many reasons, including spillover effects from technological capital, increased labour demand in the sector and the impact of training resulting in more productive workers, some of whom will 'leak' onto the domestic labour market. But how can we explain the fact that foreign-owned plants generally pay higher wages than domestically owned firms? (Incidentally, the authors point out that this differential is true even in high-income countries like the US). Lipsey and Sjöholm explain that part of the gap can be explained by the fact that FDI often takes place in industry sectors characterised by relatively higher wages, but they offer other sensible explanations as well:

> The labour market operation question is whether foreign-owned firms pay a higher price for labour, in the sense they pay more for labour of a given quality, at least as measured by education and broad skill categories. They might do so for several reasons. One is that they might be forced to do so by host-country regulations or home country pressures. Another might be that workers have a preference for locally-owned employers. A third is that foreign-owned firms might wish to reduce employee turnover, because they invest more in training than locally-owned firms, or because they fear leakage of their technological advantages if employees move on to other employers. Finally, foreign firms may, because of a lack of knowledge of the local market, pay higher wages to attract good workers. In other words, domestic firms might be in a better position to identify and attract good workers without paying a wage premium.[33]

So, if the case of Indonesia is typical (and there is no reason to suspect that underlying considerations would be markedly different elsewhere), it seems we have ample evidence that, in general, foreign TNCs pay workers appreciably more than domestically owned companies do.

For all of these 'hot' social issues, there will always be exceptions, like the Chinese MCC operation in Papua New Guinea discussed earlier, but it does seem that we should recognise that TNCs, through their global supply chains, are not only employing an enormous number of workers in the developing world, but they are also paying higher wages than local firms,

---

[32] Lipsey and Sjöholm, 'Foreign Direct Investment', p. 13.   [33] Ibid., p. 1.

contributing to the emancipation of women in traditional patriarchal societies and helping to change the way the world thinks about respect for internationally recognised labour standards.

Policy-making and capacity-building priorities: economic growth and good governance

A dynamic global economy not fully understood

Poverty reduction is only feasible in the context of economic growth. Countries seeking economic growth have no realistic option today apart from participation in the modern globalised economy. Membership in the WTO has reached 150 countries and customs territories, with another two dozen countries in some stage of accession to the WTO, so this fact of life seems to be widely acknowledged. International trade in goods and services, FDI and economic growth are inextricably tied together, and in the centre of it all are some 77,000 TNCs. These firms' 770,000 affiliates employed 62 million workers and exported over US$4 trillion in goods and services in 2005. And these statistics are likely a gross understatement of the contribution to the global economy of supply chains linked to TNC operations because they do not include the many independent subcontractors not owned by TNCs but which are still fully integrated into the supply chain. Remember, Nike owns none of the factories in developing countries contributing to its sportswear and footwear lines. TNCs and their supply chains are therefore an inescapable part of any economic growth strategy seeking to reduce poverty.

Why TNCs fragment their global production among their own subsidiaries and independent subcontractors has been the subject of considerable study. Prema-Chandra Arthukorala explains:

> the expansion of international product fragmentation as a new facet of international production has been largely underpinned by three mutually reinforcing developments over the past few decades. First, rapid advancements in production technology have enabled the industry to slice up the value chain into finer 'portable' components. Second, technological innovations in communication and transportation have shrunk the distance that once separated the world's nations and have improved the speed, efficiency and economy of coordinating geographically dispersed production processes. This has facilitated the establishment of 'services links' to combine various fragments of the production process in a timely and cost

efficient manner. Third, liberalisation policy reforms in both home markets and host countries have considerably removed barriers to trade and
investment.[34]

In his own discussion of the causes for and implications of what he
terms 'the second unbundling', economist Robert Baldwin characterises
the current wave of globalisation as one in which different tasks associated
with the production of goods and services can now be performed in
different locations. In a September 2006 paper, he asserts:

> Globalisation means unbundling. All sorts of economic relationships
> were bundled spatially to avoid or minimize transportation; this situa-
> tion implied that the price of many goods, services and wages were set
> in local markets, not global markets. This bundling meant that workers'
> pay was tied to the bundle's average productivity. By pure logic, we know
> that the link to the average dragged down the wage of some workers while
> pulling up the wages of others. Unbundling breaks the link to the bundle's
> average. Workers will increasingly get paid what they are worth on the
> world market. This will lead to gains and pains from trade.[35]

Clearly, as noted in the *Economist* article (cited earlier) discussing the
views of Baldwin and others, we need to develop new ways of thinking
about the economics of globalisation. But however one looks at it, the
primary actors in this global game are the TNCs, and any government
seeking help in reducing poverty in its country is going to want a piece
of the action. This implies adopting investment-friendly policies while at
the same time deploying elements of good governance (including sound
regulatory policies) that ensure that workers reap both economic and
social benefits from the TNCs' involvement in the local economy. Earlier,
we looked at how the Chinese environment may not now be as attractive to
foreign investors as it once was, and how a change in Malaysia's political
attitude toward Australia had contributed to a big shift in investment
patterns.

Stability is clearly an important factor that TNC investors will take
into account. Over the years, Thailand has been a major beneficiary of
FDI by TNCs, but since the 2006 coup d'état in the country, Bangkok
has been moving in directions that have foreign investors re-thinking

---

[34] Prema-Chandra Arthukorola (2006), 'Product Fragmentation and Trade Patterns in East
Asia', Asian Economic Papers 4.3, The Earth Institute at Columbia University and the
Massachusetts Institute of Technology, p. 4.

[35] Richard Baldwin (2006), 'Globalisation: The Great Unbundling(s)', a paper delivered on
20 September 2006 as part of the project 'Globalisation Challenges for Europe and Finland',
p. 45.

their strategies for the country. In an article published in the *Australian Financial Review* on 13 February 2007,[36] a journalist details Ford Motor Company's announcement in January 2007 that it might scrap plans to build a small car plant; Unilever's decision not to proceed with the planned move of its Australian dry-foods operation to Thailand and the fact that the value of applications by foreigners to invest in the country in 2006 were down by 40 per cent compared to 2005. The authorities in Bangkok would do well to recognise that the gains from globalisation are not irreversible, particularly with competitors like Vietnam in the neighbourhood.

Without any doubt, individual countries' experiences with particular TNCs might be considerably at variance with the norm, but there are a number of things we can say about the relative role of TNCs with a fair degree of certainty. As Wolf pointed out, we know these companies are efficient at identifying opportunities and knowing how to add value when these opportunities are identified. It makes sense, as Lodge and Wilson argue, that TNCs facilitate access to those things local business needs to grow but might not otherwise be able to find. Clearly, their economic power makes them important agents of change. Economists have demonstrated through exhaustive studies that foreign-owned firms typically pay substantially higher wages than domestically owned firms and that, over time, their impact on the local labour market will bring about a rise in the wages paid by local firms as well. The employment of women in factories owned or subcontracted by TNCs has often assisted the women of patriarchal societies to begin to emerge from lives of servitude and dependence. Finally, it is increasingly the case that TNCs and the responsibility they must take for actions of companies throughout their global supply chains are making important contributions to enhanced workplace conditions and greater respect for internationally recognised labour standards.

Transnational corporations want good governance in a host country

Through news articles, research by academics and first-hand accounts, we know that decision makers in TNCs are swayed by more than cheap labour when they come to decide where to locate elements of their global supply chains. Good governance matters. And good governance ensures

---

[36] Anne Hyland, 'Thai Troubles a Headache for Foreign Investors', *Australian Financial Review*, 13 February 2007, p. 61.

that the operations of TNCs contribute positively to the wellbeing of local populations, including through poverty reduction.

Attempting to bribe TNCs to locate in a country through direct subsidies, tax holidays and similar inducements is certainly not the right way to ensure that the FDI will make a sustainable contribution to poverty reduction. Also, trade-related investment measures, some of which are already prohibited for WTO members, are similarly ill-advised. Companies are not impressed by export taxes or quotas that interfere with their business models. Studies by the Organisation for Economic Cooperation and Development (OECD) and others have demonstrated that government actions to void fair labour standards in export processing zones in an effort to attract investment does not work – and from the accounts of TNCs' efforts to protect their brands, we can see why.

A trade-friendly environment is more likely to attract investment by TNCs than one riddled with protectionist devices. This is part of the reason why Southeast-Asian countries have been so successful in attracting FDI, and helps to explain the explosion in China-destined FDI since that country's accession to the WTO. Trade facilitation measures that speed customs clearance and reduce opportunities for corruption at the border are very important as well. A November 2005 survey of member companies of the European Round Table (ERT) showed that 65 per cent of the respondent companies look more favourably at new investments or additional business in markets where trade facilitation measures had been substantially improved. In 23 per cent of the ERT responses, companies reported having foregone or abandoned investment opportunities of local business expansion because of trade facilitation shortcomings in developing countries.

Rule-of-law issues and the enforceability of contracts figure very importantly in companies' decisions on where to locate their investments, and the rule of law protects local citizens as well, helping to ensure that they benefit from TNC investments. The right approach to regulation is important, and it is critical to make a distinction between liberalisation and de-regulation. The benefits of liberalisation in the telecommunications services sector, for example, cannot be realised effectively in the absence of sound, pro-competitive regulation by an independent regulator. The only thing worse than a government-owned monopoly that abuses its position in the market is a privately-owned anti-competitive telecommunications operator. Competition policy and competition law are complex legal areas, and today a large number of developing countries have only very weak or non-existent regulations on domestic competition.

Implementation of positive policies like those mentioned above varies widely around the world and in the developing countries of the Asia-Pacific region. Where governance is weak, international efforts to undertake capacity-building work in the area are often given a high priority, and for good reason. Trade-related capacity building can also be important, particularly in the areas that are so important to business, like trade facilitation. With the right regulatory environment and an equitable legal environment, governments can set the stage for attracting TNC FDI that will contribute to poverty reduction in a sustainable fashion.

The case studies

The individual case studies in this section of the book are intended to bring the discussion of the role of TNCs and their global supply chains down to the level of individual firms and their stories in particular communities. As one would expect, there are both good stories and bad stories, as well as some of more ambiguous outcome. In all cases, there are lessons to be learned from the experience of others. It is hoped that these lessons can inform government policy makers, community leaders and even the management of TNCs as they consider future investments in the supply chain.

AusAID's Peter Van Diermen describes in his case study how the garment industry in Cambodia struggles to overcome challenges posed by impending competition from China and elsewhere. The sector is owned almost exclusively by foreign TNCs, mainly from other Asian countries. The sector employs more than 300,000 women, most of whom come from rural areas and who earn above-average wages, about 60 per cent of which are routinely remitted to their families in home villages. Built on serving a niche market where it exploits its adherence to internationally recognised core labour standards, the industry's future viability may be imperilled by the coming end of safeguard measures limiting Chinese exports and Cambodia's unnecessarily high cost of doing business. The author suggests that government action on trade policy issues that would streamline customs procedures would make an important contribution to cutting the cost of doing business and helping the sector remain competitive in global markets.

In her fascinating account of how the Yazaki company came to be one of the most important employers of Samoans, Margaret B. Malua details the history of this TNC's automobile electric-harness factory in the South Pacific. Prior to the establishment of the plant, the opportunities open to the company's 1,900 local employees were limited by Samoa's smallness and remoteness from major markets. The auto-parts firm set up its subsidiary in the early 1990s to supply the Australian market under a preferential access scheme. Samoa was chosen as the location because it was politically more stable than its neighbours, had a welcoming approach to foreign investment, had a reasonably good infrastructure and had cheap and available labour. Over the years, the company's operations have made a substantial contribution to poverty reduction and to the employment of women, who tend to spend large amounts of their pay checks on improving the lot of their family members. Now, a change in the way Australia implements the SPARTECA (South Pacific Regional Trade and Economic Cooperation Agreement) scheme may call into question Yazaki's continued operation in Samoa, with serious consequences for the local community.

In an even more dramatic case that illustrates the importance of the textile and clothing sector for developing countries, Omas Bulan surveys workers in Indonesia on their views on working conditions and describes the challenges facing the sector in a country where it directly and indirectly employs more than 5.5 million people. If the sector is to survive into the future in Indonesia, it has to deal with problems relating to very old manufacturing equipment, serious competition from China in export markets as well as in the Indonesian market, and trying to obtain bank credit from local banks that seem to already have written off the sector as a high risk 'sunset sector'. The Indonesian Government seems to recognise that something needs to be done, and has embarked on a programme to help manufacturers replace their outdated equipment, train textile workers and facilitate loans to companies. If the assistance does not work and the sector collapses, not only will Indonesia stand to lose 15 per cent of its non-oil exports, but the already high (39 million plus) level of poor in the country could be swelled by those who lose their jobs in textiles and clothing production.

A colleague of Omas Bulan, also at the University of Indonesia, Beta Gitaharie Laksono, contributes a case study of the sports footwear sector in the country. In this most labour-intensive of manufacturing sectors, multinational companies based in China and Vietnam are increasingly investing in Indonesia to produce sports footwear under contract to Nike, Reebok and similar branded shoe retailers. The sector has a big impact on contributing to poverty reduction, as experienced workers are paid considerably more than local minimum wages, and a strong multiplier effect has been observed in communities where footwear production facilities are located. The author describes the challenges facing the sector where its competitive position is threatened by high transportation costs and infrastructure bottlenecks.

Contract production of sporting equipment is also the subject of Safdar Sohail's case study in Pakistan, recounting the arrival and departure of Nike. The case study discusses the important contribution hand stitching of soccer balls makes to the people of Sialkot, where half of the soccer-ball stitchers come from landless families in rural areas, and a further third from small farms with less than two hectares of property. When Nike ends its relationship with a local producer on grounds that the latter failed to abide by the labour standards set by Nike, the consequences for the local population are enormous.

A final case study in this section of the book discusses the evolution of the electronics sector in Vietnam and its role in helping to lift local people out of poverty. Phan Van Sam and Andrew Stoler show how Vietnamese Governments' acceptance of the need for a stable investment climate and good governance has encouraged Intel Corporation and others to make billions of dollars worth of investment in the country, employing thousands of people in good jobs with important side benefits for the workers and their families.

The themes that run throughout these real-life accounts are that foreign-owned TNCs and the employment they provide to local, often rural, populations can be a substantial factor in achieving poverty reduction goals, and that the continuing viability of the companies' operations (or of the locally owned firms contracting for these TNCs) often depends importantly on the national and global trade-policy environment.

1.1

Cambodia's textile and garment industry

PETER VAN DIERMEN[*]

Introduction

During the late 1970s, Cambodia emerged from a period of conflict with very little of its economy intact. It suffered tremendous humanitarian and economic hardship. Even then, it was not until almost a decade later that the domestic economy really began to grow. In a primarily rural economy, the garment sector was an early and large-growing export industry. Without question, it added substantially to the trade position of the country and its foreign exchange reserves. It also contributed significantly to the growth of wage labour. Much of the original growth was driven by preferential access to the two main markets of the US and EU. But more recently, as the country moves further into the post-2005 free garment trade environment, and as the end of the safeguards imposed on China loom, Cambodia faces an uncertain future.

Garments are a global market, with a large number of developing and least-developed economies competing in two giant markets: the US and the EU. China dominates the global garment market and must be considered in any strategy. But once we move beyond this generality, it is possible to observe that the Cambodian garment market is made up almost exclusively of foreign regional investors that generally own several production sites in the region. A number of small locally owned factories also operate in Cambodia, primarily as subcontractors to the large export firms.

Women account overwhelmingly for employment in the industry, most of them working long hours for low wages.[1] In Cambodia, more than

---

[*] Peter Van Diermen is the Economic Adviser for the Australian Government aid agency, AusAID. The views expressed in this publication are those of the author. The publication does not necessarily reflect the views of AusAID or the Australian Government.

[1] Wages for women in the garment sector are low relative to the Organisation for Economic Cooperation and Development (OECD) standards, but generally are above Cambodia's annual per capita income of US$430.

300,000 women are employed in the industry.[2] These women come mostly from subsistence rural areas. They remit significant amounts of money back to their villages and are part of extended families' livelihood and survival strategies.

In this context, and with a particular focus on women, the chapter explores how trade regime changes have had an impact on poverty. It does this by exploring the role of the global garment value chain and its implications for Cambodia's future prospects and impact on poverty and women.

Cambodian context

Cambodia's transition to a market economy began in the 1990s. From its low base, industrial output has grown rapidly, as has gross domestic product (GDP), averaging 8% per annum between 1995 and 2005. The economy continues to grow, with real GDP growth in 2006 estimated at about 10.5%, which will make a third consecutive year of double-digit growth. While per capita income remains low at US$430, there has nevertheless been a significant impact on poverty. Between 1993 and 2004, the World Bank estimates that poverty fell by 10 to 15%, to be around 35% when measured by national poverty indicators (or 18.5% when measured by the 'dollar a day' indicator).

Despite the rapid growth, Cambodia remains primarily an agrarian economy, with 80% of the population living in rural areas and 60% of the workforce employed in the agricultural sector. Over the past decade, agriculture has declined in importance as a result of poor harvests and booming construction, garment and tourism sectors (see Table 1A). In 1995, agriculture made up 50% of output, but by 2000 it accounted for only 38%, and by 2005 it had declined further to 34%, now accounting for less than the share of services. Along with the changing growth has been a shift in the labour force. Between 1998 and 2004, the share of employment in industry tripled to 12%. Even greater growth occurred in the services sector, which by 2004 accounted for 27% of the labour force.

A key driver of these changes has been the growth of the garment sector, which dominates the formal economy. In 2006, the sector accounted for 14% of GDP, close to 80% of exports and 10% of the labour force.

The rapid rise of the garment sector can be traced back to the mid 1990s when Cambodia began a period of political and economic normalisation

[2] ILO (2007) identified 337,000 workers.

Table 1A *Cambodia's real GDP growth by sector (%, 2000 prices)*

	2001	2002	2003	2004	2005	2006
Agriculture	4.5	−2.1	11.9	1.1	16.4	4.4
Paddy	0.7	−7.8	22.3	−12.2	43.6	1.0
Industry	11.7	17.7	12.5	16.8	12.3	17.1
Garments	28.4	21.3	16.8	24.9	10.3	21.9
Services	8.7	6.3	4.4	11.7	12.1	11.4
Tourism	22.6	18.8	−16.7	23.4	17.3	23.2
Non-agriculture GDP	9.5	10.7	7.0	14.5	10.3	13.2
Total GDP	**7.7**	**6.2**	**8.6**	**10.0**	**13.4**	**10.4**

Source: National Institute of Statistics for 2001–06.

with the international community. While some foreign-owned factories had existed in Cambodia during the 1970s, almost all of the growth occurred from around the mid 1990s onwards. Spurred on by initial low production costs (primarily cheap labour) and a period of relative stability, a large number of regional investors built garment factories in and around the capital, Phnom Penh. Following the industry's initial take off, further growth occurred in response to Cambodia's position in the international trade regime. In contrast, and perhaps a slightly oversimplified characterisation, it can be argued that the local business environment has primarily acted as an inhibitor to even more rapid growth of the garment sector (Leung, 2006, p. 20). Table 1B provides a broad overview of the sector, and shows just how significant the growth in the sector has been.

Between 1995 and 2005, the sector grew rapidly in terms of both its contribution to exports and employment.

Table 1B shows that while the growth of exports to the US and the EU increased, they increased much faster to the US than the EU. Both growth patterns, however, started from a very low base, and were a response to preferential access. The much faster growth of exports to the US was not as a result of substitution from the EU. Rather, the pattern is explained by very rapid growth over a very short time, and the dominance of a few brand names making up the majority of Cambodia's export market. For example, The Gap accounts for 40 per cent of Cambodia's garment exports. A further explanation for the differential growth pattern is that, during the same time period, Europe also opened access to other producers closer to the EU region, for example Turkey.

Table 1B   *The garment sector in Cambodia*

	1995	2000	2005
Exports (US$ million)	26	965	2,169
Exports as a % of total exports	2.98	69.32	–
US share of exports (%)	0.23	76.27	71.37
EU share of exports (%)	97.71	22.90	22.54
Factories	20	190	247
Employees	18,703	122,644	283,906

Source: US Embassy in Cambodia (2006).

The ability of the Cambodian garment sector to respond to future changes in the trade environment and policy initiatives will be heavily influenced by a number of key features, including the position of Cambodian factories in the value chain. The key features of the industry that will influence their ability to adjust include:

• manufacturing being limited primarily to cut-and-assemble
• lack of domestically produced textiles for use in garment factories
• low productivity when compared to competitors
• importance of the US as a final destination (75%)
• concentration on a few buyers (approximately 30% of production for The Gap brand name)[3]
• garment export firms almost exclusively foreign-owned (with 28% of owners originating from China or Hong Kong)
• International Labor Organization (ILO) 'Better Factories Cambodia' branding.

Trade policy changes

Key trade reforms that have improved Cambodia's position include its participation in the WTO Integrated Framework (IF) process. This started in 2001 with the Diagnostic Trade Integration Study (DTIS). Since the IF process was completed, several trade reforms have been implemented. Table 1C provides a brief list of some of the reforms carried out since the

---

[3] USAID (2005). Other companies that source from Cambodia include: Adidas Group, Eddie Bauer, H&M Hennes & Mauritz, Liz Claiborne, Nike and Phillips-Van Heusen.

Table 1C   *Trade reform in Cambodia since the IF was completed*

2001	• The government reduced maximum tariff rates from 120% to 35% and reduced the number of tariff bands from twelve to four. The structure of the four tariff bands are 0%, 7%, 15% and 35%, of which about 95% of the tariff lines are under three bands: 7%, 15% and 35%. • The average un-weighted tariff rates were lowered to 16.5% from 17.3% in 2000, and 18.4% in 1997.
2002	• The government moved forward with its tariff restructuring programme by reducing the un-weighted average tariff rate to below 15% in 2002 to 2003. • The government initiated a Triangle Economic Cooperation strategy between Cambodia, Vietnam and Lao PDR, focusing on: (i) commerce, (ii) industry, (iii) public works and transportation, and (iv) tourism.
2003	• Cambodia became the 147th WTO member at Cancun's 5th WTO Ministerial Conference following five successful rounds of working party negotiations with its multilateral and bilateral market partners. • The Cambodia-Canada Memorandum of Understanding, signed by the two countries in March 2003, has given Cambodia, along with other least developed countries (LDCs), quota- and duty-free access to its markets.
2004	• The National Assembly ratified Cambodia's accession package to enter the WTO. One hundred out of 107 law makers present raised their hands to approve the package (on 31 August). • The Special Trading Agreement signed with the US in 1999 expired (31 December 2004). The agreement that the US granted Cambodia guaranteed a garment export market under special Generalised System of Preference (GSP) and Most Favoured Nation (MFN).
2005	• The Tariff Relief Assistance for a Development Economy (TRADE) bill was introduced in both the US Senate and the House of Representatives. The bill would grant Cambodia and fourteen other developing countries duty-free access to US markets. It has been modeled after the Africa Growth and Opportunity Act (AGOA), which provides special access of textile and clothing exports from lesser developed countries in Sub-Saharan Africa to US markets.
2007	• The DTIS update was completed in May 2007 with the support from a number of donors and agencies. Discussions are taking place on establishing a trade donor basket fund for effective implementation of the updated DTIS. • The TRADE bill has been reintroduced to the US Senate.

IF process was started. A high priority that has not yet been implemented is the development of a 'single window' for customs. Under a single window, the handling of quarantine, health and immigration documentation would be computerised and done through a single agency. The Association of Southeast Asian Nations (ASEAN) group is also committed to achieving a single window, as are the World Bank and several other regional and multilateral bodies. The cost in time and money at clearing imports and exports at the Cambodian border remains a key bottleneck in the trade reform agenda.

Following on from the IF process, Cambodia's accession to the WTO provided significant and ongoing benefits to its trade regime position. In 2004, Cambodia was the first of the least developed countries to join the WTO. Its accession to the WTO provided several immediate benefits. More generally, accession to the WTO provided a boost to Cambodia's image and made it more attractive to foreign investors. In the long term, Cambodia hopes that accession will diversify foreign direct investment (FDI) out of its two primary export-earning sectors of garments and tourism.

Cambodia benefited from the development of the Multi-Fibre Arrangement (MFA) under the General Agreement of Tariffs and Trade (GATT). The MFA imposed a quota system on most large garment-exporting countries, attracting foreign investors from Hong Kong, Taiwan, Malaysia and Korea to Cambodia, taking advantage of its original quota-free status. Soon after, exports rapidly grew so that by 1998, the US started to negotiate to bring Cambodia into the quota system. By 1999, quotas were imposed on twelve categories of garments produced in Cambodia, but with special allowances made for additional quotas subject to compliance with international labour standards. Conditions were monitored and verified by the ILO under what became known as the Better Factories Cambodia programme. These conditions have been consistently met. At the same time, garment categories not under the US quota system have also grown rapidly.

Parallel to this has been the growth in the EU market. While not as large as the US, the EU nevertheless represents the second largest market for Cambodian garment exporters. In 1997, Cambodia signed a framework of cooperation with the EU under the Generalised System of Preferences (GSP). This was followed in 1999 with a three-and-half-year EC-Cambodia agreement that gave Cambodian garment exports duty- and quota-free access to EU markets. This agreement was known as the 'Everything But Arms' Agreement. In 2002, Canada followed by removing quota restrictions and allowing Cambodia duty-free access to its garment and textile market.

Competitive considerations

The end of the MFA quota system led initially to the cessation in the growth of Cambodia's garment exports to the US (EIC, 2007, p. 30). However, after the US imposed safeguard measures against China, exports from Cambodia started to grow again. Nevertheless, the safeguards are only short term, and Cambodia will then need to compete directly with China, as it will face similar conditions for entry into the US and EU markets. With the end of the MFA, Cambodia's garment exports to the US now face tariffs ranging from 10 to 20 per cent. At the same time, Cambodia faces stronger competition from Vietnam, which joined the WTO at the beginning of 2007. Like Cambodia, the largest market for Vietnam garment exports is the US. However, Vietnam's investment climate is generally considered more attractive in terms of lower energy costs, better investment security and more skilled workers (EIC, 2007, p. 24). Vietnam's entry into the WTO and its competitive edge over Cambodia also brings to the fore the issue of Cambodia's high-cost domestic economy. In addition, the country is also hampered by poor and inadequate infrastructure, which further hampers its competitive position and attractiveness for FDI. Thus, the future of Cambodia's garment exports is far from clear.

In the past, Cambodian garment production has grown largely because investors have taken advantage of the country's special quota arrangements with the US. Regional investors, particularly ethnic Chinese firms (from Taiwan (sixty-nine garment factories in 2006), Hong Kong (sixty-five factories), Korea (twenty-nine factories) and Malaysia (twenty factories), as well as factories from China (thirty-seven in 2006)), have set up in Cambodia to take advantage of the quota system. The majority of these investors own other garment production centres in the region. Their Cambodian investments represent part of their regional production strategy. Investors have multiple production sites in order to reduce the risk of disruption and to take advantage of different incentives and conditions. Consequently, orders for particular lines of garments may be shared between several different production centres owned by a single investor within the region. For example, a line of garments consisting of matching tops and bottoms may see the tops produced in one country and the bottoms produced in Cambodia. Although preferential access to the

US market is not assured, The Gap (the largest single buyer in Cambodia) has indicated that a significant reason for continuing to buy from the country continues to be the ILO 'Better Factories Cambodia' branding.[4] Also, under the US's WTO (Doha Round) agreement to provide duty- and quota-free access to the poorest countries, there continues the possibility of the US offering preferential treatment to Cambodia's garment sector.

Thus, while the garment sector in Cambodia dominates the formal economy (with tourism and agriculture as the other two pillars), it represents only a small part in the global garment sector, and is highly vulnerable to changes given its concentration on a few final destinations and its high foreign ownership and higher costs than its immediate rivals located in Bangladesh, China and Vietnam (EIC, 2006, p. 13). Furthermore, in an industry that is largely driven by costs and product quality, reliance on 'Better Factories Cambodia' branding as the primary means to give it a comparative advantage may prove to be a high-risk strategy.

Impact on women

The growth in female garment workers has also had spillover effects on the rural sector and the wider economy. In 2007, the garment sector employed over 300,000 people in some 300 factories. More than 90 per cent of all workers in the industry are women, predominantly from the rural sector who have migrated to find work in the factories. Most of them occupy the lowest levels in the industry, with supervisory roles often carried out by men, and managerial positions mainly occupied by expatriates from the factory's country of origin. It has also been estimated that an additional 150,000 jobs are created indirectly in support services (Neak and Yem, 2006, p. 11). This includes street vendors, beauty parlours, moto-taxis and piece-workers, as well as many other informal activities.

The impact of the garment sector can also be measured using more quantitative economic tools. Using a preliminary input/output model, the Economic Institute of Cambodia estimated that a 10% increase in demand for garment products would result in a 17.5% increase in total domestic production. This can be broken down into a 2.4% increase in trading business, a 0.5% increase in transportation, a 0.4% increase in electricity consumption and a 0.3% increase in hotel and restaurant activity (Neak and Yem, 2006, p. 8).

---

[4] The organisation named Business for Social Responsibility, which represents The Gap, as well as several other major buyers, wrote on 2 March 2007 to the ILO Better Factories programme.

Women in the industry typically remit back to their rural subsistence families between US$20 to 40 per month (ADB, 2004). These remittances support on average four to nine family members in the village (ILO, 2006, p. 3). Remittances are used both for consumption and investment purposes. Remittances supplement subsistence farming and allow families to purchase consumer goods otherwise not available to them. But the money is also used to invest in children's education, buy fertiliser or livestock, renovate homes and dig wells (World Bank, 2006). Thus, the garment sector supports, directly and indirectly, more than a million people out of a total population of just over 14 million (Bargawi, 2005).

Impact on garment workers and value chain

In order to illustrate and provide anecdotal evidence of the impact on changes in the trade regime on female garment workers in Cambodia, over fifty female garment workers were interviewed, as well as donor, union, industry and government representatives.[5] The following vignette illustrates the impact the garment sector has on women.[6]

Sitting in a small room shared by three women, we talked to Sem Pheak, a sixteen-year-old garment factory worker from a small village in Kampong Chhnang.[7] She started work in the industry eighteen months ago. That morning, however, when the supervisor discovered that her identity card was forged, she was fired from her job on the assembly line. She explained that many young underage women obtain fake identity cards to work in the industry. Before she was fired, she earned a base salary of US$55 per month, but sometimes more with overtime (US$50 minimum wage and US$5 attendance bonus). Her share of the rent is US$5 per month, and she sends home around US$30 each month to her family. The remaining US$20 plus is used for living costs, mostly food and household essentials. She explains that sometimes the money is not enough to live on, and she borrows from friends. Her monthly remittances pay for her younger brother to go to school, and pay for food

---

[5] Interviews were held and information was obtained from the Ministry of Women's Affairs, Ministry of Industry, Mines & Energy, Coalition of Cambodia Apparel Workers Democratic Unions, Free Trade Union of Workers of the Kingdom of Cambodia, The Garment Manufacturers Association in Cambodia (GMAC), ILO Better Factories Cambodia and the Garment Industry Productivity Center.

[6] Khin Pisey, a research assistant from the Economic Institute of Cambodia, provided support and assisted in the fieldwork conducted in Phnom Penh during May and June 2007.

[7] The interview with Sem Pheak from Kampong Chhnang was held on 26 May 2007, on the outskirts of Phnom Penh near her factory.

and other items for her subsistent farmer parents. Until that morning, her work week consisted of six days, starting at 7 a.m. and finishing at 4 p.m., with an hour off for lunch. When there is overtime, she is expected to work the additional hours.[8] The factory has a water-cooled fan but no air-conditioning, and they are allowed four bathroom breaks during the day. She was not sure if the factory had a union representative, nor had she heard of the ILO's Better Factory Cambodia programme.

Sem Pheak's story is at once unique and similar to many of the women working in the garment industry. It is unique in that each of the more than fifty women interviewed had their own individual story to tell. But throughout their individual stories, common themes emerged. Consistent among the women was the remittances of money back to subsistent families in the village. Also remarkably consistent among the workers' stories was the level of remuneration and conditions of employment.

During the interviews, the living conditions observed at various locations around Phnom Penh were also very similar. All the women who migrated from the rural area to the city had made an economic decision and, as a result, had increased their income and standard of living. The majority of women interviewed for this study, and the larger surveys done by other studies, show that women choose to migrate and work in the garment sector because it increases their income and provides a wider range of livelihood strategies for their families (see, for example, the survey by the Cooperation Committee for Cambodia, 2005). Almost all the women interviewed came from subsistence farming families that owned small holdings of land which did not produce enough to sustain the extended family. The remittances from the women provided an important source of income, and for many rural families, the only source. When asked what they saw as their long-term future plan, only a few mentioned going back to the village from where they had come. Asked where they would like to bring up their family after they were married, most preferred to stay employed in the garment sector and bring up their family in Phnom Penh. Their ambitions were often related to moving into better accommodation, earning higher wages and becoming small market traders or working in beauty salons.

The impact of trade regime changes on the growth of the garment sector and its implications for women's livelihood is connected to Cambodia's

---

[8] Shift work is paid at approximately US$0.25 per hour. The labour laws are currently being revised (May 2007), and it is proposed to revise downward the penalty rate for night work from 200% to 130%.

position in the global value chain of garment production. Cambodia has explicitly sought to place itself in a niche position of guaranteeing adherence to specific international labour standards set out in government legislation, and by providing a legal framework conducive to FDI. In relation to labour standards, the monitoring and verification of these standards has been independently carried out through the ILO's Better Factories Cambodia programme of factory inspections and reports. By law, all exporting garment factories must be registered with the ILO programme. Labour laws in Cambodia guarantee garment workers a minimum wage, specific conditions tied to hours worked, overtime allowances, compensation for injuries sustained at work and paid and unpaid leave entitlements. Interviews with the Garment Association and the Better Factories programme indicated that in the post-2005 quota system, the primary benefit of the programme was to provide buyers with confidence that minimum standards of labour practice were being adhered to by the factories located in Cambodia.

This strategy, however, needs to be seen in light of the global, regional and domestic aspects of the value chain. Almost all of the 300 registered export factories are owned by regional investors that have multiple production centres within the Asian region.[9] Therefore, large single-production lines of garments that may consist of several different individual garments are often distributed among the different production centres. These orders can then be further spread in-country by subcontracting to local firms. In Cambodia, there exist a number of unregistered and smaller locally owned subcontracting firms that take on work from the larger registered export firms. Thus, the Better Factories certification provides a guarantee for workers in Cambodia's foreign-owned export firms, but not for those that work for locally owned subcontractors or for other parts of the same manufactures' value chain located outside Cambodia. Even within the export segment, not all firms comply, and it is estimated that some 20 per cent of the 300 export factories do not meet the Better Factories standards.[10] Firms that do not comply with the Better

---

[9]   In 2006, of the 284 factories that were members of GMAC, sixty-nine were from Taiwan, sixty-five from Hong Kong, thirty-seven from China, twenty-nine from Korea, twenty-two from Cambodia, twenty from Malaysia, ten from Singapore, seven from the US, six from Macau, five from Canada, three each from Britain and Australia, two from Indonesia and one each from Germany, Vietnam, the Philippines, Bangladesh, Denmark and Japan.

[10] This estimate is based on the most recent report produced by the ILO Better Factories Cambodia programme (June 2007) and interviews with various stakeholders, including the Garment Association and the Better Factories programme.

Factories standards are publicly named on the ILO website and risk losing export orders, or where compliance is related to Cambodia labour laws, risk prosecution.

The issue of whether this market strategy has provided substantially better conditions for women in comparison with countries that compete in the same market segment is debatable. Vietnam is often referred to as a natural competitor to Cambodia. Cambodia's niche market strategy is often misinterpreted to mean that women are guaranteed 'better' working conditions. It does not. What it does do is guarantee independent verification that factories adhere to international labour standards that are encoded in national Cambodian law. Consumers can have greater confidence in the independently verified results as opposed to buyers doing their own inspections.[11]

In contrast, Cambodia's open FDI regime, encoded in laws, regulations and procedures, are often poorly adhered to or, at best, unevenly enforced and provide opportunities for rent-seeking. In an industry where production costs primarily drive competition, costs cannot be ignored. Productivity studies show that Cambodia lies in a group of countries – which includes China and India – where labour costs are about US$1 per operator hour (USAID, 2005, p. 26). Interviews with the Garment Manufacturers Association of Cambodia (GMAC) also indicate that input costs (labour, water, electricity, rent etc.) are only slightly higher for Cambodia than its near neighbours. However, labour productivity is significantly lower when benchmarked against regional standards (USAID, 2005, p. 31). In addition, when considering the total cost of doing business, which includes bureaucratic, regulatory and infrastructure costs, as well as production costs, Cambodia's competitive position becomes much worse.[12]

To draw the different strands together, we can summarise that changes in the global trade regime and Cambodia's positioning in it, through its allocation of additional quota and its openness to foreign investment and meeting international labour standards, has seen the growth of a sizeable domestic garment industry, but a small one in global terms. An ongoing concern for the industry will be the ability to improve productivity through incorporating best practices and reducing the transaction cost of doing business in Cambodia.

[11] Note, however, that the Better Factories inspections do not replace buyers' own inspections. Buyers have their own global systems that they continue to use in Cambodia.
[12] See, for example, Cambodia's 143rd ranking in the World Bank *Doing Business 2007* report (World Bank, 2007).

Policy implications and options

Given the above scenario and analysis, and with specific emphasis on women, what then are the most effective trade-policy strategies and trade capacity-building measures for the growth of the garment sector and poverty reduction?

First and foremost, any policy discussion must consider what role there is for continuing to use the ILO Better Factories Cambodia programme for adhering to international labour standards and appealing to buyers' corporate social responsibility strategies and ultimately to consumers' preferences. Given that this strategy is already in place, and has attracted a good reputation for the country as a whole, it should continue to be used and to form part of future negotiations for preferential market access to the US and the EU. Allowing the programme to fall into disuse would have significant long-term negative implications. Having said this, it cannot go on as it is. The end of the preferential quota system and the ILO's separation in October 2007 from the Better Factories Cambodia programme all require a rethink of how it might work in the future.[13]

Perhaps the most significant policy option that would have the greatest direct impact on the industry would be to reduce the cost of doing business. This can be divided into two parts. Studies have shown that the productivity of the country's garment factories is well below benchmarks for similar industries in other countries (USAID, 2005). Furthermore, under the heading of improving the country's competitive position and more directly related to trade, the following options can be considered:

- Follow up on the 2002 and 2007 World Bank work on the DTIS. The 2002 work led to most non-trade barriers being eliminated. An update on the DTIS was completed in late 2007, and commits the government to further trade-related reforms.
- Implement the Single Window project, aimed at establishing an electronic system for lodging import and export documents, paying fees, duties and taxes. This would significantly reduce the opportunities for illegal and unofficial levies and would increase the efficiency of the process.

---

[13] The direct relationship between Cambodia's labour standards and preferential quota access to US markets ended when the Agreement on Textiles and Clothing (ATC) quota system ended in December 2004. This has also prompted the ILO to develop an exit strategy from its Better Factories programme. The existing strategy is meant to ensure the sustainability of the programme, and will lead to the programme being staffed primarily by local experts.

- Increase efforts on regional integration. Through the ASEAN group, Cambodia is actively negotiating free trade agreements with Japan, China, Korea, India, the EU, Australia and New Zealand. It is also actively moving to closer integration with Vietnam and Laos.
- Diversification in FDI should be encouraged. FDI is mostly found in garments followed by tourism. Diversification can be encouraged by the passage of a number of laws required under Cambodia's WTO accession commitment. Many of these laws are critical to improving investors' confidence.

A defining characteristic of the Cambodian garment sector is its lack of vertical integration. Most textiles are imported and come direct from the buyer or the factory at which the main order is placed. Moreover, most of the work is cut-and-assemble work, with very little else done in-country. While greater productivity in the sector would encourage further investment, it may not lead to greater vertical integration. Some policy consideration should be given as to how to develop market-friendly policies for encouraging investment along the value chain.

The link between rural women coming to the city to work and remitting money to poor impoverished villages should be further explored for building development options for the rural sector as well as more directly for the 300,000 women. Any policy consideration for improving women's lives needs to take account of the impact on the garment sector, and should not add to garment producers' production costs. But given the large number of donors and the importance of gender for most of these organisations, the appropriate ministries should take ownership and lead in identifying ways in which women's health, housing and safety and opportunities can be improved, not just in the factory but also outside in the wider community.

References

Asian Development Bank (ADB) (2004), *Cambodia's Garment Industry: Meeting the Challenges of the Post-Quota Environment*, prepared for the Ministry of Commerce, Phnom Penh.

Bargawi, O. (2005), *Cambodia's Garment Industry – Origins and Prospects*, ESAU Working Paper 13, Overseas Development Institute.

Cooperation Committee for Cambodia (2005), *Impact of the Garment Industry on Rural Livelihoods: Lessons from Prey Veng Garment Workers and Rural Households*, Cooperation Committee for Cambodia: Cambodia.

Economic Institute of Cambodia (EIC) (2006), *Economic Review* 3(3): all articles.

(2007), *Cambodia's Garment Industry Post-ATC Human Development Impact Assessment*, Economic Institute of Cambodia, in partnership with the UNDP Regional Centre in Colombo.

International Labour Organization (ILO) (2006), *Women and Work in the Garment Industry*, Better Factories Cambodia: Phnom Penh.

(2007), *Eighteenth Synthesis Report on Working Conditions in Cambodia's Garment Sector*, Better Factories Cambodia, Phnom Penh.

Leung, S. (2006), 'Integration and Transition – Vietnam, Cambodia and Lao PDR', paper prepared for the seminar 'Accelerating Development in the Mekong Region – The Role of Economic Integration', Siem Reap, Cambodia, 26–27 June 2006, NCDS/APSEG, The Australian National University: Canberra.

Neak, S. and Yem, S. (2006), 'Trade and Poverty Link: The Case of the Cambodian Garment Industry', draft report, EIC: Phnom Penh.

USAID (2005), *Measuring Competitiveness and Labour Productivity in Cambodia's Garment Industry*.

US Embassy of Cambodia (2006), *Economic Significance of the Garment Sector in Cambodia*, US Embassy of Cambodia: Cambodia.

World Bank (2006), *Cambodia: Halving Poverty by 2015? Poverty Assessment 2006*, World Bank: Phnom Penh.

(2007), *Doing Business 2007*, World Bank: Washington, WA.

1.2

Australia's WTO trade-policy changes and the future of a Samoan car-parts investor*

MARGARET B. MALUA**

Introduction

Samoa is one of the five[1] least developed countries (LDCs) in the Pacific. Samoa's inherent characteristics of smallness, remoteness from major markets of the world and its vulnerability to natural calamities contribute significantly to its ability to compete globally, and impacts on its economic development. Through a substantial foreign-investment package, the Government of Samoa was able to attract a major foreign investor in 1991. Yazaki Western Samoa was set up in 1991 as a subsidiary of Australian Arrow Pty. Ltd (AAPL). It was later formed as a separate entity with full production in 1995; and in 1997, it took on the name Yazaki EDS Samoa Limited (YES). Today, YES is a manufacturing base for AAPL (formerly Yazaki Australia).

YES is a TS16949- and ISO14001-certified manufacturing plant that assembles and produces wiring harnesses for most of the Australian vehicle manufacturers. It is the largest multinational company operating in Samoa, as well as the single major private-sector employer in the country.

The utilisation of YES of Samoa's eligibility to export to Australia under a non-reciprocal trade agreement (SPARTECA) was an important factor in the company's decision to invest in Samoa. In the years since its establishment in Samoa, YES has become an important industrial player, employing thousands of Samoan men, and especially women, and contributing to the local economy through a significant multiplier effect. Recently, partly as a result of Australia's longer-term plans to modify its import policy for the automobile industry, and partly as a result of the

---

* Also see case study 2.3 in this book, on Samoan agricultural policy.
** Margaret Malua is an independent Economic and Trade Consultant in Samoa, and a Partner in Pacific Trade Consult.
[1] Other Pacific LDCs are: the Solomon Islands, Vanuatu, Tuvalu and Kiribati.

way in which SPARTECA may be implemented, there is a chance that YES may close its operations in Samoa, with important consequences for the local economy. This case study examines the Samoan economy, the background to the investment in Samoa by YES, and some of the factors influencing the decision as to whether a small Pacific LDC may lose its most significant foreign investor.

Samoa in the global context

It is, at first, quite surprising to discover that a major national export of this country is a category of automotive parts destined for Australia. When we look at the island in context, this does not seem to fit what one would expect to see as the international trade profile of Samoa. Samoa is a small island country in the Pacific, with a population of 179,186 (figure from Samoa's 2006 Census). The country's 2005 nominal gross domestic product (GDP) was measured at just AU$600 million, translating into a GDP per capita of AU$3,072. As noted earlier, Samoa is one of five LDCs in the Pacific. Despite Samoa's efforts to justify its vulnerability, and the impetus graduation may give to foreign investment by lowering the financial risk factors associated with LDC status, the UN has now recommended Samoa's graduation to developing country status come 2010.

Samoa experienced major economic disruption in the early 1990s due to poor economic management and successive natural disasters. However, strong political leadership and pragmatic economic policies have formed the basis for sustainable economic policies since 1995.

Economic challenges

Samoa's economy and economic development are faced with many challenges. Samoa's smallness limits its domestic market size. Its remoteness restricts the movement of both exports and imports in association with high transportation and shipping costs. The freight capacity and frequency of transportation by air and sea do not provide for a favourable infrastructure for trade.

Development is also hindered by its narrow resource base, with land being the major natural resource. With an economy heavily dependent on agriculture, about 80 per cent of the land is owned customarily by extended families. Very little land is available for commercial activities other than that leased by the government.

Table 1D   *Sex/age distribution per age group*

Age group	Male (%)	Female (%)
10−14	11.9	11.9
15−19	10.3	9.6
20−24	8.2	8.0
25−29	7.5	7.4

Source: Government of Samoa (2002).

Samoa's workforce is one of its most valuable resources, although it is largely dominated by a semi-skilled and unskilled work force. Samoa has a very young population. Table 1D shows that over 50 per cent are young people between the ages of twelve and thirty.[2] This makes it a challenge for the government to provide education for the younger population as well as employment opportunities for about 10,000 school leavers each year.

The median age in Samoa is 19.7 years old. This is a very young median age when compared, for example, to the median age in developed countries, for instance Japan, where the median is over 30 years of age. The above factors contribute to the limited foreign-investment opportunities available in Samoa, despite having a politically stable government and an enabling environment for investments.

National policies and strategies

Since the first Statement of Economic Strategy (SES) 1998–99, the government has continued to view the private sector as the engine for development and growth, and has placed great emphasis on the importance of developing the private sector. Today, the Strategy for the Development of Samoa (SDS) 2005–07 sets out the government's key economic and social sectors and priority areas for development. It has in place strategies to achieve these developmental goals. The SDS identifies six key development priorities: the private sector; agriculture; tourism; community; education; and health. The government remains committed to macroeconomic stability and the implementation of measures to contain government expenditure. The ultimate goal for stimulating private-sector

[2] Figure from the Samoa National Youth Policy 2001–2010.

investment is to create employment opportunities in addition to providing goods and services, and generating a solid source of government revenue. Promoting private-sector investment, therefore, is a key prerequisite for achieving the national vision of a better quality of life. The broad key areas for promoting private-sector investment include continued strengthening and refinement of the enabling environment for private-sector development and, in particular, promoting investment in areas where Samoa has strong comparative advantage.

Samoan investment policy

Through the Enterprises Incentives and Export Promotion Act 1992–93 (EIAPA), the government operated a tax-incentives scheme to assist with the development of enterprises in Samoa until its abolishment in June 1999. This was in line with the aim to stimulate investment by liberalising the economy and stimulating competition, rather than by granting special incentives to investors. At the same time, Samoa was also undergoing substantial tax and tariff reforms. Approval orders granted under the EIAPA between 29 May 1998 and 25 June 1999, together with export enterprises approval orders, were grandfathered until they reached the expiry date stipulated in their respective orders.

The Foreign Investment Act 2000 now governs foreign investment in Samoa, including the sectors in which foreign investment is restricted, and those business activities that are reserved only for locals. The Samoan Government's intention that the private sector should have the leading role in developing a competitive national economy is difficult given its small size and underdeveloped industries. It is therefore important that it provides for an environment that will attract foreign investment into the country. Such foreign investment is expected to enhance the domestic economy through the provision of employment opportunities, the inflow of new capital, technology and management skills in all sectors of the economy, as well as the contribution to export earnings to offset the balance of payment deficit.

Investment policies and guidelines needed to be adjusted to be in line with global changes. Samoa's recent WTO accession, bringing the island into the multilateral trading system, is one of the tools to adjust to globalisation. Samoa is also committed to other regional trade agreements, such as the Pacific Island Countries Trade Agreement (PICTA) and current negotiations for an economic partnership agreement (EPA) between Pacific ACP (PACP) countries and the European Community (EC).

Participation in these trading arrangements will contribute to Samoa's efforts in providing a more conducive investment environment, particularly access to duty concessions of Samoan products into major markets of the world.

One of these key trading arrangements, particularly for YES, is the South Pacific Regional Trade and Economic Cooperation Agreement (SPARTECA).

SPARTECA

SPARTECA is a non-reciprocal arrangement between Australia and New Zealand on one hand, and Forum Island Countries (FICs) on the other, which came into force on 1 January 1981. The current members of SPARTECA are Australia, New Zealand, the Cook Islands, the Federated States of Micronesia, Fiji, Kiribati, Marshall Islands, Nauru, Niue, Papua New Guinea, Solomon Islands, Tonga, Tuvalu, Vanuatu and Samoa. SPARTECA was notified to the WTO on 20 February 1981 under paragraph 2(c) of the Enabling Clause, in spite of it including two developed members (Australia and New Zealand) and being a non-reciprocal agreement. The issue of legal cover does not appear to have been debated, nor any concerns. However, a reference to this question was made at the Council Meeting on 2 February 1988 (Doc. C/M/217), which had under item 7 of its agenda the consideration of SPARTECA's biennial report (Doc. L/6279). At that meeting, the US considered that Australia and New Zealand should seek a waiver for SPARTECA. However, New Zealand noted that seven years had lapsed since the presentation of the Agreement to the General Agreement of Tariffs and Trade (GATT), and the matter was not pursued further.

The Agreement seeks to promote and accelerate development of the FICs through the promotion of economic, industrial, agricultural and technical cooperation among them. Under the Agreement, Australia and New Zealand offer duty-free, unrestricted or concessionary access for virtually all products originating from the developing island member countries of the Forum, as long as the stipulated rules of origin (ROO) are met.

The ROO for SPARTECA are separately defined by both Australia and New Zealand to determine that the goods produced in FICs are eligible for preferential access. The ROO are currently based on a value-added approach of 50 per cent local content ascribed to materials and/or operations performed in the exporting FIC country.

At present, most exports from the FICs to Australia and New Zealand enter under SPARTECA. Technical support for trade and export development are also available for FICs through the commitment by Australia and New Zealand to the Pacific Island countries (PICs) through the funding of the South Pacific Trade Commissions in Auckland and Sydney, as well as market-support assistance through the Forum Secretariat.

Why invest in Samoa?

When the Australian Government introduced the Button Plan in the mid 1980s, it provided for a favourable environment for the automobile industry due to incentives in the form of progressive removal of tariff quota assistance to allow and encourage industry rationalisation. The features of the plan included:

- an annual import tariff quota being set at 22% of domestic demand, with a penalty duty of 100% for imports that exceeded the quota (to be phased down to 57.5% by the end of 1992)
- the 85% local-content scheme being retained and the export facilitation scheme being extended and broadened.

However, the plan was reviewed in the mid 1980s due to the substantial depreciation of the Australian dollar with corresponding increases in prices for imported cars. The review resulted in many changes, which included the abolishment of some of the features of the plan that had given much protection to the car manufacturing industry. Import quotas and the local-content scheme were abolished, with car producers only entitled to import 15 per cent of content duty-free.

SPARTECA offered the opportunity for Yazaki Australia to import 100 per cent of content duty-free into Australia. It needed to establish a content-manufacturing plant in one of the FICs that was eligible under the agreement. The opportunity to manufacture in low-cost countries was also a major factor in considering SPARTECA as an alternative.

Yazaki Australia first looked at establishing operations in Fiji, but was greeted with a union strike march in 1989 and 1990, and the country was still recovering politically from the 1987 coup. In Tonga, they found the infrastructure was weak, and they were unfamiliar with the political structure in terms of operating a business. Other FICs such as the Solomon Islands and Papua New Guinea were experiencing political unrest.

Samoa, however, offered a more conducive environment for operations:

- Reasonably sound infrastructure: electricity and telephone lines reached almost all parts of the islands. Water projects to supply all parts of the country were rapidly progressing. Eighty per cent of the roads were tar sealed.
- Political stability: Samoa has been the safest and most stable government in the South Pacific since its independence in 1962, with only five Prime Ministers elected over this period, in contrast to other PICs in the region. The steady growth of its economy and improving standard of living was a favourable factor.
- Cheap and available labour: at the time, the minimum labour rate was SAT$1 per hour, compared to the minimum wage in Australia and New Zealand of AU$20 per hour and NZ$22 per hour.

Although the skill level of the Samoan workforce was low, and it would be the first time that they would be introduced to production/assembly-line work, Yazaki Australia considered the Samoans working at their Auckland subsidiary operation as very efficient and reliable. In addition, the Government of Samoa welcomed Yazaki and offered much support and many incentives, even at the initial discussions, at the high level of government authority. Yazaki would in turn maintain a certain level of employment and other commitments. A Memorandum of Understanding was drawn to this effect.

Employment and income

Since YES commenced operations, its workforce has averaged around 1,800 employees, with about 1,941 workers employed today (2007). Figure 1D illustrates the number of YES employees from 1991 to 2004.

YES' workforce is largely dominated by female workers, as (Samoan) women are perceived to work more skillfully with their hands and that they work more efficiently than men.

In 1995, the pre-assembly arm of the operation was transferred from Melbourne to Samoa. This was a major task, as many machine operators were required to be trained on the many and varied processes involved; hence 1996 saw the highest number of employees for YES. As the skill levels improved, Yazaki adopted a sinking-lid policy as production became more efficient. For instance, from 1995 to 1996, overall efficiency was approximately 33%, and in 1997 to 1998, it rose to about 80%, which led to a reduction in employment numbers. In the following years,

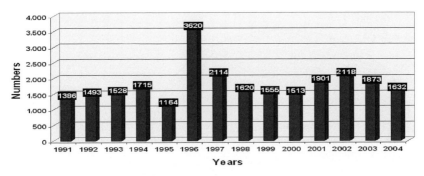

Figure 1D   Number of employees at YES (1991–2004). *Source:* YES (2007).

Table 1E   *Pay-per-week breakdown analysis of 2007*

Number of staff with <SAT$100 per week	Number of staff with SAT$101–300 per week	Number of staff with >$301 per week
382	1,026	533

Source: YES (2007).

as demand for products increased, more employees were recruited as required.

There were teething problems relating to employment and production. The new work methodologies introduced by YES were challenging, which led to high staff turnover, which impacted productivity. YES had to adjust to the cultural and social factors surrounding Samoan workers in order to provide a more friendly working environment. YES has since entered into a partnership with the government through the Ministry of Women's Affairs and the Committee on the Elimination of Discrimination Against Women (CEDAW). This partnership provided YES with guidance on how to develop and implement policies on women, which it has achieved successfully. YES is now working on a project on sex and reproductive education for its workers.

In 2004, there were 687 males and 1,997 females employed at YES, with a combined salary of SAT$14.8 million. As most of YES workers are from the rural area, this is an important source of income, which contributes to the development and welfare of the rural communities. Table 1E is a summary analysis of the breakdown in employment as per pay/wage brackets, with just over 50 per cent earning no more than SAT$300 per week.

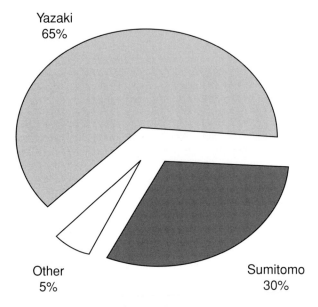

Figure 1E   YES Australian market share. *Source:* YES (2007).

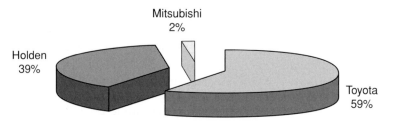

Figure 1F   YES customer breakdown. *Source:* YES (2007).

YES sales and market share

YES sales have been growing steadily over the past years. It continues to dominate the Australian market for wire harnesses. Figure 1E provides a breakdown of the Australian market share for YES products. In terms of buyers, YES exports to three car manufacturers in Australia, with Toyota being its major export buyer. Figure 1F provides an illustration of YES Australian buyers.

In order to maintain this market share and competitiveness, YES has kept up with global market requirements. In meeting overseas standards, YES managed to get ISO 9000 and ISO 14001 Certifications in 2004.

This contributed towards producing high-quality products to meet its customers' requirements. This move by the company coincides with the move by the Australian car-manufacturing industry to improve standards of their products in order to become competitive in the global market.

Government assistance and support to YES

The Government of Samoa, in line with its investment policy objectives, welcomed Yazaki's proposal to set up operations in Samoa, with the vision that this large investment in the Samoan economy defies its inherent unfavourable investment conditions, and that it would benefit the country in the long term. To facilitate this new investment, in 1992, the government committed to provide building facilities to house the company, and in 1994, two buildings were provided for all of the company's operations.

YES is currently operating on government land, with two of its three main buildings provided by the government. The last stage of the new YES building was built by YES after declining the government's offer to construct this third building. This was an investment on their part, to further improve the working conditions and atmosphere of the company.

Under the EIAPA Incentive Scheme, the government awarded YES with packaged fiscal incentives. The first package was approved on 10 January 1991, with the last approval order issued on 14 August 1996. Fiscal incentives awarded to YES include:

- duty-free and excise-tax-free imports of machinery, plant, equipment, vehicles, raw materials and building materials up to the value of over SAT$250 million
- income tax holiday granted in November 1994 to expire in November 2009
- termination for last customs-and-excise duty concession in July 2010.

Implementation of SPARTECA / a derogation for YES

Due to global market changes, including unexpected currency fluctuations, YES has not been able to meet the SPARTECA 50 per cent ROO criteria for a number of its exports to Australia, and its products have become subject to a 15 per cent duty. YES applied for derogation from the ROO, in which the Samoan Government negotiates with the Australian authorities (Customs).

The first derogation was granted in 2001 for two years before the expiry date in 2003. YES requested derogation in 2003 and were granted eighteen months, which expired in June 2005. The third derogation was requested by YES due to a change in the nature of the new models of Toyota, Holden and Mitsubishi in 2005 and 2006. These new models followed a global design platform initially incorporating many imported components. The request was granted through political support. For YES' part, they needed to provide information and proposed strategies on how to bring their local value content up to 50 per cent.

As the world's economies are integrating, industrial production has become fragmented, with many companies challenged by the fact that products and necessary components are produced in different parts of the world where there is a competitive advantage. These modern production-sharing arrangements were not contemplated or provided for in the ROO of the SPARTECA.

Forum Trade Ministers in June 2006 called for a review of SPARTECA ROO so that they are made easier, more accessible and meaningful to FICs. The review includes a look at alternate rules, including the Change in Tariff Classification (CTC) approach. The CTC looks at each product line, and can be used in conjunction with other methods, such as the value addition currently in place. Samoa is in the forefront of negotiating a review of the rules to allow duty-free importation of the final products into Australia under a different tariff heading. Raw materials, although sourced from outside the region, should be under a different tariff heading, and therefore qualifies the product as 100% locally manufactured. YES is the major reason the Samoan Government is keen on negotiating this.

A move to change the ROO is necessitated by the erosion of preferences under SPARTECA, as Australia is giving lower percentage local-content criteria to products from Asian countries. With the change in the Australian Government, it would be interesting to know if the new Rudd's government, as part of the review of the motor vehicle industry in Australia, will consider a derogation for Samoa to continue its market access for YES wire harnesses to Australia.

How has YES contributed to poverty reduction in Samoa?

Table 1F shows YES overall contribution to GDP for the period 1998 to 2005. YES alone contributed an average of 8% to the overall GDP, and made up about 80% (average) of the 'other manufacturing'[3] sector's

---

[3] Excludes food and beverage manufacturing.

Table 1F *YES contribution to GDP (1998–2005)*

	1998	1999	2000	2001	2002	2003	2004	2005
Overall GDP (value addition at 2002 market prices)	728,184	750,730	804,652	869,459	885,000	913,030	943,427	992,225
Other manufacturing	75,004	82,270	91,545	112,630	107,654	114,337	106,613	99,892
Yazaki	48,143	55,949	63,098	82,473	79,017	85,009	75,316	67,154
Yazaki / other manufacturing (%)	64	68	69	73	73	74	71	67
Yazaki / overall GDP (%)	6.61	7.45	7.84	9.49	8.93	9.31	7.98	6.77

Source: Ministry of Finance, Apia, SAMOA.

contribution to the GDP. This is a substantial contribution by a single operation, and its absence would make significant changes to the sectoral contributions and economic outlook for Samoa.

In 2004, YES contribution contracted as a result of a decline in demand from Australian markets, resulting in a –1 per cent contribution to growth.

Samoa's private sector is dominated by YES, with the remainder of Samoa's light industrial sector concentrating on providing local substitutes for imports. Samoa has had little success in attracting foreign direct investment, despite its stable political environment and extensive economic reforms.

YES has also contributed substantially to the Samoan economy through value addition to the GDP.

It is estimated that YES pays around SAT$2.5 million for utilities such as electricity, water and telecommunication. It is also estimated that YES pays around SAT$4.6 million for other supporting services such as transportation and meals.

YES has helped to up-skill the workforce

YES' capacity-building efforts and staff training have contributed to the up-skilling of a large part of Samoa's otherwise unskilled labour force. YES has provided a training ground to up-skill Samoa's workforce both physically and psychologically. Although YES' principal skills would be irrelevant to any other existing industry, the knowledge and the ability to transfer knowledge or apply this to related industries is important.

Community assistance

YES also offers much assistance to the Samoan community in terms of donations and sponsorships to schools, universities, health organisations, churches, sports, the environment, government and individuals with special needs etc. YES' contribution to the general community in the form of donations, sponsorship and assistance etc. will be voided if its operations in Samoa are shut down.

Threats to YES operations in Samoa

From a recent YES proposal to the Samoan Government, and also from interviews conducted by the author,[4] a number of concerns and challenges faced by YES have been identified.

---

[4] See the end of this chapter for a list of interviews that took place.

Wages in Samoa

The national minimum wage has been reviewed four times over the past decade, changing from SAT$0.92 to SAT$1.25 in 1995 to SAT$1.40 in 1998. In 2002, the minimum wage was raised further to SAT$1.60. The public-sector minimum wage was increased to SAT$2.40, which led to pressures in the private sector to increase its minimum wage to SAT$2.00, which became effective 26 September 2005.

The pressure induced by this increase in the minimum wage (SAT$0.9 million per annum) has resulted in YES submitting a proposal for further incentives from the government. The proposal by YES reflects this as additional costs of doing business in Samoa (increase in minimum wage and others such as National Pension Fund contribution).

Based on the assumption that 2,000 YES workers are currently being paid SAT$1.80 and working for 40 hours a week, then it will cost YES around SAT$0.9 million to raise these workers' salary from SAT$1.80 to SAT$2.00 per hour.

Logistical and infrastructure issues

Samoa's geographical isolation from its suppliers and customers signifies major potential problems in terms of time-related issues. Lead-times between customer orders and delivery does not allow much room for YES to order its raw materials and produce the customer orders, and not be subjected to changes in orders or design by customers.

There have been many challenges to YES with regards to the efficiency in the provision of utility services since its inception. These challenges have been addressed from time to time, and the company has also made investments in ensuring that quality power and water supplies are available throughout the production.

Competitive pressures

Other Yazaki affiliates operating out of China, Indonesia, Thailand and the Philippines are operating at production costs five to ten times lower than YES. This is due to the huge labour cost variance between these countries and Samoa. The government increased its minimum rates by 50% and the private sector by 25%. YES, then, is faced with people moving to the public service and labour costs increasing substantially, making YES even less competitive against its Asian counterparts.

These companies manufacture all the raw materials either in the same company or not far from their operations in the same country. Shipping services out of these countries are very competitive and therefore costs are economical compared to Samoa. Some analysts predict that if the oil prices continue at this high level, then by 2010, there is a great possibility that the industry will no longer exist. The more lucrative options are that of the smaller-engine and more attractive imported cars.

SPARTECA rules of origin

The ROO requirements have been the most difficult to meet, especially for the manufacturing sector, where labour is the major input and the majority of raw materials are being imported from outside Australia and New Zealand. YES is disadvantaged as its raw materials are 100% sourced from overseas, mostly from countries outside the region. Australia is now enforcing the 15% tax on products with less than 50% local content. Sourcing from within the region is more costly, and sometimes components are not manufactured or available.

The future for YES in Samoa

Ceasing operations in Samoa is under serious consideration by YES as this chapter goes to print. According to YES officials interviewed, YES needs to address the challenges it faces, and its concerns are coupled with unknown effects of globalisation before it realises its next move.

The future of YES depends on its ability to overcome its operating and market challenges. The development and survival of the Australian car-manufacturing industry will certainly impact on YES operations, and the eventual disposition of SPARTECA ROO will be important. With the review of SPARTECA ROO, the outcome is unknown as to whether a change in the rules to CTC will be favourable for YES. As such, YES needs to consider this and determine whether operations in Samoa remain competitive.

Samoa without YES

Samoa would not have reached this stage of economic development without the contribution made by YES. YES brought the answers to Samoa's prayers in terms of employment and business opportunities.

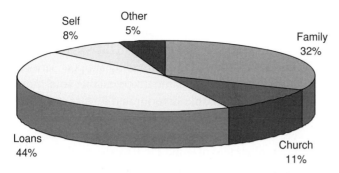

Figure 1G   Average spending of YES income by staff. *Source:* YES (2007).

Unemployment and income loss

The most certain and most direct impact would be the unemployment of some 2,000 Samoans currently with YES. This unemployment would mean the loss of income earned by these workers, and would result in a trickle-down effect on other sectors, especially those in which this income is spent on.

A small survey was conducted as an attempt to gather information on YES staff income earned and their key expenditures. The survey identified the servicing of loans/debt (loan repayments) as the major spending item, which accounted for 44% of total pay – these loans were said to have been taken out for family commitments; 32% of the income was spent on family expenses; 11% towards church contributions; 8% for personal needs; and 5% on other expenses. The survey also revealed that averages of six to seven persons per household are dependent on the YES earnings. The survey results are depicted in Figure 1G. In total, an estimate of 14,000 people depend on the wages paid out from Yazaki directly to its employees. This does not include other service providers and part-time employees.

In its sixteen years of operation, YES has created new market opportunities for a range of local businesses, which have expanded or come into existence to provide support services demanded by YES' existence. These include the development of new/expanded retail outlets in the Vaitele area, inclusive of stalls and street-side vendors/stalls, bus and taxi transportation etc.

As the major expenditure of YES' 2,000 workers' income goes to servicing debts and loans with financial institutions, the absence of this income (due to unemployment) would mean loan-repayment defaults.

This would then lead to outstanding repayments and arrears, mounting interests charged and an increasing principal-loan balance to pay off. This not only applies to YES employees but also extends to the loss of income of employees and businesses that have been providing support services to YES' existence. The Central Bank of Samoa reports that total non-performing loans at the commercial banks deteriorated further at the end of 2006, with a total of SAT\$23.1 million in problem loans. This is an increase of 30.9 per cent from 2005. The reasons for the big increase are not specified, but the unemployment of some 2,000 workers will certainly be a cause of (some) concern to commercial banks and their arrearage levels.

Furthermore, it will not impact positively on the overall liquidity position of commercial banks, especially at a time when the overall monetary conditions in Samoa remain tight, with only a slight improvement in commercial bank liquidity at the end of 2007.

The Vaitele Industrial area where YES is located with other industries has developed its own little township and business centre comprising a number of small- and medium-sized retail outlets, banking facilities, restaurants and small eatery outlets (e.g. BBQ vendors), Laundromats etc. to cater for the industrial operations in the area. YES is the largest of these, and includes other operations such as the brewery, a meat manufacturer and branches of the Electric Power Corporation and Ministry of Works Transport and Infrastructure. YES employees undoubtedly dominate the working population at Vaitele, and the absence of YES will result in the closure of many of these small-scale outlets as sales may not sustain their operations.

Similarly, transportation services through bus and taxi operators have been able to benefit from business opportunities derived from YES existence, through the transportation of its employees both for work shifts as well as for social occasions. With an estimated YES annual spending of SAT\$4.6 million on these support services, this would have a substantial impact on these private small-scale operators.

By April 2008, it appeared that the company would definitely reduce its labour force as a result of the closure of the Mitsubishi manufacturing plant in Australia. In view of potential government pressure, if YES were to immediately cut staff, the company has apparently adopted a policy whereby an employee is dismissed immediately if they make a mistake, such as missing work without notice or using a work phone without authorisation etc. The company will likely have to cut at least 120 workers on a monthly basis. If six to seven people per household rely on one YES employee salary, then there would be between 700 and 800 people facing severe financial difficulties.

Concluding observations

Samoa would be greatly impacted if this multinational company moves its operations offshore, as this is the only major private-sector employer in the country employing those ranging from unskilled, semi-skilled and those with specialised skills.

One question that remains a nagging issue for policy makers and trade watchers is: would Samoa be better off if Yazaki had not moved in? One could argue that Samoa would have been better off socially or culturally – even though Samoa would have been poorer as a result of less employment – if Yazaki had never set up in Samoa. On the other hand, the Samoan Government and most people would only give praise to the contribution that the company has made to Samoa, and that life must therefore go on in searching for more opportunities. The country's expectations have been raised as a result of the economic contributions of this company to the lives of the Samoan people, and so there is much support for this latter view.

As Samoa continues to negotiate access to become a member of the WTO, it will need to carefully assess the real benefits to the country if it becomes a member, given that even without WTO membership the country is already affected by globalisation. The future of SPARTECA is definitely a non-issue, with current regional discussions and negotiations already underway on PACER plus. The Pacific Islands Forum is now faced with the challenges of PICTA implementation, a disappointing experience in negotiations for an EPA with the EU and the ongoing national consultations and missions to determine the main trading issues in a PACER Plus agreement with Australia and New Zealand. The hot topic in relation to trade with Australia and New Zealand is the seasonal labour schemes provided by New Zealand that now Australia is considering closing.

Unfortunately for multinational companies like YES, it appears to be downhill for them, and their best option will likely be to move operations offshore. This could be the best time for them as well, as Samoans rush to send their workers to pick fruit and vegetables in New Zealand. The future of trade between Australia and Samoa could be unfavourable for Samoa unless there is significant progress on labour mobility, greater flexibility in ROO and a strong commitment to trade-related capacity building.

Therefore, an integrated trade framework for Samoa is still a long way from addressing our objectives towards poverty alleviation and economic sustainability.

The Samoan Government really needs to work together with the private sector, non-governmental organisations, the donor community and international organisations to develop an integrated approach to lift the country's trade regime to a level so that, in the future, it remains competitive in a globalised economy.

Bibliography

Australian Manufacturing: A Brief History of Industry Policy and Trade Liberalisation, by Michael Emmery, from the Economics, Commerce and Industrial Relations Group. 2005 Government of Samoa, Budget Speech 2007/08, Ministry of Finance.

Government of Samoa, Strategy for the Development of Samoa 2005–2007, Ministry of Finance.

Government of Samoa (2002), *Report on the Census 2001*, Ministry of Finance, Statistics Division.

Samoa Memorandum on Foreign Trade Regime – WT /ACC/SAM 01: Accession Division.

Trade Liberalisation: Opportunities for Australia 2002. Trade Development Branch, Department of Foreign Affairs and Trade.

Yazaki EDS Limited (YES) (2007), presentation to the Government of Samoa, April.

Interviews

Mrs Nella Tavita-Levy, Ministry of Foreign Affairs and Trade, Samoa.
Mr Lyndon Chu Ling, Ministry of Commerce, Industry and Labour, Samoa.
Mr Oliva Vaai, Yazaki EDS Limited.

Surveys

Employees of Yazaki EDS (fifty employees were interviewed).

1.3

The textile and clothing sector in Indonesia

OMAS BULAN SAMOSIR[*]

Background

The textile and clothing sector plays an important role in Indonesia's economy. In 2005, this sector contributed roughly 15 per cent to Indonesia's non-oil exports, and accounted for 3.5 million jobs.[1] Although the business climate was weak and the Multi-Fibre Arrangement (MFA) quotas had expired, exports of Indonesian garment and textile producers increased 3.5 per cent in 2004 to US$7.28 billion. The US and Europe are the main destinations for mid- and high-end Indonesian textile and garment exports.

Poverty has been one of the main population and development problems faced by Indonesia. In 2006, nearly 18% of the population, some 39 million people, were classified as 'poor'. This represented a big increase from the previous year, when 16% of Indonesians were classified as 'poor' (Statistics Official News, 2006). Most of the poor live in rural areas (63.41%). In 2005, the unconditional cash transfer scheme was implemented by the government in a bid to reduce poverty. However, the impact has not been significant. It seems that this money was used by the poor as a source of income to cover increased expenditure caused by an increase in the price of basic essentials. Another scheme is under development that would give money to the poor conditionally.

The textile and textile product sector in Indonesia

The structure of the textile and textile product (TTP) sector in Indonesia involves manufacturing industry-sector business activities

---

[*] Omas Bulan Samosir is a senior researcher at the Demographic Institute, Faculty of Economics, University of Indonesia.
[1] Figures taken from the US Embassy of Jakarta website: www.usembassyjakarta.org [last accessed 22 February 2007].

from downstream to upstream, ranging from fibre, filament, thread and cloth production to the production of ready-to-wear garments. The TTP sector has been a key activator of the national economy. In 2005, the contribution of this sector to non-oil export foreign-exchange acquisition was US$8.60 billion, with the net-export being US$6.99 billion. In the period of January to October 2006, that figure increased 7.19% to US$7.82 billion. This increase put the TTP sector in first position of non-oil export foreign-exchange earnings, with a 12.65% contribution. It is estimated that the export value of the Indonesian TTP sector will reach US$10.6 billion in 2007.

From a macroeconomic perspective, the contribution of the TTP sector to the national gross domestic product (GDP) in 2006 reached 3%, (about US$9.65 billion). Besides its overall economic impact, the TTP sector also has an important social impact, as it absorbs large numbers of employees, both directly and indirectly. In 2005, it absorbed 1.84 million workers, or 15.7% of total workers in the manufacturing sector, plus 3.68 million indirect workers. In total, labour absorption of this sector in 2005 was 5.52 million workers.

In 2005, Indonesia was one of the largest exporters of TTP in the world. For cloth and thread, Indonesia's market share was 1.7% at 11th position. For ready-made garments, Indonesia's market share was 1.9% at 8th position. The largest overseas market for TTP is Europe. In 2005, total imports of TTP into the EU reached US$194.53 billion. It increased 2.58% from the previous year (US$189.63 billion). Indonesia's TTP exports in 2005 for thread and cloth reached 0.46 billion at 11th position, and for ready-made garments the figure was US$1.54 billion at 10th position.

The US is the second most important importer of TTP. In 2005, the US imported US$102.61 billion, an increase of 6.45 per cent from US$96.39 billion in 2004. Indonesia is one of the largest sources of imports of TTP products into the US. In 2005, for thread and cloth, Indonesia exported as much as US$210 million, and for clothing, US$3.16 billion. In the US, Indonesia was at 11th position for textiles and 8th for cloth as a source of imports.

Although China is the world's largest TTP exporter, it is also the largest market for imports of thread and cloth. In 2005, China imported US$15.50 billion of these products. Indonesia's exports to China for thread and cloth were US$192 million, putting Indonesia in 10th position with a 1.2 per cent market share.

In general terms, there is always a surplus in TTP trade in Indonesia. In the last five years, the surplus was US$5.75 billion on average. The surplus was highest in 2005, when US$6.99 billion was contributed by garments and US$4.85 billion from thread exports, as well as US$1.35 billion from cloth sheets and other textile products.

TTP sales in the domestic market have tended to decline in the last five years, by 17.71% on average. For garments and other textile products, there was a decline in market share, caused by the increase in imports (both legal and illegal) that saw increases of 121.78% per year on average. Both the volume and value of illegal imports increased 132% and 35% from 2004 to 2005 respectively. Illegally imported TTP are generally low-quality products. There was a difference between China's TTP exports to Indonesia (US$11.599 million) and China's TTP imports from Indonesia (US$55.953 million) according to a record by the UN in 2004.

Inter-regional free trade agreement

In order to protect its important external markets, Indonesia has made and is negotiating several trade agreements, including the:

• ASEAN-China Free Trade Area (ACFTA)
• Indonesia-Japan Economic Partnership Agreement (IJEPA)
• comprehensive trade economic partnership (CTEP) between Indonesia and Iran
• comprehensive economic partnership (CEP) between Indonesia and Pakistan
• ASEAN-Korea Free Trade Agreement (AKFTA)
• ASEAN-India Regional Trade and Investment Area (AIRTIA).

ACFTA is an economic agreement that was signed by the leaders or country heads of ASEAN (Association of Southeast Asian Nations) countries and China on 4 November 2002 in Phnom Penh in Cambodia. ACFTA includes rules on goods and services trade and the negotiation of an agreement on investment. Up to now, ACFTA has produced tariff reductions and agreed rules of origin (ROO) since its initial implementation in 2006.

The IJEPA was first initiated by the two countries' leaders in November 2004. It was agreed in December 2004. IJEPA was then agreed and signed on 24 November 2006 in Tokyo by chief negotiators. IJEPA will mark a new era for Japan-Indonesia collaboration through an approach that covers trade in goods, trade in services, customs procedures, investment, movement of natural persons, energy and mineral resources, intellectual property, government procurement, competition, improvement of business environment and promotion of business confidence, and cooperation.

The CTEP between Indonesia and Iran was signed by Trade Ministers of both countries on 21 June 2005. Based on the roadmap, the agreed agenda in 2006 was to arrange a preferential trade agreement in goods and ROO.

The CEP between Indonesia and Pakistan was signed by the Trade Ministers of each country on 24 November 2005. Based on the roadmap, the arranged agenda in 2006 was to arrange a preferential trade agreement in goods and ROO.

ASEAN and Korea implemented a free trade agreement (FTA) covering trade in goods (AKFTA) in June 2007. In November 2007, a complementary FTA covering trade in services was signed.

On 15 September 2002, ASEAN and Indian Economic Ministers assigned economic senior staff to form a task force to arrange a Framework Agreement on Comprehensive Economic Cooperation between ASEAN and the Republic of India, which is in the AIRTIA. The long-term objective of AIRTIA is to achieve a free trade region between the two economies.

These six agreements show that trade liberalisation between Indonesia and other regional countries was motivated by a shared understanding of the important role of trade in improving people's welfare in each country. Besides economic integration objectives, the agreements' coverage is not only focused on goods traded between countries, but is also focused on production factors and service traffic, development and standardisation of telecommunications and transportation infrastructure, and relevant institutions that coordinate, manage and regulate that economic integration process.

Furthermore, the existence of global production-sharing arrangements means that these agreements can be expected to deliver benefits to sectors such as TTP in terms of the reduction of import duties and excise taxes, increased export quotas and other trade-facilitation benefits in destination countries.

Garment and textile working conditions

Demographic and socioeconomic background characteristics

As part of this project, the author successfully interviewed seventy-two workers of the TTP sectors, where thirty-five were male (48.6%) and thirty-seven were female (51.4%). By region, twenty-four (33%) were from DKI Jakarta, twenty-six (36%) were from West Java and twenty-two (31%) were from Banten. By age group, most of them were aged twenty-six to thirty-four years (50%), followed by aged eighteen to twenty-five years (31%) and thirty-five to forty years (12.5%). Only 5.6% were aged forty-one to fifty years, and there was one worker aged above fifty years.

Most workers in the garment and textile sector had middle-school education: 62.5% had senior-high-school (*Sekolah Menengah Atas*/SMA) education and 31.9% had junior-high-school (*Sekolah Menengah Pertama*/SMP) education. The other 5.6% had graduated from primary school. In addition, male workers had better education than female workers, where 71% of male workers had SMA education while the figure was 54% for female workers.

For marital status, 42% were not married, 54% were married and 4% were divorced. Of those who were married, 61.5% had working spouses and 38.5% had unemployed spouses. All of those who were married lived in the same house with their spouses. By place of residence, most workers in the study lived in rented houses (55.6%), 19.4% lived in their own houses and 23.6% lived with their parents/relatives.

Employment conditions

By type of work, the percentage of workers who worked at jobs requiring physical strength was higher for male workers than for female workers. Meanwhile, female workers usually worked at jobs that need carefulness, such as sewing. These results indicate that in the garment and textile sector, there is a work division between male and female workers based on the strength needed to do the job.

In the study, the workers were asked whether they knew about the market destination of the products they produced. This is important because it may affect their working spirit and assist in their production of quality products, affecting the reputation of their employers. In addition, this knowledge is also important in order to have bargaining power for the workers' own rights for better pay. The results of the study show that most workers knew the market orientation of their companies (94%). Most stated that their companies exported their products (56%) and 34% stated that their companies exported more of their products than were destined for the domestic market. In addition, the percentage who knew about the market orientation of the companies was higher for male workers than for female workers.

In the companies covered by the survey, the greatest number of workers (38%) had been in the employment of their current company for between

Table 1G   *Years of employment with company*

Years of employment	Percentage of workers surveyed (%)
1 or less	24
2–5	38
6–10	22
11–15	7
15 or more	10

two and five years (see Table 1G). Whether the workers were counting time in the company generally or in a particular section of the company, the percentage breakdown was more or less the same.

One important indicator of workers' social welfare is the pay received to live a better life. The results of the study show that most workers (62.5%) received between Rp 816,100 and Rp 1,500,000 monthly (between AU$125 and AU$231 with the exchange rate of AU$1 = Rp 6,500). A substantial percentage of them received less than AU$108 monthly (18%), where most of them had worked for less than five years. Another 18% of the workers received between AU$125 and AU$108 monthly. These findings indicate that, despite the involvement of their companies in global production-sharing arrangements, the salary of workers in the garment and textile sector remains at subsistence level. There was no significant difference in salary received by male and female workers. The percentage of those who received higher than the provincial minimum wage was slightly higher for female workers than for male workers (62.5% versus 60%).

Employment status is another critical issue in the discussion of decent employment in Indonesia. As a strategy for reducing costs and raising efficiency of production, many companies in the country have increased their reliance on short-term contract workers with no real security of employment. This study found that a substantial percentage of work-ers were contractual workers (39%) and 4% were weekly workers. The percentage of permanent workers, however, was 56%. Those who were contractual workers mostly had one-year contracts (78.6%), 17.9% had three-month contracts and 3.6% had six-month contracts. Furthermore, female workers were more likely to have temporary working status, either contractual or weekly. The results indicate that the situation of these workers is far from secure.

In terms of working hours, the situation can be categorised as 'decent', as most worked for seven hours a day (87.5%), followed by eight hours a day (9.7%) and six hours a day (2.8%). However, most workers enjoyed one day off for six working days a week (90.3%) with only 9.7% working just five days a week. In addition, the percentage of those who worked eight hours a day was higher for female workers than for male workers (16.2% versus 2.9%). There was no significant difference in the number of days worked between male and female workers.

Payment for workers usually comprises a salary and some overtime salary, as well as transportation and meal money. Although workers often receive payments from their employer intended to cover transportation and meal costs separately from their salaries, the workers, in many cases, lump these payments with their salaries and use the money for purposes other than for that intended, for example saving the money or using it to cover other living costs. This way, many are able to improve their living conditions. However, this is not always the case. The results of the study show that most workers did not receive transportation or meal money (67% for both) since their companies provide the transportation facilities to assure on time arrival at the work place; and their companies provide meals at the work place in order to keep workers around the work place during break time. Most of those who received transportation and meal money received the money monthly together with their salaries (71% and 58% respectively). Meanwhile, 81% of workers stated they received some overtime salary and most received it monthly (81%). There was no significant difference between male and female workers in terms of salary, meal, transportation and overtime payment systems.

With subsistent income, it can be understood that most workers cannot save money from their income, or, if they can save money, the amount is not significant. The results of the study show that 62.5% of workers could not save money from their salaries. Among those who could save money, most could save less than AU$23 monthly (41%), followed by between AU$23 and AU$31 monthly (37%) and more than AU$31 monthly (22%). In addition, female workers were more likely to save from their salaries than male workers (43.2% versus 31.4%). However, of those who could save money, male workers were more likely to save a greater amount of money (more than AU$31) than female workers (27.3% versus 18.8%).

Rights at work

Knowledge of the exact amount of the provincial minimum wage (AU$138 in DKI Jakarta, AU$109 in West Java and AU$123 in Banten) as well as the maximum weekly overtime hours (ten hours or less) is important to workers so they know about their rights. The results of the study show that most workers knew the provincial minimum wage as well as maximum overtime hours. Male workers had better knowledge about these two issues than female workers, indicating a higher concern of male workers on these matters, particularly since they were or they would be the head of a family.

Work safety and good facilities are also a worker's right at the work place. In the study, workers were asked about the availability of health facilities, toilet facilities and safety facilities and training. Most workers stated that they sometimes had health problems when working (86%), and of them, 75% stated that those health problems related to working conditions, with headaches being the most cited health problem (68%), followed by tiredness (32%) and backache (21%). In their responses to the survey about problems encountered in the workplace, a greater number of females (89%) than males (83%) indicated work-related health problems.

The availability of first aid facilities was almost universal: 98.6% of workers stated that there was a first aid facility in their company. However, the availability of health clinics was lower: 86% stated that there was a health clinic in their company, with most stating that they were not asked to pay for health services they received at the company's health clinic (98%). It seems that, in terms of health at work, workers obtained their rights. There was no significant difference between male and female workers in terms of the availability of health facilities at the work place.

Most workers received work-safety training at the work place (86%), meaning that only a small percentage of them did not (14%). However, only 7% of those trained had a work-safety training certificate. None of the female workers in the study had work-safety training certificates, while the figure was 14% for male workers, calling into question the quality of the training. In addition, female workers were more likely to report that they had no work-safety training (19% versus 9%).

In terms of the availability of drinking water at the work place, all stated that drinking water was provided. In addition, almost all stated that the toilet facilities were clean (98.6%), and 89 per cent stated that work safety equipment was available, with masks being the most cited equipment (86%), followed by gloves (63%), head cover (42%) and footwear (32%). Female workers were more likely to report the availability of work-safety equipment than their male counterparts (92% versus 86%), particularly that of head cover.

Social protection

Another aspect of a good working environment is the presence of social protection. This includes equal treatment at the work place, social security and on-leave and holiday pay (*Tunjangan Hari Raya*/THR). Workers' overall appreciation of whether their work was 'decent' also depended on their perceptions of the fairness of their salary and working hours and the adequacy of other payments for meals, transportation and THR, as well as whether work place facilities were suitable for their needs. The results of the study show that most workers stated that there was no unfair treatment at their companies (79%). Male workers were more likely to report unfair treatment at the work place than their female counterparts (29% versus 14%). In addition, 60% of the workers stated that the treatment was appropriate, with no significant difference between male and female workers on this matter.

A large portion of workers in the study (88%) stated that they were members of the Worker Social Security Scheme (*Jaminan Sosial Tenaga Kerja*/JAMSOSTEK). Only 18% stated they also had extra health insurance other than JAMSOSTEK, with male workers being more likely to report having extra health insurance than female workers (23% versus 14%).

In terms of annual leave, most stated that they received twelve days a year (74%) and all stated they received a normal salary when they were on leave. Female workers were more likely to report that they never took annual leave than male workers (57% versus 49%), mainly because they were not permanent workers (53% versus 27%). In addition, 89% of workers received THR, mostly in the form of money (63%) and as much as one month's salary (67%).

Social dialogue

Social dialogue is an important method of communication between workers and manufacturers in order to promote good-quality work. Usually it is channelled through a workers' union within the company. The results of the study show that most workers stated that there was a workers' union in their company (72%). However, most workers were not members of the workers' union (65%), with female workers being more likely not to be union members than male workers (70% versus 60%). Of those who were members of a workers' union, most stated that the workers' union was useful for them (88%) and that their working conditions were better (60%). However, most stated that the salary level of union members and non-union members was the same (52%). Female workers were more likely than male workers to report that a workers' union was useful (91% versus 86%), that working conditions were better (64% versus 57%) and that salary levels were better (64% versus 36%).

Another manifestation of the social dialogue is through the Mutual Employment Agreement (*Kesepakatan Kerja Bersama*/KKB). The results of the study showed that most workers stated there was a KKB in their company. However, among those who stated there was a KKB, only 25% of workers knew the contents of the KKB, 34% knew it only partly and 41% did not know the contents of the KKB. In addition, most stated that with a KKB, working conditions had improved somewhat (52.5%), with 15.3% stating that working conditions had improved a lot and 32.2% stating that there was no improvement. In addition, female workers were more likely to state that there was a KKB than their male counterparts (87% versus 77%). Male workers were more likely to know the contents of a KKB than female workers (30% versus 22%).

Financial support from and to workers

Although they lived with subsistent salaries, some were able to support their families: 57% of workers in the study stated that they sent money to their relatives and 54% of this group did it routinely. Most sent between AU$15 and AU$46 on average (49%), 39% sent less than AU$15 and 12% sent between AU$39 and AU$77. When asked about how their relatives used the money sent home by the workers, most cited food and clothing purchases. The next most important use was to pay for education, followed by health-related payments. Female workers were more likely to send less than male workers (48% versus 30%). Meanwhile, male workers were more likely to send between AU$15 and AU$46 more than their female counterparts (60% versus 38%).

Three workers in the study received support from their relatives, but only one received routine support, with the amount being between AU$8 and AU$15.

Workers' evaluation of their welfare conditions

When asked to compare their working conditions to other company working conditions, 21% stated that their conditions were better, 53% stated conditions were the same and 26% stated conditions were worse. Male workers were more likely to report that their conditions were better

(26% versus 16%) or worse (34% versus 19%) than their female counter-parts, while female workers were more likely to report that their conditions were the same (65% versus 40%).

In the study, workers were also asked to evaluate their current wel-fare conditions compared to their welfare conditions two years ago. Most stated that their current welfare conditions were the same as their condi-tions two years ago (49%), 36% stated conditions were worse and 15% stated conditions were better. Increasing cost of living was the most cited reason for deteriorating welfare conditions (92%), followed by unchanged salary (31%). Furthermore, male workers were more likely than their female counterparts to state that their welfare conditions were better (23% versus 8%) or worse (46% versus 27%). Male workers were more likely to report that the increased cost of living was the cause of their worsened welfare conditions (75% versus 10%).

In summary, the study reveals that the conditions of Indonesian work-ers in the garment and textile industries involved in the global production supply chain were far from decent. However, despite the situation, they were able to save money as well as support their relatives financially. Cer-tainly, workers' participation in the TTP sector helps to reduce poverty at the familial level. In other words, the TTP sector makes a positive contri-bution to poverty reduction in Indonesia since it absorbs a substantial pro-portion of workers. Compared to having no job at all, workers in the TTP sector in Indonesia are better off having a job with subsistence salary levels.

Hindering and supporting factors

According to Mr Inov (API General Secretariat), there are eleven problem areas in the TTP sector:

(1) cotton material
(2) monetary and banking
(3) labour force
(4) illegal TTP imports
(5) environment
(6) infrastructure
(7) port tariffs
(8) energy
(9) regional autonomy
(10) machine restructuring
(11) anti-dumping accusations.

Of these eleven problem areas, the crucial problems are energy and machinery restructuring. The State Electricity Company (*Perusahaan Listrik Negara*/PLN) implemented the maximum energy policy.[2] As stated by a staff member from the Ministry of Industry, the implementation of this policy was considered a massive blow to the TTP sector because, usually, textile machines work twenty-four hours continuously. However, with the support of the Ministry of Industry, companies that have 350 operational hours per month are freed from this maximum energy policy.

The situation described above may bring on a decline in workers' welfare. As stated by Mr Syukur, a staff member from the Workers Association (*Serikat Pekerja Seluruh Indonesia*/SPSI), there is a tendency toward a decline in workers' welfare because of the decline in production in the TTP sector. In addition, Indonesian workers are falling behind Chinese, Vietnamese and Indian workers in terms of efficiency, professionalism and productivity. This is often because the manufacturers also worked inefficiently and depended upon land or facilities inherited from their parents and upon financial support from political and tribal groups that was not dependent on an evaluation of the manufacturers' competitive position.

Another obstacle, according to the staff member of SPSI, is significant corruption in the government. This is about collusion, corruption and nepotism (CCN) – Indonesia's 'disease'. In order to run an industry and to get legal permission easier and more quickly, business people in Indonesia have to deal with the staff of relevant government institutions as well as Members of Parliament. And these all require pay-off money. An application regarding a business matter might not be considered if someone does not 'bribe' the persons who would be dealing with it.

However, despite all of these woes, many manufacturers believe that the TTP sector in Indonesia has a bright future. World conditions are conducive for TTP-sector expansion, as stated by the General Secretary of API. Garment trends have changed: people not only talk about clothing for summer, winter, autumn and spring, but also clothing for winter 1, winter 2, summer 1, summer 2 and so on. Because he sees a favourable future climate for the development of international sales, the General Secretary argues that resources should be made available to

---

[2] Maximum energy policy meaning that PLN charges industries a higher rate if they use electricity beyond the maximum energy allowed.

improve the sector's capital equipment and increase the productivity of its labour force so that it is in a position to take full advantage of market opportunities.

However, the recent bright spots do not mean that the TTP sector in Indonesia does not have a problem. As stated by Mr Sumanto, a staff member at a textile firm, the main problems faced are: (i) aged machinery (on average fifteen to twenty-five years), in particular in the spinning/weaving sector; (ii) the difficulties in entering world markets because of declining competitiveness, in particular from new emerging competitors that use new technology, causing Indonesian export values to stagnate (between US\$7 to US\$8 billion per year); (iii) cheaper and varied products from China's TTP sector flooding Indonesia's domestic market, both with legal and illegal goods; and (iv) in general, the banking sector considering the TTP sector to be a sunset sector with high risks.

Policy recommendations

In order to facilitate the sector's employment of additional workers, the Department of Industry is providing low-interest loans to companies for the purpose of renovating plant and equipment or for restructuring their production to become more competitive. The loans are financed from the government's national budget and are generally offered at rates comparable to those provided by other ASEAN governments to their industries (*Anggaran Pendapatan dan Belanja Negara*/APBN). This programme has an indirect impact on workers and is handled by the Ministry of Manpower and Transmigration. With this policy, the TTP sector is expected to grow and will be able to absorb more workers. On the manufacturing side, economic upgrading has been effected through improving machine technology.

On the other hand, labour problems have often created long industrial relation conflicts regarding payment and welfare systems. This cannot be separated from the manpower surplus problem in Indonesia. Mr Sahat, a staff member from the Ministry of Manpower and Transmigration, stated that the government has intervened in industrial relations through the implementation of regional minimum wages to ensure workers' welfare. The government needs to determine provincial minimum wage and good living conditions in order to resolve the disagreement between workers and manufacturers.

The government has a strong interest in the development and long-term sustainability of the TTP sector in Indonesia and has backed up this interest with funding in support of the sector's efforts to obtain new and more efficient machinery and to renovate older machines. The government, through the Department of Industry supported through a Technology Improvement Programme for the TTP sector, plans to replace part of or all production equipment, including supporting machines, with better technology in order to improve productivity, quality and competitiveness of the products. In principle, the direction and goals of the programme are to give low interest rates to all TTP industries that want to improve their machinery and technology. However, because of the limited budget, the government is currently not in a position to assist all firms in the sector. Taking into account the broader national interest, the government allocates public resources first to those firms that make the greatest contributions toward employment, or firms that produce goods having a higher value addition and which contribute more to national export earnings.

Last but not the least, coordination and consolidation among all stake-holders should be improved, such as through the Department of Industry, API, SPSI, the Department of Manpower and Transmigration, the International Labor Organization (ILO) and the community. API suggested that the government should pay attention to the real situation of the TTP sector and not only pursue political goals. The business climate should also be improved through support from the banking system. The broader community should also be encouraged to invest in the TTP sector since the presence of industry in a region has multiplier effects to support economic activities in the region.

In terms of workers' welfare, the Ministry of Manpower and Transmigration should collaborate with JAMSOSTEK to improve workers' welfare. This can be done by building hospitals, transportation facilities and education facilities for workers and their families. With this approach, greater access to basic needs will be given to workers and their families. In turn, it will open the way to poverty reduction amongst garment and textile workers.

Conclusions

From the discussion above, it can be concluded there are three main factors hindering the continuation of the Indonesian textile sector: (i) an unsatisfactory financial and investment climate; (ii) limited infrastructure; and (iii) a complex and corrupt bureaucracy. The government should improve its roles as well as performance to support the development of the TTP sectors in the country. The government is one of the key players. In particular, if it can successfully combat CCN in the country, improve government performance and improve the infrastructure, investment in the country will grow significantly, thus creating more jobs and increasing the welfare of workers. The point is that not only will these sectors contribute to poverty reduction, but also to employment opportunities in other areas as the investment climate improves.

Maintaining the textile and garment sector in Indonesia is necessary for poverty reduction because of the very large number of workers employed in the sector. At the same time, the government must perform its role in the facilitation and promotion of good-quality work, i.e. protecting the workers and creating a conducive investment climate through good infrastructure and supporting policies.

Bibliography

Asosiasi Pertekstilan Indonesia (API) (2007), *Revitalization Competitiveness of Textile and Textile Products in Indonesia* (*Revitalisasi Daya Saing Industri Tekstil dan Produk Tekstil*/TPT), API.

Embassy of the United States (2007), Indonesia Garment Sector Post-Multi Fiber Agreement, Embassy of the United States: Jakarta, Indonesia, available at www.usembassyjakarta.org [last accessed 25 March 2009].

Statistics Official News (2006), 'Poverty Rate in Indonesia in 2005–2006' (*Tingkat Kemiskinan di Indonesia Tahun 2005–2006*), Statistic Official News (*Berita Resmi Statistik*) 47(9).

1.4

Transnational corporations and the footwear industry: women in Jakarta

Introduction

The manufacturing sector holds an important role in the Indonesian economy. The sector's contribution to total national production increased from 37% in 1988 to 46% in 2005. Four major industries dominate manufacturing. They are: food, beverages and tobacco (International Standard Industrial Classification (ISIC) 31); textiles, garments, leather and footwear (ISIC 32); chemicals and rubber (ISIC 35); and transportation equipment and machinery (ISIC 38). These four industries account for nearly 79% of the total manufacturing output.

The textiles, garments, leather and footwear industry has unique characteristics, for it is, among the above four, the most export-oriented and primarily labour intensive. As a result, it holds a special place in a surplus labour economy like Indonesia. Employment in this industry absorbs more than 20 per cent of the total workforce in Indonesia.

Table 1H indicates that footwear exports are one of the ten most important Indonesian export categories. Exports of footwear have grown by a yearly average of 8.8% over the period of 2002 to 2006. The US and EU countries are the two most important markets for Indonesia's footwear exports and account for 75% of total Indonesian footwear exports. Remaining export volumes are distributed to Japan (4%), Mexico (1%) and other countries (20%). Analysts predict that the EU will become Indonesia's single most important export destination.

Investment figures for the footwear industry also show a trend of increased investment in the period of 2003 to 2006. The growth rate of investment in the industry demonstrated a very slight increase (0.4%)

---

* Beta Yulianita Gitaharie Laksono is a senior researcher at the Demographic Institute, Faculty of Economics at the University of Indonesia.

Table 1H   *Indonesia's top ten export categories*

Commodity	Jan–Oct (US$ billion) 2005	Jan–Oct (US$ billion) 2006	% of total exports 2006
Electrical tools	6.06	6.05	9.36
Coal	3.56	5.26	8.13
Rubber and rubber products	4.13	4.83	7.47
Machinery/mechanical tools	2.94	4.80	7.42
Cooper, ash and residues	3.79	3.55	5.49
Garment, not knitted	2.55	3.51	5.43
Wood and wood product	2.62	2.81	4.35
Household and lighting	2.65	2.70	4.18
Footwear	*1.32*	*1.54*	*2.38*
Fish and shrimp	1.31	1.49	2.30
Total top-most ten products	**30.93**	**36.54**	**56.51**
Other	23.93	28.12	43.49
Total non-oil and gas exports	**54.86**	**64.66**	**100.00**

Source: Indonesia: Trade and Investment Highlights, September–November 2006.

in 2003 to 2004, but a drastic increase (at an annual average of 22% per year) for the 2004 to 2006 period. Particularly important investments in this period came from Chinese and Vietnamese sources. Eleven new producers established operations in Indonesia in 2006, with the value of additional investment reaching Rp 466.2 billion. The production-capacity utilisation rate also jumped significantly from 68.6% in 2002 to 73.8% in 2006.

In the world market, China, Vietnam and Indonesia are recognised as the three largest footwear exporters, with global market shares of 35%, 30% and 22% respectively; and for all three, the most important markets are the US and EU countries. China dominates 60% of the US market. China's export of leather shoes to EU countries increased 450% from 2004 to 2005 (an enormous increase in only one year), putting domestic production of these EU countries at risk. In a safeguard action, the EU imposed import quotas and increased duties on Chinese footwear products in April 2006. The US also took action against Chinese exports of footwear that same year. The imposition of anti-dumping and import quota policies forced some 3,000 Chinese shoe factories to shut down.

Vietnam is now ranked as the second most important producer of shoes in the world market – taking over Indonesia's earlier position as number two. Vietnam's exports to EU countries increased 100% from 2004 to 2005. In the same way it reacted to Chinese shoe-export surges, the European Commission took safeguard actions and imposed new import taxes of 10% *ad valorem* on shoes imported from Vietnam.

From the above description, we can see that Indonesia has opportunities to expand its footwear industry – demonstrated by its potential to increase production, investment, export, utilisation, productivity and employment – and is also in a position to benefit externally from the safeguard actions in place against its competitors in both China and Vietnam. Indonesia is also the beneficiary of GSP (Generalised System of Preference) preferential rates from the EU (in the form of tariff reductions from 17% to 13.3%), which makes its exports of footwear more competitive in Europe. However, taking advantage of these opportunities requires the footwear industry (under government supervision) to ensure that it complies with rules of origin (ROO), local added requirements of 25% or minimum local content of 40% and changes in goods classification.

The Indonesian Government and external aid agencies should strive to ensure the continued existence of the footwear industry in Indonesia because it contributes to the reduction of local poverty, both directly through employment and indirectly through its multiplier effect in deriving creation of jobs through higher levels of production. Greater output will increase employment, induce higher labour demands and further reduce poverty. It is a challenge to the Indonesian Government to stimulate, endorse and support the further development of the footwear industry in the country.

Nature of the footwear industry in Indonesia

The footwear industry in Indonesia is the most labour-intensive sector among manufacturing industries, and is characterised by a specific operation pattern: the subcontracting pattern. A brief description of the nature of the industry follows.

Labour intensity

One unique characteristic of the footwear industry is that it is the most labour-intensive manufacturing industry where, to date, it has not proved technologically feasible for machines to replace the role of humans in the production process. Every part of the production process – designing, cutting, sewing, pressing, gluing, polishing, quality controlling and packaging – requires human skills. The quality of the shoe is dependent on the skill and experience of the workers. It is widely admitted that the sewing quality of Indonesian workers is superior to that of workers in other countries where shoes are made. This is a good selling point and adds value to the products of Indonesia's footwear industry.

Current statistical data indicate that some 150,000 workers are employed in the industry. The growth rate of employment in the industry increased quite significantly in recent years – statistical data show employment growth of 0.06% in 2004, 3.8% in 2005 and 6.4% in 2006. Field findings indicate that firms characterised as 'small' (with 200 workers or less) typically employ more than 50% of the production workforce as contract-based workers, whereas larger firms (sometimes employing as many as 7,000 workers) tend to have larger numbers of permanent employees. If Indonesia continues to ramp up shoe production to fill the gaps created by restrictions on Chinese and Vietnamese exports, there is the potential to see the number of workers in the industry double to 300,000.

Subcontracting pattern

The footwear industry is one where many transnational corporations (TNCs) have the power to coordinate and control operations in more than one country, even if they do not own the companies actually producing the shoes. Among the world's most known firms for sport shoes that have such subcontracting operations are Adidas, Nike, Puma and Reebok. These branded shoes are produced in Asian countries like China, Vietnam and Indonesia. The principal TNCs have the ability to take advantage of geographical positions in the distribution of factors of production.

The subcontracted mode of production in individual cases very much depends on the particular international brand owner/holders. Indonesia's subcontracted branded sport-shoe producers usually take orders from brand owners. Brand owners/holders generally make the designs and frequently require specific input materials. Domestic shoe producers are cultivated as 'shoe tailors'. Under these circumstances, the Indonesian firms are unlikely to develop innovation and creativity in producing shoes. On the other hand, it is clear that global demand for branded footwear is considerably higher than demand for non-branded footwear. Non-branded footwear faces considerable barriers to enter world markets.

Because these branded-shoe TNCs do not own factories in the producing countries, and because they have the ability to take advantage of geographical positions affecting shoe production, they would, to a large extent, be indifferent as to where to produce or who to subcontract. They will place orders to whoever charges less for the cost of production under subcontract. Normally, factory identities are not indicated on shoe labels; instead, the country where the shoe is produced is denoted along with the brand name.

As already stated, the footwear industry has a very labour-intensive characteristic, and because of this, branded-shoe TNCs mostly select outsourced modes of production. With this mode of production, they do not have to tie up the large sums of money needed to directly employ workers to make the shoes. By way of example, a typical shoe producer in Indonesia subcontracting to a branded-shoe TNC may employ an average of 5,000 to 10,000 workers. In an outsourcing model, the company will likely not engage in employing workers permanently, and is likely to disregard important commitments to workers. Workers in such circumstances do not have working contracts with owners or management and are thus at risk. A more serious problem recently seen in Indonesia involves shoe producers who summarily close up shop and leave the country, leaving their workers unpaid. This type of player does not consider workers as an important element in the production process. This is unfortunate, because experience has demonstrated that workers who spend considerable time specialising in one or more specific production processes become more skilled and valuable to the company. Most importantly, the creation over time of good employer-employee relations creates a situation where workers will support their employers, and vice versa.

Home-production (piece work) modes are not suitable for footwear manufacturing firms – particularly those with high international quality standards. Such production modes are risky in terms of being able to ensure strict adherence to quality standards. Shoes, both sport and casual types, *must* be produced in a factory where sequential tasks in the production process can be perfected and monitored.

Contribution to poverty reduction

The nature of the footwear industry is different from technology-intensive industries. The existence of a labour-intensive footwear factory in fact produces direct, positive economic impacts to local surroundings (attracting in-migrants and creating other employment opportunities), hence supporting the reduction of local poverty. Technology-intensive industries normally employ only twenty to thirty workers, and therefore do not absorb nearly as many workers as a footwear factory. Technology-intensive industries do contribute to the national economy, but not so directly to local surrounding areas because of their limited direct-employment impact, and therefore they tend to have less of an impact on poverty reduction.

The existence of a footwear industry in Indonesia contributes to the reduction of local poverty through its multiplier effect in deriving creation of jobs. Taking advantage of opportunities mentioned earlier, the industry has the potential to generate a higher demand for shoes produced in Indonesia – implying a higher level of production and a larger number of workers employed. This will generate derivative demands for other goods and services, which then will create other formal and informal job opportunities such as small food and utilities kiosks, telephone booths and transportation/logistics businesses. In addition, the existence of the factory will also make a contribution to the whole village/municipality/district where the factory is located, and even to neighbouring villages. For these important reasons, closing down a shoe-producing factory would have dire consequences because it will throw thousands of workers out of work and will affect the life of their families – wives and children – and will affect other local businesses' chances for survival (e.g. motorcycle rental services (*ojek*), food kiosks etc.).

Aside from job creation, the existence of a footwear factory also affects workers' level of welfare. Workers in a typical footwear factory who have worked for more than one year are paid much more than the required minimum wage. The minimum wage at the national level is set at approximately Rp 700,000. It is based on the proper life needs (*KHL = Kebutuhan Hidup Layak*), which is indexed to the market value for food, shelter, education, health and recreation.

Workers should also be provided with social protections on health, old age or pension, accident and death. In its efforts to increase all sector workers' welfares, the Ministry of Labour coordinates with Jamsostek (*Jaminan Sosial Tenaga Kerja*/Labour Social Security) to construct low-priced houses, hospitals, transportation and free education provisions. It is recognised in Indonesia that workers' welfare is not only about wages, but is about other social aspects as well.

Field findings

Summaries of field findings from surveys in the three provinces of Banten, West Java and DKI Jakarta indicate that the footwear industry contributes to savings and poverty reduction. Workers with a high level of education did not rule out work as production workers in shoe factories. For them, being employed was more favourable than staying unemployed. Moreover, our survey found that 61.4% of the total respondents were married, and 84.4% of them already had between one to four children. They had to work to support and take care of their families. Almost 70% of the married respondents were prime income earners (most were men), with around 20% of their spouses also working. Most male workers (79%) had wives who did not work, whereas among female workers, 79% said their husbands also worked. Clearly, women working in the industry contribute to domestic financial affairs.

Regarding residential arrangements, all female workers in the field survey were living with their husbands, but about 25% of male workers were not residing with their wives (of these, 20.8% of the wives lived outside the province, and 4.2% lived in different regions of the same province). The data demonstrate that there is worker in-migration to these regions due to the existence of opportunities for employment and higher wages in the footwear industry.

Most of the workers surveyed were permanently employed (62%), with a considerably smaller number (32%) being contract-based workers. All were working within normal working hours and days – seven to eight hours a day and five to six days a week. There was no discriminatory treatment for women, who worked on the same days and for the same periods as the men covered in the survey.

More than half of the workers were paid on a monthly payment system (55.7%). Others were paid on weekly (20%) and two-weekly (24.3%) payment systems. Field findings indicate the lowest wage was Rp 700,000 per month, which is equal to the national level of minimum wage, whereas the highest was Rp 1,752,000 per month. It implies that all workers in the three observed provinces receive their wages either at or considerably above the provincial minimum requirement.

Half of the total workers interviewed could realise some savings out of their total earnings. In an interesting finding, it appeared that more female workers were able to save from their earnings than male workers. Of course, this was in line with the survey's findings that male workers were generally the prime income earners. The data also proved that prime income earners saved less than non-prime income earners because they had to support and finance their families' needs and expenses. Another interesting finding from the survey indicated that married workers (28.6%) saved more than single workers (21.4%), and those who lived with their spouses and whose spouses were working could save more.

Almost half of the workers (48.6%) who could make monthly savings put Rp 100,000 of their incomes aside as savings. This finding was also confirmed with firm owners the author interviewed. They said that workers saved around 30% of their total earnings every month and transferred their money via banks to their home villages. Some of the workers used postal services to send their money, and some took their savings home on Idul Fitri personally.

Sixty seven per cent of the total workers surveyed transferred or sent their money to their parents/siblings/relatives. This was mostly done by workers in the East Java and Banten regions. More married workers (40%) transferred or sent their money than single workers (27%). However, the transfers were in general not routinely made, except for workers in Banten. The amount of monthly financial support sent to their families was mostly between Rp 50,000 and Rp 200,000. Only a few workers sent between Rp 300,000 and Rp 500,000. The money they transferred was mainly to support their parents'/siblings'/relatives' basic needs, particularly for food (61%), and only in a few cases to support educational expenses (11%) or to provide basic shelter (1%). The findings indicate that workers in the footwear industry in Indonesia distribute their incomes to their home villages, provide support financially to their families and, overall, make a contribution through their employment to the reduction of poverty in the country.

The survey also found that the overall welfare of a significant number of workers had improved (49%) within the last two years. The higher the level of overall welfare the worker had, the higher the amount of earnings sent home, and the more they therefore contributed to poverty reduction. However, some workers (27%) were found worse off than they were two years ago. These workers reported that living costs were getting more expensive, and wage increases were insignificant and insufficient to cover the rising living costs. In the case of a few workers, they indicated that their condition worsened because of changes in worker status (usually from permanent to contract-based), changes that seem to be increasingly applied by many factories. Others indicated that their wives no longer worked and could not contribute to their financial needs.

In general, the field findings indicate that workers are paid fair wages and receive incentives, allowances and benefits. Work hours and health and safety conditions are found to be in compliance with the existing regulations. There is no sex discrimination in treatment and job assignment.

Barriers to the footwear industry in Indonesia

Despite the contribution it makes to poverty reduction, the footwear industry in Indonesia still experiences barriers that impede the industry from near-term expansion – both in terms of internal and external constraints.

Internal barriers

Among the perceived problems with Indonesia's relative competitive position in this sector is that Indonesian workers are less productive than their counterparts in China. Part of the productivity gap is ascribed to different work cultures in the two countries.

Many Indonesian manufacturing industries are not operating efficiently. In a globalised world, industries must be managed professionally and efficiently. In Indonesia, many entrepreneurs do not run their companies professionally – they depend too much on the faculties of their relatives; and they rarely undertake developmental or innovative work in the plant. It is a fact that many companies in Indonesia are not internally run in an efficient way.

It is also true that, in most cases, the condition of the machinery in the manufacturing sector is often old or obsolete. The newest machines are often at least fifteen years old. These must be replaced, for they cannot operate efficiently; they demand more energy and are less productive. Even though labour costs are relatively less expensive, old machines can seriously undercut the productivity of the plant.

The absence of an efficient infrastructure, professional management and high-quality standards demanded by branded shoe retailers also impede small- and medium-sized shoe producers in their efforts to compete in the international market. Small- and medium-sized shoe producers should be supported by the government (i.e. through facility upgrades that improve health and safety in the workplace), while marketing, management and technical assistance could be supported by the footwear association. After some time, these small- and medium-sized producers could be certified as ready to participate in domestic and international exhibitions. They could then take orders from abroad, with strong confidence of delivering a quality product on time.

Another important limitation to the footwear industry's further development in Indonesia stems from the fact that it is still dependent on imported leather. Leather comprises 60 per cent of the total raw material required for footwear production. In addition, foreign footwear buyers or importers require particular leather input specifications that mostly cannot be satisfied by domestic leather producers. The famous leather tanning in Indonesia known as Java Box is concentrated in Java regions. The leather quality is demanded not only by the footwear industry but also by other industries, such as bag and garment industries. No countries produce leather as high-quality as the Java Box. Regrettably, production levels are not sufficient to fulfil all of demand due to the limited growth of the cattle population in the country. As a result, leather-tanning firms import leather from other leather-producing countries, for instance Australia. Recently, the situation has been complicated by the discovery of foot and mouth disease in some major leather-producing countries. For that reason, the Government of Indonesia put restraints on imported leather from endemic countries for some weeks. This, of course, will augment cost and time, which in turn will lessen the industry's competitiveness. Some of Indonesia's shoe production uses a combination of leather and non-leather (fabrics, denims) for the upper parts of the shoes. To support sufficient domestic leather supplies, the government has also decided to impose an export tax on raw and half-done leathers. The export tax has created a less than constructive impact on the footwear industry.

A final internal limitation stems from the fact that domestic shoe producers are often feeble with designs; in fact, shoes are merchandised products whose models and designs evolve quite rapidly. Some producers do not understand how to utilise diversification of inputs on one hand and combine inputs on the other hand. Innovation is important in the industry due to its quick-changing fashions.

External barriers

The cost of transportation in Indonesia is still a barrier to the footwear industry's development. Transportation costs in Indonesia are four times higher than those in China, both in terms of money and time, which creates inefficiencies. To be competitive in the world market, Indonesia's footwear industry should operate in a more efficient way. Indonesia's industry should increase its productivity and improve the business climate. The latter badly needs the government's support.

Another constraint is delays in imported-leather input delivery due to problems of shipment arrival at the port, arrangement of departure and release documents and other reasons. This lack of effective trade-facilitation measures is a real problem, and it results in serious difficulties for the industry, including lost time, delays and rescheduling in production, suspended deliveries to buyers and impugning the producers' credibility.

Government policies, particularly at the regional level, are contributing to high costs in the industry. Local charges can add up to 20 to 30% of the industry's total production costs. It is also the case that non-labour costs in Indonesia are more expensive than labour costs. Labour costs in Indonesia are much cheaper in fact than in other countries (they account for just 3 to 4% of the total production cost). Labour costs, as a percentage of total production costs, are far higher in Malaysia, Singapore, the Philippines and China, where they account for about 11% of the total production costs. The situation in Japan is worse (20% of the total production cost). Indonesia's degree of competitiveness – based on wages – is being undermined by higher-than-necessary non-labour costs in the footwear industry.

There is also evidence that some foreign investors cancel plans to invest in Indonesia because of their concerns about insufficient availability of electricity, costly fees to obtain land and inadequate government support. High interest rates, taxation, charges, uncertain legal aspects, safety and security and unstable political conditions are also cited as crucial factors impeding investment in Indonesia.

Unemployment in Indonesia is a worsening problem, particularly in labour-intensive industries like textiles, garments and footwear, and the problem seems to be getting worse. Many companies are close to closing down their business operations, which could increase the current level of unemployment in the country. Even though new investments in the industry have been announced recently, it will be some time before they can come on stream and reduce the level of unemployment.

Conclusion and policy recommendations

The first step in reducing poverty is to take measures that will increase the welfare of all workers, including enhancing their standard of living. Workers must be considered as the firm's asset in the footwear industry, because the industry is well known as a labour-intensive industry and the existence of trained and satisfied workers will very much influence the performance of the industry. To induce higher productivity, workers' welfare should be improved. It must be supported by pleasant and safe working conditions. Such a work atmosphere can be created through cooperation between firms and the responsible labour union representing the aspirations of all workers in the industry. Wages, incentives and allowances should be paid fairly and should be based on existing regulations. Workers with higher incomes will be more able to support their families' financial needs. Safe and healthy working conditions (including the provision of social security by firms) must also become a consideration for footwear-producing firms in order to create conducive working conditions. Labour strikes, which obviously cause delays in the production process and distribution, will then be minimised.

Secondly, on the side of the footwear firms, businessmen have to manage their firms effectively, efficiently and professionally. Internal strategies can be considered to improve the performance of the footwear industry in Indonesia. The following are some recommendations for internal improvement:

- improvement of productivity and efficiency for a better and more professional organisation
- enhancement of product diversification – since international accounts from footwear export revenues are still dominated by branded sports shoes, local firms need to improve the quality of non-sport (casual) shoe products, including design improvement
- efforts made to penetrate world markets, particularly the EU markets, which are known for their strict rules
- better promotion of Indonesian footwear products on international markets – participating in product exhibitions abroad and utilising trade promotion centres abroad and Indonesian embassies
- participation in trade missions with the government to introduce Indonesia's footwear products.

In fact, businessmen need support from the government in many aspects, both at national and regional levels. The footwear industry is one of the country's foreign-exchange generators. It contributes significantly to the country's economy, both as a labour absorber and a revenue generator. GSP granted to Indonesia and anti-dumping policies imposed on China and Vietnam should be considered as external stimuli that help to expand market share; however, Indonesia cannot depend only on these external stimuli for success. To support the footwear industry, the Government of Indonesia has to take steps to remove the internal constraints on the industry. Some recommendations, in which the role of the government is important, are proposed for the improvement of the footwear industry:

- Limited access and capacity of highways (toll and non-toll highways) are impeding the transportation from the factories (industrial centres) to the port; therefore, it is important for the government to improve infrastructure quantity and quality and to overcome the traffic jam problems. The government should also create an alternative mode of transportation for import and export purposes.
- Delays in product shipment should be minimised, for they are causing additional costs for storage.
- High-cost economy practices, including legal and illegal charges, should be reduced, or better, eliminated. These practices undermine Indonesia's competitiveness in international and domestic markets.
- Improved labour conditions – by revising regulations and laws that are more business favourable – are needed to attract foreign investors.
- The investment climate should be promoted – together with improvements in infrastructure and energy availability – to support the industry.
- Illegal footwear imports must be stopped, for they are impeding domestic production and trades.
- Indonesia's product designs are relatively out of date compared to other countries' products. The industry needs government support in terms of technical assistance in improving designs and quality.
- Indonesia's dependency on imported materials, particularly leather input, has made itself less competitive in the world market; the government has to immediately eliminate import duty for leather used in footwear production.
- The government has to facilitate and integrate production network/supply chains in order to ease input supplies.

Appendix 1A   survey methodology

The case study included the conduction of field surveys of the footwear industry's main stakeholders; namely, the workers and the employers/firms. The author interviewed seventy workers of export-oriented shoe producers – comprising thirty-five men and women workers – and firms/shoe producers of small- and large-scale firms and the Indonesian Footwear Association. The sample size included 10 per cent of over-sampling. The firms' locations, both for the purpose of worker and firm respondents, were obtained from the Indonesian Footwear Directory published by the Indonesian Footwear Association. To obtain perspectives from government officials, the author also interviewed officials from the Ministry of Labour and Transmigration (Directorate General of

Table 1I   *Frequency of workers interviewed based on factory location*

Province	District/municipality	Number of workers interviewed	%
DKI Jakarta	North Jakarta	4	5.7
	South Jakarta	10	14.3
	West Jakarta	4	5.7
West Java	District of Bogor	6	8.6
	Municipality of Bekasi	6	8.6
	District of Karawang	2	2.9
Banten	Municipality of Tangerang	11	15.7
	District of Tangerang	23	32.9
	District of Serang	4	5.7
	Total	**70**	**100.0**

Supervision on Industrial Relations and Labour Social Protection) and the Ministry of Industry (Directorate General of Metal, Machinery, Textile and Other Industry – 'footwear industry' is under 'Other Industry' of the Directorate General). Each interview was meant to describe workers' and firms' conditions from the government point of view.

The worker questionnaire was designed to be semi-structured/quantitative, and the others to be in-depth interview/qualitative questionnaires. The worker interviews took place in three provinces: DKI Jakarta (North Jakarta, South Jakarta and West Jakarta), West Java (District of Bogor) and Banten (District of Karawang, Municipality of Tangerang, District of Tangerang and Municipality of Serang). Whilst conducting the surveys, some factories were discovered to be closed down. Altogether, seventy workers in twenty-eight shoe factories were interviewed. The choice of who to interview was determined in proportion to the number of factories existing in a province. In the case of this case study, footwear factories were mostly found in Banten; therefore, the largest number of workers interviewed were in Banten. To analyse the data from the quantitative questionnaires, some cross-tabulation was performed. Table 1I indicates the frequency of workers interviewed according to factory location.

1.5

Pakistan: the arrival and departure of Nike

SAFDAR SOHAIL*

Introduction

One aspect of globalisation is the dispersion of supply chains around the world. The socioeconomic benefits of global outsourcing cannot be denied. But the conditions that can make global outsourcing work more for the world poor are hotly contested, and are getting more academic and political attention than ever, putting the spotlight on the multinational corporations (MNCs) controlling the global supply chain. Nike International made headlines in November 2006 by announcing its decision to pull out of a production agreement with a Pakistani company that was meeting almost the entire requirement of hand-stitched soccer balls for Nike.

Sialkot, Pakistan's soccer ball-stitching capital, received the news of Nike's decision to pull orders from the city's largest producer, Saga Sports Sialkot, with disbelief and dismay. At the time of suspension, Saga Sports was supplying on average 20,000 balls to Nike per day. Nike alleged that Saga Sports had hired outside makers and part-time workers who worked in non-approved stitching centres, and paid them on a per-ball basis for supplying the firm, which was a violation of their contract. The sacking of Saga Sports by Nike, however, put at stake the means of sustenance of thousands of families who were directly affected. The making and unmaking of the partnership between Nike and Saga Sports has important implications for the deepening of corporate social responsibility (CSR) in a country like Pakistan, and for the efforts aimed at making global outsourcing work for the poor of the world more than ever, which the author proposes to present as a case study in the following pages.[1]

---

* Dr Safdar Sohail works with the Commerce and Trade Group, Social Studies Centre of Pakistan.
[1] The author consulted vast literature published in Pakistan and elsewhere on social compliance issues, particularly child labour issues and other aspects of outsourcing of the

Pakistan's soccer-ball industry

The roots of soccer-ball production in Pakistan are very old. Around 1860, sporting goods like tennis and badminton racquets, cricket bats and polo mallets (and since the beginning of the twentieth century, soccer balls too) had been produced in the Indian subcontinent for the members of the British army and colonial administration. Later on, both in India and Pakistan, the sector's orientation toward an external, well-funded demand by British soldiers and administration staff was expanded toward export. The special setting of the Sialkot district, with experienced craftsmen and the close cooperation of traders with the colonial administration and the British army, who were positioned in Sialkot as well, led to the emergence of large-scale manufacturing enterprises before the partition of the Indian subcontinent in 1947. Together with numerous small enterprises, they grew into a sporting-goods cluster. Thereafter, soccer-ball production and Pakistan's sporting-goods production remained concentrated in and round Sialkot. In the jargon used by the Trade Development Authority of Pakistan (the National Trade Promotion Organization of Pakistan), Sialkot has the two 'traditional' export sectors, i.e. sports goods and surgical instruments, both of which are more than 100 years old, accounting for around half a billion US dollars worth of export earnings. In the sports-goods industry, more than two thirds of the exports are accounted for by the soccer-balls sector alone. Soccer-ball production is also the sector in which the brands are the most active and visible, due to heavy importation from Nike and Adidas.

Soccer-ball production

A soccer ball is made up of two components: (i) the external part, made of synthetic materials; and (ii) the internal part, made of natural rubber. The soccer balls are produced using synthetic leather, i.e. PVC and PU. This is both imported and locally produced. For a better quality and better price for a ball, usually demanded by the big brands, the imported material is used after mutual agreement. In most of the cases, brands do not supply

soccer-ball industry of Sialkot, with special reference to the Nike case. The author also held extensive discussions on the possible causes and implications of the breakdown with the management of Saga Sports, the Sports Goods Exporters Association of Pakistan, labour leaders, CSR-related inspection agencies, NGOs, labour directly affected by the cancellation of the contract, representatives of ILO, and government officials related to the case, such as the District Labour Office, Trade Development Authority of Pakistan, Punjab Employees Social Security Institution and the representatives of the District Government of Sialkot.

their own material.[2] In addition to synthetic leather, the other inputs are coarse cloth and latex for lamination. As latex is not produced in Pakistan, it is always imported. Specialised factories in Sialkot usually produce the internal rubber part.

Soccer-ball production is labour intensive and time-consuming, involving many steps and processes. Firstly, the synthetic material panel is tailored and multiple layers of cloth are glued. Two workers produce about fifty such panels per day, which are the basis for around 300 balls. The textile inner layer ensures that the ball keeps its round form even during hard exposure. Therefore, the kind of synthetic material and the number and quality of the inner layers are the major criteria for quality. In the next stage, pentagonal and hexagonal patches are stamped out with an electric-driven machine. At the same time, these patches receive small slits for the seam. Small machine manufacturers in Gujarat, a neighbouring city of Sialkot, mostly produce these machines, developed especially for soccer-ball production. One worker can stamp out patches for 300 to 400 balls per day.

A soccer ball commonly requires a cover of twenty hexagonal and twelve pentagonal patches. According to this presetting, the patches need to be arranged for the stitchers. The thread and wax are bought locally and are provided to the stitchers as well. Before stitching, the polyester thread is rubbed with wax in order to make the seam waterproof. The 'makers', responsible for getting the ball stitched, deliver the materials to the stitchers and collect the stitched balls. The balls are stitched together by hand in stitching centres. The stitching requires strength and skill because the seam runs inside. One ball requires around 650 stitches. The last few stitches must be placed with great finesse so that one cannot recognise them on the finished ball.

An experienced worker manages to stitch three soccer balls during an eight- to nine-hour working day. The stitchers' wages depend on the number of soccer balls stitched; as a result, there are no minimum working hours at most of the smaller working centres. At the export company's office, the balls undergo quality inspections and are checked on roundness, weight and possible air loss. The application of brand labels and special designs according to the foreign contractor is the last stage before the balls are packed and shipped.

A high-quality ball fetches around US$5 to US$8 for the exporting company. The supply chain of a football starts with research and

[2] Nike did not supply any raw materials to Saga Sports.

development on the design at the main office of the brand, and the balls are sold by the brand through a marketing strategy developed, again, by the brand's office located somewhere in the developed world. At the bottom of this globally sourced supply chain is the stitcher, who brings the handsewn ball into being.

Social profile of stitchers

Two out of five of the working population in the region depend directly or indirectly on the sports-goods industry.[3] The soccer-ball stitching in Sialkot is predominantly a man's business. Half of the soccer-ball stitchers in the rural areas of Sialkot come from landless families. The agriculture in Sialkot is rain-fed and provides only limited opportunities for farm labour, in the presence of fairly high levels of mechanisation. They usually work in small-scale industries, in workshops or as mobile providers. Due to the high seasonality of work in export-oriented sectors, these families depend strongly on the additional income of other family members. A further third of soccer-ball stitchers come from families with less than two hectares of land and who typically lack capital to grow high-income vegetables, etc. Such families are also usually under economic distress. Just 14 per cent of rural soccer-ball stitchers come from families where direct economic pressure is not the reason for their involvement in stitching. Sialkot is one of the most densely populated districts of Pakistan, resulting in the parcellisation of land. Eighty-seven per cent of farmers in the Sialkot district own less than five hectares of farming land. In Sialkot today, agriculture is the main source of income for a third of the working population.

Arrival of brands and re-organisation of soccer-ball production in Sialkot

Brands in the sports industry started playing an important role in the world with the aesthetic shift to the mass consumption of 'brands' in the late 1980s and early 1990s. At the same time, in Pakistan, the sports-world giants like Adidas and Nike became active in procuring different sports items, especially soccer balls. Sialkot was already a big centre for the exportation of soccer balls before the arrival of the brands. The brands

---

[3] 'Football Production', report by Network of European World Shops, Germany, 2005, available at www.worldshops.org [last accessed 10 February 2009].

gradually started impacting upon the organisation of the production process.

Sialkot's soccer-ball sector has been, in parts, integrated for a long time to the global market through a consumer-driven commodity chain. The re-organisation engendered due to the brands' mass demand wiped out some of the existing jobs and entrepreneurial opportunities for small enterprises. But, in the medium and long term, it improved the lot of the poor as it brought a significant expansion to the sector, and a more efficient organisation and higher per-unit value, as brands were importing more expensive balls. As far as wages are concerned, there is little evidence in Sialkot that workers would have got lower wages and fewer jobs in the presence of MNCs, compared to what they would get in their absence, other things remaining the same. Contrary to the impression created by the campaigns in affluent countries against 'sweatshops' run by transnational companies in poor countries, it is abundantly clear that the poor were keen to get into the gates of those factories producing for the brands, since their alternatives were much worse, i.e. inferior jobs or work conditions or unemployment. The brands helped bring a cultural change in which, these days, there is a deepening abhorrence against child-labour usage.

Development of a model ethical partnership

Before signing the contract with Saga Sports, Nike ordered social audits of many stitching units in Sialkot. Nike's choice of Saga Sports was well thought out, as Saga Sports had the best CSR record in the entire soccer-ball industry in Pakistan.[4] Saga Sports had developed their own voluntary CSR strategy, which was offering much more for the welfare of workers as compared to the workers' welfare demanded by local labour laws. The owner of Saga Sports, Sufi Khurshid Ahmad, hailed as a visionary because he had set his eyes on future CSR demands from the soccer-ball industry from the brands, in an atmosphere of 'labour union criminalisation', had played an important role in the finalisation of the Atlanta Agreement in 1997. On the other hand, Nike was very conscious of its corporate image, and wanted a successful partnership to prove its assertion that,

---

[4] Ambreen Waheed, 'Evaluation of the State of Corporate Social Responsibility in Pakistan and a Strategy for Implementation', report for the United Nations Development Programme and Security Exchange Commission of Pakistan, 2005, available at www.rbipk.org [last accessed 10 February 2009].

'when Nike enters a country to manufacture products, wages increase and poverty decreases.'

The Nike-Saga Sports partnership grew very fast, both in business and in trust. In 1999, Nike informed Saga Sports that it was also interested in finding a second source for the production of soccer balls somewhere outside Pakistan. Saga Sports offered to establish a factory in a foreign country, and looked at the possibilities of putting up a factory in countries such as Bangladesh, Vietnam, Indonesia, Morocco, Dubai and China, and finally decided, in consultation with Nike, to set up a factory in China.[5]

Gains of the Nike-Saga Sports partnership

At the time of signing the Agreement in 1998, the CSR in the soccer-ball industry in Sialkot was equated with the abolition of child labour. Nike's code of conduct, in any case, included all the core labour standards, but child labour had high importance. The successful implementation of their contract, integrating Nike's code of conduct, over a period of nine years, improved the general working conditions of workers in and around Sialkot, and particularly helped a large number of women and tremendously curtailed the menace of child labour. As agreed in the contract, Saga Sports put in place a manufacturing system of 'approved stitching centres' with attendant facilities for workers, replacing exploitation-prone family-based informal work places, scattered around Sialkot in a radius of around 50 km. Nike started buying big volumes after its agreement with Saga Sports, in the context of the Atlanta Charter.[6]

The agreement by all accounts functioned very well, and Nike kept on increasing its orders to Saga Sports until the end of 2005, when it reached 6 million balls per month. Nike had, in fact, expressed its intention to increase its orders gradually to 9 to 10 million by 2009. The agreement between Nike and Saga gave an important contribution to the community,

---

[5] The factory started its operations in 1999 with a production capacity of 30,000 balls per month. In 2001, this capacity was enhanced to 50,000 balls per month. Along with giving business to Saga Sports China, Nike also established business relations with some Chinese companies. However, this business was limited to machine-stitched balls and some mini ball products. Saga Sport's China unit was closed down about three-and-a-half years ago. The main reason was that Saga Sports could not manage it as per China's laws, and it was going into loss.

[6] The Atlanta Charter was signed by the ILO, the Sialkot Chamber of Commerce and Industry and UNICEF on 14 February 1997. It was announced at the Sports Super Show in Atlanta, Georgia. Its goal was to combat high rates of child labour in the Pakistani soccer-ball industry.

as it made possible the return of the 'factory', which had disappeared in
the late 1970s. In a factory stitching centre, it is possible to get better
productivity and better wages and social protection to the workers at the
same time.

From the start, there was a clear, though verbal, understanding between
Nike and Saga Sports that Saga Sports would pay its workers more than
the legal minimum wage in Sialkot. All the available evidence shows that
Saga Sports lived up to its promise. Saga Sports also promised to gradually
develop its capacities to house its stitchers in factory-constructed stitching
centres. For this purpose, Saga Sports initially planned to construct five
state of the art stitching centres accommodating about 500 stitchers each,
for which, at the request of Saga Sports, Nike also agreed to make some
financial contribution. This contribution was in the shape of an increase
in price on each ball produced for Nike. Later, Saga Sports constructed
about ten more similar facilities on its own.

Unravelling of the Nike-Saga Sports partnership

Nike announced to the press in November 2006[7] that it had found, after
an investigation of six months, that Saga Sports was outsourcing many of
the balls to outside 'makers' and part-time workers who worked in non-
approved stitching centres in their homes around the city of Sialkot, and
paid them on a per-ball basis, which was a violation of its contract. Nike
also asserted it had found numerous labour, environmental and health
and safety compliance violations within Saga Sports' facilities, including
serious allegations by trade union representatives and other Saga Sports
employees of worker harassment, wrongful termination and inaccurate
payment of wages.

Additionally, Nike quoted an unannounced audit of Saga Sports, unre-
lated to Nike's investigation, compiled in October 2006 by an audit team
sent by the Fair Labour Association (FLA), which supposedly found at
least a few similar violations. While lamenting the inaction of Saga Sports
on significant labour concerns, Nike asserted that they were forced to take
the decision after exhaustive efforts. Nike presented the severance of the
contract with Saga Sports as a 'milestone', as with this, Nike was entering
into the third phase of CSR, characterised by 'social enterprise' concerns.

The author's extensive interviews with different stakeholders in Sialkot,
Lahore and Islamabad and their survey of literature has helped the author

---

[7] Andrew Clark, 'Nike Sacks Premiership Ball Maker over Labour Fears', *Guardian*, 21 November 2006, available at www.guardian.co.uk [last accessed 10 February 2009].

identify the principal causes of the eventual failure of the agreement between Nike and Saga Sports. It is hard to give priority to any one possible explanation given below, but the author believes that a systematic exploration of the possible reasons for the break down of the Nike-Saga Sports partnership is very instructive for designing and implementing CSR-centred agreements, which could last longer and could be replicated by other companies, not only in the soccer-ball sector but also in other export sectors where brands are outsourcing from countries like Pakistan, such as ready-made garments, etc.

Short-term causes of the break-up

Ineffective remediation

A photograph, taken around May 2006, showing a child working in a home-based stitching centre, seems to have awakened Nike to the possibility of its competitors accusing it of being soft on CSR violations by their suppliers. When confronted by Nike, Saga Sports did promise to consolidate all the stitching and to do away with home-based stitching once and for all, but it appears Nike had lost faith in the will and capacity of Saga Sports to do it. The dismissal by Saga Sports of managers in the gloves section of Saga Sports, reported on by the FLA, gave Nike a suitable opportunity to take the final step to the severance of the agreement, as the involvement of the FLA had given an added credence to their argument. Instead of taking an extreme step, which was justified by Nike as a pre-emptive action, the remediation should have been given a better chance. IMAC[8] records show that Saga Sports stitching centres increased from 2002, without being certified by Nike (see Table 1J).

With the help of an efficient monitoring system, Nike should have discovered this problem much earlier. Instead, Nike continued increasing its demands on Saga Sports, knowing full well that the thirteen certified stitching centres alone could not meet the increasing demand on production capacity.[9]

---

[8] IMAC (the Independent Monitoring Association for Child Labour) is a not-for-profit organisation, set up as a successor organisation to the ILO–IPEC's Workplace Monitoring Programme in the Soccer Ball Industry in Sialkot. ILO-IPEC (International Program on the Elimination of Child Labour) ran this programme from 1 October 1997 to 28 February 2003. On 1 March 2003, it handed the programme over to IMAC.

[9] Saga Sports' exports, 85 per cent of which were going to Nike, rose from US$20 million in 2001 to US$32 million in 2006.

Table 1J   *Saga's registered stitching centres in Sialkot*

Year	Registered centres
2001	13
2002	132
2003	131
2004	143
2005	219
2006	96

Source: IMAC website: www.imacpak.org
[last accessed 10 February 2009].

Deficiencies in the monitoring system

Nike, despite importing huge volumes, did not establish an office in Sialkot (as was done by Adidas earlier) or a liaison office (as Adidas has in Sialkot even now). Nor did Nike engage IMAC for inspections of the social compliance violations. Even when Saga Sports asserted its 'home-based' centres were registered with IMAC and were certified by IMAC to be free of child labour, Nike did not contact IMAC to verify the veracity of its claims. IMAC did not, on its own, expand the scope of its inspection to include social compliances other than child labour. In this sense, the Sialkot Chamber of Commerce and Industry and ILO Pakistan, the major sponsors of IMAC, did not fully appreciate the importance of a more comprehensive code of conduct by Nike, and did not try to prepare the industry to embrace the worker welfare-related social compliances. Now, after the crisis with Nike, the scope of inspection by IMAC has been expanded, and they have added other social compliances to be in line with the 'decent work conditions' of the ILO.

Management weaknesses of Saga Sports

The founder of Saga Sports and the main organiser of the Atlanta Charter on behalf of the soccer-ball industry died in 2001. There is a common perception in industry circles that, from that point, communication gaps started growing and that the new managers did not, perhaps, take their CSR obligations that seriously. Saga Sports management did not, perhaps, have the management capacity to understand the nature of inter-organisational relations and to take it forward. In one of the major studies on the soccer-ball industry of Sialkot, the difficulties the Pakistani companies are facing in managing inter-organisational relations is considered one of the most important potential threats that Pakistani companies will face in the coming days, where globalised supply chains offer an opportunity in the global economy as well as a challenge to maintain acceptable conditions in the workplace.[10]

CSR as a tool of 'competition'

Sialkot is one of the busiest commercial export cities in Pakistan, with exporters operating in an atmosphere of cut-throat competition for export orders. In the presence of this bare-knuckle competition, the possibility of competitors using alleged CSR lapses to their own advantage cannot be ruled out.

Longer term causes of the break-up

'Informalisation' of the labour market

The 1970s saw the introduction of much pro-poor legislation. The Sialkot soccer-ball industry reacted by resorting to cottage/family-based production. The predominance of informal production arrangements has become an established way of doing business over the years, and is like a culture. However, CSR compliance requires a formalisation of the work. But this re-formalisation can only take place with strong institutional support from governmental agencies and civil society organisations. The former in this case proved very weak in enforcement and inducement. As far as the CSRs are concerned, there is a serious trust deficit in Sialkot in the role of non-governmental organisations (NGOs), limiting the influence of the latter.

Nuanced dissonance on the issue of child labour

Many researchers have pointed out the complexity of the child-labour issue in Sialkot. Ali Khan has elaborated on the process of the acceptance of the dominant developed country development theory, coming from the West, by the local stakeholders, especially NGOs, to use it to their own advantage.[11] The possibilities of such a misuse of the child-labour issue

---

[10] Rafi Farzad Khan, 'Beyond Child Labour in Pakistan's Soccer Ball Industry', PhD thesis, Faculty of Management, McGill University, Montreal, 2004.

[11] Ali Khan, 'Representing Children', PhD dissertation, submitted to Corpus Christi College, Oxford, 2002.

notwithstanding, it is true that one does find cynical approaches to the child-labour issue in Sialkot, raising the scepter and consequent fear of the re-emergence of child labour.

Trade union capacity

Much of the literature on the labour movement in Pakistan is partisan in nature. There is, in any case, some truth to the allegations by the employers that the trade union leaders get used to benefits from their position at the cost of employers' legitimate interests. The deep mistrust between the trade unions and the employers in general does not allow for the emergence of optimum win-win situations. The strengthening of labour unions needs to be accompanied by the inculcation of responsibility in workers in general and in the managers in particular.

Difficulties in indigenisation of CSR imperatives

The codes of conduct of brands have standard provisions on labour welfare such as compensation and freedom of association. Both these prescriptions have to operate in local contexts. In terms of compensation, the Pakistani Government periodically fixes the minimum wage. Every brand and their manufacturers claim to pay at least this minimum wage. All the available evidence proves the same. In fact, Nike insisted on wages higher than the minimum wage. Therefore, as far as the formally employed worker is concerned, there have usually been few wage-related problems. In the case of the stitchers engaged by the 'makers'/subcontractors, Nike or other brands expect their contractors to pay a sustainable or 'living' wage to these workers. The majority of such workers either work on a piece-rate basis or are employed on a contract basis, and usually don't work for a continuous period of time and may have other sources of income. In their case, it is not easy to determine whether the wages being paid to them by the 'makers' are 'living' wages. Different manufacturers in Sialkot provide different forms of social protection; therefore it can become debatable as to whether the code of conduct is being implemented in letter and spirit.

As far as freedom of association is concerned, Nike has been trying to expand factory-based stitching, where it should be possible for the unions to operate. In the case of these centres, managers claim that since artisans are piece-rate subcontractors, they do not qualify as 'employees' and hence do not fall under the freedom of association clause in Pakistani law. Brands have responded to this situation differently. Reebok believes its group managers work as representatives; Adidas refers to the independent

PAKISTAN: THE ARRIVAL AND DEPARTURE OF NIKE 171

'maker' as a representative of the artisans, while Nike/Saga Sports used to claim that its elected representatives – more like a representative committee instead of a traditional trade union – fall within the definition of workforce representatives. The Puma representative, according to Puma, spends one hour every month meeting with artisans and workers to handle complaints through an established mechanism. As far as the workers in factories and bigger stitching centres are concerned, at the moment there are some labour unions in the soccer-ball sector.

Impact of Nike's withdrawal from its deal with Saga Sports

Nike stopped receiving soccer balls from Saga Sports after the latter completed the orders in the pipeline by March 2007. Eighty five per cent of the total production of Saga Sports was going to Nike. Unable to find alternate arrangements for exports, they phased out their production. Their factories and offices were shut down in May 2007. Saga Sports was providing work to 7,000 workers at the time of the suspension of the contract. As most of the Saga Sports workers, especially those working in the approved stitching centres, were well trained, other factories have reportedly re-employed many of them.

After a dip in total exports subsequent to the last World Cup, exports have picked up during 2007. Nike is also reported to be importing indirectly from other companies in Sialkot. The large companies in particular are individually benefiting from more orders. But as far as workers are concerned, the withdrawal of Nike has created a wave of lay offs in different factories and stitching centres due to an over-supply of trained stitchers. The most vulnerable, i.e. women and the seasonal workers coming from rural areas, have been hit the hardest due to these lay offs, and a large number of home-based stitching centres now have little work. As Nike had created monopsonic conditions, in which workers were being paid relatively high wages, its withdrawal has reduced the income of stitchers as their average piece-rate wage has gone down, even if the export figures might remain unchanged.

In the case of Sialkot's soccer-ball industry, the average income of a stitching household is inversely proportional to the employment of child labour. Therefore, the possibilities of the return of child labour cannot be ruled out. In the case of Sialkot, various studies have confirmed that the prevalence of child labour is a genuine proxy for the vulnerability of a stitcher's family. The withdrawal of Nike has the potential of reversing the gains it had generated with its partnership with Saga Sports in reducing child labour, as the better returns to the stitchers acted as an incentive for them to send their children to school.

The effects of Nike's withdrawal could be catastrophic, especially for workers, if similar clients walk out on their Pakistani suppliers, crippling the sector of hand-sewn soccer balls, already threatened by cheap and/or machine-made soccer balls.

A way forward for the soccer-ball industry of Sialkot

Given the high visibility of the Nike-Saga Sports partnership, the lessons and insight produced by this partnership in its making as well as breaking can go a long way in strengthening the positive relationship between compliance with labour standards and poverty reduction, contrary to the popular assumption that the developed countries can use compliances and standards to reduce market access. In Sialkot, the author's interviews reveal that there is an awareness that the focus is now not only on child labour. The industry needs a much more robust programme of social investment. After the Nike-Saga Sports spat, the industry seems to be more acutely aware of a whole range of issues. The industry appears to have realised the potential gains and threats of a repeat of the Nike-Saga Sports break-up, and have expanded the scope of the inspection and monitoring of IMAC. If brands also use this opportunity to strengthen their own as well as industry-wide mechanisms of inspection and monitoring, more than 20,000 families can come out of the worst form of poverty and exploitation.

The Nike-Saga Sports case has emphatically brought the issue of poor and inadequate monitoring to the fore. It is not an easy task as the stitchers are scattered around hundreds of villages surrounding Sialkot. The best form of monitoring will come from community or worker representatives themselves. The industry is mulling over the new strategy of Nike, which is aimed at establishing durable links between trade and poverty in the future, and they assert they would come up with a better response across the soccer-ball industry. In February 2007, all the stakeholders, including the representatives of Nike, gathered at Lahore and signed the Sialkot Initiative, which basically re-affirms the resolve of the industry and other stakeholders to address the issues of child labour and the implementation of other core ILO conventions. Following the Sialkot Initiative and contacts between the Prime Minister of Pakistan and Nike management at Davos, Nike has announced that it will resume importing from Pakistan, and Nike has signed a contract for a small order with another Sialkot-based company. But it must be added that no lasting solution to child labour and labour development can be found by focusing on the soccer-ball sector alone. A revitalised agreement on child labour and other labour rights, led by the Sialkot Chamber of Commerce and Industry, must reach out to other businesses, with the help of the ILO, such as the surgical instruments and leather-garments sectors, so that a uniform standard of compliance can be established across the region, eliminating the migration of child labour from one sector to another.

Consumers and the media in the developed countries have made a significant contribution to increasing the social dividend of global outsourcing arrangements. Workers in far-off places, working in poor working conditions, hope they can impact on the brand's business. But a globalised supply chain has also increased the distance between the worker at the bottom of the supply chain and the consumer. Ensuring effective, standardised social audits and promoting a culture of disclosure across the board remain the most precious tools for making verifiable information available within its correct context for remediation or denial of market access.

Making outsourcing work for the poor

Global outsourcing is an important characteristic of globalisation, making possible an internationalisation of the supply chain. The presence of MNCs in a developing country does bring economic benefits to the workers and people of that area, but the nature and net value of these benefits can be variable. The possibility of a big gap between the minimum benefits accruing to the workers and the community, and the optimum benefits that ideally should be there, have been a principle focus of CSR activism in the developed world regarding MNCs' 'sweatshops'.

Investment by MNCs in a country like Pakistan makes an initial contribution to poverty reduction through higher wage rates, more secure employment and sometimes improvements in healthcare facilities. Over the longer term, higher incomes realised by workers will make it possible for their children to be better educated and to have higher skill levels than their parents, contributing to a virtuous circle where poverty levels decline with each successive generation.

Pakistan has signed all eight of the core ILO Standards, but the enforcement of most of these Standards remains rather weak, diluting the poverty reducing potential of these Standards.[12] Like in many other countries, pro-market and pro-FDI policies being pursued since the early 1980s have resulted in the gradual erosion of 'labour rights infrastructure', especially in export-oriented sectors. The expansion of the informal sector, the shift from permanent labour to contractual labour, consolidation of large land holdings resulting in an exodus of share-cropping tenants towards cities, and low growth rates in the 1990s and early 2000s have further eroded the working conditions of workers in Pakistan. In these circumstances, the expectations from the government to referee the arrangements between the workers and the employers as stipulated under the code of conduct of the brands could be rather limited. There is a need for the brands to work equally closely with the trade unions/representative bodies in the process of labour development. Through the empowerment of workers, the globalisation of the supply chain can reduce more poverty and misery in the world. It would be a labourious task, but there are few other options but to work with the labour representatives to increase the capacity of labour welfare institutions, instead of working only with NGOs, as Judith Tendler puts it forcefully:

> No matter how hard we work to dream up a better approach to reducing poverty and no matter how much we bring economists to the table to sit with other social scientists, we are making the task even more difficult by allowing the subject of labour, organizing within countries, to slip into oblivion. We also lose thereby a scarce ally to stand behind the poverty-reducing agenda, and miss the opportunity to build essential institutions for the mediation of conflict between management and workers.[13]

[12] Alan Coudouel and Stefano Paternostro, *Analysing the Distributional Impact of Reform*, World Bank, Washington, DC, 2006.
[13] Judith Tendler, 'Why Social Policy is Condemned to a Residual Category of Safety Nets and What to Do About It', draft for the Thandika Mkandawire 'Social Policy in a Development Context' project, United Nations Research Institute for Social Development, Geneva, 2000.

1.6

Vietnam: Intel and the electronics sector

ANDREW L. STOLER AND PHAN VAN SAM*

Introduction

Vietnam is one of the world's poorest countries, with a large rural population and gross domestic product (GDP) per capita (PPP basis) in 2006
of just US$3,100. However, agriculture's share of economic output has
declined steeply in the first years of the twenty-first century, and strong
economic growth in non-traditional sectors has played a major role in
transforming the country into a modern economic success story. When
he visited Vietnam in mid 2007, World Bank President Robert Zoellick
was quoted as saying:

> Vietnam has the potential to be one of the great success stories in devel-
> opment. It has already achieved one of the fastest improvements in living
> standards in the world, with a great reduction in poverty. Driven by the first
> stage of reforms and the benefits of trade and WTO accession, Vietnam is
> on pace to become a middle income country by 2010.[1]

This case study is about the changes in Vietnamese policy that have created an environment in the country that is attractive to foreign investors
who, because of the access that Vietnam now enjoys in foreign markets,
can be certain that the lion's share of their production can be successfully exported to overseas buyers. The operations of these companies are
making possible the employment of large numbers of young Vietnamese
in skilled, well-paid jobs – something that is critically important in a

* Andrew L. Stoler is Executive Director of the Institute for International Trade at the
University of Adelaide. Phan Van Sam is Dean at Mekong University, Vietnam. The authors
are especially appreciative of the assistance provided to this project by Ms Uyen Ho, who is
Corporate Affairs Manager at the Intel Corporation, Ho Chi Minh City, Vietnam.
[1] 'Vietnam "Success Story": World Bank Chief', press release on the website of the Embassy
of the Socialist Republic of Vietnam in the United States, 7 August 2007 (available at
www.vietnamembassy-usa.org/news/story.php?d=20070807122021 [last accessed 10 June
2009]).

country where the median age is 26.4 years and the domestic labour force is growing by more than 1 million people every year.[2] The electronics sector is developing rapidly in Vietnam, where it is making a very significant contribution to the country's economy, and within this sector, Intel Corporation is an important part of the picture.

This case study discusses how a mainly agrarian economy develops the human resources required to participate in high-tech manufacturing; the reasons why Intel and other foreign investors chose to locate in the country; government policies positively influencing these decisions (as well as remaining aspects of the centrally planned command economy that continue to interfere with the market economy's operation); and the contribution of open-trade and investment policies to poverty reduction in Vietnam.

Starting from a low base, and building blocks to a hi-tech future

In the period following the end of the Vietnam War (which the Vietnamese refer to as the 'American War'), the national economy was in a shambles. Government efforts to establish a viable command economy through collectivisation of farms and factories failed to meet the nation's needs over the ten-year period to 1985. Famine was widespread, with food and even bicycles subject to government rationing. An already bad situation was considerably exacerbated by serious domestic corruption and external economic restrictions and foreign embargoes. Vietnamese officials could see that conditions in most of their nearby neighbours were dramatically better and, not surprisingly, the government came to the conclusion that economic development would only be possible in a different policy context.

A key event seems to have been the 1986 Sixth Party Congress of the Communist Party, where Communist Party officials embarked on a series of reforms designed to liberalise Vietnam's economy. The reforms are known as *doi moi* (meaning 'renovation'), and they opened Vietnam up to the outside world with new and liberal rules for investment and trade. The promulgation in 1986 of the Law on Foreign Investment was a key step. In their efforts to transform an agrarian society into a modern industrial and services-oriented economy, the Vietnamese appear to have learned lessons from others' experience. Early on in the reform process, the

---

[2] Central Intelligence Agency (USA) (2007), *The World Factbook – Vietnam* (available at www.cia.gov [last accessed 10 February 2009].

Vietnamese authorities assigned a priority to the information technology sector.

The importance of education and training

Government authorities recognised that in order to provide highly qualified engineers and skilled workers for the hi-tech sector, the country would need to boost technical education by establishing vocational schools, technical colleges and universities. There would need to be efforts not only by the central government and ministries but also from provincial level, industrial parks, hi-tech parks and hi-tech companies. An important part of the project would be encouragement of foreign investors to invest in hi-tech projects, and through these projects, local people would be able to benefit from technology transfer opportunities and training.

Many Vietnamese looked at the case of Costa Rica as an example to follow. Costa Rica could have been little more than another banana republic, because in earlier years, its GDP depended heavily on exports of banana and sugar. Following the Costa Rican Government's success in persuading Intel to invest in the country, a series of electronics companies like Taiwan's Acer Group, Microsoft Corp., Motorola Inc., DSC Communication Corp. and Sawtek Inc. followed with important investments in Costa Rica. Currently, Lucent Technologies Inc. is negotiating a deal for production facilities. Today, more than 20 per cent of Costa Rican GDP originates in the high-tech sector.

Costa Rica's pitch to businesses emphasises that English courses are mandatory for all Costa Rican students. The country is setting up a nationwide network of computer labs in high schools and universities. Costa Rica has a literacy rate topping 94 per cent, an educated work force with 12,000 engineering students, and one of the highest rates of computer usage in the Western Hemisphere after the USA and Canada.

Vietnam faces a big challenge in providing a qualified workforce for the hi-tech industry. Most of its young workforce is inexperienced. Consequently, the government has devoted considerable attention to the problem of training workers, technicians and engineers for this industry. In 2006, Vietnam had roughly 9,000 IT graduates and 150,000 IT and electronics workers. The government hopes to double the number of qualified workers to 330,000 by 2015 (including 240,000 who will be electronics and telecom specialists). It aims to have 15,000 hi-tech workers with Masters and Doctorate degrees.

To achieve this goal, Vietnam needs to strengthen and enhance the educational system, especially technical education. Currently, Vietnam has more than 100 universities and colleges, most of which have IT and technology departments. In addition, Vietnam also has more than 300 vocational schools and centres throughout the country. However, in order to create conditions where the sector can benefit from enough qualified people, these institutions and schools must internationalise their syllabus and curricula. Recently, the Ministry of Education and Training, Ministry of Science & Technology and Ministry of Labour, Invalid and Social Affairs have updated their programmes and facilities to meet this challenge. In addition, Vietnam is making efforts to attract foreign educational institutions to set up joint ventures and wholly owned training-related subsidiaries in Vietnam, working with partners like RMIT, APTECH, Microsoft, IBM etc. Intel has programmes collaborating with Vietnamese universities to train Vietnamese students. Foreign-owned electronics and IT corporations also provide a lot of in-house training and workshops for local technicians and engineers. It is also likely that Vietnam could become a stronger player in the sector more quickly if it could tap into the pool of more than 3 million talented overseas Vietnamese.

Lessons from other agrarian economies like India, Thailand, Korea, Taiwan, China, Malaysia, Indonesia and the Philippines also show that through strengthening the educational system, especially in technical and technological education, countries have been successfully industrialised. Especially important have been open-door policies to attract foreign direct investment, which demonstrably brings with it the improvement of human resources in these countries (both in quantity, and quality through technology transfer, vocational training and in-house training).

Locking in reforms through trade agreements

Following its decision to move in the direction of liberalising the trade and investment climate, the Vietnamese Government embarked on a series of trade agreement initiatives that collectively play a key role in locking in domestic reforms and guaranteeing access to key foreign markets. Discussions with the USA led to the lifting of the American trade embargo in 1994, followed later by a bilateral trade agreement. In 1995, Vietnam joined the Association of Southeast Asian Nations (ASEAN), cementing its relations with neighbouring countries. In the same year, Vietnam began the process of accession to the WTO.

The bilateral request-offer negotiations with key trading partners that are at the core of the market access aspect of WTO accession were wrapped up by Vietnam in July 2006. The accession package was adopted by the WTO General Council in November 2006, and Vietnam formally became a member of the WTO in early 2007. With membership came a long list of further reforms in the country, beginning with the end of restrictions on trading rights and revisions to twenty-four laws and hundreds of government regulations addressing intellectual property rights, product standards etc. The country also joined the Information Technology Agreement providing for duty-free trade in information technology products – an important step for any country seeking to encourage investment by foreign IT companies. The overall WTO package is impressive for its size as well: 560 pages of schedules of concessions on industrial and agricultural products; a 60-page schedule of commitments on trade in services; and a 260-page working party report detailing Vietnam's commitments in non-scheduled areas.

Joining the WTO brought Vietnam fully into the modern global economy with all of the legal guarantees, opportunities and challenges associated with participation in the liberal world trading system. It was a necessary and desirable complementary step to the country's other trade agreements and the domestic reforms it had set in place.

Government policies in favour of the information technology sector

According to Dr Bui Van Quyen, General Director in the Ministry of Science and Technology,[3] the Vietnamese Government began according special status to the information technology sector (along with biotechnology, new materials, automation and machine building) in 1990, long before it even started the process of acceding to the WTO. A special concessional tax regime was introduced for foreign-invested electronics firms where, in general, a low corporate tax rate of 15 per cent applies – but not in the early years of an investment where it is normal to provide a complete tax exemption for the first three or four years of a new company's operations, followed by another five years in which the normally applicable tax rate is halved. Dr Phan Hien Minh, Head of the Taxation Section on Foreign Companies in Ho Chi Minh City,[4] described the considerable

---

[3] Interviewed in his office in Ho Chi Minh city on 21 September 2007.
[4] The Taxation Section on Foreign Companies in Ho Chi Minh city, Ministry of Finance. Interview conducted in Ho Chi Minh city on 15 November 2007.

BOX 1A   SELECT TAX-INCENTIVE MEASURES BENEFITING THE ELECTRONICS SECTOR

- Stipulation in Law on Foreign Investment in Vietnam (Modification and Amendment) – 9 June 2000
- Decision No. 24/2000/ND-CP stipulating details in regard to the Law on Foreign Investment – 31 July 2000
- Decision No. 27/2003/ND-CP – 19 March 2003
- Law on Corporate Tax – 16 June 2003
- Decision No. 99/2003/ND-CP – 28 August 2003
- Decree No. 53/2004/QD – 5 April 2004

---

number of tax incentive-related decrees and decisions providing for preferential tax treatment of hi-tech investment projects, including those in the electronics sector (see Box 1A). He confirmed what we had already heard from others: that this sector is seen as essential to the modernisation of the country's industrial base and is also recognised as a key contributor to a solid modern infrastructure on which other industries can be built.

The government has been following a structured strategy on the development of the communications sector, which incorporates policies designed to greatly increase the number of internet users in Vietnam. In addition, new laws have been passed to enhance the legal environment for the hi-tech sector. The Vietnamese National Assembly recently enacted the Law on Information Technology and the Law on Electronics Transaction and Intellectual Property (which provides, inter alia, for copyright protection for software and integrated circuit layout designs). A new law on technology transfer entered into force in July 2007.

Another government project (Project 112 in 2006) was aimed at building up 'e-government' in Vietnam. Dissatisfied with progress made under this project, government officials have revamped the original concept and assigned it to a newly created Ministry of Information and Communication for implementation in the period 2007 to 2010.

Local universities are encouraged to work closely with foreign-invested IT companies, and the government has taken steps to organise 'bridging classes' for engineers and other training activities, including Japanese language courses for those hoping to work with Japanese companies involved in the Hoa Lac Hi-Tech Park.

In exchange for favourable tax treatment and other policies designed to promote investment in the IT sector, the government requires foreign

investors to bring clean, state-of-the-art technologies with their investments in Vietnam. Dr Bui Van Quyen observed that Vietnam is adamant
that it will not be the garbage heap of manufacturing technology. Foreign
investors are also required to be environmentally sensitive and provide
good conditions and dormitories for their workers.

Ho Chi Minh City (Saigon) Hi-Tech Park

We spoke to Mr Pham Chanh Truc, former General Director of the
Saigon Hi-Tech Park and current senior advisor to the Hi-Tech Park
on 25 September 2007. He claimed he was a major force in initiating the
idea for the Hi-Tech Park when he was Vice-Chairman of Ho Chi Minh
City in the 1990s, and later was appointed to head the project. From
the start, he worked hard to convince companies like Intel to invest in
the Park. Under the direction and guidance of Vietnamese Government
Decisions Nos. 99 and 53, signed by the Prime Minister, the Hi-Tech Park
in Ho Chi Minh City provides the following preferential treatment for
foreign investors in the IT sector:

- The government provides Park infrastructure, including water and electrical power. The Park has its own dedicated power-generating station
  with a large and stable generating capacity.
- The government contributes importantly to the training of human
  resources working with firms in the Park, and cooperates with foreign
  investors, national universities and plans to introduce cooperation on
  training with American-based universities in the future.
- Shuttle-bus services are provided to pick up workers and take them to
  and from their job sites.
- Low price housing is built by the government for workers in the Park.
- Foreign investors in the Park benefit from the very best preferential tax
  rates available in the country. In general, an initial period of four years
  of total corporate tax exemption is followed by five years where the
  tax rate is halved. A company considered as a 'pioneer' might even be
  accorded a reduced corporate tax rate of just 10 per cent for a period as
  long as fifty years from the date on which they become profitable.

As noted earlier, foreign investors in the Park are expected to contribute to
Vietnam's technological development by performing research and development in the country, and employing state of the art technologies in
their production processes.

The current Director of Science and Technology at the Saigon Hi-Tech Park, Dr Duong Minh Tam,[5] told us that tax revenues realised by the government from foreign-invested enterprises in the Park are not considered important to the country's economic development. A much more important objective is the creation of jobs, technology transfer and gaining local experience in the management of technology. Policy makers consider that if the country's IT development strategy works, it will some day have its own home-grown electronics companies. This is the objective of the government when it offers preferential treatment to foreign-invested electronics firms.

Intel Corporation's investment in Vietnam

Intel Corporation has been in Vietnam for over ten years, and it has made considerable investments in building out IT infrastructure with local government agencies.[6] Despite this long presence of the company in the country, it was two corporate press releases issued in 2006 that dramatically alerted the world to the scale of Intel's planned involvement in Vietnam. On 28 February 2006, the corporation announced it would build a US$300 million semiconductor assembly and test facility in Ho Chi Minh City. In making the announcement, Intel Chairman Craig Barrett said:

> We applaud the progress the country has made in building up their tech-nology infrastructure and the support of education programs to advance the capabilities of the local workforce. Intel looks forward to working with the government and public sector in Vietnam to grow their technology capabilities and competitiveness.

The February announcement was followed in November[7] by an even more dramatic press release, in which the company announced that it would increase the size of the assembly and test facility it was building in Vietnam from 150,000 square feet to 500,000 square feet, and raise its investment in the project from $300 million to $1 billion. Rick Howarth,

---

[5] Interviewed in his office in Ho Chi Minh City on 28 September 2007.

[6] The information on Intel's investment in Vietnam contained in this section of the case study (unless otherwise footnoted) has been provided to the authors by Ms Uyen Ho, Corporate Affairs Manager, Intel Corporation, Ho Chi Minh City, Vietnam. The authors are deeply appreciative of the cooperation shown to them by Ms Ho and by other officials of the Intel Corporation.

[7] Intel press release of 10 November 2006: 'Intel Expands Investment in Vietnam'.

General Manager of Intel Products Vietnam, is quoted in the press release as stating:

> Intel has enjoyed a strong, constructive working relationship with the Vietnam Government, both at the local and national levels. We are very pleased that the discussions with the local authorities went smoothly so we could significantly expand the facility's size.

The November announcement also indicated that Intel Products Vietnam would be participating in the Intel World Ahead programme, which aims to enhance lives by accelerating access to technology for everyone, anywhere in the world. Focused on developing communities, the programme integrates and expands Intel's effort to advance progress in four areas: accessibility, connectivity, education and content.

The Intel investment decision is clearly a major coup for Vietnam that promises to contribute importantly to the realisation of the government's goals for the electronics sector and, through its impact on the country's economic development, poverty reduction. What were the reasons behind Intel's decision to make this investment in Vietnam? How will the facility be integrated into Intel's operations, and where will the products made in the plan be sold? How will this important transnational corporation (TNC) treat its workers?

Factors influencing Intel's decision to invest in Vietnam

The assembly and test facility that Intel is building in Vietnam is part of the company's worldwide expansion of production capacity, and when completed, it will be the seventh such facility in Intel's global network. Other sites include Penang and Kulim, Malaysia; Cavite, Philippines; Chengdu and Shanghai, China; and San Jose, Costa Rica. The decision to invest in Vietnam was not made due to the country's membership in WTO, in ASEAN or the bilateral trade agreement with the USA, although Vietnam's strong, market-driven economy (which is certainly influenced by these trade agreements) was an important factor in the company's decision. Political stability also had a role in the company's selection of the location for this facility. The specific factors enumerated by Intel officials as influencing the decision to locate the investment in Ho Chi Minh City are:

- access to infrastructure (including airport services, ample water supplies, land and reliable electrical power)

- a rapidly growing economy, where annual growth averages in excess of 8 per cent per annum
- a large population of more than 84 million people with a very low level of computer penetration
- the Vietnamese people's desire for education and interest in learning more about the high technology sector
- Saigon High Tech Park's proximity to relevant educational institutions
- Vietnam's young and energetic workforce
- Ho Chi Minh City's proximity to Intel's other assembly and testing facilities in Malaysia, China and the Philippines.

The company also acknowledges that incentives are a common practice in the high-tech industry, where they are used to help offset part of the huge costs associated with new facilities. While corporate officials have indicated that the exact incentives provided to Intel are confidential, our interviews with Vietnamese officials suggest that Intel's investment in Saigon High Tech Park has been accorded 'pioneer' status – which would guarantee it preferential tax treatment for perhaps as long as fifty years.

Another very interesting aspect of the Intel relationship with the host government is the anti-corruption memorandum of understanding signed in mid 2007 between the company and Saigon Hi-Tech Park. Recognising that the Intel project, involving thousands of suppliers and contractors, would likely be the target of some degree of graft, the MOU evidently provides for each party to inform relevant agencies, subsidiaries, agents or contracts in the event of improper behaviour being discovered.[8] The MOU obviously serves the interests of the company, which would like it to serve as a model in its dealings with officials in other parts of the world. It also serves the interest of Vietnam, which is high on the list of the most corrupt countries maintained by Transparency International, and where the Prime Minister is committed to an anti-corruption policy.

The new assembly and test facility

The new billion dollar assembly and test facility that Intel is building in Ho Chi Minh City will eventually employ as many as 4,000 people, with a significant multiplier effect in the local area as a supply base

---

[8] Lan Anh Nguyen (2007), 'Intel's Vow in Vietnam', *Forbes Asia* 26 (November): 85–6.

locates near the facility and other services develop to work with the company. The 500,000 square foot plant will produce chipsets using Intel's latest fabrication technologies. There will be no differences of any significance between this plant and other Intel assembly and test facilities, as the company leverages a 'copy exact' philosophy for its operations.

The chipsets to be assembled in Vietnam once the factory begins production in 2009 are one of the key components used in the production of motherboards for the computer industry. They will be used in desktop and laptop computers, servers and numerous embedded applications. The global supply-network aspect of this plant is demonstrated by the company's planned imports and exports associated with the facility. Both raw materials and capital will be imported to support the manufacturing of Intel's chipset products. Typical raw materials include: substrates, capacitors, solder paste and flux, tape and reel packaging and epoxy underfill. Intel's substrates come from sources in Japan, Taiwan and the Philippines. Capacitors and tape and reel packaging come from China. Epoxy comes from Japan. Solder paste and flux comes from Japan and the USA. Intel's capital tools come from all over the world. As an estimate, approximately 99 per cent of the plant's chipset production will be exported outside of Vietnam, with the products shipped to original equipment manufacturers and subcontractors for assembly into computers. Since most computers today are assembled in China, Intel expects that the vast majority of the chipsets will be exported to that country. When the plant is ramped up to its full production capacity, the value of the products made in the Intel plant and shipped to export markets is expected to be between US$5 to 6 billion per year.

As noted earlier, the plant is also expected to have a significant multiplier effect on the local economy. According to company officials, a look at other 'greenfield' sites where Intel has started up similar operations provides a clear picture of what is possible in Vietnam. Intel does not expect to see its global suppliers move their operations close to the factory, because the piece parts are small and easily air freighted. However, there will certainly be a large supply base that will be located close to the chipset assembly and test facility. This supply base will include equipment vendors, packaging suppliers, tooling vendors, logistics suppliers, nitrogen gas suppliers, as well as motherboard subcontractors and computer assembly subcontractors that will integrate the Intel chipsets into finished motherboards and computers. In addition, Intel expects to see a growth in local support to its operations in areas like food vendors, furniture

vendors, landscaping services, facilities management companies, relocation companies and packaging (boxes) suppliers.

The new plant's contribution to the Vietnamese economy and its
employment of many thousands of workers – directly and indirectly –
will be felt for a long time. Intel officials indicate that assembly and test
facilities like the one currently under construction have very long life
spans, because the capital tools and facilities tools are easily upgraded
to support the company's latest assembly and fabrication technologies.
Intel expects the Ho Chi Minh City factory to operate for thirty to fifty
years.

Employment with Intel Products Vietnam

Up to 4,000 workers will be employed by Intel Products Vietnam's Ho Chi
Minh City assembly and test facility when it becomes fully operational.
Only about 50 to 100 of the positions created will be filled by expatriates,
drawn from around the world, so Vietnamese will be hired for the vast bulk
of the jobs in the plant. The company will be recruiting workers across a
wide range of disciplines. Professionals will be needed to support the site
from finance, staffing, human resources, construction, facilities management, engineering, manufacturing, information technology, purchasing
and legal and public affairs. The company is of the view that for all of the
positions other than engineering, there appears to be a sufficient number
of local resources to support the operation. In the case of engineering,
until recently, employment prospects for Vietnamese were limited, so few
Vietnamese graduated from local universities with engineering degrees.
To better equip all of its employees for work at Intel, the company will put
them through a multitude of training programmes designed to acclimatise
them to the unique culture of Intel. Intel's specialised courses cover everything from business ethics training to structured problem solving, from
presentation skills to job-specific training. The company has established
'Intel University', which provides over 3,000 different courses taught by
Intel employees.

All of the jobs in the new Intel facility in Vietnam will be capable
of being performed equally by both men and women. Intel's policy is
to design its processes to ensure that there are no barriers that prevent men or women from doing the required work. According to Intel's
Ms Uyen Ho, hiring the best and brightest people helps drive Intel's pas-
sion for innovative technology, and the company believes in sharing that
success with employees who have helped earn it. Bonuses are an important

element of cash compensation, as they link a portion of each employee's pay directly to Intel's performance and profitability. Intel has two bonus programmes to recognise employee contributions to the company's success. Firstly, the Employee Cash Bonus Plan (ECBP) is a profit-sharing programme tied directly to Intel's financial performance. Secondly, the Employee Bonus is based on individual and business group performance, as well as corporate earnings per share.

At Intel, employees are able to own a stake in the company. Through Intel's stock programme, full- and part-time employees may be eligible to receive restricted stock units and options based on their past performance and anticipated future contributions. Additionally, all employees are encouraged to enroll in the Stock Participation Plan, a programme that offers employees an opportunity to purchase Intel stock at a price lower than the fair market value through convenient payroll deductions. In addition to these compensation programmes, Intel offers a variety of important benefit programmes to protect the wellbeing of employees and eligible family members. Starting on the first day of employment, Intel offers comprehensive medical and other insurance coverage for employees.

Intel's comprehensive compensation and benefits package is designed to attract, retain and reward the people necessary to create Intel's longer term growth and profitability. According to company officials, wherever possible, the company provides the ability for employees to participate in a range of compensation programmes, which allow employees to share in Intel's financial success, and innovative benefits that help employees and their families achieve improved quality of life and financial security. Base pay for each job at Intel Products Vietnam is determined by several factors, including: what competitors generally pay for a similar job (based on regular local-market surveys that ensure competitive wages); how the responsibilities compare with other jobs at Intel; and the employee's relevant education, skills, experience and job performance. Intel's stated goal is to pay above-average total cash compensation when Intel has an average year and, with bonus payouts, well above average when Intel outperform their competitors.

Other electronics firms operating in Vietnam

As part of the research for this case study, the authors interviewed local officials from Sony Vietnam, Toshiba Electronics Company, Panasonic Vietnam Company, JVC Vietnam Limited and the Samsung Vina

Company.[9] Most of these Japanese and Korean companies have been in Vietnam years before Intel, and most are mainly concerned with the assembly of consumer electronics products such as televisions, digital cameras, digital music players, DVD players, computer printers and drives and occasionally white goods like washers and dryers. To a large extent, these firms' factories' outputs are destined for domestic consumption inside Vietnam, although in one or two cases there are exports of a limited range of items to other ASEAN countries. None of these firms employ more than 850 workers in their operations, and several employ only 200 to 300 workers in their Vietnamese plants. All of those who the authors interviewed indicated that they enjoyed tax benefits specifically oriented to the encouragement of the high-tech electronics sector in Vietnam, although it would seem that these firms' operations are likely qualitatively different from the Intel investment in terms of the potential for technology transfer and engineering training. All of the firms provide generous salary and benefit packages to their employees that compare favourably to what would likely be on offer from a non-foreign employer in Vietnam.

What is certainly clear is that in an economy characterised by very rapid growth, the electronics sector – even before the Intel plant comes on stream – is making a very important – and rapidly growing – contribution to Vietnamese exports. According to the Vietnam Electronics Industry Association, exports of electronics from Vietnam grew by 166 per cent in the 2003 to 2006 period. The Government of Vietnam has unveiled a plan to more than double annual electronics exports by 2010 (which should be an easy target to meet, given Intel's expectations for the company's own exports). Table 1K demonstrates how the growth in Vietnam's electronics exports accelerated over the four-year period – rising at an annual rate of 77 per cent in 2006 compared to 2005.

Electronics, poverty reduction and the future

The authors asked representatives of the Asian Development Bank (ADB) and the World Bank for their views on the contribution of the electronics

[9] Ms Pham Xuan Anh Thi, Public Relations Director, Sony Vietnam (10 November 2007); Ms Do Thanh Suong, Director, Administration and Human Resources, Toshiba Electronics Company (11 November 2007); Mr Phan Thanh Trung, Sales Manager, Panasonic Vietnam Company (12 November 2007); Ms Nguyen Thi Nguyen, Director of Human Resources and General Affairs, JVC Vietnam Ltd (14 November 2007); and Ms Chau Kim Ngan, Human Resources Manager, Samsung Vina Company Ltd (19 November 2007).

Table 1K   *Vietnamese electronics exports*

Year	Electronics sector exports (US$ millions)
2003	528.1
2004	663.1
2005	793.1
2006	1,400.0

Source: Vietnam Electronics Industry Association, 2007.

sector in Vietnam to poverty-reduction strategies. At the ADB, Mr Omkar Shrestra, Deputy Country Director in the Vietnam Resident Mission,[10] opined that the development of the electronics sector in Vietnam has helped to diversify local industry and the services sector, and that this greater diversification is laying the foundations for sustained growth in output and employment, and helping to reduce poverty in the country. Mr Shrestra believes that sustaining rapid economic and employment growth requires focused efforts to increase national competitiveness and attract increased investment to maximise the potential benefits from greater regional and international integration. In Vietnam today, businesses are seeking support to: accelerate infrastructure development and address remaining policy and institutional bottlenecks to private investment; improve financial intermediation; and enhance human-resources development. These are areas in which the ADB plans to support the Government.

In the ADB's view, in order for Vietnam to attract further investment in this sector, clearly it must further improve the business environment through cutting red tape, simplifying further procedures and ensuring compliance with intellectual-property protection statutes. One of the most important factors is to ensure the availability of human resources, particularly skilled human resources. According to the ADB, a shortage of skilled resources is cited as the most serious problem in a recent Business Forum conference. Ongoing reformation of the education system, including encouragement by the government of private participation in education, is a good step.

At the World Bank office in Hanoi, we heard a similar message from Mr Doan Hong Quang, Senior Economist in the Poverty Reduction and

---

[10] Interviewed in Hanoi on 11 October 2007.

Economic Management Unit.[11] He said that, significantly, the electronics sector is one of the few sectors of high value-added in which Vietnam has comparative advantage, and that this could be seen by the rapid growth rates of investment, especially foreign direct investment and the resulting dramatic increase in export turnover. Apart from generating employment and higher income for a large number of employees, this impressive growth in the sector would also have some indirect effects through backward and forward linkages, as well as through the consumption channel. This situation was helping Vietnam develop infrastructure for hi-tech industries, and laid a good foundation for the process of the industrialisation and modernisation of Vietnam. In the World Bank's view, it will contribute to the poverty reduction process by improving the living standard and quality of life for Vietnamese people. When asked whether government policies and/or laws were still in need of reform in the future in order to ensure that investment and production in the electronic sector is sustainable, he opined that Vietnam should speed up the administrative reform to reduce bureaucratic procedures in state management, and to facilitate the operation of enterprises in general and of the electronics companies in particular. In addition, the government must have an appropriate strategy on education, science and technology to provide enough skillful workers, technicians and engineers for the sustainable development of this sector (a familiar message heard throughout this case study's development).

Concluding observations

In the course of Australia's hosting of APEC in 2007, a meeting held in Melbourne in April showcased work on the OECD's Policy Framework for Investment (PFI). At this session, Dr Nguyen Thi Bich Van[12] made a presentation to the group on how Vietnam had acted in recent years to improve the general climate for governance in the country and the investment climate in particular. Vietnam has got the message: good governance and a welcoming investment climate, combined with educational and training and infrastructure development policies and programmes can attract high-quality investment in key sectors like the high-technology electronics sector. While there are still certain aspects of Vietnam's former command-economy mentality that could be usefully reformed, Intel's

[11] Interviewed in Hanoi on 5 November 2007.
[12] Deputy Director of Foreign Investment Agency, Ministry of Planning and Investment, Government of Vietnam.

decision to invest a billion dollars in its assembly and test facility are a testament to how far the country has come.

Intel's investment is also a clear demonstration of how a major global TNC is contributing through its global supply network and geographically diversified operations to poverty reduction and economic growth in an important developing country in the Asia-Pacific region.

II

Trade in agriculture and poverty reduction

Agriculture and trade solutions for rural poverty

LEE ANN JACKSON[*]

Introduction

Nearly 70% of the world's poor live in rural areas, and most depend on agriculture for their livelihoods (World Bank 2007b). In many poor countries, agriculture accounts for at least 40% of gross domestic product (GDP) and 80% of employment. Thus agriculture plays a potentially crucial role in poverty reduction strategies. During the Green Revolution (in the 1960s and 1970s), development and aid communities stressed the relevance of this sector as an engine of growth for countries with a high proportion of rural population. However, in the 1980s and 1990s the attention given to agricultural policies as catalysts for development and poverty reduction decreased significantly. Currently, agriculture is once again on the forefront of development debate, as recent work on the role of agriculture in development has confirmed the importance of this sector in reducing poverty (World Bank 2007b, von Braun 2007, Food and Agriculture Organisation 2005).

The set of opportunities and challenges affecting agriculture's contribution to poverty reduction have changed dramatically over the past few decades. Developing-country food demand is expected to increase over the next few decades, driven by moderate economic growth, although these increases are expected to differ across products. For example, some studies have shown that economic growth in South Asia will lead to increases of nearly 100% for meat, eggs and fish, and of 70% for milk and vegetable products (Kumar and Birthal 2007). At the same time, the resource base upon which agriculture is built will shrink due to resource degradation, climate change and competition from urban expansion.

* Lee Ann Jackson is Economic Affairs Officer in the Agriculture and Commodities Division of the WTO Secretariat. The views expressed in this publication are those of the author. The publication does not necessarily reflect the views of the WTO, its members or the Secretariat.

Investments in the agricultural economies of developing countries are required, but the impact of policy interventions in terms of poverty reduction will vary depending upon country-specific characteristics. One policy approach will definitely not fit all countries.

Country characteristics, particularly the current contribution of agriculture to the national economy and the development status of the country, will influence the optimal types of strategies for agriculture-based development. In low-income countries, agriculture is likely to remain a major source of growth and development, and thus the priority may be investment in productivity enhancements and improvements in marketing. In rapidly developing countries, rural poverty may best be addressed through strategies that offer improvements in non-farm income. For urbanised countries, agriculture's role may be to reduce the number of rural poor through establishing marketing links with high-value urban markets.

Trade and market integration can enhance the potential positive impacts of investments in agriculture by generating market-access opportunities. However, as with agricultural policies more generally, trade liberalisation has complicated impacts on national economies, and without the right enabling conditions, trade liberalisation does not guarantee rural poverty reduction (Hertel and Winters 2006). Each country's unique characteristics will determine available policy choices, as well as the outcome of policies focused on linking domestic and international markets.

This chapter highlights domestic policies that can enhance the potential synergies between trade policies and agricultural development. The next section provides an overview of the role of agriculture in development in the Asia-Pacific region. The chapter then uses examples from the case studies to describe situations where trade opportunities catalysed agricultural activities and supported poverty reduction, and highlights factors that limit the potential development of opportunities. The section starting on p. 211 identifies issues that are expected to have increasing importance in the area of agricultural production and trade in the future. The last section draws out lessons for future policies in this area.

Current state of agricultural development and trade in the Asia-Pacific region

According to World Bank estimates, poverty in East Asia and the Pacific has declined over the past decade. The number of rural poor has decreased from 1,036 million in 1993 to 883 million in 2003 (World Bank 2007b).

Nevertheless, this overall picture of poverty reduction masks the outcomes within individual countries where rural poverty has worsened.
Declines in the total number of rural poor have been concentrated in
East Asia and the Pacific. In South Asia, the number of rural poor has
increased over the past decade, and is expected to stay at higher levels than
the number of urban poor until 2040 (World Bank 2007b). Although the
Asian agricultural sector is expected to continue to grow, its contribution
to Asian economic growth both in terms of contribution to GDP and
share of the workforce is declining. Urbanisation is increasing rapidly
in East and Southeast Asia (ratio of urban population to total population) but has proceeded much more slowly in South Asia and the Pacific
Islands.

Agriculture will fill several roles in the economy, including serving as
a source of investment opportunities for the private sector, the driver of
the rural non-farm economy, and a source of livelihood for rural people.
The countries profiled in the set of case studies following this chapter have begun the transformation from agriculture-based economies to
economies in which manufacturing and services are also playing important economic roles. Typically, during this transformation, agriculture's
contribution to economic growth decreases, but poverty remains concentrated in rural rather than urban areas.

Taking a look at the countries profiled in the following case studies, a
gap is evident between the share of agriculture in GDP and the share of
agriculture in the workforce. In China, the share of agriculture in employment declined from 47.4% in 1997 to 44.1% in 2002, but the proportion
of the population employed in agriculture remains relatively high. In
Indonesia, the share of agriculture in employment has not maintained a
consistent trend over the past decade, instead varying between 41.2% in
1997 and 46.3% in 2003 (World Bank 2007a).

Table 2A provides an overview of the annual change in agriculture
value added and the annual change in rural population for the countries
profiled in the following case studies. For some countries, the rate of
decline in the share of agriculture in GDP is much greater than the rate
of decline in the rural population. For example, between 2002 and 2004,
Samoa's agriculture value-addition was shrinking while rural population
was growing. This implies that policies were not leading to poverty reduction in rural areas, since the shift out of agriculture into non-agricultural
production has not coincided with a corresponding decrease in the number of people depending upon agriculture for their livelihoods. In contrast,
both China and India have over the past five years experienced shrinking

Table 2A *Annual change in agriculture value-addition and the annual change in rural population for selected countries*

	2002	2003	2004	2005	2006
China					
GDP per capita (constant 2000 US$)	1,106.0	1,209.0	1,323.1	1,448.8	1,594.9
Agriculture value-addition (% of GDP)	13.5	12.6	13.1	12.5	11.9
Agriculture value-addition (annual % growth)	2.9	2.5	6.3	5.2	4.5
Rural population growth (annual %)	−0.8	−0.9	−0.9	−0.9	−1.0
Indonesia					
GDP per capita (constant 2000 US$)	843.8	872.4	904.0	942.5	983.1
Agriculture value-addition (% of GDP)	16.4	16.2	15.4	13.1	11.9
Agriculture value-addition (annual % growth)	3.2	4.3	4.1	0.6	3.7
Rural population growth (annual %)	−0.8	−0.9	−0.9	−1.0	−1.1
Nepal					
GDP per capita (constant 2000 US$)	225.9	228.7	232.4	233.9	233.8
Agriculture value-addition (% of GDP)	39.4	39.1	38.6	38.2	39.5
Agriculture value-addition (annual % growth)	2.2	2.5	3.9	3.0	1.7
Rural population growth (annual %)	1.6	1.5	1.5	1.4	1.3
Samoa					
GDP per capita (constant 2000 US$)	1,432.2	1,443.0	1,478.0	1,547.4	1,577.9
Agriculture value-addition (% of GDP)	14.8	13.3	13.1	13.6	–
Agriculture, value-addition (annual % growth)	−0.1	−4.9	−9.3	5.7	–
Rural population growth (annual %)	0.8	0.7	0.6	0.5	0.1

Source: World Bank 2007a.

rural populations, while maintaining positive annual growth in agriculture value-addition. The potential impact of changes in agricultural policy will differ for these countries than for those countries in which the rural population is declining at about the same rate as the decline in the share of agriculture in GDP. Through careful management of this process of change, countries can create long-term solutions to rural poverty (see the discussion in the last section, p. 223).

What types of domestic factors constrain the potential for agricultural growth? In many parts of Asia, challenging natural conditions such as declining farm sizes, land degradation and production on marginal lands limit the expansion of agricultural areas and constrain the potential contribution of the agricultural sector to poverty reduction. While the small size of Asian farms may be one factor that contributed to the success of the Green Revolution techniques, there is concern that the continued decline in size could create market imperfections that would inhibit productivity improvements. For example, imperfect credit markets prevent small farmers from adopting more productive capital-intensive techniques or higher value products. In some areas, insecure property rights, particularly those of marginalised populations, create disincentives for farmers to invest in land improvements that would limit potential land degradation.

Over the past twenty years, improvements in infrastructure and communications technology have enhanced Asian rural communities' capacity to link to markets (see Table 2B). While the total distance covered by roads has increased steadily over time in most countries, the proportion of roads that are paved varies by country. Nearly 80 per cent of China's road network is paved. In contrast, Nepal still has less than a third of its road network paved as a result of the highly mountainous Nepalese terrain. Furthermore, communication networks have also improved over the past decade, with the number of telephone mainlines per 1,000 people and the number of mobile phone subscribers per 1,000 people increasing steadily in all cases.

Existing links with external markets and historic trading patterns have also influenced the ways in which Asian economies have developed their agricultural sectors. Countries will have diverse concentrations of exports and imports, with some countries, such as Nepal and Samoa, having just a few major products representing a significant proportion of the value of their agricultural exports. China's agricultural exports are less concentrated, however; Chinese imports of soybeans represented in 2005 more than 70% of the total value of agricultural imports (see Table 2C).

Table 2B *Infrastructure and communication networks*

Country	1997	1998	1999	2000	2001	2002
China						
Roads, total network (km)	1,226,405	1,278,474	1,351,691	1,402,698	1,698,012	1,765,222
Telephone mainlines (per 1,000 people)	57.15	70.39	86.71	114.70	141.81	167.31
Mobile phone subscribers (per 1,000 people)	10.76	19.21	34.531	67.52	113.87	160.89
Indonesia						
Roads, total network (km)	341,467	355,363	342,700	355,950	361,780	368,360
Telephone mainlines (per 1,000 people)	25.14	27.74	29.877	32.30	34.54	36.59
Mobile phone subscribers (per 1,000 people)	4.62	5.31	10.91	17.79	31.20	55.24
Nepal						
Roads, total network (km)	–	–	13,223	–	–	15,308
Telephone mainlines (per 1,000 people)	6.15	8.93	10.60	10.92	11.93	12.84
Mobile phone subscribers (per 1,000 people)	0	0	0.230	0.42	0.69	0.86
Samoa						
Roads, total network (km)	790	790	–	–	2,337	–
Telephone lines (per 100 people)	4.967031	4.956215	4.940134	4.924077	5.557471	6.722322
Mobile cellular subscriptions (per 100 people)	0.450213	0.865000	1.413459	1.444858	1.436782	1.539986

Source: World Bank 2007a.

Table 2C *Main agricultural imports and exports by value (2005)*

Import products	Import value (US$ 1,000)	% of total agric. imports	Export products	Export value (US$ 1,000)	% of total agric. exports
China					
Soybeans	8,498,335	75	Crude materials	2,071,122	17
Cotton lint	3,580,651	31	Food prep nes	1,449,996	12
Palm oil	1,901,859	17	Maize	1,096,581	9
Rubber nat dry	1,846,508	16	Cigarettes	805,507	7
Hides wet salted cattle	1,413,137	12	Other fruit and parts of plants	690,514	6
Indonesia					
Wheat	799,003	32	Palm oil	3,756,286	34
Cotton lint	576,002	23	Rubber nat dry	2,577,563	23
Cake of Soybeans	474,166	19	Palm kernel oil	587,748	5
Sugar, refined	364,040	14	Coffee, green	498,372	5
Soybeans	308,010	12	Cocoa beans	467,826	4
Nepal					
Rice, milled	32,220	20	Crude materials	150,866	60
Wool, degreased	15,218	9	Animal or vegetable fats and oils, hydrogenated	45,427	18
Bever, dist. alc.	5,895	4	Bever. non-alc.	14,757	6
Goats	5,227	3	Lentils	7,273	3
Lentils	4,817	3	Cmpd feed, Oth. or nes	6,633	3
Samoa					
Non-Food alc.	47,016	52	Fruit juices, nec	3,261	45
Coffee extracts	9,058	10	Coconut (copra) oil	1,479	20
Chicken meat	4,992	6	Food prep nes	849	12
Food prep nes	3,164	4	Fruit dried nes	445	6
Flour of wheat	2,348	3	Oil, fish, mar. mamm.	335	5

Source: Food and Agriculture Organisation 2007b.

Table 2D *MFN-applied agricultural duties*

Product groups	China	India	Indonesia	Nepal	Vietnam	Fiji
Animal products	14.8	33.0	4.2	10.9	20.1	14.4
Dairy products	12.2	35.0	5.0	14.3	21.9	10.7
Fruit, vegetables, plants	14.9	31.5	5.1	12.9	30.6	5.8
Coffee, tea	14.6	56.3	4.8	23.8	37.9	12.4
Cereals and preparations	24.4	37.3	5.6	16.1	27.4	16.8
Oilseeds, fats and oils	11.0	52.5	4.2	11.2	13.4	5.6
Sugars and confectionery	27.4	48.4	8.3	15.3	17.7	27.0
Beverages and tobacco	22.7	68.9	56.0	55.0	66.6	263.1
Cotton	22.0	17.0	4.0	0.0	6.0	3.0
Other agricultural products	12.0	27.1	4.3	7.9	7.8	3.3

Source: WTO and International Trade Centre 2007.

Explicit trade policies will distort prices and hence lead to inefficient market outcomes, including the suppression of agricultural output growth. Historically, agricultural policies have tended to shift from net taxation of the agricultural sector to subsidies in support of agriculture as a country's income rises. While these distortions have been decreasing over the past few decades, especially in developing countries, their perpetuation continues to impede poverty reduction efforts. Reliance on market-price support dominates in the non-OECD area, and may even be increasing in some countries.[1]

Table 2D presents a summary of applied agricultural duties in the case of several of the case-study countries, as well some other countries in the region. This table indicates that, in general, the product groups with the highest average applied Most Favoured Nation (MFN) duties are beverages and tobacco. Three of the case-study countries (China,

[1] However, current estimates of producer support for non-OECD countries indicate that current support for producers remains well below the OECD average (OECD 2009).

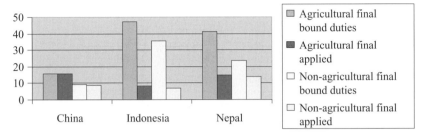

Figure 2A   Simple average agricultural and non-agricultural duties. *Source:* WTO and International Trade Centre 2007.

Indonesia and Nepal) have MFN-applied duties that are on the low end of the range in these product groups.[2]

In terms of the impact of trade liberalisation on an individual economy, it is the relation between the bound MFN duty indicated in WTO members' schedules and MFN-applied duties that determines how much of an impact negotiated tariff reductions will have. Figure 2A shows the difference in the tariff regimes of several of the case-study countries. The transition to a more open economy may create, in the short run, price or import volatility, particularly for countries like China, where bound and applied rates are nearly the same. For example, China's average bound and applied rates are the same, and therefore any reduction in bound rates will lead to a real reduction in applied rates. Reduction in bound rates is unlikely to have a substantial impact on applied duties in the case of Indonesia and Nepal.

In addition to tariffs, sanitary and phytosanitary measures (SPS) are increasingly influencing market-access opportunities, creating both barriers and potential opportunities for exporters in emerging markets. One indication of the types of SPS policies that have created friction among Asian exporters and their trading partners is the list of 'specific trade concerns' which are raised in the context of SPS Committee meetings at the WTO. Thirty-eight concerns have been raised by developing countries in the Asia-Pacific region (see Table 2E). Food safety issues (including maximum residue limits for pesticides and specifications for food additives) have led to nineteen out of the thirty-eight trade concerns raised in the committee by countries in the region. In addition, recent fears

---

[2] Since Samoa is still in the accession process, the WTO database of applied duties used for this table does not contain Samoan data.

Table 2E   *Specific trade concerns raised by WTO members from the Asia-Pacific region (1997–2007)*

Title	Members raising the concern	Members maintaining the measure	Date
Import ban on frozen poultry	Thailand	Korea, Republic of	1997
Import prohibition of milled rice	Thailand	Mexico	1997
Maximum levels for certain contaminants (aflatoxins) in foodstuffs	Argentina, Australia, Bolivia, Brazil, Gambia, India, Indonesia, Malaysia, Philippines, Senegal, Thailand	European Community	1998
Import prohibition of coconut palms and related products	Philippines	Brazil	1998
Restrictions on imports of sauces containing benzoic acid	Philippines	Australia	1998
Quarantine requirements for chicken meat	Thailand	Australia	1998
Prohibition of poultry meat imports from Thailand	Thailand	Czech Republic	1998
Interim rule affecting solid wood packaging material	Hong Kong, China	USA	1998
Measures regarding canned tuna in oil	Philippines	Belgium, European Communities	1999
Restrictions on imports of tropical fresh fruit	Philippines	Australia	2000
Restrictions on canned tuna	Thailand	Egypt	2000
Import restrictions on durian	Thailand	Australia	2000

(cont.)

Table 2E   *(cont.)*

Title	Members raising the concern	Members maintaining the measure	Date
Import restrictions on prawns and prawn products	Thailand	Australia	2001
Import restrictions on soy sauce	Thailand	European Communities	2001
Geographical BSE risk assessment	Canada, Chile, India	European Communities	2001
Restrictions on importation of sugar-cane top from Indonesia	Indonesia	Japan	2001
Notification on Chinese fruit imports	China	Philippines	2002
Restrictions on shellfish	Indonesia	European Communities	2002
Amendment of the food sanitation law	China	Japan	2002
Restrictions on imports of Chinese potted plants in growing medium	China	USA	2002
EC-proposed regulation on maximum residue levels of pesticides	Argentina, China	European Communities	2003
Notification on maximum tolerance levels for Ocratoxin A in coffee	Colombia, Papua New Guinea	Germany, European Communities	2003
Revision of standards and specifications for food and additives	China	Japan	2003
Maximum residue levels for pesticides on food	China	European Communities	2004

(cont.)

Table 2E   *(cont.)*

Title	Members raising the concern	Members maintaining the measure	Date
EC regulation on aflatoxins and Ocratoxin A in foods for infants and young children	China	European Communities	2004
Standards and specifications for food additives (boscalid)	China	Japan	2004
US rule on materials derived from cattle and record-keeping requirements	Argentina, China	USA	2004
Directives on residual pesticide tolerance and inspection methods for tea	China	European Communities	2005
Positive list system for pesticides, veterinary drugs and feed additives MRLs	China, USA	Japan	2005
Restrictions on Ya pear imports	China	USA	2005
Proposed regulations for piper methysticum (kava-kava)	Fiji	European Communities, UK	2005
Safety insurance and quality improvement standards for feed and feed additives	China	Japan	2005
Import suspension of heat-processed straw and forage for feed	China	Japan	2005
Import requirements for Indian mangoes	India	Japan	2005

(cont.)

Table 2E   *(cont.)*

Title	Members raising the concern	Members maintaining the measure	Date
Import restrictions on Enoki mushrooms from China Taipei	Taipei, China	Canada	2005
Restrictions on cinnamon	Sri Lanka	European Communities	2005
Import restrictions on wooden Christmas trees	China	USA	2006
Revised generic IRA for prawns and prawn products	Thailand, China	Australia	2007

about the spread of avian influenza have led countries to implement trade restrictive measures, which can have significant temporary impacts on poultry-producing countries in the region. These types of restrictions on the poultry trade are being raised more frequently since reports of the highly pathogenic variety of the disease have increased (see discussion at p. 214). At the same time, SPS measures may contribute to the evolution of high-value product markets, which could also offer opportunities for Asian producers.

Understanding trade–poverty linkages in the context of agricultural development

Trade offers potential opportunities in the way of new, higher value markets; however, at the same time, if these trade opportunities are not uniformly available to all households, enhanced trade can exacerbate existing inequity. The various effects from trade liberalisation, including income effects, portfolio effects and effects on the variability of existing income sources, overlap and interact depending upon pre-existing socioeconomic conditions at the community level. Thus, understanding the system of economic incentives and impacts and the relevant feedback mechanisms that influence farm household-level decision-making is essential for policy development in this area (see, e.g., discussions in Hertel and Winters 2006 and Winters *et al.* 2006).

For farm households, the immediate impact of shifts in relative prices will be twofold. Firstly, trade-induced changes in food prices alter budget allocations. If prices increase, net consumers of a particular commodity may experience declining welfare. Poorer households will feel a bigger consumption impact from increasing prices since they devote a larger proportion of their household budget to food items. Secondly, farm households that produce food crops to sell on the domestic market will benefit from increased income-generation as prices increase. While it is difficult to determine *a priori* how these price changes will affect individual households, resource endowments, market linkages and labour market characteristics clearly can impact outcomes. The case studies following this chapter highlight the importance of local conditions in creating successful development paths that capitalise on trade opportunities.

At the most basic level, the condition of the land used for agricultural cultivation will determine both the suitability of crops and the possibility of successfully adopting productivity-enhancing strategies. In areas with steeply sloped lands, such as those described in the Nepal case study, low productivity and unsustainable production methods can rapidly lead to soil erosion and land degradation. Hilly areas are particularly susceptible to soil erosion if the agricultural practices are not carried out in ways that limit the disruption of soil structure and vegetative cover. Thus, agricultural production choices require sustained management techniques to mediate the potential degradation. In other areas, the resource-constraining factor is water availability. For example, the case study on Indonesia highlights the importance of sustained public support for irrigation and water supply in order to maintain irrigation ditches and related physical structures over time. Since many poor communities live in marginal areas, resource endowments are more likely to be a constraining factor in relation to the potential options for shifting to new types of agricultural production.

Even if the resources and land characteristics are suitable for new types of agricultural crops and production strategies, producers still require necessary inputs, information and credit in order to respond effectively to price signals (Winters *et al.* 2006). Farmers may be constrained in their abilities to shift easily among crops to take advantage of shifting prices, particularly where high transaction costs have limited the foreign investment and trade that might support diversification efforts. Without appropriate policies to address economic rigidities that inhibit people from adjusting flexibly to changing economic signals, trade liberalisation can lead to a poverty trap. In the rural sector, inertia of farmers and a reluctance to shift from traditional farming practices may require extra efforts from the public sector to promote the maximisation of potential benefits from comparative advantage. The Bali ornamental-fish case study provides an example of one fishing community that was able to capitalise on eco-tourism interests in order to transform its fishing techniques to less-environmentally damaging methods, while at the same time enhancing its revenue. However, these successes have not been replicated in other fishing communities.

Linking to domestic and international markets is equally important, especially for farmers who are seeking to capitalise on new and emerging market opportunities. Declining farm size may create barriers to market integration since small farmers may be at a disadvantage in terms of integrating with the commercialised economy (Pingali *et al.* 2005). For example, small farmers may not have the physical capacity to store their perishable products so that they can sell these products when the prices are higher. Again, the Nepalese case study provides a useful example of agricultural producers who have had difficulty linking to domestic markets due to the extreme variability in elevation of the Nepalese landscapes. This case study suggests that support to farmers, through upgrading existing roads and encouraging the collective ownership by farmers of transportation vehicles, would help them overcome these challenges. Physical infrastructure should also be complemented by enhanced communication to ensure that producers receive accurate and timely price signals, which enable them to adjust their production activities.

Existing market conditions and patterns of protection that may have insulated domestic markets from international price signals will also determine the impacts of market liberalisation in agriculture. Competitive markets are not likely to have large outcomes from improving market conditions since the changes in economic conditions will be incremental rather than abrupt. Governments may have implemented distorting policies with the intention of addressing the needs of poor communities. If policies were originally put in place to create a safety net for poorer communities, then the removal of these policies is likely, at least in the short run, to exacerbate poverty. The case study on Indonesia's rice economy describes such a case, in which the Indonesian Government's rice policy had been motivated by a desire to ensure food security. Modifications of these policies, which created price rigidities in the Indonesian rice market, will lead to an adjustment to new relative prices and will require policies to support poor households who may in the short term be adversely affected by increasing rice prices.

The rural poor have difficulty managing risks due to lack of resources and access to financial markets. Economic risks, such as price volatility, create one set of challenges. Trends towards higher food prices in general could have a significant impact on households' access to inputs and resources for production and their resulting income (see discussion in the next section). The extent to which households are able to buffer themselves against potential risks associated with market exposure will influence the impact of trade liberalisation on poverty reduction. Farmers' vulnerability to environmental risks can exacerbate these economic risks. For some small, physically isolated communities, as noted in the case study on Samoa, the high risk of weather-related disruptions to agricultural productivity, as well as to infrastructure, can create conditions of vulnerability. In the small Pacific Islands, for example, typhoons can wipe out annual agricultural production, reduce the efficiency of the domestic transportation networks and damage port infrastructure. The overlapping vulnerabilities can deepen the severity of the impacts in terms of future economic growth paths. To the extent that households have access to coping mechanisms, such as assets to store wealth, access to remittances or access to micro-credit, their consumption impacts can be smoothed (Meyers 2006). Thus, for example, the relative importance of remittances as inputs to rural household incomes can be quite large for small Pacific Island countries.

Trade liberalisation is more likely to lead to poverty reduction when households can take advantage of new market opportunities, both in the context of opportunities within the agricultural sector but also with respect to opportunities to shift labour to alternative activities. The labour endowment and rigidities in the labour market will influence the extent to which trade will impact growth in the rural sector.[3] Shifting wages will create incentives for farmers to alter their production portfolio, or even to leave the agricultural sector. Closer examination of income effects of

---

[3] Theory suggests several alternative labour-market responses to trade liberalisation. Since, in the case of developing countries, the abundant factor is low-paid unskilled labour, traditional theory would conclude that when borders open, the wages of skilled and unskilled labour should converge (Wood 1997). Alternative theories, which focus on firm behaviour under monopolistic competition, note that efficient firms are more likely to enter the export market and expand, implying that the extent of pre-existing labour market distortions will condition responses to liberalisation (Manasse and Turrini 2001). If technological change is factored into the story, it is possible that as skilled labour migrates from developed countries, developing countries could find that their high-wage skill-intensive sector grows, which increases the wage differential in developing countries (Zhu and Trefler 2005).

trade liberalisation in specific markets reveals that labour market effects can be important channels for trade reforms to affect welfare.[4] Most developing countries typically do not have full-employment conditions in their agricultural labour markets, so the level of unemployment prior to liberalisation will also influence the extent to which trade liberalisation affects domestic wages and resulting poverty levels. The critical factors that will determine the potential poverty impacts that act through labour markets are the impact of liberalisation on the demand for labour and the elasticity of labour supply.

As noted in the previous section, standards in export markets that specify particular product characteristics, such as pesticide residue content, create market-access hurdles for many agricultural products. Poor farmers face a complex array of public and private SPS-related standards, which often differ dramatically between domestic and export markets. In order for farmers to benefit from market opportunities, they must satisfy the requirements of their markets. This requires flexible and efficient markets for inputs, and often investments to ensure that their production processes can achieve the required levels of quality and safety. In order to justify these types of investments, farmers need confidence in the reliability of future market demand for their output. Furthermore, access to current information regarding relevant measures of potential trading partners is essential in order for farmers to anticipate product requirements. In many cases, public food safety and plant and animal health measures overlap with private-sector systems of standards, contributing to the challenge of gathering and analysing the relevant market information. While there are possible benefits for small farmers related to accessing private-sector networks, they may also be excluded from opportunities due the challenges of negotiating contracts with large firms (see the discussion in the next section).

The 'hot issues' for the future

Future shifts in global economic, political and environmental conditions will have significant impacts on agricultural production and trade and the potential for agricultural trade to ameliorate poverty. These trends will alter consumption and production patterns and will affect the market linkages that determine the ultimate impact on rural poverty.

---

[4] See, for example, the case studies in this book on Bangladesh, Tonga and Kerala, India.

Table 2F   *Evolving Asian diets (1979–2001)*

	Product	1979–81	1984–86	1989–91	1994–96	1997–2001
Consumption	Rice	82.3	88.7	89.2	86.0	84.1
(kg/cap/yr)	Wheat	54.3	62.5	65.8	69.8	66.7
	Milk	26.1	30.2	32.1	37.5	41.6
	Meat	11.4	14.0	17.1	22.4	26.3
	Beef	2.0	2.3	2.6	3.8	4.1
Calorie	Total calories	2,286	2,463	2,550	2,637	2,680
consumption	% from cereals	65.53	64.68	63.25	59.73	56.27
(cal/cap/day)	% from animal sources	7.92	8.85	9.96	12.14	13.66

Source: Adapted from Pingali 2007, based on FAOSTAT data.

Changing consumer preferences

Changes in global food preferences and diets, higher incomes, increased awareness of food safety and environmental issues and increased urbanisation will alter consumer preferences and consumption patterns. Changing consumer preferences (related to rising incomes) create incentives for market differentiation and value chain development. The emerging agricultural retail network offers opportunities for entrepreneurial small-holders, if they are supported by adequate organisations, to link to these value chain markets (see the discussion below). Producers of staple crops and traditional commodities can also benefit from product differentiation targeted at changing global consumer demand.

The main trends in the transformation of Asian diets include reduced per capita consumption of rice, increased consumption per capita of wheat and wheat-based products and a rise in high protein diets. The rising share of daily consumption of meat, milk and other animal products of Asia is particularly striking (see Table 2F). Across Asia, per capita meat consumption has more than doubled, from 11.4 kg per person from 1979 to 1981 to 26.3 kg from 1997 to 2001. In addition to the growing importance of meat in consumption patterns, convenience foods and beverages are also becoming increasingly popular.

In response to rapid urbanisation and the Westernisation of diets in Asia, food-supply systems will dramatically transform (Pingali 2007). Already there is strong evidence that the composition of imports is changing. Some FAO estimates indicate that by 2030 the agricultural trade deficit of developing countries could reach an overall net import level of US$31 billion (Food and Agriculture Organisation 2003).

Food prices and biofuels

Most agencies predict that prices will eventually stabilise after 2009/2010 at a higher plateau due to both demand and supply factors (FAO, OECD and the World Bank). Economists identify several factors contributing to this growth, including changing weather patterns, strong expected demand growth in developing and emerging economies (China and India) (Minder and Leahy 2008), the Westernisation of Asian eating habits and stronger biofuel demands.

The rapid evolution of the crop-based biofuels industry has been triggered by efforts to alleviate oil shortages through the development of alternative fuels. In theory, biofuels could displace imported oil while at the same time lowering the amount of greenhouse gases released into the atmosphere. In practice, the implications of biofuels are much more complicated. Demand for land to support increased production of crops for biofuels may contribute to deforestation of tropical rain forests. In addition, the production of biofuel crops requires synthetic inputs and fossil fuels to fuel machinery. As the initial rush to promote these products has tapered off, shifts in attitudes are leading to biofuel-constraining policies. For example, the EU has recently begun considering official policies that would ban the import of particular biofuel crops that do more harm than good in addressing climate change (Kanter 2008). In any case, in the medium term, the expansion of biofuel production will have diverse impacts on agricultural markets. For example, the expansion of biodiesel use in the EU raises demand for vegetable oils in global markets. The large increases in corn-based ethanol production in the USA affect the production, use and prices of farm commodities throughout the sector, as meat production will be negatively affected by the increased cost of feed-stuffs.

The extent to which trade policies amplify already-high food prices is of particular concern for poor households, for whom food represents a disproportionately large share of their household budget. However, while most poor are net buyers of food, others are net sellers. Thus, any change in price will produce winners and losers among the poor, and the distribution of winners and losers will be country specific.

SPS issues

Food safety and quarantine issues can have a significant impact on the stability of agricultural productivity, and these SPS issues are expected to shift in the future as a result of climate change. Recent food scares stemming from zoonotic diseases such as BSE have resulted in a growing political awareness regarding the need to reduce the incidence of food hazards in agricultural commodities. Consequently, this has led to the establishment of food safety standards and regulations for products along the supply chain, regardless of whether they are destined for informal, formal or export markets. Increasingly, the institutions involved in the provision of supply-chain management play important roles in the delivery of high-value perishable agricultural and livestock products to distant markets.

Avian influenza is a major food-safety and animal-health concern in Asia. The incidence of highly pathogenic avian influenza in the region has remained high over the past few years. Since December 2007, Bangladesh, Benin, China, Egypt, Germany, India, Indonesia, Iran, Israel, Myanmar, Poland, Russia, Ukraine, Turkey and Vietnam have confirmed new outbreaks of the highly pathogenic strain of avian influenza in poultry stocks. Except for a few cases in wild birds in China, Poland and the UK, most of the confirmed outbreaks occurred in domestic poultry, including chickens, turkeys, geese and ducks (Food and Agriculture Organisation 2008). Indonesia continues to have a high level of reported outbreaks of the disease, which is in part due to an enhanced monitoring and surveillance programme.

Avian influenza will have economic impacts throughout the poultry sector, starting from the livelihoods of smallholders and poultry farmers and including regional and international trade. Studies of impacts in the region indicate that large commercial producers specialising in poultry production for the domestic market sustain short-term economic losses related to loss of consumer confidence. Small-scale producers lose relatively more in relation to their overall level of assets and income (Food and Agriculture Organisation 2007a). The policy challenge is to maintain a balance between protecting poultry from the disease and thus ensuring human health while minimising disruption of the livelihoods of the millions of people involved in producing, processing and selling poultry. The chain for food safety begins on the poultry farm, and thus the most effective entry point in managing this disease is through enhanced food safety measures in the poultry-farming and production processes.

Productivity enhancements and constraints

Productivity enhancements are crucial in the context of increasing land degradation and water constraints. However, while biotechnology innovations may potentially offer the most poverty reduction impacts to developing countries, the landscape of trade in biotechnology products is currently dominated by large developed countries. Developing countries may be hesitant to adopt biotechnology products if they fear that this adoption will limit their access to biotechnology-averse markets in the future. Productivity-driven production increases are expected to continue in developing countries, but continued public investment in appropriate technologies is essential, and the danger is that the broader political setting for biotechnology products may inhibit the optimal level of investment in these technologies.

On the other hand, land and water resource constraints may cap potential productivity increases. Agricultural production may be influenced by climate change both through variability of temperature and precipitation. In the future, it is expected that demands on water will increase in order to satisfy the demand of growing urban populations and to fill the irrigation needs of growing agriculture.

Climate change

Most current climate-change models consider changing weather patterns, temperatures and water availability and their impacts on overall agricultural productivity (see, e.g., Cline 2007). In the long term, climate change may lead to an adjustment in the distribution of agricultural production, creating opportunities for regions where temperature and precipitation changes lead to enhanced potential productivity. At the same time, if climate change leads to rising sea levels, as expected, small island economies could face severe economic adjustment challenges.

Increased variability of weather patterns may also create obstacles to agricultural productivity improvements, particularly for the food-insecure producers. Small-scale producers may be at a higher risk in the short term, given their limited resource reserve to respond to extreme unexpected events. Governments can address potential climate change-induced reductions in productivity through investing in improved agricultural inputs and improved varieties. Environmental monitoring and early warning systems would also enable governments to take effective and timely action to support poor farmers who depend upon thin production margins (Brown and Funk 2007).

Climate change will also have important impacts on the distribution of agricultural production by altering the relative competitiveness of pests and diseases and catalysing permanent ecological change. Populations of

pests that could not survive over winter in certain colder regions of the
world might begin to have increasing ecological impacts as a result of
increasing temperatures. Shifts in seasonal temperatures and humidity
can have population-level impacts by altering the lifecycle in ways that
disturb the balance of predator–prey relationships. These types of outcomes are particularly difficult to predict, as they depend upon complex
relationships of organisms and physical conditions and the way these
change over time.

Water

Agriculture accounts for 90% of consumptive water use in the Asia-
Pacific region (Food and Agriculture Association 2005). Irrigated areas
in the region increased by 15 million hectares between 1993 and 2003.
In general, irrigated agriculture covers 18% of the cultivated land in the
developing world, but represents nearly 40% of the value of agricultural
output. Irrigated production will continue to be an important component of agricultural growth strategies, yet the potential for mismanagement of water resources and competition among user groups over this
increasingly limited resource exacerbates future uncertainty in this area.
Poor water management can lead to land degradation through salinisa-
tion, resulting in declining productivity and diminishing agricultural land
areas.

Standards

The system of public and private standards is growing increasingly complex in response to consumer preferences, and these standards will place
additional requirements on suppliers (Henson and Reardon 2005). In
the public sector, new and revised regulations and the development of
institutions have changed the landscape of public policies and the relationship between public and private sectors. The WTO's SPS Agreement
has also catalysed institutional responses by WTO member countries,
who are seeking optimal approaches to managing their SPS obligations
while maximising their benefits from trade and minimising their risks
associated with trade in agriculture and food products.

In parallel, the role of private standards has also evolved dramatically
in recent years, driven by responses to regulatory developments and consumer concerns, and as a means of competitive positioning in markets
for high-value agricultural and food products (Fulponi 2006). Markets

for organic and specialty products are likely to increase. Although they are not legally binding in a regulatory sense, private standards can be de facto mandatory for suppliers. As a result, private standards are becoming important drivers of agri-food systems in both developed and developing country agri-food markets. In order to understand the implications of private-standards development on market access by small-scale farmers, a clear understanding of the nature and magnitude of market-entry costs is crucial. The incentives and capacity of retailers and processors to implement private standards will also influence the potential distributive outcome of private-standards development, and this issue is of particular importance to developing countries with limited resources.

Retail expansion

The growing role of transnational supermarkets over the past two decades has led to dramatic changes in food production and marketing systems around the world. Retail transformation in Asia has been consistently advancing since 2000 (Reardon *et al.* 2003, Reardon *et al.* 2004). By 2002, supermarkets accounted for 33% of the processed/packaged food retail market in Southeast Asia. In East Asia, this number is 30% (Reardon *et al.* 2003). The supermarket share of Chinese urban food markets rose to 48% in 2001 from 30% in 1999. Thus, this trend, which has been accompanied by rapid consolidation and multinationalisation of the supermarket sectors in developing countries, has mixed outcomes for suppliers.

The combined impact of a changing urban food demand and a more consolidated retail sector has led to increased vertical integration along the food production and processing chain. Transnational supermarkets seeking to enhance the efficiency of their operations typically have a more centralised system of procurement based upon specialised wholesalers and contract farmers. In some developing countries, supermarkets are dominating the retail food sector, displacing traditional retailers such as central food markets and local food sources in urban areas. Evidence suggests that vertically integrated food systems are meeting domestic demands, as well as export market demands.

The process of commercialisation presents many challenges to small farmers. Production costs associated with meeting requirements of output markets are typically higher than those associated with subsistence farming. Costs of entry into the new commercialised food systems are exacerbated by the need to adjust to new players, regulations and relationships and the increased frequency of these interactions. Given the complex contracting relationships that are often the foundation of vertical agricultural integration, large retail firms may prefer to enter into contracts with a smaller number of medium-sized producer groups. These scale effects put small farmers at a disadvantage in terms of commercialisation opportunities.

The way forward: developing policies to encourage rural poverty reduction

A clear understanding of future global trends in the agricultural economy can provide a vision of potential opportunities, including for economic growth. At the same time, a thoughtful domestic-policy framework is necessary to ensure that the vulnerable are not disadvantaged by policy actions. Policy makers will need to prioritise relevant trade policy and trade-related capacity-building activities in order to deal with the challenges of addressing poverty reduction over time. This section discusses the factors that will influence the likelihood for success of these policy choices. As noted previously, the case studies highlight specific factors that lead to success or failure of poverty reduction efforts in the context of individual countries and communities. While the optimal ways forward for developing countries will differ depending upon country characteristics, lessons can be drawn from the case studies presented here. Countries will need to manage a portfolio of policy interventions and social investments to address immediate needs with long-term development programmes to increase productivity, create employment and increase the value of the poor's assets. Creating an enabling environment for smallholder production is essential.

While trade policies will have an impact on both international and domestic prices, domestic policies are likely to have a more significant influence on how market liberalisation impacts flow through the domestic economy. Consideration of the risk implications of policies that align domestic prices more closely with international prices is important, since an open market is more susceptible to price changes as an outcome of global events. Furthermore, price volatility is also often associated with low-volume markets, implying that small farmers who are shifting to producing for new markets may face an increased exposure to risk. Measures to lower transaction costs, improve market linkages and provide value-added services can contribute to buffering of risks by reducing the potential rigidities in the economic system.

Provision of public goods

The public sector will play a key role in terms of provision of public goods. Under-investment in rural areas limits a country's ability to capitalise on opportunities generated through market liberalisation (Byerlee *et al.* 2006). Furthermore, long-term inefficient allocation of public resources to urban areas (due to the distortions in public policy making) has disadvantaged rural areas. Some evidence suggests that core public investments are crowded out by public expenditures on subsidies (for inputs) and expenditures to serve the interests of large producers. Core public investments need to focus on the production of public goods such as infrastructure (both physical and communication), education and research and development. Countries or regions that are vulnerable to external shocks, such as Small Island economies like Samoa, will benefit from investment in infrastructure, which can buffer physical effects of extreme weather events as well as investments in monitoring and advanced warning technologies to anticipate these shocks. All of these will have positive spill-over impacts on the economy.

The creation of rural employment opportunities both through enhanced agricultural activities and through the development of alternative non-farm employment is essential. A rapidly growing agricultural sector and a good investment climate will contribute to the establishment and maintenance of a dynamic rural economy (World Bank 2007b). Public investment in improved educational opportunities will provide farmers with skills to respond to potential market opportunities both on and off-farm and will support agricultural growth. Educational enhancements should be targeted at disadvantaged groups, such as women, to compensate for existing chronic low levels of education.

The generation of new technologies to improve sustainable productivity growth can contribute to acceleration in growth in the rural economy (Pingali 2007). Productivity growth is lagging but necessary to create or strengthen international competitiveness and stimulate agricultural exports, or, if exports are not competitive, to at least feed a growing local population. In order to encourage rapid growth in the agricultural sector, agricultural research priorities should be re-oriented towards the generation of new technologies to enhance yields and to smooth out production (Byerlee *et al.* 2006). There is significant potential for new technological innovations and improved handling and distribution systems that could support relatively high future productivity growth rates in non-OECD countries. Nevertheless, innovation will require continued investment in research and development in this area, as well as appropriate investment and business policies and an enabling environment.

An increased demand for higher product standards may generate market opportunities that could contribute to rural growth. The strategic development of SPS-capacity to promote export opportunities would allow producers to capitalise on niche markets and specialised production. These types of strategic investments require a clear understanding of the export markets in order to be able to predict export market requirements. To the extent that these types of capacity building require private sector involvement and investment, the stability and predictability of the investment climate is also crucial. The public sector can promote this type of climate through policies that encourage the development of stable and predictable financial markets.

Public and private partnerships

The actors involved in agriculture and rural development and the ways in which they act have changed over the past few decades. New relationships between public and private sectors and civil society are required to encourage entrepreneurial responses to opportunities and challenges. Institutional innovations that support more collaborative and efficient interaction between public and private actors may take a long time, but can be supported through public sector planning and support (Nogueira 2006).

One aspect of the benefits associated with the effects of public and private partnerships relates to the possibility of reducing smallholder transaction costs, i.e. through the development of supply chains for high-value exports produced by small farmers. Small producers, like the fishermen described in the Bali case study, may benefit from coordinating with similar producers to invest in necessary physical capital resources. In addition, through well-managed producer organisations, small producers may be able to profit from more effective integration into marketing chains linking to external markets. Coordinated marketing chains will be increasingly important with the spread of retail stores. There is an incentive for large private firms to enter into contracts with medium firms because this reduces their transaction costs in terms of contracting over a smaller set of companies to provide inputs. Public policies need to ensure that smallholders are not excluded from marketing chains (Henson and

Reardon 2005). Public-sector efforts could contribute to the organisation of producer groups, which would then be able to contract more efficiently.

The complex system of public and private standards will challenge policy makers in determining appropriate responses to food quality and safety issues. Private standards may complement existing public regulations by filling in gaps in risk management systems. Or, private standards may have evolved primarily in response to consumer demands for differentiated products, and may provide a redundancy with respect to public standards addressing risks. It is also possible that a particular system of private and public standards work in synergy to maintain the optimal product safety. The example of policy approaches for managing avian influenza illustrates the importance of developing functional working relationships between the private-sector poultry producers and public-sector regulatory officials. The implementation of good husbandry practices for safe poultry production requires joint efforts by national and local authorities and communities, animal-health workers, agriculture and veterinary health authorities, farmers and other stakeholders, including consumers.

Institutional reform

Institutional reform is also crucial for pro-poor growth. These reforms include improving the efficiency of factor markets, especially land and labour markets since, effectively, functioning markets can enhance farmers' ability to exit from the agricultural sector. The development of water markets may also provide a more efficient allocation of this increasingly scarce resource.

As noted in the conclusions of the case study on Nepal, an increased participatory policy process could catalyse these reforms. In order to rebalance the distribution of public investments to compensate for past suboptimal rural investment, it is essential that local governments, producer organisations and consumers are integrated in the policy process in order to generate political will to redistribute public resources. Stakeholder deliberations on policy design and implementation could provide a new approach to discuss ways forward for historically disadvantaged sectors and regions. If stakeholders have the ability to hold the public sector accountable for their actions, their voices will have a stronger impact in shaping potential reforms. The credible commitment of donors to reward better governance in public agencies would lead to more effective local participatory processes.

Strengthening civil society and improving representation of the rural poor should be a priority when seeking to implement an agenda that bases macro-economic development policies on the foundation of agricultural growth (World Bank 2007b). Towards this end, effective producer organisations can give voice to small farmers and enhance their ability to integrate into marketing chains.

Safety nets and sequencing

The timing of benefits and costs is not always overlapping. For example, in Bangladesh, the average landless, poor household may lose welfare from an increase in rice prices in the short run, but may gain in the long run as wages rise over time (World Bank 2007b). The importance of transitional measures was noted in the case study on the rice economy in Indonesia, and these types of measures are particularly important given the small farmers' risk aversion in the context of rapidly changing global markets for agricultural products. Increased diversification also gives farmers the ability to withstand negative shocks (Food and Agriculture Organization 2006). Food aid may offer one potential type of safety net, but as noted in the case study, there are many factors that make implementing effective food aid challenging. In many situations, a more sustained approach to supporting the poor is preferred to dependence on food aid for a safety net.

The sequencing of policies that alter labour markets is particularly important in shaping alternative approaches to rural development based upon trade as a catalyst. Some authors have identified a common pattern to successful pro-poor rural-development strategies. Typically, the first step includes basic investments in public goods to develop technologies to enhance the product base. The second step includes investments to improve farmers' access to financial services and input and output markets (Hazell et al. 2007). These types of services would provide mechanisms for farmers to manage their economic risks rather than simply reacting to unpredictable shocks. In the final stage, the private sector would ultimately replace the public sector in the provision of these investment services; however, this transitional step can be difficult to implement.

Conclusion

Given the complexity of policies that affect poverty reduction and development in rural areas, no single approach will guarantee success. Policy makers should bear in mind the conditioning factors that will shape the outcome of policy decisions, recognising that these factors will also be changing over time. As noted above, economic policies need to be balanced with appropriate institutional innovations in order to increase the likelihood that policy implementation will lead to impacts at the local level. By keeping an eye on the actual constraints for farmers, policy makers can target public resources to those areas that are more likely to lead to positive results.

Each of the cases profiled in the following case studies demonstrates the fact that country-specific characteristics play a critical role in determining the poverty reduction impact of policy interventions. From the situation of traditional Nepalese farmers, and that of the fishermen in Bali seeking sustainable harvesting techniques, we note that one key aspect of poverty reduction is the extent to which the producers' socioeconomic environment is conducive to innovation. Part of the challenge of developing poverty reduction policies is to enhance the flexibility of producers to adapt to shifting market conditions. Since some of the rigidities in these countries may arise from social or cultural views, plans for economic policy change are more likely to succeed if they include a long-term perspective of the social and cultural changes required.

In an environment that adequately transmits market-price signals and has limited constraints to producer decisions, producers can adjust their behaviour effectively to maximise income. Of course, other case studies in this book point out particular situations of market failure, such as the lack of price transmission to the producer level (i.e. the Indonesian rice case study) or the need for insurance mechanisms for countries who may be more vulnerable to price swings (i.e. Samoa). In these contexts, an emphasis on interventions that specifically target these types of market failures may be more likely to yield results, shifting the context of producers' decision-making in such a way as to encourage innovative approaches to income generation.

While some policy interventions emphasise one-dimensional policy levers, such as removing border measures to enhance effective transmission of price signals to domestic producers, an implicit lesson from most of the following case studies is the importance of cooperation and coordination. The food aid case study in particular draws out this theme, highlighting the importance of international and national coordination. The importance of understanding the multi-faceted nature of policy intervention is perhaps more obvious in the food aid case study. However, it is no less important than addressing poverty through local interventions. The layers of local, national and international factors that influence poverty reduction vary across countries and communities, but the lesson that context is important in determining the impact of particular policies is consistent.

Within this complex array of policies, trade can offer both opportunities and challenges for the rural poor. The role of the policy maker is to support policies that will encourage agricultural growth while paying attention to labour markets and non-farm activities to enable the poor to move flexibly into alternative economic activities. With a strategic vision regarding market opportunities, policy makers can invest in productivity enhancement while supporting organisational development at the local level in order to link poor producers to markets. In order for trade opportunities to provide sustained benefits to the rural poor over time, policy makers will need to engage with local populations to ensure that the relevant specific constraints to market integration and growth are addressed. While these efforts will require time and resources, the potential benefits merit sustained investment in these areas.

References

Brown, M. and Funk, C. (2007), 'Food Security under Climate Change', *Science* 319: 580–1.

Byerlee, D., Diao, X. and Jackson, C. (2006), 'Agriculture, Rural Development and Pro-poor Growth,' 21: 1–72, Agriculture and Rural Development Discussion Paper 21, World Bank: Washington, WA.

Cline, W. (2007), 'Global Warming and Agriculture: New Country Estimates Show Developing Countries Face Declines in Agricultural Productivity', CGD Brief, September 2007, Center for Global Development, Washington, WA.

Food and Agriculture Organisation (2003), 'FAO', in J. Bruinsma (ed.), *World Agriculture: Towards 2015/2030*, Earthscan Publications: London.

    (2005), *State of Food and Agriculture 2005*, Food and Agriculture Organisation: Rome.

    (2006), *The State of Food and Agriculture in the Asia-Pacific 2006*, Food and Agriculture Organisation: Rome.

    (2007a), 'Economic and Social Impacts of Avian Influenza', Food and Agriculture Organisation: Rome, available at: www.fao.org/avianflu/documents/Economic-and-social-impacts-of-avian-influenza-Geneva.pdf [last accessed 11 February 2009].

    (2007b), *FAOSTAT*, Food and Agriculture Organisation: Rome.

    (2008), 'New Avian Influenza Flare-ups', Food and Agriculture Organisation, Rome, 24 January 2008.

Fulponi, L. (2006), 'Private Voluntary Standards in the Food System: The Perspective of Major Food Retailers in OECD Countries', *Food Policy* 31(1): 1–13.

Hazell, P., Poulton, C., Wiggens, S. and Dorward, A. (2007), 'The Future for Small Farms for Poverty Reduction and Growth', 2020 Discussion Paper, IFPRI: Washington, WA.

Henson, S. and Reardon, T. (2005), 'Private Agri-food Standards: Implications for Food Policy and the Agri-food System', *Food Policy* 30(3): 241–53.

Hertel, T. and Winters, L. A. (2006), *Poverty and the WTO: Impacts of the Doha Development Agenda*, World Bank: Washington, WA.

Kanter, J. (2008), 'EU Shifts to Tougher Stance on Biofuels', *International Herald Tribune*, 15 January 2008.

Kumar, M. P. and Birthal, P. S. (2007), 'Changing Composition Pattern in South Asia', in P. K. Joshi, A. Gulati and R. Cummings Jr. (eds.), *Agricultural diversification and smallholders in South Asia.*

Manasse, P. and Turrini, A. (2001), 'Trade, Wages, and "Superstars"', *Journal of International Economics* 54(1): 97–117.

Meyers, R. (2006), 'On the Costs of Food Price Fluctuations in Low-income Countries', *Food Policy* 31(4): 288–301.

Minder, R. and Leahy, J. (2008), 'Asia Battles with Surging Food Costs', *Financial Times*, 10 January 2008.

Nogueira, R. M. (2006), 'New Roles of the Public Sector for an Agriculture for Development Agenda', Background Paper for the *World Development Report 2008*, World Bank: Washington, WA.

OECD (2009), *Agricultural Policies in Emerging Economies: Monitoring and Evaluation 2009*, OECD: Paris.

Pingali, P. (2007), 'Westernization of Asian Diets and the Transformation of Food Systems: Implications for Research and Policy', *Food Policy* 32(3): 281–98.

Pingali, P., Khwaja, Y. and Meijer, M. (2005), 'Commercializing Small Farms: Reducing Transaction Costs', East and Southern Africa Working Paper No. 05–08, Agricultural and Development Economics Division, Food and Agriculture Organization: Rome.

Reardon, T., Timmer, P., Barrett, C. and Berdegue, J. (2003), 'The Rise of Supermarkets in Africa, Asia, and Latin America', *American Journal of Agricultural Economics* 85(5): 1140–6.

Reardon, T., Timmer, P. and Berdegue, J. (2004), 'The Rapid Rise of Supermarkets in Developing Countries: Induced Organizational, Institutional, and Technological Change in Agri-food Systems', *Electronic Journal of Agricultural and Development Economics* 1(2): 168–83.

von Braun, J. (2007), 'The World Food Situation: New Driving Forces and Required Actions', Food Policy Report No. 18, International Food Policy Research Institute: Washington, WA.

Winters, L. A., McCullogh, N. and McKay, A. (2006), 'Trade Liberalization and Poverty: The Empirical Evidence', *Journal of Economic Literature* 62(1): 72–115.

Wood, A. (1997), 'Openness and Wage Inequality in Developing Countries: The Latin American Challenge to East Asian Conventional Wisdom', *World Bank Economic Review* 11(1): 33–57.

World Bank (2007a), *World Development Indicators*, World Bank: Washington, WA. (2007b), *World Development Report 2008: Agriculture for Development*, World Bank: Washington, WA.

WTO and International Trade Centre (2007), *World Trade Profiles 2007*, WTO/UNCTAD: Geneva.

Zhu, S. C. and Trefler, D. (2005), 'Trade and Inequality in Developing Countries: A General Equilibrium Analysis', *Journal of International Economics* 65(1): 21–48.

Food aid: commitments and oversight

JOHN FINN*

Introduction

Food aid is needed to address hunger, but it is not always the best way. The main cause of hunger in the world is poverty, and development and increasing wealth will reduce hunger. However, natural and man-made disasters can and will occur, and food aid may be needed to prevent or reduce hunger during emergency situations.

There are, however, instances when food aid can harm development and trade. For instance, aid donations may be motivated by a desire to dispose of surplus production in the donor country, and can displace commercial imports in the receiving country – that is, reduce imports from other countries.

Thus, food aid can have both positive and negative effects on both trade and development. Over the past few years, a considerable body of academic work has developed that looks at how to improve the efficiency and effectiveness of aid and how to minimise or prevent any harm it may cause. Many papers have stressed the importance of targeting, selecting the right type of food aid, choosing the most effective means of delivery and reducing the number of conditions attached to aid by the donor. A lot of criticism has been directed at tied food aid, particularly aid tied to procurement – that is, to food aid donated in the form of commodities. The point is that in-kind food aid often takes longer to arrive at the place of the emergency, and may not be the most appropriate type of food for the situation, as well as effectively being an export subsidy for the donating country.

* John Finn is a counsellor in the WTO Agriculture and Commodities Division. This article was written in his capacity as a Visiting WTO Fellow with the Institute for International Trade at the University of Adelaide. The opinions expressed in this paper are those of the author and do not represent the WTO, its members or the Secretariat.

However, food aid needs greatly exceed supply, and the biggest donor (the USA) gives its food aid in kind (as is also the case for China, Korea and Japan). It may be correct to state that, in principle, aid should be in cash form, but it may be wishful thinking to believe that switching donations to cash-only would not result in smaller donations. On the other hand, cash-based food aid is usually more efficient and gives more flexibility to food aid agencies to deliver the most appropriate type of food in the most appropriate way.

However, different situations require different responses. In slow-onset emergencies, there may be enough time for planning, creating the infrastructure and delivering aid. In other cases, a natural disaster may require immediate response and regardless of cost. In other cases, the response to the emergency may change over time, from supplying food aid at the beginning to reconstruction and development later on. The big differences between different situations and the responses required mean that any rules that cover food aid need to allow the agencies involved in delivery the flexibility to address each situation in the most appropriate way.

There are a number of international agencies that have a role in food aid, but despite the large number of entities involved in overseeing and assessing food aid, there are no clear enforceable rules. At the same time, there must be enough flexibility to permit the appropriate response to each situation.

The need for food aid

About 850 million people in the world do not have enough to eat (FAO 2006b).[1] In most cases, this is not the result of a shortage of food, but rather because many people lack the resources to buy enough food. In these cases, development assistance is a better response than food aid. However, even in situations of food shortage caused by disasters, the UN reported that funds committed in response to appeals corresponded to only 43 per cent of requirements (OCHA 2007).

The shortage of food aid is likely to get worse in the future because food prices are increasing, as shown in Figure 2B. Unlike price peaks that happened in the past, current prices are unlikely to fall because they are not the result of a shortage but are caused by higher demand in some of

---

[1] However, it has been pointed out that in-kind aid is often slower in delivering food in emergencies than cash donations used to buy food locally – although it should also be noted that the United States Department of Agriculture (USDA) and the United States Agency for International Development (USAID) are taking steps to improve the timeliness of deliveries.

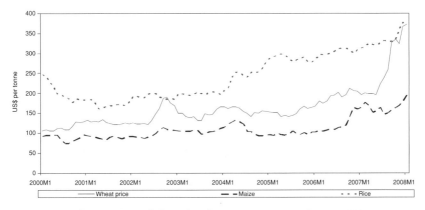

Figure 2B   Wheat, maize and rice prices from January 2001 to January 2008.
Source: IMF prices for the following: wheat, No. 1 Hard Red Winter, ordinary protein,
FOB Gulf of Mexico; maize (corn), US No. 2 Yellow, FOB Gulf of Mexico, US price;
rice, 5% broken milled white rice, Thailand nominal price quote.

the world's biggest countries. In addition, food demand is shifting from
basic cereals to higher value meat and other animal products, and animal
products are not as efficient as crops in delivering calories. To get a pig to
gain one kilogram of live weight requires 2.4 kilograms of feed (Red Meat
Industry Forum 2007); poultry require less, but grain-fed cattle need a
lot more, and even if the bovine is grass-fed, that can still mean land is
taken from crop production and put into pasture. At the same time, in
some other countries land is being taken out of food production and into
bio-fuels.

Thus, growing wealth in countries like China and India is leading to
increased consumption of food, particularly of meat and other animal
products, which either directly reduces land available for cereals or uses
cereals to feed the animals. The impact of this, along with the production
of bio-fuels, is pushing up food prices.

The impact of higher prices is not all bad news. It means many farmers,
farm labourers and agricultural service suppliers will see incomes and
living standards improve. But for those living in urban areas and for
many landless people in rural areas, and even for those farmers who
consume more food than they produce, it means more money must be
spent on food.

High prices for food will mean greater need for assistance to acquire
food. That does not mean food aid is the right response to every case of
hunger. Indeed, in many cases the most appropriate form of assistance
is not food delivered directly to those that cannot afford it, but rather

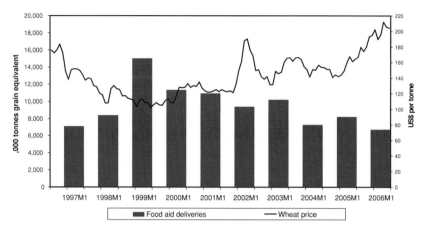

Figure 2C   Wheat prices and food aid deliveries. *Note:* no data on deliveries for 2007. *Source:* IMF wheat prices for wheat, No. 1 Hard Red Winter, ordinary protein, FOB Gulf of Mexico; WFP database (http://one.wfp.org/interfais [last accessed 10 June 2006]) for deliveries of food aid.

development assistance or the redistribution of resources in order to reduce poverty. However, the number and extent of emergencies are unlikely to decline, and may increase as a result of climate change (von Braun 2007). Responding to these crises will cost more because food prices will be higher, but past trends show food aid deliveries tend to fall as prices increase, as shown by Figure 2C.

An additional factor is the impact of new trade rules through the Doha Round on trade negotiations in the WTO. Several issues under negotiation will have an impact on food aid. The most important of these are the rules being developed for food aid itself, which are likely to influence what types of food aid can be provided in different situations, with restrictions on in-kind food aid, sale of in-kind food aid (monetisation) and tying aid to commercial transactions, particularly in non-emergency situations. In addition, the elimination of export subsidies and export credits of more than 180 days (although longer periods may be allowed for export credits to least-developed and net food-importing developing countries) will have a direct impact on food-import bills of many developing countries.

Indirect impacts from the Doha Round may also arise from reductions in domestic support and improvements in market access. Reducing subsidies that encourage production will, presumably, lead to reduced production. Reducing tariffs in countries like Japan, Korea and the member states of the EU will increase their imports, which will also mean less product is available (and at higher prices) for other countries. That does not mean that reducing distortions to agriculture trade is a bad idea. Indeed, improving trade opportunities for agriculture will benefit developing countries and will reduce poverty, and it could also mean that the decline in production in some countries will be met by increased production in other countries. However, when coupled with reductions in production subsidies and the elimination of export subsidies, it could also mean that higher prices will result.

Although the need for food aid may increase in the next few years, that does not mean that food aid should be delivered without regard to its impact on the donor's, recipient's or regional markets. Indeed, how food aid is procured and delivered can have a significant impact on a lot of people. Procured one way could mean that producers in the donor country benefit because their grain crops are bought and delivered as food aid. It can also mean that when the food aid arrives in the country of need, it depresses local prices and reduces farmers' incomes. Thus, food aid can cause problems by displacing or competing with sales of food both in the country receiving the aid and for countries that would normally export to the country receiving the aid. This can mean that other people suffer from lower prices or lower sales for the food they would normally sell.

Definitional issues and types of food aid

Not surprisingly, many people get emotional about food aid, but discussion and debate are not helped by the large number of technical terms used and misunderstandings of the specific definitions of these terms. It is also very easy to make generalisations, which are usually correct but may not apply in every case. For example, it may be generally correct to say that food aid donations should not be tied, should be in grant form and should be acquired locally or through triangular transactions. But what does all that mean, and is this statement realistic in all cases? What if the aid is required in an emergency that can best be responded to through in-kind donations from stockpiles?[2]

Humanitarian, programme and project food aid

Broadly speaking, food aid can be divided into three distinct categories: humanitarian, programme and project.

---

[2] www.fas.usda.gov/excredits/FoodAid/Reports/reports.html [last accessed 12 February 2009].

Humanitarian food aid is aid delivered in response to an emergency or humanitarian crises. It is usually delivered as a grant from the donor country either as cash or in kind. The concept of an emergency is clear to most people, and some organisations, like the World Food Programme (WFP), have definitions (WFP 2005). However, there are different definitions in different organisations, and these are subject to change. Furthermore, many publications write about 'emergency situations' rather than 'emergencies' partly because, legally, the only entities entitled to declare an emergency are sovereign governments and, in some cases, the Secretary General of the UN. Unfortunately, some governments are unwilling to declare an emergency even though, by any normal definition, there is one.

Programme food aid is a bilateral transfer of food commodities from the donor government to the recipient government, often in fully grant form but sometimes at concessional prices or on credit terms. It can have an important role in providing net-importers with food in times of economic shocks when the country cannot get access to foreign exchange or commercial credits to cover the cost of imports. In some cases, programme food aid may be useful, but it can also have negative repercussions such as depressing local markets. Furthermore, it is an unpredictable resource that can be turned off or on depending on the donor country's objectives and needs. Following negative reviews of food aid during the 1990s, the use of programme aid has declined (OECD 2006).

Project food aid can be transferred through the government of the recipient country or through other channels. In many cases, the food provided is sold in the recipient country and the money is used to fund government or non-govermental organisation (NGO) programmes (a practice called monetisation). Thus, project food aid can be divided into two subcategories: aid used to finance local food acquisition for direct distribution in support of a project, like food for work or food for education schemes; and in-kind aid, which is monetised by an organisation to generate funds for its development activities. Given the widely different types of projects, targeting and delivery mechanisms, it is not surprising that opinions differ widely on the efficiency and effectiveness of project food aid.

Figure 2D shows that, over the past few years, there has been a significant shift in the proportion of aid given to emergencies (humanitarian) and taken away from programme and project food aid, although this is the result of reductions in the latter two categories rather than any increase or shift in total donations to the former.

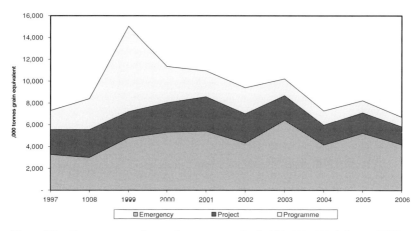

Figure 2D   Emergency, project and programme food aid (1997–2006) *Source:* WFP database (http://one.wfp.org/interfais).

Tied aid: in-kind, direct transfers and triangular transactions

The way in which food aid is delivered can be divided into three categories: in-kind or direct transfers, triangular transactions and local purchases. In-kind food aid is delivered by the donating country as food, which is then distributed in-country. Triangular transactions involve the donor country contributing funds that are used to buy the food aid in another country for delivery in the recipient country. Local purchases also involve the donor making cash donations that are used to buy the food in the country for delivery to the receiving people in the same country.

To some extent, these divisions based on mode of delivery are artificial because, at some point in the donor-to-recipient chain, food aid must be converted from cash to food for the simple reason that you cannot eat cash. This obvious fact is not always clear, partly because assessments focus on the donor's means of donation – which can be in kind or as cash – and partly because aid given in other forms, such as farming tools or cooking utensils, may be called 'food aid' although the final product is not food. This is not to suggest that such forms of aid are in any way inferior to food or cannot be vital to food production or consumption, just to note that you cannot eat a spade. Although a spade may be essential for planting seeds, it is not 'food' and therefore should not be called food aid.

Thus, cash must be converted to food, and the conversion can take place: (i) in the donating country by buying stocks from domestic producers; (ii) in a third country, such as under a triangular transaction; or (iii) in

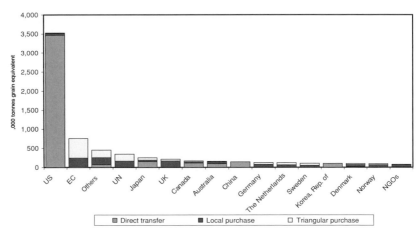

Figure 2E   Food aid by mode of delivery and donor (2006). *Source:* WFP database (http://one.wfp.org/interfais).

the country where the food aid is needed if the shortage is localised within the country. Figure 2E shows the amount of aid given by different donor countries in each of the three categories: direct transfer (in-kind aid), local purchases and triangular transactions. In some cases, the purchase is actually made some time before delivery and is stockpiled in the donating country or through regional stockpiles, such as the ASEAN Food Security Reserve. In some cases, the in-kind aid is converted back to cash through monetisation, as the funds are needed for non-food purposes.

Commercial displacement and additionality

Commercial displacement occurs when some or all of the food aid does not result in new consumption, but rather reduces market-based sales. Ideally, food aid should result in consumption that would not have taken place if the aid had not been delivered – that is, food aid should not compete with domestic or regional production. However, the reality is that food aid always has some commercial effect. Even in emergencies where all food aid results in additional consumption in the recipient region, it will distort the market in the region where it was acquired. Once again, this is not to suggest that the commercial effect should not be minimised, or that some forms of aid could not be more efficiently acquired, just that there is an inevitable commercial effect.

It is unlikely that food aid has much global impact on the world market. Total aid levels represent only a small proportion of production and an

Table 2G *World wheat exports, production and food aid*

	Wheat exports, (,000 tonnes)	Production, (,000 tonnes)	Food aid (,000 tonnes)	Food aid as % of exports	Food aid as % of production
1996	106,086	584,559	3,763	3.55	0.64
1997	104,650	612,279	3,776	3.61	0.62
1998	98,030	593,134	3,984	4.06	0.67
1999	110,961	587,544	9,326	8.41	1.59
2000	100,647	585,494	5,824	5.79	0.99
2001	107,102	587,657	5,548	5.18	0.94
2002	106,735	572,113	4,332	4.06	0.76
2003	105,673	560,056	5,034	4.76	0.90
2004	109,689	628,289	3,144	2.87	0.50
2005	110,288	624,554	3,518	3.19	0.56
2006	106,833	595,977	2,925	2.74	0.49

Source: Food aid – WFP database (http://one.wfp.org/interfais); production and exports – OECD 2007b.

Table 2H *US: wheat exports, production and programmed food aid*

Year	Exports (,000 tonnes)	Production (,000 tonnes)	Food aid (,000 tonnes)	Food aid as % of exports	Food aid as % of production
2001	26,190	53,000	3,517	13.43	6.64
2002	23,139	43,706	2,277	9.84	5.21
2003	31,524	63,813	2,303	7.31	3.61
2004	29,012	58,740	1,766	6.09	3.01
2005	27,472	57,287	2,243	8.16	3.92
2006	23,814	49,315	1,263	5.30	2.56

Source: Food aid – USDA (for fiscal year); production and trade – OECD 2007b.

even smaller proportion of trade in agricultural products. Table 2G shows the level of wheat food aid compared to global production and exports.

However, in terms of individual country donors, the ratio of food aid donations and exports can be much greater. Programmed US food aid for wheat and wheat flour in 2001 was 3.51 million tonnes (USDA 2001) compared to total exports of 26.19 million tonnes (OECD 2007b), which is the equivalent to 13.4 per cent of exports. Table 2H shows the quantity of wheat and wheat flour programmed for food aid for the years 2001 to 2006 and compares them with the total production in the USA.

Although food aid may represent only a small portion of production of the biggest donor of in-kind aid, it can cause problems in the receiving country if it depresses local prices, which would then discourage local production – something that was recognised as long ago as 1960 (Schultz 1960). Although this is probably not the case in emergency situations where a crisis creates the need for food in a region, it would be more likely to occur for project and programme aid, which may be sold on local markets by monetisation by the government or by NGOs (OECD 2006).

Tied food aid

Food aid is always tied in the sense that it is tied to the donation being for a particular purpose, for example cash donations are tied to the purchase of food or to services, products or infrastructure related to food aid. Similarly, in-kind food aid is tied in the sense that its procurement is tied to production in the donor country.

The Development Assistance Committee (DAC) defines tied aid as aid that 'includes loans, grants or associated financing packages with a grant element greater than 25 per cent and defined as aid which is in effect (in law or in fact) tied to the procurement of goods and/or services from the donor country and/or a restricted number of countries' (DAC 1987) and untied aid as grants and loans that 'are freely and fully available to finance procurement from substantially all aid recipient countries and from OECD countries' (DAC 2001).

This issue is, however, confused by the WTO Agreement on Agriculture, which prohibits aid tied to commercial exports of agricultural products to recipient countries. Although it is likely that this prohibition will be extended to cover food aid tied directly or indirectly to commercial exports of agricultural products or of other goods and services (WTO 2007), it is still significantly different to the definition used by DAC.

According to DAC, and based on its definition, 90 per cent of food aid is tied in some way:

- to procurement, processing, packing or to shipment by the supplying country
- through restrictions on the form of contracting or tendering process (such as commodity type or size of shipment)

- through administrative decisions such as a donor procuring aid without a competitive tender (e.g. in emergencies)
- by requirements to acquire food locally or regionally.

Therefore, it is not surprising that almost all food aid is subject to some kind of restriction and is thus defined as 'tied'. DAC notes that the inefficient cost of tying food aid in terms of direct transfers is at least 30%, and that the actual costs of tied food aid transfers were, on average, about 50% more than acquisition through local food purchases, and 33% more costly than through triangular transactions. However, the DAC study goes on to note that 'there are substantial cost inefficiencies associated with tying food aid although some tied aid was quite efficient. The levels of inefficiency are context specific, depending on the commodity, destination and whether the commodity was to be sold, to be monetised or to be directly distributed' (OECD 2006).

Role of international organisations and the WTO

There are several international organisations that have some role or responsibility for managing, controlling and delivering food aid:

- the World Food Programme (WFP) of the UN
- the Consultative Subcommittee on Surplus Disposal (CSSD) of the Food and Agriculture Organization (FAO) of the UN
- the Food Aid Convention (FAC) of the International Grains Council (IGC)
- the Office for the Coordination of Humanitarian Affairs (OCHA) of the UN, which coordinates humanitarian relief operations and works with all major institutions involved, including the Red Cross and NGOs
- the Development Assistance Committee (DAC) of the Organisation for Economic Cooperation and Development (OECD)
- the Agreement on Agriculture of the WTO, which includes rules concerning food aid and requires donor governments to provide annual notifications of food aid deliveries.

In addition, there are many NGOs that work independently and in cooperation with the international organisations, and others in supporting, providing and delivering food aid. The USA is the largest donor of international food aid, donating more than half of all food aid, followed by the European Commission, Japan, the UK, Canada and Australia. The UN is also an important donor of food aid.

Table 21   *Food aid donations to the WFP from 2002 to 2006 in US$*

	2002	2003	2004	2005	2006
US	939,348,716	1,458,913,241	1,065,403,760	1,175,725,989	1,123,646,475
EC	177,326,417	200,874,450	200,500,745	263,940,274	265,762,058
UN	861,995	1,028,715	629,507	7,181,919	159,748,173
Canada	52,661,860	114,705,056	88,872,126	152,464,083	149,413,829
UK	95,717,938	135,734,363	115,883,885	114,263,605	100,371,690
The Netherlands	58,794,913	50,421,733	77,738,387	115,347,615	79,985,360
Japan	92,895,679	130,135,637	135,729,626	160,528,867	71,169,633
Australia	50,387,958	39,204,682	41,496,882	61,883,805	60,554,058
Germany	60,920,190	46,503,475	65,330,766	70,866,797	59,621,622
Other	292,725,002	377,593,275	449,207,944	603,510,929	634,240,919
Total	**1,821,640,668**	**2,555,114,627**	**2,240,793,628**	**2,725,713,883**	**2,704,513,817**

Source: WFP database (http://one.wfp.org/interfais).

The World Food Programme (WFP)

The UN's WFP started operations in 1963 and is the main UN agency for delivering food aid. Today, it is the world's largest humanitarian agency, through which it, along with governments, other UN agencies and other organisations, provided 4 million tonnes of food aid to 87.8 million people in 78 countries.[3] Donations are almost entirely from governments in both cash and in-kind form.

The WFP relies entirely on voluntary contributions to finance its humanitarian and development projects. Donations can be made either as cash, in-kind food aid or as the basic items necessary to grow, store and cook food. In 2006, a total of about 4 million tonnes of food were delivered, of which about 2 million tonnes were from in-kind contributions and 2 million tonnes were purchased with cash donations (WFP 2007). Details of donations, in terms of US dollars, by different countries are set out in Table 21.

The WFP does not have a formal oversight role in terms of food aid deliveries, but it does conduct, oversee and participate in studies on the effectiveness and efficiency of different kinds of food aid, and the role of food in achieving different objectives. In addition, through the International Food Aid Information System (INTERFAIS), it maintains a database on food aid. It also works with the FAO and others on needs assessments, and with IFPRI to assess food aid programmes.

[3] www.wfp.org/aboutwfp/introduction/index.asp?section=1_section=1 [last accessed 12 February 2009].

Consultative Subcommittee on Surplus Disposal (CSSD)

The CSSD is part of the FAO, although its headquarters are in Washington and not in Rome, which is the headquarters of the FAO. It was created in 1954 at a time when there were increasing surpluses of food in some countries and chronic shortages in others. At the same time that the CSSD was created, thirty-seven FAO member countries adopted the Principles of Surplus Disposal and Consultative Obligations (hereafter 'the Principles'). In 1970, the FAO adopted the mechanism of Usual Marketing Requirements (UMR) as a way to try to ensure that the recipient countries maintained normal levels of commercial imports in addition to the aid received – that is, the food aid received should result in additional consumption and not act as a substitute for normal imports.

The Principles have been likened to a code of conduct for governments in the provision of food aid (FAO 2006a). Although article 10.4 of the Agreement on Agriculture of the WTO requires donors to respect the UMR, the actual wording used in the Principles indicates that donors are not obliged to follow them. For example, the general principles in paragraphs 1 to 3 of the Principles state as follows:

(1) The solution to problems of agricultural disposal *should* be sought, wherever possible, through efforts to increase consumption rather than through measures to restrict supplies.

(2) Member Governments which have excess stocks of agricultural products *should* dispose of such products in an orderly manner so as to avoid any undue pressure resulting in sharp falls of prices on world markets, particularly when prices of agricultural products are generally low.

(3) Where surpluses are disposed of under special terms, there *should* be an undertaking from both importing and exporting countries that such arrangements will be made without harmful interference with the normal patterns of production and international trade.

(FAO 2000)

It has also been noted that the CSSD has no enforcement powers and that notifications of aid transactions are voluntary. Indeed, notifications do not cover all aid, and it has been claimed that the CSSD is 'routinely ignored by its donor members', that the CSSD does not have the legal status of a treaty (Barrett and Maxwell 2005) (although it is recognised by the Agreement on Agriculture, which does have treaty status). It has also been stated that its link to the Agreement on Agriculture is weak because there is no mechanism for notifications by the CSSD to the WTO's Committee on Agriculture (Konandreas 2005). However, WTO members are required to make notifications on the food aid they provide

(WTO 1995) – although this legal obligation is not taken too seriously by many WTO members.[4]

Food Aid Convention (FAC)

The first FAC was negotiated in the context of the Kennedy Round of trade talks in the General Agreement on Tariffs and Trade (GATT). In contrast to the period of oversupply in the 1950s that led to the establishment of the Principles of Surplus Disposal, the FAC was negotiated when supplies were low and donors sought to share the burden with other countries.[5] The result was the adoption of the Wheat Trade Convention and the first FAC.

The FAC has been renegotiated a number of times. The current Convention was established in 1999 to run until 30 June 2002 but has been extended a number of times. A full renegotiation of the FAC is expected to start after the current round of trade negotiations in the WTO has been concluded. In the meantime, FAC members have agreed to extend the existing Convention with effect from 1 July 2007. Under the current FAC, members have undertaken to provide 4.795 million tonnes of aid (wheat equivalents) plus €130 million for the European Communities. Although FAC members' commitments are listed in terms of tonnes of wheat equivalent, the actual aid can be given as other cereals, edible oil, skimmed milk powder or as cash. Commitments by different countries under the FAC are listed in Table 2J.

In addition to commitments on minimum levels of food aid, the 1999 FAC also requires its members to improve the monitoring evaluation of the impact and effectiveness of food aid operations. This requires an evaluation of the needs by the recipient countries. In addition, all food aid to least-developed countries that are covered by these minimum commitments should be in the form of grants, and grant-form aid should represent at least 80 per cent of total food aid and should not be tied to commercial exports of goods or services to the recipient country.

The FAC has been criticised for a number of reasons. Firstly, although the commitments to provide a minimum quantity of food aid should ensure a minimum quantity of aid, these minimum quantities are, in fact, well below actual deliveries through the FAC, and further below food aid needs (see Figure 2F).

---

[4] See, for example, the summary of the Chairman's statement to the 48th meeting of the regular Committee on Agriculture in the WTO (G/AG/R/48, 6 July 2007), paragraph 46.
[5] www.igc.org.uk/en/aboutus/default.aspx#fac [last accessed 11 June 2009].

Table 2J   *Members' minimum annual contributions (tonnes wheat equivalent)*

	1986 Convention	1995 Convention	1999 Convention
Argentina	35,000	35,000	35,000
Australia	300,000	300,000[1]	250,000[2]
Austria[3]	20,000	–	–
Canada	600,000	400,000	420,000
European Communities	1,670,000	1,755,000	1,320,000 +€130 million
Finland[3]	25,000	–	–
Japan	300,000	300,000	300,000
Norway	30,000	20,000	30,000
Sweden[3]	40,000	–	–
Switzerland	27,000	–	40,000
US	4,470,000	2,500,000	2,500,000
Total	**7,517,000**	**5,350,000**	**4,895,000 + €130 million**

Source: WTO 2006.

[1] Austria, Finland and Sweden acceded to the EC in 1994.

[2] Australia's commitment was reduced to 250,000 tonnes with effect from 1 July 1998.

[3] Australia's commitment was reduced to 150,000 tonnes with effect from 1 July 2003.

World Trade Organization (WTO)

The WTO is not an aid agency. Its role in food aid is focused on: (i) the extent to which a member might use food aid to circumvent export subsidy commitments;[6] and (ii) how least-developed and net food-importing developing countries might be affected by an increase in food prices, which might result from reduced production and export subsidies.[7]

Under the current Agreement on Agriculture, article 10.4 obliges food aid donors to ensure that food aid not tied to commercial exports of agricultural products and to comply with the FAO Principles of Surplus Disposal and the system of UMR. In addition, the Results of the Uruguay

[6] See article 10 of the Agreement on Agriculture.

[7] See article 16 of the Agreement on Agriculture and the Marrakesh Decision on Measures Concerning the Possible Negative Effects of the Reform Programme on Least-Developed and Net Food-Importing Developing Countries.

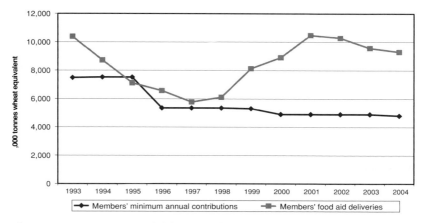

Figure 2F   Commitments and deliveries of food aid through the food aid convention by FAC members. *Note:* The minimum annual contributions do not include the commitment by the EC, under the 1999 FAC, to provide 130 million in addition to its quantity commitment. *Source:* WTO 2006.

Round include the Marrakesh Decision on Measures Concerning the Possible Negative Effects of the Reform Programme on Least-Developed and Net Food-Importing Developing Countries. This Decision was taken because of a fear that reductions in production and export subsidies could result in higher prices for agricultural products. Under it, WTO members agreed:

- to review the level of food aid established under the FAC
- to adopt guidelines to ensure that more aid was provided to least-developed and net food-importing developing countries in fully grant form and/or on appropriate concessional terms
- to give full consideration to requests for improving agricultural productivity
- that any agreement on export credits would make appropriate provision for special treatment for least-developed and net food-importing developing countries.

The WTO rules on food aid have never been tested in dispute settlement. However, members have used the Committee on Agriculture in the WTO to put questions to other WTO members on food aid. Out of the first forty-eight meetings of the Committee on Agriculture, issues related to food aid were raised thirty-nine times. Most of these were questions from one member to another asking for details of food aid deliveries or programmes.

It has been stated that the Marrakesh Decision has not been implemented (Mamaty 2002, Oxfam 2002, Murphy 2007). These claims ignore the fact that this is a legal issue, which can only be answered by the dispute settlement system of the WTO, and that it could also be argued that, technically, all obligations under the Decision have been met. After all, levels of food aid have been reviewed, the FAC has reached agreement on commitments and most food aid is given in fully grant form. Presumably, what these commentators mean is that the provisions are, in their opinion, inadequate to meet the needs of least-developed and net food-importing developing countries.

From the negotiations on the Doha Round, it is clear that WTO member governments will adopt new rules on food aid and export credits. The Hong Kong Ministerial Declaration of December 2005 states:

> On food aid, we reconfirm our commitment to maintain an adequate level and to take into account the interests of food aid recipient countries. To this end, a 'safe box' for bona fide food aid will be provided to ensure that there is no unintended impediment to dealing with emergency situations. Beyond that, we will ensure elimination of commercial displacement. To this end, we will agree effective disciplines on in-kind food aid, monetization and re-exports so that there can be no loop-hole for continuing export subsidization.[8]

More recently, the Chairman of the negotiations put forward a paper that outlined possible modalities for the negotiations, and included a detailed section on possible rules for food aid.[9] However, the objective of these rules is to prevent circumvention of export subsidy commitments and, while doing so, to ensure that rules on food aid do not cause any unintended impediment to dealing with emergencies. Therefore, the focus of the Chairman's suggestions was to establish some basic rules that would cover all food aid, what conditions would have to be met for an 'emergency' situation when only the basic rules would apply, and what additional rules should apply in other situations.

---

[8] The full text of the Ministerial Declaration can be found www.wto.org/english/thewto_e/minist_e/min05_e/final_text_e.htm [last accessed 12 February 2009].

[9] Annex F of TN/AG/W/4, the full text of which can be found at www.wto.org/english/tratop_e/agric_e/agchairtxt_1aug07_e.doc [last accessed 12 February 2009], and a new version distributed on 6 November 2007, available at: www.wto.org/english/tratop_e/agric_e/workdoc_excomp_e.doc [last accessed 12 February 2009].

Organisation for Economic Cooperation and Development (OECD)
and the Development Assistance Committee (DAC)

The DAC was established in 1960 as a forum for consultation among aid donors. It covers all kinds of official development assistance (ODA). While food aid is an important (though declining) element of ODA, it also includes other kinds of aid, such as debt forgiveness and technical cooperation.

The DAC publishes guidelines on development assistance and monitors assistance and the effectiveness of aid given by donors through peer reviews and publications of aid statistics. Although it cannot enforce compliance with commitments, it does carry out extensive studies on development aid, including food aid, and it does oversee its members' performance compared to their commitments, such as under the Paris Declaration on Aid Effectiveness. This Declaration was also the product of work undertaken by the DAC, and is an international agreement to improve aid effectiveness and accountability (OECD 2005).

The DAC is the fifth body to which food aid flows are reported (the others being the FAC, the CSSD, INTERFAIS of the WFP and the WTO Committee on Agriculture). In addition to ODA data, DAC statistics also cover private aid flows through NGOs.

Efficiency of food aid

Given the general concern that food aid donations fall far short of needs, efficiency of delivery is essential to achieving the most from limited supplies. However, the extent to which efficiency can be achieved depends greatly on the mode of delivery, the degree of targeting and how food aid fits into the overall recovery plan.

The DAC of the OECD assessed the efficiency of aid transfers by different donors to various recipients and by different forms of aid – direct transfer, local purchases and triangular transactions.[10] Efficiency was assessed by comparing the actual cost of providing aid with the cost of provision through an alternative commercial transaction. The study was based on a survey of 1,119 food aid transactions to fifteen recipient countries[11] by sixteen donors, including all major donors except Korea

---

[10] This section draws on OECD 2006.
[11] The recipient countries were: Bangladesh, Cape Verde, Eritrea, Ethiopia, Georgia, Haiti, India, Jordan, Kenya, Korea (Democratic Republic of), Malawi, Mauritania, Mozambique, Peru and Zambia.

and China.[12] The results show big differences between donors, recipients and modes of delivery. Overall, the best levels of efficiency were achieved when food aid was part of a more comprehensive scheme aimed at poverty reduction or disaster relief, and when least restrictions were applied to the donation. One caveat that may apply to the results is that relatively few donors dominate different forms of aid. In terms of total aid provided in 2006:

- the USA provided 83% of total aid through direct transfers
- the EC and the UN provided 56% of total aid through triangular transactions
- the EC, UN and UK provided 53% of aid through local purchases.

Thus, the general results for each mode of delivery will depend on the schemes and programmes operated by these donors. Another factor that may affect efficiency is that provisions attached to aid by some donors are meant to ensure that the aid is used as intended. While these provisions may reduce efficiency and flexibility to address different situations, they may be necessary to reduce cases of misuse of aid, which could seriously undermine future efforts if they are not controlled.

As expected, in-kind or direct transfers of aid were the least efficient of the three modes of supply, at 134% of the cost of the alternative commercial transactions. Triangular transactions were less efficient than the alternative commercial transactions – although only very slightly at 1% more expensive – and much less efficient than local purchases, which were 12% less expensive than alternative commercial transactions. However, the data that go towards these general statistics show considerable variability between donors, modes of supply and recipients. Thus, local purchases under Denmark's food aid projects were found to be less efficient than direct transfers from Japan, Germany and the Netherlands. Similarly, Canada, Germany, Italy and Switzerlands' triangular transactions were more efficient than their local purchases, although, in general, the opposite was the case. However, for any given donor in the survey, direct transfers were the least efficient form of food aid.

Given the poor efficiency of direct transfers, it is not surprising that those donors that provided most of their food aid by this method were the least efficient, with Australia, Canada and the USA all being worse than average.

---

[12] The donors covered by the survey were: Australia, Belgium, Canada, Denmark, the European Commission, Finland, France, Germany, Italy, Japan, the Netherlands, Norway, Sweden, Switzerland, the UK and the USA.

Although local purchases are usually the most efficient, there are big differences between efficiency levels in different recipient countries, which ranged from 64% in Zambia (that is, it was 36% cheaper than an alternative commercial transaction) to as high as 206% in Haiti. This is not really that surprising, as local costs will vary a lot depending on location. It would be expected that imports into a land-locked country with poor infrastructure would be more expensive than local sourcing. However, this is not always the case because it will also depend on local production conditions and the proportion of the country in need of food aid. Thus, local purchases in Zambia and Malawi (64% and 85% respectively) were quite efficient, while local purchases in Mauritania were inefficient (136%).

Conclusions and policy considerations

With the large number of entities overseeing food aid and analysing and reporting on levels and delivery, it would seem that food aid is over-regulated. However, it might be more a case of over-assessment but inadequate enforcement. No single organisation has the means or the ability to enforce aid commitments or rules on delivery. However, the structure already exists for both. The FAC provides for commitments on the minimum level of aid provided by its members, and the CSSD already provides for rules on delivery of food aid. But the terms of these rules mean that they represent guidelines rather than enforceable rules. In addition, the WFP of the UN and the DAC of the OECD gather, compile and present a lot of data and analysis of food aid.

That does not mean that these organisations have been unsuccessful in changing the delivery of food aid. Needs assessments are now seen as essential for the targeted delivery of food aid, and form a critical element of the draft rules on food aid under negotiation in the WTO. In the face of criticisms relating to the efficiency and effectiveness of in-kind aid compared to cash, and tied aid compared to untied aid, there has been an increase in cash aid and a greater emphasis on local and regional purchases. However, this change has been gradual, and the rate of change varies considerably from one country to another.

These changes have also been reflected in the 1999 FAC and the 2005 Paris Declaration on Aid Effectiveness. The current negotiations on agriculture in the WTO also show that the research and monitoring by international organisations, national organisations and NGOs are having an effect.

It does seem to be a good idea to have strong and straightforward rules relating to food aid that set out what can and cannot be done, but this may not always be practical. Food aid needs differ widely from one situation to another, so that clear simple rules will not be applicable in all cases at all times. Flexibility is needed by donors, recipients, international organisations and aid workers to be able to address these different situations. That does not mean that there shouldn't be stronger oversight of food aid or stronger rules relating to commitments of food aid. Given that higher prices for food are likely to persist for some time, and that food aid commitments in the FAC cover neither all donors nor current needs, and given that OCHA appeals are rarely met, there is scope for some improvement in coverage of the FAC (products and donor countries), commitments under the FAC and enforcement of those commitments.

Commitment levels are one thing, but means of delivery are also important. Tying food aid makes it less efficient, more likely to cause commercial displacement and slower in being delivered than cash-based aid. However, it may also be that in some cases, the tying of food aid is essential to ensuring it is not wasted or misused. Complete flexibility for an agency to use funds how it sees fit in every circumstance may work for many agencies, but, human nature being what it is, it also means someone somewhere will misuse funds. In addition, for food aid to address emergency situations, financial efficiency may not be that important. In some cases, when local infrastructure is destroyed or very poor and the need is immediate, air delivery may be the only practical means of getting aid to the place of need. It may be extremely inefficient financially, but there may be no choice. It has also been claimed that targeting, including timeliness, is more important than tying status in terms of development effectiveness and market disruption effects (Barrett and Maxwell 2005), although not all would agree (Clay 2006). However, it would seem to be the case that even if food aid is donated in-kind it does not mean it is inappropriate.

In addition, it is likely that if all food aid had to be untied from procurement, it would result in a decline in aid. Not everyone is as cynical as the former chairman of the Committee on Agriculture of the US House of Representatives, who instructed a representative of the Department of State: 'we are primarily interested in getting rid of these surpluses and we don't care how you do it and under what authority. We have told you we want the commodities sold for dollars, first and then for foreign currencies or then donate them' (Cooly 1959), but the reality is that some people need a reward for doing good deeds.

While new WTO rules may go some way towards reducing or eliminating commercial displacement and improving the targeting of food aid, they do not, and are not intended to, address non-trade-related issues like adequate levels of aid and enforcement of related commitments. As these are not trade issues, this should not be surprising. A number of different proposals were made by various people on improving the FAC (Barrett and Maxwell 2007, Hoddinott and Cohen 2007, Clay 2006). Others have suggested it should be the CSSD of the FAO (Konnandreas 2005). Some of these have suggested that the international agency responsible for food aid should have access to the WTO's system of dispute settlement, but this is probably unrealistic. The WTO is an intergovernmental organisation, and that rules out other agencies having access to its dispute settlement system as complaining parties.

One solution might be to create a technical agency for food aid that is not intergovernmental. After all, some donor and recipient governments have not been very responsible and are unlikely to improve their behaviour, so it might be better to keep politics out of the agency entirely. A technical arbitration agency could be set up, which would take decisions that would be binding unless there was a consensus against it by the governments that make up the parent organisation, be it the FAC, the UN or the FAO. There is certainly no shortage of expertise in the world; from the international organisations involved in food aid, the aid agencies of national governments and the NGOs actually involved in food aid delivery, it should be possible to select a panel of experts that could decide on minimum commitment levels, what constitutes a needs assessment, if in-kind food aid is the right way to go and so on. But, like any entity responsible for setting commitments, all that is meaningless unless some means of enforcement can be agreed upon.

Alternatively, the current systems, with all their imperfections, may be more realistic. Food aid has changed. Evaluation and criticism from many sources has helped it to evolve for the better. The pace of this evolution is slow, but it may not happen any faster under a centralised entity created to try to enforce standards and rules. With rising food prices, the current critical weakness is ensuring adequate levels of aid, and the record of national governments in meeting ambitious objectives for aid is not great. In 2006, only five of the twenty-two DAC members met the goal of providing ODA of 0.7 per cent of gross national income (OECD 2007a), in spite of the many symbolic commitments of UN members to meet the Millennium Development Goals by 2015. The enforcement of stronger commitments like these will not be achieved through the WTO dispute settlement system. It will only be achieved through public awareness, political will and the monitoring and publicity given by international and national organisations, individuals and NGOs.

References

Barrett, Christopher B. and Maxwell, Daniel G. (2005), 'Towards a Global Food Aid Compact', *Food Policy* 31 (2006) 105–18, available at: www.sciencedirect.com [last accessed 10 June 2009].

Clay, Edward (2006), 'Food Aid and the Doha Development Round: Building on the Positive', Overseas Development Institute Background Paper, ODI: London, available at: www.odi.org.uk/events/food_aid_sept05/background_note.html [last accessed 10 June 2009].

Cooley, H. D. Hon. (1959), US House of Representatives, Hearings before the Committee on Agricultural, 'Extension of Public Law 480', Series X, 15 July 1959, p. 207, quoted by T. W. Shultz (1960), 'Value of US Farm Surpluses to Underdeveloped Countries', *Journal of Farm Economics* 42(5): 1025 (Proceedings of the Annual Meeting of the American Farm Economic Association).

DAC (1987), *Revised Guiding Principles for Associated Financing and Tied and Partially Untied ODA*, OECD: Paris.

(2001), 'DAC Recommendation on Untying Official Development Assistance to the Least Developed Countries', Annex 1, 25 April 2001, DCD/DAC(2001) 12/FINAL, amended 15 March 2006, DCD/DAC(2006)25 and DCD/DAC/M(2006)3.

FAO (2000), *Reporting Procedures and Consultative Obligations under the FAO Principles of Surplus Disposal*, Annex G ('Principles of Surplus Disposal') and Annex H ('Procedures for the Establishment of Usual Marketing Requirements'), available at: www.fao.org/ world/lowa/docs/CSSDHandbook1.pdf and www.fao.org/world/lowa/docs/CSSDHandbook2.pdf [last accessed 12 February 2009].

(2006a), *The State of Food and Agriculture: Food Aid for food Security?* FAO: Rome.

(2006b), *The State of Food Insecurity in the World 2006*, FAO: Rome.

Hoddinott, John and Cohen, Marc J. (2007), 'Renegotiating the Food Aid Convention: Background, Context, and Issues', IFPRI Discussion Paper 00690, IFPRI: Washington, WA.

Konandreas, Panos (2005), 'Multilateral Mechanisms Governing Food Aid and the Need for an Enhanced Role of the CSSD in the Context of the New WTO Disciplines on Agriculture', FAO: Geneva.

Mamaty, Isabelle (2002), 'Integrating Agriculture Trade and Food Security Policy', Joint ICTSD/FES Round Table, 2 December 2002, available at: www.ictsd.net/downloads/2008/08/mamatypaper_final.pdf [last accessed 12 February 2009].

Murphy, Sophia (2007), 'The WTO Agricultural Negotiations and the Least Developed Countries: Limitations and Options', in N. Koning, P. Pinstrup-Adnersen and R. J. Bogers (eds.), *Agricultural Trade Liberalization and the Least Developed Countries*, Springer Science and Business Media: Wageningen, available at: http//library.wur.nl/frontis/trade_liberalization/13_murphy.pdf [last accessed 12 February 2009].

Oxfam (2002), 'Boxing Match in Agricultural Trade', Briefing Paper, available at: www.oxfam.org.nz/resources/AgriculturalTrade.doc [last accessed 12 February 2009].

OCHA (2007), 'Humanitarian Appeal 2007, Mid-year review', United Nations, available at: www.humanitarianappeal.net [last accessed 12 February 2009].

OECD (2005), 'Paris Declaration on Aid Effectiveness', available at: www.oecd.org/dataoecd/11/41/34428351.pdf [last accessed 12 February 2009].

(2006), *The Development Effectiveness of Food Aid – Does Tying Matter?*, OECD: Paris.

(2007a), 'Development Aid from OECD Countries Fell 5.1% in 2006', 3 April 2007, available at: www.oecd.org/document/49/0,3343,en_2649_201185_38341265_1_1_1_1,00.html [last accessed 12 February 2009].

(2007b), *OECD.Stat, Agriculture and Fisheries, Agricultural Outlook, Commodities Balance 1970–2016*, OECD: Paris, available at: www.oecd.org/statsportal/0,3352,en_2825_293564_1_1_1_1_1,00.html [last accessed 10 June 2009].

Red Meat Industry Forum (2007), 'Introduction to Pig Production in the UK', 25 May 2007 (information available at www.redmeatindustryforum.org.uk/supplychain/PigProduction.htm [last accessed 10 June 2009]).

Schultz, Theodore W. (1960), 'Value of US Farm Surpluses to Underdeveloped Countries', *Journal of Farm Economics* 42(2): 1019–30, available at: http://chla.library.cornell.edu/c/chla/browse/title/5033566.html#1960 [last accessed 12 February 2009].

USDA (2001), 'US Food Aid Tables, Table II – Programmed US Food Aid for FY 2001', March 2002, USDA, Foreign Agriculture Service: Washington, WA, available at: www.fas.usda.gov/excredits/FoodAid/Reports/fy01tableii.pdf [last accessed 10 June 2009].

von Braun, Joachim (2007), *The World Food Situation: New Driving Forces and Required Action*, IFPRI: Washington, WA.

WFP (2005), Executive Board, First Regular Session, Decisions and Recommendations of the First Regular Session of the Executive Board, Rome, 4 February 2005 (WFP/EB.1/2005/13).

(2007), *WFP Facts and Figures*, available at: http://documents.wfp.org/stellent/groups/public/documents/newsroom/wfp095401.pdf [last accessed-12 February 2009].

WTO (1995), 'Notifications Requirements and Formats, Adopted by the Committee on Agriculture on 8 June 1995' 30 June 1995, G/AG/2.

(2006), 'Implementation of the Decision on Measures Concerning the Possible Negative Effects of the Reform Programme on Least-Developed and Net Food-Importing Developing Countries, Note by the Secretariat' 10 January 2006, G/AG/W/42/Rev.8.

(2007), 'Revised First Draft of Modalities', Annex F, 1 August 2007, TN/AG/W/4.

2.2

Indigenous Nepalese and trade liberalisation

PURUSHOTTAM OJHA*

This chapter looks at a case study of an indigenous community in the Byas municipality in order to explore the linkages between trade and poverty reduction strategies in western Nepal. It identifies local and national strategies for linking small farmers and entrepreneurs to existing and future trading opportunities.

An overview of trade and economy

Nepal is one of the least developed countries in the world, with a per capita gross domestic product (GDP) of US$350 (MOF 2007). Being a landlocked, agrarian economy,[1] Nepal's economic development and trade-sector promotion are largely dependent upon agricultural and forest-based products. Nepal's high mountains and hills possess potential for growing various kinds of fruit, vegetables, medicinal herbs, spices and aromatic plants. Tourism, hydropower, traditional cottage and small industries and remittances can also play an important role in poverty reduction in Nepal.

Nepal has been pursuing liberal economic policies since the mid 1980s, with increased efforts since the establishment of a democratic system of government in 1990. At this time, the licensing system was fully abolished and import and export regimes were liberalised. The new trade policy, foreign investment and industrial policies were formulated in 1992, creating growth opportunities for the private sector and encouraging investment. The Nepal–India trade treaty signed in 1996 provided unilateral duty-free access for Nepalese-manufactured articles in the Indian market. Accession to the WTO in April 2004 and membership of the South Asian Free

---

* Purushottam Ojha is Secretary of the Ministry of Industry, Commerce and Supplies for the Government of Nepal.
[1] Agriculture is the main source of livelihood for over 80% of the population and accounted for 36% of GDP in the fiscal year 2005–06 (MOF 2007, p. 81).

252

Trade Area (SAFTA) and the Bay of Bengal Initiative for Multi-Sectoral Technical and Economic Cooperation (BIMST-EC) in the same year created a staunch political base in support of free trade. In the process of WTO accession, Nepal undertook new initiatives to improve legal regimes related to import and export, customs valuation, transportation and trade facilitation and intellectual properties. Service sectors were also being liberalised in line with the WTO General Agreement on Trade in Services (GATS) commitments made during WTO accession.

The competitiveness of Nepalese trade has been constrained by several factors, including weak physical infrastructures, inadequate mechanisms and incentives for firms to acquire new technology, an unfavourable business climate created through rigid labour legislation and inadequate bankruptcy and foreclosure provisions (MOICS 2004). Price competitiveness has been further constrained due to inadequate infrastructure and the high transit transportation cost. An inadequate regulatory framework combined with unpredictable implementation policies have further added to the cost of doing business in Nepal.

The lack of an adequate transportation infrastructure within the country has inhibited market integration of interior parts of the country. Road transportation is the primary mode of transportation, with a total road length of 17,280 kilometres (MOPPW 2006). Forty-nine airports provide short take-off and landing services, catering to smaller aircrafts and the transportation of passengers rather than traded goods. Rail services are limited to passenger traffic movement in 50-kilometre stretches, and cargo train services to a multi-modal terminal built inside Nepal, 400 metres away from the international border and connected to the Indian Railway system.

Nepalese trade reform initiatives have not adequately addressed the issue of trade facilitation. Simplification and standardisation of trade-related documents and procedures and improvement in transit transportation operations are crucial to trade facilitation. Poor physical infrastructure hinders the production and sale of farm products. For example, lack of cold storage facilities in airports and dry ports is constraining the export of agricultural and forest products.

The basic strategy for Nepal's global economic integration is the expansion of trade opportunities through increased market access and competitiveness in order to trigger economic development (NPC 1998 and 2003). Trade liberalisation can affect poverty indirectly through its effect on economic growth, and directly through its effect on factor markets (income and employment), product markets (prices and availability of commodities) and government revenue and expenditure.

Trade policy reform was expected to contribute to high and sustained growth and poverty reduction. But evidence to date suggests that the benefits of Nepal's trade reform were confined to a few manufacturing industries and largely failed to address the problems of the agricultural sector and rural communities (Bhatt and Sharma 2006, Khatiwada 2005). Available studies describe the macroeconomic linkages between trade and poverty; however, no attempts have been made to find these linkages at the micro (grassroots) level. Therefore, this chapter will explore the linkages between poverty reduction strategies and trade by using a case study of indigenous communities living in the Byas municipality of Nepal.

Capacity building for trade

Supply-side bottlenecks often limit a least developed country's (LDC) ability to benefit from globalisation. Limited internal resources constrain investments in infrastructure, institutions and human resources. Various initiatives are being undertaken – at bilateral, regional and multilateral level – to mobilise more external funding, with a view to enhancing the supply-side capacity of trade. Some of the important donor-supported programmes in this regard are: the EU-ITC-sponsored Asia Trust Fund (identification and development of export-potential products), the GTZ's Private Sector Promotion Project (supply- and value-chain management for handmade paper, coffee, orthodox tea, etc.), the microenterprise development programme of the UNDP (United Nations Development Programme) and the Integrated Framework (IF) supported projects of the WTO. Currently, an IF-supported project, Enhancing Nepal's Trade-related Capacity (ENTReC), is under implementation. The project, among others, focuses on the capacity building of government and private sectors, trade policy analysis and identification of new areas of comparative advantage. However, the link of the project with grassroots communities is not very strong, and the resources available under the project are insufficient to expand activities to achieve wider coverage. Similarly, at the regional level (like SAFTA and BIMST-EC), member countries agreed to implement capacity-building measures and provide technical assistance, particularly for LDC members to help them adjust their economic structure and expand their trade and investment opportunities. However, most of the commitments are made on a voluntary basis and are not implemented properly.

At the domestic level, the Government of Nepal has embarked on trade-related capacity-building initiatives like increasing public spending in agriculture, a special package for the development of small and medium enterprises (SMEs) and handicrafts, and the formulation and enactment of various pieces of legislation (the Company Act, Competition Act, Insolvency Act and Multi-modal Transport Act). The government is initiating measures for building sanitary and phytosanitary measures (SPS) and technical barriers to trade (TBT) capacity with the help of its development partners (particularly from the United Nations Industrial Development Organization (UNIDO) and the German Government), including upgrading the national laboratories and testing facilities, realigning national standards and building human capacity. The Government of Nepal is also implementing the Business Incubation Project to promote innovations, focusing on SME development. These innovations can create new business opportunities and entrepreneurship, triggering the growth of enterprises at the grassroots level; however, resource limitations have constrained efforts to scale this project up to the national level.

The multilateral, regional and national initiatives noted above are important for supply-side capacity building; however, additional efforts and increased funds or technical support are needed in order to redirect the benefits of such initiatives to grassroots level, particularly for the indigenous and disadvantaged communities.

Trade and poverty linkages: a case study approach

Introduction to the Byas municipality case study

The Byas municipality is the headquarters of a historical district of Tanahun in western Nepal. The municipal area, with a population of 28,245 (DDC Tanahun 2001), was traditionally but sparsely inhabited by indigenous/ethnic communities of Derai, Bote and Kumal (who have remained poor for generations), depending upon subsistence farming and fishing for their livelihoods. In addition, men from these communities migrate on a seasonal basis to major urban centres in Nepal and India. The planned settlement of the municipality was started in the District headquarters in 1970, with subsequent development of physical infrastructures and services. The site was given municipality status in 1992 as a result of a fast growth of in-migration and the development of urban-related services.

While initially dominated by the indigenous community, the settlement's demographic composition has evolved over time due to outmigration of the native people and a continuous inflow of people from outside. The arable land owned by the indigenous people was either purchased by the government for public construction or sold to the new immigrants of the town. Displaced households from the growing urban area began living in the outskirts of the settlement, cultivating available agricultural land.

Urbanisation and the availability of alternative sources of livelihood, rather than farming, have affected cropping patterns and farm management systems. The development of road, electricity and telecommunication infrastructures has improved the accessibility of agricultural extension services. The availability of new crops, new varieties and fertilisers have induced transitions to new cropping schemes and have increased cropping intensity. Moreover, as the trade and service sectors have grown over time, options for off-farm employment have improved.

The Byas municipality produces agricultural products like ginger, black pulses (lentils), honey and citrus fruits, which are sold in the domestic markets and also exported outside the country. Traders collect products in small quantities from the individual households and sell them in large markets, where the products are ultimately exported. Farmers mostly sell farm goods in unprocessed forms at low prices. No effective measures have been adopted for adding value to the farm products that could benefit the poor. The poorer sections of society, particularly the women of the indigenous communities, are badly integrated into the market economy. Hence there is a need to examine the adequacy of trade policy, infrastructure availability and other systemic issues with a view to establishing a coherence between human development and trade.

The emergence of the municipal area triggered the migration of indigenous communities from the city centre to the outskirts. Modern transportation facilities and urbanisation brought significant changes in the living standards of these communities, which had been traditionally engaged in agriculture and fishing (see Box 2A). However, the changes varied across households. Therefore a survey was conducted to assess the causal link between changes in settlement and production patterns and their impacts on income and trade.

There are 6,511 households in the Byas municipality, with a total population of 28,245. Of these, the ethnic groups of Darai, Kumal and Bote comprise 18 per cent of the population, and they are settled in seven

BOX 2A   FROM FERRYING TO DAIRYING: THE SUCCESS
OF LAL BAHADUR

Lal Bahadur Bote (age 50), an inhabitant of the Byas municipality-5, belongs to an indigenous ethnic group that has traditionally been dependent on fishing and ferrying people across the river by canoe. Fishing had become less lucrative over time due to over-fishing. Similarly, the construction of suspension bridges over the rivers eliminated the need for ferrying across the river. Thus Lal Bahadur lost his traditional jobs due to the development of infrastructures and the modernisation of society. However, he was left with a small parcel of land that he had inherited from his late parents. Initially, he worked enough to make a living out of the land, which was nearly taken by the Municipal authorities for the expansion of the city. However, Lal Bahadur was able to sell the property for a good price.

Out of the proceeds of the sale of land Lal Bahadur managed to purchase 0.75 hectares of cultivable land in the outskirts of the area, and built an irrigation channel from a nearby spring to provide irrigation facilities. Lal Bahadur started planting vegetables and raising chickens and water buffaloes on the newly purchased land. These new businesses paid him well, as there were opportunities to sell fresh vegetables, milk, eggs and chickens in the market. Lal Bahadur is now a successful farmer who has been able to bring about qualitative changes in his lifestyle with increased income. Now his elder son is helping him to do farm work while the younger son is attending the university in Kathmandu, and their only daughter is doing her Bachelors Degree in Arts at the local college in Damouli. He owns a motorbike, a colour television and a telephone, and is able to pay the hospital bills for the treatment of his family members.

When asked about the external factors behind his success, Lal Bahadur replied that the support of the UNDP-funded project called the Rural Urban Partnership Programme (RUPP) over the past five or six years was quite helpful. The project focuses on establishing rural–urban linkages though enhancement of productivity at the farm level and helping rural communities to sell their products in nearby urban centres. Through the support of this project, Lal Bahadur had developed essential skills and established how to link in with the markets. 'Indeed, hard work and honesty to the profession are the key factors behind my success,' says Lal Bahadur. In addition, he believed that the irrigation facilities and transport linkages were the two key elements for enhancing productivity, diversification and access to nearby markets.

wards of the municipality[2] (DDC Tanhun 2001). Ward No. 5, selected for the study, consists of 250 households with a total population of 1,700, the average family size being 6.8. All of them depend on agriculture in one way or other. The ratio of male to female is 49:51. Sixty per cent of the population are economically active or employable. Ten per cent of the total households were selected as a sample for the study.

Socioeconomic status and access to basic services

Survey results show that the indigenous community has comparatively good access to basic services. Around 88% of households have access to safe drinking water within 500 metres of their home, and 16% of families have water taps within their home. All households have electricity and sanitation facilities within their home. For 84% of the households, the primary school is located within 500 metres. The secondary school is located at the same distance for 56% of the households. The health centre is located at less than one kilometre for 12% and at two to three kilometres for 76% of households. Access to transportation and a rural market is also quite good as the feeder road passes in the vicinity of these settlements.

Around 23% of the people surveyed cannot read or write. Out of the literate population, 64% have completed only primary level education; the remaining 13% have completed secondary education.

Land holding and use

The average land holding in the surveyed area is 0.36 hectares, while 28% of households occupy comparatively large holdings (0.5 hectares and above) and 36% of households possess less than 0.25 hectares of land. Household size is generally large compared to the national average: 36% of households have five or fewer family members while 20% of the households have eight or more members and 44% of the households have between six and seven members. All the households surveyed were engaged in agricultural activities, with 67% of them fully dependent on agriculture for their livelihood. Besides agriculture, 4% of households are engaged in wage labour, and 29% are employed in the services sector. Among the surveyed households, two households claim that they are food sufficient all year round. Among the remaining households, 24% claim that the duration of food sufficiency is six to nine months, 60% claim that

---

[2] The municipality is comprised of eleven wards.

the food is sufficient for only three to six months, and the remaining 8% report that their food production is sufficient for less than three months.

The area under study (Ward No. 5 of the municipality) covers 700 hectares, of which around 150 hectares is under forest cover and is managed and regulated by the local community. The forest provides firewood, fodder and timber for use of community households. Farmers seem to be aware of the problems of over-extraction of forest resources and encroachment to the forest area and hence follow the Forest Use Plan, which allows sustainable use of resources. Fruit and fodder tree plantations are commonly included in the area, contributing to the area's forest cover. In addition, livestock production and bee farming have the potential to contribute to improving local livelihoods. Implementation of an integrated agro-forestry programme for additional supply of fodder, forage and flowering plants provide enhanced opportunities in this area. The use of farmland at the household level shows that around 80% of the land is cultivated, 10% is covered by homesteads and the remaining 10% is used for other activities, such as livestock and chicken raising, bee-keeping and off-farm activities.

Impact on agriculture: new migrants vis-à-vis the indigenous community

One third of the surveyed families were migrants, displaced from the municipality due to either urban growth, family separation or relocation in pursuit of better opportunities. Newly arrived immigrants are more likely to produce and transact on cash crops and commercial items. The cropping pattern has shifted in favour of cash crops and high-yielding varieties. Ginger and summer and winter vegetables have replaced the traditional cereal crops such as paddy, wheat and corn. Rearing of farm animals, particularly water buffaloes and cows for dairy products, goats and chickens for meat products, and bee farming are the preferred farm activities. As migrant and indigenous farmers learn from each other, the farming behaviour of the community changes over time. Box 2A, above, illustrates the story of one farmer able to make the transition successfully.

Off-farm business works to reduce poverty. Around 30 per cent of households are engaged in off-farm businesses such as running teashops, bee-keeping, making bamboo baskets, making furniture and repairing bicycles. Carpentry, production of local handicrafts, wood works and bamboo works are the preferred off-farm activities. The net income[3] from agricultural produce is generally less than the income of households that draw their collective incomes from agriculture *and* off-farm business. The survey revealed that households which are totally dependent on agriculture earn US$659 per year on average, while the households that are engaged in other off-farm activities vis-à-vis agriculture earn US$944 per year on average.

Remittances

Out of the twenty-five surveyed households, ten households had family members (usually the unskilled) working in Malaysia and Gulf countries. The survey shows that an average remittance from an individual worker is around US$1,500 per annum. Thus the share of the remittances in net income for a household can be worth 60 per cent or more of a household's net income, contributing significantly to poverty reduction at the household level. The focus group discussions carried out during the survey revealed that the migrant workers were more attracted to the labour markets of the Republic of Korea and Japan due to the higher average pay (US$7,000 to 8,000 per year).

Agricultural production and niche products

Focus group discussions and surveys on the sale of agricultural products in the community showed that some products could capture local markets and also be exported out of the country. These were:

- Bee-keeping and honey production – the local farmers of the municipality sell about 2,500 kilograms of honey at the local market; the products are then taken to bigger markets by the trader and exporters.
- Ginger and dried gingers – 15,000 kilograms per year are collected by the traders and exported to India.
- Winter and summer vegetables – these mainly cater for the nearby district centre and capital city, with an approximate quantity of 1,000 metric tonnes per year.
- Milk and milk products – approximately 800 metric tonnes per year are collected by the local cooperative and sold to the milk-processing industries, mainly in Pokhara and Kathmandu.

---

[3] Net income does not include the agricultural produce consumed by the farmer himself.

- Poultry and meat – these products are sold at the local market (approximately 100 metric tonnes per year).
- Sub-tropical fruits – fruits such as banana, mango, litchi, pineapple and guava are mainly sold at the local markets.

Bamboo products, particularly baskets, and furniture-making and wood-carvings, were also seen as important off-farm activities. However, at present, production is now limited to supply at the local market.

Infrastructure

The development of physical and social infrastructures can contribute significantly to the integration of poor communities with the market place. The settlements under study are well connected by the road network mentioned earlier, and from electricity and telecommunication services. The national highway is just five kilometres away from the settlements, which has made the life of farmers and settlers easier both for travel and the sale of farm products. However, the road needs regular upgrading; currently, out of 20 kilometres of the road, only five kilometres are gravelled, and the rest is earthen. Telephone services are available from two public booths, and the electricity supply, although connected to the national grid, is not dependable due to power shortages during the winter season.

Despite the persistence of social hierarchy systems in the community (common to Nepalese society), there is strong social harmony and a good feeling of cooperation among people within the locality. Several social institutions functioning in the communities are instrumental in promoting unity among the diverse ethnic groups. Fifty per cent of households were members of local dairy cooperatives. Local people and farmers were also running various social institutions, like the water users group, the school management committee and the forest users group. The traditional cultural group (called the Rodhi Club) of the community has been an effective instrument in preserving the traditional songs, music, dance and cultural heritage of the indigenous community.

Findings of the study: implications to trade policies

The trade regime in Nepal has been substantially transformed since the beginning of the new millennium. Tariff rates have decreased (the average weighted tariff reported in 2007 was 12.5 per cent) as part of a commitment towards gradual reduction of tariffs in the wake of membership to regional and multilateral trading systems. Service sectors, which were largely restricted to foreign investors, have been gradually opened (a commitment has been made to open seventy subsectors during accession to the WTO).

However, in the face of more liberalised trade, Nepali entrepreneurs are struggling to compete in international markets. For example, after the phase-out of the Agreement on Textiles and Clothing (ATC), Nepal lost market share in exports of garments and woollen carpets. Higher production costs, outdated technologies, low productivity of labour and rigid labour laws are some of the factors affecting production and corresponding exports. Ten years of internal conflict has put a significant strain on production and export.

The case study cited above highlights the various opportunities that exist if value addition, diversification, infrastructure, remittances and capacity building can be put to good use in favour of lower-income farmers and indigenous groups. The implications to be drawn for trade policy makers are summarised below.

Enhance supply side and capacity building

Enhancing supply-side capacity can assist in developing vital links between agricultural trade and poverty reduction as follows:

- through the identification of niche products
- through their development at the commercial level
- by their quality improvement
- through market promotion with appropriate marketing and market-access strategies.

Increasing supply-side efficiency of production will require an overall improvement in agricultural productivity and, if appropriate capacity-building and economic inclusion measures are in place, will assist rural livelihoods and ultimately leverage benefits to the rural poor.

Enhancing the knowledge of farmers in modern farming practices, including the improvement of farm-related services, is particularly important for capacity building for farmers. Farmers should be well informed about the benefits of adopting new production patterns and new agricultural business so that they can make rational choices regarding the types of products and production methods used. The introduction of new varieties of vegetables and fruits, switching to bee farming and poultry raising and switching to new products from the traditional crops will require more technical knowledge and support of farmers.

Irrigation can obviously enhance production and productivity of crops. Local farmers are aware that access to irrigation facilities can increase the number of potential annual crop rotations and enhance the possibilities for diversification of agricultural products. Farmers realise that even in the absence of community-level irrigation channels, vegetable farming, fruit plantation and chicken and pig rearing can be promoted if individual water-tap connections are available to the farmers at the household level. Hence, the government needs to focus on facilitating the construction of community irrigation and water-supply schemes to the benefit of rural farmers and producers.

Byas municipality communities have recognised that fresh vegetables, dairy products, honey, ginger, cardamom and poultry products are important cash crops. The export of ginger to India, albeit in small quantities, from the locality is facing problems with quarantine checks at the Nepal–India border. There are issues related to the residue of pesticides or antibiotics in some of the export farm products, particularly in exports to EU countries. Farmers need to be well informed about SPS measures and other TBTs in order to anticipate and mitigate these border measures.

In fact, there are a range of 'behind the border' barriers that constrain agricultural development. The incidence of multiple taxes while transporting goods across administrative boundaries of districts, the scattered number of small growers, the higher cost of banking transactions, weak market information and market intelligence, insufficient testing and laboratory facilities for food safety and standards and the lack of cold chain storage and warehousing facilities are just some of the vexing problems that need to be addressed in order to promote trade in agriculture and forest products.

Attention is needed in providing export credits to exporters and effective extension services along with easy access to credit for farmers. Organising farmers to form cooperatives, identifying potential niche products and investing in the development of these niche products so as to move them to higher-value chain exports are some of the initiatives requiring immediate attention. The promotion of the Nepalese brand and trademark is equally important for enhancing market access for Nepalese indigenous products.

Encourage value-added exports in agriculture, forest and SME products

As we have discovered, the Byas municipality has the advantage of producing a range of important agricultural and forest-based products like honey, milk and milk products, ginger, cardamom, banana, mango, wood carvings and bamboo works. The development of value-added processing facilities could contribute to the successful marketing of niche export markets in India and South Asia. Setting up export houses with tax relief and duty draw-back facilities would help small producers and farmers to reach out to the markets in an effective way. Farmers should be encouraged to form joint cooperatives with the local chambers of commerce in order to promote agriculture trade.

Local communities possess traditional knowledge in producing textiles, woodcarving, paper work, bamboo craft, woodcraft, metal craft and folklore items, but these items compete with cheaply manufactured articles and consumable goods. Local communities could directly benefit if the traditional products were modified through design improvements and the adoption of new technologies and innovations to enhance the productive capacity and satisfy evolving market preferences. Rural credit programmes can provide adequate financial support to the community for such initiatives. Institutional support in improvement of design and the registration of trademarks and patents would be required for protecting the intellectual property rights of traditional knowledge.

Explore services-trade potential

Trade in services has significant growth potential in the Byas municipality and in Nepal generally. Skill development and apprenticeship training for a young workforce would help to generate self-employment opportunities in the sectors of tourism, transportation, information technology, SMEs, construction and industry. Trade policy should be able to correctly identify the most needy areas for skill development and also facilitate the services trade, including the movement of labour. If impediments in labour mobility and labour market restrictions are lifted in conjunction with trade reform, labour may move from the informal to the formal sector. This could have a strong impact on poverty reduction.

The temporary migration of young workers to the Gulf countries and Malaysia has become a part of life in many rural communities in Nepal; 30 to 40 per cent of young people from the Byas municipality work abroad in pursuit of better incomes to supplement their household incomes.

However, there are problems in labour migration because the migrant workers often suffer at the hands of middlemen who collect exorbitant fees but do not guarantee employment. In order to streamline the processes of temporary migration, the government could introduce youth employment and protection policies, and at the same time pursue advocacy in the international trade-negotiation forum to liberalise mode 4 services under the GATS. It is equally important to prepare and implement Nepal's human-resources development plan with a focus towards enhancement of the skills training and knowledge of the potential migrant workers so that such migrant workers could benefit from better remuneration and working conditions abroad.

Emphasise transportation and transit facilitation

Transportation infrastructure plays an important role in facilitating the replacement of the traditional crops by cash crops. Farmers are unable to fully harness the benefits of the major highway system across the country due to the absence of feeder and subsidiary roads linking to national highways. The development of roadways and inland waterways could contribute to farm produce transportation. This requires a comprehensive transportation plan by the national government that addresses the needs of farmers living in marginal areas. Further facilitation of transportation to the community should include the upgrading of existing roads, encouraging farmers to own transportation vehicles collectively or through the cooperatives and creating road links to interior parts of the district for promoting intra-district trade.

Enhancing the transit-transportation infrastructure is equally important in order to provide access to the overseas markets. Regional markets are important destinations of exports; however, the lack of an adequate infrastructure limits potential integration to these markets. For example, the only highway passing through Kathmandu to Lhasa has severe operational limitations due to inadequate maintenance and rehabilitation in order to address annual landslide and flood damage. Nepal's transit transportation relies on one road and one rail corridor connected to the Kolkata port in India. The corridor currently in use is constrained by port inefficiency, slow customs processing and clearances, bad road conditions and outdated vehicles. Rail traffic is limited by insufficient wagon availability – a single track for a 200 km stretch that requires locomotives to wait for passenger trains to cross this section. The improvements in transit operation require large financial investments for the modernisation of fleet and tracks, which would require collaboration between countries at the bilateral or subregional level.

Link trade policy reform with poverty reduction strategies

Mutually supportive policies are required to encourage trade-related growth, particularly in the areas of macroeconomic stabilisation, pro-competition regulatory institutions and laws, investment policies, human resources development, governance and the rule of law. Developing linkages between markets and local agricultural production within the country will help to increase the productive capacity of farms, thereby enabling the farmers to be a part of a monetised, more prosperous economy. Trade policy (by creating a bridge between domestic policies and global market conditions) can therefore contribute to achieving Nepal's national development goals.

Appropriate policies need to be adopted in order to cope with price volatility of tradable commodities. Negative price shocks, when they occur, can undermine an important market and are likely to have poverty implications. Hence, integrating agro-based products vertically (forward and backward linkages) and horizontally (establishing linkages with services and manufacturing sectors), adding value in the supply chain and hedging farmers against the risk of failing market prices are some of the important mechanisms to be pursued through the trade and agriculture policies.

Concluding remarks: the voice of farmers

The decade-long conflict and violence in Nepal has contributed to poverty and unemployment. Asymmetries in rural and urban development and between geographical regions have exacerbated social discrimination and exclusion, which have persisted in Nepalese society for centuries. With a new political scenario due to the Peoples Movement-II since April 2006, there are growing demands for inclusive development in social and economic spheres, particularly targeting the indigenous, tribal Dalits and Madhesi peoples. The government has increased spending on social programmes in current years to improve the level of human development. Multilateral agencies, bilateral donors and NGOs are also providing development assistance in supplementing the government initiatives. However, there is a need for greater coordination in their efforts in order to enhance the process of development cooperation. When asked to give their opinions on how best to address poverty and unemployment, community leaders surveyed gave the following views.

An active and caring government is needed to lead the agenda

Government has a crucial role in assisting farmers through support for irrigation and a transportation infrastructure, the setting up of agricultural marketing centres and the construction of warehouses. In addition, there is a need for targeted subsidies for agricultural inputs (particularly fertilisers and seeds) in order to assist local farmers to compete with imports from neighbouring countries.

The increasing oil price in the international market and the shortage of electricity in domestic markets has hindered farmers' efforts in managing their farms and selling farm products. Special dispensation to farmers towards meeting their energy needs would help maintain and enhance productive capacity.

A proactive and energetic business community is needed for better results

The indigenous community and the local inhabitants of the Byas municipality have felt the need for forging an effective alliance with the business community in the district. The businesspeople who are involved in trade also provide informal, financial market services to the farmers, but they charge exorbitant interest rates. The local chambers of commerce may facilitate the supply of agricultural inputs to the farmers and purchase their farm products in return. A joint cooperative between the local chamber of commerce and the farmers' group may be formed so that the issues of production, marketing and distribution could be streamlined in a more coherent manner.

Development partners: focus on decentralised implementation

Development projects and programmes prepared and implemented centrally are often unable to address local-level problems due to inadequate information and a lack of understanding of the problems faced by the local community. There is a need for community participation at all levels during project development that would help in bringing a sense of ownership and building a sustainable base for development initiatives.

Farmers prefer that development cooperation follows the decentralised approach in implementation, particularly in the sectors of health, transportation infrastructures, school buildings, drinking water and irrigation. The decentralisation model would further help in building local capacity to manage projects at the community level.

NGOs: focus on providing support to agriculture

NGOs are important vehicles to educate people and carry on development activities at the community level. There are few NGOs in this municipal area, most of them taking up activities related to the environment, forest protection, literacy, public health promotion and related awareness-raising programmes. Support for the promotion of agriculture and trade would be a new and important functional area for professional NGOs. These organisations could provide training to farmers in new methods and technologies of farming, help to identify niche products, share information on SPS and TBT measures and market-access opportunities under various trading arrangements and could help farmers to commercialise their farming practices.

Final summary

Overall, the story of the indigenous peoples of the Byas municipality in Nepal is one of cautious optimism as farmers like Lal Bahadur Bote manage to embrace the transition from a traditional agricultural community to a more prosperous market-based community. This will require significant investment and time to reduce barriers to productivity and allow for more efficient supply-side export solutions. However, with the involvement of the local community and support from the Nepalese Government, Nepalese migrants and the international donor community, there are a range of ways forward for low-income farmers to consolidate, add value and diversify farm productivity, off-farm production and services trade. If development strategies can succeed in linking small farmers and entrepreneurs to existing and newly emerging trading opportunities, there is significant potential for greater wealth creation in the future.

References

Bhatt, S. R. and Sharma, P. (2006), 'Trade Liberalization and Poverty: The case of Nepal', *Trade Insight* 2(3).

DDC Tanahun (2001), *District Profile*, District Development Committee: Tanahun.

Khatiwada, Y. R. (2005), 'Linkages between Trade, Development and Poverty Reduction: A Study on the Short Term Impact of Trade Liberalization on Poverty in Nepal', a report submitted to South Asia Watch on Trade, Economics and Environment (SAWTEE): Kathmandu.

Ministry of Finance (MOF) (2007), *Economic Survey: Fiscal Year 2006/07*, MOF, Government of Nepal: Kathmandu.

Ministry of Industry, Commerce and Supplies (MOICS) (2004), *Nepal: Trade and Competitiveness Study*, MOICS, Government of Nepal: Kathmandu.

Ministry of Physical Planning and Works (MOPPW) (2006), *Statistics of Strategic Networks, SSRN 2004*, MOPPW, Government of Nepal: Kathmandu.

National Planning Commission (NPC) (1998), *Ninth Plan*, NPC, Government of Nepal: Kathmandu.

(2003), *Tenth Plan/PRSP*, NPC, Government of Nepal: Kathmandu.

2.3

Samoan agricultural policy: graduating from least developed country status

HAMISH SMITH AND LEE ANN JACKSON*

Introduction

The Independent State of Samoa (Samoa) is located in the South Pacific approximately half way between Hawaii and New Zealand. With a land area of just 2,934 square kilometres, a small population of less than 200,000 people, and per capita gross domestic product (GDP) of little more than US$2,200 in 2006 (World Bank, 2007), Samoa exhibits the typical characteristics of small island developing states (SIDS). In addition to these economic features, Samoa faces development challenges due to a lack of natural resources, remoteness and susceptibility to natural disasters.

Through a gradual improvement in economic development, Samoa has met the criteria for least developed country (LDC) graduation, and in 2003 Samoa began the process of LDC graduation and formally became a candidate for graduation in 2006. In July 2007, the UN Economic and Social Council (UN ECOSOC) endorsed a recommendation for Samoa's graduation. This chapter looks at some of the concerns that have been expressed by Samoa regarding their LDC graduation and the possible implications for Samoa's agricultural trade and policy from this graduation.[1]

Background

Since reforms in the mid 1990s, Samoa has recorded strong economic growth relative to its Pacific Islands neighbours, including the doubling of GDP per capita (Goverment of Australia, New Zealand and Samoa, 2006).

* The authors are Economic Affairs Officers at the WTO Secretariat. This case study was written in their personal capacity. The views expressed in this chapter are their own and do not represent an official position of the WTO, its members or the Secretariat.
[1] Also see Chapter 1.2 on Samoa's car parts industry.

Table 2K   *Main components of GDP (percentage of total, constant 2002 prices)*

Sector	2000	2001	2002	2003	2004	2005	2006
Agriculture	15.8	14.7	13.7	12.3	12.3	11.5	15.8
Manufacturing	15.9	15.5	15.8	14.5	13.4	11.9	15.9
Construction	6.2	6.1	6.0	7.9	8.5	8.6	6.2
Trade	20.9	22.2	22.0	21.9	22.0	22.8	20.9
Transportation and Communications	12.6	11.8	12.4	12.8	12.8	12.9	12.6
Government and Finance	16.1	16.6	17.3	17.9	18.7	20.0	16.1

Source: Asian Development Bank, 2007.

Samoa achieved real GDP growth of 3.5% in 2003, 3.9% in 2004 and 5.5% in 2005 (Economist Intelligence Unit, 2007), though this was down on growth of 7% in 2000 and 6.8% in 2001. Despite these economic advances, its economy remains heavily dependent on the agriculture sector, official development assistance (ODA) and remittances. Furthermore, poverty continues to be prevalent in Samoan society (Economist Intelligence Unit, 2007). Over 20% of Samoa's population were living below the basic-needs poverty line[2] in 2002, while 5.5% survived on less than US$1 per day (Abbott and Pollard, 2004). Continued poverty in Samoa is exacerbated by continued damage to the economy as a result of the impact of tropical cyclones.

Like many SIDS and other developing and least developed countries, agriculture plays an important economic and social role in Samoan society. The agricultural sector has traditionally accounted for a large share of GDP, though this has declined over recent years (see Table 2K). In 2005, agriculture accounted for 11.5 per cent of GDP. Approximately half of Samoa's population lives in rural areas and at least two-thirds are engaged in predominantly subsistence agriculture (Government of Australia, New Zealand and Samoa, 2006).

A high dependence on agricultural production renders Samoa's economy vulnerable to external shocks, especially natural disasters and fluctuations in world agricultural commodity markets, which can significantly

[2] The basic-needs poverty line (BNPL) measures the incidence of basic-needs hardship. The BNPL includes not only food but also a basket of other essential non-food expenditure (goods and services) that each household/individual needs to maintain a basic standard of living (Abbott and Pollard, 2004, p. 25).

set back long-term development strategies.[3] Samoa anticipates experiencing an average of six cyclones per year, and each of these events has the potential to alter the composition of agricultural production for years (UNCTAD, 2006). Despite the agricultural sector's distinct vulnerability, the Samoan Government views this sector as a key element of development potential, particularly the creation of employment opportunities (Government of Australia, New Zealand and Samoa, 2006).

Samoa's agricultural development objectives combine two main approaches: (i) increasing agricultural production to aid food security; and (ii) increasing commercial investment through improved productivity levels, diversified farming systems and new plant species (Government of Australia, New Zealand and Samoa, 2006). Samoa has a long-term livestock improvement programme, including investments in local processing industries to ease the reliance on imported meat. In addition, Samoa has recently invested in quarantine and regulation services to enable Samoan fruit and vegetable growers to realise the economic potential of access to other markets in the Pacific, as well as helping to protect the local industry from imported plant and animal diseases. Table 2L indicates the value of the agriculture sector relative to the manufacturing and services sectors.

Although agriculture is seen as a key element of Samoa's development strategy, government spending on the sector has declined from 1.1% of GDP in the late 1990s to 0.8% between 2001 and 2005 (Government of Samoa, 2006). The government has continued to assist with the development of agriculture through a variety of approaches, including investments in research capacity, market development missions and the encouragement of production diversification away from traditional crops to non-traditional crops and other high value-added products. Institutional strengthening of agricultural sector management continues in the area of standards-setting and quarantine procedures to facilitate export of fruits and vegetables, while a micro-credit scheme has been established for small business development in collaboration with two NGOs through a facility from the Asian Development Bank (ADB) (Government of Samoa, 2002).

Samoa has a small manufacturing industry, based primarily on processing agricultural products; the production of import substitutes such

---

[3] In collaboration with regional organisations and non-governmental organisations (NGOs), the Government of Samoa is establishing an early warning system to reduce some of this vulnerability from natural disasters. There are also ongoing discussions regarding a special insurance scheme to facilitate post-disaster reconstruction (Government of Samoa, 2002).

Table 2L   *Relative importance of key sectors*

	2000	2001	2002	2003	2004	2005
Rural population (% of total population)	78.1	78.0	77.9	77.8	77.7	77.6
Agr. – value-addition per worker (constant 2000 US$)	1,857.7	1,799.6	1,797.7	1,710.3	1,628.1	–
Agr. – value-addition (% of GDP)	16.8	14.9	14.8	13.3	13.1	13.6
Agr. – value-addition (annual % growth)	0.1	–3.1	–0.1	–4.9	–9.3	5.7
Food exports (% of merchandise exports)	–	32.1	25.3	17.3	22.5	–
Manufacturing – value-addition (% of GDP)	14.8	16.0	15.8	16.3	15.9	14.7
Manufacturing – value-addition (annual % growth)	8.8	16.5	3.6	3.9	–0.6	–3.3
Merchandise trade (% of GDP)	51.8	60.5	58.5	49.6	48.5	49.3
Services, etc. – value-addition (% of GDP)	57.2	58.0	58.5	59.8	59.4	59.1
Services, etc. – value-addition (annual % growth)	6.6	7.8	5.5	3.2	5.6	5.9
Trade in services (% of GDP)	–	–	–	–	38.2	40.6

Source: World Bank, 2007.

as soft drinks, beer and snack foods; and the production of automotive electrical systems (wire harnesses) for the Australian market through a joint venture with the Japanese company Yazaki. Yazaki Samoa is the single largest private-sector employer in Samoa, with more than 2,000 employees. In 2004, production from Yazaki Samoa's operation accounted for over 20% of Samoa's total manufacturing output, or approximately 3% of Samoa's GDP (Economist Intelligence Unit, 2007).

External trade plays a large role in the Samoan economy, contributing close to one quarter of GDP (see Table 2K on p. 271). However, the value of imports significantly outweighs the value of exports, resulting in a large merchandise trade deficit (see Tables 2M and 2N). Exports of fish, beer and coconut cream remain important for Samoa (Table 2M). Table 2N indicates that imports are dominated by food and live animals, mineral

Table 2M   *Exports by SITC section and principal commodity (US$ million)*

	2002	2003	2004	2005	2006
SITC section					
Food and live animals	15.0	11.1	12.9	11.8	11.1
Beverage and tobacco	1.7	2.0	2.4	2.9	2.0
Mineral fuels, etc.	0.5	0.4	2.5	3.2	2.0
Animal, vegetable oil and fats	1.1	2.0	1.4	1.6	1.1
Basic manufactures	3.6	2.0	2.3	0.8	0.8
Other	49.1	69.9	63.8	66.8	51.0
Total	**71.1**	**87.5**	**85.3**	**87.2**	**68.0**
Principal commodity					
Fresh fish	8.60	5.30	4.94	4.27	5.56
Beer	1.16	1.28	1.56	1.78	1.25
Coconut cream	0.92	1.01	1.06	0.84	0.86
Taro	0.30	0.44	0.52	0.31	0.21
Garments	1.32	4.48	4.78	0.13	–

Source: Asian Development Bank, 2007.

Table 2N   *Imports by SITC section (US$ million)*

SITC section	2002	2003	2004	2005	2006
Food and live animals	34.06	39.46	37.64	39.36	41.45
Mineral fuels, etc.	17.21	20.42	29.93	36.86	43.51
Chemicals	9.48	10.87	13.67	15.53	15.99
Basic manufactures	25.94	28.42	52.44	65.01	63.61
Other	45.83	52.19	76.09	82.10	110.52
Total	**132.53**	**151.37**	**209.75**	**238.87**	**275.08**

Source: Asian Development Bank, 2007.

fuels, chemicals and basic manufacturing products. Australia and New Zealand are the most important export destination and source of imports respectively (see Table 2O).

To help offset its large merchandise trade deficit, Samoa relies heavily on trade in services, as well as on remittances from the large number of Samoans living in Australia, New Zealand and the US. In 2004, trade

Table 20   *Main trading partners (exports by 2005 and imports by 2006, percentage of total)*

	2002	2003	2004	2005	2006
Main export destinations					
Australia	60.3	64.2	65.7	75.9	–
American Samoa	2.3	2.2	3.1	13.6	–
United States	9.1	4.8	5.6	6.5	–
New Zealand	2.3	1.5	1.1	2.0	–
Indonesia	0.1	14.7	5.2	0.0	–
Main sources of imports					
New Zealand	23.7	19.7	24.8	31.0	21.0
Fiji Islands	20.6	18.3	21.3	6.0	13.7
Singapore	0.5	4.4	8.4	2.9	12.9
Australia	15.9	15.3	8.8	22.6	10.9
Japan	13.3	11.8	7.5	7.5	8.9
Other	25.9	30.3	29.1	30.0	32.5

Source: Asian Development Bank, 2007.

in services accounted for 38% of GDP (see Table 2L on p. 273) while remittances were worth around 24% of GDP, making it a critical component of Samoa's national accounts. Remittances provide an important safety net, increasing household income and contributing to enhanced personal consumption, including housing, social obligations, household goods and education. Samoa's tourism industry is the second-largest source of foreign exchange after remittances (Economist Intelligence Unit, 2007).

As an LDC, Samoa depends on foreign aid to support its development goals. Between 2001 and 2003, Samoa received approximately US$40 million in foreign aid annually. This fell to just US$21 million in 2004 before a sharp rise to US$73.5 million in 2005. Australia, Japan and New Zealand have traditionally been the largest bilateral donors to Samoa (US$14.1, US$12.9 and US$4.3 million respectively in 2005). Generally, most multilateral aid has come via the EC (US$2.8 million in 2005), but in 2005 the International Development Association provided US$8.0 million. The vast majority of Samoa's aid receipts are used for social infrastructure and services, including investments in education and health (OECD, 2007).

LDCs and graduation

According to the UN classification system, LDC status is based on three criteria (UNCTAD, 2006). For the 2006 triennial review, the following three criteria were assessed:

(1) per capita gross national income – 2002 to 2004 average
(2) a human assets index
(3) an economic vulnerability index.

A triennial UN review examines whether any existing LDCs should be removed from the list of LDCs (or 'graduated') or if other countries should be added to the list of LDCs based upon evaluation of these indicators. Once an LDC has met two of the three criteria thresholds in two consecutive reviews, it may be recommended for graduation. A non-LDC country meeting all three criteria at the time of any review may be awarded LDC status.[4] Graduation from LDC status signals that durable and undisputed socioeconomic progress has been made (UNCTAD, 2006). The loss of LDC treatment and benefits typically entails lower levels of international development support.

Various changes to the graduation process have been made over the years. Initially, any country meeting the criteria for graduation in two successive reviews could be considered for 'immediate' graduation, subject to a decision by the UN ECOSOC and the UN General Assembly. In 1999, a new economic vulnerability criteria was adopted to replace the previous economic diversification index. At the same time, the UN Committee for Development Policy (UNCDP) considered that an economic vulnerability index (EVI) could only give a partial and approximate measure of the relative level of vulnerability faced by a country, and recommend that a country-specific 'vulnerability profile' be prepared for each potential graduation case.

Samoa first met the necessary conditions for graduation in 1997. Nevertheless, as a result of the change in graduation criteria, Samoa failed to meet the requirement of achieving adequate levels in two out of three criteria at the 2000 review. As a result, Samoa was no longer a candidate for graduation. In the 2003 review, once again Samoa was found to exceed two of the three criteria thresholds – exceeding the low-income and human-assets thresholds, but failing to meet the economic vulnerability threshold. As a result, a vulnerability assessment was carried out for

---

[4] For each of the three criteria, there is a margin established between the threshold for conferring LDC status and the threshold for graduating a country from LDC status.

Samoa for the 2006 review. At the time of the 2006 review, Samoa continued to meet the necessary two out of three criteria. However, Samoa's EVI had declined since the previous review, primarily as a result of cyclone Heta in 2004 (UNCTAD, 2006). In July 2007, UN ECOSOC endorsed the CDP's recommendation to graduate Samoa. Therefore, Samoa will begin its three-year transition period from 1 January 2008 before graduation takes effect from 1 January 2011.

The results of Samoa's review suggest that Samoa exhibits the elements of the island paradox: while relatively prosperous in terms of its income and social performance, Samoa remains economically highly vulnerable. In discussing Samoa's vulnerability to natural disasters, a senior Samoan government official remarked that most sectors of Samoa's economy would be adversely affected if a hurricane was to strike Samoa, and this was why Samoa had argued that a 'vulnerability index' be adopted as a means of determining whether or not Samoa should graduate from LDC status.

Possible implications for Samoa from LDC graduation

LDC status can provide potential benefits to LDCs in at least three main areas: (i) trade; (ii) finance for development; and (iii) technical assistance. The following section examines the extent to which LDC graduation will impact these three policy areas.

Trade

Compared to other developing countries, LDCs have always benefited from specific advantages under the Generalised System of Preferences (GSP).[5] While the advantages provided to LDCs under GSP schemes vary by product coverage and country of origin, many countries are moving towards full duty- and quota-free access for imports from LDCs. Australia, New Zealand, Norway and Switzerland already provide this, while the EC provides duty- and quota-free access for all products originating in LDCs except military goods since 2001.[6] Therefore, as an LDC, Samoa is eligible

---

[5] The GSP allows developed countries to provide non-reciprocal tariff concessions to developing countries.

[6] Under the EC's Everything But Arms (EBA) programme, full liberalisation of sugar, rice and bananas is being phased in over the period of 2006 to 2009 depending on the product.

to receive the best preferential trade access to a number of markets.[7] This does not, however, imply that Samoa necessarily benefits from a margin of preference over non-LDC suppliers, as the Most Favoured Nation (MFN) duty may already be zero.

The loss of LDC status might have a negative impact on Samoa's export revenue as a result of either lower competitiveness and/or requirements to pay import duties. However, this may not necessarily be the case. For example, while, clearly, Samoa would cease to be eligible for access under the EC's EBA programme, Samoa's trade profile indicates that trade with the EC is very limited. In 2004, only one per cent of Samoa's exports were destined to EC markets. Thus the impact of the loss of duty- and quota-free access to the EC could be considered insignificant. Furthermore, as a member of the African, Caribbean and Pacific (ACP) group of countries, Samoa receives preferential access to the EC market via an alternative path.

Currently, the ACP and the EC are negotiating a new reciprocal trading arrangement called an Economic Partnership Agreement (EPA).[8] At the time of writing, it was not clear whether Samoa had initialled an interim EPA with the EC. According to the EC, where interim agreements had been signed, they included duty- and quota-free access to the EC market from 1 January 2008 (with short transition periods for sugar and rice). ACP countries were provided with long transition periods to phase out duties on imports from the EC as well as certain exclusions. Therefore, on the assumption that Samoa signs an EPA on the basis of duty- and quota-free access to the EC market, even if Samoa graduated from LDC status it would still be entitled to the same level of preferential access to the EC market that it currently has, albeit with a requirement to gradually liberalise Samoa's market to EC goods. Therefore, in terms of market access for Samoan goods to the EC, LDC graduation is unlikely to have significant negative consequences. In addition, the EC has committed to

---

[7] While import duties may be zero for LDCs, they are still required to respect country of origin rules and other import standards, which can make it difficult for LDCs to actually realise the potential benefits of such access. Nonetheless, such access can provide the beneficiary with a competitive advantage over their competitors, which, for a small island country with limited scope to realise economies of scale, can be a significant advantage.

[8] Although the Cotonou Agreement contains provisions through to 2020, it required a waiver from WTO members to certain WTO provisions. The EC was not prepared to request another waiver to allow the continuation of the Cotonou Agreement to be exempt from various WTO provisions. Rather, in order to avoid the need for such a waiver, the EC decided to negotiate reciprocal trade agreements with ACP countries.

providing €23 billion in development assistance to ACP countries over the next seven years.

With respect to the EPA negotiations, a senior Samoan government official noted that, from the outset, the Pacific countries had stressed the importance of putting in place a development chapter to address adjustment costs. Noting the perception that the EC had not adequately addressed this issue, and with limited trade to the EC, the official questioned how Samoa could be expected to open its market by lowering tariffs on products from the EC when Samoa hardly exports to the EC. Also, given the Pacific Agreement on Closer Economic Relations (PACER), the official noted that by lowering tariff barriers to products from the EC market, Article VI of PACER would become operational. This article specifies that free trade arrangements may be negotiated between the Forum Island Countries (FICs)[9] and Australia and New Zealand on an early timeframe should FICs begin negotiations of a free trade agreement with other developed countries.

Under the South Pacific Regional Trade and Economic Cooperation Agreement (SPARTECA), Australia and New Zealand offer duty-free and unrestricted or concessional access for virtually all products originating from the FICs. Under SPARTECA, New Zealand provides duty-free and unrestricted access to all products originating in the FICs, while Australia allows duty-free and unrestricted entry to all FIC products except for sugar. To qualify for duty-free and unrestricted or concessional access benefits, goods exported to Australia and New Zealand must meet the Rules of Origin set out in SPARTECA. Thus, even with the loss of LDC status, Samoa would retain the same relative access opportunities from which it already benefits. It is also quite possible that any new PACER agreement would extend similar market-access arrangements as with SPARTECA.

On 15 July 1998, a working party was established to oversee the accession of Samoa to the WTO, following its application for membership three months earlier. In 2003, WTO members agreed that negotiations for accession of LDCs to the WTO be facilitated and accelerated through simplified and streamlined accession procedures, with a view to concluding these negotiations as quickly as possible.[10] In this respect, members agreed to exercise restraint in seeking concessions and commitments on trade in goods and services, while transitional periods or arrangements shall be accompanied by a plan of action supported by technical assistance

---

[9] Pacific Forum countries minus Australia and New Zealand.
[10] WTO (2003), paragraph 1.

and capacity building. Moreover, targeted and coordinated technical assistance and capacity building, including under the Integrated Framework (see the section on technical assistance on p. 282), shall be provided on a priority basis.

Six years after the first meeting of the working party, questions remain as to the effectiveness of the General Council Decision. Graduation would technically imply a loss of these LDC accession provisions for Samoa. A senior Samoan official remarked that some WTO members may use the LDC graduation timeline to put more pressure on Samoa to give into their requests. However, Samoa would not rush its accession process by agreeing to all requests just to beat the LDC graduation deadline. Of the opinion that the goal posts for Samoa's accession continued to shift, the official questioned whether Samoa had been fully treated as an LDC. That said, as an interested member of Samoa's WTO accession working party, New Zealand Aid (NZAID) noted that it was the New Zealand Government's view that graduation was not expected to impact on the nature of New Zealand's bilateral negotiations with Samoa regarding the terms and conditions New Zealand would seek under the accession process.

In the case of New Zealand (and Australia) with the provision of SPARTECA and a possible future reciprocal trade agreement under PACER, there would seem little incentive to seek greater concessions from Samoa since if they were 'multilateralised' under the MFN principle, it would have the effect of eroding any future preferential access to the Samoan market over its main competitors. But in a more general sense, graduation could alter both the negotiating parameters and the dynamics of Samoa's WTO accession, though Samoa will retain LDC status for the next three years.

Despite concerns over various ongoing trade negotiations, Samoa remains committed to trade liberalisation as shown by recent trade policy changes, which have reduced import tariffs from 60% to 20%. To help businesses adjust to the evolving trade regime, the government has established a scheme to assist businesses and industries that may have been adversely affected by the reforms (Government of Samoa, 2002). In response to these changes, the Samoan Government is increasing assistance to agricultural producers to meet sanitary and phytosanitary standards in order to realise market access opportunities that will help with the development of a profitable agricultural sector. But Samoa's remoteness from major markets means that high transportation costs will remain a hurdle in the ability to be competitive.

Finance for development

Benefits in the area of finance for development typically involve voluntary commitments made by developed countries. As noted earlier, as an LDC, ODA remains an important element of the Samoan Government's ability to pursue its developmental objectives. Although donors have pledged to provide a minimum level of ODA to LDCs, it is not apparent that this would have any adverse impact on the level of ODA that Samoa receives from its main bilateral donors. Discussions with both the Australian and New Zealand aid agencies, AusAID and NZAID respectively, indicated that graduation from LDC status would not affect the way in which either country determined their aid levels for Samoa.[11] These decisions were not related to LDC status. AusAID has bilateral programmes with individual Pacific Island countries, along with a regional programme. In the case of the provision of aid to Samoa, AusAID holds regular consultations (together with New Zealand) to discuss its aid strategy, which is based on a broad range of issues. Although the issue of LDC status had come up during recent discussions, graduation would not impact on the provision of aid to Samoa from Australia.

NZAID noted that the provision of aid was guided by the OECD Development Assistance Committee (DAC). Although Samoa is listed as an LDC country under the DAC's list of countries eligible for ODA, LDC graduation would simply mean a shift to the 'other low-income countries' under the DAC list but no change in the guidelines for the provision of ODA. Several countries are included in the DAC list of ODA recipients but have never had LDC status.

Although Samoa's development strategy seeks to increase agricultural activity for local consumption and food security, commercial investment through improved and diversified farming systems and species and generating employment opportunities in the agricultural sector, agriculture does not feature as a specific element of New Zealand's development programme for Samoa. However, development of the agriculture sector could be supported indirectly as part of private-sector and tourism development. As confirmed by AusAID and NZAID, the Samoan senior government official was of the view that bilateral aid flows – past and present – to Samoa were not dependent on LDC status. Rather, aid flows tended to depend on historical ties with the developed donors as well

---

[11] Australia and New Zealand have adopted a joint development strategy for Samoa in order to provide a more harmonised donor programme. The joint strategy is based on Samoa's own development strategy.

as the groupings Samoa identifies with (e.g. the Pacific Forum and the Commonwealth).

However, according to senior Samoan officials, LDC status allows Samoa to receive concessional interest-rate loans from international financial institutions such as the World Bank, the International Monetary Fund (IMF) and the ADB. As nearly all of the loan funds needed for development projects, particularly for infrastructure and agriculture, have been sourced from the World Bank and the ADB, any loss of LDC status could negatively effect Samoa's ability to maintain present concessionary terms, and thus could potentially limit the level of funding it would obtain for future development projects. If Samoa's loan conditions become less favourable, potential funding could be restricted and the place of agriculture in Samoa's development priorities altered.

Technical assistance

A key aspect of technical assistance for LDCs is provided through the Integrated Framework (IF) for Trade-Related Technical Assistance to LDCs. The IF aims to improve the capacity of LDCs to formulate, negotiate and implement trade policy so as to be able to fully integrate into the multilateral trading system. Six multilateral agencies – the IMF, the International Trade Centre, UNCTAD, the United Nations Development Programme, the World Bank and the WTO – offered support (WTO, 2006).

The IF has since been enhanced with an aim of maximising the benefits LDCs can derive from the technical assistance provided by the cooperating institutions. The IF has two main objectives: (i) to mainstream trade into national development plans; and (ii) to facilitate the coordinated delivery of trade-related assistance, thereby assisting LDCs to address their supply-side constraints and more generally become active players and beneficiaries in the world trading system.

Samoa is already an IF beneficiary country, having started the process of preparing its Diagnostic Trade Integration Study (DTIS) to identify areas where Samoa needs to build trade capacity through the identification of constraints to traders, for example sectors of greatest export potential. Once the DTIS is completed, the findings will be elaborated through an action matrix to fund priority projects (see the IF website: www.integratedframework.org [last accessed 22 February 2009]). Despite being a facility for LDCs, as an existing beneficiary member of the IF it is expected that graduation will have no impact on Samoa's ability to use the IF.

The Samoan senior government official commented that overseas training missions and meeting attendance, for example, were fully funded by multilateral institutions, and such opportunities could reduce as a result of graduation. This would reduce Samoa's ability to fully benefit from such technical assistance opportunities or participate in international meetings.

Conclusion

As a nation on the verge of graduating from LDC status, Samoa should celebrate its success in increasing its level of development and prosperity. However, it remains profoundly aware of its vulnerability to external shocks outside of its control, particularly the damaging forces of tropical cyclones. Samoa clearly demonstrates the features of a so-called 'island paradox': relatively prosperous through its income and social performance while remaining economically highly vulnerable. Indeed, most of Samoa's key economic sectors – agriculture, fishing and increasingly tourism – are vulnerable to significant disruption from natural disasters. Disruption to these sectors alone has the potential to set back Samoa's developmental objectives several years.

But Samoa's vulnerability to external economic and natural shocks will remain irrespective of graduation, and therefore the key question regarding LDC graduation is to what extent graduation will negatively impact on Samoa and its agricultural and trade policy.

With a large proportion of the population engaged in the agriculture sector, it is unsurprising that Samoa views development of the sector as an important part of government policy. It is apparent that the government is putting a significant level of resources into assisting with the development of the agricultural sector, including through efforts to increase productivity and employment and realise the opportunities presented through trade and market-access opportunities. But the Samoan Government relies not only on ODA to assist with these policy objectives, but also on concessional financing provided by international financial institutions such as the World Bank and ADB. Although graduation is not expected to change the conditions of aid from two of Samoa's largest bilateral donors, the same cannot necessarily be said for international financial institutions. A potential rise in the cost of borrowing or a reduction in the level of financing could have implications for Samoa's ability to continue to assist with the development of the agricultural sector. Given that the impact of a severe cyclone could reduce Samoa's ability to fund necessary reconstruction and set back the development of the sector many years, Samoa should make strategic decisions about funding and investments that would allow it to build up its capacity to withstand shocks.

One approach could be to increase options for crop insurance, which would provide a buffer for agricultural producers in the face of risks associated with extreme events. By buying insurance, farmers could smooth out uncertain production levels due to climatic variation. This type of insurance would also be important in the event that, as expected, climate change exacerbates unpredictability of climate. Typically, private-sector insurers are able to provide insurance efficiently and effectively if the variation between good and bad years is not too large. There could be a role for the Samoan Government to develop an insurance programme, given the extreme nature of cyclone events; however, the government would need to guard against pricing insurance premiums at levels that do not accurately reflect the risks. Low premiums can distort the incentive of farmers to cultivate particular crops or cultivate in particular areas.

Samoa could also direct available funding to the development of physical infrastructure for ports, telecommunications and roads that would be less vulnerable to the impact of a cyclone. In the mid 2000s, the World Bank implemented an Infrastructure Emergency Recovery Project, which included three main components:

(1) the repair and improvement of seawalls, renourishment of beaches and restoration of the lagoon and reef systems in shoreline areas damaged or threatened by erosion
(2) road rehabilitation or reconstruction, including drainage improvement in affected areas
(3) implementation support through specialist consulting services for the investigation, design, justification and supervision of the recovery of coastal protection measures.

Investments in these areas have increased the resilience of infrastructure assets against natural hazards. However, sustained investments are needed, albeit at lower levels than those immediately following a cyclone, to ensure that infrastructure capacity does not erode over time.

In other areas such as trade and technical assistance, the implications of graduation are less pronounced. The impact on existing market-access arrangements is likely to be negligible with its main trading partners. Though Samoa is likely to be required to open up its own market to competition via various means (e.g. EC–ACP EPA negotiations, WTO accession), it is worth bearing in mind that the size of the Samoan economy and its remoteness from major international ports is likely to have a bearing on the attractiveness of Samoa as an export destination. Although one study estimates that Samoa could lose up to US$10 million annually in lost tariff revenue under a PACER agreement, because of the nature of the negotiations, such losses can not be attributed to LDC status. That said, Samoa has already committed to tax reform and the expansion of services, which in time will significantly offset any loss of import revenue. As a beneficiary of the IF for LDCs, Samoa is likely to retain trade-related capacity-building benefits after graduation because it has already started its process of developing an action plan to serve as the basis for trade-related technical-assistance delivery.

Despite its vulnerability, over the past decade Samoa has increased its competitiveness and productivity through targeted reforms. While Samoa is unlikely in the near future to dramatically alter the sectoral composition of its economy, the government can develop targeted policies to enhance the contribution of agriculture, tourism and remittances to economic growth. To remain on this progressive path, it will need to continue to focus on strategic diversification of agriculture in order to capitalise on new and emerging market opportunities. In addition, given Samoa's island setting, tourism will continue to play an important role in Samoa's economy. With investments to reduce the risk of infrastructural damage and measures to protect the natural reef environment from extreme climatic events, Samoa could further develop the tourism sector as a source of economic growth. With respect to remittances, new technologies can help reduce the cost and reinforce the security of international transfers. The government could encourage banks to develop services relating to remittances, life and health insurance, and education of children to future immigrants. These types of social policies would enhance the flow of resources to Samoa's economy from abroad and would contribute to economic growth.

Samoa has made substantial progress in achieving economic development goals, and with continued reforms can move farther out of poverty.

However, it will need strong, reliable support from external donors in order to continue this reform – particularly if it does graduate from LDC status. The sustained access to concessional loans and ongoing support for capacity building will enable Samoa to foster resilience to climatic shocks and to support flexibility and innovation in the agricultural sector.

References

Abbott, D. and Pollard, S. (2004), *Hardship and Poverty in the Pacific*, Asian Development Bank, Pacific Department: Manila.

Asian Development Bank (2007), *Key Indicators (of Developing Asia and Pacific Countries)*, Asian Development Bank: Manila.

Economist Intelligence Unit (2007), *Country Profile of Samoa*, Economist Intelligence Unit: London.

Government of Australia, New Zealand and Samoa (2006), *Joint Samoa Program Strategy 2006–2010*.

Government of Samoa (2002), *Samoa's First Report on the Implementation of the Brussels Program of Action for Least-Developed Countries*, United Nations: New York, NY.

(2006), *5 Year Report on the Implementation of the Brussels Program of Action for Least-Developed Countries*, United Nations: New York, NY.

OECD (2007), *Geographical Distribution of Financial Flows to Aid Recipients 2001–2005*, OECD Development Assistance Committee: Paris.

UNCTAD (2006), *Vulnerability Profile of Samoa*, UNCTAD: Geneva.

World Bank (2007), *World Development Indicators 2007*, World Bank: Washington, WA.

WTO (2003), *General Council Decision, Accession of Least-Developed Countries* (WT/L/508).

(2006), *An Enhanced Integrated Framework – Report of the Chairman of the Task Force on an Enhanced Integrated Framework, Including Recommendations* (WT/IFSC/W/15).

Bali's ornamental fishing industry

LYDIA NAPITUPULU*

Background

Aquarium fish, corals and other biota (collectively known as 'ornamentals') are traded internationally. Between 1.5 to 2 million people worldwide are estimated to keep marine aquaria, an industry worth US$200 to $330 million annually. An estimated 20 to 24 million individual fish, 11 to 12 million coral pieces and 9 to 10 million individual invertebrates were traded on this market in the early 2000s. In total, this trade encompasses more than 1,000 species. Fishermen in Southeast Asian countries, including Indonesia, are the main source of this supply (Wabnitz *et al.*, 2005).

An archipelago spanning about 85,000 km of coastline, Indonesia has the world's largest coral reef system, straddling an estimated 50,000 km^2, or around 18 per cent of the world's total reef resources – the habitat of marine ornamental species (Reefcheck, 2005). Unsurprisingly, Indonesia is the second largest exporter of ornamental fish (by number of fish exported – second only to the Philippines), and was the largest exporter of ornamental corals and ornamental invertebrates in 2001.[1] It has been estimated that Indonesia can sustainably supply 60 per cent of the total world demand of ornamental fish (Bruckner, 2001).

In Indonesia, ornamental fish trading is concentrated in Jakarta and Bali. Direct flights from these cities carry fish and other biota to destinations in North America and Europe (TICR Foundation, 2006). Bali is the largest exporting port for ornamental fish. There is a large concentration of exporters, numbering between thirty and sixty outfits, half of which are registered in Bali and the other half in branch offices. In 2005,

---

* Lydia Napitupulu is a Research Fellow in the Faculty of Economics at the University of Indonesia.
[1] Reporting of volume for live ornamental fish is less relevant since packaging and water make up the bulk of the volume/weight of fish destined for export.

ornamental fish was one of the top ten exports of Bali, worth US$5.1 million in value, up more than thirty fold from US$16.3 million in 1997. The trend, however, has fluctuated, and exports (in terms of value) have not reached their 2000 peak of US$5.8 million[2] (see Table 2P).

In response to the rapidly growing international demand for ornamental fish, unsustainable practices have sprung up, including the use of poisons such as cyanide, a particularly effective technique for capturing live reef fish. Cyanide is used in the form of pellets or, more commonly, in liquid form placed in bottles. Target species exposed to cyanide are temporarily stunned and easily captured. These techniques began in the 1960s in the Philippines in order to supply the growing market for ornamental fish; later, fisherman also used these methods to capture live reef food fish (LRFF) destined for restaurants in Hong Kong and other Asian cities (Bryant et al., 1998).

In the early 1980s, Filipino fishermen in North Sulawesi introduced the use of cyanide to capture ornamental fish to fishermen in Indonesia. By the late 1980s, the method had spread widely to other parts of Indonesia, not only to capture live ornamental fish but also LRFF (such as groupers and Napoleon wrasses) and rock lobsters (Pet-Soede and Erdmann, 1998). In the mid 1990s, it was estimated that 90% of vessels transporting live fish in eastern Indonesia had cyanide on board, and that 80% of ornamental fish caught in Indonesia were caught by cyanide (Pet-Soede and Erdmann, 1998). While the social costs are high, the use of cyanide to capture ornamental fish yields significant benefits to operators. Typically, the initial 'invasion' is led by large cyanide catcher-boats, financed by well-capitalised and connected firms. These boats take large amounts of fish and cause major damage to local reef ecosystems. As fish stocks dwindle and return on capital declines, they move on to new untapped areas (Pet-Soede and Erdmann, 1998; Bentley, 1999).

The negative environmental impacts of cyanide use include over-exploitation of the fisheries and the physical destruction of reef structures. Over-exploitation results from intensive harvesting of certain species, including direct targeting of spawning sites, and from the (unnecessary) impacts on other non-target species in the vicinity (Mous et al., 2000).

---

[2] Note that these numbers are obtained from reports by wholesale exporters and grossly underestimate the volume of trade since only a fifth of all wholesalers operating globally contributed to the statistics for 2001 (Wabnitz et al. (2005).

Table 2P *Ornamental fish exports from Bali (1997–2005)*

Description	1997	1998	1999	2000	2001	2002	2003	2004	2005
Marine ornamentals	162,701	6,377	3,041,836	5,818,203	5,270,065	4,979,583	5,238,521	4,015,449	5,071,000
As percentage of total primary commodity (%)	0.17	0.01	3.64	5.85	5.59	5.77	6.64	4.53	–
Total primary commodity	95,037,554	43,735,923	83,672,867	99,430,460	94,261,395	86,295,625	78,917,041	88,724,742	–

Source: BPS 2006.

Additionally, since high mortality is inevitable among a catch of live reef fish (mortality rates estimated at 80% for ornamental fish and 50% for LRFF), fishermen collect even more specimens to fulfil demand.

Exposure to cyanide also kills corals, leading to physical destruction of reef structures. In Indonesia, fishermen work in teams, bringing about two to five litres of cyanide on each fishing trip; each squirt (20 cc) can kill 25 m^2 of corals within three to six months, leading to a loss of live coral cover at a rate of 5 to 6 per cent per 100 m^2 of reef per year (Mous *et al.*, 2000; Bryant *et al.*, 1998). The loss of coral reef structures also means the loss of the services they provide, for example shoreline protection, habitat and spawning grounds and other ecological services (see Moberg and Folke (1999) for a discussion of the economic benefits of coral reefs).

A 1996 World Bank study estimated that cyanide fishing in Indonesia yielded a net present private benefit of about US$40,870 per km^2 a year over a period of twenty-five years, while generating losses of double that amount in lost tourism and deteriorated fisheries (Cesar, 1996). A more recent study found that cyanide fishing and coral collecting generate environmental costs that are almost ten times their benefits (Fahrudin, 2003).

Over the last few decades, the condition of Indonesian reefs has reflected these growing threats, including the threat from cyanide fishing methods. More than 70% of reefs have been rated 'fair' and 'poor', and less than 7% were described as being in 'excellent' condition, in 2003 (Ministry of the Environment, 2006).

Faced with the continued growth of the ornamental fish market and the spreading of cyanide fishing techniques, the Indonesian Government, non-governmental organisations (NGOs) and other stakeholders have developed regulatory, institutional and livelihood measures directed at creating a more sustainable ornamental fish industry.

Current trade agreements and/or trade-related poverty reduction policies affecting the sector

Harvesting has led to over-fishing and the destruction of habitats in the marine ornamental fisheries of Indonesia, generating large social costs. Domestic attempts at correcting these market failures include raising awareness of non-sustainable fishing practices; institutional and regulatory fishery reform; community capacity building and promotion of alternative livelihoods; and trade facilitation/expansion. There have been fewer international measures, those including measures under the Convention on International Trade in Endangered Species of Wild Fauna and Flora (CITES) and the development of industry standards. Importing countries also implement phytosanitary measures for the importation of marine ornamentals.

Domestic measures

Awareness raising

The Asian financial crisis from 1997 to 1998 depreciated Indonesian currency and increased the profitability of the export market (see Table 2P on p. 290). As a result, exporters became more aggressive at sourcing products from local fishermen. The author observed first hand, in the Riau Islands on the western part of Indonesia in 1998, a holding net in the middle of the sea where fishermen could sell their catch, for pick up by boats coming directly from Singapore. During this time, Indonesian fishermen responded to changing market forces and increased demand by rapidly adopting new fishing methods, i.e. the cyanide fishing mentioned above. Fishermen increasingly targeted spawning aggregations since enforcement of the regulations had decreased due to a lack of funding for the enforcement agencies (Pet-Soede and Erdmann, 1998).

Around this time, the Government of Indonesia implemented a large-scale programme for coral reef conservation and management (called Coremap) funded by loans from multilateral agencies. This programme included national awareness-raising campaigns about coral reefs and the threats facing them. Similar efforts were also made at subnational levels, spearheaded by bilaterally funded projects and NGOs.

Institutional and regulatory reform

Before 1999, the responsibility for coastal and marine resources in Indonesia was fragmented between different ministries (e.g. fisheries were under the Ministry of Agriculture and marine/coastal conservation under the Ministry of Forestry). The creation in 1999 of a ministry specifically responsible for Indonesia's coastal and marine resources has been hailed as a 'true watershed' for enhanced fisheries management in Indonesia (Dutton, 2005). The Ministry drafted several bills, including a bill on fisheries, which was finally adopted in 2004 (Law No. 31 on Fisheries), replacing a 1985 law. The new law declared destructive fishing methods, including the use of cyanide, illegal; prohibited inter-ship transfer at sea; and set out harsher punishments for the financiers of illegal activities as opposed to the boat crew.

Another set of watershed regulatory reforms was the 'big bang' decentralisation of Indonesia, where authority and responsibility for many public functions were devolved from the central government to the local government (i.e. to the provincial and municipality/district) level, including responsibility for and jurisdiction over natural resource management (see Patlis (2005) for a discussion).

Community access to natural resources

In parallel with the spirit of decentralisation and political reform, the property-rights systems of poor communities for resources have also improved. Recognition and efforts at strengthening those rights have occurred at the local level (e.g. community consultations on zonation and the development of alternative livelihood options), regional level (e.g. recognition of traditional rights) and at the national level (e.g. rights to natural resources and the environment as a form of basic need in Indonesia's national Poverty Reduction Strategy Papers (PRSP)) (Fox *et al.*, 2005; UNEP, 2006).

Market expansion

Indonesia exports a large volume of ornamental fish. Nevertheless, with less than 8% of global market share in terms of value, it is still far behind Singapore, whose exports account for about 23% of the global market. Singapore imports 90% of its ornamental fish from Indonesia and there is no export tax for ornamental fish. For species not protected under CITES (see below), exporting involves only the provision of sample specimens for inspection at designated fish quarantine stations.

The Government of Indonesia has invested in a large-scale holding facility located close the Indonesian capital, Jakarta. The main purpose of the facility is to provide a more dependable supply of ornamental fish, in terms of quality, quantity and price, and thus to act as a buffer between small-scale local suppliers and the international market. The facility can stock up to 26 million individual ornamentals per month, and mostly sources fish bred in captivity, with only about 10 per cent comprised of fish caught in the wild. The premises also houses quarantine and research facilities (Ministry of Marine Affairs and Fisheries, 2004).

International and bilateral measures
CITES

The Convention on International Trade in Endangered Species of Wild Fauna and Flora (CITES) is a multilateral environmental agreement administered by the United Nations Environment Programme (UNEP), to which Indonesia is a signatory. CITES works by subjecting international trade in select species to certain control and licensing systems. Species are categorised into three groups (or 'appendixes'); Appendixes I and II are, respectively, species threatened with extinction and species not endangered but which may become so if trade is not regulated. Some species in the Syngnathidae family (pipefish and seahorses) are included in these categories (Sadovy, 2003). Appendix III contains species that are protected in at least one country (which has asked other CITES parties to assist in controlling their trade). Seventy species of wild coral and sixty-one species of cultured corals are listed in Appendix III. Three ornamental stony corals (also termed 'coral rocks'), both wild and cultured, are included in this category, and quotas are in place for these.

Industry standards

The Marine Aquarium Council (MAC) began developing industry standards for the ornamental fish industry in the early 2000s, and it is currently the only system in place for ornamental fish. The standard – a type of 'eco-label' – is intended to promote the sustainable production of good quality fish, addressing all activities along the supply chain, including the condition of the habitat, capture of fish, transport and handling and culture activities (see the Marine Aquarium Council website for more details – www.aquariumcouncil.org [last accessed 22 February 2009]).

Import measures

National requirements for the importation of marine ornamental fish differ among countries. The US, as the largest importer of Indonesian marine ornamentals, does not impose import tariffs on live fish, and only fairly recently implemented import permit requirements for freshwater

ornamental fish, mainly to guard against disease (US Department of
Agriculture, 2006). Similar phytosanitary measures are in place for the
importation of live ornamental fish to the European Community.

The ornamental fishery of a small Balinese hamlet: Minabakti Soansari Fishing Group

The evolution of the fishing group Minabakti Soansari reflects the dynamics of the marine ornamental fisheries sector in Bali.

Initial condition

The province of Bali had a population of about 3.4 million people in 2006,
with an average population growth between the years 2000 and 2005 of
less than 1% (0.86% to be exact). The regional gross domestic product
(GDP) per capita in 2006 was US$1,136,[3] slightly lower than the national
GDP per capita of US$1,345. Fisheries comprise 3.27% of the regional
GDP. About one-third of the working population (34%) is employed in
the agricultural sector. The unemployment rate is relatively low, at 5.32%
in 2006 (compared to the national average of 10.45%), and only about 7%
of the population can be categorised as 'poor' (as opposed to the national
average of 17%) (BPS, 2006).

Buleleng Regency is located on the northern coast of the Bali Island. It
has a reputation for being one of the poorer amongst Bali's nine regen-
cies/municipalities. In 2005, its per capita GDP was US$763, the second
lowest in Bali (Statistics Indonesia, 2006).

Les Village lies in the Tejakula subdistrict of Buleleng, about 90 km
north of Denpasar, the capital. It has a population of more than 7,000,
about 1,500 of whom work as fishermen, either full time (around 60%) or
part time. Its coastline is about 2 km long. More than 650 boats have been
registered in Tejakula, but only three have in-board engines; the others
are non-engine and out-board powered boats. Les Village has seventy-five
households, mostly involved in catching ornamentals.

Aquarium fishing as a means of livelihood began in the early 1980s when
fishermen from Les Village started to catch aquarium fish to supplement
their income from pelagic fish and octopuses. During these early years,
Les Village fishermen had used nets before being introduced to cyanide

[3] US$ worked out at an exchange rate of Rp 8,828 per US$1 (Bank of Indonesia middle rate as of 31 May 2007).

to capture fish. The role of the local leader, in this case the village chief, was instrumental in introducing the new, more 'efficient', technology for capturing ornamentals. Fishermen were taught to dive to depths of eight to ten metres to squirt cyanide on a localised area of the reef to stun fish hiding inside. The fish lost consciousness and were then easy to collect.

Ornamentals have taken over as the main source of livelihood in Tejakula. The switch from pelagic fishery to ornamental fishing was due partly to the over-fishing situation in northern Bali, making it harder for fishermen to catch enough fish, and partly due to the higher returns available from the new trade. Beginning as a sideline, ornamental fishing soon attracted most fishermen at Les Village as a full-time activity. In 1982, there was only a single local collector with three to five fishermen working under him in Tejakula. This grew to two collectors and twenty-six fishermen by 1986. By 1990, there were twelve local collectors employing 200 fishermen and boats with fifteen tonnes of capacity able to travel to off-shore waters.

Over the years, however, it became apparent that there were serious problems associated with the use of cyanide for capturing ornamentals. A typical fisherman would use up to 50 g of cyanide a day, with up to 2.5 kg of the poison used by a fishing group during each trip, enough to destroy 1,250 m^2 of reef. The coral reefs close to the village began dying off, and were soon destroyed completely. The numbers of fish and types of species were dwindling, and some species could no longer be found. Fishermen soon had to travel further and further away to catch enough fish of good value,[4] even as far away as Sulawesi and Kalimantan. Even though they had to travel further, incurring higher costs, the volume of catch was not significantly higher.

In addition to being harmful, the new method was revealed to actually be economically inefficient. With cyanide use, between 5 and 75% of fish caught die within hours of capture, and between 20 and 50% in the following hours. Importers in the US reported that 30 to 50% of aquarium fish imported from Southeast Asia die shortly after arrival (Mous et al., 2000). Only 50% of all fish caught this way could be expected to reach the exporter, and only 40% were expected to be sold to the final consumers.

---

[4] Some of the long-distance travel can be explained by bigger boats and more equipment being used, hence more fish needed to be caught to obtain a profit.

It was also apparent that the new fishing method caused serious health risks. The harvesting of ornamentals was aided by surface air being pumped through a hose to the diving fishermen. Since air compressors are expensive, many fishermen used large inflated tyres to store their air supply. This was risky because the fishermen were prone to decompression sickness, leading to light deafness, complete paralysis or even death.[5]

There were also social consequences associated with the use of cyanide, especially as stricter law enforcement began. Cyanide fishermen were routinely apprehended by law enforcement agencies, necessitating bribes or even jail time. As tourism gained a foothold in those parts of the island, fishermen were increasingly in conflict with tourist operators and resorts.

Transformation of the fishery

After conducting an investigative assessment of destructive fishing practices in all of the coastal villages in Bali, a group of concerned individuals formed the Bahtera Nusantara Foundation (Bahtera) with the idea of introducing more sustainable fishing practices to fishing communities. Bahtera first introduced the idea of catching ornamentals using nets to the fishermen of Les Village in 2001, coupled with improvements in the handling and transporting of fish. Fishermen were receptive to the offer and, over time, Bahtera and the fishermen of Les Village, with the support of volunteers and some international donors, have improved fishing, handling and transportation methods and have initiated activities to take advantage of opportunities for coral culture and tourism.

Foremost, the group has demonstrated that using nets does not reduce the number of fish caught. In fact, all varieties, even the most difficult to catch, proved catchable. Soon cyanide was completely eliminated from use in the village, and the reefs started to improve. Villagers were also taught how to dive more safely using decompression techniques. Fish handling improved and therefore mortality rates and the associated waste were

---

[5] A former cyanide fisher based in Gilimanuk at the western end of Bali admitted he lost twenty-seven men to this form of harvesting in a period of two years.

minimised, and fishermen's incomes were maximised. One study indicated that a reduction of 5% mortality can improve fishermen's revenues by 25% (Schmidt and Kunzman, 2005).[6]

Given these successes in transforming the harvesting process, Bahtera and the fishermen later formed a limited liability company. The company is professionally managed and has come up with an additional innovative business expansion, known as coral culture. Initially, coral culture was undertaken to both rehabilitate the reefs as well as provide additional revenues. Over time, their labour-intensive mode of coral 'breeding' attracted the attention of the private sector, which initiated an 'adopt-a-coral' programme to help finance breeding and rehabilitation expansion. This novel technique has attracted tourists. Some dive operators and resorts have developed dive packages especially for the site, providing additional income for the group.

Women in the village have also benefited from transformation to a 'business' model. Fishing groups now undertake more handling and maintenance of fish caught (instead of handing fish directly to local buyers when they reach the shore). Handling and maintenance of fish is labour-intensive work, and women have taken over portions of it, such as the routine changing of water. Increased numbers of visitors have also created income-generating opportunities for women who can earn money from providing food and refreshments to visitors.

Improvement in the economics of fish harvesting has also followed, after some years, by improvement in the village's coral reef ecosystem. It may still take a few years before coral cover significantly improves; however, currently more than 200 species of fish can be seen in the waters off Les Village, including cardinal fishes, damsel fishes, angel fishes, wrasses and blennies. One fish that disappeared for a period after 1985, the blue-ringed surgeon fish, has made a comeback, with a current population standing in the thousands.

The success of Les Village fishermen has also enhanced their social standing. National senior officials and international dignitaries often visit the area to observe this success story. Given that this community was previously a local embarrassment, the new social standing is a dramatic improvement.

---

[6] Using a sample of fish shipments from East Java, South Sulawesi and Bali, Schmidt and Kunzmann (2005) showed that the reason behind the high level of mortality, despite good holding facilities, is that many fish and biotas are not suitable for the ornamental fish trade.

Effective trade policy strategies and trade capacity-building measures for poverty reduction in the future for the sector

Despite Indonesia's importance in the global marine ornamentals trade, participation in this industry has not significantly improved the plight of fishermen. Moreover, environmental degradation caused by destructive fishing methods is threatening fishermen's livelihoods and wellbeing in the long term. There are some who conclude that cyanide use will persist given the open-access nature of fishing grounds, increasingly fierce competition amongst fishermen, weak law enforcement and a lack of technical capacity to evolve. Ornamental fishermen operating in northern Bali seem to concur with these conclusions.

Domestic measures

Firstly, the opportunity cost of *not* engaging in cyanide fishing is high, since others are very ready to engage. Some fishermen operating in the vicinity of the West Bali National Park, for example, readily admit to still using cyanide, indicating that others also do so. Some fishermen who say that they do not use cyanide nevertheless indicate that cyanide use is still rampant, mostly blaming other fishing groups (e.g. from a neighbouring village, from other ethnic groups, etc.).

In addition to the environmental externalities associated with using cyanide as a harvesting technique, there is also the problem of agency failure. Surveillance and control procedures are lacking, and (surveillance) personnel carry out their functions according to their own interests rather than according to the interest of the public (Weimer and Vining, 1999). Fishermen in a small fishing community in Bangsring Village, East Java, notorious for widely practicing cyanide fishing, always carry cellular telephones with them, since they have made arrangements with officials patrolling the north-western coast of Bali whereby they will be given advance notice of patrolling activities (Napitupulu, 2006).

Secondly, there are barriers to technical skills, as information on better fish-handling and transportation and alternative methods of fishing are scarce. One fisherman in East Java was very enthusiastic about the 'alternative' methods being implemented in Bali. He does not have the means, however, to seek out the information himself. Thus far the proponents of sustainable harvesting techniques have been small NGOs who also lack the resources to undertake large-scale interventions.

Table 2Q   *Prices at various levels of the ornamental fish supply chain*

	Price at various points of the supply chain (Rp)				
Type of fish	Fisher	Local collector(s)	Exporter	Importer	Retail at country of destination
Butterfly fish	100–1,200	150–5,000	4,400–88,280	25,000	63,000
WWF	50–350	750	132,420–264,840		
CCIF	1,000	2,000	7,200	40,000	94,000

Source: Mous *et al.*, 2000.

Thirdly, trade facilitation measures have, to date, focused on the exporting end of the supply chain rather than the harvesting, handling and transportation of fish at the fishermen's end. At the fishermen's end, there is abundant supply, a limited number of buyers and symmetric information, so fishermen have weak bargaining powers. Between the fishermen and the exporter, there could be several chains of custody (local and regional traders), and fishermen receive only a small fraction of the price at the exporter or retailer end of the chain, as shown in Table 2Q for the commonly traded Butterfly fish and Clownfish. It is not surprising, then, that fishermen feel disconnected from government planning and programmes. If fishermen could earn a higher proportion of the ornamentals' value-addition, then there would be more incentive to ensure the long-term viability of the resource stock.

Fourthly, government programmes in research and development have continued to focus on freshwater ornamental fish rather than marine ornamentals, and on food reef fish (e.g. groupers). For example, some seahorse species can be cultured, but such technology has never been disseminated to the fishermen (Ministry of Marine Affairs and Fisheries, 2004). Another market to be tapped into is that of live coral, and coral breeding would be a sustainable option, as demonstrated by the fishermen at Les Village. The primary limitation for coral breeding is the length of time it takes for the coral to reach a size suitable for trading (between six months and three years); thus far, however, fishermen have not had any assistance in this matter.

Lastly, many local governments have used regional autonomy as an opportunity to raise revenues for the local budget through a convoluted set of regional fees and taxes, which vary across regions, making it more

Table 2R   *Trend in reported fish export (2005–2007)*

Year	Number of fish	Value (US$)	Average value per fish (US$)
2005	12,972,982	4,701,734.98	0.36
2006	5,204,156	1,941,530.70	0.37
2007 up to May	1,545,105	613,183.25	0.40

Source: Bali Fishery Service, various years.

complex and costly for collectors and exporters. This is in addition to 'informal' taxes (e.g. security fees and bribery) already being collected (Fahrudin, 2003). One exporter is even considering getting out of the business altogether because she finds it hard to compete in the international market. The consequence of this situation is unclear, but there is at least one possible outcome: that Indonesian collectors and exporters may need to reduce the prices offered to fishermen to make up for the higher costs, and, in turn, fishermen will prefer to sell directly to buyers at sea (through inter-ship transfer) who will be able to offer higher prices and who do not export through formal channels (and therefore do not pay local fees and taxes). Data from the Bali quarantine stations (self-reported by exporters in order to determine the number of specimens they need to submit for quarantine) indicate a large decrease in the number of fish exported between 2005 and 2007 (see Table 2R).

The consequences of depressed prices at the fishermen's level are unclear. A limited engagement of these fishermen in the international market due to their lack of competitiveness may be good for the environment. Nevertheless, in the short term, ornamental fishermen will suffer a reduction in income, with the potential for negative effects on the environment.

International measures

The impact of international measures on inducing more sustainable harvesting have been nominal at best, and so far have not contributed to a significant improvement in the long-term welfare of fishermen. Firstly, the number of species being monitored and controlled through CITES is very small, and implementation is lagging. For example, even though

Table 2S   *Export of ornamental fish from January to May 2007*

Month	All exporters			Three MAC-certified exporters		
	Number of fish	US$	Value per fish (US$)	Number of fish	US$	Value per fish (US$)
January	231,220	94,533	0.41	96,850	17,883	0.18
February	393,835	138,700	0.35	95,160	17,903	0.19
March	282,155	115,483	0.41	52,800	11,423	0.22
April	327,905	127,650	0.39	94,025	15,981	0.17
May	309,990	136,817	0.44	58,320	17,915	0.31
Total	1,545,105	613,183	0.40	397,155	81,105	0.20
Certified exporters as percentage of total exporters (%)				*26*	*13*	*50*

Source: author's calculation from quarantine self-reporting data.

trade in seahorses is restricted, reported imports are relatively large (Wabnitz *et al.*, 2005). Quotas have curbed official exports of coral species and created incentives for coral breeding; however, they have not altered the highly unsustainable way that corals are harvested from the sea.[7]

Secondly, industry standards have so far been limited in scope, and judging from the experience of the eco-labelling of timber products and other agricultural commodities (e.g. organic, bird-friendly, fair trade, etc.), the desired large-scale impact may be a long time coming, if at all. It should be noted that industry standards have only been operational since the early 2000s.

From the fishermen's point of view, however, the main weakness of the industry standards has been the lack of price premium that can be earned from enrolling in these programmes. In early 2007, several Indonesian exporting agencies were certified by MAC. Three of those companies regularly export through Bali, and have tabulated the information they provided for quarantine purposes (see Table 2S, above). The average value per individual ornamental fish for the certified exporters is actually about half of the average for all exporters for the first five months of 2007.

---

[7] One estimate indicates that the removal of 10 cm^2 of coral leads to damage of 100 cm^2 (Mous *et al.*, 2000).

Other measures

In general, tariff and non-tariff barriers are lacking for the marine ornamental fish trade, which, given the large-scale negative externalities the industry is causing, may not be optimal. Given that exporters are already incurring large fees, it is fairly unlikely that export tariffs would be supported. However, a range of sanitary and phytosanitary (SPS)[8] measures in the form of more stringent inspection for traces of cyanide residues, combined with an expansion of the quota system, seems to be warranted.

Fishermen at Les Village indicated that some type of phytosanitary measures should be in place both in the importing as well as exporting countries, as a way of providing incentives for other fishermen to switch to sustainable harvesting measures. However, given widespread collusion and corruption, they are also sceptical of such measures being well implemented in Indonesia.

Precedents for technical barriers to the trading of environmentally harmful commodities are well known. Such measures aimed at the marine fishery of Indonesia include SPS measures against Indonesian shrimp exports (for its antibiotics content) and the suspension of Indonesian tuna exports to the US for inadequate installation of by-catch exclusion devices.

Conclusion

International trade in marine ornamental species is important for small-scale coastal fishermen in Indonesia, and large volumes are being harvested to meet the demand. However, harvesting methods continue to include the use of cyanide, a method that is highly destructive, leading both to over-fishing and the loss of ecological conservation in the reef's ecosystem.

This case study has focused on one community of fishermen that has successfully made the transition into sustainable harvesting and breeding of marine ornamentals. A similar transition has not, however, been forthcoming in other communities. Fishermen point to entrenched systemic barriers to such transformation. Domestic market and agency failure, the nature of international trade in marine ornamentals and the limited impact of international measures to promote more sustainable harvesting

---

[8] Sanitary and phytosanitary measures are aimed at ensuring food is safe for consumers, and to prevent the spread of pests and diseases among animals and plants.

have also contributed to the continued use of unsustainable harvesting practices.

Domestic (national and subnational) measures aimed at curbing cyanide fishing are largely ineffective because surveillance and controls are lacking and there are insufficient disincentives to the use of cyanide. The current trading system places fishermen at a disadvantage because they bear a disproportionate percentage of the risks associated with fishing for ornamentals (e.g. health and safety risks and risks from livelihood impacts of degraded reef resources) while others in the supply chain reap most of the benefits. Government facilitation of poverty alleviation and market expansion has focused less on the fishermen's needs and more on the needs of the bureaucracy and the exporters.

International trade in marine ornamentals is very liberal, with almost non-existent barriers to trade, either tariff or non-tariff, in place. To date, the impact of CITES and of international standards on methods of harvesting marine ornamentals has been negligible. Even the limited industry standards that do exist do not enable certified producers to reap any price premiums. Such measures could, however, be developed to be more effective in the future. In addition, there may be scope for the effective use of SPS standards – for example stricter inspections for traces of cyanide residue – to induce more sustainable harvesting.

References

Bentley, N. (1999), *Fishing for Solutions: Can the Live Trade in Wild Groupers and Wrasses from Southeast Asia be Managed?*, TRAFFIC Southeast Asia: Petaling Jaya, Malaysia.

BPS (2006), *Statistics of Bali Province, Bali in Figures*, BPS: Denpasar.

Bruckner, A. W. (2001), *Proceedings of the International Workshop on the Trade in Stony Corals: Development of Sustainable Management Guidelines*, NOAA: Jakarta.

Bryant, D., Burke, L., McManus, J. and Spalding, M. (1998), *Reefs At Risk: A Map-based Indicator of Threats to the World's Coral Reefs*, World Resources Institute, Washington, WA.

Cesar, H. (1996), *Economic Analysis of Indonesian Coral Reefs*, *Environment Department, Work in Progress*, World Bank: Washington, WA.

Dutton, I. M. (2005), 'If Only Fish Could Vote: The Enduring Challenges of Coastal and Marine Resources Management in Post-reformasi Indonesia', in *The Politics and Economics of Indonesia's Natural Resources*, ed. B. P. Resosudarmo, ISEAS: Singapore.

Fahrudin, A. (2003), *Extended Cost Benefit Analysis of Present and Future Use of Indonesian Coral Reefs: An Empirical Approach to Sustainable Management of Tropical Marine Resources*, Department of Agricultural Economics, Faculty of Agricultural and Nutritional Science.

Fox, J. J., Ahuri, D. S. and Resosudarmo, I. A. P. (2005), 'Unfinished Edifice or Pandora's Box? Decentralisation and Resource Management in Indonesia', in *The Politics and Economics of Indonesia's Natural Resources*, ed. B. P. Resosudarmo, ISEAS: Singapore.

Ministry of the Environment (2006), *Status Lingkungan Hidup Indonesia 2005*, Ministry of the Environment, Jakarta.

Ministry of Marine Affairs and Fisheries (2004), 'Raiser ikan hias Cibinong momentum kebangkitan bisnis ikan hias Indonesia', press release.

Moberg, F. and Folke, C. (1999), 'Ecological Goods and Services of Coral Reef Ecosystems', *Ecological Economics* 29: 215–33.

Mous, P. J., Pet-Soede, L., Erdmann, M. *et al.* (2000), 'Cyanide Fishing on Indonesian Coral Reefs for the Live Food Fish Market – What is the Problem?', *SPC Live Reef Fish Information Bulletin*: 20–6.

Napitupulu, L. (2006), 'Economic Valuation of Bali Barat Coral Reef Ecosystem: Fisheries and Tourism Benefits to Stakeholders in West Bali and East Java', unpublished report submitted to WWF Indonesia Friends of the Reef-Climate Change Programme.

Patlis, J. M. (2005), 'New Legal Initiatives for Natural Resource Management in a Changing Indonesia: The Promise, the Fear and the Unknown', in *The Politics and Economics of Indonesia's Natural Resources*, ed. B. P. Resosudarmo, ISEAS: Singapore.

Pet-Soede, L. and Erdmann, M. (1998), 'An Overview and Comparison of Destructive Fishing Practices in Indonesia', *SPC Live Reef Fish Bulletin* 4: 28–35.

Sadovy, Y. (2003), 'CITES, Santiago and Conservation in the Live Fish Trades', *SPC Live Reef Fish Information Bulletin*: 52–4 (11 April 2003).

Schmidt, C. and Kunzman, A. (2005), 'Post-harvesting Mortality in the Marine Aquarium Trade: A Case Study of an Indonesian Export Facility', *SPC Live Reef Fish Bulletin*: 3–12 (13 January 2005).

Statistics Indonesia (2006), *Gross Regional Domestic Product Regencies/Municipalities in Indonesia 2001–2005*, Statistics Indonesia: Jakarta, p. 165.

TICR Foundation (2006), *Status Review of Indonesian Marine Ornamental Fish Trade*, TICR Foundation.

UNEP (2006), *Indonesia: Integrated Assessment of the Poverty Reduction Strategy Paper with a Case Study on Sustainable Fishery Initiatives*, UNEP: Geneva, p. 52.

US Department of Agriculture (2006), *Spring Viremia of Carp; Import Restrictions on Certain Live Fish, Fertilized Eggs, and Gametes*, US Department of Agriculture: Washington, WA.

Wabnitz, C., Taylor, M., Green, E. and Razak, T. (2005), *From Ocean to Aquarium: The Global Trade in Marine Ornamental Species*, Biodiversity Series No. 17, UNEP-WCMC: Cambridge, p. 66.

Weimer, D. L. and Vining, A. R. (1999), *Policy Analysis: Concepts and Practice*, 3rd edn, Pearson Prentice Hall: Upper Saddle River, NJ.

2.5

The rice sector in West Java

MILDA IRHAMNI AND CHAIKAL NURYAKIN*

Introduction

As a result of Indonesia's integration into the global economy over the past three decades, imports have expanded. Despite a generally open economic policy, Indonesian policy makers are reluctant to open up their agricultural sector due to the perceived negative impacts of trade liberalisation on poor domestic producers of agricultural products. Agriculture significantly influences the livelihood of poor rural households through employment and income effects, and poor households typically allocate a large share of consumption expenditure for agricultural products. Therefore, any trade policies that influence agriculture will affect the welfare of poor rural households.

Policies that affect staple crops, such as rice for Indonesia, are particularly sensitive. Rice holds a strategic position in Indonesia's agricultural policy. Food policy in Indonesia focuses mainly on increasing rice production to ensure food security, a goal that was formulated in the early years of the country's independence (Mubyarto, 1971), based on the significance of rice to the livelihood of the population. Rice represents about 7.2% of average consumer expenditure, and 7.1% of the farm-level workforce is employed in rice production (Warr, 2005). The role of rice is even greater for the lowest income group. For example, 18% of the workforce with primary school education or less is employed in the rice-production sector (Warr, 2005). Therefore, poverty discourse in Indonesia is closely related to rice policy issues.

Indonesia is the third largest producer of rice, but it is also the largest rice importer. In 2002, even though the country produced nearly

* Milda Irhamni and Chaikal Nuryakin are Research Fellows with the Faculty of Economics at the University of Indonesia. The authors would like to acknowledge the help from Sulastri Surono from Lembaga Penelitian Ekonomi Masyarakat with the Faculty of Economics at the University of Indonesia and Andi Muh. Alfian Parewangi from the Faculty of Economics at the University of Indonesia.

52 million tonnes of paddy rice (Surono, 2006; Rakotoarisoa, 2006), it also imported around 1.8 million tonnes of rice (UN Comtrade, 2007). Rice imports varied from year to year from as high as 4.75 million tonnes in 1999 to as low as 0.19 million tonnes in 2005 (UN Comtrade, 2007). Despite such variation, rice imports have consistently created a major stir in Indonesia's political environment, which partly explains why the rice sector remains highly protected.[1] The aim is to control the quantity and price of imports to protect producers of rice, in particular producers of low-milling-quality rice (Rakotoarisoa, 2006).

The global market for rice is generally thin, volatile and segmented. For example, from 1961 to 2000, rice trade volume comprised only 4.5% of world rice production, compared to wheat (18%) and maize (13.6%) (Gulati and Narayanan, 2002). In addition, the global rice market is dominated by several major players. Among the major exporters are Thailand, Vietnam, India, China, Pakistan and the US (Gulati and Narayanan, 2002). Indonesia, the Philippines, Bangladesh, Malaysia, East Asia and the Middle East are the major importers (Gulati and Narayanan, 2002). The rice market is also segmented by type and quality. For example, East Asian demand for japonica rice was met by imports from the US, Australia and China, while Africa imported indica rice from India and Thailand (Gulati and Narayanan, 2002). This indicates that there is a low degree of substitution across rice varieties.

The global rice market is highly distorted. Many countries employ domestic and external controls and, collectively, these distortions explain the thinness and volatility of the world rice market. Taken together with the concentration of the global rice market, these characteristics suggest that the impact on world prices of production or consumption changes in major trading/producing countries will be magnified (Gulati and Narayanan, 2002). This is because an increase in import demand in major importer countries is unlikely to be met with an equal increase in export supply. Instead, these changes translate into major price fluctuations. The strong linkages in rice economies explain the interaction of rice policies among trading partners. An increase in export subsidies by a rice-exporting country might trigger the imposition of a higher tariff

---

[1] There are no available data on the rice lobby. However, agents for the lobby typically include the Indonesian Farmer Association (*Himpunan Kerukunan Tani Indonesia* – HKTI), members of the legislature, several non-governmental organisations (NGOs) and independent observers (Basri and Patunru, 2007). Furthermore, the Indonesian press frequently reports on the impact of rice trade liberalisation on farmers' welfare, which has shaped the national psyche on the issue.

by its trading partner (Rakotoarisoa, 2006). Since countries design their rice policies strategically, trade reforms in the rice sector typically move at a slow pace. Countries tend to behave in an oligopolistic manner: no individual country will liberalise its trade before other countries.

The Uruguay Round yielded the first multilateral agreement dedicated to agriculture: the WTO Agreement on Agriculture (Huan-Niemi, 2005; Hanrahan and Schnepf, 2007). The Doha Development Round of negotiations, launched in 2001, emphasises the integration of developing countries into the world trading system. The Doha Ministerial Declaration mandate for agriculture specifically calls for 'comprehensive negotiations aimed at: substantial improvements in market access; reductions of, with a view to phasing out, all forms of export subsidies; and substantial reductions in trade-distorting domestic support' (WTO, 2001). Furthermore, the declaration acknowledges that special and differential treatment for developing countries will be an integral part of the negotiations.

The impact of the current negotiations on agricultural products remains to be seen. Indonesia is negotiating the inclusion of several sensitive agricultural commodities, including rice, into special products exempted from tariff reduction (WTO, 2005). Under the current proposals by the Chairman of the Committee on Agriculture, Crawford Falconer (2007), there would still be special treatment for developing countries, and the tariff reduction cut for these countries would be two thirds of the cuts for developed countries.

If rice is designated as a special product, the immediate impact of the Doha Development Round on Indonesian rice-producing households will be minimal. Nevertheless, the issue of trade and poverty in the rice sector remains significant since the current regime of rice protection will influence long-run agricultural development. This leads to several important questions: despite the current levels of protection in the rice market, should Indonesia liberalise its rice imports further? What would the impact and policy implications be for poor rural households whose livelihoods depend on rice?

Background: reforming Indonesian rice policies

Several distinct trade-poverty linkages can be examined. In the short run, the first impact of liberalisation will be on the border price. A study by Sulastri Surono (2006) implies that, given the global rice-trade environment, in which developed countries subsidise their rice exports, rice trade liberalisation will depress the domestic price in Indonesia. In 1998,

Indonesia opened its domestic market to rice imports and the resulting import surge led to lower domestic prices. While a price reduction would benefit consumers of rice, it would most likely decrease the income of producers. The net impact of the price changes thus depends on the net welfare loss between producers and consumers. This impact would also depend on the extent of price transmission to households, which will in turn depend on infrastructure quality, distributional margins and geographic location (Hertel, 2006). For example, households in remote areas are less likely to be influenced because price changes are not readily transmitted to them.

Price changes will modify production and consumption behaviour, with corresponding implications for the labour market. Following import liberalisation, some rice producers might adjust their working hours (to produce more to fulfil their budget outlays) or switch occupations to cope with the changes. However, the degree of adjustment will depend on various basic market and infrastructure characteristics (FAO, 2005). In the long run, the impact on poverty from rice trade liberalisation will depend on economic growth. If trade reform could bring about steady economic growth, in particular agricultural growth, it will most likely reduce the incidence of rural poverty. However, because the potential opportunities associated with liberalisation might be lost in the absence of critical infrastructure to support producers (Winters, 2000), liberalisation needs to be supported by adequate and sound 'behind the border' policies.

During the early life of Indonesia's New Order Regime (late 1960s), the issue of food security was considered to be of great importance. In the 1970s, a comprehensive food policy was introduced to increase rice production, including enhanced inputs and financing mechanisms. The goal was to ensure food security and promote poverty alleviation by ensuring the availability of affordable rice at all times, in all locations (Sidiki, 2004). The National Food Logistic Agency, Bulog (*Badan Urusan Logistik*), managed policy interventions during this period to stabilise prices. It adopted a buffer-stock strategy by buying paddy rice during harvest season at a specified floor price to prevent price decline, storing the purchases and selling its stock when the wholesale price reached the preferred ceiling price (Sidiki, 2004; Pearson, 1990). The band between the floor and ceiling price was designed to be large enough to encourage private storage and distribution participation (Pearson, 1990).

In relation to international trade, the government insulated the domestic market from the highly unstable world prices by making Bulog the sole agency controlling trade in rice. It would import when the country had a rice deficit, and export when there was a rice surplus. Indonesia did export rice for a short period in the 1980s, when production increased significantly. In 1984, Indonesia announced that the country had attained rice sufficiency. At the time, Bulog's rice stock had reached its largest ever amount, in excess of 30 million mt (Sidiki, 2004). Over the next half decade, Indonesia continued to experience rice surpluses, which allowed Bulog to release its stock in the world market (Amang *et al.*, 2000).

The 1970 to 1995 period was thus characterised by high intervention in the rice market. Nevertheless, Bulog effectively maintained stable prices throughout the period prior to the Asian Economic Crisis (Warr, 2005). However, an econometric assessment for the same period conducted by Timmer (2004) shows that the advantages of Bulog's policy diminished over time.

A combination of the Asian economic crisis, currency devaluation and government budget issues led to the adoption of a more market-oriented price policy. The government abolished the general price subsidy and adopted a targeted subsidy programme by conducting special market intervention (*Operasi Pasar Khusus Beras* – OPK), which later changed to a 'rice for the poor' (*Beras untuk Rakyat Miskin* – Raskin) programme (Perum Bulog, 2007).[2] Both programmes were created to ensure food security for low-income households (Sidiki, 2004; Perum Bulog, 2007). The crisis also caused changes in Bulog's role in the rice trade. Bulog no longer holds a monopoly right for rice imports (Perum Bulog, 2007).

However, these reforms seem to be superficial, as Bulog still accounted for 75 per cent of total rice imports (Warr, 2005). Furthermore, the monopoly power of Bulog was re-established due to the failure to maintain the rice price floor (Rakotoarisoa, 2006). This failure resulted from a surge in rice imports to 4.75 million mt in 1999, from only 0.3 million mt in 1997, following the zero import tariff imposed by the government (UN Comtrade, 2007). Under the new scheme, private imports were allowed only under a specific tariff of Rp 430 per kg, which was around 25 per cent of the 2002 import price (cost, insurance and freight) and conditional on 'red lane' customs treatment (Warr, 2005). Together, the tariff and non-tariff barriers explain, in part, the widening gap between the border prices

---

[2] Despite providing a more targeted subsidy to the poor households, the programme is under media scrutiny due to the alleged rampant corruption and mistargeting in the implementation.

of imported rice and domestic prices (Warr, 2005). Between 2000 and late 2004, the domestic rice price reached levels of 40 to 50 per cent above import prices (Warr, 2005). In addition, bumper harvests in 2004 led the government to impose a seasonal ban on rice imports, where rice imports were strictly forbidden one month before and two months after peak harvest (Sidiki, 2004).

Difficulties in reforming rice trade policies also come from the perception that rice imports would have negative impacts for poor agricultural households. One argument for protection that was frequently cited by Bulog and the Ministry of Agriculture was that protection reduces poverty by raising poor farmers' income (Warr, 2005). However, several studies show that rice price increases have had a deleterious effect on poorer households. A study by Warr (2005) found that the incidence of poverty increased by almost 1 per cent with a rice import ban. Furthermore, among farmers, a ban would benefit only the richest farmers. World Bank (2006) estimates show that rice price increases between February 2005 and February 2006 increased poverty by 3.1 million people. The case study below therefore investigates the contrasting perceptions of the link between poverty and trade in the rice sector through examination of a specific rice-cultivating society in Karawang.

Case studies of Pedes subdistrict, Karawang Regency, West Java

In order to understand the impact of rice import liberalisation, a small-scale survey in the Pedes subdistrict of the Karawang Regency was conducted. A qualitative approach was used to identify the costs and benefits of rice trade liberalisation to farmers.

For the purpose of this analysis, and using the definition employed by Warr (2005), farmers in Indonesia can be categorised as net producers and net consumers. Net producers are sellers of rice, including farmers who own land and some who rent land. Net consumers include farmers who own no land, farmers who produce agricultural products other than rice and urban residents, unless they are the absentee owners of a paddy field. The latter group also includes farmers who produce some rice but also purchase additional rice from the sale of other commodities.

Karawang Regency was chosen due to its status as a rice storehouse. It consists of twenty subdistricts with various levels of poverty incidence. We chose one subdistrict, Pedes, because it has a high incidence of poverty, and because around 80 per cent of households work in the agricultural sector. Five villages out of thirteen in the subdistrict were chosen to represent different poverty incidence levels: Laban Jaya, Purpasari, Karang Jaya, Kertamulya and Kertaraharja. Fifty farmers from these five villages were then randomly chosen to be interviewed. For the purpose of this study, the poverty head count is determined using the Biro Pusat Statistic poverty line, except for five farmers who did not want to disclose their income.[3]

Karawang is a famous industrial and rice-production district in West Java. Due to its close proximity with Jakarta and Bekasi, it has one of the largest industrial areas in Indonesia. Nevertheless, 51% of the district area is devoted to agricultural purpose. This area serves as a rice storehouse (*Lumbung Beras*) for West Java, with production reaching 1 million tonnes per year in 2001. Of the total paddy fields, 86% is irrigated and 14% is rain-fed.

Despite its role as an industrial and major rice-producing area, rural poverty is still prevalent in Karawang. The average percentage of poor households was around 52% in 2005 (PODES, 2006).[4] About 80% of the population works in agricultural activities (see Table 2T). These figures confirm that agriculture is the backbone of these poor households' livelihoods.

The fifty farmers interviewed in Pedes can be divided into five types according to ownership of land and human resources employment. Firstly, ownership of land divides farmers into landless farmers (*buruh tani*) and farmers with land. *Buruh tani* may be further divided into two categories: the first is *buruh tani upahan*, who receive income from the land owners on a daily, weekly or monthly basis – this kind of farmer has little influence on the input and production decisions of rice farming; the second type is *buruh tani penggarap*, who either rent the land from or use a sharing system with the land owner. This type of farmer has a greater influence on production and input decisions. Land owners or farmers who have land can be categorised into three groups: those who have land and employ household members to work on the farm; those who employ *buruh tani upahan*; and those who employ *buruh tani penggarap*. The first and second type control production and input decisions, while the third has less influence on decisions regarding farm work.

---

[3] To identify their welfare condition, the Raskin criteria were employed. It was also taken into account whether these five farmers had ever benefited from any pro-poor-related governmental programme. Despite the relative incomparability of the two poverty measures, the employment of Raskin criteria for determining poverty conditions of the five farmers was considered to be adequate since this study does not involve a quantitative approach.

[4] PODES data is village-level data. The respondents interviewed are the head of the villages, thus the poverty incidence from PODES data is different from what we use for categorising the farmers.

Table 2T *Stylised data for the Pedes subdistrict*

Village	Total population	Number of poor households	Percentage of poor households	Number of agricultural households	Percentage of agricultural households	Number of buruh tani (persons)	Percentage of buruh tani from the total population
Jatimulya	8,012	1,844	75.0	1,956	80.0	2,632	32.9
Kertaraharja	6,323	827	50.0	1,328	80.0	1,868	29.5
Karangjaya	7,786	1,285	67.0	1,541	80.0	2,352	30.2
Malangsari	3,158	484	58.0	666	80.0	982	31.1
Kertamulya	6,574	915	55.0	1,335	80.0	1,997	30.4
Payungsari	7,406	1,612	80.0	1,614	80.0	2,489	33.6
Randumulya	5,514	923	61.0	1,214	80.0	1,803	32.7
Labanjaya	5,217	1,089	83.0	1,055	80.0	1,543	29.6
Sungaibuntu	8,165	1,179	58.0	1,618	80.0	2,267	27.8
Kedaljaya	4,320	676	59.0	921	80.0	1,364	31.6
Dongkal	3,581	572	52.0	873	80.0	1,308	36.5
Puspasari	3,616	823	76.0	867	80.0	1,334	36.9

Source: PODES (2006).

These five types of farmers then can be categorised as 'net consumers' and 'net producers'. The survey categorised as net producers twenty-three of the twenty-four landowners, who said that they sell all the rice they produce, as well as all sixteen *buruh tani penggarap*. Thus, in total, thirty-nine of the fifty interviewed farmers are net producers. Only five can be considered net consumers.[5] Whether they are net producers or consumers, all the interviewed farmers preferred stable rice prices to increasing rice prices.

The market structure of the Indonesian rice economy can explain these preferences. Farmers sell their harvest in the form of wet, threshed paddy rice to rice collectors, or *tengkulak*.[6] The *tengkulak* absorb the farmers' production at a higher price than the ceiling price imposed by the government. The ceiling price imposed by the government acts as the benchmark for price negotiations between farmers and *tengkulak*. Because their small size makes it inefficient to process the paddy rice individually, farmers prefer to operate through the *tengkulak*. Farmers also face time constraints to maintain harvest quality. The lack of drying and storing facilities at the individual farm level and the fact that only *tengkulak* are willing to come and buy the harvest (and have the capacity to carry out the drying process) also explain why farmers prefer to sell their harvest to *tengkulak*. Price is rarely the main factor behind farmers' decisions to sell their harvest since net producers do not capture the full benefits of price increases.

Furthermore, protection does not benefit net consumers since they are forced to purchase rice at higher prices. Moreover, most of the interviewed farmers can be categorised as poor and may switch to become net consumers depending on the living needs and quality of production. The ownership of adequate land or other economic means to support farming plays a more significant role in determining the welfare of these farmers rather than rice price protection (see Table 2U). Many of the farmers are not 'pure' net producers as they sell the rice production mostly because of the need for cash to purchase food, repay debt and other needs. Many of the farmers also sell their produce because the paddy rice produced is of a better quality than they themselves consume.

At the same time, price interventions have created a bias in farmers' cultivation decisions, preventing diversification of agricultural production to

---

[5] Six farmers cannot be categorised as net consumers or producers.
[6] *Tengkulak* are rice collectors who collect rice from individual and small-scale farmers and then sell it in a larger batch to consumers or retailers.

Table 2U   *Poverty incidence distribution among the five categories of farmer*

			Poor	Not poor	Total
				Poverty condition	
	Own land and employ	Frequency	8	2	10
	household members	Row percentage	80	20	100
		Column percentage	21.62	15.38	20
	Own land and employ	Frequency	5	6	11
	Buruh Tani Upahan	Row percentage	45.45	54.55	100
		Column percentage	13.51	46.15	22
	Own land and employ	Frequency	2	1	3
	Buruh Tani Penggarap	Row percentage	66.67	33.33	100
		Column percentage	5.41	7.69	6
Farmers'	*Buruh Tani Penggarap*	Frequency	14	2	16
categories	(landless and rent from or	Row percentage	87.5	12.5	100
	share land with land owner)	Column percentage	37.84	15.38	32
	Buruh Tani Upahan	Frequency	4	0	4
	(landless and receive	Row percentage	100	0	100
	income from land owner)	Column percentage	10.81	0	8
		Frequency	4	2	6
	NA	Row Percentage	66.67	33.33	100
		Column Percentage	10.81	15.38	12
		Frequency	37	13	50
	Total	**Row percentage**	**74**	**26**	**100**
		Column percentage	**100**	**100**	**100**

Source: Timmer (2004).

higher-value crop and livestock systems (Timmer, 2004). Trade liberalisation will lead to price shifts and a reallocation of farmers' resources in the long run. Thus, the long-term benefit (cost) of liberalisation depends on the willingness and capability of the farmers to reallocate their resources, either in terms of crops produced or labour time allocated. Rigidity in the reallocation of labour in particular could exacerbate the potential negative impact of rice trade liberalisation on rural poor households.

Rigid resource allocation seems to be quite prevalent among the interviewed farmers. Among the respondents, 54 per cent of them were not willing to switch crops even when other crops have relatively higher prices. This may be because most farmers lack the knowledge and capital needed to switch to other crops. In addition, this rigid behaviour also extended to labour decisions, despite the fact that the Karawang Regency was strategically chosen for the study since it has one of the largest industrial areas in Indonesia and is thought to provide opportunities for off-farm employment.

Given alternative jobs, only twenty farmers stated they would be willing to change jobs so long as the job was in their hometown, and only a handful would be willing to migrate to other areas. The existence of farmers who also hold other jobs besides farming to make ends meet does not preclude this reluctance to move out of rice farming. The farmers interviewed highlighted their limited transferable skills and low education base as reasons why it would be difficult for them to switch to other jobs outside the agricultural sector (see Table 2V). The government needs to take these employment rigidities into account when liberalising the rice market.

The result of the study also highlights farmers' dependency on government agricultural programmes. Farmers' main concerns were the uncertainty of production and increasing production costs. Therefore, all farmers agreed that government agricultural programmes, such as training on agricultural productivity and support for fertiliser subsidies, would improve their skills, productivity and welfare. Among these programmes, farmers consider policies regarding fertiliser prices to be among the most important, since fertiliser costs constitute the largest share of rice production costs. Irrigation systems are also perceived to be a priority area, as a lack of irrigation means farms can only be harvested twice a year. In addition, policies to strengthen financial support for the farmers need to be improved as most farmers still choose to borrow from sources other than banks, including from the *tengkulak*.

The farmers' views toward imported rice are mixed. Most perceive that rice imports will be harmful for their welfare. Nevertheless, only twenty stated that increased imports have adversely influenced their welfare by inducing rice production contraction. Moreover, only seven of them identified a ban on imports as a high priority in government rice policies. Most farmers highlighted the need for improved agricultural infrastructure, an agricultural credit scheme and training. Table 2W provides a list of policies that the farmers believe needs to be pursued by the government.

The results of this study highlight the mixed impact of trade liberalisation. For many of the farmers, trade liberalisation would provide benefits in terms of a lower price for consumed rice. Furthermore, as argued by Timmer (2004), rice protection is simply not sustainable in the long run.

Table 2V   *Poor households' distribution based on educational attainment*

			Poverty condition		
			Poor	Not poor	Total
	No schooling	Frequency	5	0	5
		Row percentage	100	0	100
		Column percentage	13.51	0	10
	Primary school	Frequency	27	7	34
		Row percentage	79.41	20.59	100
		Column percentage	72.97	53.85	68
	Junior high school	Frequency	2	3	5
		Row percentage	40	60	100
		Column percentage	5.41	23.08	10
Highest educational attainment	Senior high school	Frequency	2	2	4
		Row percentage	50	50	100
		Column percentage	5.41	15.38	8
	Diploma	Frequency	1	0	1
		Row percentage	100	0	100
		Column percentage	2.7	0	2
	University	Frequency	0	1	1
		Row percentage	0	100	100
		Column percentage	0	7.69	2
	Total	Frequency	37	13	50
		Row percentage	**74**	**26**	**100**
		Column percentage	**100**	**100**	**100**

Source: Timmer (2004).

The government therefore needs to enhance its role in smoothing out the liberalisation process through transition and complementary policies that help the farmers cope with liberalisation by improving rural infrastructure, increasing training for farmers and facilitating reduced production costs, such as the cost of borrowing.

Policy recommendations

Given the previous discussion, should Indonesia liberalise its rice imports? Different underlying conditions will influence household responses

Table 2W　　*Important government rice policies perceived by respondents*

Policies	Frequency	Percentage of total %
Provides training and village co-operation (*Koperasi Unit Desa* – KUD)	3	6
Provides credit support	4	8
Provides capital support and training	4	8
Provides government support for farmers	2	4
Reduces the price for rice seeds	1	2
Provides better quality seeds (*bibit unggul*)	1	2
Improves irrigation systems	16	32
Increases the price floor for husked rice	1	2
Reduces the price for pesticides	1	2
Provides a safety net for when harvests fail	1	2
Designs an import policy that is pro-farmers	1	2
Reduces the price and increases the quality of fertilisers	6	12
Provides a policy that balances producer and consumer interests	2	4
Provides a stable price	1	2
No response	6	12
Total	**50**	**100**

Source: Timmer (2004).

to changes in prices. Given the development of appropriate complementary policies, trade liberalisation could offer improved food security.

Several studies argue that trade reforms accompanied with proper 'behind the border' policies could have a positive impact in poverty reduction strategies (Dorosh, 2001; Gulati and Narayanan, 2002; Anderson, 2004; Winters *et al.*, 2004; Timmer, 2004), even for a large importing country like Indonesia. Timmer (2004) in particular argues that the large differential between world and domestic rice prices has not provided incentives to raise productivity because new technology is not available for the farmers. The benefit to net producers' welfare caused by increasing prices is substantially offset by its adverse impact on net consumers' welfare. He argues therefore that lower prices and a certain degree of rice price variability are acceptable, as this provides a signal to farmers to diversify their production and allocate their resources more efficiently.

Given the long-term declining trend in world rice prices, the diversification of farmers' income sources will be critical to increase agricultural income and smooth out the liberalisation process. Furthermore, many farmers do not own land or they have to produce on small plots of land. These farmers can rarely be categorised as net producers and thus will not benefit from higher rice prices. Timmer's argument therefore implies that the current regime of protection is unsustainable in the long run. He further reasons that rural poverty should be solved not by confining farmers to farm work, but rather by creating supporting policies that create off-farm alternative employment.

The results from our case study seem to support Timmer's argument that much of the benefit of high rice prices due to protection seems to elude farmers. Nevertheless, farmers' inertia and inflexibility in the labour market will, in the short run, result in some losers from freer trade. Therefore, along trade liberalisation, complementary policies should be established to enable farmers to fully participate and benefit from international trade while at the same time providing better rice-price levels for poor net consumers of rice. The twin-track policy approach developed by the FAO (2005) could serve as a basis for these complementary policies.

Track 1: creating opportunities

Creating opportunities involves policies that stabilise macroeconomic conditions and provide a favourable environment for savings and investments. This stability should be accompanied by a substantial increase in the agricultural share of government budgets to reduce the prevalence of poverty in the agricultural sector.

The success of policy design and implementation is highly influenced by civil society and the functioning of markets. Therefore, the government should engage farmers, consumers and the private sector in constructing and executing comprehensive policies. In this regard, the role of civil society organisations, such as Rural Unit Cooperative (*Koperasi Unit Desa* – KUD) or farmers' associations, needs to be expanded and strengthened. Well-functioning markets will ensure fair competition, protect market access for agricultural households and transmit appropriate price signals to influence household resource allocation. To ensure price transmission to the farmer level, the government also needs to enhance agricultural infrastructure facilities and reduce supply-side constraints. This should also be accompanied by an improved supply of irrigation water, which would significantly improve the productivity of farming activities (see Table 2W on p. 318).

In designing comprehensive policies, the government needs to account for environmental impact, which will influence land productivity in the long run. Future agricultural intensification should focus on new technology, such as new and improved varieties of rice and organic farming. The government and NGOs can contribute to the managing and monitoring of the environmental impacts of agriculture activities and ensure that such activities are developed in a sustainable manner and that poor households are afforded equitable access to improved agricultural technology. This implies that public support is required to complement the private sector in agricultural research and technology.

Policies to increase non-farm rural activities and diversify food crops supplied in the local market are also needed to provide alternative occupations and income sources, and to create risk management opportunities in the face of trade reform impacts. The government needs to ensure that rural financial markets are working adequately and that the poor have fair access to this market. One such policy to ensure capital access for the poor is by promoting micro-financing schemes. Increased support for post-harvest operations will also enhance the value addition in the agricultural sector. Thus, investment in food handling, processing, distribution and marketing should be made to ensure the greatest participation of small-scale rural producers and to avoid post-harvest production loss.

Track 2: ensuring access

Since the effects of protectionist policies on poverty are diffuse, many benefits are captured by only a small section of the communities. Trade liberalisation could serve as a basis to push the economy towards transparency and efficiency. Rather than providing blanket protection (restricting import and price stabilisation policy) for rural households, direct assistance is generally more desirable. One obvious advantage of such a policy is the transparency of derived benefits and costs. However, the presence of rampant corruption might undermine the success of this type of programme. To ensure that the poor get maximum benefits from such programmes, the government needs to conduct impact evaluation and improve the institutional foundations of the country. Regular monitoring and evaluation of the effectiveness of programmes, within a system of appropriate laws and regulations, supported by civil society, fair competition and high-quality governmental bodies, will increase the government's capacity to provide assistance, prevent corruption and ensure that the poor have fair access to programmes. Such conditions will enhance the operation of domestic markets, which will in turn provide correct signals for decisions regarding agricultural activities.

It is also important to mention that there are several examples of directly targeted programmes for food security that can also assist in the liberalisation adjustment process:

(1) Direct feeding programmes can provide direct access to food for poor households. For example, the Raskin programme, conducted by Bulog, involves the distribution of rice at a low price (IDR 1,000/kg) to poor households identified using poverty criteria. A recent assessment conducted by Perum Bulog and the LIE Department of Economics (2006) identified several problems related to the programme, including confusing criteria, which created difficulties in identifying relevant households, a smaller supply of rice than needed to satisfy the demand of the identified households and distribution difficulties that led to increased costs to the beneficiaries.

(2) Income-transfer programmes, which included in-kind transfers, such as subsidised rations and food stamps, as well as cash transfers. In Indonesia, examples of such programmes include the Health Card and Direct Cash Transfer. An unconditional cash transfer programme, *Bantuan Langsung Tunai*, was launched by the government in October 2005 as a response to increased fuel prices. Under the programme, IDR 100,000 was given to poor households every month. A rapid appraisal of the programme conducted by SMERU (an independent institution for research and public policy studies on various socioeconomic and poverty issues in Indonesia) in 2005 highlighted several aspects of the programme. Firstly, it concluded that the level of mistargeting was quite low. Secondly, the distribution of funds was impeded by the minimal number of officials involved, high transportation costs for recipients who live far from the place of distribution and long queues during the first day of funds disbursement. Thirdly,

the programme created certain misperceptions and social friction. Despite the problems associated with it, in general, recipients' level of satisfaction with the programme was quite high.

Conclusion

In summary, this case study and other studies examined suggest that the impact of rice trade liberalisation might initially be somewhat limited, and opposition from some producers can be expected. However, it is also noted that the price of rice is rarely the main driver of farmers' decisions to sell or diversify their production, and that, in fact, the lower prices that liberalisation would bring would benefit farmers who are net consumers of rice. While liberalisation could have a negative impact on some farmers in the short term, this impact could be minimised with good support for 'behind the border' government policies. The main challenges in the Indonesian context seem to be in easing the adjustment process through improvements to supply-side productivity and by supporting those who are adversely affected by liberalisation. A 'twin-track' approach of creating opportunities and ensuring access to benefits offers suggestions for achieving these goals. Consultation and rural empowerment should take centre stage in Indonesia's agricultural policy by ensuring that the benefits of trade reform are adequately transferred to rural households.

References

Amang, B., Soetrisno, N. and Sapuan (2000), 'Can Indonesia Feed Itself?', in B. Arifin. and H. S. Dillon (eds.), *Asian Agriculture Facing the 21st Century: Proceedings of the Second Conference of Asian Society of Agricultural Economists (ASAE)*, Asean Society of Agricultural Economists: Jakarta, pp. 91–103.

Anderson, K. (2004), 'Agriculture, Trade reform and Poverty Reduction: Implications for Sub-Saharan Africa', Policy Issues in International Trade and Commodities Study Series No. 22, UNCTAD.

Basri, M. C. and Patunru, A. A. (2007), 'How Keep the Policy Open: The Case of Indonesia', paper to be published by the Forum on Debt and Development (FONDAD).

Dorosh, P. A. (2001), 'Trade Liberalization and National Food Security: Rice Trade between Bangladesh and India', *World Development* 29(4): 673–90.

Falconer, C. (2007), 'Communication from the Chairman of the Committee on Agriculture, Special Session', available at www.wto.org/english/tratop_e/agric_e/agchairtxt_30apr07_e.htm [last accessed 23 February 2009].

Food and Agriculture Organization (FAO) (2005), 'The State of Food and Agriculture: Agricultural Trade and Poverty', FAO Agriculture Series No. 36, FAO.

Gulati, A. and Narayanan, S. (2002), 'Rice Trade Liberalization and Poverty', MSSD Discussion Paper No. 51, International Food Research Institute (IFPRI).

Hanrahan, C. E. and Schnepf, R. (2007), 'WTO Doha Round: The Agricultural Negotiations', CRS report for Congress, Order Code RL.33144.

Hertel, T. W. (2006), 'A Survey of Findings on the Poverty Impacts of Agricultural Trade Liberalization', *Journal of Agricultural and Development Economics* 3(1): 1–26.

Huan-Niemi, E. (2005), 'Special and Differential Treatment under the WTO Agreement on Agriculture', Agrifood Research Working Papers 98, Agrifood Research.

Mubyarto (1971), 'Food Price Policy in Indonesia', paper presented at the SEADAG Conference: Honolulu, Hawaii.

Pearson, S. (1990), *Indonesian Rice Policy*, Cornell Press: Ithaca, NY.

Perum Bulog (2007), 'Sejarah Bulog Sebelum menjadi Perum', available at www.bulog.co.id/sejarah.php [last accessed 23 February 2009].

Perum Bulog and LIE Department of Economics (2006), 'Evaluation on the Rice for Poor Program', report prepared for the Bulog Assessment of the Raskin programme, University of Indonesia.

PODES (2006), *PODES Statistical Data*, BPS: Jakarta.

Rakotoarisoa, M. A. (2006), 'Policy Distortions in the Segmented Rice Market', MTID Discussion Paper No. 94, IFPRI.

Sidiki, M. (2004), 'Indonesia Rice Policy in View of Trade Liberalization', paper presented to the FAO Rice Conference, Rome, 12–13 February.

Surono, S. (2006), 'Kondisi Perberasan dan Kebijakan Perdagangan Beras di Indonesia', *Jurnal Kebijakan Ekonomi* 2(2): 183–96.

Timmer, C. P. (2004), 'Food Security in Indonesia: Current Challenges and the Long-run Outlook', Center for Global Development Working Paper No. 48, Center for Global Development.

UN Comtrade (2007), 'Database', available at http://comtrade.un.org/db [last accessed 23 February 2009].

Warr, P. (2005), 'Food Policy and Poverty in Indonesia: A General Equilibrium Analysis', RSPAS Working Papers, RSPAS ANU.

Winters, L. A. (2000), 'Trade Liberalization and Poverty', Discussion Paper No. 7, Poverty Research Unit, University of Sussex: Sussex.

Winters, L. A., McCulloh, N. and McKay, A. (2004), 'Trade Liberalization and Poverty: The Evidence So Far', *Journal of Economic Literature* 42(March): 72–115.

World Bank (2006), *Making the New Indonesia Work for the Poor: Overview*, World Bank: Jakarta.

WTO (2001), 'Doha WTO Ministerial 2001: Ministerial Declaration', WT/
     MIN(01)/DEC/1, available at www.wto.org/english/thewto_e/minist_ e/min
     01_e/mindecl_e.htm [last accessed 23 February 2009].
     (2005), 'Summary Report on The Thirty First and Thirty Second Formal Special
     Sessions of The Committee on Agriculture', Committee on Agriculture Spe-
     cial Session held on 19 April and 3 June, available at www.wto.org/english/
     thewto_e/countries_e/indonesia_e.htm#top [last accessed 23 February 2009].

Chinese agricultural policy: central and western province

SHUNLI YAO[*]

Introduction

Reform in agriculture and in other areas of the Chinese economy in the past thirty years has contributed to rural poverty reduction. Agricultural reform has removed distortions inherited from the era of central planning and early industrialisation. As a result, the extent of policy bias towards industry at the expense of agriculture and within agriculture, towards grain production at the expense of horticulture and other labour-intensive crops, has been substantially reduced, and the livelihood of Chinese farmers has improved. In the 1980s, the emergence of township and village enterprises led to rural income improvement, enabling farmers to avoid urban migration. In 1992, when Deng Xiaoping made his tour to the south to re-activate China's reform, foreign direct investment (FDI) in China started to gain momentum. In the coastal cities, foreign-funded enterprises have set up processing and assembly operations for exports, creating job opportunities for millions of rural migrant workers. From 1981 to 2002, the population under the poverty line in China was reduced from 490 million to 88 million.[1]

Trade reform, most notably the phase-out of the Multi-Fibre Arrangement, is believed to have been helpful with rural poverty alleviation. The expansion of China's textile and clothing exports, together with the surge of FDI-induced processing exports, created more job opportunities for migrant workers. In contrast, agricultural trade reform is generally perceived as being detrimental to rural development. In WTO and free trade agreement (FTA) talks, China considers agricultural market access the

---

[*] Shunli Yao is Associate Professor at the School of International Trade and Economics, University of International Business and Economics.
[1] Numbers cited in Wang *et al.*, (2004). The poverty line is defined by the World Bank definition as US$1 per day.

most sensitive defensive interest due to fears that a surge of grain imports could displace low-income Chinese grain growers. In fact, Chinese negotiators have cited rural poverty as a key concern to justify its reluctance to make major concessions in agricultural market access.

However, in the long run, market access for grain imports is expected to improve as a result of WTO and FTA negotiations and production constraints from water shortages in China's grain belt. Market access liberalisation will make it more financially difficult to maintain grain production through its domestic support programme. Future adjustment in agricultural production is inevitable and will release agricultural resources from the grain sector and possibly move them to horticultural and other labour-intensive agricultural sectors. Horticultural crop exports face Sanitary and Phytosanitary (SPS) requirements. Therefore, policies that would help upgrade the quality of Chinese horticultural exports to meet the stringent SPS requirements in the high-end overseas markets would contribute to promoting Chinese agricultural trade.

Over the next ten to fifteen years, China's newly launched New Rural Development (NRD) programme calls for substantially increased investment in rural areas. This NRD programme is designed to combat the stagnation in agricultural and rural development, widening the rural/urban divide. It aims to boost rural development in the coming fifteen years and is part of a larger picture of re-orientation in Chinese development strategy to emphasise the 'scientific development' approach to building a 'harmonious society'.[2] The NRD programme goals include raising farmers' income, enhancing agricultural production and improving rural environment.

While the NRD programme is ambitious, it is expected to be underfinanced. This chapter examines approaches for aligning and adjusting Chinese agricultural trade policy to make better use of resources available to the agricultural sector and, therefore, to help achieve those NRD goals. In the following section, the chapter provides a background on the economic and social environment under which Chinese agricultural trade policy develops. The chapter then goes on to describe two cases: (i) the province of Shandong's success story of horticultural exports; and (ii) the dilemma faced by a poverty pocket in a Beijing suburb. The chapter then discusses policy recommendations drawn from the case studies and the

---

[2] These key words have been included into the Party Charter in the Seventeenth Chinese Communist Party Congress, convened in October 2007.

possible application of a similar approach to other under-developed rural areas, followed by concluding remarks.

Background

Pre-reform era

In the mid twentieth century when the People's Republic was founded, China was an agrarian economy with an under-developed industrial sector.[3] Like most developing countries at that time, China adopted a strategy that emphasised industrial development.[4] Agriculture was intended to serve as an input to this development strategy. In addition to budget outlays and bank loans, the bulk of which went to industrial investment, the government set a low wage for industrial workers, a high price for industrial products and a low price for agricultural products as an implicit tax to divert agricultural revenues and private savings into industrial sectors. As such, the agricultural sector was depressed.

Meagre investments in the agricultural sector were heavily biased towards grain production to ensure adequate food supply for the country. Farmers were required to fulfil the grain production quotas assigned to them by the government, and grain bureaus were set up across the country to enforce the grain procurement.

On the international trade front, the US-led UN embargo against the new communist regime in the 1950s and the policy-induced 1958 to 1960 famine reinforced the conviction of the Chinese leadership that the principle of 'grain self-sufficiency' should lead agricultural trade policy decisions. This was the general setting of the Chinese agricultural economy before the reform started in 1978.

Reform

Chinese agricultural reform started with the introduction of the household responsibility system in the late 1970s and early 1980s, to boost farmers' incentives in agricultural production. As a quasi privatisation measure, a land tenure system was instituted to ensure farmers of the rights to keep the land for twenty years. Most agricultural commodity prices were liberalised through the removal of price controls. Instead of a

---

[3] This section is drawn in part from Yao (2007), which also discusses the political economy of Chinese agricultural trade policy.

[4] For a thorough analysis of this 'catch up' strategy, see Lin *et al.*, (2003).

mandatory production quota sold to the government at lower than market price (the procurement practice during most of the reform years), a price support programme was put in place to encourage grain production, though most of the time market prices are higher than the minimal procurement prices. These changes in the procurement policy helped transfer grain revenue from grain marketing bureaus to farmers. During the reform years, Chinese agricultural liberalisation did not change the patterns of taxing agriculture to subsidise industry. This practice was only stopped in 2006 when China launched the NRD programme.

Implementation of China's WTO accession commitments has made China one of the most liberalised countries in agricultural trade. Grain tariff rate quotas (TRQs) have been expanded and both in-quota and out-quota rates lowered. Cotton and soya imports have been opened up to meet the rising domestic demand.

Outcomes

Agricultural liberalisation has unleashed the potentials of labour-intensive production in agriculture. The development of horticulture, poultry, dairy and animal husbandry sectors has helped diversify the diet of the population and has also increased farmers' income. As a result, distortions due to over-emphasis on grain production in the pre-reform era have been substantially reduced.

Nevertheless, grain production is still the priority in agriculture. With a slight increase in the total sown area, additional land use for horticulture has been met mainly by a modest shrinking of the sown area for grain, a reflection of China's changing policy on 'grain self-sufficiency' (from 100% down to 95%). The declining grain acreage coincided with productivity gains in the sector. The Household Responsibility System gave a boost to grain production in the early 1980s. Agricultural research and development (R&D) investment, concentrated mostly in the grain sector and some in the pre-reform era, started to show its impact in the reform years. However, since the 1990s, grain yield has been mainly fuelled by a higher intensity of input use rather than by productivity improvement. The grain sector fatigue suggests that the marginal return on investment in the grain sector is shrinking.

The reform does not change the patterns of intensive farming in Chinese agriculture. Each year, Chinese agriculture consumes about 46 million mt of fertilisers and 300,000 mt of pesticides, with only 30% and 40% utilisation rates respectively. Water shortages in China's grain belt and the over-use of farm chemicals also raise the environmental concerns of agricultural production (Murphy, 2004). While farm chemical use helps improve yields, pesticide residues have made it difficult for Chinese agricultural exports to enter overseas markets, especially high-end Japan, Korea, US and EU markets, which maintain stringent SPS requirements for farm imports.

The viability of the price support programme that had been instituted to ensure 'grain self-sufficiency' and the 'grain self-sufficiency' target itself require a protectionist grain-trade policy. The economic logic is that liber-alising border measures (improved market access in China's case) would make it more costly to maintain the price support programme. For Chi-nese agriculture, domestic liberalisation has left the market as the sole regulator of grain production, and WTO accession commitments have opened the door for imports through the TRQ system. Ongoing WTO and FTA negotiations are likely to further liberalise agricultural trade. All these developments would make it difficult to maintain sufficiently high domestic grain prices. To boost grain production through farm sub-sidies, though allowed under China's accession protocol, is not a finan-cially viable option given its sheer size and the large number of farmers engaging in grain production. Therefore, land-intensive grain produc-tion can hardly enrich farmers, and poverty pockets are more likely to appear at the margin of grain production in the wake of agricultural trade liberalisation.

New policy initiatives

Despite the overall economic growth after thirty years of reform, which in general is in favour of urban and coastal areas where most FDI has gone, the rural/urban divide has further increased (the urban/rural per capita income ratio reached over 3:1 in 2005!). To correct this disparity and also create a rural market for the demand-driven economic growth, China's Eleventh Five-Year Plan has included the NRD programme into its platform. One immediate policy reform is to abolish all fees and taxes associated with agricultural production. This is a very significant move, because it is the first time in several thousand years that no tax or fees are being imposed on Chinese farmers.

The NRD programme carries a price tag. It is estimated by Justin Yifu Lin, Chinese economist and the mastermind of the NRD programme, that over the fifteen years timeframe (2006 to 2020), it would require addi-tional annual investment in the rural areas of 270 billion yuan, equivalent to China's annual defence budget and four times as much as its annual FDI inflow. This price tag should be interpreted as an indicator of the difficulties, rather than actual financial ability, to achieve the NRD goals. Funds available to the ambitious programme will be limited. The politically powerful state-operating enterprises (SOEs) still receive huge amounts of subsidies through loans and from the state budget, which leaves the government with little room for financial manoeuvring. FDI has played a vital role in Chinese urban and industrial development, but as a commercial operation, little has gone, and will go to, the rural area. The NRD programme would help with rural poverty-alleviations, but it is not specifically designed for that purpose. Instead, it consists of a long list of projects that will compete for funds with rural poverty-alleviation operations.

Given the limited resources available for the Chinese agricultural sector, one feasible approach is to correct remaining distortions in the factor market between agriculture and industry, as well as within agriculture. This includes equal opportunities to credit, inputs, R&D funds and logistic support for all agricultural productions. In poor areas, resources in the grain sector should be re-directed to more productive or profitable use in agriculture.

The life cycle of the NRD programme overlaps with the ongoing WTO and FTA negotiations and the implementation period of possible trade agreements. Therefore, the two parallel events would have close interaction with each other.

China is abundant in farm labour but scarce in arable land. Therefore, with free trade it would become a potential net importer of grain and other land-intensive crops and would become a net exporter of horticultural and other labour-intensive agricultural products. Politically, China supports agricultural liberalisation in the WTO. On top of the significant concessions made in its accession negotiations, China is ready to make further concessions in market access in the ongoing WTO agriculture negotiations. Of course, China's offer in market access is conditional on substantial concessions in the areas of domestic support and market access by OECD (Organisation for Economic Cooperation and Development) countries. China is also seeking differential and preferential treatment for developing countries and for the newly acceded members, which would allow China to lower the tariffs or expand TRQ quotas for fewer tariff lines by a smaller amount, with later implementation dates and a longer implementation period. This would have an impact on grain imports. Market access reform in other countries, however, does not help with China's horticultural exports, as tariffs for horticultural products have been low and the key hurdles for China's agricultural exports have been SPS measures. The prospects of Chinese agricultural exports are not promising, unless efforts are made to upgrade the quality of its products, much of which are grown with the heavy use of pesticides and other farm chemicals.

Substantial progress has been made in China's FTA talks with ASEAN (Association of Southeast Asian Nations), Australia and New Zealand, all with significant agricultural components. The China-ASEAN FTA agreement excludes rice, but in the ongoing China-Australia FTA talks, China is under pressure from Australia to open up its grain trade. The proposed China-Australia FTA is significant for China, as it is the first FTA with a developed country, which is again the first developed country to recognise China's market economy status. Since China's accession to the WTO, anti-dumping investigations of Chinese products in the US and EU have often been conducted with invocation of the non-market economy status clause in China's accession protocol. Seeking recognition of its market economy status has been a top priority in Chinese foreign-trade diplomacy. Australia sees this recognition as a down-payment for a comprehensive FTA, i.e. an FTA that would give it unfettered access to the Chinese market for its minerals, energy and agricultural exports. To strengthen the trade relations with Australia also conforms to China's need for a secure energy supply to fuel its fast-growing economy. Stakes of a successful conclusion of the FTA negotiations are high for both China and Australia.

Implication for poverty alleviation

The NRD programme and the outcomes of the WTO/FTA negotiations will be the dominating forces that shape the development of Chinese agricultural trade in the coming decade. Agricultural trade reform will generate pressure for further adjustment of agricultural production through market access liberalisation. Given that grain production is not in line with China's comparative advantage, it cannot enrich farmers. On the other hand, domestic support for grain production has its own financial constraints. As a result, poverty pockets exist in China's grain belt, and future agricultural adjustment is likely to generate more at the margin of grain production.

The NRD programme will create favourable opportunities for eradicating these rural poverty pockets. With better roads, schools and healthcare and other infrastructure upgrading in rural areas, it would be easier for farmers to identify and explore more profitable businesses in agriculture, and for resources to move to areas with higher returns. Still, the general rural infrastructural improvements brought by the NRD programme also need to be coupled with initiatives specific to the promising agricultural sectors that would help absorb the shocks of agricultural liberalisation. In the absence of a rural safety net, those initiatives could serve as de facto trade-adjustment assistance programmes. In the case of horticulture, its expansion would create more employment opportunities; the adoption of new technology in horticulture to meet the SPS requirements in high-end overseas markets would reduce pesticide use; and the income generated in the sector would help lift farmers displaced by the grain-sector adjustment out of poverty and put them in a sector expected to sustain its growth and generate high income for farm labourers in an increasingly globalised Chinese economy.

What problems are facing the horticultural sector in China, and what can be done to foster a vibrant export horticultural sector in China? The following section examines the development of horticultural production in China and the province of Shandong's success story of horticultural exports. Lessons will be drawn for poverty alleviation in China's grain belt and in metropolitan suburbs.

Horticulture and poverty alleviation: case studies

General patterns: interview with Professor Zhong Funing

Industrialisation of the Chinese horticultural sector is the driving force behind its rapid growth in recent years, according to Professor Zhong Funing of the Nanjing Agricultural University. Japanese and Korean companies in Shandong province and large domestic agri-business groups in the southern provinces have entered the horticultural sector. Farmers' participation in the industrial horticultural production takes two forms: (i) as company employees; and (ii) as landlords. Thus, farmers receive salaries and rents from the companies as income, and they generally earn more than they did in traditional grain production. Over the past few years, horticultural prices have been declining as more farmers and companies enter the business. But still, the newcomers earn a better income than they did as grain growers.

Horticultural production is labour-intensive, but it also requires access to quality seeds, market information and marketing channels. Farmers often are constrained by lack of funds for initial investment, which usually takes years to show any return. The horticultural sector cannot compete with the grain sector in receiving bank loans. As a result, despite the liberalisation of the Chinese agricultural sector, lack of funds can act as a barrier to the movement of agricultural resources into more profitable sectors. In terms of public spending on agriculture, generally there is no crop-specific support programme except for grain production.

With respect to the environmental consequences of farm chemical use, Professor Zhong Funing suggests that, in China, the use of pesticides and other farm chemicals in horticulture is heavier than in grain production. In cross-country comparison, for per-unit output, China uses more farm chemicals than the EU and US. This has not only contributed to rural environmental deterioration, but it has also made it difficult for Chinese horticultural products to enter the overseas market.

Shandong's experiences: interviews with Mr Qu Guoqiang and Mr Su Jianchang

Mr Qu Guoqiang, Director of the International Cooperation at the Agricultural Agency of Shandong Province, explained that Shandong has a long tradition in horticultural production. Two factors contributed to its recent export surge. Firstly, domestic agricultural liberalisation allows farmers to choose the crops they grow on their farmland. As a matter of policy, conversion of farmland to non-agricultural use is subject to scrutiny by the government, which, for food-security reasons, sets strict conditions for the conversion. However, as long as the land is for agricultural use and the minimal level of grain production is guaranteed, the farmland can be used to grow any crop.

Secondly, foreign investors, mainly from Japan and Korea, are encouraged to engage in export-oriented horticultural production. According to Mr Qu, the local government has been providing foreign investors with networking and other logistics services, as well as subsidies for land use, etc. But it has a role in a firm's operation only at the early phase of its presence in Shandong.

Shandong's horticultural exports help with local employment, and they also fetch very high prices at Japanese retail markets, sometimes ten times as high as domestic retail prices. Though it is not clear exactly how the income is distributed among the various parties involved, local framers who are part of the foreign-funded horticultural production normally earn more than farmers who do it alone.

The positive impact of the NRD programme is visible, as more roads are being built in the region. But, except for grain, there is no special support programme for specific crops. Some local preferential policies towards foreign investors serve as incentives for horticultural production, but they are not a national policy and are in no way comparable in magnitudes with subsidies given to grain production and its related operations.

Foreign-funded firms in horticultural production and exports do have a spill-over effect on local firms, which have learned from the experiences of the foreign firms in management, production and marketing. The Qihe Green Foodstuff Company[5] is a privately owned agri-business firm located in Zibo, Shandong Province, specialising in mushroom-breeding. Compared to Japanese firms, which started earlier with strong capital backing and aimed for the Japanese market, Qihe targets the Korean market, setting up mushroom-breeding and production facilities there to further process the semi-finished products shipped from its home base in Zibo.

Qihe chooses the Korean market mainly because it is easier to get visas for its employees. According to its general manager, Mr Su Jian-chang, by exporting semi-finished rather than final mushroom products, the company has been able to meet SPS requirements, which are gener-ally less stringent for the former. Of course, the quality improvement of its products is also attributable to the company's efforts to standardise the production procedures and to enforce quality control over all aspects of production and the sourcing of materials.

Qihe's operations require heavy initial investment. At the early stage, it was very difficult to get loans, and they had to raise money themselves, like many other domestic private enterprises. They did receive various support from the local government, but only as awards after the firm had become successful rather than as much needed start-up capital. Even for the late-arrived nominal amount, its availability had to rely on the firm's personal connections within the government. Nevertheless, Qihe's success enables it to pay its employees well. The forty to fifty Chinese employees at its Korean facilities picking mushrooms earn salaries three times as high as local farm workers in Shandong.

When asked if Qihe would like to set up operations in a poor region, Mr Su said there is no policy to encourage this move, though he believes that labour costs in the poverty region are low, and mushroom production techniques would be a valuable asset to fight poverty.

[5] Company website: www.qihe.cn [last accessed 24 February 2009].

Mentougou: a poverty box in Beijing suburb

To promote horticultural production and non-traditional agriculture can sometimes be the only way out for some poverty boxes in developed regions of China. Mentougou is a rural mountainous suburb west of Beijing. According to a report released by the Peking University Institute on Poverty Research (Dong, 2006), traditionally a mining town, Mentougou's economy heavily depended on its role as a supplier of coal for the city and for the nearby steel-maker, the Capital Steel and Iron Company. In recent years, in preparation for the Beijing Olympic Games, the polluting steel-maker was shutdown and moved out of Beijing. The region's small coalmines are also in the process of being closed. As a result, Mentougou's economy is in shambles. An attempt has been made to develop the sheep-raising industry, but it has not been successful and has only left its vegetation damaged, which dealt another blow to the already deteriorating environment.

Mentougou's strategy of fighting poverty has been to develop environmentally friendly horticulture and agricultural tourism. The community produces pears, walnuts, cherries and other quality local specialties and since it is part of a metropolitan city it can access a big market for its horticultural and tourist products. However, the intended areas have not currently been developed into full-blown industries that are strong enough to pull the community out of poverty.

Like many other regions in China that have difficulties in tapping the potentials of horticultural production as a means of poverty alleviation, lack of funds and local expertise are the reasons for Mentougou's slow progress. To restore the damaged environment and build schools and other rural infrastructures would take a bulk of the public funds coming through the NRD programme. Obviously, more needs to be done to craft policies that would attract resources and talents from the agricultural research institutions and successful agri-business firms in Beijing to Mentougou.

Solutions and ways forward

Most of China's poverty alleviation attention is on its western region, where economic development lags far behind other parts of the country. However, poverty boxes do exist in its grain belt, mostly in the central part of China,[6] and even in metropolitan suburbs, as a result of trade

[6] See report by French (2008) for the *New York Times*.

liberalisation. Poverty occurs in the wealthy region because there is no social safety net or adjustment assistance programme, and also because proper policies are not in place to encourage horticultural production as a way to smooth the transition. Based on the above analysis, the following three areas can be explored for solutions and ways forward.

Firstly, the FDI policy should be linked with horticultural development in poverty regions. Preferential policies for foreign investment should be developed to encourage their participation in horticultural production and should not be included in the ongoing reform to unify the country's tax codes for domestic and foreign-funded firms. Unlike western regions, China's central and coastal areas have good infrastructure, which should attract FDI. Indeed, in recent years, FDI in China is moving to inland areas for new investment opportunities.

Secondly, horticulture does not enjoy the same political status as grain. However, the current administration is targeting rural poverty through the NRD programme. As part of this programme, policies could be developed to give agri-business companies preferential access to bank loans and other government subsidies if they engage in horticultural production in a poverty region.

Thirdly, a strict testing and certification system should be developed to provide consumers with information on agricultural products in the market. Mr Su of the Qihe Green Foodstuff Company has complained that the current system does not work, as one can actually buy a certificate for organic products. Professor Zhong Funing suggests that this also has something to do with high information costs associated with the system. The lack of strict testing and of a certification system not only raises the food safety concern but also denies genuinely good producers of domestic market expansion before they expand overseas. Perhaps food safety concerns of participants in the Beijing Olympics and the Shanghai World Expo may prompt the government to increase investment in testing and certification systems for agricultural products in the two cities – and eventually to extend these investments to other major cities in China.

References

Dong X. (2006), 'Release of the Investigative Report by the PKU Project Team on Mountainous Poverty Region in Beijing', presentation at the Inaugural Forum on Sustainable Development Strategy for Poverty Region in China, Tianjin, 13 to 14 May (in Chinese).

French, W. H. (2008), 'Lives of Grinding Poverty, Untouched by China's Boom',
    New York Times, 13 January.
Lin, Y., Cai F. and Li Z. (2003), *China's Miracle: Development Strategy and Economic
    Reform*, Chinese University of Hong Kong Press: Hong Kong.
Murphy, D. (2004), 'A Fearsome Thirst', *Far Eastern Economic Review*, 22 July 2004.
Wang S., Li Z. and Ren Y. (2004), *China's 87 Project on Poverty Alleviation: National
    Strategy and its Impact*, case study prepared for the World Bank poverty
    conference in Shanghai (in Chinese).
Yao, S. (2007), 'Chinese Agricultural Reform and the WTO and FTA Negotiations',
    in *Agricultural Trade: Planting the Seeds of Regional Liberalization in Asia*,
    United Nations: Bangkok, Thailand.

III

Trade in services and poverty reduction

3

The future of trade in services for
developing countries[1]

JOY ABRENICA,* CHRISTOPHER FINDLAY**
AND AIK HOE LIM***

Introduction

The question in this theme chapter is: what is the impact of services policy reform on the welfare of poor households? As explained below, there is a variety of channels through which services can be provided, and it is important to consider the whole portfolio of options in order to identify the ways in which poor households might be affected. Hoekman (2006) reviews the nature of services trade liberalisation and its scope to generate welfare gains.

The framework adopted here is to combine a discussion of the nature of trade and investment in services, and the associated impediments to integration in the world economy, with a series of issues that Winters (2000a, 2000b) identified with respect to liberalisation more generally. These issues include:

- how reform affects prices and how these price changes are passed through the rest of the economy
- whether the reform will destroy currently effective markets or create new ones, allowing consumers access to new forms of services

[1] Work on this paper was also supported by a grant from the Australian Research Council (LP0775245).
* Joy Abrenica is Associate Professor at the School of Economics, University of the Philippines.
** Professor Christopher Findlay is Head of the School of Economics at the University of Adelaide.
*** Aik Hoe Lim was on sabbatical leave as a visiting WTO Fellow at the Institute for International Trade when writing this paper. The views expressed are his alone and do not necessarily represent the views of the WTO Secretariat or its members and therefore cannot be attributed to it.

- the nature of the second-round effects of these first two effects, and their particular effects on poor households
- the characteristics of the factors of production used in services production and the elasticity of their supply
- the impact of the reforms on government revenue
- whether the new business environment will be significantly riskier and how that will affect incentives for investment
- the links between reform and growth
- whether there are particular local effects to be taken into account
- whether any transitional unemployment will be concentrated among the poor households.

In the sections below, the chapter reviews these issues and their application to services reform. The focus of the discussion is the impact of domestic policy reform with respect to these issues. Also of interest to developing countries, and with great significance to poor households, is the effect of the liberalisation of the movement of people to provide services in other developed countries. In a separate section, the chapter considers the opportunities associated with this type of reform. However, before turning to the above issues, it is useful to review the nature of trade and investment in services.

Trade and investment in services

A services transaction requires contact between consumers and producers. Services production involves a value-adding activity but its output cannot be stored, and instead is consumed as it is produced. Services firms create capacity to supply these activities, and in many cases their provision is highly differentiated. A number of options exist for international transactions depending on whether the consumer moves (mode 2) or the services firm relocates (mode 3), or whether neither move physically but make contact in other ways (mode 1). Also, services might be provided not within a business structure but through the movement of people (mode 4).

It is difficult to find data on the relative significance of these different modes. The data available on the extent of mode 4 transactions is discussed in more detail below. Karsenty (2000) provided some estimates of the scale of the other modes. More recent estimates are shown in Table 3A. These data highlight the importance of mode 3. The total worldwide value of mode 3 transactions was estimated to be in the order of US$3,500–US$3,600 in 2004.

Table 3A *Relative importance of mode of supplies in international services transactions*

Mode	Importance (%)
Cross-border supply (BOP)	35
Consumption abroad (BOP travel)	10–15
Commercial presence (foreign affiliates)	50
Presence of natural persons (BOP compensation)	1–2

Source: Maurer *et al.,* (2006).

Services firms are not restricted to use of one of these modes; they might use a combination, and the nature of the mix may change as the business matures or as the policy environment shifts. As in the case of goods, services production could be broken up into a series of steps (as in a supply chain) and various steps could be located in different countries.

A range of policy measures affect trade and investment in services. Measures that affect the movement of consumers and producers are relevant, and measures that affect the operations of firms in various markets are also important. Some measures apply to foreign providers only (e.g. rules concerning the extent of foreign ownership of local services firms) and some apply to both local and foreign suppliers (e.g. licensing schemes). Some policies apply to establishment and some are more important to operations. This suggests a 2 × 2 classification of policy measures (foreign only or foreign plus domestic, against establishment and operations).[2]

These measures differ in their effects: some that restrict entry are likely to add to rents, but others may add to costs rather than rents (Dee and Sidorenko, 2006). It is important to continue work to isolate these impacts, since the results determine the political economy of reform and its welfare effects. Brown and Stern (2001) and Deardorff and Stern (2006) review work done on measuring barriers to trade in services and their effects.

Impacts of reform

The chapter now turns to the issues identified earlier. Following this, the special issues of mode 4 delivery of services are discussed. (Refer to Figure 3A, which illustrates the four modes of supply of services.)

---

[2] See Pauwelyn (2005) for a discussion of the treatment of the first of these distinctions in the General Agreement on Trade in Services (GATS).

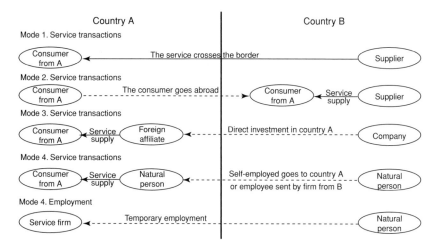

Figure 3A   The four modes of supply: an illustrative model. *Source:* UN manual on statistics of international trade in services.

How reform affects prices and how these price changes are passed through the rest of the economy

Removing barriers to entry to all suppliers will add to capacity and competition, leading to lower prices in those markets where services are not tradable in other forms. This might occur, for example, with the removal of restrictions on mode 3 delivery in telecommunications, health or retail. In goods reforms, where barriers to trade are removed, foreign-sourced quantity supplied increases, prices fall and domestic output falls. But in services reform, when the increments to supply occur via mode 3, local output can *increase* because of the rise in foreign investment, at the same time as local prices falling. As Dee and Sidorenko (2006) point out, these effects change considerably the political economy implications of managing services reform compared to that for goods.

In other cases, removal of impediments to international business via modes 1, 2 or 4 would align domestic and international prices, and with effects more familiar with goods reform: falling prices for previously protected sectors and a decrease in local output, and rising prices for exportable services where impediments to export are removed. These price changes feed through to real income effects for poor households, depending on whether they are net buyers or sellers (which is less likely) of the relevant services.

In economies whose service sectors have been relatively closed to domestic private suppliers as well as to foreign participation, services liberalisation has been found to lower prices, with significant welfare effects. Konan and Maskus (2006), for instance, in their simulation of the Tunisian economy, found that gains from services liberalisation would be more than three times the magnitude of estimated gains from goods trade liberalisation alone.[3] Moreover, 75% of services liberalisation gains are to be achieved from the liberalisation of mode 3 barriers on commercial presence, which impede foreign investment, and real household income also stood to gain by 4% by granting the right of establishment to foreign firms (Konan and Maskus 2006, p. 19).

Price reductions following services liberalisation are also found in Dihel and Kalinova's (2004) study on banking and telecommunications services in transition economies.[4] In telecommunications, the removal of barriers to commercial presence lowered prices of fixed and mobile telephone services and improved fixed-line penetration. Reforms would, however, need to remove both general restrictions on competition as well as barriers to foreign equity participation. Partial removal of barriers to foreign participation without parallel lifting of restrictions on new entry would shift monopoly rents to foreign operators, with limited benefits to domestic consumers. Should both fronts be liberalised, Dihel and Kalinova (2004, p. 19) estimate that the price of fixed-line telecommunications could be reduced by up to 20% in Bulgaria and Romania and by 30% in Macedonia. For the banking sector, the impact of removing market access and national treatment restrictions on prices was more limited. This was in part due to the fact that the banking sector was already fairly contestable for many of the countries studied, and also because other critical factors such as macroeconomic instability and lack of other complementary structural reform were inhibiting banking-sector performance.

---

[3] Konan and Maskus (2006) used a computable general equilibrium model of the Tunisian economy with multiple products and services and three trading partners. Restraints on services trade were defined as those on cross-border supply (mode 1) and commercial presence (mode 3).

[4] Dihel and Kalinova's (2004) sample included the Baltic States and eight South Eastern European countries (for telecommunications and banking) and Russia (for telecommunications). Restrictiveness indexes are computed for countries under study and used to estimate the impact of existing policies on the sector's performance and price levels.

Whether the reform will destroy currently effective markets or create
new ones, allowing consumers access to new forms of services

Services reform may destroy some pre-reform marketing systems and at the same time create markets for services that previously did not exist.

An example of the former may be the effect of opening up markets for retail and wholesale services on traditional food ('wet') markets. Poor households' welfare, particularly as producers or net sellers of agricultural products, may be closely tied to traditional marketing channels: examples of the adjustments they face are examined in a series of papers including Natawidjaja *et al.* (2007) and Hernández *et al.* (2007). New forms of retail services, on the other hand, offer all households access to combinations of price and quality in a wider range of goods. The impact of supermarkets on nutrition is also debated, and their effects may be mixed despite their strong consumer appeal.

New markets for services might be created. The package of services defined as logistics is one example. Logistics is the process of planning, implementing and controlling the efficient flow and storage of goods, services and related information from the point of origin to the point of consumption to meet customers' requirements. The provision of logistics services requires input from a number of service providers, including the providers of transport and warehousing as well as other value-adding activities. Luo and Findlay (2004) report the experience of WTO accession in China on the provision of logistics services. They estimate that logistics costs as a share of total wholesale prices might have fallen by 10 to 14 percentage points in association with China's commitments on various services as part of accession to the WTO. The gains came mainly from new ways of organising the component activities, rather than reforms within the component activities of the service. In other words, the gains came from the creation of a new market.

The incidence of these gains may favour producers, which in the case of agricultural products are more likely to be poor households. For example, poor households providing products whose local prices are determined in world markets (e.g. agricultural products), and from which transportation margins are deducted to determine a 'farm gate' price, may receive the majority of the gains.

There are other examples of new services being created, for example the variety of services associated with telecommunications reform, the provision of mobile phones and access to the internet and its associated benefits of access to information services. Torero and von Braun (2005,

2006) stress the value of information and communications technology (ICT) in the provision of public services for poor households, but they also stress that:

> ICTs offer an opportunity for development, but not a panacea. For the potential benefits of ICTs to be realized in developing countries, many prerequisites need to be put in place: prompt deregulation, effective competition among service providers, free movement and adoption of technologies, targeted and competitive subsidies to reduce the access gap, and institutional arrangements to increase the use of ICTs in the provision of public goods.
>
> (Torero and von Braun, 2005, p. 6)

The nature of the second-round effects of these first two effects, and their particular effects on poor households

Services transactions via mode 3 increase the stock of capital flowing into the economy and thus raise national income. They may also bring better integration into international markets through improved management, new production techniques, quality control and access to foreign markets. Foreign direct investment (FDI) may enhance productivity by providing goods and services that are either not produced by the economy or are produced inefficiently.

Access to transactions via other modes of supply can also facilitate adjustment and structural change. Technological change and facilitation from the liberalisation of complementary services such as telecommunications leads to a finer division of supply chains, which can offer new export and employment opportunities for labour-rich developing countries. Developed countries, for example, can relocate services activities to developing countries through outsourcing and off-shoring (Bhagwati *et al.*, 2004). The labour demanded in these activities may be relatively skilled compared to other local endowments of labour; however, UNCTAD (2005) argues for the opportunities for small and medium enterprises (SMEs) in business processing.

From the perspective of poverty reduction, cheaper and more abundant services enhance the welfare of the poor. More efficient intermediate services such as finance, telecoms, transportation and business services would also improve economic performance overall and could potentially generate more jobs. Services such as education and health are also important for developing human capital.

Better access to services also supports productivity growth in other sectors. In sub-Saharan Africa, findings from Arnold, Mattoo and Narciso (2006) are consistent with the view that access to services inputs of competitive quality and price matter for the productivity of firms, and are thus an essential element of a strategy for promoting growth and reducing poverty. Using data from over 1,000 firms in ten sub-Saharan African countries, their results show a significant and positive relationship between firm productivity and access to telecommunications, electricity and financial services.[5] Arnold et al. (2006) examine the link between services-sector reforms and the productivity of manufacturing industries. They focus on manufacturing industries that use services inputs. They use firm-level data from the Czech Republic for the period of 1998 to 2003, which show a positive relationship between services-sector reform and the performance of domestic firms in downstream manufacturing sectors.

These productivity effects are not only important for manufacturing. Services firms themselves are large services consumers, for example tourism's use of air transport, data processing's use of telecommunications, etc. Small island economies are especially sensitive to these issues (Findlay et al., 2005).

Markusen et al. (2000) highlight that it is not only the availability of producer services that is important to downstream economic activities, but also their localised proximity. Drawing from economic geography literature, they point out that producer services tend to agglomerate around manufacturing sectors since firm performance is enhanced by the local availability of such services.[6] What this suggests is that, in the case of producer services, FDI through commercial presence is qualitatively different to cross-border supply in its productivity impact. Close availability of producer services is important because the service provider and client generally benefit from personal contact and discussions. The prohibition of commercial presence may thus hamper the productivity gains to downstream economic activities from such services.

---

[5] Arnold et al. (2006) used data from the World Bank Enterprise Survey to calculate the total factor productivity of firms and to develop objective and subjective indicators on how the performance of services sectors constrain a firm's activities.

[6] Producer services are defined by Markusen et al. (2000) as including managerial services, engineering services, financial services, marketing services and information services.

The characteristics of the factors of production used in services production and the elasticity of their supply

When domestic output increases in the services sector following reform, demand for labour will also increase. It is not clear, however, what the effects will be on various types of labour, and whether the demand for labour supplied by poor households will increase. The Chinese experience of urbanisation suggests that growth in some services activities does increase demand for labour previously employed in agriculture, for example in construction and other local services. Whether this increase in demand also affects wages depends on the elasticity of the supply of that labour. Incomes may be higher as a result of working longer hours.

Markusen *et al.* (2000) found that policies that aim to protect domestic skilled labour against competition from imported services can have the perverse effect of lowering the returns to domestic skilled labour. Modelling the impact of FDI in services on the domestic market, they find that even when foreign firms use less domestic labour, the positive productivity and scale effects on downstream industry can be sufficiently powerful that the real wage of skilled labour increases after the liberalisation of FDI in service industries.

The impact of the reforms on government revenue

Protection of local production of goods through tariffs generates government revenue. Reform reduces government revenue and may affect government capacity to fund the provision of services that raise the real incomes of poor households. This direct effect of reform is less likely in the case of services reform because of the nature of the policies that are changed. These are more likely to involve regulatory reform than the removal of impediments that generated government revenue.

There is one case in which the revenue effects are significant from the perspective of poor households. This occurs in markets where barriers to entry are used to create rents that then finance the provision of services to poor or isolated areas. This cross-subsidy model breaks down if markets are opened to competition, which will attract entry into the profitable sections of the market. Alternative fiscal forms of support would have to be developed to maintain services previously provided. These issues are particularly important in telecommunications, and may also be important in health.

*Whether the new business environment will be significantly riskier and
how that will affect incentives for investment*

The effects of services reform on risks in the investment environment are
not clear. Exposure to world prices and the risks of competition from new
providers may be a challenge for incumbents. Entrants may, however, have
access to complementary services to help manage these risks (e.g. through
their financing arrangements[7]) or have developed business strategies for
doing so (e.g. production differentiation based on higher levels of local
knowledge). Access to competitive complementary services will therefore
be important in making the transition to the new more open environment.

There are special issues associated with the reform of the financial sector and its openness to foreign participation. Kiyota *et al.* (2007) examine the argument for financial liberation in Ethiopia. The benefits, they
stress, are the positive effects on the efficiency of the banking sector,
the improvement of bank supervision through the regulatory spillover
of foreign bank entry and the possible positive effects of foreign banks
on wages and employment. They also note the risks involved, including
'financial fragility': the likelihood of a banking crisis is greater when the
financial system is liberalised and where the institutional environment
is weak. Prasad *et al.* (2004) find that: (i) good institutions and quality
of governance; (ii) macroeconomic stability; and (iii) relatively flexible
exchange rate regimes and (success) in maintaining fiscal discipline add
to the probability of both the potential growth and stabilisation benefits
of financial globalisation.

Mishkin (2007) stresses the importance of managing financial liberalisation properly.[8] Mishkin also argues that participation of foreign banks
in the financial system contributes to financial development, which in turn
helps poor households get access to credit. His conclusion of a review of
work in the field is that 'the income of the poorest fifth of the population actually grows faster than average gross domestic product (GDP) per
capita' in countries with better financial development.

The links between reform and growth

Economic growth is the most important long-run mechanism for poverty
reduction, and services reform makes a contribution in a variety of ways.

---

[7] See Svaleryd and Vlachos (2002) for more discussion of the relationship between protection
and the development of markets for risk.
[8] Mishkin also notes the work of Kaminsky and Schmuckler (2002), that even with the risk
of instability (the short-run 'pain') or crises, the long-run gain is significant.

Its various links to productivity growth in the rest of the economy have already been stressed. In addition, it provides access to additional capital, which adds to national income, as also already noted. Reform and openness brings new technology in a physical sense (e.g. digital technologies associated with telecommunications) but also new structures of organising businesses (as in the case of logistics), and adds in the process of their adoption to productivity and thereby growth. Openness of local markets adds to the threat of entry of new competitors and to actual entry, leading to better levels of efficiency, greater productivity and incentives to innovate. Furthermore, better quality education and health systems that are associated with the reform of those markets add to rate of accumulation of human capital and thereby growth.

Acemoglu and Johnson (2005) have stressed the links between the enforcement of property rights and long-run growth, and many of the services-sector activities, particular professional services, are key parts of the enforcement process. Reform will add to the capacity to provide those services supports to the development and operation of these institutions.

There are some studies on linkages to growth. Mattoo *et al.* (2001), for instance, in a study of sixty countries over the 1990 to 1999 period, found that openness in the financial and telecommunications sectors influences long-run growth performance. Eschenbach and Hoekman (2005) also document a positive correlation between the extent of services liberalisation and economic growth in transition economies for the period 1990 to 2004.

Whether there are particular local effects to be taken into account

In some countries, there may be particular local impacts of reform, leading to pressure for the relocation of households for example. In other cases, it is the local application of policy that is more important. Some countries (e.g. China) have scheduled services reform with variations across regions. Local firms were protected for longer in less well-developed areas. This delay also delays the receipt of the sorts of benefits discussed here, and may actually widen rather than maintain income gaps.

In some countries, the impacts of reform are geographically concentrated. This may be related to the provision of complementary services such as infrastructure. For example, the Indian information technology sector is commonly referred to as an example of a growing sector in a developing country that has benefited from reform, but its requirements for access to infrastructure services has led (alongside a local policy environment that facilitates its development) to its geographic concentration around Bangalore.

Whether any transitional unemployment will be concentrated among the poor households

There may be transitional effects that are important. Konan and Maskus (2006) found that adjustment costs were less for services liberalisation as compared to the liberalisation of goods trade. Gains were more evenly distributed across factors and did not lead to dramatic changes in the composition of production as in the case of pure goods-trade liberalisation.

Rutherford *et al.* (2005), in their model on the poverty effects of Russia's WTO accession, also demonstrate this point.[9] Despite the estimated gains for virtually all households, with more than 70 per cent of the total value of gains accounted for by services liberalisation, during a transition period it is possible that many households will lose jobs.[10] However, they also find that while gains are unevenly distributed across income groups, the poor gain slightly more than the wealthy because the wage rate of unskilled labour increases more than the rate of return on capital.[11]

Movement of people and poverty reduction

Liberalising the supply of a service through the temporary movement of natural persons could generate very large mutual gains to both developing and developed WTO member countries.[12] At the outset, it is important to note that movement of natural persons under mode 4 of the GATS relates only to the services sector and explicitly to the temporary movement of

---

[9] Rutherford *et al.* (2005) used a dataset with 55,000 households. Surveys were commissioned on barriers to FDI in telecommunications, banking, insurance and securities, and maritime and air transportation services.

[10] Rutherford *et al.* (2005), p. 4.

[11] Rutherford *et al.* (2005), p. 24. The poorest decile of households gain 7.6% while the richest gain 6.8%.

[12] Mode 4 is defined in Article I of the GATS as the supply of a service 'by a service supplier of one Member, through presence of natural persons of a Member in the territory of any other Member'. The GATS Annex on Movement of Natural Persons Supplying Services specifies that two categories of natural persons are covered: (i) natural persons who are 'service suppliers of a Member' (i.e. self-employed suppliers who obtain their remuneration directly from customers); and (ii) those affecting natural persons of a member who are 'employed by a services supplier of a Member in respect of the supply of a service'.

service providers to provide specific services rather than to permanent migration and entry into the labour market.[13] However, on the premise that the economic consequences of movement of natural persons under mode 4 are akin to labour migration, most studies take a wider view and examine not only the movement of service providers but of labour on a permanent and temporary basis.

Walmsley and Winters (2005) estimate that an increase in developed countries' quotas on the inward movements of both skilled and unskilled temporary workers equivalent to 3 per cent of their workforces would generate an estimated increase in world welfare of about US$156 billion.[14] Further work by Walmsley *et al.* (2005) confirm these results and show that permanent residents in developed countries would also be major beneficiaries with real incomes increasing by an average of US$200 per person as compared to US$24 per person for developing-country permanent residents.

Despite the potentially huge gains from liberalising mode 4 and the commonality of interest between developing and developed countries, little has so far been achieved within the framework of the GATS. In existing GATS schedules, commitments for mode 4 tend to be far more restrictive than for other modes of supply.[15] Of the commitments that have been made, there is a general bias in favour of highly skilled labour as compared to low or unskilled labour. About 280 out of a total of 400 schedule entries relate to the temporary movement of executives, managers and specialists.[16] Close to 70 per cent of the commitments are also for 'intra-corporate transferees'. This category is of limited interest to developing countries as they are linked to FDI through the commercial presence of firms from the same home country.

Current estimates suggests that mode 4 accounts for less than 2% of world services trade, which points to the potential for further liberalisation of the temporary movement of natural service providers.[17]

---

[13] In the GATS Annex on the Movement of Natural Persons Supplying Services, it is stated that: 'The Agreement shall not apply to measures affecting natural persons seeking access to the employment market of a Member, nor shall it apply to measures regarding citizenship, residence or employment on a permanent basis.'

[14] The model used by Walmsley and Winters (2005) uses a much wider mode 4 definition of temporary movement of natural persons than the GATS as it uses data on workers' remittances, which includes transfers by permanent migrants as well as by foreign workers in non-services sectors, as an input. Workers' remittances are used because the mode 4 definition in the GATS does not correspond to any data that is collected in trade statistics.

[15] Figures are from WTO (2002), p. 2.

[16] WTO (2002). Estimates are as of April 2002.   [17] WTO Secretariat (2005), p. 8.

Remittances to developing countries, which include transfers from both permanent and temporary migrants in all economic sectors, were estimated at US$206.3 billion in 2006 (or 40% more than total overseas development aid).[18] For many low-income countries, remittances are already a significant part of capital inflows. In Bangladesh and Lesotho, for instance, remittances accounted for 27% of total GDP in 2001.[19] Remittances are also significant for large developing countries. In India, remittances by the expatriate labour force of the state of Kerala accounted for more than 20% of the state's income domestic product.[20] The €2.9 billion remitted by Moroccans and Egyptians abroad in 2002 represented the largest source of foreign exchange for both countries.[21]

In terms of poverty-related impacts, the effects are complex and may differ widely between sectors, economic activities and skill levels. Nevertheless, virtually all studies on the temporary movement of natural persons show that the greatest absolute and poverty-related gains for developing countries come from the liberalisation of the low and unskilled.[22] Greater liberalisation of mode 4 would allow developing countries to exploit their relative abundance of low and unskilled labour. Mode 4 service providers would benefit directly from higher wages, some of which would flow back to the sending country in the form of remittances.[23] While mode 4 service providers are not migrants, they are also likely to benefit from increased incomes. Other less tangible but potentially important benefits may be productivity gains from exposure to new working methods and ideas that could be transferred upon return to the home country.

Much of the concern regarding the downsides of mode 4 liberalisation for developing countries have focused on the outflow of skilled professionals depleting the country of the human capital needed for economic growth at home. Given that skilled manpower is relatively scarce in developing countries, the negative effect of their departure is likely to be considerable. Skeldon (2005), however, argues that, given the inability of many developing countries to optimally absorb their skills, the negative effect of the outflow of skilled professionals may be overstated. Moreover, apart

---

[18] See World Bank (2007).   [19] Kategekwa (2006).
[20] See Jha et al. (2005), p. 79.   [21] Figures are quoted by Collyer (2005), p. 8.
[22] See Winters (2003), Walmsley and Winters (2005) and Walmsley et al. (2005).
[23] Walmsley et al. (2005) estimate that skilled and unskilled service providers themselves gain in real terms by US$9,200 and US$9,400 respectively.

from the contribution of remittances, from the perspective of poverty alleviation, the outflow of skilled professionals is less relevant as they are unlikely to be poor.

Clearly, the movement of low and unskilled labour provides greater potential for poverty alleviation. For one, the positive economic impact of their remittances would more than offset the economic loss of their contribution to the home economy. The reality is also that many developing countries face a large surplus of low or unskilled labour, which they are unable to absorb. Collyer (2004) noted that Maghreb countries will require more than 1 million jobs a year.[24] Egypt will require between 600,000 and 800,000 jobs to maintain employment at current high levels. Due to aging populations and other demographic factors, developed countries, on the other hand, face a reverse situation, with growing scarcity of labour in their markets. The paradox, however, is that despite this correlation of interest, policies on the movement of the lowly skilled are far more restrictive than for the highly skilled.

While simulations on the temporary movement of natural persons appear conclusive that liberalisation of mode 4 even within the narrow remit of trade in services is welfare-enhancing, an account must also be taken of the conditions under which the movement takes place. Barber *et al.* (2005), in their examination of temporary mobility schemes in the UK, illustrate how the cycle of movement from recruitment to working, remitting money and the subsequent return may undermine the gains from higher income abroad, and thus reduce the positive impact on poverty.[25] For instance, exploitative practices by recruiters or employers may erode any income earned. If working conditions are abusive, it is also unlikely that there will be any training that would allow temporary movers to gain new skills that could then be taken home. Barber *et al.* (2005) note that empirical evidence is discouraging, with results of various studies showing that low-skilled temporary workers typically do not acquire formal skills during their time abroad.[26] Collyer (2004) also highlights that skilled foreign workers may take jobs or provide services below their training and capacity, thus undermining the notion of skills

[24] See Collyer (2004), p. 4.
[25] While temporary mobility schemes such as those operating in the UK go beyond the scope of mode 4 of the GATS, their experiences in terms of the benefits gained by the individual and his or her country of origin are helpful in understanding the types of problems that may undermine the gains from providing services abroad.
[26] See Barber *et al.* (2005), p. 11.

being improved whilst abroad. In terms of remittances, difficulties with opening bank accounts and gaining access to the formal financial sector may result in higher transfer charges being paid, thus reducing the net capital flow home. In sum, to be of maximum benefit, temporary mobility schemes, including those for service providers, would have to be designed in a way that regulates recruitment, establishes minimum work or service conditions and facilitates financial flows.

Some of the ways to resolve the problems highlighted by Barber *et al.* (2005) would be to allow formal entry into the labour market by temporary movers, as this would allow them to benefit from domestic labour laws and regulations. However, this is unlikely to occur, since a hallmark of temporary mobility schemes is that the foreign worker is excluded from the formal labour market. A better avenue (despite the difficulties in making progress) that would mitigate some of the concerns about temporariness and entry into the domestic labour market, whilst providing greater transparency and predictability to the temporary mover, would be to utilise the GATS mode 4 scheme.

Permanent migration is politically fraught. GATS mode 4 has the advantage of being explicit: that temporary movement is to provide specific services rather than formal entry into the labour market. GATS mode 4 also does not impinge on national visa and work permit regulations. From the home country point of view, temporary migration under mode 4 implies a return of skills, thus alleviating problems of 'brain drain'. Of course, the question is how to ensure that the move is temporary. Clearly, there remain a number of important issues to resolve within the framework of the GATS. Managing a GATS mode 4 scheme is also likely to be complex and will require regulatory innovations in both the home and host country. Chaudhuri *et al.* (2004), for instance, provide an in-depth examination of the shortcomings of the GATS framework in relation to mode 4, and propose a model for overcoming them. At the time of writing, while the likelihood of a breakthrough in the negotiations on mode 4 commitments, especially for low-skilled and unskilled service providers, may appear remote, progress here would be key to maximising the poverty alleviation effects of trade in services.

Conclusion

There is significant potential for low-income economies to gain from services trade and investment liberalisation, and in the process for low-income households to gain as well. There are particular benefits from the introduction of foreign investment in these services into these economies, including for poor households. It adds to capacity, lowers domestic prices and creates new services. Poor households gain as consumers of these services, and some research suggests the income effects for those households are more significant than for the average household (the case of financial development, for example, and access to ICT may be another). Poor households also gain indirectly as services reform adds to the productivity of other sectors, reducing the costs of intermediate inputs that raise their income. The impact of reform on the transportation and logistics sectors is one example of these sorts of effects. Poor households may also gain through the labour market effects of reform, which lead to higher output and additional demand for labour.

These effects refer to the impact of reform in the home country. Reform in export markets also matters, particularly for people movement. The potential for gains from these forms of services transactions are very large for the labour-exporting countries.

Transactions in other modes offer access to new lower-cost services to households as consumers, or provide complementary inputs adding to productivity in various service sectors that poor households consume directly or indirectly. The growth of outsourcing is one example of this mode of doing business, which adds further to the demand for labour in developing countries. The skill orientation of that labour demand and the implications for poor households is a topic for further work.

Poor households can gain therefore from services trade and investment liberalisation, which occurs both in their home countries and in the rest of the world. However, there are significant challenges in the implementation of reform.

The nature of trade in services and the nature of the impediments to international business mean that capturing the gains from domestic reform requires attention to matters that are often 'behind the border', for example regulatory processes. In those cases, the manner in which the policy is administered is often as important as the specification of the policy itself. Gains to poor households depend on the success of the national reforms. Successful reform requires attention to both design and implementation of policy, and that may be challenging for a developing economy with relatively scarce endowments of skills to manage the regulatory processes, and which lacks institutions that support a commitment to a high quality of governance.

These issues are acute with respect to financial-sector reform, which offers significant efficiency gains and national benefits, including for poor households, but also leads to greater risks of instability. Opening up the infrastructure sector to foreign participation, thereby adding to competition and capacity, also offers the scope for gain, including through access to new services delivered via ICT. However, institutions to sustain the competitive environment or regulate the natural monopoly components of it will be important to capture the gains in the host economy, rather than simply transferring rents to foreign providers. At the same time, removing the previous monopoly regimes rules out cross-subsidies. Services to poor and isolated areas then have to be funded in other ways. Similarly, mode 4 offers very significant scope for gains, but it is important to consider the case for a system in host countries that regulates recruitment, establishes minimum work or service conditions and facilitates financial flows.

Services reform itself can relax some of these constraints on the design and implementation of a reform programme. A simple example is access to international education and training, either through opening local markets or removing impediments to students studying offshore. There are other channels. The local participation of foreign banks may provide a higher level of prudential quality in the banking system, as the foreign entrants impose their home standards on their local operations. The same regulatory spillover effect applies in other service activities. Higher levels of competition or the scope for entry also opens up new options for regulatory processes, for example successful auctions for licenses in the infrastructure sector. Services reform can support the development of property rights institutions, for example, through access to a larger range of better quality professional services. Finally, more competitive markets and the reduction of the scope to earn rents reduce the gains from and incentive for corruption (Ades and Di Tella, 1999).

Successful policy reform requires consideration of packaging. For example, opening up the tourism sector to foreign investment will have a greater effect if impediments to trade in air transportation services are also removed. Services reform is an important complement to goods-sector reform as well. Efficient transportation and telecommunications services may offer options for adjustment in previously protected activities that seek to redesign their supply chains or relocate them. There are important complementarities between goods and services reforms.

The case studies that follow illustrate this theme of the ways in which complementary policy development supports the core components of reform. For example, the chapter on telecommunications reform in Vanuatu stresses the importance of establishing appropriate regulatory frameworks. Pro-competitive arrangements require, for example, arrangements to support the entry of new competitors. The work on telecommunications reform in Uganda highlights the value of paying attention to the terms of access to services by poor households in a deregulated environment, and provides fine detail on how to proceed. The chapter on India and the ICT sector examines the labour market issues, and the ways in which complementary education policies lead to a better distribution of the benefits. Likewise, the chapter on health services in Malaysia stresses the value of policies to support access in the context of higher levels of private participation: suggestions include special attention to safeguards on access and consideration of financing mechanisms for the provision of health services. The chapter on Tanzania highlights the role of policies to ease supply-side constraints among local firms, including the role of aid for that purpose.

These examples also show how both policy design and implementation in the services sector are important. Each area offers scope for international economic cooperation, as the chapter on Tanzania also discusses. Findlay (2007) argues that 'contributions arise from the three c's: the additional *capacity* to undertake and implement the recommendations of domestic policy reviews, the option to *commit* to the new policies and avoid backsliding and the value of developing methods to *capture* the spillovers in policy making in different countries'. An example of the latter is the inter-country effects of the application of competition policy, for example, in relation to mergers or anti-cartel policy enforcement.

Questions remain regarding how and where to organise the international collaborative work. Findlay (2007) notes that relevant international organisations to manage this cooperation already exist, and the WTO itself offers significant capacity. Its principles could be used by subgroups of its members to guide their work on 'behind the border' issues in smaller cooperative structures that have the capacity to implement commitments. However, no one institution is likely to provide all the forms of international cooperation for all purposes (see Soesastro and Findlay, 2006). In the short term, institutions may emerge with overlapping memberships and overlapping functions, leading to much debate about the appropriate function for a particular structure. The allocation of functions to organisations will most likely evolve as the effectiveness of different constellations becomes clear from experience, and as budget constraints on participation bind.

Bibliography

Acemoglu, D. and Johnson, S. (2005), 'Unbundling Institutions', *Journal of Political Economy* 113(5): 949–95.

Ades, A. and Di Tella, R. (1999), 'Rents, Competition and Corruption', *American Economic Review* 89(4): 982–93.

Arnold, J., Javorcik, B. and Mattoo, A. (2006), 'The Productivity Effects of Services Liberalization: Evidence from the Czech Republic', Policy Research Working Paper, No. 4048, World Bank: Washington, WA.

Arnold, J. M., Mattoo, A. and Narciso, G. (2006), *Services Inputs and Firm Productivity in Sub-Saharan Africa: Evidence from Firm-level Data*, World Bank: Washington, WA.

Barber, C., Black, R. and Tenaglia, P. (2005), 'Making Migration Development Friendly: Temporary Worker Schemes in the UK', WP T10, DRC Working Paper Series.

Bhagwati, J., Panagariya, A. and Srinivasan, T. N. (2004), 'The Muddles over Outsourcing', *Journal of Economic Perspectives* 18(4): 93–119.

Brown, D. and Stern, R. M. (2001), 'Measurement and Modeling of the Economic Effects of Trade and Investment Barriers in Services', *Review of International Economics* 9: 262–86.

Chaudhuri, S., Mattoo, A. and Self, R. (2004), 'Moving People to Deliver Services: How Can the WTO Help?', Policy Research Working Paper, No. 3238, World Bank: Washington, WA.

Collyer, M. (2004), 'The Development Impact of Temporary International Labour Migration on Southern Mediterranean Sending Countries', WP T6, DRC Working Paper Series.

Conway, T. (2004), *Trade Liberalisation and Poverty Reduction*, Overseas Development Institute: London.

Deardorf, A. and Stern, R. (2006), 'Empirical Analysis of Barriers to International Services Transactions and the Consequences of Liberalization', in R. Stern, A. Mattoo and G. Zannini (eds.), *A Handbook on International Trade in Services*, Oxford University Press: Oxford.

Dee, P. and Sidorenko, A. (2006), 'The Rise of Services Trade: Regional Initiatives and Challenges for the WTO', in C. Findlay and H. Soesastro (eds.), *Reshaping the Asia Pacific Economic Order*, Routledge: London and New York, NY, pp. 200–26.

Dihel, N. and Kalinova, B. (2004), 'Services Barriers and their Economic Impact: Examples of Banking and Telecommunication Services in Selected Transition Economies', OECD Trade Policy Working Paper, No. 7, OECD: Paris.

Eschenbach, F. and Hoekman, B. (2005), 'Services Policy Reform and Economic Growth in Transition Economies, 1990–2004', Policy Research Working Paper Series 3663, World Bank: Washington, WA.

Findlay, C. (2007), 'The Widening Agenda of Cooperation for Regional Economic Integration', in H. Soeasastro and C. Joewono (eds.), *The Inclusive Regionalist: A Festchrift Dedicated to Jusuf Wanandi*, CSIS: Jakarta.

Findlay, C., Forsyth, P. and King, J. (2005), 'Developments in Pacific Islands' Air Transport', in S. Chand (ed.), *Pacific Islands Regional Integration and Governance*, ANU E Press and Asia Pacific Press: Canberra, pp. 168–92.

Hernández, R., Reardon, T. and Berdegué, J. A. (2007), 'Supermarkets, Wholesalers, and Tomato Growers in Guatemala', *Agricultural Economics* 36(3): 281–90.

Hodge, J. and H. Nordas (1999), *Liberalization of Trade in Producer Services: The Impact on Developing Countries*, Chr. Michelsen Institute.

Hoekman, B. (2006), 'Liberalizing Trade in Services: A Survey', World Bank Policy Research Working Paper 4030.

Jensen, J., Rutherford, T. and Tarr, D. (2005), 'Telecommunications Reform within Russia's Accession to the World Trade Organization', World Bank.

Jha, V., Gupta, S., Nedumpara, J. and Karthikeyan, K. (2005), *Trade Liberalization and Poverty in India*, Macmillan: New Delhi.

Kaminsky, G. and Schmuckler, S. (2002), 'Short-Run Pain, Long-Run Gain: The Effects of Financial Liberalizations', World Bank Working Paper 2912.

Karsenty, G. (2000), 'Assessing Trade in Services by Mode of Supply', in P. Sauve and R. Stern (eds.), *GATS 2000: New Directions in Services Trade Liberalisation*, Brookings Institution: Washington, WA.

Katagekwa, J. (2006), 'Extension of Mode 4 Commitments to Include Unskilled Workers in the WTO: A Win-win Situation, Especially for LDCs', OECD Development Centre Panel on Migration and Development, WTO Public Forum 2006, Geneva, 25–26 September 2006.

Kiyota, K., Peitsch, B. and Stern, R. (2007), 'The Case for Financial Sector Liberalization in Ethiopia', Working Paper 565, Research Seminar in International Economics, University of Michigan: Michigan, IL.

Konan, D. E. and Maskus, K. E. (2006), 'Quantifying the Impact of Services Liberalization in a Developing Country', *Journal of Development Economics* 81(1): 142–62.

Luo, W. and Findlay, C. (2004), 'Logistics in China: Implications of Accession to the WTO', in D. Bhattasali, S. Li and W. Martin (eds.), *China and the WTO Accession, Policy Reform, and Poverty Reduction Strategies*, World Bank and Oxford University Press: Washington, WA.

Marion, J. and R. Piermartini (2005), 'The Impact of Mode 4 Liberalization on Bilateral Trade Flows', WTO.

Markusen, J., Rutherford, T. F. and Tarr, D. (2000), '*Foreign Direct Investment in Services and the Domestic Market for Expertise*', World Bank: Washington, WA.

Mattoo, A., Rathindran, R. and Subramanian, A. (2001), *Measuring Services Trade Liberalization and Its Impact on Economic Growth: An Illustration, Volume 1*, World Bank: Washington, WA.

Mattoo, A. and Sauve, P. (eds.), *Domestic Regulation and Service Trade Liberalization*, World Bank and Oxford University Press.

Maurer, A., Magdeleine, J. and d'Andrea, B. (2006), 'International Trade in Services: GATS, Statistical Concepts and Future Challenges', paper presented to the 2006 Conference of the International Association for Official Statistics, Ottawa, Canada, available at www.iaos2006conf.ca/pdf/Andreas%20Mauer.pdf [last accessed 24 February 2009].

Mishkin, F. S. (2007), 'Is Financial Globalization Beneficial?', *Journal of Money, Credit, and Banking* 39(2–3): 259–94.

Natawidjaja, R., Reardon, T., Shetty, S., Noor, T. I., Perdana, T., Rasmikayati, E., Bachri, S. and Hernández, R. (2007), *Horticultural Producers and Supermarket Development in Indonesia*, UNPAD/MSU Report No. 38543, World Bank: Indonesia.

Pauwelyn, J. (2005), 'Distinguishing Domestic Regulation from Market Access in GATT and GATS', *World Trade Review* 4(2): 131–70.

Prasad, E. S., Rogoff, K. S., Wei, S.-J. and Kose, M. A. (2004), 'Financial Globalization, Growth and Volatility in Developing Countries', NBER Working Paper No. W10942.

Rutherford, T., Tarr, D. and Shepotylo, O. (2005), *Poverty Effects of Russia's WTO Accession: Modeling 'Real' Households and Endogenous Productivity Effects*, World Bank: Washington, WA.

Skeldon, R. (2005), 'Globalization, Skilled Migration and Poverty Alleviation: Brain Drains in Context', WP T15, DRC Working Paper Series.

Soesastro, H. and Findlay, C. (eds.), *Reshaping the Asia Pacific Economic Order*, Routledge, Taylor & Francis Group: Oxford and New York, NY.

Svaleryd, H. and Vlachos, J. (2002), 'Markets for Risk and Openness to Trade: How are They Related?', *Journal of International Economics* 57(2): 369–95.

Torero, M. and von Braun, J. (eds.) (2005), 'Information and Communication Technologies for the Poor', IFPRI Brief, available at www.ifpri.org/pubs/ib/ib40.pdf [last accessed 24 February 2009].

Torero, M. and von Braun, J. (eds.) (2006), *Information and Communication Technologies for Development and Poverty Reduction: The Potential of Telecommunications*, John Hopkins University Press and IFPRI: Baltimore, MD.

UNCTAD (2004), *Handbook of Statistics*.

UNCTAD (2005), 'Business Process Offshore Outsourcing: Untapped Opportunities for SMEs', UNCTAD/SDTE/TIB/2005/6, UNCTAD: New York, NY.

Walmsley, T. and Winters, L. A. (2005), 'Relaxing the Restrictions on the Temporary Movement of Natural Persons: A Simulation Analysis', *Journal of Economic Integration* 20(4): 688–736.

Walmsley, T., Winters, L. A., Parsons, C. and Ahmed, S. A. (2005), 'Quantifying the International Bilateral Movements of Natural Service Providers', paper presented at the 8th Annual Conference on Global Economic Analysis, Lubeck, Germany, June 2005.

Winters, L. A. (2000a), 'Trade and Poverty: Is there a Connection?' in D. Ben-David, H. Nordstrom and L. A. Winters (eds.), *Trade, Income Disparity and Poverty*, WTO, 43–69.

    (2000b), 'Trade, trade policy and poverty: what are the links?' Discussion paper No. 2382, Centre for Economic Policy Research, London, (also available from http://siteresources.worldbank.org/INTPOVERTY/ Resources/WDR/winters1.pdf).

    (2003), 'The Economic Implications of Liberalizing Mode 4 Trade', in A. Mattoo and A. Carzaniga (eds.), *Moving People to Deliver Services*, World Bank and Oxford University Press: Washington, WA, 59–92.

World Bank (2007), *Migration and Remittances Factbook*, World Bank: Washington, WA.

WTO (2002), 'GATS, Mode 4 and the Pattern of Commitments: Background Information', Joint WTO–World Bank Symposium on the Movement of Natural Persons (Mode 4) under the GATS, WTO: Geneva.

WTO Secretariat (2005), *International Trade Statistics 2005*, WTO: Geneva.

Information and communications technology services in Uganda

SIDDHARTHA PRAKASH[*]

Globalisation has reduced barriers between countries in areas that extend beyond the realms of conventional trade. Incorporating intellectual property rights and services into the ambit of the WTO has given birth to the knowledge economy. A 'knowledge economy' is defined as a greater reliance on human intellect than on physical inputs and natural resources (Dahlman, 2005). Knowledge, ideas and experience are intangible assets with economic values, augmented by innovation and technology. Information and communications technology (ICT) provide the necessary infrastructure for the knowledge economy to function efficiently. This case study seeks to demonstrate how the use of ICT can help to empower the poor.

Lack of knowledge, experience and know-how often conspire to keep poor people poor. ICT can help to bridge the knowledge deficit by leveraging the best of local and global knowledge systems to serve the poor. They are helping governments to achieve the Millennium Development Goals (MDGs) through enhancing livelihoods, better delivery of services and allowing local stakeholders a voice in the planning process. According to UNDP,[1] ICT can promote pro-poor growth through: (i) catalysing private-sector investment and increasing the sustainability and reach of small- and medium-scale enterprises; (ii) facilitating the delivery of agricultural extension and financial and business support services in under-served rural areas; and (iii) facilitating learning and exchange and thereby helping to scale up the delivery of education.

---

[*] Siddhartha Prakash is Senior Manager of Government Regulation and Institutional Development at PricewaterhouseCoopers Pvt Ltd, India. The paper is based on the author's experiences at the World Bank in Washington and the WTO in Geneva. The views are those of the author's alone.

[1] See the UNDP website at www.undp.org [accessed in 2005].

This case study examines the linkages between the liberalisation of the ICT sector in Uganda and its impact on the poor. The study will navigate between the policy reforms implemented at the national level in the ICT sector and the subsequent growth of the Nakaseke Telecentre[2] in a remote town of Uganda. The combination of a positive regulatory framework and donor support led to the growth of the telecentre, which in turn transformed the lives of the local farmers, women and youth. The case study will present their stories and offer lessons to guide policy makers undertaking ICT-sector reforms in the Asia Pacific region.[3]

Poverty in Uganda

Uganda's economy is based on agriculture: in fact, 70 per cent of the population are farmers living in rural areas. Although Uganda is endowed with rich natural resources such as coffee, tin and cobalt, it remains a least developed country (LDC), defined by low levels of human and economic development. Thirty per cent of the country's 30 million people remain in extreme poverty. Recent studies indicate that poverty is highly feminised, implying that women form a dominant section of the poor (WOUGNET, 2006). The country's LDC status can largely be attributed to the economic mismanagement of Idi Amin's brutal regime that reversed all development indicators between 1971 and 1985.

Trade and economic reforms

In 1987, a new government led by President Museveni adopted a wide range of economic and institutional reforms to liberalise the trade regime and encourage foreign direct investment (FDI) into Uganda. The most notable achievements have included:

- strengthening fiscal policy to improve expenditure allocations
- civil service restructuring to reduce the drain on public finances
- privatisation of state enterprises to reduce state subsidies
- financial-sector reforms to improve banking services
- modernised marketing of agricultural products
- a free exchange system and an open capital account.

---

[2] A telecentre is a centre that provides access to information and communications services using various technologies such as phone, fax, computers, email, the internet and library services.

[3] See the 'Interviews' section at p. 381 for a list of interviews conducted with stakeholders involved in the ICT sector in Uganda.

In 1997, the government transitioned from post-conflict recovery towards poverty reduction, with the support of the World Bank. Uganda became the first country to receive debt relief under the Heavily Indebted Poor Countries Initiative (HIPC). Uganda's gross domestic product (GDP) growth has averaged 6% per year between 1987 and 2006. The country seems to be in a position to achieve several of the MDGs. Poverty levels have fallen from 56% to 31% between 1992 and 2006. Uganda's experience provides a framework to integrate trade liberalisation into a comprehensive poverty reduction strategy at the policy and project levels.

ICT-sector reforms

Background

Uganda's ICT journey began with the liberalisation of the telecommunications sector in the 1990s. The rationale for reform was that the state-owned monopoly operator Uganda Posts and Telecommunications Corporation (UPTC) suffered from a poor performance record. The public undertaking was heavily subsidised. Revenue generation was ineffective. Telephone services were limited to basic telephony. Consumers had to wait eighteen months to acquire a new telephone line. Corruption mounted as consumers paid bribes to get services ahead of the queue.

Most investors were reluctant to invest in telecommunications until the sector was reformed. The process began with the adoption of a Telecommunications Policy in 1996. The policy aimed to increase the level of telecommunications-service penetration and availability at affordable prices. The objective was to increase tele-density from 0.26 lines per 100 persons to 2 lines per 100 persons and to add new services, including email, paging and voice messaging (Kaggwa, 2005).

An independent regulator

The policy was implemented through the 1997 Uganda Communications Act, which established the Uganda Communications Commission (UCC) as an autonomous regulator.[4] The Commission regulates the telecommunications market and generates revenue through licenses. The licensing system was used to establish an appropriate market structure for licensing ICT services and conditions for enforcement, inspection and investigation (Tusubira, 2003). UCC has promoted equal treatment between the

---

[4] See the UCC website at www.ucc.co.ug [last accessed 28 February 2009].

rates, terms and conditions for national operators and foreign companies, thus complying with the General Agreement on Trade in Services (GATS). In this way, the regulatory environment promotes transparency and accountability.

Privatisation

The Communications Act began the process of privatising the state-incumbent UPTC. The postal and telecommunications sectors were separated, with the creation of Uganda Telecom Ltd (UTL) in 1998. It took the government twelve years and three attempts to successfully privatise UTL. The delays were caused by resistance from UPTC employees, problems pertaining to the valuation of the company's assets and discomfort with the initial bidders. In 2000, UTL became Uganda's first national operator. The government balanced the interests of different stakeholders through allowing gradual liberalisation and retaining a 49 per cent stake in the company. However, the management of the company was left in the hands of private investors to increase efficiencies.

The process of privatisation was delayed by many factors. In 1993, Celtel was granted a license, with services restricted to the provision of mobile telephony. The government granted a second license to a private telecommunications operator MTN Ltd in 1998. Despite parliamentary opposition, the government went ahead with the reform, which reflected the maturity, tenacity and strong political commitment of the reformers.

While government policy was at times bold, it was equally cautious, allowing limited competition to control the pace of liberalisation. This was achieved primarily through the creation of a duopoly. An exclusivity period was granted to the two main national service providers, UTL and MTN. For the first five years, only these two operators were entitled to provide a wide range of telecommunications services.

Liberalisation led to the development of effective public-private partnerships. The government spent US$20 million in 1992 to upgrade the telephone cable network. The private sector invested US$550 million into the sector between 1999 and 2002, without which the sector would not have taken off (Tusubira, 2003).

Rural telecommunications

The government realised that the telecommunications policy and the Communications Act would not in themselves lead to universal access.

A Rural Communications Development Policy (RCDP) was adopted in 2001 to provide access to basic communications services in under-served areas that were not commercially viable for the two national telecommunications operators to service. The RCDP aims to ensure that the rural population has reasonable and affordable access to communications services. The policy attempts to strike a balance between ICT content and infrastructure development.

The policy established a Rural Communications Development Fund (RCDF) to promote ICT in rural areas and leverage investment for rural communications development as a viable business (Moshiro, 2005). Licensing fees are the main source of revenue for the UCC and the main source of funding for RCDF projects. All telecommunications operators contribute 1 per cent of their gross revenues to the RCDF. The fund disperses grants to local entrepreneurs for the provision of basic communications and internet services in rural areas. The UCC complemented the RCDP's rural communications strategy by waiving license fees on public-payphone service providers and internet cafes (Kaggwa, 2005). In addition, the government has exempt all ICT equipment from customs duties to help make computers affordable. These are good examples of pro-poor initiatives to enable the poor to benefit from the reforms.

Several challenges emerged during the implementation of the RCDF. These included low demand for ICT services, high costs and lack of grid electricity. The RCDF has provided SMART subsidies to catalyse the start-up of ICT facilities in rural areas. The subsidies are intended to offset the extra costs of setting up and operating ICT facilities that are less viable in rural areas than urban settings. The fund provides energy grants to meet the alternative energy needs of a given rural area to all project implementers.

ICT policy

The Uganda National Council for Science and Technology (UNCST) started raising awareness about the potential contribution of ICT towards development in 1999. The Council organised a series of workshops and consultations to sensitise civil society and policy makers on ICT issues. UNCST's efforts led to the formulation of a National Information and Communications Technology Policy in 2003, with the aim of promoting the development of ICT infrastructure in the country. The policy seeks to 'stimulate industrial growth, commerce, infrastructure and linkage of rural and urban communities as well as uplifting disadvantaged groups, while taking care of gender balance' (WOUGNET, 2006). The policy builds on the work of previous telecommunications reforms to help mainstream the use of ICT in Uganda.

The government established an ICT Ministry in 2006 to implement ICT activities at the policy, project and local levels. The move reflects a strong political commitment towards promoting ICT for development in Uganda. The Ministry is developing the institutional capacity of national institutions to use and generate ICT services. Five agencies, such as the Uganda Investment Authority, have been selected to mainstream ICT applications within government institutions and promote economic activities such as e-commerce. The Ministry's second priority is to develop Uganda's ICT infrastructure through the establishment of a national transmission backbone. The Ministry also extends budgetary support to rural telecentres for the provision of ICT services to the poor.

Foreign investment in telecommunications

Uganda required large capital investments worth US\$600 million to overhaul the telecommunications sector in the 1990s, which underscored the importance of attracting private and foreign investment. The liberalisation of the Ugandan economy paved the way for improved market access and FDI inflows. Macroeconomic reforms such as the deregulation of exchange controls in 1991 eased the movement of foreign capital in and out of the country. The government developed an Investment Code to provide a fast-track mechanism to process foreign business applications within forty-five days.[5]

The government has encouraged foreign competition in the ICT sector by eliminating restrictions on foreign ownership of local firms. Under the GATS, Uganda has undertaken full market-access commitments on the supply of telecommunications services through consumption abroad. The government, however, has made limited commitments in crossborder supply and commercial presence. It has not undertaken commitments on the presence of natural persons, except for technical personnel.

As for national treatment, Uganda has made full commitments on the supply of services through cross-border consumption abroad and commercial presence. It remains unbound, however, in relation to the presence of natural persons (Trade Policy Review 2001[6]).

---

[5] See the Uganda Investment Authority website at www.ucc.co.ug [last accessed 28 February 2009].

[6] See www.wto.org/english/tratop-e/tpr-e/tp182.htm [last accessed 8 April 2009].

Uganda had imposed some limitations in its GATS commitments with the aim of complementing internal policy reforms. For example, during the initial five-year duopoly period, cross-border supply of telephone and mobile services had to be provided through one of the two national telecommunications operators. Similarly, all FDI inflows had to be channeled through UTL or MTN (WTO, 1999).

Sectoral impact

Carefully sequenced trade and economic reforms have transformed Uganda's ICT sector. Uganda's Communications Commission effectively regulated and monitored the growth of the private sector, which has improved service delivery, lowered tariffs and enhanced customer care. Liberalisation has brought in much-needed private-sector investment and competition. The government's sale of its majority stake in UTL generated US$30 million, which was invested in developing the country's telecommunications infrastructure. The ICT sector has attracted over US$350 million since 2001 as a result of the policy reforms.[7]

A number of global and regional telecommunications companies decided to invest in Uganda to exploit new business opportunities arising from the reforms. Celtel was the first foreign investor in the telecommunications sector to provide mobile services. In 1998, MTN (operated by a consortium from South Africa, Sweden and Rwanda) entered the Ugandan market by introducing pre-paid subscriptions. MTN is 90% foreign owned and controls 55% of the mobile market (Novatech-ProInvest, 2007). In 2000, a consortium led by the German firm Detecon won the bid to claim a 51% stake in UTL. The Consortium comprised of Swiss-based Telcel and South Africa's Ikwezi Group. By 2003, MTN had invested close to US$185 million in Uganda, with an additional US$100 million by UTL (IFC, 2004).

These new players have injected foreign capital, technology and human-resource capabilities to build local capacity within Uganda's ICT sector. For example, the privatisation of UTL has improved the management of the company. The entire operations were overhauled, attracting fresh talent from abroad. Detecon and Telcel installed modern technologies by digitising the whole network. Celluar and internet technologies were introduced and the company has grown profitable, year after year.

---

[7] See the Uganda Investment Authority website at www.ucc.co.ug.

Lower tariffs

Innovative services and pricing schemes have included optimising calling charges, dropping connection charges and eliminating subscription charges to benefit the consumer. For example, Celtel was the first to offer free roaming services within East Africa (WOUGNET, 2007). By 2000, competition had driven down local and international tariffs by over 50 per cent. These measures have made ICT services accessible and affordable to a larger number of people. In addition to consumers, Ugandan firms in other sectors have also benefited from lower tariffs, which have contributed towards reducing operating costs (Ssewanyana and Busler, 2007).

Uganda, being a landlocked country, continues to suffer from high internet costs compared to neighboring countries, due to poor internet bandwidth coverage. The lack of an integrated fibre-optic network throughout the country means that voice data and the internet have to be delivered via satellite links. Cyber cafes are a cheaper option to personal subscription, which requires a personal computer, fixed telephone line and an internet subscription. Critics of the government's duopoly argue that it hindered the growth of the ICT sector at the start of the reform process. Competition did not materialise in basic telephony, and prices remained high.

Better services

The government completely opened up the telecommunications sector by ending the duopoly in July 2005 and revising the telecommunications policy to encourage further foreign investment in ICT services and infrastructure development. The ICT Ministry has facilitated the process through investing in the expansion of fibre-optic connectivity between towns and cities. To level the playing field, UCC has banned the practice of allowing the national telecommunications operators to offer subsidised services. Removing these barriers to entry has attracted new market entrants such as Warid and HITS, backed by Middle Eastern investors. The revised telecommunications policy has led to more companies being licensed to provide any service using any technology, ranging from VoIP to VSAT. The different activities of all operators have been harmonised.

Today there are twenty-three ICT service providers in Uganda, comprising five internet service providers, fifteen public service providers and three national telecommunications operators. The tele-density has risen from 0.3% to 13% over the past decade. For instance, the number of fixed telephone lines has grown from 45,145 in 1996 to 154,383 in 2007. The number of mobile phone subscribers has leapt from 3,000 to 3,575,263 over the same period (Masambu, 2007).

The growth in mobile services is partly attributable to the pre-paid pricing model that was adopted by service providers in Uganda. Prepaid services extended access to the poor by eliminating the need for a credit history. Access to mobile phone services has improved as a result of the complete liberalisation of the ICT sector. The ending of the duopoly has enabled regional cellular service providers to market their products and services directly to consumers.

ICT exports and GDP contribution

The software market remains unregulated in Uganda. A number of software applications developed for the domestic market have been exported to other African countries, the most popular being accounting software for small businesses and billing systems for cyber cafes (IFC, 2004). Foreign exchange inflows from exports of software and outsourcing services have increased from US$2.9 million in 2001 to over US$10 million per annum. Industry profit in the ICT sector is currently estimated at US$30 million.[8] As a result, the ICT sector contributed 4.2 per cent to GDP growth between 2001 and 2005. In 2006, the ICT sector attracted over US$73 million as FDI. These trends are indicative of the sector's significant contribution to the country's economic growth.

Global markets for local talent

Lower prices and improved service delivery have increased access to ICT services in Uganda. They have also benefited the rural poor through developing new markets for local products and services. In this way, ICT can serve a dual purpose, with the support of an appropriate enabling environment. For example, in Uganda, liberalisation resulted in an explosion of FM radio stations that jumped from 3 in 1996 to 156 by 2007.[9] The stations cover most districts using local languages, which has popularised Ugandan music and led to the growth of the local music industry. Ugandan musicians are gaining popularity across Africa through regional radio stations. Growing demand for African music has generated new income

---

[8] See the Uganda Investment Authority website at www.ucc.co.ug.   [9] Ibid.

opportunities for local musicians through exports to European and US markets.

Jobs for the poor

The rapid growth of ICT services has created employment at various levels. Several entrepreneurs have emerged to operate kiosks, public pay-phones and cyber cafes offering computer and internet facilities. These centres have themselves created jobs for people to manage and operate the services. As a result, indirect employment has risen from 116,640 in 2002 to 343,886 in 2006 (Masambu, 2007). The government's efforts to grant special incentives to promote the growth of the ICT sector in rural areas has benefited the poor. For instance, removing licenses from the small kiosk phone vendors has led to gender mainstreaming, as many women are engaged in the payphone business. Some women have been gain-fully employed in marketing telecommunications products and designing websites (WOUGNET, 2007).

Rural development

The liberalisation of the ICT sector has enhanced competition to extend services to rural areas through ordinary market forces. The policy was complemented with a universal access fund (the RCDF) to provide ICT services to the poor, who tend to be beyond the reach of the market. In addition, specific products and services have been developed to cater to the needs of the rural population, such as telecentres. The RCDF has leveraged additional resources from donors to implement its univer-sal access strategy. This includes a US$5 million credit from the World Bank, which has helped to establish: 326 public payphones in select subcounties, 771 community information centres, fifty-four ICT train-ing centres in fifty-four districts, forty-five internet cafes in forty-five districts and nine multipurpose telecentres across Uganda (Mwesigwa, 2006).

The RCDF has established internet points of presence in most rural areas, which has helped to reduce bandwidth costs, making the internet more affordable and accessible. Awareness programmes have helped to increase the user base with the net effect of reducing the unit cost per single user. The fund has created rural employment. For example, each internet cafe employs about three staff and contributes to the local economy through renting of premises and provision of services.

Critics of the RCDF argue that the majority of people who have benefited from the fund are largely private businesses and education-oriented
NGOs. The fund targeted commercially viable projects, which often left
out the rural poor with low economic returns. While women benefited
from the training offered by telecentres, such as computer and secretarial
skills, they remained absent from the ownership and management of ICT.
It is not possible to reach everyone based on market-based conditions and
select subsidies (WOUGNET, 2007). While a telecentre itself may not be
owned by the poor, the services it offers can empower women and other
marginalised groups.

Nakaseke telecentre

The Nakaseke telecentre is a donor-funded project that has benefited from
the ICT reforms in Uganda.[10] Located 50 kilometres north of Kampala,
in a remote town, the Nakaseke telecentre has introduced new ICT to
this rural area. In ten years, the telecentre has catalysed a number of
development activities in the region.

Nakaseke

The Nakaseke subcounty has a population of over 53,290, of whom 27,228
are women. The major economic activities are trading and farming. There
are about 1,103 businesses comprising retail shops, and there are 8,000
families engaged in farming and agro-processing activities. The community did not have an established reading culture. The penetration of
communications services was very low in the subcounty, which serves two
administration units (Nakaseke and Kasangombe). In 1996, there was not
a single fixed telephone line in the entire subcounty.

Telecentre project

The Nakaseke telecentre is part of a chain of five (UNESCO/IDRC/
ITU/DANIDA/British Council) donor-supported telecentre projects initiated in Benin, Mali, Mozambique and Tanzania. The overall objective
of the project was to stimulate rural development by facilitating access
to information, learning resources and communications technologies for

---

[10] See the Nakaseke telecentre website at www.nakasekecmc.blogspot.com [last accessed
28 February 2009].

the Nakaseke and Kasangombe communities. The telecentre targeted the following core user groups: women, youths, children, medical officers, workers, teaching staff, farmers and local leaders. The content and programming for the telecentre was tailored towards meeting primarily the needs and aspirations of these groups. These were met through the following select activities: computer applications training; internet, email, telephone, fax, library and photocopying services; an Open Learning Center (for outreach); a community radio, topical video shows, newspapers, and leisure and sports activities for young people.

Benefits of ICT reforms

The donors selected Uganda as the government had embarked on a reform programme and had begun to liberalise the telecommunications sector. The reforms improved the quality of services on offer and extended the coverage to rural areas. Competition lowered prices among the national telecommunications operators. Lower tariffs have made ICT services much more affordable to the rural poor. The ICT reforms helped to reduce congestion and increase call success rates, which was a major problem in remote areas like Nakaseke. The number of faults per 100 main lines dropped from 135 to 80 between 1994 and 2000 (Byaruhanga, 2004).

Every company wanted to be considered a pro-community player as a strategy for maintaining a favourable position in the rural market. UTL, for instance, waived installation fees on Nakaseke's first telephone connection to test the local market. This, coupled with government grants to promote ICT in remote areas, created the enabling environment to launch the project. Specific reforms that benefited the telecentre included tax breaks on imported computers, which helped to procure a range of desktop computers. In addition, the ICT Ministry is helping to reduce internet costs through improving bandwidth coverage in rural areas.

Empowering the poor

The telecentre has begun to change the lives of the local community. It has over 500 regular users comprising students, farmers and teachers. About fifty people access the services of the telecentre on a daily basis (ITU, 2002). The telecentre has provided internet, telephone and fax services that are being utilised to conduct local business activities. Computer training has provided jobs for youths, either in the telecentre or in local businesses. Over 1,500 people have received computer training from the centre in book-keeping, financial management, business development and marketing.

Education and health services

Donors and national research institutions have supplied various books and information materials in local languages for the community. As a result, the library has a collection of over 5,500 reading materials. The library has 245 registered users on the library book-loan scheme (Omare-Okurut, 2006). It has developed a book-box system, which provides books to meet the information needs of schools located outside Nakaseke. The school community (7,000 school children) as well as community workers and medical officers have benefited from the resource centre. The telecentre has developed a tele-medicine programme to connect the Nakaseke hospital to Mulago hospital in Kampala. ICT facilitated consultations over long distances via phone, fax and emails, which has led to timely referrals and has helped save lives (ITU, 2002).

Technology and markets for farmers

The telecentre has partnered with the National Agricultural Advisory Services to help increase agricultural productivity and incomes in the region. This is being achieved by using ICT to deliver agricultural information to poor farmers who are beyond the reach of agricultural extension workers. The project has trained extension workers, NGOs and farmers in the use of ICT. Three agricultural research institutions have been able to capture local farming technologies and disseminate relevant information about pest management and post-harvest techniques. Farmers have begun to engage in online trading, and use the telecentre to capture and disseminate information about local farming techniques and crop prices. Farmers have utilised the knowledge accessed through the telecentre to improve their livelihoods through growing new hybrid crops and practising modern agricultural techniques such as zero grazing (Omare-Okurut, 2006).

Money for women

WOUGNET, a local NGO, has developed a special CD ROM entitled *Rural Women in Africa – Ideas for Earning Money* in order to impart training and vocational skills to women. The CD ROM was piloted in the Nakaseke telecentre to provide information to local women on small-scale businesses, banking and savings schemes, farming, health issues and computer applications. The CD-ROM put a lot of emphasis on the need for rural women to work in groups in order to support and guide each other. Groups of women have since begun to engage in income generation activities such as producing and packaging indigenous medicine in the Nakaseke telecentre.

In addition, local entrepreneurs have adapted the telecentre concept to set up small ICT businesses such as cyber cafes, business centres and public phone booths in different parts of the subcounty. These are some of the ways in which telecentres have changed the lives of the rural poor in Uganda, supported by donor funding and pro-poor ICT policy reforms.

Constraints and challenges

The Nakaseke telecentre has impacted the lives of the local communities, but not everyone has been able to benefit. There are a number of factors that prevent the poor from accessing ICT services. Some of these are mentioned below and are applicable in the Asia-Pacific region:

- Low levels of education, literacy, and awareness conspire to exclude the poor from accessing ICT.
- Women's access to ICT in developing countries tends to be inhibited by several factors, including cultural constraints, distance from their homes, lack of transportation and time.
- The biggest hurdle that prevents the poor from accessing ICT is their abject poverty and lack of resources to afford the services offered by a telecentre.
- Technology poses major challenges in rural areas. Low demand and high costs of developing rural infrastructure often discourage private-sector investment.
- Most rural areas suffer from inadequate infrastructure such as broken roads, which disrupts the daily functioning of the local economy. For instance, irregular supply of electricity leads to poor connectivity and power cuts, adversely impacting ICT services and the reputation of the centre.
- The ICT sector is constantly evolving to meet the changing needs of a knowledge society through the creation of new products and services. Given the low level of education and development in rural areas, there is often a lack of local expertise and capacity to provide technical support.
- Rural-urban migration leads to a high staff turnover in rural areas, which poses major challenges for the sustainability of ICT projects.

Lessons learned

The liberalisation of the ICT sector in Uganda and its impact on helping to reduce poverty in the country provides some lessons for the Asia-Pacific region, as outlined below.

Local level

- Nakaseke is a successful example of transferring the maintenance costs from donors to the local communities, thereby moving towards sustainable local ownership. The community has contributed towards the construction of the main building for the telecentre from its tax collections. In addition, the locals mobilise funds to help cover the operational costs of the telecentre through regular fundraising activities.
- Strategic partnerships with various knowledge institutions have provided access to vital information and resources. Public-private partnerships have helped to mobilise resources to fund the technology side of the operations.
- Technological constraints meant that internet and email services were not readily available at all times due to power cuts and poor connectivity. This taught the centre to focus on other services such as the library and computer training programmes, which were functioning well.
- Instituting a lending system for information materials in the library has helped clients who cannot access the telecentre or who cannot complete their learning at the centre. Such pro-poor initiatives are important ways of providing the poor with access to knowledge.
- It is important to have an eye for the market and keep updating the range of services to meet the changing needs of the community and stay one step ahead of the competition. Nakaseke, for instance, focused on educational services at the cost of losing market share to other competitors for secretarial services (Mayanja, 2005).

Policy level

- Market liberalisation is more likely to lead to broader access than telecommunications monopolies, especially where the regulator is weak and dominated by vested interests.
- The demand for different ICT services varies. For example, there tends to be a greater demand for communications-related services such as phones, than information-related services such as the internet.

Telephone use does not require literacy, computer and language skills or training.

- It is difficult for development-oriented ICT to be sustainable if it is to provide below-market-priced services that the poor can afford, as they in turn need to be subsidised to cover the shortfall in revenue. While these telecentres can make a profit, they cannot cover their entire operational costs without additional sources of funding.
- The private sector can be a friend of the poor by bringing down prices for ICT services through competition, which has improved the quality and efficiency of service delivery in Uganda.
- Public-private partnerships are essential for the provision of universal access to ICT, especially development-oriented services targeting the poor. The government has to create the enabling environment through appropriate regulatory incentives to promote private-sector participation and infrastructure development.
- The RCDF model is a good example of how the government can leverage its resources to mobilise additional funding to promote universal access to basic ICT services. In Uganda, the model has worked well in tapping private and donor resources for establishing ICT applications in remote areas.
- User pay systems are not always appropriate for rural ICT projects in the early stages of the project. People cannot afford to pay for information-related services, which they may not yet value and afford.
- Government policy changes can benefit and adversely impact ICT. For instance, the abolition of local taxes in Uganda has reduced the financial contributions from local councils.

Policy implications

Governments need to adopt a holistic approach to policy making in order to create an enabling environment for the poor to benefit from ICT. There is a need to address the underlying roots of poverty, such as inequalities in ownership of assets, vested interest groups and power structures, lack of resources, capital, education and information. Poverty reduction requires a multisectoral approach that examines all the bottlenecks that impede the use of ICT. For instance, market information on local agricultural prices will not translate into higher farm earnings unless there are roads to transport the goods to market. Social attitudes and behaviour patterns need to be reoriented towards appreciating the value of a knowledge-driven economy to generate local demand for ICT services. Education is key to increasing access to ICT through improving literacy rates, computer skills and promoting the use of ICT applications in schools and colleges. It is equally important to understand the issues that limit ICT access for women and other marginalised groups. Accordingly, special products may be designed to ensure that people with disabilities, for instance, will be able to access information. Therefore, the type of services offered, including the times of opening and/or location, needs to be carefully considered to promote wider access to ICT. These could include innovative approaches to reach the poor, such as speech recognition and text-to-screen software for illiterate users.

ICT needs to be accompanied by other economic activities to stimulate the rural economy and curb rural–urban migration. Salaries could be comparable to urban areas to retain skilled personnel in rural ICT. One can begin with a regulation of the minimum wage in rural areas to a level that can sustain a decent standard of living. Local entrepreneurs seeking to start up small ICT businesses require technical and financial assistance related to either capital formation, equipment and technology management, market assessments or business development strategies. There is a need to provide a one-stop resource centre for these people through a universal access fund. Universal access should be integrated into national development strategies, especially in rural areas, such as Uganda's PEAP. Agricultural research and training centres can make use of ICT to capture and disseminate farming technologies.

Governments can complement ICT reforms by investing in setting up expensive infrastructure such as internet points of presence and broadband networks, and then establish specific partnerships with the private sector for its management and operations. The options for the type of infrastructure, technology and equipment should be carefully selected based on lowest costs, simplest maintenance requirements and adaptability to local context and community needs. There must be more rural electrification programmes to ensure that most of the rural areas have regular access to power. Policy makers should also explore options for developing alternative sources of energy. Further reforms to support the ICT sector could include reducing taxes on internet service providers, air time and wireless accessories to enable telecentres and cyber cafes to benefit from wireless technology and reduce their internet rental bills. Governments could partner with private firms to develop innovative ways to cover high costs for equipment and installation charges in rural areas. In Uganda, UTL has designed favourable payment plans spread over twelve months or offers free installation and equipment where local resources are lacking.

Conclusion

Uganda's experience reflects a holistic approach towards liberalisation of the telecommunications sector. It began with the privatisation of the state monopoly, which opened up the market to new players. Competition improved the quality and range of ICT services on offer. An independent regulator reduced government interference in the telecommunications sector and provided the regulatory framework to monitor the activities of all the service providers. Uganda adopted a gradualist approach towards reform to protect the interests of different stakeholders and learn through the process of undertaking liberalisation. In 1997, there were no models to follow in Africa, and the domestic ICT sector was limited to the provision of basic telephony. These factors help to explain the government's rationale for introducing a duopoly to control the pace of liberalisation in the telecommunications sector. The policy has been criticised for slowing the pace of growth in ICT services, which the regulator acknowledged by fully opening up the sector in 2006.

The overall benefits of the reforms for individuals and the economy as a whole have outweighed the losses that may have impacted vested interest groups such as UPTC staff. The telecommunications sector has been streamlined to eliminate inefficiencies and corruption in the system. The profitability, investment and output of the national telecommunications operators have continued to rise in response to competition from new players. While most targets have been met, a number of services have exceeded planned expectations, such as the explosion in mobile phone distribution and usage. In many parts of the country, these successes have helped to compensate for shortfalls in the delivery of certain ICT services.

The domestic policy reforms would not have been possible without the corresponding trade liberalisation measures that supported the growth of the telecommunications sector. While ICT reforms improved the investment climate within the sector, the deregulation of foreign exchange controls and the new Investment Code created an enabling environment for FDI to enter Uganda. Foreign capital generated the resources required to overhaul Uganda's telecommunications sector. The injection of FDI led to an inflow of international management skills and new technologies that increased automation, productivity and output across the sector.

The government went an extra step with a rural communications development policy to provide universal access to ICT services. This was supported by the RCDF to mobilise additional resources to provide basic telecommunications services to the rural poor. Such a comprehensive and well-executed reform programme has transformed the telecommunications sector in Uganda. All stakeholders have contributed to these results, including the government in setting the policy direction and the entrepreneurship of investors in improving services rapidly. The dedication of the UCC in regulating and supervising the implementation of the telecommunications reforms has been crucial to the success of the ICT sector in Uganda.

ICT can contribute to the achievement of the MDGs through enhancing livelihoods, improving the efficiency of service delivery and allowing local stakeholders a voice in the development process. They serve as a catalyst for change in rural areas, creating multiplier effects through the provision of market information, skills and training that have translated into opportunities for employment and income generation. The ICT sector reforms have brought a number of direct benefits to consumers through improved service delivery and tariff reductions that have increased affordability. However, the market cannot reach everyone in countries where a significant proportion of the population live on less than a dollar a day. A universal access fund provides a mechanism to extend ICT services to the poor. These measures must be implemented in the context of wider socioeconomic reforms to ensure access to all, especially the most disadvantaged members of society.

Interviews

The author would like to thank the following stakeholders involved in the ICT sector in Uganda for taking the time to provide detailed responses to the interviews conducted for this study:

Peter Balaba, Manager, Nakaseke telecentre.
Richard Katumba, Customer Solutions, Uganda Telecom Ltd.
John Musajja Kawa, ICT Specialist, Uganda Investment Authority.
Godfrey Kibuuka, Director of Communications, ICT Ministry.
Bob Lyazi, Director, Rural Communications Development Fund.
Meddie Mayanja, ICT Specialist, IDRC.
Joyce Muwanga, Director, Uganda National Council for Science and Technology.
Patrick Mwesiga, Technical Manager, Uganda Communications Commission.
Siragi Ngobi, ICT Consultant.
Dorothy Okello, Coordinator, WOUGNET.

Bibliography

Africa Online (2006), 'ICT Infrastructure Development in Uganda', *Africa Online.*

Byaruhanga, C. (2004), 'Managing Investment Climate Reform: Case study of Uganda Telecommunications', 2005 Word Development Report: Washington, WA.

Chronic Poverty Research Centre (CPRC) (2005), 'Chronic Poverty in Uganda, 2005 Report', CPRC: Manchester.

Dahlman, C. (2005), *India and the Knowledge Economy*, World Bank: Washington, WA.

Digital Opportunity Channel (2007), *ICTs for Poverty Alleviation*, Digital Opportunity Channel: Kampala.

Gamurorwa, Λ. (2002), *Uganda: A Success Story? – Background Note for the Government Budget*, Government of Uganda: Kampala.

IFC (2004), *ICT Investment Opportunities in East Africa, Country Specific Market Analysis: Uganda*, International Finance Corporation: Kampala.

ITU (2002), *Nakaseke Uganda – Connecting People from Timbuktu to Kabul*, International Telecommunications Union: Geneva.

Kaggwa, I. (2005), *Uganda's Experience in Sector Liberalization, Privatization and Network Status*, Uganda Communications Commission: Kampala.

Madanda, A. and Amuriat, G. (2006), *Emerging Gender Dimensions for Pro-poor Community Driven Networks*, WOUGNET: Kampala.

Masambu, P. (2007), *A Review of the Postal and Telecommunications Sector*, Uganda Communications Commission: Kampala.

Mayanja, M. (2002), *The African Community Telecenters: In Search of Sustainability*, International Development Research Centre: Ottawa, ON.

(2005), *The Nakaseke Multipurpose Community Telecenter in Uganda*, UNESCO: Paris.

Mega-Tech (2006), *The National ICT Master Plan and E-Government Network Feasibility Study in Uganda*, Mega-Tech: Virginia, VA.

Moshiro, S. (2005), *Licensing in the Era of Liberalization and Convergence, A Study of Uganda*, International Telecommunications Union: Geneva.

Mulira, H. M. (2006), *Community Driven ICT Networks for Local Development in Rural Areas*, ICT Ministry: Kampala.

MusajjaKawa, J. (2007), *Information and Communications Technology Update*, Uganda Investment Authority: Kampala.

Mwesigwa, P. (2006), *Enabling Regulatory Requirements for Community Driven ICT Networks*, Uganda Communications Commission: Kampala.

Novatech-ProInvest (2007), *The ICT Africa Marketplace, Country Profile, Uganda*, Novatech: Brussels.

Okello, D. (2006), *Community Driven ICT Networks for Local Development in Rural Areas*, WOUGNET: Kampala.

Omare-Okurut, A. (2006), *Pilot Project for the Establishment of the National Network of Community Multimedia Centres, Final Report*, UNESCO: Paris.

Organisation for Economic Cooperation and Development (OECD) (2005), 'Good Practice Paper on ICTs for Economic Growth and Poverty Reduction', OECD: Paris.

Parkinson, S. (2005), *Telecenters, Access and Development, Experience and Lessons from Uganda and South Africa*, International Development Research Centre: Ottawa, ON.

Smith, F. (2004), *Market Entry for US Firms into Developing Economies: Uganda Cellular Phone Market Case*, Pennsylvania State University: Pennsylvania, PA.

Ssewanyana, J. and Busler, M. (2007), 'Adoption and Usage of ICT in Developing Countries: Case of Ugandan Firms', *International Journal of Education and Development using ICTs* 3(3).

Tusubira, F. (2003), *Uganda, ICT Sector Performance in Africa*, International Development Research Centre: Ottawa.

Uganda Communications Commission (UCC) (2005), *Funding and Implementing Universal Access: Innovation and Experience from Uganda*, UCC: Kampala.

United Nations Economic Social Council (UNESCO) (2005), *Case Study: Nakaseke Multipurpose Community Telecenter – Uganda* , UNESCO: Paris.

Viitanen, A. K. (2003), *The Role of ICT in Poverty Reduction*, Ministry of Foreign Affairs: Finland.

VOA News (2006), *Pilot Telecenter in Uganda is Successful*, VOA: Washington, WA.

World Bank (2000), 'Poverty Reduction Strategy Paper – Uganda's Eradication Action Plan', World Bank: Washington, WA.

(2007a), 'Interview with Gerald Sendaula, Former Minister for Finance, Planning and Economic Development, Uganda', World Bank: Washington WA.

(2007b), *Uganda: Tracking Spending to Reach Development Goals, IDA at Work*, World Bank: Washington, WA.

WOUGNET (2006), *Report on the Uganda National Internet Government Forum Workshop*, WOUGNET: Kampala.

(2007), *Assessment of the Rural Communications Development Fund from a Gender Perspective*, WOUGNET: Kampala.

WTO (1999), *Uganda's Schedule of Commitments under the GATS*, WTO: Geneva.

(2001), *Uganda's Trade Policy Review*, WTO: Geneva.

Zavuga, G. and Okello, D. (2004), *Positioning for Impact: A Woman's Perspective on ICT Policy Making in Uganda*, WOUGNET: Kampala.

3.2

Health services in Malaysia

AIK HOE LIM*

Introduction

The healthcare sector is among the biggest and fastest growing service sectors in the world. Fuelled by economic growth, demographic change and globalisation, private healthcare providers are expanding rapidly in emerging markets, particularly in Asia. One interesting development has been the rise of 'health tourism', with patients from developed countries seeking cheaper treatment in developing countries. This study examines the case of Malaysia, which has recently embarked on developing exports in health tourism. The first section of this case study provides an overview of the Malaysian healthcare system and the domestic reforms that were introduced over the last decade or so. The next section reviews the key trade and health issues that have emerged. This is followed by a discussion of the risks and opportunities in liberalising trade in health services and the evidence so far on the implications of health tourism. The case study concludes with observations on some of the key policy lessons learned.

Overview of health services in Malaysia

Primary, secondary and tertiary public healthcare are provided at minimal or no cost by the Malaysian Government. Public health services in rural areas are free. Despite the high level of government financing, the actual

* This paper was written while the author was on sabbatical leave as Visiting WTO Fellow at the Institute for International Trade. The views are those of the author alone. They do not necessarily represent the views of the WTO Secretariat or its members and cannot be attributed to it. The author wishes to thank all those people who agreed to be interviewed, especially officials from the Ministry of Health, Ministry of Trade and Industry, the Malaysian Medical Association and the Association of Private Hospitals, without whose valuable inputs and insights this case study would not have been possible. Thanks also to Sharifah Hapsah, Chris Findlay, Tham Siew Yean, Rudolf Adlung, Victoria Donaldson, Stuart Harbinson and Mireille Cossy for their comments and views.

Table 3B   *Number of hospitals, medical personnel and beds in the public and private sector*

	Public		Private		
	Number	%	Number	%	Total number
Hospitals	128[1]	37	222[2]	63	350
Doctors	10,943	52	9,162	48	20,105
Dentists	1,263	46	1,488	54	2,751
Beds	32,937[3]	75	10,794	25	43,731

[1] Public hospitals are defined as those under the control of the Ministry of Health as well non-Ministry of Health government hospitals.
[2] Figure includes private maternity/nursing homes.
[3] Includes beds in non-Ministry of Health government hospitals.
Source: Calculations based on Ministry of Health (2005), *Health Facts 2005*, Ministry of Health: Kuala Lumpur.

level of health expenditure is relatively low, at 3.8% of total gross domestic product (GDP) and 6.9% of total government expenditure.[1] Currently, Malaysia does not have a compulsory national health-insurance plan. While private health insurance has made inroads in recent years, it still plays only a minor role in financing healthcare. It is, nevertheless, common for a large segment of the population (especially the urban middle class) to seek treatment in the private sector. In 2003, private expenditure on health as a percentage of total expenditure on health was 41.8%, with about 74% of that expenditure reliant on out-of-pocket financing.[2]

Table 3B demonstrates that public hospitals account for some 75 per cent of all hospital beds in the country, but the role of the private sector has been increasing over the past few decades. Of the 350 hospitals operating in Malaysia, 63 per cent are registered as private hospitals. In general, basic healthcare is widely available throughout the country.

New health challenges, privatisation and crisis

While lauded for having achieved good results at modest costs, the Malaysian healthcare system has increasingly been stretched by new

---

[1] WTO, *Core Health Indicators* database, including *World Health Statistics 2006* and *World Health Report*, 2006 edn., available at www.who.int/en [last accessed 31 March 2009].
[2] Chee, H. L. (2004), 'Current Health Care Financing Issues in Malaysia', Working Paper No. 18, Asia Research Institute, University of Singapore: Singapore.

demands.[3] Chronic non-communicable diseases as well as other lifestyle diseases are on the rise.[4] Healthcare costs are also escalating. The Ministry of Health's operating expenditure based on current prices increased by 353% from MYR 1.27 billion in 1990 to MYR 5.76 billion in 2003.[5]

Partly in response to rising costs, several initial steps were taken in the early to mid 1990s to strengthen the role of the private sector within the health sector. In 1992, the National Heart Institute was 'corporatised', but the government continued to retain control. Privatisation of the National Drugs Supply Centre, responsible for the drug distribution system in Malaysia, followed in 1994. Five non-medical hospital support services at government hospitals, as well as food supplies and catering, were privatised in 1996.

In the 1990s, private-sector investment in healthcare continued unabated, with the number of private hospitals increasing from fifty in 1980 to over 200 by the end of the 1990s. Then, in 1997, the Asian financial crisis hit the country. One of the results of the crisis was that demand for public healthcare increased as many local patients of private hospitals reverted to public hospitals.[6] Another result was that all government expenditure was curbed, including that of the Ministry of Health, which was cut by 12 per cent.[7] Initiatives to promote the role of the private sector in healthcare were given greater impetus as the fiscal situation worsened. In the Seventh Malaysia Plan (1996–2000), the government announced that it would be seeking greater involvement of the private sector in the provision of healthcare.[8]

The health sector and the GATS

As the transition and transformation of the healthcare system was taking place, Malaysia was also seeking to improve productivity in the services

[3] Ramesh, M. and Holliday, I. (2001), 'The Health Care Miracle in East and Southeast Asia: Activist State Provision in Hong Kong, Malaysia and Singapore', *Journal of Social Policy* 30(4): 637–51.

[4] Phua, K. H. and Chew, A. H. (2002), 'Towards Comparative Analysis of Health Systems Reforms in the Asia-Pacific Region', *Asia-Pacific Journal of Public Health* 14(1): 9–16.

[5] Merican, M. I., Rohaizat, Y. and Haniza, S. (2004), 'Developing the Malaysian Health System to Meet the Challenges of the Future', *Medical Journal of Malaysia* 59(1): 86.

[6] See Chee, H. L. (2007), 'Medical Tourism in Malaysia: International Movement of Healthcare Consumers and the Commodification of Healthcare', Working Paper No. 83, Asia Research Institute, University of Singapore: Singapore for an explanation of the effect of the Asian financial crisis on healthcare in Malaysia.

[7] Ching, F. (1999), *Social Impact of the Regional Financial Crisis, The Asian Economic Crisis*, Asian Updates, Asia Society, available at www.asiasociety.org/publications/update_crisis_ching.html [last accessed 28 February 2009].

[8] Chee, 'Current Health Care Financing Issues in Malaysia'.

sector and to prepare the services industry to adjust to new market conditions under the General Agreement on Trade in Services (GATS). The
Second Industrial Master Plan (1996–2005) emphasised the importance
of developing supporting services for manufacturing under its Manufacturing ++, or the cluster-based, industrial development strategy.[9] The
Ninth Malaysia Plan (2006–10) and the Third Industrial Master Plan
include the goal of expanding services to account for 60% of GDP in
2020, compared to 50% currently, and have identified healthcare services
as one of eight services subsectors for further development.

Cross-border delivery (mode 1)

Currently, Malaysia's GATS commitments are confined to private hospital
services and medical speciality services.[10] In terms of mode 1, no market-
access or national treatment limitations have been scheduled on the cross-
border delivery of health services. Starting with the Seventh Malaysia
Plan (1996–2000), there has been a series of initiatives aimed at improving the delivery of services to remote areas through telehealth projects.
These initiatives include Telehealth (or Integrated Telemedicine), one of
the flagships of Malaysia's Multimedia Super Corridor project (MSC).
To establish the infrastructure for teleconsulting within the country,
Malaysia has been an important consumer of foreign telemedicine expertise. For instance, the Malaysian Government awarded a MYR 21 million
(US$5.53 million) contract to an affiliate of the leading e-health services
company WorldCare Limited to establish a teleconsultation network linking up forty-one sites throughout the country.[11]

---

[9] Kanapathy, V. (2003), 'Services Sector Development in Malaysia: Education and Health
as alternate sources of growth', AT120 Research Conference, 20 to 21 February 2003,
available at www.tcf.or.jp/data/20030220-21_Vijayakumari_Kanapathy.pdf [last accessed
28 February 2009].

[10] Medical speciality services are defined in the Malaysian schedule as covering forensic
medicine, nuclear medicine, geriatrics, microvascular surgery, neurosurgery, cardiotho-
racic surgery, plastic surgery, clinical immunology and oncology, traumatology, anaes-
thesiology, intensive care, child psychiatry and physical medicine. The GATS excludes
'services supplied in the exercise of governmental authority', which means 'any service
which is supplied neither on a commercial basis, nor in competition with one or more
services suppliers' is exempt from the scope of the GATS. The Malaysian commitment,
which specifies 'private hospital services', emphasises this exclusion.

[11] See the Ninth Malaysia Plan (2006–10) for further details on Malaysia's Telehealth project.
The report on the award to WorldCare Limited was noted in Abidin, M. Z., Alavi, R. and
Kamaruddin, S. (2005), 'GATS and Liberalization of Healthcare Services in Malaysia', draft

Consumption abroad (mode 2)

Mode 2 covers consumers that receive medical services when abroad, and is thus relevant to health tourism. The key restrictions of interest are those that governments place on their own citizens. Mode 2 is, on the whole, relatively unconstrained. Under the GATS, the highest share of full market-access commitments (85 per cent for the hospital sector) is recorded for mode 2.[12] Moreover, virtually all relevant commitments scheduled by developed countries are without limitations.[13] Of the limitations that do exist, these mainly deal with rules regarding public health-insurance portability. Private health insurance is not covered by the GATS, as it is not a governmental measure, but the non-portability of public health-insurance entitlements across borders could be a trade barrier under the GATS.[14] In addition to portability, there may also be other obstacles that are not easily dealt with by the GATS framework. For instance, the non-recognition of foreign licenses, qualifications and standards may mean that the cost of treatment abroad is not reimbursed by health insurers on the grounds that the services provided are of a lesser quality than those provided locally.[15]

Commercial establishment (mode 3)

On mode 3 (commercial establishment), foreign-owned private hospitals are limited to a 30 per cent equity share and must enter into locally incorporated joint ventures. There is a minimum size requirement, as only private hospitals with a minimum of 100 beds are permitted, and no branching of outpatient clinics is permitted. Market access for foreign private hospitals is subject to an unspecified economic-needs test. There are also horizontal limitations on foreign acquisitions, mergers and takeovers, as well as national treatment restrictions with respect to

---

manuscript in J. Arunandchai and C. Fink (2007), *Trade in Health Services in the ASEAN Region*, World Bank Policy Research Paper No. 4147, World Bank: Washington, WA.

[12] Less than 40 per cent of WTO members took commitments in the health sector. See Adlung, R. and Carzaniga, A. (2001), 'Health Services under the General Agreement on Trade in Services', *Bulletin of the World Health Organization* 79(4): 352–64 and Adlung, R. and Carzaniga, A. (2006), 'Update on GATS Commitments and Negotiations', in C. Blouin, N. Drager and R. Smith (2006), *International Trade in Health Services and the GATS: Current Issues and Debates*, World Bank: Washington, WA.

[13] Adlung and Carzaniga, 'Update on GATS Commitments and Negotiations'.

[14] Ibid.

[15] As noted by Adlung and Carzaniga, 'Update on GATS Commitments and Negotiations', measures by private commercial insurers would not fall under the scope of the GATS.

land acquisitions and government incentives/preferences. While statistics
on the foreign ownership of private hospitals and clinics are not readily
available, various reports and studies suggest that it has been on the rise
in recent years.[16]

Movement of natural persons (mode 4)

Malaysia's mode 4 (movement of natural persons) commitments for
health services covers medical specialists in fourteen separate areas and is
subject to an unspecified economic-needs test. Foreign medical specialists
can only provide services in private hospitals with at least 100 beds, and
only at specified locations. The setting up of individual or joint group
practices is not permitted. Excluded from coverage are services provided
by pharmacists, dentists, nurses and midwives.

The GATS does not appear to have been a key driving factor in the
Malaysian strategy to reform the health sector. Recent research on health-
related services in preferential trade agreements in Asia and the Pacific also
highlight that no significant market opening has been achieved through
such agreements.[17] Much of the liberalisation of the Malaysian health
sector appears to have been driven instead by an autonomous domestic agenda of public-service reform and privatisation, which was later
supported by strategies to promote the commercial potential of the services sector in the Malaysian economy. That being said, the fact that the
Malaysian revised offer to the GATS negotiations proposes binding some
of the liberalisation that has taken place suggests that some value is placed
in locking in the commitments.

'Health tourism': from crisis management to a new export sector

During the Asian financial crisis, about 15 to 20% of private patients in
Malaysia reverted to public hospitals as companies cut back on employee
health schemes and general economic insecurity dampened consumer

[16] See Chee, 'Medical Tourism in Malaysia'; Chee, H. L. (2006), 'The Emergence of a Transnational Healthcare Service Industry in Malaysia', Working Paper No. 76, Asia Research
Institute, University of Singapore: Singapore; Kanapathy, 'Services Sector Development
in Malaysia'; and Abidin, Alavi and Kamaruddin, 'GATS and Liberalization of Healthcare
Services in Malaysia'.

[17] See Mikic, M. (2007), 'Health-related Services in Multilateral and Preferential Trade
Arrangements in Asia and the Pacific', Working Paper No. 30, Asia-Pacific Research and
Training Network on Trade, UNESCAP: Bangkok.

expenditure.[18] Private hospitals also saw their costs escalate by some 120% as the Malaysian ringgit devalued.[19] One response, following the example of Thailand's Bumrungrad Hospital, was to market its services to foreign tourists.[20] A National Committee for the Promotion of Medical and Health Tourism (renamed the National Committee for the Promotion of Health Tourism in Malaysia in 2001) was established by the Ministry of Health in 1998.[21] The Committee formulated a strategic plan: to promote 'smart partnerships' between government, healthcare facilities, travel organisations and medical insurance groups. A special unit was established in the Ministry of Health to promote health tourism and to develop Malaysia as a regional centre for healthcare services.

Government support for health tourism can broadly be said to consist of five main components. Firstly, Malaysia added health services to its already very successful 'Malaysia Truly Asia' tourism marketing campaign, positioning the country as a high-quality but low-cost location for healthcare. The branding also involved the promotion of 'cultural' advantages. Malaysia emphasised its modern medical facilities, staff with qualifications obtained from the US, UK and Australia and a comprehensive network of private hospitals and clinics, and its image as a 'Muslim country' to appeal to Islamic patients.

Secondly, three main target groups were identified: (i) middle- to high-income groups in neighbouring Association of Southeast Asian Nations (ASEAN) countries (i.e. Indonesia, Singapore, Laos, Cambodia, Vietnam and Myanmar); (ii) affluent patients from emerging markets such as China, Brazil, Chile and South Africa;[22] and (iii) patients from developed countries attracted by lower costs and the promise of faster treatment (i.e. from the UK, Singapore, Japan and Taiwan).

Thirdly, government agencies and private-sector groups have sought to create an integrated package of facilities linking health with other

---

[18] Chee, 'The Emergence of a Transnational Healthcare Service'.
[19] Malaysian German Chamber of Commerce (2007), *Market Watch: Healthcare Sector in Malaysia*.
[20] Teh, I. and Chu, C. (2005), 'Supplementing Growth with Medical Tourism', special report on medical tourism, Synovate Business Consulting, available at www.synovate.com/bc/pdf/Supplementing%20Growth%20with%20Medical%20Tourism.pdf [last accessed 28 February 2009].
[21] The description in this section of the steps taken by the government to promote health tourism is largely drawn from Chee, 'Medical Tourism in Malaysia'. See also Kanapathy, 'Services Sector Development in Malaysia'.
[22] Ibid.

consumer services. 'Malaysia Healthcare' is an online one-stop shop destination created to provide a single window for all treatment and travel
needs, allowing patients to seek pre-treatment consultations and estimate
costs, as well to book accommodation, holidays and travel in Malaysia. A
typical package would include treatment at one of the partnered specialist
facilities followed by a stay at a five-star holiday resort. A comprehensive
service is provided, which includes help with immigration, insurance,
finance and post-treatment tele-consultation between the patient's home
doctor and the doctor that provides the treatment in Malaysia.

Fourthly, the Ministry of Health sought to promote quality assurance
standards. The Ministry of Health currently recognises thirty-five private hospitals as facilities for the promotion of health tourism.[23] Private
hospitals can also seek joint Ministry of Health and Malaysian Society
for Quality in Health accreditation, and are encouraged to obtain local
and international ISO (International Organisation for Standardization)
certification.[24] The Ampang Puteri Specialist Hospital, for instance, in
addition to its Malaysian Hospital accreditation, has quality accreditation
from a German ISO certification body.[25]

Fifthly, steps were taken to improve the regulatory and policy environment for both consumers and producers of health tourism. Citizens of
most countries do not need visas to enter Malaysia. For those requiring
visas, a 'fast track clearance' process has been introduced. The patient
and next of kin accompanying the patient may also apply to extend
their stay.[26] Greater flexibility has also been provided in the advertise-
ment of medical products and services. Guidelines announced in June
2005 now permit medical practitioners and institutions to advertise their
services.[27]

While private hospitals still mainly cater to the needs of local residents,
foreign patients are expected to make up a growing proportion of the
income of private hospitals and clinics. Parkway Holdings reportedly
has plans to triple the foreign patients treated by its Malaysian hospital

---

[23] See note 21, above. See also this list of medical facilities: www.hospitals-malaysia.
org/health.cfm?&action=main&menuid=34&parentid=28 [last accessed 28 February
2009].

[24] Chee, 'Medical Tourism in Malaysia'.

[25] See the website of the Ampang Puteri Specalist Hospital: www.malaysiahealthcare.com/
AmpangPuteri/default.aspx [last accessed 28 February 2009].

[26] See the Association of Private Hospitals in Malaysia website: www.hospitals-malaysia.org
[last accessed 31 March 2009].

[27] See the website of Malaysian Medical Association: www.mma.org.my [last accessed
28 February 2009].

operator, Pantai Holdings, to reach the level of 15% of total patients.[28] Sunway Medical Centre currently receives only about 1.5% of its revenue from foreign patients but expects this to grow to 10% over the next five years.[29] The Association of Private Hospitals in Malaysia projects that foreign receipts from health tourism in 2007 will hit MYR 300 million, doubling the 2005 figure.[30]

Opportunities and risks of pursuing a strategy of health tourism

Health tourism poses a number of distributional issues. On the positive side, for the exporting country, health tourism generates foreign exchange and additional resources for investment, which can help upgrade the healthcare infrastructure. Foreign direct investment (FDI) may bring in advanced management techniques and specialised medical skills. Global competition for health tourists may also improve effectiveness in health delivery and quality standards. On the other hand, since health tourism is typically offered by private hospitals, investments may flow only to the private segment of the market. This could result in a dual market structure, with the private sector catering to foreigners and higher income nationals, and the public sector catering to lower income groups.[31]

The co-existence of private- and public-sector hospitals and clinics may not in itself be a problem. What are arguably more important are the consequences of such a co-existence on the internal allocation of resources. Due to wage differentials between the private and public sectors, doctors and other trained medical personnel may leave public hospitals to find better-paid employment in private health facilities.[32] On the other hand, foreign investment in private hospitals generates jobs and exposure to advanced, specialised medical services. This can improve human resources and the quality and productivity of health services in the long term, as foreign commercial presence creates positive externalities

---

[28] See www.mma.org.my, based on reports in *The Business Times*, 1 December 2005: 'Pantai to Tap Medical Tourism'.

[29] The *Star Online*, 'Health Tourism: a Fast-growing Market', 27 August 2007, available at http://biz.thestar.com.my/news [last accessed 28 February 2009].

[30] The *Star Online*, 'Hospitals Adapting to Foreign Needs', 27 August 2007, available at http://biz.thestar.com.my/news [last accessed 28 February 2009].

[31] Chanda, R. (2002), 'Trade in Health Services', *Bulletin of the World Health Organization* 80(2): 158–63.

[32] Chanda, R. (2001), 'Trade in Health Services', Working Paper No. 70 (revised), Indian Council for Research in International Economic Relations: New Delhi.

for national training institutions.[33] Greater government revenue due to health tourism could also be channelled back to the public health sector.

Moreover, new employment opportunities within a burgeoning private sector may help stem the outflow of health service providers abroad. 'Brain drain' in the healthcare sector has serious implications for many developing countries, particularly since medical training is often publicly funded and subsidised.[34] On the other hand, as health tourism contributes to private-sector growth, it should help increase wages. Of course, it could be argued that, initially, the external brain drain is simply replaced by an 'internal' brain drain. However, should the local labour market expand, for instance through foreign health professionals, this would reduce the strain on local resources. The net effect might be a normalisation of wages as the pool of available labour expands, thus dampening the 'internal' brain-drain effect.

In short, the impact of trade in health-tourism services on poverty is likely to be mixed. Export earnings from health tourism offer many potential economic gains. How these translate into economic growth and employment, and what the concomitant distributional effects are, however, can only be established empirically. In terms of implications on availability of health services, much will also depend on the existing state of the domestic health system, and whether there are appropriate regulations and safeguards in place to support universal service obligations to low-income, poor and remote communities.

Foreign investment and growth

Private-sector hospitals in Malaysia are predominantly locally owned. Foreign presence, although limited, is starting to grow. The largest group of foreign corporate health investors in Malaysia is from Singapore. There is also some US presence in the Malaysian market, often as a result of acquisitions or strategic alliances. In 2005, for instance, the US-based Newbridge Capital bought a controlling stake worth US$800 million of the Singaporean company Parkway Holdings, which, as explained earlier, has significant operations in the Malaysian healthcare sector.[35] US investors such as the Seattle-based Columbia Pacific Management (CPM)

---

[33] WHO (2005), 'Methodological Approach to Assessing Trade in Health Services: A Guide to Conducting Country Studies', WHO: Geneva.
[34] See Chanda 'Trade in Health Services', Working Paper No. 70 for a description of the magnitude of the brain drain problem facing developing countries.
[35] Chee, 'Medical Tourism in Malaysia'.

group have also entered into three separate joint ventures with Malaysian specialist hospitals.[36]

Foreign groups investing in Malaysia typically have hospitals and clinics in other regional markets. CPM, for instance, operates under the Columbia Asia logo and has a network of hospitals and clinics in India, Vietnam and Sri Lanka. Parkway Holdings, which operates the Gleneagles chain in Malaysia and Singapore, has operations in Brunei and India.[37] Interestingly, Malaysian operators are similarly vying for joint ventures and hospital-management contracts abroad. KPJ Healthcare manages hospitals in Indonesia and has joint ventures in Bangladesh, and intends to expand into the Middle East, Pakistan, Myanmar and Vietnam.[38] In 2004, Pantai Holdings set up a joint venture company through its subsidiary, Pantai Medivest, to explore business opportunities in the healthcare sector in Saudi Arabia.[39]

What is emerging is a complex multinational network of private hospitals and clinics. One of the advantages of being part of such a network is that it creates a global supply chain with referrals and cross-referrals being made between regionally or internationally linked hospitals and clinics, thus facilitating the flow of foreign patients between countries.[40] With each regional centre offering a different set of specialised services at different prices, cross-country referrals offer the foreign patient greater choice. For the private medical operator, this confers the advantage of a vertically and horizontally integrated supply chain that goes beyond medical facilities and includes hospitality services with partner travel agents, hotels and airline companies.

In brief, commercial presence in Malaysia is increasingly being driven not only by opportunities offered by the local market but, perhaps more importantly, by the growing regional and international market for health tourism. Out of the thirty-five hospitals that have been granted 'medical tourism' status, nineteen are fully private, in the sense that they are not government-linked. One of the positive impacts of cross-sectoral investment in health tourism is that, because there are strong linkages with other sectors, growth is generated throughout the economy. In 2006, the

---

[36] See the Columbia Asia Medical Centre website: www.hospitals-malaysia.org/health.cfm?&menuid=34&parentid=28&action=view&healthid=33 [last accessed 28 February 2009.

[37] See the Parkway Holdings website: www.parkway.com.sg [last accessed 28 February 2009].

[38] Chee, 'The Emergence of a Transnational Healthcare Service Industry'.

[39] The *Edge Daily*, 'Health Tourism to Drive Pantai's Growth', 15 September 2004.

[40] Chee, 'The Emergence of a Transnational Healthcare Service Industry', describes this as the transnationalisation of healthcare.

Table 3C *Number and percentage share of doctors and nurses in the public and private sector*

Years	Doctors					Nurses				
	Public	% of total	Private	% of total	Total	Public	% of total	Private	% of total	Total
1995	4,412	45.9	5,196	54.1	9,608	13,647	–	–	–	–
1996	4,614	45.3	5,582	54.7	10,196	14,614	72.9	5,442	27.1	20,056
1997	8,235	57.8	6,013	42.2	14,248	16,068	65.5	8,477	34.5	24,545
1998	8,555	56.9	6,461	43.1	15,016	18,134	76.6	5,538	23.4	23,672
1999	8,723	56.2	6,780	43.7	15,503	20,914	76.8	6,322	23.2	27,236
2000	8,410	53.8	7,209	46.2	15,619	23,255	74.7	7,874	25.3	31,129
2001	8,615	53.3	7,531	46.7	16,146	24,543	73.7	8,752	26.3	33,295
2002	9,424	54.0	8,018	46.0	17,442	26,029	73.8	9,251	26.2	35,280
2003	8,946	49.2	9,245	50.8	18,191	27,089	73.6	9,695	26.4	36,784
2004	–	–	–	–	–	30,002	74.6	10,218	25.4	40,220
2005	10,943	54.4	9,162	45.6	20,105	32,580	73.8	11,540	26.2	44,120

1 '–' means not available for that year.
Source: Compiled from Ministry of Health, *Health Facts.*

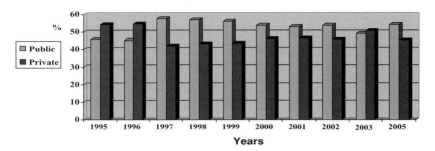

Figure 3B   Percentage share of doctors in the public and private sector (1995–2005). *Notes:* No data available for 2004. *Source:* Based on data compiled from Ministry of Heath, *Health Facts* (1995–2005 editions).

service sector expanded by 5.7%, with all subsectors registering positive growth.[41] While health services are not categorised separately, they are an important component of 'other services'. Indications are that the 4.4% increase of 'other services' in 2006 was in part driven by an expansion of private health services.[42]

Employment effects

As a result of both domestic and foreign investment, the number of private hospitals grew by nearly 350 per cent between 1980 and 2005.[43] With the rapid growth of the private sector has come significant employment growth. Indeed, it is often alleged that the growth of private hospitals has triggered a serious migration of doctors and other health professionals from the public sector to the private sector. However, a comparison of the relative shares of health professionals in the public and private sector does not show any major shift towards the private sector over the last decade.

The share of doctors who work in the public sector has fluctuated between 45 and 58% (see Table 3C and Figure 3B). The number of doctors working in the private sector increased at the end of the financial crisis in

[41] Malaysia Ministry of Finance (2006), *Economic Report 2006/2007*, Ministry of Finance: Kuala Lumpur.
[42] Ibid.
[43] Rohaizat, Y. (2004), Financing Health Care in Malaysia: Safety Net for the Disadvantaged Groups Including Pensioners, Elderly People, the Poor and the Disabled', *Bulletin of Epidemiology and Public Health on Noncommunicable Diseases in Malaysia* 3(2): 43–6.

1999, and in 2003 the share of doctors in the private sector, at 50.8%, was marginally higher than those in the public sector. However, it was still lower than the pre-Asian financial crisis figure of 54.7% recorded in 1996, and by 2005 the shares had reversed, with 54.4% of doctors working in the public sector.

What seems to be happening is a recovery in private-sector employment rather than a major change in the balance of doctors in the public and private sector. Growth in the public sector has actually outstripped that in the private sector. In 2005, there were 10,943 doctors working in the public sector, compared to 4,412 in 1995. This represents a growth of 148%. In comparison, doctors working in the private sector grew by 76% from 5,196 in 1995 to 9,162 in 2005. Nurses still work predominantly in the public sector. The relative share of nurses, apart from a sudden change in 1997, has fluctuated between 72.9% and 79.8% in the public sector and between 23.2% and 27.1% in the private sector.

Given the relatively stable share of doctors and nurses working in the public and private sector, how does one explain the anxiety that is often expressed of a brain drain of public-sector health professionals? Part of the answer lies in the shortage of health manpower that has built up in Malaysia over a number of years. The Eighth Malaysia Plan identified a deficit of some 6,796 doctors, 1,230 dentists and an alarming 15,334 nurses for the year 2000. While the total number of doctors working in Malaysia between 2000 and 2005 grew by 28% (i.e. 4,486), it was still less than the deficit identified in 2000. In 2004, it was reported that there were 3,000 vacancies for public-sector doctors.[44] In the case of nurses, there has been considerably more growth, with total numbers increasing by some 40% (i.e. 12,991) over the same period, but it still falls short of requirements. Another important aspect of the problem, which is not shown in the statistics above, is the movement of senior doctors and specialists from government hospitals to the private sector. The Malaysian Medical Association has highlighted in various reports that while public hospitals typically retain junior doctors, who must complete a compulsory three-year residency, they have had greater difficulties in stemming the flow of senior doctors to the private sector.[45]

---

[44] Materia Medica Malaysiana, debate on private wings, 27 July 2004, available at http://malaysianmedicine.wordpress.com [last accessed 28 February 2009].

[45] Ministry of Health (2000), 'Proceedings of the Workshop on the 8th Malaysia Health Plan between Ministry of Health, Malaysia, the Private Sector and NGOs', 25 and 26 January 2000, Kuala Lumpur.

Many of the problems related to the shortage of health professionals, however, predate the emergence of health tourism.[46] While the shares of doctors and nurses working in the public and private sectors do not show any big shifts towards the private sector, given the already acute shortage of health manpower, small shifts in the allocation of labour may well have a disproportional impact. What this points to is that health tourism is the proximate but not necessarily root cause of the strain on the human resources of the public sector. Indeed, health tourism could very well help address these imbalances by creating a new revenue source for the government. This income could be harnessed to improve the supply and quality of public health services, as well as the remuneration of public-sector health professionals.

Accessibility, equity and affordability

While the private sector employs about 45.6% of all doctors working in Malaysia, it only accounts for 25% of all hospital beds. This means that the public sector, which employs 54.4% of doctors, is responsible for a disproportionate share of 75% of all hospital beds. In addition to having to service more hospital beds with comparatively fewer doctors, public hospitals often have to deal with more complicated and resource-intensive cases.[47]

What this implies is that while the public- and private-sector shares of employment of doctors have remained fairly stable and are roughly equal, public hospitals may be under a disproportionate burden to meet healthcare needs. This is further compounded by the fact that private hospitals and clinics typically serve urban areas, with about 98% of private hospital beds located in urban areas with the highest concentration in the capital and surrounding urban agglomerations.[48] In addition to geographical disparities, highly skilled medical specialists also tend to be in the private sector. In 1999, 66% of surgeons and 80% of obstetricians and gynaecologists were in the private sector.[49]

These disparities must, however, be put in context. Overall, Malaysia's track record on poverty alleviation has been very good. The incidence of poverty in Malaysia has been reduced from 22.8% in 1990 to 5.7% in 2004. What remains are pockets of hardcore poor predominantly in rural

---

[46] Merican, M. I., Rohaizat, Y. and Haniza, S. (2004), 'Developing the Malaysian Health System to Meet the Challenges of the Future', *Medical Journal of Malaysia* 59(1): 84–93.

[47] Merican, Rohaizat and Haniza, 'Developing the Malaysian Health System'.

[48] Eighth Malaysia Plan (2001–05).   [49] Ibid.

areas. Official estimates in 2004 counted a total of about 67,300 hardcore
poor households, of which 79% (i.e. 53,200) are living in rural areas.[50]
The national health policy has focused on continuing to further upgrade
the rural health infrastructure and providing free healthcare to rural
communities. The overall doctor:population ratio has also improved from
1:4,132 in 1976 to 1:1,377 in 2003.[51] Health tourism and the concomitant
growth of private-sector facilities are likely to have a more direct impact
on the urban population. However, the numbers of absolute poor in
urban areas are relatively small, with about 91,600 households classified
as poor and 4,000 as hardcore poor.[52] The numbers are also decreasing,
with the incidence of urban poor declining from 3.3% in 1999 to 2.5% in
2004.

On the other hand, while absolute poverty is on the decline, income
inequality has been rising.[53] During 1999 and 2002, income inequality
widened with the Gini coefficient rising from 0.44 to 0.46.[54] The lowest
40% of income earners received about 13.5% of total income in 2002,
compared to 14% in 1990. Inequality between states and regions also
remained wide and persistent. Poverty rates for the poorest states were
Sabah (23%), Terengganu (15.4%), Kelantan (10.6%) and Kedah (7%),
compared to the national average of 5.7% in 2004.[55]

This raises a number of interesting implications in terms of the impact
of health tourism. While Malaysians enjoy a much higher quality of life
(including healthcare) than in the past, and poverty is, on the whole,
on the decline, the challenge of addressing inequality remains. During
2001 and 2005, about 450,000 foreign patients received treatment from
private hospitals in Malaysia, compared to 39,000 in 1998.[56] Further
growth is likely, as the worldwide market for health tourism is estimated at a staggering $40 billion and is expected to grow to $100 billion

---

[50] Ministry of Finance, *Economic Report 2006/2007*. Hardcore poverty is defined in the
Economic Report as households with a monthly gross income below the food poverty line,
which is based on the daily kilocalorie requirement to sustain an adequate diet.
[51] Ministry of Health, *Health Facts*.
[52] Ninth Malaysia Plan (2006–10).   [53] Ibid.
[54] Economic Planning Unit, Prime Minister's Department, Malaysia (2005), 'Eradicate
Extreme Poverty and Hunger', UN development (UNDP) programme. The Gini coefficient is a measure of inequality of a distribution of income. It is defined as a ratio with
values between 0 and 1: a score of zero indicates perfect inequality and a score of one
indicates perfect inequality.
[55] Ninth Malaysia Plan (2006–10).
[56] Figures for 2001 to 2005 are from the Ninth Malaysia Plan (2006–10). The figure for 1998
is from the Ministry of Finance, *Economic Report 2005/2006*.

by 2012.[57] This growth will certainly place greater pressure on human resources.

Competition is not limited to private hospitals but is increasingly also taking place in public hospitals. Before 1994, public-sector hospitals did not differentiate between domestic and foreign patients and charged subsidised fees to all. Fees for foreigners have since been changed but they remain low. Yet, the number of foreign patients, including work migrants and those at the lower end of the health-tourism market, has continued to increase.[58] The Ministry of Health has also approved the setting up of private wings in public hospitals that are not constrained by the government's subsidised fee structure.[59] Private wings are intended to boost the income of public-sector doctors and enable public hospitals to benefit from health tourism.

Outlook: maximising the gain and minimising the downsides

Liberalisation of a public sector that has long been protected will undoubtedly incur adjustment costs. Moreover, as inflows of foreign patients increase and competition for scarce labour intensifies, prices are likely to rise, and labour will be attracted to the more productive suppliers. Moves to privatise Malaysian healthcare have been controversial, and various civil society groups have contested the introduction of greater competition in health services.[60] Concerns range from escalating medical costs, problems of equity in access to better quality healthcare, especially for disadvantaged groups, and widening disparities in resources between the private and public sector, leading to the flight of medical personnel from the public to the private sector.

The risks of exporting health services must, however, be weighed against the benefits. Health tourism is one sector where developing countries have export potential and can earn substantial foreign receipts. In 2005, health tourism generated revenues of about MYR 151 million[61] in Malaysia,

---

[57] Figures on the size of the global health-tourist market are estimates by McKinsey & Company and are quoted in Stokes, B. (2007), 'Bedside India', *National Journal*, 5 May 2007.

[58] Ibid.

[59] The *Edge Malaysia*, 'Health Tourism to Hit RM154 Million This Year', 19 July 2004.

[60] See statements by the Coalition Against Healthcare Privatisation (an umbrella group of NGOs and trade unions) and the manifesto by Citizens Health Initiative, available at www.aliran.com [last accessed 28 February 2009].

[61] The *Star Online*, 'Hospitals Adapting to Foreign Needs', 27 August 2007, available at http://biz.thestar.com.my/news [last accessed 28 February 2009].

and this looks likely to grow, with a 30% increase in the number of health tourists recorded in the first quarter of 2007, compared to the same period in 2006.[62] Greater numbers of foreign patients need not crowd out local patients. According to the Association of Private Hospitals in Malaysia, the normal maximum occupancy rate for hospitals is 85% to 90%.[63] The average occupancy rate of local patients is about 65%.[64] Based on these figures, most private hospitals would still have a leeway of about 10% for more foreign patients.[65] Some positive knowledge-spillover effects are also possible, as growth of the sector increases the range of medical services offered. In short, greater export earnings may induce greater investment, which may in turn provide opportunities for alleviating the pressures on the domestic healthcare sector and offer local consumers greater choice. However, development benefits are not automatic and will largely depend on the policies and safeguards that are put in place.

Closing the productivity/wage gap

Clearly, the best way to respond to the lure of higher wages in the private sector is to review compensation packages and close the productivity/wage gap in the public sector. However, given that public healthcare only receives an allocation equal to 3.8% of GDP and recovers only about 2% of its operating costs, the likelihood of being able to match private-sector wages is limited. A large allocation of resources is thus needed in order to increase remuneration for health professionals and to improve the health infrastructure. In the 2007 budget, the government earmarked MYR 10 billion for the provision of health facilities and equipment, services of specialists and training programmes. Although it is unlikely that the wage gap between the public and private sector could be closed, more investment could certainly help to narrow it.[66] Economic spin-offs to other sectors from health tourism could also help increase government revenue, which could be used to further invest in the public sector.

---

[62] *Star Online*, 'Hospitals Adapting to Foreign Needs'.
[63] Figures are based on an interview with Dr K. Kulaveerasingam, the Chairman of the Committee on Database and Health/Medical Tourism of the Association of Private Hospitals on 25 July 2007.
[64] Ibid.   [65] Ibid.
[66] There was no reliable data on wage levels between public- and private-sector health professionals, though interviews conducted with the Malaysian Medical Association and the Association of Private Hospitals in Malaysia suggest that the earnings potential of private-sector specialists far exceed those in the public sector.

Integrate public and private healthcare services

The segmentation between the public and private sector will need to be addressed. Private hospitals in particular could be required to do more to meet the public healthcare burden. Although the number of doctors in the public sector is only slightly more than in the private sector, they treat three and a half times as many patients, and six to seven times as many outpatients.[67] It would not seem unreasonable to require private hospitals to treat a certain number of patients or allocate a quota of beds at subsidised rates, since they have been the major beneficiaries of the government's drive to promote health tourism. To address the urban bias of private-sector hospitals, positive incentives such as tax exemptions could be given to encourage the provision of healthcare to rural or underserved areas. There could be public-service obligations on private-sector specialists, which would require them to spend a certain amount of time treating public-sector patients. This could be complemented by schemes where private-sector specialists are encouraged to transfer skills by conducting training workshops for more junior doctors in the public sector, or to teach in university hospitals.

Strengthening the regulatory framework

The liberalisation of any service sector may require re-regulation or the establishment of new regulatory frameworks to accompany the phasing-in of greater competition. In the Malaysian context, the private sector was previously regulated by the Medical Act and Regulations (1971) and the Private Hospitals Act and Regulations (1971). That regulatory framework was strengthened by the Private Health Care Facilities and Services Act (1998). That Act sought to correct the imbalances in standards and quality of care as well as to rationalise medical charges in the private sector to more affordable levels, and it was implemented in 2006.

Adequate and appropriate regulations can help safeguard public policy objectives while harnessing the potential for trade in health services to augment resources. A greater role could be given to domestic regulation to ensure better consumer protection and quality control. In addition to the legislation, there must be institutional capacity to ensure enforcement and implementation. In this regard, should health tourism continue to grow, there may be a role for an independent regulatory body that would

[67] Chee, 'Current Health Care Financing Issues in Malaysia'.

monitor compliance of private hospitals and 'corporatised' government hospitals.

Towards a national health financing mechanism

Even without the challenges of health tourism and private-sector growth, the public sector would need to find ways to address ever-rising healthcare costs. Among the major reforms being considered in the Malaysian health system is the introduction of a national health financing mechanism. Identified in the Seventh Malaysia Plan (1996–2000), working out the details of the scheme and the institutional structure to administer it are complex, and progress has been slow.[68] If the private sector is to take up a greater share of the burden of public healthcare, there is a strong case for a comprehensive and affordable national health financing mechanism to be put in place.

Conclusion

Overall, trade in health services, including through health tourism, has mixed implications. It may enable exporting countries to earn more foreign exchange and generate additional revenue for investment in healthcare. On the other hand, increased commercialisation of health services without an appropriate regulatory framework and safeguards on access and equity, including a comprehensive national financing mechanism, may result in a dichotomy with a well-resourced private sector catering to foreigners and wealthy nationals, and an under-resourced public sector serving those who cannot afford private care. The best way to minimise the downsides of liberalising trade in services is by directly addressing the root causes of the public-private sector imbalance. In this regard, while health tourism may aggravate some existing problems it also provides the opportunity for these challenges to be corrected.

---

[68] UNDP Malaysia is currently involved in providing a consultant to study national health financing options for Malaysia.

Trade in services liberalisation in India

AJITAVA RAYCHAUDHURI[*] AND PRABIR DE[**]

Introduction

India has witnessed spectacular growth in the services sector over the past few years. The services sector has become the single largest sector in India, accounting for over half of domestic production, one quarter of international trade and two thirds of employment in the organised sector.[1] However, a significant part of India's organised services sector remains untapped and represents a very important potential export market.[2]

India's trade in services has been growing rapidly since the beginning of the last decade, following significant domestic liberalisation on the one hand and access to a growing overseas market for services on the other. Over the last fifteen years, India's services exports grew 38% faster than the country's merchandise exports and 12% faster than the global increase in trade in services. India's services exports presently equate to approximately 26% of the country's total international trade. India has succeeded in raising its penetration in global markets more rapidly in the case of services than for goods (Rakshit, 2007). Its share of world services trade is presently around 2.64% (2006–07),[3] compared to about 1% for world merchandise trade.

The crucial role of international trade in fostering economic growth, personal and social development, as well as reducing poverty and inequality, is now well recognised.[4] Multiple studies have shown that broad-based

[*] Ajitava Raychaudhuri is Professor and Coordinator at the Centre for Advanced Studies, Department of Economics at Jadavpur University Kolkata, India.
[**] Prabir De is a Fellow for the Research and Information System for Developing Countries (RIS), New Delhi, India.
[1] Estimated based on Central Statistical Organisation (2007).
[2] An 'organised' services sector is defined as jobs within the WTO's Services Sector Classification: see document MTN.GNS/W/120, Services Gateway, WTO.
[3] The Indian financial year operates from 1 April to 31 March annually.
[4] See, for example, a quick overview in Mikic and Qiu (2007).

growth in services trade is critical to accelerating poverty reduction. However, despite India's success in services exports in recent years, we know little about the empirical relationship between services trade, poverty and inequality in India.

This chapter attempts to gain some insight into the actual nature and extent of exports of services from India, and examines the underlying factors and broader implications for poverty reduction. The rest of the chapter is organised as follows. The following section provides an overview of India's mode-wise services trade. In the next section, the chapter attempts to briefly discuss India's services export competitiveness as well as multilateral and regional liberalisations undertaken by India in services trade. The discussion is centred on the role of trade in services in delivering pro-poor growth in India, with a special emphasis on India's software and information technology – business process outsourcing (IT-BPO). Next, the chapter identifies emerging challenges for India to deliver pro-poor services growth and then discusses policy implications and recommendations for a way forward. The final section provides a conclusion.

Mode-wise trade in selected services in India

Compared with other sectors, India's comparative advantage in traditional labour-intensive services sectors, such as transportation, travel and tourism, has shifted to a specialisation in technology-intensive services trade, such as financial, computer and information services. This shift in India's comparative advantage can be explained in two ways. Firstly, India's reform process, adopted in 1991, moved the country from an import-substituting industrial economy to a higher-skilled and technologically intensive services economy, resulting in the country's production and trade becoming services-driven. Secondly, the liberalisation of services sectors has facilitated efficiency (and export), encouraging economic restructuring, driven mostly by the private sector. Trade, foreign direct investment (FDI) and industrial policies have been liberalised and many restrictions have been completely dismantled. Reformed institutional, legislative and regulatory measures have helped the services sectors to grow much faster than in the pre-liberalisation period (Chanda, 2007; Rakshit, 2007).

A third point, emphasised by Gordon and Gupta (2004), is the role of splintering, whereby services-related jobs were outsourced by big manufacturing firms to domestic subcontractors on a large scale since the 1990s. As a result, India's domestic services sectors, such as software development, financial and health services, have thrived. In parallel, external demand has fuelled enormous growth in the skill- and knowledge-intensive services sectors, such as software development, leading to a massive rise in services exports. The demand has resulted in an increase from US$9.7 billion in 1997 to 1998 to US$46 billion from 2004 to 2005,[5] with an average growth of 23%, compared to a global average of 4%.

Mode 1 (cross-border trade) and mode 4 (movement of natural persons) are the two key modes of services delivery in which India has a comparative advantage. India has been playing a pro-active role in the liberalisation of services trade under the General Agreement on Trade in Services (GATS) since the launch of the Doha Round of multilateral trade negotiations.[6] Building upon its Uruguay Round commitments, in the Doha Round, India has offered commitments in thirty-three subsectors. However, a number of those commitments include limitations on market access and national treatment, consistent with India's national policy objectives.

Mode 1 export: cases of India's software and IT-BPO and higher education services

India's services trade is mostly driven by mode 1 exports of software and IT-BPO industry. The growth in mode 1 trade has been driven by two types of technological developments: (i) the computerisation and digitisation of a range of services, particularly business services; and (ii) the rapid increase in telecommunications capacity combined with a steep decline in telecommunications prices. These developments have spurred the growth of exports of software and IT-BPO services, thus pointing to the potential welfare gains of further liberalisation in this area through mode 1. Mode 1 is perceived to have very high growth potential across the globe, including within India.

---

[5] By the end of the 2006–07 financial year, services exports from India exceeded US$59 billion (RBI, 2007), mostly driven by software exports.

[6] The country has even played a pivotal role in the Hong Kong Ministerial Meeting of 2005 by incorporating Annex C into the main draft of the Agenda (see Government of India, 2006).

According to Balasubramanyam and Balasubramanyan (1997), the availability of a large pool of cost-effective, highly educated young professionals is a factor in the growth of the software sector. Starting with basic data-entry tasks in the late 1980s, the software and IT-BPO industry graduated to a high proportion of voice-based services and a range of back-office processing activities. According to the National Association of Software and Services Companies (NASSCOM), the Indian software and IT-BPO sector (including the domestic and exports segments) has grown by 28% in 2007–08, and total aggregate revenue for the software and IT-BPO sector crossed US$50 billion in 2007–08. This is nearly a ten-fold increase over the aggregate revenue of US$4.8 billion reported in 1998–99, and direct employment has exceeded 1.6 million.[7] The US and the UK remain the dominant markets for India, contributing 67% and 15% of total exports respectively in 2006–07.

In terms of higher education services, India has been active in distance learning since the early 1960s. In 2005, there were twelve open universities, including the Indira Gandhi National Open University (IGNOU), and 106 dual-mode, university distance-learning institutes and centres in the country, catering to over 2.8 million students. Today, IGNOU serves the educational aspirations of about 1.5 million students in India and thirty-five countries abroad, through eleven schools of studies and an elaborate network of fifty-eight regional centres, seven subregional centres, 1,400 study centres and forty-one overseas centres. IGNOU is already a recognised distance-learning provider in the Middle East region, particularly in Dubai, Abu Dhabi, Sharjah, Doha, Muscat and Kuwait. Its courses are also offered in Mauritius, the Maldives, Seychelles, Nepal and Sri Lanka.

Mode 4 export: movement of natural persons

Mode 4 deals exclusively with the movement of natural persons who are service providers (independent of commercial presence). India has traditionally been a large source (and also destination) for high- and low-skilled labour. Remittances inflow to India (as an indicator of mode 4 exports) is rising very fast and is a stable source of India's growing foreign exchange reserves. Total inflow of remittances to India increased to US$24.56 billion in 2005–06, from US$21.08 billion in 2004–05.[8] Remittances inflow

---

[7] See NASSCOM (2007b).   [8] Calculations based on RBI (2007).

contributed about 40% of India's total earnings from services exports, about 3% of India's gross domestic product (GDP) and about 16% of India's foreign exchange reserves in 2005–06. Globalisation and India's integration into the global economy have increased the potential for labour-mobility opportunities and increasing remittances from Indians living overseas. Trade in higher education services under mode 4 is another case of movement of natural persons (Raychaudhuri and De, 2007). For example, the Indian School of Business's (ISB) Hyderabad faculty collaboration with US management schools is a good example of mode 4 trade.[9]

Is services trade pro-poor in India?

Historical evidence across India suggests that the major factors in reducing poverty are: (i) faster growth, particularly agricultural growth that raises agricultural wages and tends to depress the price of food; (ii) lower inflation; and (iii) human resources development, notably female literacy.[10]

Owing to higher growth, India witnessed continuous rise in per capita income (PCI), from US$1,228.50 in 1981 to US$3,054.67 in 2005. This coincided with a rise in per capita income from services exports (PCISE), which increased from US$3.93 in 1981 to US$55.89 in 2005 (see Table 3D and Figure 3C). The relationship between PCI and PCISE is quite interesting: a 1% rise in PCISE is associated with about a 7% rise in PCI.[11]

Higher income has helped India in delivering pro-poor growth. For example, India has done relatively well in reducing rural and urban poverty (measured by HCR) during the period 1981 to 2004, when poverty ratios declined from 45.31% to 21.80% in the case of rural India, and from 35.65% to 21.70% in the case of urban India (see Table 3D). However, when income inequality is considered (measured by Gini coefficient), the results are rather mixed. While rural income inequality declined from

---

[9] ISB Hyderabad has faculty collaboration with the Kellogg School of Management, Wharton (University of Pennsylvania) and London Business School.

[10] See, for example, World Bank (2000) and Parikh and Radhakrishna (2005) (income elasticity of 0.6489 with robust t value of 67.458 and adjusted R^2 of 0.885).

[11] The relationship between PCI and PCISE is statistically significant at the 1% level ($t = 67.458$).

Table 3D   *Income, poverty, inequality and employment trends*

Year	PCI (US$)	PCISE (US$)	Poverty rate (%) Rural	Urban	Inequality rate (%) Rural	Urban
1981	1228.5	3.93	45.31	35.65	30.10	34.08
1991	1686.5	5.8	37.42	33.23	29.91	37.98
1992	1742.8	5.36				
1993	1791.4	5.85	37.27	32.36	28.60	34.30
1994	1888.5	6.70	43.47	33.73	29.88	35.51
1995	1993.8	7.88				
1996	2100.0	7.88				
1997	2154.3	9.77				
1998	2244.1	13.43				
1999	2362.1	15.72	27.09	23.62	26.30	34.70
2000	2415.1	16.01				
2001	2480.2	16.60				
2002	2553.4	19.80				
2003	2731.4	25.24				
2004	2885.3	40.06	21.80	21.70	26.20	34.94
2005	3054.7	55.89				

Notes: (1) poverty, inequality and unemployment rates correspond to financial year except 1983; (2) PCI is in purchasing power parity (PPP) terms, taken at constant US$2,000; (3) poverty is represented by head-count ratio (HCR) – poverty rate for the year 2004–05 is taken at a mixed recall period (MRP) basis; (4) inequality is represented by estimated Gini coefficient.
Source: (1) PCI was collected from World Bank (2007); (2) PCSE was estimated based on services exports, collected from Reserve Bank of India (2007); (3) poverty rate (HCR) collected from the National Sample Survey Organisation (NSSO); various rounds; (4) inequality rate (Gini) collected from Bhalla (2003), based on NSSO (2006).

30.10% in 1981 to 26.20% in 2004, overall urban inequality has remained flat or has even increased slightly.

The national data is interesting in that it shows a generally positive correlation between changes in national poverty and changes in PCISE (see Figure 3D). However, we found the opposite relationship between changes in growth in PCISE and national inequality (see Figure 3E). The explanation may be that, to a great extent, most export services

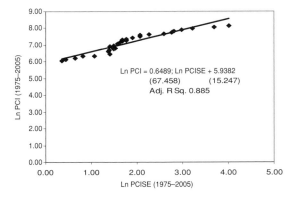

Figure 3C   Relationship between PCI and PCISE. *Notes:* (1) data in parentheses are *t*-values; (2) PCI is taken in PPP terms, at current price in US\$; (3) PCISE is taken at current price in US\$. *Source:* Calculations based on World Bank (2007) for PCI and RBI (2007) for PCISE.

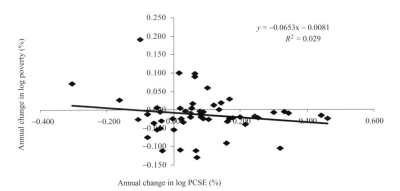

Figure 3D   Scatter of services exports and national poverty. *Notes:* (1) PCISE is taken at current price in US\$; (2) poverty is represented by HCR; (3) both poverty and PCISE are taken for the periods 1951–52 to 2005–06. *Source:* The PCISE series was calculated by the authors, based on RBI (2007), while the poverty time series was collected from Bhalla (2003).

suppliers are concentrated in urban India, where inequality appears to have increased over time. There is further evidence of this development in Table 3E.

According to Dev and Ravi (2007), the decline in urban poverty was adversely affected by changes in income distribution in states like

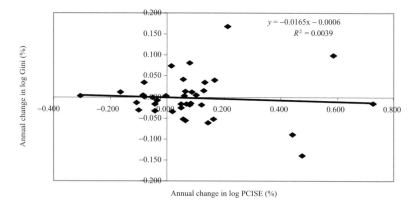

Figure 3E Scatter of services exports and national inequality. *Notes:* (1) PCISE is taken at current price in US$; (2) inequality ratio is represented by the Gini coefficient; (3) both inequality and PCISE are taken for the period 1951–52 to 1999–2000. *Source:* the PCISE series was calculated by the authors, based on RBI (2007), while the inequality time series was collected from UNU-WIDER (2007) and Bhalla (2003).

Karnataka, Tamil Nadu, Andhra Pradesh and West Bengal. These states have attracted significant investment in the IT sector. It is not entirely wrong to suggest that high urban inequality is exacerbated by the IT concentration in the capital (and metro cities) of theses states, for example Bangalore (Karnataka), Hyderabad (Andhra Pradesh), Kolkata (West Bengal) and Chennai (Tamil Nadu) – although one cannot prove causality without proper statistical tests.

As income grew, particularly in urban areas, the country's employment structure also underwent a structural shift: from agriculture and manufacturing to services.[12] Contrary to popular belief, it has been found that the rise in services-sector employment is associated with a fall in gender inequality. Female employment (per 100 males in employment) in organised services has increased from thirteen in 1981 to twenty-three in 2004 (see Figure 3F). According to the National Sample Survey Organisation (NSSO, 2006), the gender differential in the worker population ratio (WPR) in 2004–05 in the services sector was quite distinct: 25%

---

[12] It is the services sector that provides the bulk of employment in urban India, whereas the manufacturing sector was the major source of employment a decade earlier (see IAMR, 2006). The services sector in India presently contributes about 69% of the country's employment, up from 63.65% in 1981.

Table 3E *Indian state-wise urban poverty ratio (PR in %), poverty line (PL in Indian Rs) and Gini coefficient*

States	1983–84	1993–94	1999–2000	2004–05
Andhra Pradesh	PR: 36.30. PL: 106.43; Gini: 33.25	PR: 38.33; PL: 278.14; Gini: 32.31	PR: 26.63; PL: 457.40	PR: 20.70; PL: 542.89; Gini: 37.43
Karnataka	PR: 42.82; PL: 120.19; Gini: 34.46	PR: 40.14; PL: 302.89; Gini: 31.84	PR: 25.25; PL: 511.44	PR: 27.20; PL: 599.16; Gini: 36.83
Haryana	PR: 14.15; PL: 103.48; Gini: 35.40	PR: 16.38; PL: 258.23; Gini: 28.32	PR: 9.98; PL: 420.20	PR: 11.30; PL: 504.49; Gini: 36.37
Gujarat	PR: 39.14; PL: 123.22; Gini: 28.58	PR: 27.89; PL: 297.22; Gini: 29.08	PR: 15.59; PL: 474.41	PR: 10.10; PL: 541.16; Gini: 30.98
Maharashtra	PR: 40.26; PL: 126.47; Gini: 34.86	PR: 35.15; PL: 328.56; Gini: 35.69	PR: 26.81; PL: 539.71	PR: 29.00; PL: 665.90; Gini: 37.77
Punjab	PR: 23.79; PL: 101.03; Gini: 34.53	PR: 11.35; PL: 253.61; Gini: 28.02	PR: 5.75; PL: 388.15	PR: 3.80; PL: 466.16; Gini: 40.17
Tamil Nadu	PR: 46.96; PL: 120.30; Gini: 35.32	PR: 39.77; PL: 296.63; Gini: 34.74	PR: 22.11; PL: 475.60	PR: 18.80; PL: 547.42; Gini: 35.84
West Bengal	PR: 32.32; PL: 105.91; Gini: 33.78	PR: 22.41; PL: 247.53; Gini: 33.77	PR: 14.86; PL: 409.22	PR: 11.20; PL: 449.32; Gini: 38.33
All India	PR: 40.79; PL: 115.65; Gini: 34.06	PR: 32.36; PL: 281.35; Gini: 34.31	PR: 23.62; PL: 454.11	PR: 21.70; PL: 538.60; Gini: 37.51

Notes: Poverty line (PL) is calculated on a consumption basket of 1973–74 prices, upgraded according to current prices. Poverty ratio (PR) considers head-count value. Data for 2004–05 is based on MRP basis, which implies households recounted their expenditure for 30 days for food while 365 days for clothing, footwear, medical, education and other durable goods.
Source: Sharma (2004), Press Information Bureau (PIB) Note, May 2007, for the 2004–05 data (PIB, 2007) and Dev and Ravi (2007).

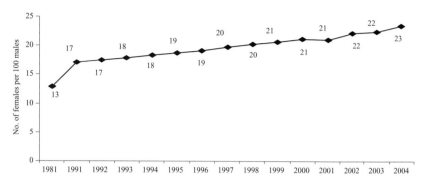

Figure 3F   Male-female ratio in services-sector employment. *Notes:* data relates to employment in the organised sector only. *Source:* Calculations based on IAMR (2006).

Table 3F   *Employment rates in India*

| | Employment rate in the services sector (%) | | | |
| | Rural | | Urban | |
Year	Male	Female	Male	Female
1977−78	12.40	5.70	61.00	38.00
1983	14.60	5.50	61.20	40.90
1987−88	17.30	7.90	63.40	42.40
1993−94	18.20	6.50	66.10	50.70
1999−2000	20.80	6.90	70.30	57.90
2004−05	25.00	8.10	69.50	53.50

Source: Calculations based on NSSO (2006).

for males versus 8% for females in rural India, and 70% for males versus 54% for females in urban India.

  While there was a distinct fall in services-sector employment for both males and females in urban India in 2004–05, compared to 1999–2000, in the case of rural India, a steep rise occurred in 2004–05, compared to 1999–2000 (see Table 3F). In other words, despite a rise in income inequality in urban India, acceleration of growth of PCI and PCISE have, perhaps, created employment opportunities for women and thereby have reduced the gender bias in employment in the services sector.

The change in skill composition and the rising wage inequality[13] (with relatively less gender bias in urban India) in services-sector employment offers a plausible explanation for the rise of income inequality in urban India, where the majority (if not 100 per cent) of India's software and IT-BPO services exports are concentrated. Growth in PCI from output and services exports appears to be another source of lower urban poverty and higher income inequality. The issue is, therefore, how much the rise in India's software and IT-BPO exports, which together presently share about 39 per cent of India's services exports, can be harnessed to contribute to the delivery of inclusive growth. Successfully tackling these challenges would require strategic choices in crucial policy making.

Making the services trade work for the poor: emerging challenges

The Indian IT industry has demonstrated its superiority and sustained cost advantages in the international market. Today, the Indian IT industry (including the domestic sector) is a US$37.4 billion market, which is expected to grow to US$47.8 billion by the end of 2007–08, an increase of nearly 28% (NASSCOM, 2007b). Software and IT-BPO exports from India grew from a meagre US$0.18 billion in 1991–92 to US$24.20 billion in 2006–07, and are expected to reach US$31.90 billion in 2007–08 (see Table 3G). They presently contribute 5.4% of India's GDP, about 29.80% of the country's services exports (2005–06) and 5.80% of the country's employment in the organised services sector (2005–06).

With this spectacular performance, the Indian IT sector is shifting its base from low-end business processes to high-value ones. While services and software exports remain the mainstay of the IT sector, increasing traction in offshore product development and engineering

---

[13] There is a general increase in inequality among wage-earners of different skills in services-sector employment in the age group of 15 to 59 in urban India. The coefficient of variation (CV) of wage rates of different skills in urban India increased from 0.48 in 1993–94 to 0.60 in 2004–05, thereby indicating a strong dispersion of wage inequality among different skills, whereas the opposite trend was found in rural India over the same period (see Appendix 3A on p. 425).

Table 3G *Software IT-BPO exports from India and its contribution to GDP and employment*

Financial Year	Software and IT-BPO exports			
	Volume	Share in GDP	Share in services exports	Share in services-sector employment
	(US$ billion)		(%)	
1991	0.18	0.11	3.50	0.31
1992	0.23	0.16	4.78	0.41
1993	0.33	0.22	6.27	0.49
1994	0.49	0.29	7.91	0.64
1995	0.73	0.44	9.99	0.76
1996	1.10	0.56	14.72	0.86
1997	1.76	0.92	18.66	0.93
1998	1.80	1.20	13.65	1.01
1999	2.70	1.40	17.19	1.21
2000	3.96	1.80	24.35	1.50
2001	6.20	2.60	36.17	2.27
2002	7.70	2.80	37.09	2.79
2003	9.80	3.20	36.47	3.59
2004	13.30	3.60	30.75	4.55
2005	18.30	4.10	29.80	5.80
2006	24.20	4.70		
2007*	31.90	5.40		

* forecasted value according to NASSCOM (2007b).
Notes: (1) exports of software and IT-BPO include revenue from computer hardware; (2) employment in the software and IT-BPO sector does not consider employment in the hardware sector; (3) employment in the services sector considers only the organised sector.
Source: (1) NASSCOM, *Strategic Review*, various issues; (2) employment figures in the organised-services sector are taken from the Ministry of Employment and Labour, Government of India.

services is supplementing India's efforts in intellectual property creation (NASSCOM, 2007b). This segment is growing at 22 to 23 per cent and is expected to report US$4.9 billion in exports in 2006–07. FDI has also reached an unprecedented scale, with over US$10 billion announced in 2006–07 to be invested over the next few years (NASSCOM, 2007b).

Unfortunately, services-sector growth did not create sufficient employment.[14] It absorbed mainly skilled labour (Gordon and Gupta, 2004). However, as Kumar and Joseph (2005) have argued, BPO (business process outsourcing) activities in information technology-enabled services (ITES) provide low value-added jobs to less-skilled persons and created 245,000 jobs in 2003–04, compared to 42,000 jobs in 1999–2000.

In India, growth in IT and ITES does create better income opportunities. However, the importance of technology in this sector results in wage inequality in the short term because higher-skilled workers gain better jobs and higher wages at the expense of the lower-skilled, thereby widening the wage gap between them. Thus, very fast growth in this sector might lead to more income inequality in society in the short term. This was amply illustrated when the statistics for Indian states were considered in Table 3E (at p. 413). At the same time, the proliferation of IT and ITES sectors that are concentrated in urban areas in some states in India might be a major cause for the growing rural-urban income disparity in India. This is clearly reflected in Table 3H.

Software exports are driven mainly by the availability of skilled manpower and local research institutions. These factors explain the development of Bangalore (capital of Karnataka), Hyderabad (capital of Andhra Pradesh) and Delhi National Capital Region (NCR – comprising states like Delhi, part of Haryana and part of Uttar Pradesh), which together shared half of India's total exports of software and IT-BPO in 2004–05 (see Table 3H).[15] This demonstrates that if a state has adequate infrastructure, it can attract more players in IT and ITES sectors. Otherwise, merely giving more support to exports does not generate the desired results. Accordingly, urban inequality, as shown in Tables 3G and 3H, has increased faster in states like Karnataka, Haryana and West Bengal, where the main urban centres are located.

Furthermore, it is clear that, globally, the rural sector receives little benefit from the IT spread as enunciated by UNCTAD (United Nations Conference on Trade and Development) regarding information and communication technology (ICT): 'The newer ICT arrives first in the main

---

[14] By this, it is meant employment in formal sectors. The result would certainly be different if the large informal services sectors were taken into account. This is not due to lack of data on informal services.

[15] See, for example, Kumar and Joseph (2005).

Table 3H   *State-wise concentration of software exports in India*

City	State	1997–98		2000–01		2004–05	
		Export# (%)	HQ* (Nos.)	Export# (%)	HQ* (Nos.)	Export# (%)	HQ* (Nos.)
Bangalore	Karnataka	22.20	84	26.64	160	28.45	172
Delhi NCR**	Delhi + Haryana + Uttar Pradesh	19.61	95	18.31	106	20.13	119
Chennai	Tamil Nadu	9.98	34	10.32	72	11.5	83
Hyderabad	Andhra Pradesh	4.25	21	6.91	61	7.49	75
Mumbai	Maharashtra	7.04	86	5.68	148	6.81	158
Pune		3.36	21	3.39	48	4.02	51
Kolkata (Calcutta)	West Bengal	1.08	26	1.31	32	4.38	42
Ahmedabad	Gujarat	0.21	13	0.33	10	0.89	14
Thiruvananthapuram	Kerala	0.09	7	0.23	14	1.03	20
Chandigarh	Punjab	0.01	3	0.01	7	0.03	11
Others		32.18	20	26.87	42	15.27	43

* Headquarters of NASSCOM members.
** Delhi National Capital Region (NCR) comprising Gurgaon (Haryana), Delhi and Noida (Uttar Pradesh).
# Shares in country's total export of software and IT-BPO.
Source: NASSCOM (2007a).

cities, and often never get to rural areas, thus creating a tension between the opportunity to integrate citizens into global society which is offered by ICTs and the threat of exclusion through the strengthening of the hegemony of the elite and widening of the urban-rural divide' (UNCTAD (2006), p. 176). India is no exception, as examples like *e-choupals*, which gives farmers information about market demand and prices, is still in its experimental stage.

Policy implications and the way forward

India continues to build on its recent record of strong economic performance. Services continue to underpin economic growth in India. India has reduced poverty substantially since the mid 1970s as growth accelerated and human-development indicators improved. India has also done extremely well in the IT and ITES sector, including BPO activities. This sector has revealed a strong comparative advantage and significant foreign-demand growth linkage. This explains India's interest in modes 1 and 4 of the GATS negotiation. However, the growth of IT and ITES are concentrated in select urban cities, and are biased to high- and medium-skilled labour. India's growth (and inward investment) brings new technology to the economy. The adoption of new technology furthers the wage divide, particularly between the skilled and unskilled, in the short run. As a result, while IT and ITES can assist in poverty reduction, it can also increase inequality within urban areas as well as inequality between urban and rural areas.

Essentially, this paper has argued that accelerated growth in the IT-services sector in India has played an important role in reducing overall poverty and, in particular, in reducing poverty amongst women. However, this has come at the cost of widening inequality, as mainly educated, higher-skilled and selected urban labour benefit from IT-services growth. As India continues to expand its IT-led services sector, both for domestic consumption and international trade, the challenge for both industry and government is to put in place measures to address these inequality gaps. Therefore, the key message is that services trade tends to aggravate inequalities in the absence of policies and programmes to guarantee 'inclusive' economic growth. By developing effective pro-poor targeting, the government can make IT-led services export better for the poor and can reduce the divide between them and the richer segments of society. There are a number of ways this can be done, with important policy implications for India. We recommend the following broad measures that the Indian Government can take to build capacity and maximise comparative advantage in skilled IT labour.

Education

Evidently, most of the growth in inequality between the highest and lowest earners is due to relatively poor education of the unskilled population.[16] In order to bridge the gap between skilled and unskilled labourers, equitable access to good-quality education at all levels, especially for the disadvantaged and lower-income groups, is a must. Linking primary education with secondary education is the biggest challenge set before the government. Curricula can be updated to include ICT education, as well as the skills and competencies required by the labour market, including analytical, communication and language skills. As more ICT is introduced in classrooms, care must be taken to ensure that the poor, who have limited access to ICT, are not left behind.

Training and employment

With rapid changes taking place in the labour market, the workplace and society, job stability and permanence of employment could decrease. Lifelong training and skill-training opportunities, particularly among disadvantaged groups, are needed to ensure that workers are able to keep up with change through retraining or continued education. Opportunities for acquiring practical employment and ICT entrepreneurship skills should be expanded.

In parallel, rural India should be empowered with an adequate social safety net. Towards this vein, the National Rural Employment Guarantee Act (NREGA), adopted in 2007, attempts to ensure a social safety net as it provides guaranteed employment in rural areas and, at the same time, has the capacity to build rural infrastructure, especially if resources from other programmes are pooled. Where appropriate, targeted subsidies can be provided to lagging and disadvantaged groups or lagging regions of the country. Women should be encouraged to continue their schooling and training. There is also a need to plan for and take action to prevent future skill shortages. The NASSCOM-McKinsey Report (NASSCOM,

---

[16] In fact, the government itself acknowledged that the *Sarva Shiksha Abhiyan* (meaning 'education for all') has expanded primary school enrolment, but it is far from providing quality education (Planning Commission, 2006, p. 6).

2005a) projections indicate that India will lack about 500,000 suitable professionals (representing an opportunity cost of US$10 billion) by the end of the decade, and in the absence of corrective action, this gap will continue to grow. However, if current trends are maintained, the IT and ITES sector (excluding the knowledge sector) will need an additional 1 million plus qualified people in the next five years, and would be likely to generate exports of US$86 billion in 2012, reported in the NASSCOM-McKinsey Report (NASSCOM, 2005a). This also suggests opportunities for public-private partnerships. A greater role for the private sector in ICT training and development would increase the supply of skilled manpower.[17]

Capacity building

Capacity building to facilitate learning for all income groups needs to be encouraged. As more efficient means of production are driven by technology, new jobs demand a higher skill and knowledge base. The poor have limited access to ICT, which in turn may aggravate income inequalities. We need to create adequate capacity for lagging regions (states) and income groups through training, education and skill-development programmes so that the poor feel comfortable in taking part in the development of the ICT sector. In this regard, more vocational education using IT and software is needed.

Planning

The government's approach to the ICT sector should be more pro-poor; it has a strong role to play in order to ease the burden of poverty and inequality. The government can contribute by removing impediments to the upward mobility of unskilled labour and by pursuing the measures outlined briefly above. These policies might also improve the country's overall services quality in the long run. Quality education, training, skill development programmes and other measures can more adequately prepare individuals for upward income mobility. In essence, the government must keep investing in human capital and new technology in order to sustain services-led growth in the long run. While a distortion-free

---

[17] While India's young demographic profile has the country favorably placed in terms of manpower availability, talent supply shortages are also fast emerging in the country (Planning Commission, 2006, p. 62).

trade in services policy alone may not cure all the problems of poverty
and inequality, it can be an important facilitator of longer-term policies,
which would allow the government to take direct action to reduce poverty
and lessen inequality. The domestic policies of the Indian Government
should not only continue to make computers available to remote corners
of the country, but must also ensure their maintenance and appropriate
use.

Participation of states

The Indian Government has to strengthen the role of state governments.
Since exports of IT services are concentrated in limited states in India,
unless the lagging states are encouraged to participate in ICT-sector development, inequalities between the states may increase. Many states (for
example, India's north-eastern states) do not have adequate capacity to
invite investment in the ICT sector, despite their higher human development. The Indian Government should build new partnerships with local
governments and civil society, in addition to the private sector. Furthermore, the government may provide subsidies (if they are WTO compliant)
to lagging states or backward regions within a state in order to strengthen
their institutional capacity and physical infrastructure in the ICT
sector.

Conclusion

In summary, the expansion of the domestic IT-services sector and growth
in trade in IT services driven by foreign trade and investment have had
a direct and positive impact on poverty reduction in India. This includes
a positive impact on a portion of highly skilled women with the capacity to take advantage of this growth. Therefore, the key issue for the
government is to address the short-term impact of IT development on
inequality.

India's services trade can work for the poor and reduce inequality even
in the short run if it generates employment opportunities for unskilled
labour and reduces the skill gap. However, it is often the case that wage
inequality is inevitable in the short term, since the demand for skilled
labour increases much more rapidly than for unskilled labour in the case
of services. Opportunities are likely to increase for unskilled labour in
the long run due to the multiplier effects of higher growth throughout
the economy. Indian Government policies must address the needs of the

groups that are largely excluded from such growth processes. The short-term impact of this will be on inequality, but its long-term impact will be on human capital development over a much larger cross-section of the population.

No doubt further detailed research will be very valuable in exploring the complex causality and linkages between the IT-led, export services-sector growth, wage inequality and poverty reduction. Particularly needed are more field surveys on urban-based IT-sector growth. On the basis of primary surveys, it is possible to look into the composition of the workforce and its dimensions, output details and sales markets, along with the wage structure of some important IT and IT-BPO companies in India.

Bibliography

Balasubramanyam, V. N. and Balasubramanyam, A. (1997), 'International Trade in Services: The Case of India's Computer Software', *World Economy* 20(6): 829–43.

Bhalla, S. S. (2003), 'Not as Poor, Nor as Unequal, as You Think – Poverty, Inequality and Growth in India, 1950–2000', final report of a research project undertaken for the Planning Commission, Government of India, entitled 'The Myth and Reality of Poverty in India', Oxus Research & Investments: New Delhi.

Central Statistical Organisation (2007), *National Accounts Statistics 2006*, Central Statistical Organisation (CSO), Government of India: New Delhi.

Chanda, R. (2007), 'Services', in K. Basu (ed.), *The Oxford Companion to Economics in India*, Oxford University Press: New Delhi.

Dev, M. and Ravi, C. (2007), 'Poverty and Inequality: All India and States, 1983–2005', *Economic and Political Weekly*, 10 February, pp. 509–21.

Gordon, J. and Gupta, P. (2004), 'Understanding India's Services Revolution', IMF Working Paper WP/04/171.

Government of India (2006), *WTO Negotiation on Trade in Services: A Backgrounder*, Ministry of Commerce and Industry, Government of India: New Delhi, available at http://commerce.nic.in/wto_sub/services/wto_service.htm [last accessed 1 March 2009].

(2007), *Economic Survey 2006–2007*, Ministry of Finance: New Delhi.

Hansda, S. (2000), *Services Sector in the Indian Economy: A Status Report*, RBI Staff Studies, Department of Economic Analysis and Policy, Reserve Bank of India: Mumbai.

Institute of Applied Manpower Research (IAMR) (2006), *India Manpower Profile 2005*, IAMR: New Delhi.

Kumar, N. and Joseph, K. J. (2005), 'Export of Software and Business Process Outsourcing from Developing Countries: Lessons from Indian Experience', *Asia-Pacific Trade and Investment Review* 1(1): 91–110.

Mikic, M. and Qiu, Y. (2007), *Achieving the MDGs in Asia and the Pacific: Where do We Stand on Trade Targets?*, Socio-Economic Policy Brief 9, UN Economic and Social Commission for Asia and the Pacific (UNESCAP): Bangkok.

National Association of Software and Service Companies (NASSCOM) (2005a), 'Extending India's Leadership of the Global IT and BPO Industries', NASSCOM-McKinsley Report, NASSCOM: New Delhi.

(2005b), *Strategic Review 2005*, NASSCOM: New Delhi.

(2007a), *Indian IT and Software Services Directory*, NASSCOM: New Delhi.

(2007b), *Strategic Review 2007*, National Association of Software and Service Companies (NASSCOM): New Delhi.

NSSO (2006), *Employment and Unemployment Situation in India, 2004–05, Vol. II*, NSS Report No. 515, National Sample Survey Organisation (NSSO), Government of India: New Delhi.

Parikh, K. S. and Radhakrishna, R. (2005), *India Development Report 2004–05*, Oxford University Press: New Delhi.

Planning Commission (2006), *Towards Faster and More Inclusive Growth: An Approach to the 11th Five Year Plan (2007–2012)*, Government of India: New Delhi.

Press Information Bureau (PIB) (2007), 'PIB Note on Indian State-wise Urban Poverty Ratio', PIB, Government of India: New Delhi.

Rakshit, M. (2007), 'Services-led Growth: The Indian Experience', *Money and Finance* 3(1): 91–126.

Raychaudhuri, A. and De, P. (2007), 'Barriers to Trade in Higher Education Services: Empirical Evidences from Asia-Pacific Countries', *Asia-Pacific Trade and Investment Review* 3(2): 67–88.

Reserve Bank of India (RBI) (2007), *Database on Indian Economy*, RBI: Mumbai.

Saith, A. and Vijayabaskar, M. (eds.) (2005), *ICTs and Indian Economic Development: Economy, Work and Regulation*, Sage Publications: New Delhi.

Sharma, S. (2004), *Poverty Estimates in India: Some Key Issues*, ERD Working Paper No. 51.

United Nations Conference on Trade and Development (UNCTAD) (2006), *Information Economy Report 2006*, UNCTAD: New York, NY.

United Nations University – World Institute for Development Economic Research (UNU-WIDER) (2007), *World Income Inequality Database V 2.0b May 2007*, United Nations University: Helsinki.

World Bank (2000), *India: Reducing Poverty, Accelerating Development*, Oxford University Press: New Delhi.

(2004), *Sustaining India's Services Revolution: Access to Foreign Markets, Domestic Reform, and International Negotiations,* World Bank: New Delhi.

(2007), *World Developmental Indicator CD-ROM 2007,* World Bank: Washington, WA.

Appendix 3A

Supply of skills and salary (wage) earnings (per day) in services sector employment in India (Rs)

	1993−94	1999−2000	2004−05
	Rural India		
Not literate	21.56	84.53	66.05
Literate and up to middle class	48.66	142.40	117.51
Secondary and higher secondary	77.39	158.37	179.66
Graduate and above	100.40	206.70	251.83
Standard Deviation (SD)	29.69	43.62	69.46
Coefficient of variation (CV)	0.48	0.29	0.45
	Urban India		
Not literate	35.22	91.57	75.45
Literate and up to middle class	54.00	120.19	132.61
Secondary and higher secondary	85.72	182.99	198.48
Graduate and above	132.39	302.26	394.15
Standard deviation (SD)	36.81	80.96	120.15
Coefficient of variation (CV)	0.48	0.46	0.60

Trade, aid and services in Tanzania

AMANDA SUNASSEE LAM[*]

Introduction: refocusing Aid for Trade on infrastructure and services

Fifteen years after the Williamson articulation of the Washington Consensus, the world has come to acknowledge that free trade is not a magic wand.[1] The world is witnessing a paradigm shift from the neoclassical focus on static welfare gains from trade liberalisation to the recognition that domestic policy interventions, institutions and infrastructure need to play a central role in capturing the benefits of trade. Trade in goods and services have the potential of fuelling growth and ultimately of alleviating poverty. However, the link between trade, growth and poverty alleviation is neither simple nor automatic. While the transmission mechanisms between trade and growth through export expansion may seem straightforward, those between trade and poverty reduction are complex. The latter depends on the way in which trade affects income distribution, employment and adjustment costs, all of which define who ultimately are the winners and losers of trade liberalisation.

Developing countries and least developed countries (LDCs) have been involved for more than two decades in implementing trade liberalisation and market-opening policies, and have been the beneficiaries of some of the most preferential market-access regimes. However, based on empirical evidence of LDCs' dismal performances in international trade, it is clear that 'making international trade a more effective mechanism for poverty reduction requires a development approach which goes beyond market access'.[2] Securing market access is not sufficient, because the private sector

---

[*] Amanda Sunassee Lam is IF Facilitator Specialist, a Consultant based at the Ministry of Industry and Commerce, Foreign Trade Policy Department, Lao PDR.

[1] J. Stiglitz and A. Charlton (2006), 'Aid for Trade', paper prepared for the Annual World Bank Conference on Development Economics, Tokyo, Japan, 29 to 30 May 2006.

[2] United Nations Conference on Trade and Development (UNCTAD) (2004), *Trade and Development Report*, UNCTAD: Geneva.

must be able to produce competitive products and services. This requires addressing the key supply-side constraints, which are known to stifle the private sectors' productive capacity. Addressing supply-side constraints requires a four-pronged approach, as follows:

(1) better national development strategies, which integrate trade objectives as a central component (mainstreaming trade into Poverty Reduction Strategy Papers (PRSP))
(2) clear national policy direction and policy reform agenda
(3) improvements in the international trade regime, including issues that go beyond the scope of improved market access to include issues of standards, rules of origin and other non-tariff measures
(4) increased and effective financial and technical assistance for the development of production and trade capacities, i.e. Aid for Trade (AfT).[3]

This chapter focuses on the role of AfT in addressing supply-side constraints. It argues that AfT is one of the requisites for unleashing the gains from trade, 'one' being the operative word. As many poorer developing countries face the prospect of very small gains, or indeed net losses, from preference erosion from the Doha Round, the revived focus on aid to build trade capacity is an opportunity for LDCs to review their policies with respect to AfT. Using Tanzania as a case study, this chapter argues that LDCs should redirect their trade and aid strategies towards addressing services and infrastructure bottlenecks. Infrastructure and services have great potential for improving productive capacities by integrating the private sector – in particular small, medium and micro enterprises (SMME) – and rural smallholders into the global supply chain. The possible scaling up of official development assistance (ODA) resulting from initiatives such as AfT, and the emphasis that the AfT debate has put on infrastructure, provides the appropriate platform for developing countries to reassess their AfT strategy and explore complementary strategies for promoting public-private partnerships.

Trade policy reform in Tanzania and economic performance

Trade in services: the poor cousin of trade policy reforms

The first market-oriented National Trade Policy (NTP) was adopted by the Tanzanian Government in 2003. The overriding theme of Tanzania's NTP

---

[3] UNCTAD, *Trade and Development Report*.

is to stimulate a process of export-led growth based on structural transformation and production, as well as market diversification.[4] This was to
be achieved through strategic trade liberalisation, combined with export
development based on implementation of dynamic, sectoral, complementary policies. The policy also emphasises the importance of proactive
engagement in multilateral and bilateral trade negotiations.[5]

Over the last five years, considerable effort has been deployed by
the Government of Tanzania to stimulate export-led growth by tackling
supply-side constraints and by undertaking major business-environment
reforms. The linchpin of the Tanzanian NTP has undeniably been the
trade policy reforms undertaken in the context of the East African Community, which brings together Tanzania, Uganda and Kenya in a customs
union. In parallel, Tanzania has been negotiating an economic partnership agreement (EPA) with the EU and has been participating in the
ongoing WTO Doha negotiations. The main policy reforms undertaken
by the Tanzanian Government in the area of trade and private-sector
development over the last ten years are highlighted below:

- Setting up export processing zones (EPZs) and special economic
  zones as the primary policy instruments for the realisation of export
  development objectives.
- Promotion of small and medium enterprises (SMEs), which is at
  the heart of the Private Sector Development Strategy.
- Promoting a conducive business environment for the private sector
  through a basket-fund programme called the Business Environment
  Strengthening for Tanzania (BEST), which focuses on regulatory
  and legislative reforms.
- The formalisation of the informal sector through a property-
  formalisation programme (known as MKURABITA), which seeks
  to ensure that all land and landed property are registered, have value
  and are usable as security for the purposes of underwriting economic
  activity.
- In the area of regional integration, the East African Customs Union
  presents one of the most advanced initiatives by Tanzania to simplify
  and harmonise import policies and tariffs. The Customs Union is
  underpinned by a common East African Community (EAC) Customs Management Act, a common external tariff and intra-regional

[4] WTO (2006), 'Trade Policy Review', reports by the East African Community Members,
WT/TPR/G/171, 20 September 2006.
[5] Ibid.

tariff liberalisation phased over a five-year transition period, where Uganda and Tanzania will gradually phase out tariffs on a selected list of Kenyan imports.

- With respect to its commitments under the WTO, Tanzania has bound many (755) of its tariff lines at 120%. However, given its commitment under the EAC Customs Union, the obligation to implement the common external tariff has the de facto effect of binding tariffs to an average of about 10.5%.[6] As an LDC, Tanzania is exempt from Most Favoured Nation (MFN) tariff-reduction commitments. Average agricultural tariffs consequent to tariff harmonisation due to membership in the EAC are an average of 22%.

With respect to reforms in the services sector, under the General Agreement on Trade in Services (GATS), Tanzania has not committed or notified to the WTO any scheduled commitment except for the tourism subsector of tourist hotels, which was made after the conclusion of the Uruguay Round of trade talks. The commitments are partial as they apply exclusively to hotels of four-star status. To date, the strategies and policies adopted by the Tanzanian Government in liberalising the services sector have been timid. With respect to the services negotiation under the WTO, the position taken by Tanzania has been to use the 'defensive' flexibilities provided in the Special Modalities for LDCs on GATS negotiations.[7] The Tanzanian Government has elaborated clear policies to support its export-led growth strategy, focusing its interventions on building a dynamic private sector and by raising the level of competencies to achieve competitive levels of productivity and quality. However, in the area of services, policy direction is less clear, and policy makers have failed to deliver a comprehensive strategy for the services sector. A number of grey areas persist with respect to the government's policies and strategies concerning: (i) the services negotiation strategy and its overall position with respect to liberalisation of the services sector; (ii) its policy direction with respect to development of the services sector as a direct export; and (iii) its strategy for boosting the services sector for building competitiveness. The services sector by virtue of its interconnection with other sectors of the economy has the potential of having a ripple effect on the economy. For example, liberalisation in the transportation and logistics sector, which is usually

---

[6] WTO, 'Trade Policy Review'.
[7] Daima Associates Limited (2007), 'Opportunities and Risks of Liberalizing Trade in Services in Tanzania', International Centre for Trade and Sustainable Development (ICTSD): Geneva.

accompanied by foreign investment, can act as a catalyst to building competitiveness of the private sector, whilst also providing consumers with efficient and affordable services that contribute directly to their quality of life.

Snap shot of the Tanzanian economy: the macro/micro mismatch

Ten years of sustained economic restructuring and market opening has unleashed an impressive supply response raising real gross domestic product (GDP) growth from 2% per annum during 1990 and 1995 to 6% per annum since 2000.[8] In 2006, real GDP growth stood at 6.7%, and it is expected to pick up to 6.8% in 2007 and to 7% in 2008 as increased investment begins to drive growth.[9] Exports of goods and services have contributed significantly to the country's overall growth and contribute 12% to GDP. The services sector in 2004 stood at 37% of GDP, and in 2005 it recorded a growth of 8.2% compared to 7.8% in 2004, consistent with increased trading and tourism activities. The current account deficit has widened from 9.5% of GDP in 2001–02 to an expected 15.5% of GDP in 2006–07, but it remains fully financed by growing external assistance (11.5% of GDP) and foreign direct investment (FDI) (4% of GDP).

Despite these strong economic indicators, per capita income in Tanzania remains very low (amongst the lowest in the East African region), and Tanzania remains one of the poorest countries in sub-Saharan Africa. The government's review of poverty in 2006 notes that progress in reducing income[10] and non-income poverty is very slow, especially in areas outside Dar es Salaam. Tanzania was ranked sixty-fourth in the UNDP's Human Poverty Index (HPI-1)[11] of 102 developing countries in 2004. Whilst international trade has expanded in Tanzania, poverty levels have been slow to ameliorate, showing that the link between 'trade expansion and poverty reduction is therefore neither simple nor automatic'.[12]

---

[8] International Monetary Fund (IMF) and the United Republic of Tanzania (2007), 'Staff Report for the 2007 Article IV Consultation and First Review under the Policy Support Instrument', prepared by the African Department, IMF Country Report No. 07/246, 12 June 2007.

[9] Organisation for Economic Cooperation and Development (OECD) and African Development Bank (AfDB) (2007), *African Economic Outlook 2006/2007*, OECD/AfDB.

[10] Overall, there has been limited improvement in the income poverty status of Tanzania since the 1990s.

[11] The HPI-1 focuses on the proportion of people below a threshold level of human development, life expectancy, education and income.

[12] UNCTAD (2004), *Least Developed Countries Report: Linking International Trade with Poverty Reduction*, UNCTAD: Geneva.

Table 3I   *Sectoral shares of GDP and contributions to growth (1990–2003 – in constant 1992 TZH)*

	Shares of GDP (%)			Average growth per annum (%)	Annual average contribution to growth (%)
	1990	2003	Average 1990–2003		
Agriculture, forestry, fishing and hunting	47.9	46.8	48.8	3.5	1.7
Trade, hotels and restaurants	16.3	16.8	16.1	4.0	0.6
Manufacturing	8.8	8.6	8.3	2.8	0.3
Transportation and communications	4.6	5.4	5.2	5.0	0.3
Public administration	8.7	7.2	8.1	2.3	0.2
Financial and business services	5.6	5.3	5.4	3.4	0.2
Mining and quarrying	0.9	3.0	1.7	13.5	0.2
Construction	5.7	5.2	4.7	3.0	0.1
Electricity and water	1.5	1.6	1.6	4.4	0.1
Total GDP				3.7	3.7

Note: Contribution to growth = shares of real GDP * real growth, and denotes what total GDP growth would have been if growth of all the other sectors were zero.
Source: Derived from data from the Integrated Framework (IF) Diagnostic Trade Integrated Study (DTIS) for Tanzania, July 2005, World Bank.

The Tanzanian economy is dominated by agriculture, which makes up nearly half of GDP (see Table 3I and Figure 3G). In 2003, the hotel and restaurant sector was the second largest contributor to growth, with a 16% GDP share, making it the second largest sector for that period.[13] In 2004, the hotel and restaurant's share in GDP fell to 11.7%, whilst that of finance and business services rose from 5.3% GDP in 2003 to match that of the hotel and restaurant sector.

Another sector worth noting is mining and quarrying, which grew at an impressive 13.5% average growth per annum between 1990 and 2003 tripling its share of GDP. However, in 2003 its contribution to growth was relatively small, with a 0.2% annual average contribution to growth. The manufacturing sector registered the worst performances, after public

---

[13] This includes tourism.

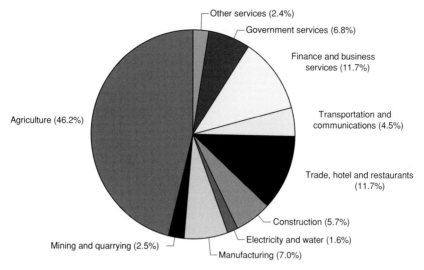

Figure 3G   GDP by sector in 2004. *Source:* ADFD (2007), *ADFD Report 2007*, ADFD.

administration, and its GDP share continues to fall, standing at 7% of GDP in 2004.

Trade in services in Tanzania is the single largest contributor to Tanzania's GDP after agriculture, contributing close to 37% of Tanzania's GDP in 2004 (see Figure 3G, above). The services sector between the periods of 1988 to 2002 grew at a rate of 4.3% per annum, compared to growth in 2005 and 2004, which respectively stood at 8.2% and 7.8%, consistent with increased trading and tourism activities. The services sector is also a major source of job creation, ranking second in employment generation after the agricultural sector, with a share of about 16% of total employment.[14] Despite its growing importance, the services sector in Tanzania has still not been performing well in international trade relative to goods exports, attracting only 30% of FDI stock in 1999 to 2002.[15]

In fact, in 2003, tourism and gold exports (43.2 per cent of the Tanzanian-goods export basket)[16] were the largest and second-largest

---

[14] J. Kweka and G. Kablewa, *Opportunities and Risks of Liberalising Trade in Services in Tanzania*, Economic and Social Research Foundation: Dar es Salaam.

[15] Ibid.

[16] Tourism receipts rose more than ten-fold between 1990 and 1995 from US$47 million to around US$500 million, and gold exports increased fifteen times between 1990 and 2003 from US$27 million to around US$400 million (World Bank (2004), *Tanzania Diagnostic Trade Integration Study*, World Bank).

Table 3J *Poverty by main source of cash income of the household (2000–01)*

	HCR (%)	Share of the poor (%)
Sales of food crops	40.6	46.9
Sales of livestock	59.1	7.2
Sales of livestock products	33.3	1.4
Sales of cash crops	38.6	20.5
Business income	24	8.4
Wages or salaries in cash	14.9	3.6
Casual cash earnings	32.8	4.9
Cash	35.2	2.3
Fishing	28.3	1.5
Other	34	3.3
Total	**35.6**	**100**

Note: HCR indicates the percentage of households that live below the poverty line for a given source of income: Share of the poor shows the percentage of poor households that derive their income from the given source. For example, around 7 per cent of the poor derive their main cash income from sales of livestock.
Source: The IF DTIS for Tanzania, July 2005, World Bank.

export items respectively. This shift in export trends has serious underlying implications on the type of export growth and its potential impact on poverty.

Most of the poor make their living in agricultural activities, and the share of the poor working in agriculture has declined only slightly over the last decade.[17] Amongst households dependent on agriculture, those most likely to be poor (highest head-count ratio (HCR)) rely on livestock sales. Agricultural households whose main source of cash income is from sales of cash crops or livestock products fare better than other agricultural households. Poverty rates are lower in households that are dependent on export income or on fishing, and are lowest for those drawing wages or salaries as the primary source of cash income (see Table 3J).[18]

These results indicate that households that are involved in export-oriented sectors are less likely to be poor. However, in practice, what is

[17] Down from 86% in 1991–92 to 80% in 2000–01.
[18] Analysis from the IF July 2005 DTIS for Tanzania, p. 9.

being observed in Tanzania is that only a minority of people are being employed in export-oriented sectors, the main reason being that despite the expansion in exports, the ability for the rural poor to integrate into the global supply chain continues to be stifled by supply-side constraints, which are mainly infrastructural or are in the services sector. In addition, export expansion in Tanzania has not contributed significantly to poverty alleviation due to the shift in composition of trade and the expansion of sectors such as mining, which have weak backward and forward linkages. The mining sector, being a capital-intensive sector, has little value-adding processes associated with it, and thus has limited ability to create complementary income-generating activities for the population.

Tanzania is possibly witnessing the beginning of an export expansion associated with enclave-led growth,[19] which is quite typical of LDCs specialising in commodity exports. The key factors that determine whether export expansion is broad-based or not are rooted in a country's economic structure: its social composition, type of enterprises and type of employment.[20] Although international trade constitutes an important proportion of total Tanzanian GDP, most jobs and livelihoods are not export-orientated; 82.11 per cent of the total employment in 2001 was in the agricultural sector. The new jobs being created in the services sector and particularly in the tourism sector have the potential for strong linkages with agro-processing. Although the services sector has a key role to play in fostering stronger supply-chain linkages, and is an important source of job creation and poverty alleviation, it has its limitations in reaching the unskilled rural poor. In order to translate the expansion of services into real opportunities, the Tanzanian Government will need to ensure that the right policies and incentives are in place to promote the necessary training and investment in capacity building.

Unleashing Tanzania's private sector: a strategy for addressing supply-side constraints

One of the main reasons that can be attributed to Tanzania's low trade performance, besides non-tariff barriers and other trade distorting practice, are problems closer to home; that is, supply-side constraints. Whilst

[19] This is a form of economic growth that is concentrated in a small part of the economy (UNCTAD, *Least Developed Countries Report*).
[20] Ibid.

there is no internationally agreed definition of supply-side constraints, it generally refers to impediments to the capacity to produce goods and services competitively and the ability to get them to the market at a reasonable price. The Diagnostic Trade Integration Studies (DTISs) that are undertaken in the context of the Integrated Framework (IF) focus on documenting and analysing the main supply-side constraints faced by LDCs like Tanzania. A review of fourteen DTISs undertaken by the WTO Secretariat[21] identifies four areas of supply-side constraints that commonly appear in DTISs:

(1)   transportation (roads and ports in particular)
(2)   customs
(3)   standards and quality requirements
(4)   export promotion.

Whilst the DTIS provides a good framework for identifying and analysing 'behind the boarder' issues affecting Tanzania's competitiveness, what the DTIS fails to do is to provide a strategy for addressing these constraints and for mobilising funding. The major building blocks for enhancing supply-side capacities are depicted in Figure 3H. The foundations of such a strategy lie in establishing an enabling policy and regulatory framework, efficient institutions and good governance, which need to be reinforced by adequate energy, transportation and information and communication technology (ICT) infrastructure, as well as a good level of general education. The two main pillars of such a strategy rely on achieving two mutually reinforcing objectives: (i) enhancing productive capacity; and (ii) reducing the cost of conducting trade.

It is clear that constraints such as poor access to finance, low productive capacity, low technology base, poor quality and standards, lack of market information and poor managerial and technical skills are all problems that keep the private sector in Tanzania from building its competitive advantage. However, with limited resources and pressing social needs, the Tanzanian Government has to prioritise sectors that are likely to have the biggest impact, and that, when addressed, are likely to provide the private sector with incentives to invest and upgrade its productive capacity. With the increasingly complex and integrated global supply chain, which is highly information-, network- and knowledge-based, services such as telecommunications, logistics, freight and cargo, marketing and

---

[21] 'Assistance to Address Supply-side Constraints' note by the WTO Secretariat, WT/COMTD/LDC/W/33/Add.1, 28 February 2005.

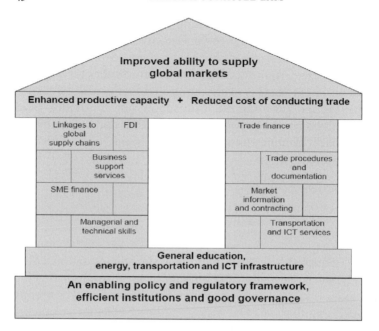

Figure 3H Building blocks for enhancing supply-side capacities. *Source:* Economic and Social Commission for Asia and the Pacific (UNESCAP) Secretariat (2004), 'Financing for Development through Trade and Investment', paper prepared by the UNESCAP Secretariat: Bangkok.

quality testing hold a central role in allowing the rural poor and the private sector in developing countries to participate fully and competitively in the market place. An approach could be to target infrastructure bottlenecks, which affect the most on the provision of key services. The Tanzanian Government can play a strategic role by focusing on providing the right policies and by channelling its investments to the main 'arteries of economic activity', which tend to be critical public goods involving big infrastructure projects and some strategic services sectors such as the following:

- the energy sector
- the water and distribution sector
- the transportation and logistics sector
- customs reform and trade facilitation
- the ICT sector.

By providing the required infrastructural investment to these key sectors and ensuring that the appropriate policy and regulatory responses are in place to stimulate them, it is likely that economic and productive activities will be able to gain sufficient scale to induce the private investments needed to ease the supply-side constraints and foster the development of key services. To illustrate the point, take, for example, the fish, horticulture and agricultural exports, which account for almost 50 per cent of Tanzania's exports. These subsectors are faced with a number of supply-side constraints that erode its competitive advantage, such as poor quality standards, the inability to adhere to sanitary and phytosanitary requirements, etc. In addition, these subsectors face high transportation costs, which, in the case of frozen fish products, account for nearly 40% of the total cost, and 80% for fresh products, which require air freighting.[22] The Tanzanian Government, by addressing the transportation and logistics constraints through a combination of investments in roads and transportation networks, coupled with policy and regulatory reforms (which will open up transportation and logistics services), could help lower transportation costs and associated services, making the sector more profitable. This increased profitability would in turn stimulate the sector, thus providing the sector with the scale needed to attract, for example, intermediary service providers such as private firms to set up inspection, verification, testing and certification services, or telecommunications providers to extend their network to remote areas.

The Tanzanian private sector is faced with innumerable constraints that stifle its productive capacity and competitiveness. In order to address these constraints, there needs to be a clear strategy for reducing these supply-side constraints and strengthen supply-chain linkages. Supply-side constraints tend to be viewed as a homogenous cluster of problems; however, on closer analysis, it is possible to see that the constraints can be grouped into different clusters. The author argues that in order to efficiently address the supply-side constraints, it is necessary to: (i) classify these constraints into distinct clusters; (ii) identify who is best placed to respond to the problems, through a division of labour between government, private sector and development partners; and (iii) find the best funding channels for addressing the specific clusters of constraints. Table 3K attempts to categorise the supply-side constraints and provides some options *on how best to address them.*

With limited resources and competing priorities, the strategy to adopt is one whereby the Tanzanian Government focuses its investment in the area of 'mega' supply-side constraints, through a combination of budget

---

[22] USAID report on the agricultural sector in Tanzania.

Table 3K *Supply-side constraints and options*

Supply-side cluster	Constraints	Lead actor	Preferred partners	Funding channels	Policy and regulatory framework
Mega cluster (infrastructure and services)	• Water resources • Energy • Transportation and logistics • ICT	Government	• Public sector • Private sector though public-private sector partnerships • Private-sector investment • Development partners	• Government budget • Loans • FDI • Development assistance	PRSP
Meso cluster (institutional)	• Access to finance • Trade facilitation and customs • Vocational and technical capacities • Business support services • R&D • Standards and quality (testing infrastructure)	Government	• Public sector • Private sector though public-private sector partnerships • Private-sector investment • Development partners	• Government budget • Loans • FDI • Development assistance	Sector master plans Regulations and laws Services offers
Micro cluster (enterprise level)	• Market information • Technology and productive capacity • Managerial and technical skills • Standards and quality requirements • Export promotion	Private sector	• Private-sector investment • Development partners	• Private equity • Development assistance	

Source: UNESCAP Secretariat, 'Financing for Development'.

allocation, public-private partnerships, FDI and development assistance, coupled with providing support to the 'meso level' reforms and policy reforms. The renewed focus of the development community on the key role that trade infrastructure and its accompanying services can play in strengthening and integrating the supply chain presents the Tanzanian Government with a unique opportunity to reassess its current investment strategy in the infrastructure and services sector. The Tanzanian Government, by focusing AfT on the 'mega clusters' of supply-side constraints, is likely to jump-start a chain reaction, allowing the private sector to make the necessary investments required to redress the supply-side constraints at the micro level. The development of the infrastructure and services sector is likely to have the biggest impact on the rural poor, who are marginalised by their remoteness to centres of production.

Transportation and logistics services in Tanzania: the weak-link case study

Transportation contributes about 7 per cent to Tanzania's GDP, and in 2001 it provided close to 120,000 jobs.[23] The subsector faces many problems and is characterised by high costs, low-quality services and inadequate institutional support. Logistics services are also known to be quite expensive in Tanzania; for example, the average cost to import one container is nearly US$1,500 – and that is three times more than in Singapore – while the operating cost per kilometer of using two-axle trucks in Tanzania is two and half times the cost in Indonesia or Pakistan. The poor standard of the road network impedes mobility and access to markets and services in the country, in particular in rural settings. The quality of road networks is also critical for transit traffic with neighbouring countries. Transit traffic made up around 21% of Tanzania's total international transport in 2003 (46% of transit traffic was by road transportation, 33% by pipeline and 20% by rail).[24] Almost all international transportation in Tanzania is by ocean freight, whilst airfreight transportation made up 0.4% in 2003. About three quarters of international transportation via ocean freight is taken by road, 17% by rail and 7% by pipeline. The unique geography of Tanzania and the fact that its neighbours are landlocked provides Tanzania with an immense potential as a transportation and logistics-services export hub within the region.

[23] Including transportation and communications. [24] IF July 2005 DTIS for Tanzania.

Regional flights are costly and have limited connections, making regional trade costly and uncompetitive. It costs as much to fly from Dar es Salaam to London as it does to fly from Dar es Salaam to Mauritius or Zambia. The maritime sector is the most open sector in the country, and it is controlled largely by the private sector, with the exception of the Tanzania Port Authority (TPA), which is a parastatal body.[25] Since the privatisation of the Tanzania Container Terminal, Dar es Salaam port now boasts the highest productivity rates of any port in eastern and southern Africa. Dar es Salaam is recognised by the World Bank as being one of Africa's most productive ports. Because of the downstream nature of road transportation activities and the increasing complexities of production methods and supply-chain management, road transportation can potentially have a much bigger impact on growth and economic activity.

AfT and public-private partnerships: harmonious cohabitation

Whilst the picture may be bleak in some areas, important progress has been made in the port and maritime services sector, with some important lessons to be learnt with respect to public-private sector partnership and government leadership and ownership of reform programmes. The road subsector in Tanzania has also benefited from substantial assistance. Over the last fifteen years, the EU has financed road projects close to €270 million. The forthcoming EU assistance for the road subsector is a transitional programme moving away from the old-style project-driven approach towards a more sector-wide response to the government's Poverty Reduction Strategy. The programme is proposed to develop a mixture of direct sector support and project support to assist existing newly created institutions and organisations to develop. The programme has four main elements, as follows:

(1)   a Road Fund (€30 million)
(2)   institutional support (€5 million)
(3)   regional road maintenance (€40 million)
(4)   paved trunk-road backlog maintenance (€30 million)
(5)   reconstruction of Zanzibar Port (€31 million).

---

[25] In May 2000, the container terminal of TPA (formerly Tanzania Harbour Authority) was divested to an international consortium of the Philippines. The divestiture transaction was historic in that it made the port of Dar es Salaam the fastest container terminal in sub-Saharan Africa, ahead of Durban, Mombasa and Mauritius.

The institutional support and direct financial contributions to the Road Fund will assist the government in developing adequate human and financial resources to effectively and efficiently deliver road-maintenance services for the entire national network.[26] Other big players in the transportation sector are the World Bank and the European Commission. However, in LDCs such as Tanzania, subsectors such as roads tend not to be particularly attractive for private capital investment, and hence it is usually sustained either by government funds or by international donors.

However, if Tanzania is to make any substantial improvements in its transportation sector and logistics services, it will need more than donor funding and government funds. The Tanzanian Government will need to find ways of making the sector profitable by leveraging public-private partnership schemes such as Build Operate Transfer (BOT).[27] Whilst the inadequate road infrastructure has been mainly funded by the Tanzanian Government and donors, a very different trend in the area of port services and other related logistics services such as the container terminal can be observed. To address some of the deficiencies in these areas, the government is promoting private-sector participation through a comprehensive privatisation programme of some of its transport-related state-operating enterprises (SOEs). Table 3L lays out the various SOEs that were under a privatisation programme in 2005.

To date, the Regional Transport Companies (RETCOS), Dar es Salaam Container Terminal and Air Tanzania Corporation (ATC) have all been privatised. Despite the impressive progress made to date and the move toward public-private partnership arrangements in the area of transportation infrastructure, the sector remains significantly under-funded and its associated services weak and dominated by only a few service providers. According to the Tanzania Investment Centre, an estimated US$3 billion will be needed over the next ten years to improve the road network.

Whilst AfT and government funding are likely to be important sources of funding for the trade-related infrastructure and services sector, the Tanzanian Government will need to aggressively promote public-private partnerships, such as BOT, and make a serious attempt to improve its investment climate.

[26] Text based on the EU website: http://europa.eu.
[27] *TanzaniaInvest* interview with Mr Fred Addo Abedi, former Chief Executive of the Tanzania National Roads Agency (TANROADS), 20 July 2006, available at www.tanzaniainvest.com [last accessed 31 March 2009].

Table 3L   *Privatisation status of transportation and logistic SOEs in 2005*

Transportation and logistics-related SOEs	State share (%)	Total value of shares (TZH)	Status
Air Tanzania Corporation	51	8,289,000,000	Joint venture
Tanzania Central Freight Bureau	*100*	*8,036,675*	*Capital structure to be firmed up*
Tanzania Electric Supply Co. Ltd	100	–	Parastatal
Tanzania Harbours Authority	*100*	*9,060,000,000*	*Parastatal*
Tanzania Posts Corporation	100	2,216,553,564	Capital structure to be firmed up
Tanzania Railways Corp.	*100*	*10,000,000,000*	*Parastatal*
Tanzania Telecommunication Company Ltd	65	191,012,000,000	Joint venture
Chinese Tanzania Shipping Company Ltd	50	7,615,256,175	Joint venture
Tanzania Zambia Railways (TAZARA)	50	4,074,000,000	Capital structure to be firmed up
Usafiri Dar es Salaam	49	348,865,100	Under privatisation
Kilimanjaro Airport Development Company Ltd	28	1,568,070,000	Joint venture

Source: The IF DTIS for Tanzania, July 2005.

Service liberalisation and its impact on the infrastructure and services sector

In order to promote and attract private-sector investment, Tanzania will need to address some of the main regulatory and legal impediments that currently deter private investment. The services sector in Tanzania is still at its infancy stage, and the general strategy for the development of the services sector has been protective.[28] With respect to the GATS negotiations, Tanzania submitted an initial schedule of commitment relating to the tourism services sector. It has also participated in a joint LDCs request on mode 4 services to trading partners. Although there are initiatives to

[28] See note 14, above.

expand the current schedule of commitments in line with national policy objectives, with a view to further opening up the economy and attracting FDI, these efforts have been timid. Whilst it is recognised that liberalisation of the services sector has the potential of benefiting the private sector and boosting export competitiveness, and can contribute to GDP through direct exports, there is still a lot of apprehension about the capacity of the indigenous private sector to participate in the services sector.[29] As discussed in Chapter 3, services liberalisation in economies that have been relatively closed to domestic private suppliers as well as to foreign participation has been found to lower prices and to have significant welfare effects.

Table 3M is a services schedule that the Government of Tanzania has been discussing in the context of the GATS services negotiations in the area of maritime transportation services. Based on a study carried out by an economic think tank, the ESRF, maritime transportation is the only service in the transportation sector that Tanzania intends to make commitments. According to the draft schedule of commitments on maritime transportation services, market access and national treatment are unbound in all modes of supply, with the exception of mode 3. For market access, a joint-venture requirement for foreign ships to trade in national waters is imposed, whereas for national treatment, citizens are given preference to operate trade in national waters (i.e. only Tanzanian ships to trade in its waters).[30] It is clear that opening is restricted and protective, with limited option for liberalisation of the sector.

Whilst the direct impact of inadequate infrastructure on economic activity is evident, what is less so is that poor infrastructure in developing countries also impedes the development of associated services, which further exacerbates low productivity and competitiveness. When road networks or port infrastructure are under-invested, it is unlikely that there will be a thriving distribution sector and logistics-services network, which all impact on the supply chain and a country's competitiveness.

Transportation and logistics services are the lifeline of all trading activities – it is what allows products and services to move from one point to another and is inextricably linked to supply-chain management. The cost and effectiveness of the sector has a direct impact on the competitiveness of a country and its exports. Weak and high-cost transportation,

---

[29] See note 14, above.   [30] Ibid.

Table 3M *Services schedule for maritime transportation services*

Sector	CPC #	Market access (MA)	National treatment (NT)	Additional commitment
(i) Passenger transportation	7211	(1) Unbound	(1) Unbound	
(ii) Freight transportation	7212	(2) Unbound	(2) Unbound	
		(3) Commitment with limitations:	(3) Commitment with limitations:	
		– Requirement on legal entity/joint venture requirement for foreign ships to trade in national waters	– Nationality: citizens are given preference to operate trade in national waters, i.e. only Tanzanian ships to trade in its waters	
		(4) Unbound	(4) Unbound	

Source: http://tsdb.wto.org/default.aspx [last accessed 15 June 2009].

energy and telecommunications infrastructure impact particularly heavily on producers of traditional products and standardised manufacturing
in poor countries[31] such as Tanzania. We have seen that this sector is a
capital-intensive sector, which will require funding from the government,
the private sector, ODA and loans in order to meet the full scale of funding
required to overhaul roads, rails, ports and maritime subsectors and their
associated services.

Rethinking Tanzania's AfT strategy and private-sector development

In 2005, Tanzania counted more than fifty active national projects in
the area of trade-related aid and PSD (private-sector development), with
more than ten active bilateral partners. Most projects are focused on
supporting poor agro-farmers in the area of production (e.g. by linking smallholders with traders and exporters via out-grower or contract
farming schemes) of mainly primary commodities (with little or no value
addition), whilst support for value adding (or vertical diversification)
such as processing, packaging and managing for quality control is less
well-covered. There are disparities and gaps between the efforts (number
of projects and resources) directed toward enhancing production and
technological advancement as distinct from those geared toward the services sector and the marketing of inputs and outputs.[32] An interview with
an Arusha-based exporter of green beans, Gomba Enterprises, pointed
out that 'all donors flock to the same areas of activities, that is the strengthening of production, but no one thinks that these products need to get
to a market – the end game is to sell!'. Donors need to coordinate their
intervention and provide support across the value chain, with clear indications and on-the-ground strategies to ensure that various interventions
augment each other.

The majority of projects in the area of PSD tend to focus on enhancing
the business and financial environment. In contrast to such programmes,
the United States Agency for International Development (USAID)
and the State Secretariat for Economic Development (SECO) tend to
set up projects that are directly targeted to private enterprises, as opposed

---

[31] IMF and World Bank (2007), 'Aid for Trade: Harnessing the Global Economy for Economic Development', paper prepared by the staffs of the IMF and World Bank, available
at http://siteresources.worldbank.org/INTEDS14/Resources/AIDFORTRADE.pdf [last
accessed 31 March 2009].

[32] A. E. Temu (2006), 'Aid for Trade and Agro Based Private Sector Development in Tanzania',
OECD Policy Dialogue with non-members on Aid for Trade – From Policy to Practice.

to the majority of current projects, which tend to be anchored in government institutions or private-sector apex bodies or in SWAPS (sector-wide
approaches)[33] or basket funds. Under the Private Enterprise Support
Activities (PESA) and Project for Rural Initiatives in Micro-Enterprise
Development (PRIME), USAID has financed a number of activities geared
to the key commodity sectors that address value-chain bottlenecks. However, the current thinking in PSD has been that support to the private
sector should be done at the macro and meso level, and that micro level
input should not be funded by ODA but by the private sector's own
resources and through the local banking system. Experience has shown
that relying on a trickle-down effect via reform in the regulatory environment and investment in infrastructure takes time, and that, in the
meantime, companies need to produce, export and make the required
investment in their capital and human resources. In the absence of a fully
functioning capital and financial market, it is difficult for private firms to
make the necessary investments to build and maintain competitiveness.
The donor community's policies in the area of PSD have predominantly
focused on avoiding market distortions by limiting the provision of subsidies (such as those provided by USAID and SECO) and have upheld
concepts such as the promotion of a level playing field with a clear exit
strategy. Unfortunately, such market-oriented approaches have limitations in a market environment where most of the principles of a perfect
market do not hold, and where market failures of all kinds predominate.
There is a growing school of thought that advocates that, in the interim
period, while the benefits from reforms in the business environment and
infrastructure kick in, there is a need for more direct intervention in the
supply chain.[34]

Donor and government policies and strategies in the area of PSD have
focused predominantly on market-oriented approaches that promote
the strengthening of an enabling regulatory environment and SMME
promotion, as well as promoting traditional smallholder production systems. In Tanzania, the majority of enterprises are SMMEs operating in
the informal sector and run by smallholder operators. Most enterprises

[33] A sector-wide approach is a way of providing development assistance that strengthens
national ownership, and helps build nationally managed systems, with the support of
development partners and lenders. In a SWAP, all significant funding for the sector supports a single sector policy and expenditure programme, under government leadership,
adopting common approaches across the sector and progressing toward relying on government procedures for all funds.
[34] Speech by Hon Dipak K. A. Patel M. P., Ministry of Commerce, Trade and Industry in
Zambia at the World Bank Programme of Seminars Aid for Trade Round Table, September
2005.

operate with rudimentary technology and management skills and are engaged in low value-addition. Small businesses in Tanzania are faced with major production-capacity constraints, which cannot be solved by merely improving the business environment. The failure to promote commercial farming, in particular the development of medium- to large-scale commercial farms, explains the low productivity growth of the country's rural sector: 'Donor funded projects are deeply rooted on food security and poverty at household level and not sufficiently on rural industrialisation.'[35] Current support as discussed above is biased toward primary production, principally for subsistence produce (food security) or for generating raw material, with very little effort to integrate comprehensive support packages to cover the entire value chain. Whilst the two approaches are necessary, what the donor community should be aiming for is a combined approach that on the one hand ensures immediate aid for primary production and food security and, on the other hand, uses AfT to build stronger trade infrastructure and services, which supports the business supply chain.

Similarly, donors and the Tanzanian Government need to recognise that policies and programmes that support the creation of medium and large firms need to be included as part of the Tanzanian Government's private-sector development strategy, and that these policies and strategies need to cohabit with the existing policies that focus on poor and small operators. There tends to be a 'prism vision' amongst the donor community, which leads to development strategies that focus on an 'either/or' approach, which is often linked to resource constraints. But the development quandary requires a complex and often paradoxical set of policies and support programmes. LDCs such as Tanzania need to rethink their AfT and private-sector strategy. Redirecting AfT to trade-related infrastructure and services needs to be coupled with various forms of private-public and private-private partnership schemes. This will require a major shift in the way AfT programmes are designed, and will also require that donors review their aid coordination, bringing together private investors, international banks, governments and donors.

Conclusion

Tanzania faces a complex set of supply-side constraints, which make producing high value-added goods at a competitive price a major challenge. The economic transformation required by Tanzania in order to integrate

---

[35] Temu, 'Aid for Trade and Agro Based Private Sector Development in Tanzania'.

fully into the global market is indeed formidable, yet it is achievable. In less than two decades, countries as diverse as South Korea, Mauritius, Chile, Vietnam and China have made remarkable progress in finding and developing their competitive advantage and transforming their economies, partly due to appropriate domestic reform programmes and greater openness to international trade. This has almost always been accompanied by a major transformation of the education infrastructure and services, which have in turn induced a surge in productive capacity. It is argued here that to unleash the potential of the private sector, AfT will have to be focused on the development of necessary infrastructure to support the expansion of services, which is key to a stronger integrated supply chain. The services sector and trade-related infrastructure have up to now been the missing link in sustaining and expanding the private sector's productive capacity. Whilst aid has been an important catalyst of reform for many LDCs, it is only part of the solution. FDI, loans and public-private partnerships will need to accompany AfT so as to reach the critical mass of investment that Tanzania will need for modernising its services sector and trade-related infrastructure. This will require bringing down the divide that seems to persist between international finance institutions, international development banks, donors and the private sector.

Telecommunications reform in the Pacific and the case of Vanuatu

CHAKRIYA BOWMAN[*]

Introduction

As small, remote communities, the Pacific Islands are constantly challenged by globalisation. Connectivity in the region – internally within countries, between countries and with the rest of the world – has always been weak. Cities like Port Moresby are far more connected with foreign cities like Brisbane or Singapore than they are with townships in Papua New Guinea's outer islands. In telecommunications, the need for cable-driven technologies has hampered deeper service penetration, and monopoly suppliers have been slow to introduce new services and cheaper technologies. By 2006, less than half of all Pacific Islanders had access to a telephone,[1] and the telecommunications-driven revolution in business services taking place in Africa and Asia had effectively passed them by.

Africa's experience with telecommunications clearly demonstrated the benefits to the poor from increased access. Markets in Africa have expanded rapidly over the last decade, a direct result of liberal regulatory environments where operators have proven highly responsive to customer needs and the potential of new technologies to drive cheaper and better services. Telecommunications is no longer a service focused on developed economies and wealthy consumers. It is the provision of services to the 1 billion plus consumers that are currently unserviced that holds the greatest promise for those companies with the foresight to develop innovative, pro-poor business models.

---

[*] Chakriya Bowman is Trade Advisor and Acting Director of the Pacific Growth Section of the Australian Government aid agency, AusAID. The views expressed in this publication are those of the author. The publication does not necessarily reflect the views of AusAID or the Australian Government.
[1] P. Budde (2007), 'South Pacific Islands – Telecoms, Mobile and Broadband 2007', paper published by C. Bowman, p. 3.

But despite the increasingly obvious benefits of competition in telecommunications seen in other developing regions, reform in the Pacific can at times appear to be a process of two steps forward, one step back. According to academic Satish Chand: 'Pacific governments . . . have been slow to embrace these developments – held back, in many instances, by public sector monopolies loath to face competition . . . The one clear lesson from this experience is that the sooner we remove the shackles from competition in these sectors (and the economy more generally), the better for regional integration, consumer welfare and growth of these economies.'[2]

However, the innovation driven in other regions is starting to reach the Pacific. Cheaper mobile technologies mean that, in stark contrast to twenty years ago when most of the region's monopolies were put in place, telecommunications companies are now clamoring to enter the market. Digicel, a Bermuda-domiciled company led by a team of Irish telecommunications executives, has been the most active in the region and clearly views the Pacific as a natural extension to its other developing country markets in the Caribbean and South America. Since it entered the Pacific Islands in November 2006, Digicel has become the fastest-growing mobile service provider in the Pacific, with operations in Samoa, Papua New Guinea, Tonga, Fiji and Vanuatu.

The Pacific Islands are now at the start of their own communications revolution, one driven by telecommunications liberalisation and the entry of competitive commercial service providers ready to service a developing country market. As the perceived wisdom of the past – that the Pacific Islands are too small and remote to attract commercial services – is dispelled, telecommunications provides an example of the benefits of service liberalisation and the entry of competition into even poor and challenging markets.

But challenges remain for liberalisation, in particular the dismantling of existing monopolies that often have years to go before expiring. This case study examines the success of Vanuatu in dismantling its monopoly telecommunications provider as a model for other countries in the region, and provides an example of the immediate benefits of reform bringing new technology and investment to previously under-serviced regions.

Background

While the potential of telecommunications has been recognised in other developing economies, its application to the Pacific has been slow, driven

---

[2] S. Chand (2008), 'Pacific Partnership for Development', *Islands Business*, 31 March 2008.

in some part by the enduring belief that small size and remoteness remain impenetrable barriers to commercial operations. A common justification for the retention of regional monopolies is the argument that, without monopolies or subsidies, and often both, services simply would not be provided.

However, a recent UNESCAP (United Nations Economic and Social Commission for Asia and the Pacific) study dispels this notion for telecommunications. It suggests that in the 'average' Pacific community, per capita funds available for telecommunications are around US$12 to US$20 per month. When combined in family or clan groupings, this could become US$25 to US$100 per month. At prices comparable with Asia, this would finance one or more mobile phones and internet access.[3] In poorer communities, services might be delivered through internet cafes, e-centres or the shared use of phones among family and clans. The use of shared facilities is common in developing countries but has been slow to reach the Pacific – internet cafes are rare and are typically provided for tourists rather than locals. An exception is the People First Network in the Solomon Islands, which manages an internet cafe in the capital, Honiara, and email stations in remote communities, but this is not a commercial venture and it relies on donor funding.

While larger businesses are clear recipients of the benefits of improved telecommunications, and are often the most vocal advocates for reform, the benefits to the poor should not be underestimated. An increasingly important feature of Pacific Island economies is remittances. Pacific Island workers are taking advantage of opportunities around the world, particularly in Australia, New Zealand and the US. Remittances to the Pacific reached US$425 million in 2005,[4] and at current trends are likely to overtake aid flows in value in 2009.

Although much of the demand for Pacific labour has been for skilled workers, programmes such as New Zealand's Recognised Seasonal Employer scheme have provided access for thousands of unskilled labourers to the New Zealand horticulture industry, and Australia is likely to follow suit with its own unskilled labour pilot programme in early 2009. These workers can remit as much as US$5,000 each through formal channels at charges that are currently in excess of 17 per cent of the remitted value.[5]

[3] UNESCAP (2007), 'Pacific Island Connectivity: The Current Situation and Opportunities for Progress', UN-ESCAP.
[4] C. Browne and A. Mineshima (2007), 'Remittances in the Pacific Region', IMF Working Paper WP/07/35.
[5] Estimates from the Reserve Bank of New Zealand (2007), internal documents.

In Africa, where there are twice as many people with mobile phones as there are with formal bank accounts,[6] mobile phones have become low-cost vehicles for remittance transfers. Safaricom Kenya, a leading mobile phone operator with around 5 million customers, has introduced a service that enables subscribers to send and receive money in an instant transaction, costing on average US$1. A pin code-protected SIM card with a money transfer menu lets the user manage funds between accounts. According to Michael Joseph, Chief Executive of Safaricom: 'within two weeks of the launch, over 10,000 account holders were registered and more than US$100,000 had been transferred'.[7] Although mobile phone banking has not yet reached the Pacific, there are over 9 million potential customers, most of whom currently have no access to formal banking products.

In the business world, telecommunications services assist not only large businesses – there is increasing international recognition of the benefits telecommunications can bring to micro-entrepreneurs. An example from the Pacific region is the story of Eduardo Belo Soares, a Timor Leste furniture maker who credits mobile telephony for the rapid and successful expansion of his business in Dili: 'Before mobile phones were available I had to travel a lot into the districts to place timber orders with growers. When mobile coverage was introduced I devised a scheme where I would lend the growers the money to buy a mobile or help them get one.'

The decision proved a turning point for the business: 'I now just ring the growers to organise my timber supplies which saves a lot of time, and have been able to expand my business. In 2002 I employed two people. Now it's nearly 50. And since I started using SMS to advertise my furniture, sales have increased even further by about 40–60 per cent.'[8] Improved telecommunications have the potential to grow small businesses and create economies of scale.

Telecommunications in the region

The chequered history of telecommunications in the Pacific region has several underlying causes. The Pacific Islands have always suffered from capacity constraints, and small populations with limited access to

---

[6] Department for International Development (DFID) (2006), 'Money Sent Home to Poor Countries Hits All Time High, New Technology Offers Potential for Further Growth', press release, 13 November 2006.

[7] M. Siddiqi (2008), 'The Global Remittances Boom', *African Business*, January 2008.

[8] E. James (2008), 'Optimism for Pacific Economies', *Islands Business*, 31 March 2008.

higher-education opportunities means that many bureaucracies lack the technical understanding needed to progress information and communications technology (ICT) initiatives. Particularly in smaller countries, it is unlikely that a coterie of bureaucrats with expertise on technological and regulatory issues could be assembled, given competing priorities within government and the degree of specialisation required to address these issues. Regional solutions are likely to be more effective in both the design of regulatory systems and the deployment of technical expertise.

The lack of progress in the region and the need for greater sharing of ICT knowledge and systems prompted Pacific leaders to develop and, in 2006, endorse the Pacific Regional Digital Strategy, with the ultimate goal of providing ICT access to every Pacific Islander. The Wellington Declaration calls for greater availability of information and communication technologies, recognising that 'while not an end in themselves, [they] have a key role as a basis for economic development, while also promoting and enhancing social cohesion, cultural enrichment and environmental conservation'.[9] The Declaration highlights the need for a competition-driven environment and the centrality of private enterprise to service provision. It also canvasses ideas such as improved cooperation between national ICT agencies, greater engagement by regional technical-assistance agencies such as the Secretariat of the Pacific Community with ICT policy development and implementation, and regional approaches to upgrading and improving broadcast content and delivery.

Yet competition has been slow to arrive, particularly in the existing fixed-line services where it is effectively non-existent (see Table 3N). There has been more success in the provision of mobile and broadband services where existing providers are less entrenched, not least due to the limited provision of these services. But, overall, the regulatory environment remains weak. Reform-minded governments such as the Lini Government in Vanuatu have fought hard-pitched battles to dismantle existing monopolies, and some, like the Somare Government in Papua New Guinea, have still not managed to banish the ghost of monopolies past – creating great uncertainty for those holding newly issued licenses and discouraging the entry of further competition.

Teledensity is generally low, particularly compared to other low-income developing countries. In sub-Saharan Africa, the average number of mobile subscribers per 100 inhabitants was 16.8 across twenty-four

---

[9] Wellington Declaration, 2006, Pacific Islands Forum Secretariat.

Table 3N   *Teledensity in the Pacific*

Country	Fixed (%)			Mobile (%)			Internet users (%)		
	2002	mid 2007*	Competition status	2002	mid 2007*	Competition status	2002	mid 2007*	Competition status (broadband)
Palau	35.0	41.0	M	10.0	52.0	C	10.0	25.0	–
Fiji	12.4	13.0	M	13.3	24.8	CP	6.6	9.4	C
Marshall Is.	6.0	8.0	M	1.1	8.5	M	2.6	14.4	–
FSM	10.0	12.0	M	3.4	19.4	M	4.4	13.0	–
Tonga	11.3	13.8	M	3.4	30.0	C	2.2	3.1	C
Samoa	6.5	11.0	M	1.5	46.0	C	2.2	4.5	C
Vanuatu	3.2	3.9	M	3.8	11.5	CP	3.5	7.5	M
Solomon Is.	1.5	1.5	M	0.2	2.2	M	<0.5	1.5	M
Papua New Guinea	1.1	1.1	M	0.3	5.1	C*	1.3	1.8	C
Kiribati	5.1	4.3	M	0.6	0.5	M	2.0	2.2	–
Timor-Leste	0.2	0.3	M	1.0	5.7	M	<0.5	<1.0	C

* 2007 or latest available. Updated subscriber data may be difficult to obtain. Where available, data are sourced directly from operators, otherwise from ITU (2006), *ICT Indicators Database*, ITU.

Notes: C = Competition; M = Monopoly; CP = Competition in progress; C* = Conflicting policy environment.

Source: N. Beschorner (2008), 'Telecommunications Background', in AusAID, *Pacific Economic Survey 2008*, AusAID: Canberra, with author's additions.

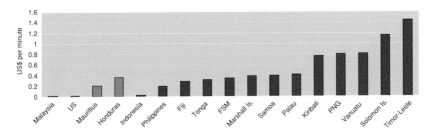

Figure 3I International call costs (2007, US$ per minute). International calls from the Pacific are among the most expensive in the world. *Note:* These are Skype-out rates: the rates charged by Skype for making a call from a computer to a phone in any other country. They are a useful, internationally comparable indicator of the cost of making an international phone call from different countries. Actual phone-to-phone international call costs may be more expensive. *Source:* Beschorner, 'Telecommunications Background'.

countries.[10] The low teledensity is reflected in high costs. Even when using low-cost technologies such as voice over internet protocol, international call costs in the Pacific are among the most expensive in the world (see Figure 3I).

Consumers in more remote locations are unable to rely on the provision of fixed lines and often use expensive technologies like Very Small Aperture Terminal (VSAT). But these costs are coming down, driven by economies of scale and some donor activity. A recent AusAID-funded project initiated and managed by the Secretariat of the Pacific Community, the Pacific Regional Internet Connectivity System (Pacific RICS) is now using VSAT and the Boeing satellite network to provide internet access to community centres in rural and remote areas. The Boeing network covers the Pacific Island region and provides access to remote areas unlikely to be serviced by commercial providers. While the satellite base station has been effectively subsidised by AusAID, community centres are expected to run on a cost-recovery basis, and use of the base station is open to small commercial operators, creating the potential for internet cafes in difficult-to-reach rural villages and outer islands. This project has the potential to provide shared access to communities previously untouched by telecommunications.

But the greatest advances have and will continue to come from the deregulation of inefficient monopolies that have to date dominated the

[10] Beschorner, 'Telecommunications Background', p. 4.

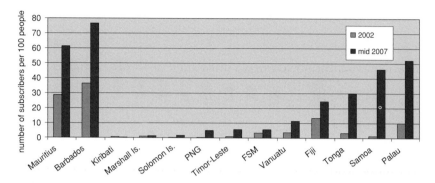

Figure 3J   Mobile phone penetration (number of subscribers per 100 people). Access to mobile phones has grown fastest in countries that have allowed competition. *Source:* Beschorner, 'Telecommunications Background' and AusAID, *Pacific Economic Survey 2008.*

Pacific Islands. Successful reformers such as Samoa and Tonga have led the way in demonstrating the benefits to other countries, but the challenges facing Pacific reformers continue to be daunting. According to World Bank Senior ICT Policy Specialist Natasha Beschorner:

> [C]onstraints to more widespread availability of affordable telecommunications in the Pacific to date include: restrictive market structures and licensing regimes (exclusive licenses, lack of competition, service-specific licenses); relatively high capital and operating costs; relatively small market size and revenues; limited and costly access to international bandwidth; legal, regulatory and institutional frameworks designed around monopolies; and limited resources and skills available to oversight institutions. These factors have hindered the investment in ICT needed in the Pacific to provide more widely available and affordable services to citizens and businesses.[11]

The lack of connectivity in the Pacific exacerbates the challenges already faced by the business community. The AusAID report, *Pacific Economic Survey 2008,* highlighted these challenges by taking the theme 'Connecting the Region' to draw attention to the need to reform key sectors such as airlines, telecommunications and shipping. 'Sea and air freight costs are among the highest in the world,' said Matthew Morris, Economics Advisor at AusAID, in interviews during the launch of the survey (see Figure 3J). 'Connectivity in the region is improving though. New entrants have had

---

[11] Beschorner, 'Telecommunications Background', p. 1.

a dramatic impact on mobile phone and aviation services. Competition has boosted services and reduced prices.'[12]

In telecommunications, the lack of hard infrastructure has allowed reforming countries to 'leapfrog' the fixed-line phase of development, and deregulation of telecommunications-service provision has seen corporate interest in the provision of infrastructure that was simply non-existent in the fixed-line days. Also, the introduction of competition has worked rapidly and effectively. According to AusAID's *Pacific Economic Survey 2008*, in 2002 just 1.5% of the population of Samoa had a mobile phone. The introduction of competition meant that this had increased to 46% by 2007. In Tonga, mobile phone use increased from 3.4% to 30% over the same period. The Papua New Guinea Government estimates that expanding its mobile phone services contributed 0.7 percentage points to gross domestic product (GDP) growth in 2007.

These successes have encouraged other countries to follow suit. Vanuatu has recently completed its own groundbreaking reform of the telecommunications market, and at the time of writing, Timor-Leste and the Solomon Islands were moving forward with their plans for reform. Vanuatu's successful negotiation of the removal of its existing telecommunications monopoly highlights the challenges facing reformers, but also shows the way forward for other small countries grappling with the liberalisation of telecommunications services.

The progress of reform in Vanuatu

Vanuatu is an economic success story from the Pacific Islands. Economic growth in Vanuatu is outpacing the rest of the region, with growth in GDP averaging 6.8% per annum between 2005 and 2007, higher than at any time in the last fifteen years. With a population of around 200,000, this has given Vanuatu a per capita income (PCI) of US$1,799.[13] Vanuatu has benefited particularly from an expanding tourism sector, spurred on by airline liberalisation that saw the entry of a second carrier, Pacific Blue, in 2004, followed by an immediate 28% increase in tourist arrivals.[14] As a result, tourism has grown steadily, averaging an increase of 11% per year since then and growing 22% in 2007.[15]

---

[12] James, 'Optimism for Pacific Economies'.   [13] AusAID, *Pacific Economic Survey 2008*.
[14] World Bank (2005), *Regional Engagement Framework for the Pacific Financial Year 2006–2009*, World Bank, p. 84.
[15] AusAID, *Pacific Economic Survey 2008* and background data from Vanuatu National Statistics Office.

Vanuatu has also experienced greater political stability since the election of the Lini Government in 2004, making it an attractive destination for tourists and encouraging foreign investment. It has sound macroeconomic policies, and its central bank is capably led by Governor Odo Tevi. Its rapidly growing property market is fuelled by Australian and New Zealand expatriates, lured by the beauty of Port Vila and the undeniable feeling that Vanuatu is about to throw off thirty years of lethargy and become a hub of Pacific business and social activity. Locals say Port Vila is 'booming'; while most tourists would have difficulty seeing Port Vila as anything other than a small country town, inhabitants and regular visitors can see the change taking place.

Unlike many countries where an independent regulatory body oversees utilities, those in Vanuatu have been regulated by contract. In 2004, when the deregulation process began with a World Bank report[16] into the management of public utilities, the Government of Vanuatu held a contract for the provision of telecommunications services throughout the country with Telecom Vanuatu Limited (TVL), owned in equal parts by the Government of Vanuatu, Cable & Wireless and France Cable and Radio. Unsurprisingly, the focus for the provision of telecommunications services had primarily been the capital, Port Vila, and to a lesser extent Vanuatu's second largest township, Luganville, on the island of Espiritu Santo. Services were expensive and benchmarking undertaken by the World Bank suggested that access levels were lower than would be expected given Vanuatu's PCI. Operational inefficiencies seemed the most likely cause of high prices, and overall performance was weak, even when measured against TVL's own low targets.

The licensing arrangement had been poorly constructed from the outset. TVL were given a license to operate exclusively in perpetuity, firmly entrenching the monopoly. In addition, the statute governing telecommunications stated that the license could only be changed with the consent of the utility. While there were opportunities for the government to terminate the arrangement in 2012, and then every three years thereafter, it would require the government to purchase TVL's assets at market value. This was a daunting backdrop to reform, and most observers anticipated no change in the operating environment until 2012 at the earliest.

In 2005, the Government of Vanuatu attempted to grant a second restricted operating license to Pacific Data Solutions for 'purposes of

[16] World Bank (2005), *Infrastructure Regulatory Review for Government of Vanuatu*, World Bank/Castalia Advisory Group.

expanding e-commerce and interactive gaming industries in Vanuatu'.[17] In December 2005, the government was ordered by the Supreme Court of Vanuatu to stop issuing licenses to any party other than TVL, but this was subsequently overturned and the license was issued. While Pacific Data Solutions installed some infrastructure, ultimately its activities were restricted to gaming customers, but it was an important psychological victory for the government and it built further momentum for reform.

In February 2006, the Minister for Infrastructure and Public Utilities, Edward Natapei, issued a press release clearly stating that the government intended to break the monopoly and open telecommunications to competition. But a speedy resolution to the situation did not seem obvious – as late as August 2006, Minister Natapei was saying that 'the franchise agreement which the Government has signed with TVL will run until 2012...therefore we have until 2012 to depend on telephone services provided by TVL'.[18] At the same time, statements suggested that there was serious consideration of a purchase by the government of the two thirds of TVL owned by Cable & Wireless and France Telecom, and that in fact an approach was made by the Council of Ministers.

By early 2007, the government was firm in its commitment to bringing TVL's monopoly to a close, and TVL's other shareholders were beginning to understand this resolve. Call costs began to fall as the threat of competition encouraged TVL to lift its game, and the government began calling for TVL to extend its coverage. It circulated a draft sector policy for public comment, which set out clear objectives for telecommunications centred on widely available, affordable and reliable services that extended into rural areas.

Donors were supportive of the government's desire to negotiate an end to the monopoly and avoid the legal actions that were beginning to accompany the push for new entrants. Donor assistance was provided by the World Bank and AusAID's then new Governance for Growth facility, an economic governance facility with an explicit focus on providing support for reform that promotes growth. In mid 2007, after an international selection process, the government hired New Zealand technology and regulatory law firm MGF Webb Ltd to represent it in negotiations to end TVL's monopoly. The World Bank subsequently mediated negotiations between the Government of Vanuatu and TVL's other shareholders,

---

[17] 'TVL Losing Grip on Monopoly over Telecommunications in Vanuatu', *The ni-Vanuatu*, 14 August 2006.
[18] Ibid.

resulting in a compensation payment of Vt 1 billion (US$10.74 million) to Cable and Wireless and France Telecom. The Government of Vanuatu used economic modelling to assist its negotiations with the parties and prepared carefully. Reports suggest that the level of preparation and expertise brought by the Government of Vanuatu to the negotiating table underpinned the success of the mediation process and resulted in a successful outcome in late February 2008, after only six months of negotiations.

On 14 March 2008, Digicel announced that it had been awarded a telecommunications license in Vanuatu and would invest US$35 million to build a state-of-the-art network that would employ more than seventy employees. It also announced a takeover of the assets of previous license recipient Pacific Data Solutions, which had restructured to focus on its online gaming business. In a media statement, government spokesman Patrick Crowby said that: 'with the introduction of competition, telecom companies like Digicel . . . can compliment TVL in connecting the rural communities to Port Vila and the rest of the world'.

But the end of the monopoly did not come cheaply, and there was some criticism from the opposition for the payment made by the Government of Vanuatu to divest its shareholding in TVL. Crowby phrased this in terms of the benefit to average ni-Vanuatu by saying:

> [I]n the long run the Government envisages a boost in the rural economies soon as all the farmers have access to phones. They can access information on market prices and can deal directly with buyers about the quantity and value of the commodity requested. This will revolutionise the communication system in Vanuatu so that instead of a farmer travelling many kilometres to make a phone call they can save that time to till their farms.[19]

Conclusion

The challenges facing services reform in small island states should not be underestimated. Existing monopolies have proven difficult to dislodge, but at the same time have proven unable or unwilling to bring new services that have the potential to dramatically improve the lives of the poor. Telecommunications is one such service that has provided demonstrable benefits throughout the developing world, but innovations have been slow to reach Pacific Island countries. However, things are changing in the region. Over the last decade, Pacific countries have moved toward greater

[19] 'Vanuatu Government Sells Interest in Telecom', *Vanuatu Daily Post*, 3 April 2008.

telecommunications liberalisation and have seen the results clearly in dramatically improved penetration rates, cheaper costs and an improved range of services.

But reforms have been difficult. Some countries, like Papua New Guinea, are still grappling with liberalisation and have yet to fully open their market. The elimination of existing monopolies is difficult – entrenched interests need to be carefully navigated to avoid costly legal action that could cripple small economies. But there have been notable successes in the region, which can provide a model for others moving forward with liberalisation, both in telecommunications and in other services sectors. Vanuatu provides a case study of how reform can be quickly and successfully negotiated through careful analysis, a sound base of economic information and by enlisting the services of an expert legal team.

Successful liberalisation of services markets has the potential to bring new business opportunities and provide services to those in remote and rural areas previously left behind in the process of globalisation. As the global economy becomes more integrated, there are increasing opportunities for those previously excluded to better connect with the global market. Ultimately, telecommunications reform in the Pacific has shown that there are operators ready to provide services to even small and remote islands, if governments give them the opportunity to enter their markets.

IV

Migration, labour mobility and poverty reduction

4

Migration, labour mobility and poverty

GRAEME HUGO[*]

Introduction

Migration has always had both beneficial and negative impacts on migrants themselves, their origin communities and their destinations. However, recently, a higher level of attention has been focused on this issue, for a number of reasons:

- The last two decades have seen an increase in the scale and complexity of international migration.
- The dominant gradient of flow has moved from north–north to south–north countries so that the potential developmental effects on south countries have increased.
- Not only have the numbers of expatriates from poorer countries in better-off nations increased exponentially, but the 'hyper-connectivity' (Dade, 2004) facilitated by modern information, communication and travel technology has allowed these expatriates to maintain stronger and more intimate linkages with their home countries than ever before.
- A shift in the global discourse around the developmental impacts of international migration away from a dominant focus on 'brain drain' toward one which recognises that the movement also has positive impacts on origin communities.

Accordingly, there has been enhanced interest not only in the relationship between migration and development but especially in the possibility of developing policies and programmes that can enhance the positive effects on origin nations but also ameliorate the negative impacts. Accordingly, multilateral agencies such as the World Bank (World Bank, 2006; Ellerman, 2003, Terry and Wilson, 2005), the UN (2006a) and Asian Development Bank (ADB) (2004), as well as national development assistance

* Graeme Hugo is University Professorial Research Fellow, Professor of Geography and Director of the National Centre for Social Applications of GIS at the University of Adelaide.

agencies such as DFID (DFID, 2007; House of Commons, 2004) and USAID (Johnson and Sedacca, 2004), are now examining the potential for intervention, which will enhance international migration's contribution to economic and social development and poverty alleviation in poor countries.

Until recently, the predominant discourse on south–north migration has been of the high degree of selectivity of that migration, which has drained poor nations of their most talented residents and hence exacerbated the constraints that low levels of human capital have imposed on development in those countries. This pejorative focus in the literature on south–north migration was reinforced by evidence of people-smuggling and trafficking. It is only in recent years that there has been a counter-view stressing some of the positive impacts of migration on origin areas. Nevertheless, it is important to not turn a blind eye to the continuing significance of brain drain. As Ellerman (2003, p. 38) points out, if the 'brain drain' literature of the 1960s and 1970s can be criticised as ignoring the complexity of migration effects by focusing only on one effect, perhaps some of the current writing 'is excessively optimistic about the impact of migration in the South'. What is required is a deep understanding of the complexity of the effects of south–north migration in order to identify areas where policy intervention can maximise positive effects and minimise negative effects.

Recent research work has indicated that 88 per cent of immigrants to Organisation for Economic Co-operation and Development (OECD) nations[1] have secondary education or higher qualifications, but that, except in relatively small nations, southern countries do not lose a high proportion of their highly skilled persons to OECD nations. They compared the numbers of skilled expatriates in OECD nations with the numbers remaining in their home nations and calculated the proportion that expatriates made up of all skilled persons from individual developing nations. Table 4A presents the fifteen nations with the lowest and highest percentages of their skilled nationals living outside the country from two separate studies. It shows that the countries with the smaller proportions of their skilled workers in foreign countries are the large nations such as China, India, Indonesia, Brazil and Bangladesh. On the other hand, those nations with the largest proportions of their skilled nationals in foreign countries are predominantly smaller. The OECD thus points out that brain drain may more adversely impact on smaller nations, preventing

---

[1] OECD unpublished data.

Table 4A *Highly skilled expatriates from selected non-OECD countries*

	Cohen and Soto (2001)	Highly skilled (aged 15+)	Barro and Lee (2000)	Highly skilled (aged 15+)
	Brazil	1.7	Brazil	1.2
	Myanmar	1.7	Thailand	1.4
	Indonesia	1.9	Indonesia	1.5
	Thailand	1.9	Paraguay	1.8
Fifteen non-OECD	Bangladesh	2.0	Argentina	1.8
countries with the	Paraguay	2.0	China	2.4
lowest percentage	Nepal	2.1	Myanmar	2.4
of highly skilled	India	3.1	Peru	2.7
15+ expatriates in	Bolivia	3.1	Nepal	2.9
OECD countries	China	3.2	Bangladesh	3.0
	Jordan	3.2	Bolivia	3.1
	Venezuela	3.3	India	3.4
	Costa Rica	4.0	Egypt	3.4
	Syria	4.3	Venezuela	3.5
	Egypt	4.4	Swaziland	3.5
	Guyana	83.0	Guyana	76.9
	Jamaica	81.9	Jamaica	72.6
	Haiti	78.5	Guinea-Bissau	70.3
	Trinidad and Tobago	76.0	Haiti	68.0
	Fiji	61.9	Trinidad and Tobago	66.1
15 non-OECD				
countries with the	Angola	53.7	Mozambique	52.3
highest percentage	Cyprus	53.3	Mauritius	50.1
of highly skilled	Mauritius	53.2	Barbados	47.1
15+ expatriates in	Mozambique	47.1	Fiji	42.9
OECD countries	Ghana	45.1	Gambia	42.3
	United Rep. Of Tanzania	41.7	Congo	33.7
	Uganda	36.4	Sierra Leone	32.4
	Kenya	35.9	Ghana	31.2
	Burundi	34.3	Kenya	27.8
	Sierra Leone	33.3	Cyprus	26.0

Source: OECD (2005), p. 129.

them from reaching a critical mass of human resources necessary to foster long-term economic development.

Clearly, there are several such nations in the Asia-Pacific region, especially in the Pacific. Moreover, we should not remain blind to the impacts of brain drain on other countries. The Philippines (2005 population of 84.8 million) is one of the nations most influenced by emigration, and it is estimated that in 2000, 18 per cent of Filipinos with college degrees were in the US alone[2] suggesting that at least one in three Filipino university graduates are lost to the nation. Particularly significant here is the net loss of doctors, nurses and other health personnel from Asia-Pacific countries. With ageing of the population in OECD nations, there have been shortages of medical workers and consequent recruitment of people with these skills from developing countries. For example, in Australia in 2001, 21.7% of the medical workforce was born in Asia, Africa and the Middle East, compared with only 7.8% of all workers (Hugo, 2005a).

In the early literature, brain drain was seen as having an unequivocally negative impact on development in the origin nations since it deprived them of scarce human resources required for achieving economic and social progress. Even the loss of small numbers could therefore be significant. While it is recognised that such effects are still strongly in evidence in Asia, there is increasing evidence that the brain drain's effects on development are not necessarily only negative. This partly derives from evidence that, in some contexts, the economies and labour markets in a number of least developed countries (LDCs) cannot effectively absorb some of the skilled people, and they can make a greater contribution to development by emigrating and remitting earnings back to the home country. Hence, an interesting econometric analysis based on Philippines data considered that, in that country, it would appear to return a net benefit to the nation to train physicians for export (Goldfarb *et al.*, 1984).

In recent years, however, some of the world's major development organisations such as the World Bank (2006), ADB (2004), International Labour Organisation (Martin, 2004), USAID (Johnson and Sedaca, 2004), DIFD (House of Commons, 2004), the UN (2006a) and the IOM (2005) argue that emigration can play a positive role in facilitating economic growth and development and poverty reduction in origin areas. It is argued that these positive effects occur through three basic processes: (i) inflow of remittances from migrants; (ii) the role played by diaspora in enhancing

---

[2] *Migration News*, July 2004, available at http://migration.ucdavis.edu/mn/more.php?id= 3033_0_3_0 [last accessed 6 April 2009].

growth and development in their origin; and (iii) the return movement of former migrants.

Remittances

Revisionist views of the impact of international migration upon development have been driven by a new appreciation of the scale and impact of remittances. Diaspora-led development in origin nations incorporates a much wider range of impacts than remittances, but there is little doubt that in development organisations like the World Bank and the ADB, remittances are at the centre of concern (Terry and Wilson, 2005). Remittances have been associated with migration from time immemorial; why is it that they have suddenly gained the attention of development economists? There are several reasons:

- Firstly, there has been a new appreciation of the scale of remittances, which have been dismissed by many as peripheral and of limited scale and effect. However, while there has been a strong appreciation that only a fraction of total global remittances are accounted for in official statistics, the level of global remittances has expanded exponentially with both the increase in migration and the increasing extent to which remittances flow through official channels. The latest estimates by the World Bank (2007) estimated global remittances in 2006 to be US$268 billion and, as Table 4B indicates, developing countries accounted for US$199 billion (74.3%) of this. Moreover remittances to developing nations increased by 17% in 2004 and 2005 and by 161% between 2001 and 2005. Some US$81 billion were received in Asia and the Pacific – over 30% of the global total. As Figure 4A shows, official remittances to less developed countries are now more than twice as great as official development assistance (ODA) and almost as large as foreign direct investment (FDI). Moreover, in considering these figures, it must be borne in mind: 'This amount, however, reflects only transfers through official channels. Econometric analysis and available household surveys suggest that unrecorded flows through informal channels may add 50 percent or more to recorded flows' (World Bank (2007), p. 1). Hence remittances are the largest source of external funding in several Asia-Pacific countries.
- In the past, the impact of remittances on development has been dismissed because field evidence indicated that the bulk of remittances were not invested in 'productive' enterprises but were spent on consumption,

Table 4B *Global flows of international migrant remittances (US$ billion)*

Inflows	2000	2001	2002	2003	2004	2005	2006e	Change 2005–06 (%)	Change 2001–06 (%)
All developing countries	85	96	117	145	163	188	199	6	107
Low-income countries	22	26	32	40	41	46	47	2	81
Middle-income countries (MICs)	63	70	85	105	123	142	152	7	116
Lower MICs	43	48	61	75	86	95	101	6	110
Upper MICs	20	22	23	30	37	47	51	9	128
East Asia and the Pacific	17	20	29	35	39	44	45	3	125
Europe and Central Asia	13	13	14	17	23	31	32	5	149
Latin America and the Caribbean	20	24	28	35	41	48	53	12	119
Middle-East and North Africa	13	15	16	21	23	24	25	5	64
South Asia	17	19	24	31	30	35	36	3	86
Sub-Saharan Africa	5	5	5	6	7	7	7	0	62
High income OECDs	46	50	52	59	66	68	68	0	37
World	132	147	170	205	230	257	268	3	83

Outflows	2000	2001	2002	2003	2004	2005		Change 2004–05 (%)	Change 2001–05 (%)
All developing countries	12	14	21	25	32	37	–	17	161
High income OECD	76	83	88	98	111	119	–	7	44
High income non-OECD	22	22	22	21	20	21	–	5	–3
World	110	118	131	144	163	177	–	9	50

Note: 'e' = estimate.
Source: World Bank (2007).

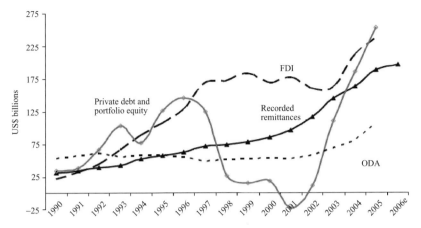

Figure 4A Remittances and capital flows to developing countries. *Note:* 'e' = estimate. *Source:* World Bank (2007).

especially the meeting of basic needs and the building and refurbishment of houses. However, it has been shown (Taylor *et al.*, 1996) that a dollar spent in such activity has multiplier effects that ripple through local and regional economies, having significant poverty reduction and developmental impacts.

- There has been a realisation that remittances are effective in poverty reduction at a grass-roots level because they are passed directly from the migrant and received by families and individuals in less developed countries so that they can be readily used to improve the situation of those people. On the other hand, FDI and foreign direct assistance (FDA) are mediated by an array of institutions, which can dilute their impact at the level of individual communities and families. Hence, of all south–north financial flows, remittances are not only the largest, but they have the greatest impact upon improving the situation of ordinary people.

- Migrants from southern nations are not drawn randomly from the entire population but tend to come from selected areas, so the impact of remittances tends also to be concentrated in particular parts of a country, where its effect is amplified. These are often peripheral areas where remittances are the only source of foreign exchange and capital inflow for development. With an increasing focus on regional and decentralised development in southern nations, there has been an enhanced realisation of the significance of remittances.

The diaspora

Much of the migration and development discourse focuses on the scale and impact of remittances. However, there is a growing realisation that the developmental effects of migration are more complex. The networks that are often set up by migrants between their destination and origin countries can be conduits for more than remittances, and the developmental implications of these other flows need to be considered. As Lucas (2001) points out, there is a growing appreciation 'that a highly skilled diaspora may play several important roles in promoting development at home'. In a rapidly globalising world, for many nation states there is a growing mismatch between their citizen population and the population residing within their national boundaries. For some countries, their diaspora is a substantial and significant part of their citizenry, and their involvement in national development effects is only part of a wider project of their incorporation in the mainstream of national life.

What are some of the ways in which the diaspora may influence economic and social development and poverty reduction in their origin country?

- through encouraging FDI either through their own auspices or through influencing the investment of companies and organisations in which they adopt leadership roles
- through acting as bridgeheads for the introduction of goods from their origins in their destinations and hence encouraging exports
- through equipping companies and organisations in the origin country with expertise in management and other areas
- to transmit information to produce rapid technology transfer from destination to origin.

It has also been argued that the diaspora may be vehicles for so-called 'social remittances'. There is some evidence that diaspora may be playing an important role in reshaping individual and social preferences as well as social norms and expectations in the country of origin (Kapur, 2001, 270). Such influences may not all be favourable for development in the origin nation and may involve the spread of 'fads, fashions and inappropriate technologies' (Kapur, 2001, 270). The potential is there too for the diffusion of attitudes toward education, change and innovation, which could be positive for development.

Diaspora may also play a role in the planning and delivery of development assistance to origin countries from destination countries (DFID, 2007).

It is necessary to stress that not all south–north migrations result in the formation of diaspora communities and transnational family networks. Moreover, the strength and function of these networks varies widely. Kapur (2001, 276) identifies four groups of factors that affect the role of diaspora in development at home:

(1) factors contributing to the potential importance of the diaspora – its size, education/skill, income and economic activity
(2) factors contributing to the realised influence of the diaspora – reasons for leaving the home country, number of generations and policies and attitudes of host and origin countries
(3) their influence – greatest when institutions incorporating the diaspora into destination societies are weakest
(4) the degree of openness of source countries to outside influences.

To this must be added intrinsic cultural differences between immigrant groups, which undoubtedly influence the degree to which diaspora are formed and transnational networks established.

Return migration

One of the enduring myths of south–north migration is that there is an overwhelming desire for people from the south to relocate permanently in northern countries. In fact, among many migrants there is a desire not only to retain valued aspects of their heritage but also to return to their homeland. The extent of circularity in international migration is underestimated. Indeed, it has been argued that return migration is often constrained by destination country policies that make frequent return difficult (Hugo, 2005b). One of the enduring features of all diaspora is return migration to the homeland, although its incidence varies greatly. It is apparent that there can be significant dividends to the home country if expatriates return, especially when they are highly skilled in areas in demand in the origin country's labour market – they will have extended their knowledge and experience while overseas and will return with a network of overseas contacts, which can benefit their work at home. There is substantial literature on return migration and studies of diaspora that indicate there is often a high level of interest among many expatriates in eventually returning to their home country. Indeed, return is often seen as being the conclusion to a successful migration.

There is a fear in some OECD nations that unskilled workers who enter on a temporary basis to meet labour shortages will inevitably become permanent settlers. We often hear the phrase 'there is nothing as permanent as a temporary migrant'. The fear that temporary unskilled workers will stay grew out of the experience of post-war Europe, when several countries opted to cope with labour shortages by importing temporary guest workers, but these groups subsequently developed substantial permanent communities. However, it is relevant to ask whether, in the contemporary situation, temporary migration is necessarily a prelude to permanent settlement. There is some evidence that this is less the case than in the past, because modern forms of transportation and communication have greatly reduced the friction of distance between origin and destination countries. This has meant that migrants are able to maintain closer and more intimate linkages with their home area than ever before. Cheapening the cost of phone calls, the introduction of email and fax and the cheapening and speeding up of international travel have not only made it possible for migrants to interact in real time with their home country on a regular basis, but they can visit home more frequently in emergencies and for breaks. This has greatly reduced the imperative for many temporary workers wanting their family to join them in the destination. Indeed, many low-skilled migrant workers see a number of advantages of maintaining a regular pattern of circular international migration in preference to permanent settlement at the destination, for the following reasons:

- They are able to 'earn' in the high-income, high-cost destination and 'spend' in the low-income, low-cost origin and hence maximise the purchasing power of their earnings.
- They seek to retain the traditional cultural, language and other associations of their homeland.
- They wish to maintain strong, wider family linkages, and this can be more easily done at home rather than at the destination.

In the contemporary situation, in the right contexts, circulation can become a permanent international migration strategy. However, this does presuppose the migrant worker being able to interact freely with her/his home country. Frequently, it is the case that such interaction is made difficult, especially where the migrant workers are undocumented. Hence, increasing policing of the Mexico-US border has resulted in a reduction in circulation and an increase of Mexicans settling permanently in the US (Cornelius, 2003).

Circular migration is increasingly seen as being especially favourable to development (UN, 2006a; GCIM, 2005; Vertovec, 2006). This is because the evidence is that short-term migrants send back a greater proportion of their earnings and that migrants may have a greater role as agents of development in their home country if they are continually moving between origin and destination. In the contemporary migration and development discourse, two opposing views on circular migration have been put forward. One group of researchers and policy makers are strongly opposed to guestworker migration. Vertovec (2006, 43) has listed the major issues that surround these programmes:

- Migrant workers can get locked into modes of dependency and exploitative relationships with employers.
- The fact that such schemes lock in migrant workers to particular employers increases the chances of exploitation and is a barrier to socioeconomic mobility.
- This migration is often associated with closing of labour markets, which cuts off opportunities for others.
- Enforcement mechanisms are often draconian.
- The rights of most workers at the destination are often restricted, so they are socially excluded.
- Such schemes foster illegal migration.

There are also other considerations:

- They can lead to the forcing down of workplace conditions, wages etc., which forces out local workers.
- They usually involve long separation from family, which can have significant negative social consequences.

However, in the recent growth in discussion on the relationship between migration and development, there has been increasing advocacy for circular migration as a mechanism that can deliver benefits for migrants and both destination and origin countries simultaneously. Vertovec (2006, 43) suggests four reasons for this:

(1) Potentially, at least, circular migration can deliver a 'win-win-win' outcome from emigration since migrant workers return to their origins and bring with them the skills, experience and money they acquire at the destination.

(2) There is a new recognition that remittances can have positive development outcomes, and circular migrants remit a much larger proportion of their income to their homes than permanent migrants.
(3) Policy makers in destinations see temporary migration as being more acceptable to public opinion than permanent migration.
(4) Many policy makers believe that new technical knowledge and improved border-control systems facilitate tracking of temporary migrants so that the problem of 'running away' and becoming an illegal settler in the destination is reduced.

Three pillars – remittances, the role of the diaspora and migrant return – are the basis on which there has been a new mantra (Kapur, 2004) around emigration having a positive role on development and poverty reduction. It needs to be said that this argument has not been without critics (De Haan, 2006; Faist, 2007), but migration is becoming an increasingly important factor in considerations of development and poverty reduction in poor nations.

One important element in the increased levels of interest in labour mobility and development is the potential for a substantial increase in the scale of south–north migration over the next two decades. As the Global Commission on International Migration concluded: 'In the contemporary world, the principal forces that are driving international migration are due to the "3Ds": differences in development, demography and democracy . . . because the differentials are widening, the number of people seeking to migrate will continue to increase in the future' (GCIM, 2005, p. 12). Despite the widening of the '3Ds', however, receiving countries have not been as willing to open their frontiers to an inflow of south-origin immigrants as they have to the other flows associated with globalisation – investment, finance, information, trade, etc. Hence, although the fundamental drivers of south–north international migration are strengthening, this is no guarantee that they will all be translated into international migration flows. One of the key elements here is the extent to which the international movement of labour is embraced in the future by nations as much they have encouraged the other flows. Here, mode 4 of the General Agreement on Trade in Services (GATS) is of relevance. Mode 4 calls for the market access for exports of human resources, especially from less developed to more developed nations. It focuses on the temporary movement of natural persons. The successful negotiation of GATS mode 4 could have significant consequences for many poorer countries in the Asia-Pacific region.

Labour mobility trends in the Asia-Pacific region

The UN (2002a) estimates that 50 million of the 175 million people world-wide who live outside the country in which they were born were in Asia. While this is equivalent to only 1.4 per cent of the total Asian population, it is a significant understatement of the impact of international migration of labour. This is partly because it severely underestimates the movement since it excludes much temporary and undocumented migration, and many countries in the region do not collect information on the stocks or flows of migrants influencing them. Moreover, migrant workers are drawn from and concentrate in particular countries and particular areas within those countries, so their impact is magnified in particular parts of the Asia-Pacific region. In addition, these data relate only to *immigrants*, and Asia is the largest supplier of *emigrants* to other regions of the world. Figure 4B shows that the foreign-born make up only a minuscule propor-tion of the population of most Asian nations. However, it also indicates that Asia has some of the world's most migrant-influenced countries, with Hong Kong having 39.4% of its population foreign-born and Singapore 33.6%. Rates of migration are generally low for the largest nations in the region, but some have argued that in China, the burgeoning internal migration, which has seen the number of rural-urban migrants in Chi-nese cities increase from 21 million in 1990 to 121 million in 2000 (Zhou and Cai, 2005), is in some ways akin to international rather than internal migration because of the *hukou* (internal passport) system (Zhu, 2004).

Any close observer of Asia over the last two decades cannot fail to have noticed how international mobility of one kind or another has entered the calculus of choice of a much larger proportion of Asian workers when they consider their life chances. Less obvious though is that inter-national movement has become much more diverse both in terms of the forms that it takes and in terms of the people who move. There has been a significant increase in movement between Asian nations but also out of and into the region. Movement is both forced and unforced, docu-mented and undocumented, permanent and temporary, work-related and non-work-related. We will now consider some of the main types of inter-national mobility of Asian workers.[3]

---

[3] For a more comprehensive treatment, see Hugo (2008).

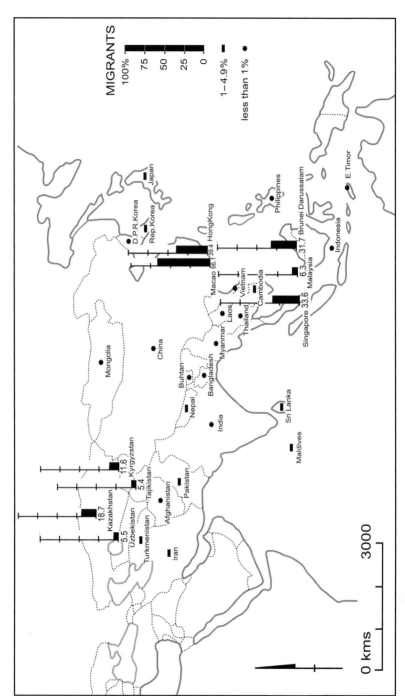

Figure 4B Asia: migrant population (2000). *Source:* UN (2002a).

Table 4C   *Australia: Long-term arrivals of Asia-born and total persons –
category of traveller by occupation (1997–98 to 2005–06)*

	Long-term arrivals			
	Asia-born		Total	
	No.	%	No.	%
Managers and administrators	48,182	18.2	165,330	15.8
Professionals	113,816	42.9	469,933	44.9
Associate professionals	32,281	12.2	100,849	9.6
Tradespersons	10,710	4.0	76,229	7.3
Advanced clerical and sales	6,041	2.3	31,135	3.0
Intermediate clerical, sales and services	32,544	12.3	126,412	12.1
Intermediate production and transportation	1,742	0.7	16,355	1.6
Elementary clerical, sales and services	18,630	7.0	47,249	4.5
Labourers	1,234	0.5	12,042	1.2
Total	**265,180**	**100.0**	**1,045,534**	**100.0**

Source: DIAC Overseas Arrivals and Departures.

Increased south–north non-permanent migration

One of the major changes in south–north international migration in recent years has been the development of temporary migration programmes in northern countries that are highly selective of skilled migrants – indeed, more selective than permanent migration programmes. These are typified by the H1B visa in the US (Martin, 2005) and the 457 visa in Australia (Khoo *et al.*, 2003). Australia shows an increase in the number of arrivals from Asia who intended to stay in Australia temporarily but who remained for a year or longer. As is the case with permanent arrivals, the long-term migrants from Asia have a high skill profile. Table 4C shows that 73.3% of long-term arrivals from Asia were in the top three occupational categories, compared with 70.3% of the total intake over the 1997 to 2006 period – hence the increased intake of skilled workers from Asia in the last decade (see Figure 4C) has not only been in the traditionally important permanent migration programme, but this has been supplemented by a large intake of temporary residents. Long-term arrivals include only those persons who intend on staying in Australia for more than twelve months, and many of the new temporary migrant-worker visa holders

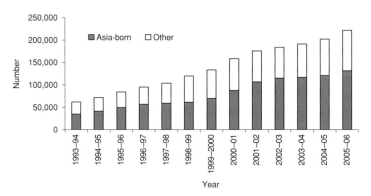

Figure 4C   Australia: Long-term visitor arrivals by birthplace (1993–94 to 2005–06). *Source:* DIAC unpublished data.

coming to Australia from Asia would be classified as short-term arrivals (those persons who intend on staying less than one year) and hence would not be included in this table. The south–north temporary migration of labour from Asia has thus increased substantially, and it is a highly skilled flow.

While much of the flow of temporary skilled workers is south–north in direction, there are two trends of increasing significance in this movement:

(1) There is an increasing flow of skilled workers between Asian nations. This is especially true of some of the more developed economies in the region. In the past, for example, most Japanese temporary migration has been of skilled people, usually employees of multinational corporations (MNCs), who move to other OECD nations. In recent years, however, other Asian countries have become the main destinations of skilled Japanese emigrants, and many of them are now moving not as an MNC employee but as part of an increasing vigorous and competitive skilled labour market within Asia. Of the 1.06 million Japanese going overseas for three months or longer in 2006, 267,064 went to other Asian nations.[4]

(2) A second temporary flow of skilled persons is coming from OECD countries outside the region. The booming economies and increasingly competitive labour markets are driving up wages in places like

---

[4] *Asian Migration News*, 16 to 31 August 2007, available at www.smc.org.ph/amnews/amnews.htm [last accessed 6 April 2009].

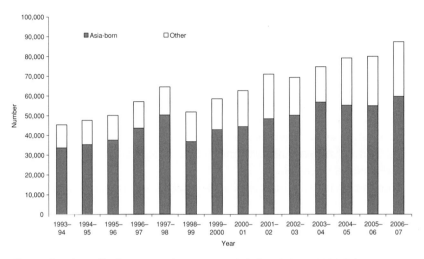

Figure 4D Australia: Long-term departures to Asia (1993–94 to 2006–07).
Source: DIAC unpublished data.

Hong Kong, Singapore and in cities like Shanghai, and this is attracting skilled workers, usually on a temporary basis, from outside the
region. Figure 4D shows the increasing flow of non-Asian-born, who
are mainly Australians, on a long-term (more than one year) but
non-permanent basis.

Remittances and development in the Asia-Pacific region

Remittances to Asia-Pacific countries come from two main types of
migrants. Firstly, there is a diaspora of permanent settlers of Asia-Pacific
origin, most of them living in OECD nations. Secondly, there are contract
labour migrants, almost all of whom remit money to their families in their
home country. Both of these groups are an important source of remittances. However, the measurement of remittances in Asia and the Pacific
is problematical, and this difficulty is exacerbated in many contexts by the
illegality of much movement, the isolation of the home areas and the long
history of remitting money to the area through non-formal, traditional
channels. In Indonesia, for example, remittances officially reported by
the Bank of Indonesia have a very narrow definition: they apply only to
transfers reported by foreign agent banks, especially in the Middle East
and Malaysia. Hence they do not include the following type of transfers,
which all appear to be significant:

- Where the migrants themselves bring the money earned back with them when they return. In Indonesia, there is a free foreign-currency exchange system, and no distinction is made between money that is changed in Indonesia by returning workers and that changed by tourists and other foreign visitors.
- There is also a considerable amount of batching[5] of remittances, with relatives and close friends bringing back money for workers still in destination areas. There is so much coming and going of workers, and the scale of movement from individual villages is so substantial, that this method is feasible.
- Some workers bring back goods (especially gold) rather than cash.[6]
- There are significant flows using postal transfers.
- There are several schemes set up by private companies to remit funds for overseas workers, several in association with particular recruitment agencies.

Accordingly, estimation of the scale of remittances is problematical.

Although official remittance data are flawed, Figure 4E shows that most nations have increased in their remittances in recent years. Only in South Korea, which has been transformed from an emigration to an immigration nation, has there been a decline. One of the major sending nations is the Philippines, where the Central Bank of the Philippines measures of formal flows of remittances have increased from US$1 billion in 1989 to US$5 billion in 1995, US$6.9 billion in 2002 and US$10.7 billion in 2005. Moreover, in 2006 remittances were growing at 15.3 per cent greater than at the same time the previous year.

Table 4D shows the pattern of growth of remittances in the various destination regions. The rapid growth of remittances is in evidence, with a current growth rate of 15.3 per cent. It is apparent that the substantial diaspora of Filipinos domiciled in foreign countries are an important source of remittances as well as the large number of overseas contract workers (OCWs). This is evident in the fact that the Americas (mainly the US) was the source of 57.4 per cent of all remittances in 2006. However, it is also interesting that remittances are growing faster than other sources.

---

[5] This is where one migrant who is returning home arranges to carry money and goods to the families of other migrant workers.
[6] Eki (2002) found that migrant workers from East Flores bring back chartered boats from their destination areas in Sabah loaded with goods, including materials to build or refurbish houses. Kapioru (1995) also notes this.

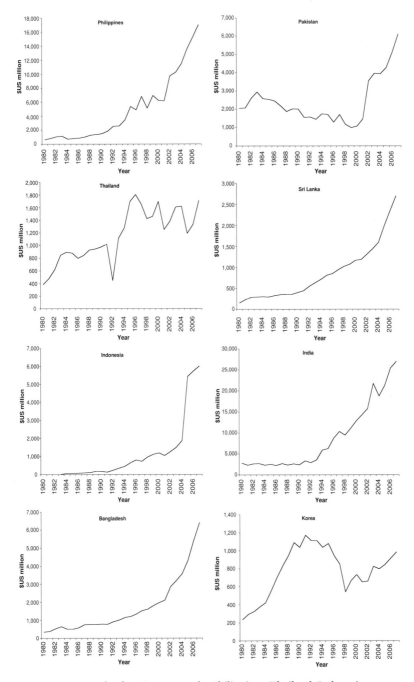

Figure 4E Growth of remittances to the Philippines, Thailand, Indonesia, Bangladesh, Pakistan, Sri Lanka, India and Korea (1980–2007). *Note:* 2007 data are estimates. *Source:* World Bank website: http://siteresources.worldbank.org/ INTPROSPECTS/Resources/334934-1110315015165/RemittancesData_Nov08 (Release).xls [last accessed 2 March 2009].

Table 4D   *The Philippines: Overseas Filipino worker remittances (2002–06 – US$ billion)*

Region	2002	2005	2005 Jan–Aug	2006 Jan–Aug	Growth rate 2005–06
Asia	1.12	1.18	0.79	0.95	21.2
Japan	0.49	0.36	0.25	0.29	14.3
Hong Kong	0.28	0.34	0.22	0.27	22.7
Singapore	0.18	0.24	0.16	0.19	19.6
Americas	3.54	6.61	4.32	4.65	7.7
Europe	0.89	1.43	0.96	1.28	33.3
Italy	0.32	0.43	0.29	0.37	30.3
Germany	0.08	0.13	0.09	0.07	−24.5
UK	0.22	0.30	0.20	0.33	66.5
Middle East	1.24	1.42	0.92	1.15	25.6
Saudi Arabia	0.99	0.95	0.63	0.69	10.9
Total	**6.89**	**10.69**	**7.02**	**8.10**	**15.3**

Source: Philippines Overseas Employment Agency.

These data only refer to money that passes through the official system, and Dimzon (2005) notes that:

• On average, 71% of worker remittances are sent home as cash, 21% are brought home personally and 8% are sent home in kind.
• Of the money sent in cash, 70% passes through banks while the rest are remitted through friends and couriers, although the proportion going through banks is increasing.

   While there is little data, it is clear that the diaspora of Indochinese, which was predominantly created by the refugee outflows in the 1970s and 1980s, has resulted in substantial remittance inflows to Laos, Cambodia and especially Vietnam. In Laos, around a tenth of the population left in 1975, with many settling in the US and other OECD nations. A survey of Vietnamese citizens in 1997–98 found that 56.5% of respondents had relatives overseas and 48.1% reported receiving money from them (Lintner, 2000, 48). There is also significant Lao labour migration into neighbouring Thailand, and a *State Planning Committee Report* in 1999 reported that remittances from abroad were the single most important source of income in the Vientiane Valley, comprising 28% of all household earnings compared with 25% from agriculture, 22% from wages and 18% from business (Lintner, 2000, 48).

The Vietnamese diaspora is playing an increasing role in the economy of their homeland. In 2002, official remittances reached US$2.4 billion,[7] double the US$1.2 billion recorded in 1998.[8] These include remittances from around 100,000 overseas contract workers in South Korea, Japan, Malaysia, Taiwan and Russia that are employed as construction workers and domestic workers, as well as the diaspora of 2.5 million *Viet Kieu* or Vietnamese who have settled permanently overseas. However, the official remittances are only part of a total flow of around US$4 billion. More than half of the remittances are sent from the US, followed by Canada, Australia, France, Germany and Japan. Some 70 per cent are directed to the former South Vietnam (Cohen, 2003, 48). The remittances are not taxed in Vietnam and there has been a proliferation of local companies and agents involved in remittances. Western Union has subagents in fifty-two provinces and cities in Vietnam (Cohen, 2003, 48).

Remittances are a major part of the economies of the South Asian countries. In Bangladesh, the official Central Bank statistics represent only part of the flow. One study has showed that 40% of remittances to Bangladesh are sent through illegal *Hundi/Hawala* systems, 4.6% through friends and relatives, 8% are carried by hand by migrants when they return and 46% go through official sources.[9] The Middle East accounts for 83% of total official remittances to Bangladesh.[10] The Pakistan figures are also substantial underestimates. Senior bankers estimate the real flow at between US$8 billion and US$10 billion, of which only US$1 billion goes through official channels.[11] It also has been suggested that in Pakistan, political and economic instability and widespread corruption has encouraged overseas Pakistanis to deposit their savings in foreign banks rather than remit them home. In some cases they have even invested their savings in India.[12] One report indicated that, on average, Pakistanis based in the Gulf region in 2002 sent home US$19 per month compared with US$230 by non-resident Indians, US$270 by Sri Lankans and US$130 by Bangladeshis.[13]

---

[7] *Far Eastern Economic Review*, 26 December 2002 to 2 January 2003, p. 11.
[8] *Asian Migration News*, 31 October 2009.
[9] 'Independent Bangladesh', in *Asian Migration News*, 7 January 2002.
[10] 'Gulf News', in *Asian Migration News*, 11 July 2002.
[11] 'Dawn', in *Asian Migration News*, 23 February 2002.
[12] 'Dawn', in *Asian Migration News*, 2 October 1999.
[13] 'Business News', in *Asian Migration News*, 14 January 2003.

India has one of the world's greatest diasporas, second in size only to that of China. In the mid 1990s, the Indian Government officially began to distinguish between 'people of Indian origin' (ethnic Indians who have non-Indian citizenship) and non-resident indians (NRIs – Indians abroad). It is estimated that the approximately 20 million ethnic Indians and NRIs have an annual income of about US$400 billion, equivalent to 80 per cent as much income as the 1 billion Indians in India.[14] About half of the NRIs are first generation immigrants born in India (Abraham, 2001). It is estimated that the 1 million Indians living in the US are equivalent to 0.1% of the total population living in India, but they earned the equivalent of 10% of Indians' national income in 2000.[15] India receives around US$14 billion each year in official remittances, mostly from semi- and low-skilled workers in the Gulf countries, and these make up an important part of the nation's US$70 billion reserves (Sharma, 2003, 29).

In Sri Lanka, the government has stated that overseas remittances 'have now become the backbone of the country's economy'.[16] Around a million OCWs (60 percent of them women) working as domestics remitted Rs100 billion in 2001 and Rs 115 billion in 2002 (US$1.2 billion).[17] The small country of Nepal received Rs35 billion (US$443 million) in remittances in 1999.

Remittances can and do have an impact on the balance of payments of nations. Table 4E relates official estimates of remittances to the value of total merchandise exports and imports over the last two decades in several major migrant-origin countries in Asia, and the effects vary considerably. Remittances are generally small in relation to export earnings in the largest countries of the region, especially China and Indonesia. An exception though is India, where remittances have represented an important share of foreign exchange earnings, especially in recent years. In all the countries of South Asia, remittances are significant, especially in Sri Lanka, Bangladesh and Pakistan. In the Philippines, remittances have made up a major share of foreign exchange earnings for many years.

In Sri Lanka, the number of OCWs abroad is now estimated to be 1.2 million (800,000 of whom are women), 14.5 per cent of the work-force (Pham and Harrod, 2008, 49). Moreover, as Figure 4F shows, the US$2.17 billion remittances are four times larger than foreign investment, twice that of international development assistance and twice the size of

---

[14] *Migration News*, 11 July 2002.   [15] *Migration News*, November 2002.
[16] *Asian Migration News*, 31 August 2001.
[17] *Asian Migration News*, 16 to 31 January 2003.

Table 4E   *Main Asian labour-exporting countries: workers' remittances (R) relative to exports and imports (1980–2006 – US$ million)*

Country	Year	Workers' remittances	Total merchandise Exports (X)	Total merchandise Imports (M)	$\frac{R}{X}$	$\frac{R}{M}$
Indonesia	1980	33	21,908	10,834	0.2	0.3
	1992	264	33,815	27,280	0.8	1.0
	2006	5,722	183,964	78,393	5.5	7.3
Philippines	1980	421	5,744	8,295	7.3	5.1
	1992	2,538	9,790	15,465	25.9	16.4
	2006	15,200	47,028	51,980	32.3	29.2
Thailand	1979	189	5,240	7,158	3.6	2.6
	1992	1,500	32,473	40,466	4.6	3.7
	2006	1,333	130,575	128,600	1.0	1.0
Bangladesh	1980	339	885	2,545	38.3	13.3
	1992	912	1,903	2,527	47.9	36.1
	2006	5,428	12,050	16,100	45.0	33.7
Pakistan	1980	2,048	2,958	5,709	69.2	35.9
	1992	1,574	7,264	9,360	21.7	16.8
	2006	5,121	16,917	29,825	30.3	17.2
India	1980	2,757	11,265	17,378	24.4	15.9
	1992	2,897	19,795	22,530	14.6	12.8
	2006	25,426	120,168	174,376	21.2	14.6
Sri Lanka	1980	152	1,293	2,197	11.8	6.9
	1992	548	2,487	3,470	22.0	15.8
	2006	2,350	6,860	10,226	34.3	23.0
China	1982	564	21,875	19,009	2.6	3.0
	1992	739	84,940	80,585	0.9	0.9
	2006	23,319	969,073	791,614	2.4	2.9

Source: Hugo (1995); *World Bank Development Report,* various volumes and remittances dataset, available at http://siteresources.worldbank.org/INTPROSPECTS/Resources/334934-1110315015165/RemittancesData_Nov08(Release).xls [last accessed 3 March 2009].

national-debt service payments. They represent 8 per cent of GDP and are the second largest source of foreign exchange after garments, and they are ahead of tea as an export earner. Moreover, it is estimated that the real flow of remittances, including those going through informal channels,

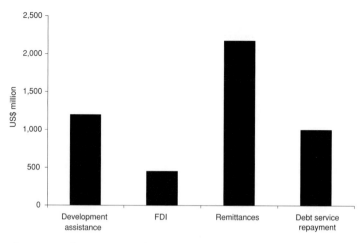

Figure 4F   The economic role of remittances in Sri Lanka (2006). *Source:* Pham and Harrod (2008), 50.

was twice as large as the official figures. Research has shown that female migrants' remittances alone support 18 per cent of the Sri Lankan population (Pham and Harrod, 2008). They have clearly acted as a safety net to cushion Sri Lanka from the impact of oil stocks and the 2004 tsunami.

Some have argued, however, that over-reliance on flows of remittances can have negative consequences in national economies. Tiglao (1997, 40), for example, argues in the Philippines case that it has insulated a backward agriculture sector from modernisation and diverted attention from the need to attract foreign investment in manufacturing. There is considerable concern in Asia (Athukorala, 1993) that labour migration, in conjunction with remittances, can lead to so-called 'Dutch disease':

> i.e. the appreciation of the real exchange rate. The Dutch disease creates a condition of greater vulnerability to external shocks by stimulating imports and reducing the incentives to develop exports. The Dutch disease also leads to an over-emphasis on capital-intensive methods of production. To avert the deleterious consequences of the Dutch disease, a number of policies can be adopted, including the depreciation of the currency, and structural reforms in the production sector to achieve greater economic efficiency.'
>
> (Quibria, 1996, 97)

Examination of remittances at a national level does not always reflect their true impact. Labour migrants are not drawn randomly from across a nation's territory. Most come from particular regions and particular localities within those regions. Hence, the impact of remittances is large in those particular areas. This has particular significance when it is considered that many migrant workers come from the poorest parts of their nations. In the large nation of Indonesia, for example, it has been shown (Hugo, 1995) that OCWs are overwhelmingly unskilled workers with poor education. Moreover, they are selectively drawn from rural areas and generally from some of the poorest rural areas such as parts of Java and Eastern Indonesia. Since there is a strong network factor involved in the migration process, these tend not just to be migration areas and regions, but migration villages from which it becomes usual for some groups to go overseas to work. This means that the economic impact of remittances is concentrated in particular areas, and its effects there are greatly magnified. Moreover, this often occurs in poor areas, which are neglected by central and provincial governments and private investors. Hence, remittances often can play a bigger role in regional development in poorer areas than in national development as a whole, especially in large nations.

Much of the argument about the impact of remittances hinges on their role in alleviating poverty. The impact of remittances on poverty in poorer countries has, however, been shown in case studies to be a complex one, with both positive and negative influences being in evidence. Nevertheless, as Khatun (2008, p. 13) points out:

> The impact of remittances through temporary movement of labour on poverty reduction has been found to be positive in several cases. Remittances can ease credit constrains and reduce risk and volatility. Besides it can promote higher levels of investment in physical and human capital which in turn foster economic growth. Remittances increase the per capita income of the remittance receiving countries and thereby can have a significant poverty reducing effect on the economy.

Certainly, a number of cross-national statistical studies would support this position. The World Bank (2006) has found that the proportion of people living in poverty is reduced by approximately 0.4% for each percentage point increase in the share of remittances of GDP. Adams (2005), in a study of seventy-one LDCs, found that a 10% increase in per capita official international remittances leads to a 3.5% decline in the proportion of people living in poverty. Moreover, studies in individual countries like the Philippines (Yang, 2004; Yang and Martinez, 2005) and Bangladesh (Siddiqui and Abrar, 2001; Afsar et al., 2002; Adams, 2005) have shown similar results. While the overwhelming weight of evidence is that in net terms, remittances have a positive impact on poverty, it is important to point out that there are also negative effects shown in the literature.

An excellent summary of the positive and negative impacts of remittances on poverty, especially as they relate to Bangladesh, has been made by Khatun (2008, pp. 13–17). Among the positive impacts identified were as follows.

An increase in income

There is little doubt that migrants earn substantially more at their destination than they could at their origin. This can be illustrated with respect to Indonesia. Fieldwork among migrants from East Nusa Tenggara in Indonesia working in Sabah (Malaysia) earned more in a month in the destination than they did in a full year at home. Similarly, migrants from West Nusa Tenggara earned eight times more in Malaysia (Hugo, 1996).

An increase in employment

Several studies (e.g. Taylor *et al.*, 1996) have shown that remittances spent in communities of origin can and do have multiplier effects in terms of creating employment for non-migrants. In Indonesia, this is seen, for example, in many OCWs investing their remittances in house building, which employs local works (Hugo, 1996). Detailed research in Mexico has shown that the second- and third-round effects of expenditure of remittances on housing are considerable where they employ local people and use local materials in the construction. Adelman and Taylor (1990) found that for every dollar remitted from abroad, total gross national product increased by between US$2.69 and US$3.17, and that the largest income multipliers were in rural communities where expenditure patterns favoured purchase of locally produced goods and services and labour-intensive production technologies. Similar findings from Bangladesh (Stahl and Habib, 1989) indicate that each migrant worker overseas creates three jobs at home through remittances. Of course, to the extent that housing materials, household goods and day-to-day items purchased from remittances are bought in from outside influences the extent of local job creation.

Reducing unemployment

Afsar *et al.* (2002) found that the unemployment rate in Bangladesh had remained stable due to the outflow of OCWs and the inflow of remittances. Similarly in East Indonesia, it was found that the exodus of migrant nations has eased local underemployment problems (Hugo, 1996).

Increased saving

Several studies have found that migrant families have a greater propensity to save than non-migrants (Nair and Pillai, 1994). Most case studies, however, have found that the dominant uses of remittances are for consumption. The overwhelming evidence from surveys in Asia is that families receive a net benefit from remittances, generally spending more on consumption than non-remittance households and having higher rates of saving (Abella, 1992). Migrant families are more likely than non-migrant families to have links with the formal financial sector. Titu Eki (2002) found in his study in East Flores, Indonesia, that savings accounted for 16 per cent of remittances among the migrant workers he studied. One important impact of remittances in East Flores has been the introduction of more cash-based activity and increased involvement with formal financial institutions – a necessary factor for development. Remittances are one of the main sources of cash for communities in East Flores, where much of the food of households is homegrown. Moreover, remittances have been the mechanism whereby people in the region have become familiar with formal financial institutions, namely banks. Banks in the migration area are much more active than in neighbouring regions, not only in receiving financial transfers and offering savings products but also as a source of loans (Titu Eki, 2002, p. 275).

Increased investment

Investment in productive activity is mainly done by migrant families who are better off, since for poorer families most remittances are spent on consumption. Nevertheless, there is evidence too of remittances being invested in productive activity. For example, Titu Eki (2002) found in his study of an East Flores village that, as Table 4F shows, while consumption was the dominant use of remittances, a substantial amount is devoted to investment-related expenditure. Some remittances are used to purchase land, but traditional methods of division of land prevent exchange of land through selling. There is some evidence of investment in transportation – through the purchase of one of the minibuses that now ply the regional, and rocky, village roads. Titu Eki (2002, p. 269) reports that forty-five

Table 4F   *East Flores Study Village: return and recent migrants: the main use made of the money sent home within the last five years (1998)*

Indicator	Return migrant	Recent migrant	Total No.	%
Household consumption	20	22	42	29.2
Debts and *adat* (customary law) costs	7	12	19	13.2
Consumptive necessities	27	34	61	42.4
Physical assets (housing, land)	15	11	26	18.0
Educational fees	16	18	34	23.6
Bank (saving accounts)	14	9	23	16.0
Investments	45	38	83	57.6
Total	**72**	**72**	**144**	**100.0**

Source: Titu Eki (2002).

minibuses had been purchased from remittances in five *kecamatan* (sub-districts) in East Flores. In some cases, groups of returned migrants have invested in the minibuses. Transportation improvement is one of the key infrastructure needs if development in the region is to progress. As yet, there are few shops in the villages, but increasing commercialisation is evident and this is a growing avenue for investment of the earnings of migration. Another productive use of remittances in East Nusa Tenggara is for the construction and maintenance of water sources, tanks and distribution infrastructure. East Flores is one of the driest areas in Indonesia, and water shortage is a major constraint on agricultural development (Barlow *et al.*, 1990). Titu Eki (2002, p. 287–8) found that remittances were used to construct public and private tanks to collect water in the rainy season and run pipes from tanks or springs to the centre of villages. Another major investment is generators, since most migrant villages are not connected to the national grid (Kapioru, 1995, 34).

Increased access to education

It will be noted in the table that in the East Flores case, almost a quarter of remittances were spent on education. Another study in the area (Goma *et al.*, 1993, 407) found that a fifth of remittances in their village study went to meet education costs. Field interviews confirm that this is a major use of money remitted from Malaysia, and an increasing amount is spent in sending teenage children elsewhere in Indonesia (especially Java) where there are better higher, secondary and tertiary education institutions. In some cases, young adults go to work in Malaysia for a few years in order to earn enough to put themselves through school in Java. Hence, some of the remittances for education are not spent in the local area but in major urban centres in Java, Makassar in Sulawesi or Kupang in Timor.

Increased access to health care

Several case studies indicate that remittances can contribute to the building up of human capital in origin areas through investing in education and health, especially of the children or siblings of migrants.

Change in the role of women

While the relationship between migration and the role and status of women is a complex multi-directional one, there are case studies which indicate that remittances have helped enhance the position of women in origin areas, especially when it is the women who are remitting money back. Siddiqui (2001) found in Bangladesh that migration could help empower women. Pham and Harrod (2008, 51) found the following in Sri Lanka:

> Women's labour migration also is having an impact on gender relations and family structures in Sri Lanka, challenging traditional gender roles and power hierarchies that may manifest in abusive husbands or a local community's confining expectations. Through the emergence of households with female breadwinners, the economic role of women in the family structure has been increased, while negative consequences reportedly relate to neglect of children and left-behind husbands whose threatened masculinity may result in alcohol abuse (not to say there is a simple causal relationship in either case). But female migration also generates positive social change: a study by Save the Children Sri Lanka found that many fathers in families of migrant mothers assumed new roles involving domestic and child-care activities. For example, 58% of fathers cooked in households where mothers had migrated, as opposed to 14% where mothers worked in Sri Lanka. However, other studies also show that returnees easily step back into their traditional household roles.

Adjustment to natural disasters

Remittances often are a form of insurance for families in the origin countries. While the dominant pattern is for remittances to be regularly sent
to families in origin countries, it is often found that they are sent when
there is an emergency in the origin. In Bangladesh, the severe flood of
2004 saw remittances sent to help relations and friends recover from the
damage (Khatun, 2008, p. 1). Similarly, the impact of the 2004 tsunami
in Sri Lanka was restricted by remittances (Pham and Harrod, 2008).

Introducing the poor to the formal financial system and community
development are two further impacts of remittances on poverty made by
Khatun (2008).

All of the above impacts of remittances in origin communities have had
positive impacts in ameliorating poverty. Against this, however, we need
to recognise that some studies have identified negative effects. Those that
have been observed are the following:

Income inequality

Although poverty can be a powerful driver of migration, it is often not
the poorest of the poor who actually move. This is because there are costs
involved in migration (World Bank, 2006). Indeed, many OCWs incur
substantial debt by selling assets or borrowing in order to finance their
migration. Hence, remittances may serve to increase income inequality
in communities experiencing out-migration between migrant and non-
migrant families. Go (2003, p. 5), for example, shows migrant families
are significantly better off than non-migrant families in the Philippines,
as have De Bruyn and Kuddus (2005) in Bangladesh.

On the other hand, Khatun (2008, p. 16) found in focus group discussions with Bangladeshi villagers that increased remittance income had
enabled poor families to close the gap with better-off families. Moreover,
there may be a time factor involved here. The initial migration out of a
community may favour better-off families since they both can afford to
pay the migration costs and are first to feel the benefits of remittances.
However, the beneficial impacts may later flow to poorer families. Stark,
Taylor and Yitzhaki (1986) argue that the uncertainty and associated costs
are likely to reduce over the period of time migrants have been leaving
the community due to the spread of information and development of
a network of contacts across a wider range of households, resulting in

increases in migration among the worse off. Moreover, over time the knock-on, multiplier impacts of migrants spending in the local community will have flowed on to non-migrants. Hence, as migration out of a village matures, there may be a reduction in income inequality.

Increased cost of living and local inflation

One impact of remittances is that the influx of income can increase the prices of commodities, land and labour (de Bruyn and Kuddus, 2005).

Impoverishment through loss of assets

As indicated earlier, many OCWs finance their migration through borrowing or sale of assets. The costs can be substantial, and in several countries there is considerable rent-taking by agents, officials and recruiters. In some cases, if there is a premature return of the worker because of illness or other reasons, the worker and their family will suffer a considerable financial loss (Hugo, 2003).

In sum, it would seem that the positive impacts outweigh the negative in terms of poverty reduction. Nevertheless, remittances from OCWs and expatriates to their home countries have been a neglected phenomena in assessments of economic development in Asia and the Pacific. The reasons for this neglect are that most remittances have flowed through informal channels, that they have been vastly underestimated in size, their greatest impacts have often been local and regional in effect rather than national, and there has been a failure to appreciate the full nature of their impacts. However, with the recent massive increase in the scale of remittances into Asia-Pacific countries, there has been a growing recognition among policy makers and researchers of their importance for economic and social development in the region. In examining redistributions of wealth between northern and southern countries, remittance flows, received in Asia, are greater than FDA flows, certainly when considered in net terms. Some also would argue that remittances are more predictable and stable than FDI and FDA flows, and they are especially effective because they are received by families. At the very least, remittances must be an important consideration in discussions of development in many countries in the region.

There is a particular concern in Asia to achieve better practice with respect to international labour migrants both in origin and destination

nations. There is considerable variation between nations in the level
of government commitment and extent of protection given to labour
migrants. For example, the Philippines has developed an array of strategies to protect its migrant workers, while Indonesia, until recently, has
done little. There is an array of international instruments available that,
if accepted by all nations, would provide a framework for international
labour migration to operate more efficiently, effectively and justly. In particular, the UN Convention on Migrant Workers (ICPRAMWF) of 1990,
finally ratified by the General Assembly in 2002, would be the basis for
improving the Asian international labour-migration system, but it has
not been ratified by most Asian nations, nor the destination countries for
Asian migrants. However, there seems little chance of ratification among
most net-receiving countries, so a more achievable goal may be improving
governance of migration in these countries.

While much Asian international labour migration remains undocumented, there will remain huge amounts of suspicion about migrants
and migration in destination nations. Nation states will be legitimately
concerned regarding their lack of control over their sovereign borders,
and migrant workers will have an aura of 'criminality' among the citizens
in the destination. Hence, there is a pressing need to regularise migration,
and this applies equally to origin as it does to destination countries. Too
often, undocumented migration is able to thrive because the documented
channels are not only too narrow and limited but also the transaction
costs involved are too high because of rampant rent-seeking by a range of
stake holders. The process is too slow and cumbersome and too difficult
and bureaucratic for potential migrant workers with little education or
skill and experience in dealing with bureaucracy. In origin countries, the
process of migration will only become fully regularised when official channels for movement are seen by potential migrants as more effective than
the undocumented channels. The common response to illegal migration
is increased policing and compliance activity against the undocumented
migration system. However, this will be ineffective unless there is at the
same time an equally concerted effort to wipe out corruption, exploitation and needless bureaucracy in the official system. In destinations, there
needs to be official and community recognition of the structural need for
migrant workers for the prosperity of local economies, and with this the
regularisation of immigration, which maintains national sovereignty and
control over who enters the country, but recognises the rights of migrant
workers and the need for them.

As was indicated earlier, civil society is playing an increasing role with
respect to migration (internal and international) in Asia, although there

is considerable variation from country to country in the nature and level of that activity. Most non-governmental organisation (NGO) activity in this area is nationally based, but there are some emerging regional NGOs that cover several nations. It is particularly important to have NGOs that are active in pairs of origin and destination countries. There are a number of examples of effective NGO activity in improving the protection of migrants, providing support for migrants but also in advocating for the rights of migrants and in lobbying to change policy in both origin and destination countries. In terms of origin countries, the Philippines has the best developed and most comprehensive NGO presence, and their role undoubtedly has improved the lot of OCWs from that country.

One of the major constraints on governments in the Asian region in the development of efficient and equitable migration systems that work for the benefit of countries of origin and destination as well as the migrants is a lack of capacity. Countries need to move from migration governance systems, which are focused on control, to ones that seek to manage people movement. Migration will continue to occur if there is a good reason for it to occur (demand for workers, persecution, environmental pressures, etc.). To seek to stop it in such circumstances is doomed to failure and simply forces the movement underground and more and more into the hands of illegal and criminal agencies. However, effective migration management requires considerable capacity and infrastructure, including the following:

- A well-trained cadre of migration officials who are not general public servants, but who have a specific background and experience across the full range of migration activities. Such a group is fundamentally important to the setting up and running of an effective migration management system, as well as in the development of emigration policies.
- Integration of all of the government activities concerned with migration – customs, police, labour and border officials.
- Appropriate migration management systems. Appropriate hardware and software have been developed at a rapid rate, especially since 9/11, and the adoption and use of these is important.
- Setting up an appropriate information system. Effective migration management is impossible without timely and relevant measurement of the scale and composition of migration into and out of the country.
- A body of policy-relevant research, which is essential not only for the continuing surveillance of the impact of migration and to make evidence-based recommendations for migration policy and practice,

but also to develop policies that can maximise the beneficial impacts of migration on development.
• A competent, well-trained national research capacity to inform policy development on migration, as well as migration and development issues.

The countries of the Asia-Pacific region vary considerably across each of these criteria, but most have shortcomings in each. Migration on the contemporary scale is a very new phenomenon in most countries, and there has not been sufficient time or resources to build up the capacity necessary for effective migration management and to facilitate migration and development processes and outcomes. It is strongly recommended here that a regional initiative be undertaken to improve capacity in this area.

There is general agreement that in the new 'age of migration', countries cannot aspire to stop migration flows, but they are best advised to develop effective management of that mobility, which maximises national interest while preserving the integrity of national borders and human rights. Effective management of migration is very much dependent on international cooperation – bilateral, regional and multilateral. It has become common place in the burgeoning number of international meetings on international migration, policy and management of international migration to conclude with a consensus of the need for such cooperation. However, the cases where such admirable intentions have become translated into operational activities on the ground remain few in number. The development of regional economic blocs such as NAFTA and the EU has seen massive shifts that have facilitated regional flows of investment, trade and finance, but initiatives regarding flow of people have been fewer. In Asia, the global trend toward regional organisation development and regional cooperation is in evidence in the development of organisations like APEC (Asia-Pacific Economic Cooperation) and ASEAN (Association of Southeast Asian Nations), which have now been in existence for more than a decade. However, little has been achieved with respect to regional agreement on international migration issues. Indeed, in ASEAN, despite the fact that all nations[18] have been strongly influenced by migration since its formation, the sensitivity of the state of Singapore to the issue prevented the issue even being discussed, until recently. ASEAN contains both major

[18] The Philippines, Vietnam, Cambodia, Laos, Thailand, Burma, Malaysia, Indonesia, Brunei and Singapore.

origin and destination nations so there would appear to be much to be gained.

It has been argued (UN, 2002b, p. 21) that:

> the adoption of the General Agreement on Trade in Services (GATS) dur-
> ing the latest rounds of the General Agreement on Tariffs and Trade (1993)
> provides a general framework for trade related temporary movements of
> people based on government to government agreements. So far, no such
> agreement has yet been worked out as GATS contains no clear specific
> rules regarding the movement of labour. However, a number of devel-
> oped countries, including the EU as a whole, have taken steps toward the
> formulation of agreements.

Hence, there are some promising signs of a recognition of the structural nature of non-permanent migration in many developed countries and its long-term significance and importance.

The UN (2002b, p. 30) also points to the acceleration of regional eco-nomic cooperation as being a positive element in developing cooperation and integration in relation to migration policy. They refer to instruments such as the Treaty of Amsterdam (1998) in the EU and the North Amer-ica Free Trade Agreement (NAFTA) of 1989. In Asia, there have not yet been similar instruments developed, although there are some promising developments. In the past, the international migration issue had been kept from the agenda of ASEAN by its sensitivity, but this is changing. The Senior Labour Officials Meeting (SLOM) in May 2003 preceding the ASEAN Labour Ministerial Meeting agreed to begin liberalising their labour markets by opening up certain sectors to workers from other ASEAN nations.[19] Nevertheless, it was also agreed that the possibility of a free labour market in the region is still remote.

It is noticeable to an observer of Asia that there has been a signifi-cant increase in meetings of officials and policy makers regarding migra-tion. ASEAN, which previously declined to discuss migration, now has the ASEAN Plan of Action on Immigration Matters. They have agreed to intensify efforts to standardise visa issuance procedures to foreign nationals. There are frequent meetings between groups of nations on trafficking. For example, in October 2004, such meetings were held by the Mekong Countries (Cambodia, China, Laos, Thailand and Vietnam) and labour officials from labour-sending nations (Bangladesh, China, Indone-sia, Nepal, Pakistan, the Philippines, Sri Lanka, Thailand and Vietnam).

---

[19] *Asian Migration News*, 1 to 15 May 2003.

Meetings took place in Manila in the previous month to share experiences, lessons learned and best practices on labour migration and finding practical means to protect migrants.[20]

The chapter now turns specifically to the implications for policy of the growing evidence that international migration can and does play a role in reduction of poverty and in facilitating economic and social development (World Bank, 2006). Clearly, the role for policy here is to 'increase the benefits and reduce the risks of migration for poor people' (DFID, 2007, p. 1) for people in low-income countries. It is necessary, however, to make a few initial cautionary remarks:

- Migration cannot be seen as a substitute for good governance and the development of a social economic development policy within Asian countries. Its role is purely subsidiary and facilitating in the development process.
- Migration is a sensitive issue in Asia and the Pacific (as it is elsewhere), and there are real sensitivities about the involvement of foreign nations in matters relating to the movement of people into countries. Over a long period, this has been a barrier to developing meaningful dialogue between pairs of sending and receiving countries.
- Migration and development policy are the preserve of different agencies or departments within national governments. Any integrated development policy needs to be inter-departmental and must cut across the sites of particular government interests.
- Consideration of migration and development initiatives involves, potentially at least, not only activities in low-income origin nations but also in destination countries, and there has been a great deal of difficulty in the past in getting origin and destination countries together to discuss joint policy implications.

Nevertheless, two basic points need to be made:

(1) People movement has increased, and is increasing, in Asia and the Pacific.
(2) The weight of empirical evidence is that this mobility can be harnessed to facilitate poverty reduction and positive developmental outcomes.

While there is much that is not known yet about linkages between population mobility on the one hand and poverty reduction and development

---

[20] *Asian Migration News*, 1 to 15 October 2004.

on the other, there are a number of areas where there is a potential role for policy to play.

Policy on brain drain

Southern nations face a real dilemma with respect to the emigration of skilled persons and students. On the one hand, such movement potentially can contribute to development while, on the other, the reality is that large numbers do not return. Human rights considerations and the realities of global migration make it impossible to prevent emigration. Nevertheless, the number of less and least development nations that reported to the UN that they had policies to reduce emigration increased from seventeen in 1976 to forty-three in 2003 (UN, 2006b, p. 47).

Turning to destinations, any unilateral attempt to selectively exclude skilled immigrants from southern nations is not acceptable from the perspective of the rights of individuals involved, and is impractical given the current demographic and labour-market situation in OECD nations. Any efforts in this direction would need to be multilateral, since a single nation could argue that if they excluded highly skilled migrants from LDCs, those migrants would simply move to an alternative OECD destination.

Nevertheless, this does not preclude OECD nations taking a more ethical approach to skilled south–north migration, and this is increasingly discussed among development assistance and professional communities in those nations. One suggestion is that receiving countries make payments of some kind – either in cash or investment in training/education in the country of origin – for every skilled migrant accepted, in recognition of the costs invested by origin nations in the development of the human capital encapsulated in each migrant. This, of course, would forge a link between immigration and development-assistance policies and ministries in receiving nations, which are currently quite separate operations. Such investments could be earmarked for the creation of training institutions to replace the skills lost. While some could argue this would simply produce more potential OECD-bound migrants, the *raison d'être* should be the recognition that destination nations have a responsibility to meet development costs of human capital paid for in origin nations. Thus the investment could be 'tied aid' in the sense that it is targeted to particular areas of activity in the origin nation. In some ways, this is analogous to the levies at present placed on migrant workers by some immigrant countries to fund domestic training programmes. Singapore, for example, imposes such a levy to be paid by the employers of skilled foreign workers, and the funds generated are put into the training/education of Singaporeans so that skill shortages in the long term can be met internally. It is not too large a jump to envisage a similar payment to and/or investment in the training/education system in origin countries.

There also have been other suggestions, such as:

- developing a code of conduct for OECD nations to follow in recruiting skilled workers
- developing circularity in this movement by encouraging temporary residence in the destination, incentives to return, portability of benefits, etc.
- at the same time encouraging the development of domestic training institutions to obviate the need for recruitment from southern countries
- imposing limits on the proportion of workers in particular sectors who are from overseas, to encourage domestic training
- imposing levies on employers of 'southern' professionals to generate funds for training both at home and abroad.

Policy on remittances

The World Bank (World Bank, 2006; Terry and Wilson, 2005) is placing considerable emphasis on the development of policies to maximise the amount of money remitted by migrants to their home area and the effective capturing of these resources to facilitate poverty reduction and development. There are therefore two areas of policy concern:

(1) to maximise the inflow of remittances
(2) to mobilise remittances to enhance development.

With respect to the first, one issue is the exorbitant costs that have often been involved in the process of sending money home. In 2000, the average cost of sending remittances to Latin America was 15 per cent of the value of the transaction. However, since then, greater competition, advances in technology and greater awareness among relevant government agencies has halved the costs and made available an additional US$3 billion each year to receiving families (Terry, 2005, p. 11). The fact remains, however, that transaction costs are often too high and remitters are at the mercy of predatory institutions and individuals at both the sending and receiving end. There is much that can be done by governments at both ends of the process to maximise the proportion that gets through and the speed and security of the process. As Orozco and Wilson (2005, p. 380) point out: 'remittances remain financial flows in search of financial products. Too few financial institutions offer transnational families affordable financial products and options.' Terry (2005, p. 11) also makes the point that remittances are often the initial point of entry of poor families into the formal financial system: 'to open a savings account, or obtain a loan or mortgage. This is the critical first step to entering the financial mainstream for individual families and reaching the goal of financial democracy for a country.'

Turning to the second issue of how to mobilise remittances to enhance development, it has been shown that there is significant developmental impact if there is an increase in the proportion of remittances that flow through formal financial systems (Terry, 2005, p. 12). Yet what is clear is that government authorities (national, regional and local) in origin countries have often failed to create contexts that can lever remittances to achieve developmental goals. Some countries have attempted to tax remittances at various times, but the main effect has been to divert more remittances through non-official channels. In 2002, Sri Lanka announced that it would impose a 15 per cent tax on the US$1.2 billion received each year, but was quickly forced to withdraw the measure when there was a public outcry.[21] A number of innovative programmes have been successfully introduced in Mexico. These include programmes where federal and state governments match remittances to undertake developmental activity in depressed regions (Zárate-Hoyos, 2005). However, these target remittances sent by *groups* of migrants from the same area, the so-called 'hometown associations', and the bulk of remittances are still received by individual families.

In some contexts there has been a failure to realise the potential role of remittances in regional development. For example, in an Eastern Indonesian case study (Hugo, 1998), there have been few flow-ons from migrations that have involved investments generating local production for export to other regions or expanded local job opportunities. While there can be little doubt that households and villages with migrant workers have benefited considerably, the region remains among Indonesia's poorest areas. It is a peripheral area with limited agricultural potential, and low levels of education, and which is neglected by the central government (Hugo, 1998). The reasons for the limited impact of remittances on regional development are:

---

[21] *Migration News*, January 2003.

- the remittances are focused on an isolated peripheral area
- the illegality of the migrants sending the remittances
- the lack of sufficient physical infrastructure, especially transportation infrastructure, which would create a favourable environment for small investors
- the lack of integration of the remittance recipients into regional planning efforts
- the lack of appropriate training/education programmes to assist returning migrants in making effective investment decisions.

It is somewhat paradoxical that while the export of labour has been explicitly incorporated into national planning efforts in Indonesia (Hugo, 1995), in a poor province where labour migration is one of the few sources of funding into the region, it is not being considered at all in regional development planning. Hence, it is not only at national levels that public authorities have failed to lever remittances for development. Orozco and Wilson (2005, p. 386) have argued that an adequate policy response for improving the development impact of remittances will involve an effort and partnership between an array of stakeholders – transnational families, money transfer companies and financial institutions, public authorities, civil society and international organisations. They advance a number of core principles for three of these stakeholder groups.

Remittances institutions

- Improve transparency.
- Promote fair competition and pricing.
- Apply appropriate technology.
- Seek partnerships and alliances.
- Expand financial services.

Public authorities

- Do no harm.
- Improve data.
- Encourage financial intermediation.
- Promote financial literacy.

Civil society

- Leverage development impact.
- Support social and financial inclusion.

Most tellingly, they conclude: 'remittances remain private flows in search of public opportunity... for so long the sign of a broad problem, now (they) have potential to be part of a far reaching solution'.

Australia, for example, can develop effective policies to assist in migration in Asia and the Pacific, playing a positive role in development and poverty reduction without any modification or change to Australian immigration policy. However, there is increasing international consensus that, in order to maximise the benefits of international migration for development, there is a need for co-operation between origins and destinations.

What would be the elements in a 'development sensitive' immigration policy for a developed country like Australia? Such questions are being increasingly raised in Europe and North America (DFID, 2007), but there are a number of elements that can be put forward in a preliminary way:

- Fundamentally, it involves examining and considering the benefits and impacts of a particular migration policy, not only from the perspective of the destination country but also that of the origin countries.
- One consideration relates to issues of brain drain, especially that of medical workers. The potential for such elements as codes of practice or providing medical-training development assistance to origin areas needs to be considered in a pragmatic and realistic way. It needs to be considered that not all skilled emigration is negative in its effects on low-income countries, but it is true that some is, and where this is the case, effective, workable ways of counter-balancing its effect need to be considered.
- Another consideration relates to circular migration. There is a pressing need to explore the development and extension of these programmes. Australia presents a good example of this need. It has developed one of the most effective temporary migration programmes in the world, focusing on skill (Khoo *et al.*, 2003). Although there have been abuses of the programme, it has overwhelmingly had a positive effect in Australia (Khoo *et al.*, 2003). There has been increasing discussion in Australia as to whether this programme should be extended to unskilled workers (Senate Standing Committee on Employment, Workforce Relations and Employment, 2006). The justification has been both from the perspective of the positive benefits this will have for the poor in low-income nations, especially in the Pacific (Maclellan and Mares, 2006), but also that it would meet labour shortages for unskilled and semi-skilled workers in particular sectors. Hitherto, this suggestion has been rejected by the government for a number of reasons:

- the unskilled labour shortage has been questioned and attributed to employers refusing to pay appropriate wages and conditions or seeking to drive these down
- a questioning of the benefits of remittances and return migration
- a fear that the negative experience of other earlier unskilled labour migration schemes have resulted in permanent settlement, especially in the schemes of the 1950s in Europe
- a fear that such schemes are exploitative of the migrants themselves.

It is recommended here that this issue needs to be confronted squarely in Australia and a comprehensive and authoritative investigation made into it. It needs to be established if there are real sectoral labour shortages for unskilled or semi-skilled workers who do not meet correct criteria for temporary entry or permanent settlement and if so, in what areas? Moreover, this analysis should not be confined to the contemporary situation but should be projected over the next two decades in the light of ageing of the workforce and structural change in the economy. It has been shown, for example (Hugo, 2007), that Australia faces an increase in the number of paid care workers of 3.0% per annum between 2001 and 2011 and 3.2% and 3.9% per annum over the next two decades. In all, over the three decades there will be an extra 69,954 workers needed in the residential area and 136,457 in the non-residential area. This investigation also needs to not only look at the *past* experience of temporary labour-migration schemes but also look at the potential for Australia to develop best practice in such schemes using all of the tools available in migration management in the twenty-first century. The question needs to be asked as to whether all unskilled, temporary labour migration is bad or whether it is the way such extremes have been managed that has caused its negative effects. The fact is that they are often beneficial to the movers and their families. Perhaps a pilot scheme could be initiated in a sector that has proven labour shortages and which is limited to a few countries of origin. The New Zealand and Canadian experience in this area should be invaluable, as is evident in the chapter on Tonga labour mobility by Taukolo, Redden and Esau, one of the case studies that follow.

Consideration needs to be given to ways in which, at the Australian end, positive diaspora linkages with home nations can be facilitated. This would involve examination of dual citizenship, portability of entitlements and facilitating joint activities in business or research.

To introduce a developmentally sensitive immigration policy would require a 'whole of government' approach rather than being the responsibility of a single government department or agency. Australia has been an important and influential global player in post-war international migration. It has been at the forefront of innovation and the development of best practice in this area. Australia now has the opportunity to continue and enhance this tradition by showing how effective migration policy and management can not only deliver dividends to receiving countries but through sound, well thought-through and delivered policies and programmes can at the same time produce benefits for low-income origins as well.

Conclusion

One of the key relationships in the contemporary discourse on migration development relates to that between temporary mobility (especially of low-skilled workers) and poverty reduction. The evidence is that labour mobility has the potential to achieve poverty reduction in low-income countries, although that potential is not always fulfilled. It is generally true that it is not the poorest of the poor who move, because they often do not have access to the financial resources required for international labour migration, nor do they have the margin to undertake the risk of that migration. However, there are three ways in which poverty reduction can be achieved by communities sending out temporary migrant workers:

(1) through the workers themselves and their families directly receiving an enhanced income, which they can use for purchase of goods and services and investment
(2) through the second and third multiplier effects that migrant spending in the village creates for non-migrants
(3) over time, the poorer elements of a community migrating as migration out of that community becomes more general and the perceived risks involved in migration are reduced.

Moreover, there is evidence in some countries (e.g. Indonesia) that international labour migrants are drawn from some of the poorest areas of the country. The individual case studies that follow provide further clear examples and case-study insights into the labour migration–poverty reduction relationship.

References

Abella, M. I. (1992), 'Contemporary Labour Migration from Asia: Policies and Perspectives of Sending Countries', in L. L. Lim and H. Zlotnik (eds.), *International Migration Systems: A Global Approach*, Oxford University Press: Oxford.

Abraham, J. (2001), 'Global NRI/PIO Community – A Perspective', talk delivered at the Overseas Indian Conference, organised by the Indian Merchant Chamber in Mumbai on 7 January, 2001, available at www.gopio.net/NRI_PIO_Talk_Mumbai.html [last accessed 3 March 2009].

Adams, R. (2005), 'International Remittances and the Household: Analysis and Review of Global Experience', paper presented at the Plenary Session of the African Economic Research Consortium, Nairobi, 29 May.

Adelman, I. and Taylor, J. E. (1990), 'Is Structural Adjustments with a Human Face Possible? The Case of Mexico', *Journal of Development Studies* 26(3): 387–407.

Afsar, R., Yunus, M. and Islam, A. B. M. S. (2002), *Are Migrants after the 'Golden Deer'? A Study on Cost-benefit Analysis of Overseas Migration by the Bangladeshi Labour*, IOM, Regional Office for South Asia: Dhaka.

Asian Development Bank (ADB) (2004), 'Developing the Diaspora', paper presented at Third Co-ordination Meeting on International Migration, Population Division, Department of Economic and Social Affairs, United Nations Secretariat, New York, 27 to 28 October 2004.

Athukorala, P. (1993), 'International Labor Migration in the Asia-Pacific Region: Patterns, Policies and Economic Implications', *Asian-Pacific Economic Literature* 7: 28–57.

Barlow, C., Gondowarsito, R., Birowo, A. T. and Jayasuriya, S. (1990), 'Development in Eastern Indonesia: The Case of Nusa Tenggara Timur', *International Development Issues*, 13.

Cohen, M. (2003), 'Overseas Bounty', *Far Eastern Economic Review*, 16 January, 48.

Cornelius, W. (2003), 'Mexico, New Security Concerns, and Implications for Development', presentation at the MPI Meeting on Remittances and Circular Migration as Drivers of Development, University of California at San Diego, 3 April 2003.

Dade, C. (2004), 'Transnationalism, Foreign Assistance, Domestic Communities: New Opportunities and New Challenges for Canada and the United States', *Focal Point* (Spotlight on the Americas Special Edition, March): 1–2.

De Bruyn, T. and Kuddus, U. (2005), *Dynamics of Remittance Utilisation in Bangladesh*, International Organisation for Migration (IOM): Dhaka.

de Haan, A. (2006), 'Migrations in the Development Studies Literature: Has it Come Out of its Marginality?', WIDER Research Paper No. 2006/19, UNU-WIDER: Helsinki.

Department for International Development (DFID) (2007), 'Eliminating World Poverty: A Challenge for the 21st Century', White Paper on International Development.

Dimzon, C. S. (2005), 'Philippine Migration, Remittances and Development in the Philippines', paper presented at the Workshop on International Migration and Labour Market in Asia, organised by the Japan Institute for Labour Policy and Training, Japan Institute of Labour, Tokyo, 20–21 January.

Ellerman, D. (2003), *Policy Research on Migration and Development*, World Bank: Washington, WA.

Faist, T. (2007), 'The Transnational Turn: Migration and Politics', in A. K. Sahoo and B. Maharaj (eds.), *Sociology of Diaspora: A Reader*, Rawat Publications: Jaipur.

Global Commission on International Migration (GCIM) (2005), 'Migration in an Interconnected World: New Directions for Action', report of the Global Commission on International Migration: Switzerland.

Go, S. P. (2003), 'Recent Trends in International Movements and Policies: The Philippines', paper prepared for the Workshop on International Migration and Labour Markets in Asia, organised by the Japan Institute of Labour, Tokyo, Japan, 5–6 February.

Goldfarb, R., Havrylyshyn, O. and Mangum, S. (1984), 'Can Remittances Compensate for Manpower Outflows?', *Journal of Development Economics* 15: 1–17.

Goma, J. N., Mantra, I. B. and Bintarto, R. (1993), 'Labour Force Mobility from East Flores to Sabah Malaysia and the Extent of the Influence in the Village Origin: A Case Study at Nelereren Village', *BPPS-UGM* 6(4A): 401–12.

House of Commons (2004), *Migration and Development: How to Make Migration Work for Poverty Reduction*, The Stationery Office: London.

Hugo, G. J. (1995), 'Labour Export from Indonesia: An Overview', *ASEAN Economic Bulletin* 12(2): 275–98.

(1996), 'Economic Impacts of International Labour Emigration on Regional and Local Development: Some Evidence from Indonesia', paper presented at the Annual Meeting of the Population Association of America, New Orleans, LA, May.

(1998), 'International Migration in Eastern Indonesia', unpublished paper prepared for the East Indonesia Project, University of Adelaide: Adelaide.

(2003), 'Information, Exploitation and Empowerment: The Case of Indonesian Contract Workers Overseas', *Asian and Pacific Migration Journal* 12(4): 439–66.

(2005a), 'Demographic Trends in Australia's Academic Workforce', *Journal of Higher Education Policy and Management* 27(3): 327–43.

(2005b), 'Migrants in Society: Diversity and Cohesion, Thematic Project 4: Global Commission on International Migration', report for the Global Commission on International Migration: Geneva.

(2007), 'Contextualising the "Crisis in Aged Care" in Australia: A Demographic Perspective', *Australian Journal of Social Issues* 42(2): 169–82.

(2008), 'Asian Labour Migration Trends', first draft of a report to the Asian Development Bank.

International Organisation for Migration (IOM) (2005), 'Engaging Diasporas as Development Partners, for Home and Destination Countries: A Policy Roadmap', paper of the IOM: Geneva.

Johnson, B. and Sedaca, S. (2004), *Diasporas, Emigrés and Development, Economic Linkages and Programmatic Responses*, a special study of the US agency for international development, Carana Corporation: Washington, WA.

Kapioru, C. (1995), *Mobilitas Pekerja Yang Berstatus Suami, Dan Dampaknya Terhadap Perubahan Status Wanita Dan Kondisi Sosial Ekonomi Rumah Tangga*, UNFPA: Kupang.

Kapur, D. (2001), 'Diasporas and Technology Transfer', *Journal of Human Development* 2(2): 265–86.

Khatun, F. (2008), *Temporary Movement of Low Skilled Labour: Implications for Poverty Reduction in Bangladesh*, Centre for Policy Dialogue (CPD): Bangladesh.

Khoo, S. E., Voigt-Graf, C., Hugo, G. and McDonald, P. (2003), 'Temporary Skilled Migration to Australia: The 457 Visa Sub-Class', *People and Place* 11(4): 27–40.

Lintner, B. (2000), 'Living on the Edge', *Far Eastern Economic Review*, 27 July, 48.

Lucas, R. E. B. (2001), 'Diaspora and Development: Highly Skilled Migrants from East Asia', report prepared for the World Bank, Boston University: MA.

Maclellan, N. and Mares, P. (2006), 'Remittances and Labour Mobility in the Pacific', a Working Paper on Seasonal Work Programmes in Australia for Pacific Islanders, Institute for Social Research, Swinburne University of Technology: Victoria.

Martin, P. (2004), 'Migration and Development: Toward Sustainable Solutions', International Institute for Labour Studies Discussion Paper DP153/2004.

(2005), 'Managing Labour Migration: Professionals, Guest Workers and Recruiters', UN Expert Group Meeting on International Migration and Development, United Nations, New York, NY.

Nair, P. R. G. and Pillai, P. M. (1994), '*Impact of External Transfers on the Regional Economy of Kerala*, Centre for Development Studies: Trivandrum.

Organisation for Economic Cooperation and Development (OECD) (2005), '*Trends in International Migration 2004*, OECD: Paris.

Orozco, M. and Wilson, S. R. (2005), 'Making Migrant Remittances Count', in D. F. Terry and S. R. Wilson (eds.), *Beyond Small Change: Making Migrant*

Remittances Count, Inter-American Development Bank: Washington, WA, pp. 375–94.

Pham, M. H. and Harrod, K. (2008), 'Sri Lanka's Forgotten Heroines', *Far Eastern Economic Review* (January/February): 49–51.

Quibria, M. G. (1996), 'Migration, Remittances and Trade: With Special Reference to Asian Developing Economies', in P. J. Lloyd and S. Williams (eds.), *International Trade and Migration in the APEC Region*, Oxford University Press: Melbourne, pp. 84–98.

Senate Standing Committee on Employment, Workforce Relations and Employment (2006), '*Perspectives on the Future of the Harvest Labour Force*, Senate Printing Unit, Department of the Senate, Parliament House: Canberra.

Sharma, A. (2003), 'Come Home, We Need You', *Far Eastern Economic Review*, 23 January 2003, 28–9.

Siddiqui, T. (2001), *Transcending Boundaries: Labour Migration of Women from Bangladesh*, The University Press Limited: Dhaka.

Siddiqui, T. and Abrar, C. R. (2001), *Migrant Worker Remittances and Micro-Finance in Bangladesh*, ILO: Dhaka/Geneva.

Stahl, C. and Habib, A. (1989), 'The Impact of Overseas Workers' Remittances on Indigenous Industries: Evidence from Bangladesh', *The Developing Economies* 27(3): 269–85.

Stark, O., Taylor, J. E. and Yitzhaki, S. (1986), 'Remittances and Inequality', *The Economic Journal* 96(383).

Taylor, J. E., Hugo, G. J., Arango, J., Kouaouci, A., Massey, D. and Pellegrino, A. (1996), 'International Migration and National Development', *Population Index* 62(2): 181–212.

Terry, D. F. (2005), 'Remittances as a Development Tool', in D. F. Terry and S. R. Wilson (eds.), *Beyond Small Change: Making Migrant Remittances Count*, Inter-American Development Bank: Washington, WA, pp. 3–19.

Terry, D. F. and Wilson, S. R. (eds.) (2005), *Beyond Small Change: Making Migrant Remittances Count*, Inter-American Development Bank: Washington, WA.

Tiglao, R. (1997), 'The Global View', *Far Eastern Economic Review*, 19 June, 40.

Titu Eki, A. (2002), 'International Labour Emigration from Eastern Flores, Indonesia to Sabah, Malaysia: A Study of Patterns, Causes and Consequence', unpublished PhD Thesis, Population and Human Resources Department of Geographical and Environmental Studies, University of Adelaide: Adelaide.

United Nations (UN) (2002a), *International Migration Report 2002*, UN: New York, NY.

(2002b), *National Population Policies 2001*, UN: New York, NY.

(2006a), 'International Migration and Development, Report of the Secretary-General', Sixtieth Session, 'Globalization and Interdependence: International Migration and Development', 18 May 2006.

(2006b), *World Population Policies 2005*, UN: New York, NY.

Vertovec, S. (2006), 'Is Circular Migration the Way Forward in Global Policy?', *Around the Globe* 3(2): 38–44.

World Bank (2006), *Global Economic Prospects 2006: Economic Implications of Remittances and Migration*, World Bank: Washington, WA.

 (2007), 'Remittance Trends 2006', Migration and Development Brief 2, Development Prospects Group, World Bank: Washington, WA.

Yang, D. (2004), *How Remittances Help Migrant Families*, 1 December, available at www.migrationinformation.org/Feature/display.cfm?id=270 [last accessed 3 March 2009].

Yang, D. and Martinez, C. (2005), 'Remittances and Poverty in Migrants' Home Areas: Evidence from the Philippines', in C. Ozden and M. Schiff (eds.), *International Migration, Remittances and the Brain Drain*, World Bank: Washington, WA.

Zárate-Hoyos, G. A. (2005), 'The Development Impact of Migrant Remittances in Mexico', in D. F. Terry and S. R. Wilson (eds.), *Beyond Small Change: Making Migrant Remittances Count*, Inter-American Development Bank: Washington, WA, pp. 159–91.

Zhou, M. and Cai, G. (2005), 'Migrant Workers' Adaptation to Urban Life', paper prepared for the Urban China Research Network Conference: 'Urban China in Transition', New Orleans, Louisiana, 15–16 January.

Zhu, Y. (2004), 'Changing Urbanization Processes and In Situ Rural-Urban Transformation: Reflections on China's Settlement Definitions', in A. Champion and G. Hugo (eds.), *New Forms of Urbanization*, Ashgate: Aldershot.

4.1

Migrant labour and remittances in Bangladesh

FAHMIDA KHATUN*

Introduction

The movement of service providers from developing and least developed countries (LDCs) has increased at a fast pace due to global trade liberalisation, which has dismantled barriers to trade and integrated the global economy rapidly over the last fifteen years. Temporary movement of labour has particularly increased from these countries to high-income countries since the early 1990s (UN, 2004). This is also due to the fact that demographic structures of population in many countries, particularly in the developed countries, is such that trade in labour services has become absolutely necessary to facilitate and complement their economic activities.

International labour migration yields significant benefits in both the recipient and sending countries. Winters (2003) demonstrated that an increase in developed countries' quota on the inward mobility of skilled and unskilled temporary workers equivalent to 3 per cent of their workforces would generate an increase in world welfare of over US$150 billion per year. Movement of persons, temporary or long-term in nature, can provide high employment opportunities to all kinds of people and can easily be translated into real social, educational and economic development. The income earned by migrants increases both the migrants' and their families' welfare and strengthens the national economy.

It is in this context that movement of labour is being integrated into the trade-related and overall development strategies of several countries. It is also considered an important tool for poverty alleviation in the country of origin of workers through reducing unemployment. However, unlike trade in goods and services, barriers to the movement of natural

* Fahmida Khatun is Additional Director at the Centre for Policy Dialogue (CPD), Bangladesh.

persons across borders is still high. This is particularly true for less-skilled temporary migrants from poor countries. Access to markets is being reduced due to increased competition with supplies from several countries.

In view of the increased migration and the potential for further mobility of labour across borders, the issue has attracted significant importance in the WTO. Thus, temporary movement of natural persons under mode 4 of the General Agreement on Trade in Services (GATS), which calls for market access for exports of human resources, particularly from developing countries and LDCs, is one of the most important modes of supply of services for labour-abundant countries such as Bangladesh. The development dimension gets more pronounced with the movement of low- and semi-skilled people from these countries.

Bangladesh is one such country that has been able to benefit significantly in terms of continued increase in remittances through the movement of its human resources. The abundance of labour supply in Bangladesh has given it a comparative advantage over other countries in the global market. Bangladesh earns huge amounts of foreign exchange through remittances of its workers abroad. These remittances have not only been able to reduce the current account deficit and stabilise the balance of payments of the country for the last few years, but they also have helped in improving the standard of living of a large section of the population through employment of its workers. However, labour mobility from Bangladesh has never been a smooth process due to several external and internal constraints. Had there been a comprehensive policy in the country to facilitate the movement of all categories of workers from Bangladesh, and fewer barriers by the importing countries, Bangladesh could benefit more through the movement of low- and semi-skilled workers. Hence, opportunities lie for Bangladesh in a successful negotiation of GATS mode 4.

Though international migration is a well-researched topic in Bangladesh, the issue of labour mobility in the context of GATS mode 4, with a view to identifying the possibilities of poverty reduction through increasing the temporary movement of labour, has not been investigated. The issue is not adequately managed, partly due to poor understanding of the impact of temporary movement of labour in Bangladesh's economic development. Though professionals and skilled workers also face several problems in entering the global market, it is the low-skilled workers who face more obstacles in various forms. However, given the abundance of labour in this category in Bangladesh and the global-market demand for such labour, the country has tremendous potential to gain through exporting its low-skilled human resources.

Design of the case study

Objectives and scope

The objective of this case study is to understand the importance of temporary movement of low-skilled workers for the Bangladesh economy and to assess the role of their remittances in assuring livelihoods for the poor communities in Bangladesh. This is because the share of semi-skilled/unskilled workers abroad is more than 65 per cent of the total overseas employment of Bangladeshis.[1] The study examines the concerns and complexities of labour mobility under GATS mode 4. Issues such as the need to amend, strengthen and better enforce domestic regulations to gain from liberalisation of mode 4 have been discussed. The inter-relationship between gender and trade under mode 4 is examined because the role of women is critical for economic and human development. There is also a global demand for female labour in a few specified services, such as nurses and household staff.

More specifically, the study aims to explore the following questions related to the temporary movement of low-skilled labour:

- how has migration helped in reducing poverty at the community level?
- what are the issues and concerns for the poor whose welfare is dependent on migrant labour and remittances?
- will greater market access under GATS mode 4 assist in reducing poverty?
- what are the challenges in terms of trade policy to find ways of poverty reduction through mode 4?

The ultimate goal of the study is to design appropriate trade policies that could address the attendant problems that continue to undermine the growth potential of low-skilled workers from Bangladesh. As the focus of the study is to understand the poverty issues of the remitting communities, low-skilled temporary migrants have been targeted for the analysis.

Methodology and sources of data

The study is based on both primary and secondary information. Members of the remitting workers' families were interviewed in order to understand

[1] Bureau of Manpower Employment and Training (www.bmet.org.bd [last accessed 2 April 2009]).

how labour mobility and remittances have impacted their lives in terms of poverty reduction. Two focus group discussions (FGDs) were held with the members of the remitters' families in each of the two villages called Balia Bill and Char Ghosta in the Manikganj district of Bangladesh, from where the exodus of workers as temporary workers to various destinations has been common since the early 1990s. A total of fifty people participated in four FGDs, with thirty people from the first village and twenty from the second. A few individuals from each village were interviewed separately to have detailed discussions on various aspects of the migration and their lives.

Information has also been collated through debriefing experts, policy makers, bank officials, representatives from non-governmental organisations (NGOs) and migrant welfare associations on issues such as trade and migration.

Secondary data and information were collected from the Bangladesh Bank, the Ministry of Expatriates' Welfare and Overseas Employment (MOEWOE), the Bureau of Manpower Employment and Training (BMET), Bangladesh Overseas Employment Services Limited (BOESL), the Refugee and Migratory Movements Research Unit (RMMRU) of the Dhaka University, the Welfare Association of Returnee Bangladeshi Employees (WARBE) and the Bangladesh Ovibashi Mohila Sramik Association (Bangladesh Women Migrants Association) (BOMSA). The study has also used insights from published books, reports and journal articles on international migration, remittances, poverty and GATS mode 4.

Study area

The villages under study are located in the district of Manikganj, close to the capital Dhaka. The total population in each village is about 2,500. The majority of villagers are farmers by profession. Others are either rickshaw-pullers or fishers. A small number of villagers are running small business too. Though the majority of women from these villages do not work outside their homes, women from the extremely poor families work as day labourers in rich families. Though several NGOs, including the Grameen Bank, Bangladesh Rural Advancement Committee (BRAC), Association for Social Advancement (ASA) and Proshika, operate in the villages, only a few took out loans with these NGOs. Surprisingly, most of the respondents are found to be unaware of such loans. The migrant workers or their family members did not take any loans with these NGOs either before or after migration.

Workers from both villages started to migrate temporarily in the early 1990s. So far, about 200 villagers from both villages have migrated to countries such as Saudi Arabia, Bahrain, Malaysia, Singapore, Dubai and Italy. Among them, around ten are female migrants. The majority of male migrants are working in agricultural farms and gardens while some of them work in the shipyards. Some are also involved in small businesses. Female migrants are working as housemaids in Saudi Arabia. Most of the migrants are illiterate and are from poor families. Only a few are educated, but only up to primary level. As reported, the educated ones who are from slightly better-off families can go to countries like Italy to earn more.

Layout of the study

Following the introductory and study design sections, a brief overview of the economic significance of labour mobility for Bangladesh in terms of the volume and flow of remittances is presented in the next section. Following that, the destination of temporary workers from Bangladesh is discussed. A literature review of the studies on migration, remittances and poverty reduction is then undertaken, with a view to understanding the issue both in a global and Bangladesh context. The next section presents the findings from the case study based on the discussions with the migrant families. The impact of migration has been discussed both at the household and community levels. Given the importance of gender issues in migration, this section also provides gender perspectives of migration based on the interviews. Key problems identified by the villagers as regards short-term international migration are discussed. Finally, the last section presents some important conclusions and major trade policy implications based on both primary and secondary information.

Economic significance of temporary movement of labour from Bangladesh

The economy of Bangladesh has been quickly integrating with the global economy as a result of increased international trade. This has been due to various economic and trade policy reforms in the mid 1980s and in the 1990s. Trade integration in Bangladesh's economy has registered a remarkable rise from about only 17% in 1991 to about 43.3% in 2008. The share of overseas development assistance (ODA) in gross domestic product (GDP) has declined from 5.6% in 1991 to 2.4% in 2008. Compared to exports, ODA is only 13.3% of the total exports of the country.

518 FAHMIDA KHATUN

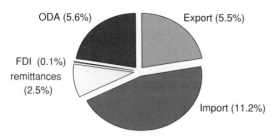

Figure 4G Share in GDP (FY 1991). *Source:* Bangladesh Bank, www.bangladesh-bank.org [last accessed 2 April 2009].

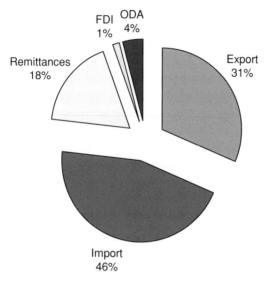

Figure 4H Share in GDP (FY 2008). *Source:* Bangladesh Bank, www.bangladesh-bank.org.

Figures 4G and 4H compare the share of various components of GDP of the country in the financial years 1991 and 2008. The ratio of ODA and total exports and remittances has increased from 1:1.4 in 1991 to 1:12 in 2008. Total exports stood at US$14.1 billion and total imports at US$20.2 billion in 2008, compared to US$1.7 billion and US$3.5 billion respectively in 1991. Table 4G presents the trade openness in Bangladesh over the years.

The performance of remittances has also been overwhelming. It has increased from US$764 million in 1991 to US$7.92 billion in 2008. The export sector, including export of human resources, has played a key role

Table 4G   *Bangladesh's degree of openness and the extent of globalisation (US$ million)*

	FY 1981	FY 1991	FY 2001	FY 2007	FY 2008
1. Export (X)	725	1,718	6,467	12154	14088
2. Import (M)	1,954	3,472	9,335	17157	20217
3. Remittance (R)	379	764	1,882	5978	7915
4. ODA disbursed	1,146	1,733	1,369	1565	1873
5. FDI (net)	0	24	550	793	650
Total (1–5)	4,204	7,711	19,603	37646.3	44743.8
GDP (current price)	19,812	30,975	47306.0	67714.0	78996.9
Degree of openness (X+ M as % of GDP)	13.5	16.8	33.4	43.3	43.4
Extent of globalisation (%)	21.2	24.9	41.4	55.6	56.6
X as % of M	37.1	49.5	69.3	70.8	69.7
(X+R) as % of M	56.5	71.5	89.4	105.7	108.8
ODA as % of GDP	5.8	5.6	2.9	2.3	2.4
ODA as % of X	158.1	100.9	21.2	12.9	13.3

Source: CPD Trade Database compiled from the Bangladesh Bank, www.bangladesh-bank.org and Export Promotion Bureau, www.epb.gov.bd [both last accessed 3 April 2009].

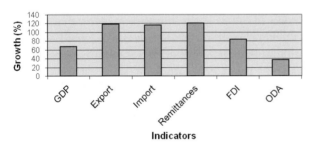

Figure 4I   Growth during 1991 and 2008. *Source:* Bangladesh Bank, www.bangladesh-bank.org.

in the improvement of the macroeconomic performance of the country. In addition to increased remittance flow, it has contributed in terms of incremental employment generation and investment. Figure 4I shows the growth of GDP and external sectors.

Bangladesh is an exporter of professional, skilled, semi-skilled and unskilled workers to more than twenty-two countries. The number of

Table 4H   *Remittances and other flows to Bangladesh (in US$ million)*

Fiscal year	Export	FDI	Remittances	Foreign aid (disbursement)
1995	3,472.56	92.25	1,197.63	–
1996	3,882.42	231.61	1,217.06	–
1997	4,418.28	575.31	1,475.42	–
1998	5,160.46	576.46	1,525.43	–
1999	5,312.21	309.14	1,705.74	–
2000	5,748.05	578.65	1,949.32	–
2001	6,467.50	354.47	1,882.10	1,369.00
2002	5,986.39	328.30	2,501.13	1,442.00
2003	6,545.05	350.25	3,061.97	1,585.00
2004	7,598.77	460.41	3,371.97	1,034.00
2005	8,654.52	845.26	3,848.29	1,491.00
2006	10,526.16	743.00	4,802.41	1,280.00
2007	12,177.86	793.00	5,978.47	1,099.52
2008	14,110.80	650.00	4,151.25	1,376.54

Source: CPD Trade Database, compiled from various sources such as the Bangladesh Bank, www.bangladesh-bank.org, the Export Promotion Bureau (www.epb.gov.bd) and the Economic Relations Division of the Ministry of Finance, Government of Bangladesh (www.erd.gov.bd) [all last accessed 3 April 2009].

Bangladeshi workers going abroad per year has increased from only 6,087 in 1976 to 875,055 in 2008. If the number of dependent families is accounted for, the beneficiary of these remittances would be even larger – around 3.4 million. In 2008, remittances received by Bangladesh constituted 10% of its GDP. From 1991 and 2008, wage earners' remittances to Bangladesh registered a growth of 13.8% per year, which is far above its annual GDP growth (around 6%). Remittance flow to Bangladesh was always higher than the inflow of foreign direct investment (FDI). The gap between remittance inflow and foreign aid disbursement has been increasing since 2001 due to the consistent growth of remittance inflow and the deterioration in foreign aid disbursement. Table 4H and Figure 4J show the flow of export income, remittances and FDI in Bangladesh.

Markets for temporary workers

From 1976 to 2008, about 6.2 million Bangladeshis went abroad for temporary work, providing services in the Middle East, Asia, Africa and

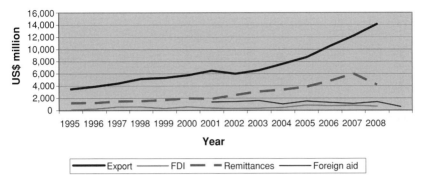

Figure 4J Remittances and other flows to Bangladesh. *Source:* Bangladesh Bank, www.bangladesh-bank.org.

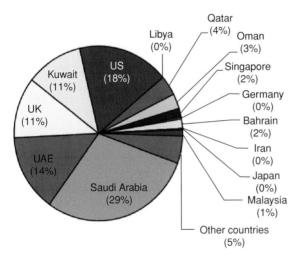

Figure 4K Share of remittances to Bangladesh by country (2005–08). *Source:* Bangladesh Bank, www.bangladesh-bank.org.

Europe. This is about 12.7 per cent of the total labour force of the country. In 2008, the total number of migrant workers overseas has reached an all time high. Figures 4K, 4L and 4M show the remittance inflow to Bangladesh by country and the annual flow of workers from Bangladesh.

An analysis of the dynamics of labour mobility from Bangladesh shows that the buoyancy of remittances during 1991 and 2008 is mainly due to an increase in the number of short-term migrants to countries such as Saudi Arabia, Kuwait, the United Arab Emirates (UAE), Qatar, Oman, Libya,

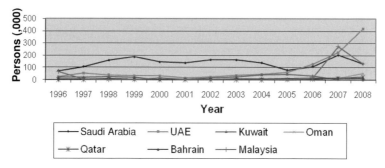

Figure 4L   Annual distribution of Bangladeshi workers in major countries (1976–2007). *Source:* BMET, www.bmet.org.bd [last accessed 2 April 2009].

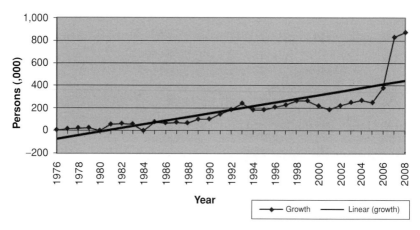

Figure 4M   Overseas employment from Bangladesh (1996–2008). *Source:* BMET, www.bmet.org.bd.

Bahrain, Iran, Malaysia, South Korea, Singapore, Hong Kong and Brunei. From 1976 to 2008, Saudi Arabia was the largest importer of workers from Bangladesh, accounting for 40.8 per cent of total workers who went abroad during this period (BMET, 2008). Apart from Saudi Arabia, the UAE and Malaysia, Bangladeshi migrants were also working in the US, and the UK, Australia, Canada, Germany, France, Italy, Switzerland, New Zealand, Belgium, the Netherlands, South Africa, Japan, Mauritius, Jordan and Lebanon. Figure 4N shows the top destinations of overseas employment from Bangladesh.

Bangladesh exports four types of human resources: professional, skilled, semi-skilled and less-skilled. For the period of 1976 to 2008, the share of unskilled workers in total overseas employment was about

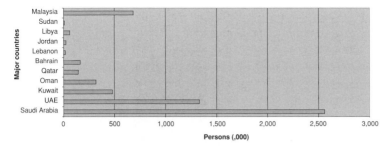

Figure 4N   Top destinations for overseas employment from Bangladesh (1996–2008). *Source:* BMET, www.bmet.org.bd.

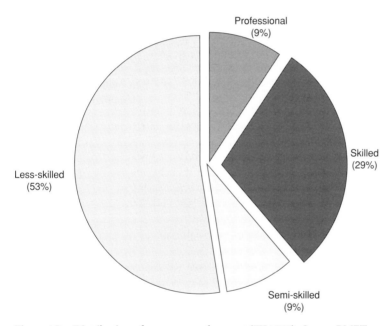

Figure 4O   Distribution of overseas employment (FY 1976). *Source:* BMET, www. bmet.org.bd.

50%, while the share of professionals was only 2.9% (see Figures 4O, 4P and 4Q).

Most of the countries where Bangladesh sends its workers are members of the WTO. Therefore, it is critical that Bangladesh takes up the issue of liberalisation of GATS mode 4 with these countries so that meaningful market access can be ensured through the successful completion of the Doha Round.

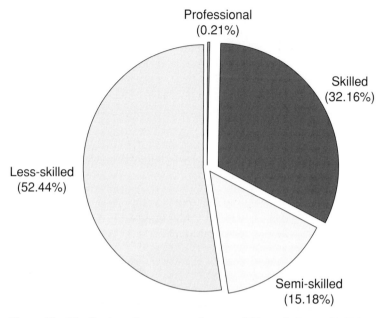

Figure 4P   Distribution of overseas employment (FY 2008). *Source:* BMET, www. bmet.org.bd.

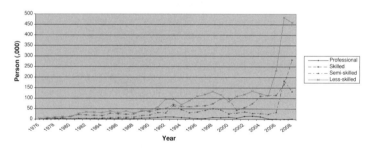

Figure 4Q   Flow of labour migration from Bangladesh under different categories (1976–2008). *Source:* BMET, www.bmet.org.bd.

Temporary movement of labour and poverty-reduction evidence from micro studies in Bangladesh

Increased movement of labour may affect the welfare of a country through remittances, and it has been viewed as a stimulus to the development process of developing countries. Remittances, which are basically the payment for services of labour exported from a country, can generate multiplier effects in the economy through the expenditure made out of this income. Such expenditure increases the aggregate demand. Though part of this demand may be met by imports, the increase in the effective demand may also be an important stimulus to local industry. This process presupposes that remittances help reduce poverty and thus increase effective demand.

Though migration has obvious developmental impacts on the economy through an increased flow of remittances, its impact on poverty is less known in the context of Bangladesh. While there is a surge of work on migration and remittances,[2] the poverty dimension of migration has not been explored. The following discussion on the poverty impact of temporary labour mobility has been based on the case study conducted in two villages and has been substantiated by the existing studies on remittances in Bangladesh. The poverty impact of labour mobility can be analysed by investigating the positive and negative impacts of remittances at the household and community levels.

Positive impacts

The impact of remittances through temporary movement of labour on poverty reduction has been found to be positive in several cases. Remittances can ease credit constraints and reduce risk and volatility. Besides, it can promote higher levels of investment in physical and human capital, which in turn fosters economic growth. Remittances increase the per capita income of the remittance-receiving countries, thereby having a significant poverty-reducing effect on the economy.

The cross-country and micro-based estimates support the above claim, suggesting that the fraction of the population living in poverty is reduced by about 0.4 per cent for each percentage point increase in the share of remittances to GDP (World Bank, 2006). By examining poverty, migration and remittances for seventy-one developing countries, Adams and Page (2005) concluded that a 10% increase in per capita official international remittances leads to a 3.5% decline in the number of people living in poverty. Similar findings have been revealed in the study conducted by the International Monetary Fund (IMF), which uses a sample of 101 countries for the period of 1973 to 2003 (IMF, 2005). Household surveys in low-income countries reveal that remittances have reduced

---

[2] Some of the recent studies include Bryun and Kuddus (2005), Siddiqui (2002a, 2002b, 2003), Murshid et al. (2002), Siddiqui and Abrar (2000, 2001), Afsar et al. (2002), Abrar (2000), Mahmood (1998, 1996, 1994), Ahmed and Zohra (1997) and Gardner (1995).

the incidence and severity of poverty in those countries. For example, international remittances have reduced the poverty head-count ratio by 11 percentage points in Uganda, 6 percentage point in Bangladesh and 5 percentage points in Ghana (Adams and Page, 2005). Several country-spacific studies have demonstrated a positive impact of remittances in reducing poverty in the recipient region.[3] Bangladesh has also experienced a number of positive effects due to increased labour mobility and thus remittances.

Income and employment

The change in family welfare of the migrants is reflected through the significant change in income of migrant workers. Murshid *et al.* (2002) estimated that an increase of remittances by Taka 1 would increase national income by Taka 3.3. The migrants from the villages in the case study have also been able to increase their income significantly. Prior to migration, the average monthly income of migrants who used to be either farmers or were day labourers would range between Taka 1,500 and Taka 12,000. As a migrant worker, at present they earn between Taka 25,000 to Taka 150,000 per month depending on their skill and type of work, and remit about Taka 10,000 to Taka 120,000 per month to their families back in the village, which contributes to the overall increase in their family income. This reinforces previous findings that migrants remit more than 80% of their income, and this is reflected in a higher income of the recipient households (Mahmud and Osmani, 1980). Siddiqui and Abrar (2001) find in their study that 51% of total income of families is derived from remittances.

Studies reveal that remittances have not only been able to reduce the deficit in the current account balance and stabilise the balance of payments of Bangladesh, but they have also helped to improve the standard of living of a large section of the population through employment of its workers. As a matter of fact, temporary labour migration from Bangladesh to the Middle Eastern and Southeast Asian countries occurs mainly in order to look for better opportunities and to escape unemployment and poverty. Afsar *et al.* (2002) state that the unemployment rate has been stable due to the continuous outflow of workers and inflow of remittances.

---

[3] For example, Adams (2004) for Guatemala, Yang (2004) for the Philippines, Gustafsson and Makonnen (1993) for Lesotho, Wodon *et al.* (2003) for Mexico, Taylor *et al.* (2005) for Mexico and Yang and Martinez (2005) for the Philippines.

The FGD for this case study shows that increased possession of land by some families due to increased remittances has been claimed to create employment opportunities for the marginalised villagers. The returned migrants hire labour to work for them in the field for cultivation rather than cultivating the field themselves. However, this has not significantly improved the unemployment situation of the village – this is due to the insufficient number of returnees and lack of opportunities.

Savings and investments

Several region-specific micro-studies reveal that remittances are used for consumption, investment and savings. All these methods of utilisating remittances have impacts on poverty reduction. The majority of remittances are used for food and clothing, home construction and repair, marriages and ceremonies, loan repayment, education, healthcare and purchase of land (Siddiqui and Abrar, 2001; Afsar *et al.*, 2002). Such use of remittances prevents the migrants' families from falling into poverty. As remittances are considered to be a transitory source of income rather than a permanent one, most families try to save out of this for the future. Mahmood (1991) found that households who received remittances saved 50 to 75% of their income, compared to 5% by households who did not receive any remittance.

Investment out of remittances is mainly done by those who are better off, particularly by Bangladeshis living in the US and the UK (Kuddus, 2003; Siddiqui, 2003). As a matter of fact, the initial socioeconomic conditions and demographic characteristics of remittance-receiving households, the skill and position of migrants and the length of stay abroad also determine the type of expenditure and investment of remitters and remitting families. For example, marital status of the migrant was found to be negatively related to investment in trade and business (Mahmood, 1991). Investments can also be in the form of buying land or education for children and other younger family members.

Access to education and healthcare

Investment in human capital may be induced by remittances, which has an impact on the wellbeing of households. However, the effect of migration on education and healthcare in the context of this case study is poorly understood. Though education and primary healthcare have improved in the migrant families, it cannot be linked directly to migration, as there has been a general improvement in enrolment at schools and primary healthcare in rural Bangladesh due to the intervention of both the Government of Bangladesh and NGOs. With the existence of a number of NGOs, particularly BRAC, which has education and health programmes, it is more difficult to assess the social impact of remittances without any household-level survey. However, in a few cases it was found that sons or younger brothers of the migrants were going to highschools and colleges, which can be related to remittances sent by their elder brothers. An anthropological study in a Bangladeshi village in the district of Sylhet found that international migration has transformed the economic and social fabric of the society (Gardner, 1995).

Role and position of women

The improved economic condition of the remitters' families has an impact on the status of women in the family in terms of more responsibilities and increased decision-making authority in the absence of the husband. The number of female migrants from Bangladesh is insignificant, and so is their impact on the family and on society. However, there is a huge potential for the low-skilled women and for the country to gain from temporary migration. This will also help empower women both in the family and in society. Siddiqui (2001) reveals that an important motivating factor behind women's migration is to possess a sense of empowerment in addition to an increase in economic status.

Adjustment to natural disasters

Families receiving remittances in the case study used the money mainly for consumption, while a few purchased agricultural land with the money. Though some had saved a portion of the money, no significant investment had been made. About 50 to 60 per cent of families used the money either for construction or for repairing houses. During the severe flood of 2004, remittances sent by the migrant workers were particularly useful when there was disruption in their livelihood and destruction of houses and properties.

Given the incidences of natural calamities and the poverty situation in Bangladesh, the role of migration and remittances is important as a coping strategy for the distressed families. During severe natural catastrophes, it is not only the migrant families that receive support from the migrant workers, but the whole nation gets assistance from the migrant communities abroad. Gardner (1995) found that remittances have saved families from entering into debt during vulnerable periods.

Community development

Migrants from the US and the UK contribute to community development through philanthropic activities. Such initiatives not only contribute to the reduction of income poverty through the construction of roads and culverts, charity and helping the victims of natural disasters, but also human poverty through activities such as healthcare, educational projects and scholarship programmes for poor students. However, these are done by long-term or permanent migrants through the formation of trusts and associations.

Negative impacts

As opposed to the positive impacts of remittance on poverty, it is also believed that remittances may impact the society negatively through effects on income distribution, employment and cost of living. The whole process of migration from countries without appropriate, adequate institutional structure is a difficult one, which may not yield the expected outcome from migration.

Income inequality

It is mainly members from the better-off segment of a society who are likely to migrate in the nascent state of migration, as the uncertainty and the associated costs are likely to be high. Therefore, remittances would have an unequalising effect on poverty reduction at that point in time. However, the uncertainty and the associated costs are likely to reduce over time due to the spread of information and contacts across a wider range of households, resulting in increases in migration among the worse off. This would subsequently have favorable effects on poverty and income inequality (Stark et al., 1986).[4]

Though income disparity between migrant and non-migrant poor families has been observed in some areas in Bangladesh (de Bruyn and

---

[4] The relationship between remittances and inequality has been considered to be not so important except for in situations where inequality interferes with the functioning of the economy or the political system (Banerjee and Newman, 1993; Alesina and Rodrick, 1994; Persson and Tabellini, 1994). On the other hand, evidence on the relationship between remittances and inequality in other countries is also inconclusive. The Gini coefficient has been found to drop as a result of remittance receipts in Sri Lanka (De and Ratha, 2005), and income inequality is estimated to drop for Mexican communities with relatively high levels of past migration (McKenzie and Rapport, 2004). However, remittances tended to make the distribution of income more unequal where international migration was a relatively new phenomenon (Stark et al., 1986).

Kuddus, 2005), the FGD with the villagers reveal that an increased income of the poor families from remittances has improved their living conditions and has reduced inequality, compared with the better-off families. Increased income in the remitting families also has an income effect on remittances in the area, as it is now hard to find a sufficient number of day labourers due to the higher income of the villagers.[5]

Though improved economic conditions of the migrant families has encouraged other villagers to migrate, only a few have successfully worked abroad due to lack of resources. Those who migrated had to pay more than required to the labour-exporting agencies, even though the rates are fixed by the government. Sometimes, due to unscrupulous acts of the corrupt recruiting agencies, the poor workers cannot migrate and therefore lose everything. This may worsen the economic conditions of poor families, widening the income gap between themselves and well-off families.

Cost of living and local inflation

Increased income among a certain section of people due to remittances may contribute to increases in price of commodities as well as daily wages of labour. Land prices in the villages in the case study went up at a faster rate in the remitting villages compared to other villages, due to remittances. Earlier studies found that remittances from the Middle East to the Chittagong district are used to buy social status and to purchase land, which has led to a concentration of land ownership and a sudden increase in land prices (de Bruyn and Kuddus, 2005). During the FGD, the villagers mentioned high inflation, but the existence of high inflation at the moment cannot be explained by an inflow of remittances since prices have gone up all over the country.

Impoverishment through loss of assets

Though migration is often the result of poverty, it is not the poorest who migrate, as there is a cost involved in it (World Bank, 2006; Asis, 2002). These costs include fees for recruitment, skills certification, a passport, a visa and travel. This has been true for Bangladesh, where the extreme poor cannot afford to migrate to other countries, only to other parts of Bangladesh, to earn their livelihoods. These people who belong to the extreme poverty level and who cannot earn even a dollar a day are landless

---

[5] In Nicaragua, a rise in remittances reduced labour-force participation but increased self-employment (Funkhouser, 1992), while Yang (2004) mentions that remittances reduce the supply of child labour but increases that of adult labour.

and lack skills and resources for international migration. Studies show that international migration involves huge costs, ranging from Taka 95,000 to Taka 500,000 (discussion with members of migrant families; Afsar *et al.*, 2002), depending on the destination and type of job. However, the poor who do migrate abroad through various ways, such as acquiring work visas through relatives, friends and neighbours, are slightly better off than the extreme poor.

Migration and gender

Migration is not gender neutral, and gender-based discrimination of low-skilled workers is common in the case of Bangladeshi migrants. As women are in a less advantageous situation in the job market due to their reproductive role and domestic occupations, there is also institutional bias against women's employment in various occupational sectors. They are employed only in a few low-paid jobs, including as domestic workers and care givers.

Female migrants are working as housemaids in Saudi Arabia and Dubai. They have had to sell all assets to go to work abroad, as these women are from the extreme-poor families and their husbands are mostly day labourers or marginal farmers. However, they have had to pay only about one third of what the male migrants pay to go to these countries. This is because the employers in the destination countries have taken care of most of the expenditures related to their migration, since finding housemaids is very difficult in those countries. Female migrants earn significantly less than male migrants. Their average income varies between Taka 7,000 to Taka 15,000. They remit around 70 to 80 per cent of their income to their families back home.

There is also fear of trafficking, rape, sexual harassment and various kinds of abuse and exploitation that restricts the migration of women workers. Gender-based discrimination in the Gulf countries has resulted in the exclusion of less-skilled women from legal access to labour export opportunities. This has been effective with the application of Article 8 of the Emigration Ordinance 1982 of the Government of Bangladesh,[6] which restricted less-skilled women from regular employment overseas.

---

[6] Article 8 of Ordinance No. XXIX of 1982 reads: 'If the Government, having regard to the occupation, profession, vocation or qualification of any person or class of persons is satisfied that emigration of such person or class of persons is not in the public interest, it may, by order, prohibit the emigration of such person or class of persons and thereupon the departure of such person or class of persons otherwise that in accordance with such order shall not be lawful.'

More recently, less-skilled female labour is restricted according to age; women over twenty-five years are not allowed to go for overseas employment. Only a few less-skilled women can avail this opportunity, since many women in Bangladesh are married and have young children at this age. This policy has in fact made the situation of female migration more vulnerable, since less-skilled women are migrating through irregular processes, which increases the threat of trafficking and exploitation in various forms for which they cannot resort to any governmental assistance. The Government of Bangladesh is also deprived of the benefits of a functional labour force as it uses irregular remittance channels.

Though families of female migrants are better off now, the villagers do not find it decent for women to work abroad. This is partly due to their outlook towards women and partly due to the fact that women are vulnerable to exploitation, harassment and abuse by the employers.[7] However, some of the returnee female migrants feel that their work abroad made them feel empowered. As the number of female migrants is not significant, and they are engaged only in low-paid jobs, the impact of remittances on education and healthcare of children is not clear. The social impact of female migration has been mixed in Bangladesh in the sense that, in some cases, the migration of women gave better educational opportunities to children, while in others, children's education suffered due to the absence of their mothers (Siddiqui, 2003).

Policy recommendations

International migration has received increasing attention from the Government of Bangladesh over the years, which has been reflected through various efforts taken by the government. Some of the initiatives include the creation of the BMET in 1976 to ensure the welfare of migrant workers, the formulation of a new Emigration Ordinance in 1982 and the establishment of the Ministry of Expatriate Welfare and Overseas Employment in 2001. However, short-term international migration of low-skilled workers is still an area beset with several bottlenecks that need to be addressed by the policy makers.

---

[7] In addition to low wages and working conditions, gender-specific physical and sexual harassment are common for female migrants in many countries. This sometimes leads to serious health consequences and results in termination of the contract (ILO, 2004; UNGA, 2004).

Domestic policies

The need for a comprehensive policy is urgent in order to facilitate short-term migration and to benefit from the experience and knowledge gained by Bangladeshi workers abroad and remittances sent by them. Such a policy should focus on the following issues.

Facilitate short-term migration of the poor

The objective of poverty reduction would be better materialised by increasing the number of low-skilled workers. The poor lack resources to acquire training and take up jobs as migrant workers in developed countries. The government and micro-finance institutions may take initiatives to provide credit and training to potential poor migrants. This will help poor people as they do not have to borrow from local moneylenders at a very high interest rate. The Government of Bangladesh and NGOs should also take initiatives for imparting basic training in terms of skills, language, rights and obligations, savings and money transfers before the departure of the migrants. Poor workers could be issued passports free of cost and without hassle.

Access to information

Most low-skilled migrants decide to migrate without adequate information, which is often risky and costly. The government should provide information on opportunities of migration and the risks associated with them. There should also be a mechanism to stop poor people from remote areas receiving prospective job information. Information on labour markets and their trends can be provided through institutions set up towards this end.

Improve efficiency of remittances

Gains from the temporary movement of workers are subject to low remittance cost and high returns on migrants' savings. Most of the migrants from the villages in the case study remit money through banking channels. However, they send money through informal channels such as *Hundi*[8] if the money is needed urgently. They prefer *Hundi* over banking channels

---

[8] In the *Hundi* system, the migrant gives money to an intermediary who informs the agent in the country of origin of the amount and instructs them to pay the equivalent of the money to the recipient. The recipient collects the money from the agent by using the code that s/he receives from the migrant. An informal exchange rate is used to determine the amount of money in local currency.

because of the lower processing cost and the instant delivery facility. Only on rare occasions do migrants send money through friends visiting Bangladesh.[9] As *Hundi* is an informal method and is based entirely on trust, without any official documents in the process of remitting money, there is always a risk involved in the method. However, the low-income remitters have no alternative but to adopt this method to save their hard-earned money. Some have mentioned harassment and various types of cheating at the airport after their return to Bangladesh. Therefore, efforts must be taken to reduce costs of sending remittances in order to encourage remittances going through legal channels. Banks should monitor timely delivery of remittances to the migrants' families.

Maximise utilisation of remittances

The remitters should be encouraged to save their wages and send more to their home country. Doing so will not only help their families but may also help in reintegrating the migrants into the economic activities of their home countries upon their return. Information on various savings instruments and investment opportunities and schemes should be disseminated among them.

Special attention of female migrants

Policies should be formulated for greater inclusion of women in migration since there is growing evidence that female migrants can play a crucial role in poverty reduction through food security, education and healthcare by using remittances. Poor women should be provided with better access to banking and loans. The labour attaché in foreign missions of Bangladesh should monitor that work visas of women should allow mobility to enable them to escape abuse and exploitation.

Monitoring labour-exporting agencies

The poor mostly sell assets (such as land) or borrow money from friends and relatives at high interest rates to avail the opportunity to migrate and earn better wages. However, migration or attempts to migrate may lead to impoverishment of workers if they are defrauded. Incidences of such fraudulence are common in Bangladesh. The migrants complain that after migration, they do not get the jobs, payments and benefits they are

---

[9] A study on the migrants in the UAE found that 46% of the total volume of transactions had been channeled through official methods, approximately 40% going through *Hundi*, 5% through friends and relatives and 8% was hand-carried by migrants themselves (Siddiqui and Abrar, 2001).

promised by the recruiting agencies before migration. Lack of accommodation facilities and humiliation and assault from locals in the destination countries are other problems for the migrants. They also reported that there exist discrepancies in salary levels between migrants from different countries, and migrants from Bangladesh get the lowest wages compared to migrants from other countries. The government should strengthen the monitoring mechanism of the labour-exporting agencies to prevent fraud and exploitation.

Improving social and human rights conditions

Foreign missions in destination countries should provide counseling services, welfare assistance, information and advisory programmes and orientation on arrival and should monitor working and living conditions of migrants. Labour attachés at Bangladesh missions abroad should receive training in dealing of migration issues and problems of Bangladeshi workers.

Institutional support to the returnee migrants

Absorption of the skilled returnees in the local economy is also important. Once the migrants are back in the country, they have to be reintegrated into the domestic labour market. Reintegration may be done through supporting the returnees in various forms, such as providing loans to invest in self-employment activities.

Negotiation at the global level

Bangladesh has an active interest in the temporary movement of semi-skilled and low-skilled workers under GATS mode 4, while the commitment of developed countries covers mainly professionals. On the other hand, Bangladesh's interest in mode 4 is somewhat different from other developing countries that like to export skilled labour. Mode 4 has received less attention during the post-Hong Kong meetings at the WTO, and there has been little substantive progress in the mode 4 negotiations under the GATS. The bilateral and plurilateral negotiations have not made any significant progress in mode 4 liberalisation. Developed countries have not made any discernible departure from their position on opening up their markets under mode 4.

In this context, Bangladesh has to continuously push the agenda of mode 4 in the WTO so that negotiations for formulating necessary disciplines for mode 4 are concluded before the conclusion of market-access negotiations during the Doha Round. Desired market access of workers from countries such as Bangladesh is restricted by a number of provisions made by developed countries. Bangladeshi migrants face several problems in overseas markets in terms of immigration restrictions, recognition and licensing requirements, the requirement of social security, wage disparity, lack of transparency in classification of natural persons, stringent qualification norms for various professional services and the requirement for an economic-needs test. Moreover, for the low-skilled worker, it is particularly difficult to enter some developed countries, as they have undertaken Most Favoured Nation (MFN) exceptions to allow labour into their countries only from those countries that are geographically close or have some colonial, cultural or linguistic relations. As Bangladesh does not have such an agreement with any developed country, the removal of MFN exceptions will help Bangladesh to seek market access for low-skilled labour.

Outside the GATS process, Bangladesh should also pursue the issue of short-term labour migration in various trade and economic cooperation agreements. Bilateral agreements can improve the benefits of temporary movements of workers for countries of origin through greater certainty of access and enabling conditions. Such agreements can ensure that credentials of migrant workers are accepted in the destination countries. Information on demand for labour in various sectors in destination countries and adequate bargaining power to negotiate terms and conditions of employment are pre-requisites for successful agreements. Bilateral agreements can include provisions such as monitoring and managing migrations.

Conclusions

Given the advantageous situation of Bangladesh in terms of being a labour-abundant country, Bangladesh has the potential of becoming a key global player as a source country for the supply of less-skilled human resources to developed countries. Therefore, the temporary movement of low-skilled workers can be an important strategy for poverty reduction through maximising the outflow of workers and the inflow of remittances. The findings of this case study suggest that, for effective migration management, adequate institutional structures and mechanisms have to be in place. The developmental impact of migration depends to a great extent on the policies concerning labour outflows, education, training, capacity building, remittances and protection of interests of workers. Hence, well-developed and institutionalised overseas employment regulation can have economic and social impacts. In order to maximise the benefit of the temporary movement of low-skilled workers, a well-planned and holistic approach has to be adopted to support low-skilled migrant workers from the pre-departure stage to their stay in destination countries, and even to the period after their return home.

Bibliography

Abrar, C. R. (2000), *On the Margin: Refugees, Migrants and Minorities*, Refugee and Migratory Movements Research Unit (RMMRU): Dhaka.

Adams, R. H. (2004), 'Remittances and Poverty in Guatemala', World Bank Policy Research Working Paper No. 3418, World Bank: Washington, WA.

Adams, R. H. and Page, J. (2005), 'Do International Migration and Remittances Reduce Poverty in Developing Countries?', *World Development* 33(10): 1645–69.

Afsar, R., Yunus, M. and Islam, A. B. M. S. (2002), *Are Migrants after the 'Golden Deer'? A Study on Cost-benefit Analysis of Overseas Migration by the Bangladeshi Labour*, IOM, Regional Office for South Asia: Dhaka.

Ahmad, Q. K. and Zohara, F. (1997), *Utilization of Remittances from Abroad for Local Employment Promotion: The Case of Sylhet Division*, ILO and Bangladesh Unnayan Parishad (Mimeo): Dhaka.

Alesina, A. and Rodrik, D. (1994), 'Distributive Politics and Economic Growth', *Quarterly Journal of Economics* 109(2): 465–90.

Asis, M. M. B. (2002), 'International Migration: An Emerging Opportunity for the Socio-Economic Development of the ESCAP Region', Social Policy Paper No. 6 (United Nations Publications Sales No. E.02. II. F.40).

Banerjee, A. and Newman, A. (1993), 'Occupational Choice and the Process of Economic Development', *Journal of Political Economy* 101(2): 274–98.

De, P. and Ratha, D. (2005), 'Remittance Income and Household Welfare: Evidence from Sri Lanka Integrated Household Survey', unpublished paper, Development Research Group, World Bank: Washington, WA.

de Bruyn, T. and Kuddus, U. (2005), *Dynamics of Remittance Utilisation in Bangladesh*, International Organisation for Migration (IOM): Dhaka.

Funkhouser, E. (1992), 'Migration from Nicaragua: Some Recent Evidence', *World Development* 20(3): 1209–18.

Gardner, K. (1995), *Global Migrants, Local Lives: Travel and Transformation in Rural Bangladesh*, Clarendon Press: Oxford.

Gustafsson, B. and Makonnen, N. (1993), 'Poverty and Remittances in Lesotho', *Journal of African Economics* 2(2): 49–73.

International Labour Organization (ILO) (2004), *Gender and Migration in Arab States: The Case of Domestic Workers*, International Labour Office: Geneva.

International Monetary Fund (IMF) (2005), *World Economic Outlook*, IMF: Washington, WA.

Kuddus, U. M. (2003), 'Channeling Diaspora Remittance into the Securities Market of Bangladesh', internship report for IOM, Institute of Business Administration, University of Dhaka: Dhaka.

Mahmood, R. A. (1991), *Employment of Bangladeshis Abroad and Uses of their Remittances*, Bangladesh Institute of Development Studies: Mimeo.

(1994), 'Analysis of Present and Future Emigration Dynamics in Bangladesh', paper presented at the IOM/UNFPA meeting on Emigration Dynamics of Developing Countries, Bellagio, Italy, October 1994.

(1996), 'Immigration Dynamics in Bangladesh: Level, Pattern and Implications', paper presented for the Asiatic Society of Bangladesh, Dhaka.

(1998), 'Globalisation, International Migration and Human Development: Linkages and Implications', United Nations Development Programme (unpublished): New York, NY.

Mahmud, W. and Osmani, S. R. (1980), 'Manpower Export from Bangladesh to the Middle East: A Cost Benefit Analysis', Bangladesh Institute of Development Studies: Mimeo.

McKenzie, D. and Rapport, H. (2004), 'Network Effects and the Dynamics of Migration and Inequality: Theory and Evidence from Mexico', Working Paper No. 201, Stanford Center for International Development: Stanford, CA.

Murshid, K. A. S., Iqbal, K. and Ahmed, M. (2002), *A Study on Remittance Inflows and Utilization*, IOM, Regional Office for South Asia: Dhaka.

Persson, T. and Tabellini, G. (1994), 'Is Inequality Harmful for Growth?', *The American Economic Review* 84(3): 600–21.

Siddiqui, T. (2001), *Transcending Boundaries: Labour Migration of Women from Bangladesh*, The University Press Limited: Dhaka.

(2002a), 'Migration Challenges of Bangladesh: Options and Policy Recommendations', paper presented at a conference on Orderly and Humane Migration: An Emerging Development Paradigm, organised by IOM and IBS of Rajshahi University, Rajshahi, 6 August 2002.

(ed.) (2002b), *Beyond the Maze: Streamlining Labour Recruitment Process in Bangladesh*, RMMRU: Dhaka.

(2003), 'Migration as a Livelihood Strategy of the Poor: The Bangladesh Case', paper presented at the Conference on Migration, Development and Pro-poor Policy Choices in Asia, Dhaka, 22–24 June, available at www.eldrs.org/go/livelihoods [last accessed 3 April 2009].

Siddiqui, T. and Abrar, C. R. (2000), 'Contribution of Returnees: An Analytical Survey of Post-return Experience', IOM and UNDP: Dhaka.

(2001), *Migrant Worker Remittances and Micro-Finance in Bangladesh*, ILO: Dhaka/Geneva.

(2003). *Migrant Worker Remittances and Micro-Finance in Bangladesh*, Refugee and Migratory Movements research Unit, Dhaka.

Stark, O. J., Taylor, E. and Yitzhaki, S. (1986), 'Remittances and Inequality', *Economic Journal* 96(383): 722–40.

Taylor, J. E., Mora, J. and Adams, R. (2005), 'Remittances, Inequality and Poverty: Evidence from Rural Mexico', annual meeting, 24 to 27 July 2005, Providence, RI 19245, American Agricultural Economics Association (new name as of 2008: Agricultural and Applied Economics Association): Milwaukee, WI, available at http://arelibrary.ucdavis.edu/working_papers [last accessed 2 April 2009].

United Nations (UN) (2004), *World Economic and Social Survey*, UN: New York, NY.

United Nations General Assembly (UNGA) (2004), 'World Survey on the Role of Women in Development', report of the Secretary General, addendum on 'Women and International Migration', September, UNGA: New York, NY.

Winters, L. A. (2003), *The Economic Implications of Liberalising Mode 4 Trade*, School of Social Sciences, University of Sussex: London.

Wodon, Q., Lopez-Acevedo, G. and Siaens, C. (2003), 'Poverty in Mexico's Southern States', MPRA Paper No. 10578, University Library of Munich: Munich, available at http://mpra.ub.uni-muenchen.de/10574/1/MPRA_paper_10574.pdf [last accessed 2 April 2009].

World Bank (2006), *Global Economic Prospects*, World Bank: Washington, WA.

Yang, D. (2004), 'International Migration, Human capital and Entrpreneurship: Evidence from Philippine Migrants' Exchange Rate Shocks', research programme on International Migration and Development, DECRG, Policy Research Working Paper No. 3578, World Bank.

Yang, D. and Martinez, C. A. (2005), 'Remittances and Poverty in Migrants' Home Areas: Evidence from the Philippines', Serie de Documentos de Trabajo. No. 257, Departamento de Economía, Universidad de Chile: Chile, available at www-personal.umich.edu/~claudiap/yangmartinez_poverty.pdf [last accessed 2 April 2009].

4.2

Migrant remittances in the state of Kerala, India

SAIBAL KAR[*]

Introduction

Migrant remittances are increasingly recognised as an instrument of development for a large number of countries in the developing world. Several studies are available that devote substantial attention to the welfare implications of migration and inward remittances.

This case study focuses on the impact of migrant remittances on the level of poverty in the state of Kerala in India, which is well known for its large stock of migrant workers. The major impact of such migration operates through the remittances sent home.[1] The non-migrant members of these households purchase better living standards, school attendance, access to healthcare facilities and provisions for the future with the aid of such remittance receipts. Therefore, the impact of remittances on development, and more specifically poverty, are considerable for low- and middle-income countries.

Kerala produces a heterogeneous group of migrants, living and working virtually all over the world. Migrants from Kerala range from medical practitioners, accountants, lawyers and other highly skilled professionals, to vehicle drivers, mechanics, construction workers and semi-skilled or unskilled workers, with many located in different countries of the Middle East. In fact, of the large number of migrants of Indian origin working in the Gulf countries, a considerable proportion originate from Kerala (approximately 45 per cent, according to the Bureau of Labour, Government of India). Figure 4R shows the stock of migrants of Indian origin working in the Middle East. The figure clearly shows that during the Gulf wars there was a reduction in the number of migrant workers in the

---

[*] Saibal Kar is a Fellow in Economics at the Centre for Studies in Social Sciences, Calcutta, India.

[1] Of course, there are several other sources through which migration affects development and welfare, such as higher human capital formation (see Stark and Wang, 2002).

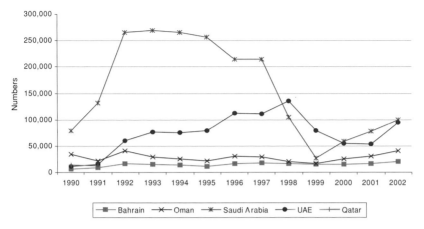

Figure 4R   Indian immigrants in the Gulf countries. *Source:* Labour Bureau, Government of India, various years.

Middle East. However, both pre-war and post-war migration trends have been significantly high, which naturally attracted attention from various quarters trying to comprehend the impact of such a large exodus on the regional and national levels. This particular case study offers some specific assessments in relation to Kerala and the impact of remittances on poverty.

Recent literature on remittances and poverty

It is generally observed that a large portion of remittances are received in kind and transferred through unofficial channels, and are therefore not accounted for in overall impact assessments. While further research is needed to reach a general consensus, some studies show that larger and more regular remittances originate from among the relatively unskilled migrant groups. Stark Taylor and Yitzhaki (1986) found that migrants from Mexico to the US, who were less skilled than internal rural-urban migrants in Mexico, remitted less than those having little or no education (Stark *et al.*, 1986, p. 732). The relatively more unskilled migrants remitted regularly to sustain their low- or middle-income households in the origin countries. Consequently, the impact of remittances on poverty at the household level is a very important issue.

A few recent studies do offer interesting observations on migrant remittances and poverty. For example, Adams and Page (2003) consider a large group of low- and middle-income countries. Using country-specific studies on remittances, income distribution and poverty, they conclude that a 10% increase in the share of remitting migrants in a country's population would lower the poverty level in the home country by 1.6%.

They also establish that the poverty head-count ratio (HCR), the poverty gap index (measuring depth of poverty) and the squared poverty gap index (measuring severity of poverty) all respond negatively and significantly to both emigration and inward remittances: as emigration and remittances go up, the poverty indexes go down. This should imply that if more remittances flow into the originating economy (or if the country produces more remitting emigrants), this is capable of reducing not only the absolute number of poor people in that country but also the mean distance below the poverty line.[2]

Individual country studies also largely corroborate these results in addition to raising other issues of considerable importance for many poorer economies. Quartey and Blankson (2004) show that migrant remittances help to reduce the impact of macroeconomic shocks, as evidenced in Ghana, through the application of consumption-smoothing policies.[3] Similarly, Aredo (2004) observes the effect of remittances on the extent of urban poverty in Ethiopia, and concludes that remittances help manage risk for members of households in adverse situations, such as during food shortages, drought, flood or unemployment.

All of these studies note that migrant remittances have been steadily increasing for many developing countries, including India, which is well known for its large annual remittance receipts.

Remittances in India and Kerala

Official remittances to India in the 2005–06 financial year reached US$21 billion, and a large part of this flowed into Kerala, a southern province, producing the largest share of emigrants in the country.[4] While migrant remittances contribute about 3% to India's gross domestic product (GDP) presently, the share of remittances to the net state domestic product (NSDP) of Kerala is quite large at 25% since 2000. This, and of course the impact such large transfers create for the local economy, may be one of the reasons why the state of Kerala, unlike any other province in the country, maintains a systematic record of emigration and a moderately

---

[2] For India, the poverty gap index for the year 2003–04 was 8.1.

[3] Migrants' departures may serve, directly or indirectly, to enhance or possibly worsen the consumption, incomes and wellbeing of those who remain in the rural areas.

[4] A district-level map of Kerala is available in Appendix 4A (Figure 4T).

long time-series of data on official remittances received. This has been accompanied by more micro-level data accumulated through a survey of 10,000 households throughout Kerala with members who have emigrated. Zachariah *et al.* (1999) offer information on a large number of demographic dimensions associated with migration and remittance receipts for these households. These data have subsequently been used for reflecting on the socioeconomic and demographic implications for Kerala.

The focal point of this case study is the causal implications of inward migrant remittances on poverty. This constitutes an in-depth analysis of the role of remittances on urban and rural poverty levels in Kerala. One would expect a rise in the flow of remittances to reduce the number of people living below the poverty line in both urban and rural parts of the province.

The rest of the case study is organised as follows. The following section offers a brief discussion on the evolving fiscal and financial conditions in India, which helps to locate the issue of migrant remittances in a relevant context. This section also includes a brief description of the changes in trade and capital-market policies that may have been significant in affecting both emigration and remittance inflows. The chapter then focuses on the important remittance-poverty nexus, where we offer observations on structural changes and cyclical tendencies of real remittances. Data for all these exercises are obtained from various issues of the *Economic Review*. The final section concludes with general observations and policy implications.

Reforms and fiscal conditions in India

The 1970s ushered in sweeping changes in the economic environment – the collapse of the Bretton Woods pegs, the first oil shock and the beginning of massive private-capital flows. In India, the move to an adjustable, pegged exchange-rate regime, based on a trade-weighted basket of currencies, corrected for the overvaluation of the exchange rate. Simultaneously, the national authorities undertook measures to provide financial incentives to draw earnings from Indian migrant labour into banking channels. These policy measures took the form of foreign and local-currency denominated deposit schemes, with significant interest rates vis-à-vis international and domestic interest rates.

Foreign currency deposits were provided with exchange rate guarantees, and both foreign and local currency deposits were provided with tax benefits. Explicit in these policy measures was a clear understanding that earnings from Indian labour deployed abroad were sent home through a variety of channels, and that there were policy instruments that could garner these flows to overcome foreign exchange constraints. Over the following years, net inflows into non-resident Indian deposit accounts in India grew significantly.

India was denied access to international financial markets by the downgrading of sovereign credit ratings throughout the 1990s. During this difficult period, India issued foreign currency bonds, directed specifically at the Indian diasporas abroad, with attractive interest-rate differentials, exchange guarantees, fiscal concessions and facilities for local transfers.

Foreign currency bonds have brought in US$11.3 billion since 1991 and have helped the economy to tide over the crisis of 1991, the sanctions imposed by the US in 1998 and the adverse global environment mainly fuelled by the recession in the US in 2000. A predominant portion of these bonds re-entered the country on redemption either as currency transfers or as inflows into the deposit schemes.

Importantly, inflows of labour earnings into the financial account have occurred without diminishing inflows into the current account. This implies that foreign currency bonds lured large investments (into the financial accounts) from residents abroad while they continued sending remittances towards maintenance of families back home (current account). In other words, this suggests that there has been a switching of some funds from extra-legal (unrecorded remittances) to legal channels. Therefore, for the recorded balance of payments statistics, there has been an addition, rather than substitution, of workers' remittances.

Migrant remittances recovered from the stagnation of the second half of the 1980s to reach US$8 billion by the mid 1990s. As the premium commanded by the unofficial exchange rate declined significantly and trade and payment restrictions eased, workers' remittances were channelled through new routes other than the traditional categories described earlier. For instance, with the liberalisation of bullion imports, allowing them to be brought in as baggage by returning Indians under a nominal customs duty, remittances took the form of gold and silver, which rose from US$1 billion in 1992–93 (the year of liberalisation) to nearly US$3 billion before the practice completely ended, subject to full relaxation of bullion imports under open general license.

Migrant remittances

Under Indian law, workers who remain outside India for more than 186 days during a financial year are regarded as non-resident Indians, and the remittances received from such sources are recorded under current transfers. In India, workers' remittances comprise transfers towards family maintenance, personal donations and gifts to charitable trusts and repatriation of savings by Indian residents abroad. These can be distinguished from capital movements, which involve transfer of ownership of fixed assets and forgiveness of liabilities by creditors.

Since 1997–98, the official statistics have clubbed together various entries into the generic heading 'inward remittances from Indian workers abroad for family maintenance'. These official transfers, however, capture only a small portion of the total receipts, since it is widely known that a significant volume of workers' remittances transit through informal channels, such as goods, precious metals and gems or as cash brought in by returning Indians. Another route of inward remittance from workers has traditionally been through local withdrawals from deposit accounts offered to non-resident Indians. In recent years, this method of remitting has gathered enough importance to warrant separate classification.

In retrospect, the attractive financial concessions for Indians working abroad, instituted during the 1990s, turned out to be effective avenues for the consolidation of workers' remittances, as the bulk of these bonds were redeemed locally. The changing profile of workers' remittances under private transfers clearly shows that transfers in the form of unrequited one-way flows not involving quid pro quo, such as gifts and donations, are only a miniscule portion of India's private transfers. Evidently, at a time of capital constraints, these avenues often provided useful funds to the state to be channelled as development expenditure. Nevertheless, since a major share of transfers was in the form of gifts and donations, remittances largely benefited a select group of households without much spill-over socially. This means that, until recently, remittances had a limited role in poverty reduction or an increase in welfare for a large number of residents in India. With extensive inflow of remittances, the present conditions seem more equitable and conducive to future general improvement due to the effects of remittances on the wider society, which we explore next.

Migrant remittances and poverty in Kerala

We begin by a brief characterisation of the structural changes and cyclicality involving emigrants and migrant remittances for Kerala. Figure 4S provides evidence on the magnitude of emigration from Kerala and the remittances received.

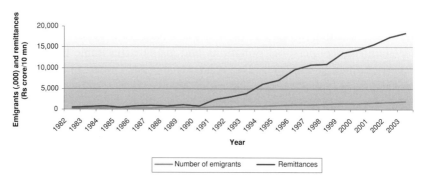

Figure 4S Total number of emigrants and remittance receipts in Kerala.
Note: 1 Billion = 100 crores. *Source:* Kerala State Planning Board.

Structural changes in emigration and remittances

Identifying structural changes for a variable observed over a period of time helps us to understand whether there has been any movement in the trend line it generally follows. We notice that both emigration behaviour and remittance receipts display identifiable shifts from the trend, to the extent that both may be deemed 'unstable' during some periods covered under the study. In terms of poverty, this can be an important finding, since a sudden increase or decrease (differing from the projected trend) in variables can effect policy formulations in a significant manner. For example, if the migration trend follows a positive structural shift in the post-reform decade in Kerala, higher remittance receipts as a consequence would now provide a larger cover for family needs, thus minimising the role of directed subsidies offered by the state. The reverse applies when events like the Gulf War force repatriation and lower the emigration flow, triggering a need for larger subsidies from the government.

Do migrant remittances move with the income cycles in Kerala?

We can identify if the trend in remittances goes hand-in-hand with income at the state level by using the technique of cyclical fluctuations. A pro-cyclical movement of real remittances implies a strong correlation between macroeconomic upswings or downswings in the state and the flow of remittances, meaning that as state income increases, so too do incoming remittances. Counter-cyclical tendencies refer to situations where remittance flow is observed to decline as the household income or state-level income increases. A counter-cyclical movement of remittances should imply that emigrants remit more when the household is facing a downturn, mitigating the income risk facing households.[5] Finding such evidence may have direct implications for poverty alleviation programmes.

Using econometric analysis,[6] the evidence suggests some correlation between these two series, leading us to conclude that real remittances flowing to Kerala are strongly pro-cyclical with the real NSDP between 1973 and 2003. In other words, there is a correlation between macroeconomic upswings or downswings and the flow of remittances: as state income rises, so too do incoming remittances.

In terms of policy, this should mean that a rise in state income attracts more remittances in the province, and therefore the entire economy can attain higher levels of both simultaneously. Of course, we do not estimate the causality in this case; however, there is a popular supply-side explanation of why higher domestic income may attract larger remittances. A higher income often relaxes the financial constraint on migration decisions and might culminate in larger emigration and consequently higher remittance receipts.[7]

However, this pro-cyclical trend also indicates that a downturn in state performance may cause a lower inflow of remittances (other than the family maintenance component), causing further distress. In short, migrants may choose to keep their money offshore until the domestic economy improves. If this is true, then migrant remittances do not play the role of insurers against downturns in the economy. Clearly, this has significant implications for poverty alleviation arising out of remittance movements.

Effects of migrant remittances on urban and rural poverty in Kerala

Finally, let us concentrate on analysing the impact of migrant remittances on urban and rural poverty levels in Kerala between 1973 and 2003. Given the fact that migrant remittances received in Kerala have increasingly constituted a large percentage of the NSDP (a rise from 0.57% in 1973 to

---

[5] A well-known method, namely the Hodrick-Prescott filter (Hodrick and Prescott, 1980), separates the trend of each series (i.e. de-trends) from its cyclical (fluctuating) components. The test of pro-cyclicality or counter-cyclicality between two variables is in obtaining the correlation between the cyclical components of the variables and not the trends. At the regional or state-level, this requires de-trending the real remittances and the real NSDP and isolating the cyclical counterparts.

[6] We have recalculated the aggregate remittances and the NSDP as real remittances (nominal remittances divided by the Consumer Price Index (CPI)) and real NSDP, by using CPI for industrial workers (base year 1993) as the price deflator.

[7] Kar and Beladi (2004) discuss such effects.

about 23% in 2000; Kannan and Hari, 2002), it is expected that the impact of remittance earnings (both cash and in kind) is positive and significant on the income and consumption levels of not only the direct recipients of the remittances but also for wider society. As noted previously, it has been estimated that a rise of 10% of remitting emigrants in a country's GDP can lower the share of people living in poverty by up to 1.6%.

While a detailed connection between remittances and poverty at the aggregate level is unavailable for India, despite large remittance inflows into the country, region-specific data and analyses for Kerala have been considerable. Zachariah *et al.* (1999) and Zachariah *et al.* (2002) claim that the outreach of remittances received is substantial – contributing to educational, health and other conspicuous consumption expenditures. The benefits of remittances are also expected to be more widely dispersed for Kerala than what is observed in most other regional or country experiences because the emigrants originate not from one or a few major locations but from all over the state, covering both urban and rural districts.[8]

In fact, the rural districts of Malappuram and Kannur separately produced more emigrants in 2004 than the capital city of Thiruvananthapuram (Table 4I). Also, the percentage change in emigrants from several rural districts is quite high compared to the state capital. (Kottayam registers a 200 per cent increase within a five-year period.) If such emigration leads to transfer of remittances, then it is quite plausible that the impact of remittances is considerable for both rural and urban poverty levels in the state.

It is documented in several other studies on poverty and inequality in India that national- or state-level surveys report the percentages of poor people and the level of inequality[9] only intermittently over various periods of time. The poverty and inequality measurements available for our purposes have thirteen entries for the state of Kerala between 1973 and 2003. The major findings of this study include the following.[10]

Both the urban and rural HCRs register negative sensitivities with both per capita NSDP and remittances as a proportion of NSDP. This implies

---

[8] See the map of Kerala in Appendix 4A.
[9] The statistic used to describe the degree of inequality in a distribution is called the Gini coefficient.
[10] The complete econometric exercise may be made available to the interested reader on request. A longitudinal panel data set was used with variables of HCR, poverty gap, squared poverty gap, Gini coefficient for Kerala, average per capita expenditure and remittances as a proportion of NSDP.

Table 4I *Distribution and change in total number of emigrants for districts in Kerala (1999–2004)*

District	Emigrants			Emigrants per 100 households			Return emigrants		
	2004	1999	% change	2004	1999	% change	2004	1999	% change
Thiruvanantha-puram	168,046	130,705	28.57	21.5	19.9	8.04	103,059	118,878	−13.30690
Kollam	148,457	102,977	44.17	24.4	18.4	32.61	69,314	74,106	−6.46641
Pathanamthitta	133,720	97,505	37.14	44.3	33.1	33.84	83,502	54,537	53.11073
Alappuzha	75,036	62,870	19.35	15.2	13.2	15.15	43,109	34,572	24.69339
Kottayam	106,569	35,494	200.25	24.0	9.1	163.74	28,368	18,164	56.17705
Idukki	7,880	7,390	6.63	2.9	2.9	0.00	3,766	5,017	−24.93520
Eranakulam	121,237	103,750	16.85	16.9	17.0	−0.59	74,435	45,028	65.30825
Thrissur	178,867	161,102	11.03	27.2	25.6	6.25	86,029	116,788	−26.33750
Palakkad	177,876	116,026	53.31	32.6	21.8	49.54	55,008	39,238	40.19063
Malappuram	271,787	296,710	−8.40	45.0	49.2	−8.54	141,537	123,750	14.37333
Kozhikode	167,436	116,026	44.31	28.6	22.0	30.00	109,101	60,910	79.11837
Wayanad	7,704	4,552	69.24	4.4	2.9	51.72	3,852	3,327	15.77998
Kannur	202,414	88,065	129.85	43.2	19.0	127.37	45,394	28,263	60.61282
Kasaragod	71,449	38,747	84.40	30.6	19.1	60.21	47,468	16,667	184.80230
Total	**1,838,478**	**1,361,955**	**34.99**	**26.7**	**21.4**	**24.77**	**893,942**	**739,245**	**20.92635**

Source: Kerala State Planning Board, *Economic Review 2004.*

that a rise in both per capita NSDP and remittances as a share of this lowers the HCR in urban and rural districts. Thus, a rise in remittances directly reduces poverty in both rural and urban areas.

The sensitivity of HCR to the remittance share in NSDP is quite small for both urban and rural areas. However, the absolute value of the level of sensitivity of rural HCR is higher than that of urban HCR. This implies that a 100% increase in remittances as a share of NSDP will reduce the rural head-count poverty ratio by 8% compared to a possible reduction in urban head-count poverty ratio by 7%. In other words, if remittances (as a share of state domestic product for each person in the population) double, 8 out of every 100 poor people in the rural districts will be lifted out of poverty, compared to 7 out of every 100 people in the urban areas. Thus, a rise in remittances entails a larger benefit for the rural poor compared to their urban counterparts.

The sensitivity of both rural and urban poverty estimates, with that of the level of inequality, is close to one and statistically significant. In other words, the higher the level of inequality, the higher the level of poverty, and this follows an almost one-to-one correspondence. In isolation, such a result is neither novel nor unexpected. What is special about this finding is the fact that we consider such changes in rural and urban poverty measures in the presence of remittance receipts by respective households, when remittance receipts by themselves can alter the level of intra-household inequality. These findings show that it is quite likely that we can expect rising income inequality between households owing to the inflow of remittances, and this in turn can temporarily exacerbate the poverty situation.

In brief, therefore, the relationships explored in this section clearly identify that remittances can help to reduce rural and urban poverty in a significant manner. The negative relationship between remittances as a share of NSDP and both rural and urban HCRs implies that a higher relative contribution from migrant remittances directly reduces poverty levels.

General observations and policies

Externality and social spillover

While the direct impact of remittances leads to a reduction of both rural and urban poverty, its individualistic nature makes an understanding of the extent of the impact on social spillover difficult. Spillover, or externality, implies something that affects wider society, and is not just concentrated in a few quarters. A positive externality arises from, for example, enjoying the view of a garden that one's neighbour maintains. Air pollution, on the other hand, is an example of a negative externality for those who are not directly, or are indirectly, responsible for it. While remittances have definite direct impacts for the receiving households, this study has not explored their externality or social spillover impacts for the wider society within Kerala. So although it is generally understood in the literature that they are a positive externality, the limits of this study have not allowed it to be proven so here. If externalities are closely accounted for in other studies dealing with the overall impact of remittances, it is possible that the present predictions of change in poverty levels are underestimates.

Consider a poor village that regularly sends migrants to a foreign country, who then send back remittances in cash or kind. The prime beneficiaries are obviously the members of that migrant's household. The increased wealth in that household would spill over to the local markets, financial intermediaries and so on. However, if the village was initially devoid of adequate educational or healthcare facilities, this substandard infrastructure would not necessarily improve with such income effects.

It is possible that private facilities may develop to cater to these richer remittance-receiving households, but this would not be automatic and would hardly be inclusive, and the general problem of market failure may continue (consider the unavailability of paved roads, covered sewage systems, street lights or clean drinking water). The households that could afford to might even move to a location where better facilities were available, creating both interpersonal and inter-regional disparities in income. Without voluntary and concerted efforts among the rural beneficiaries to set up these facilities, or active involvement of the state in providing the same by suitable taxation schemes on remittance receipts, the benefits of remittances can be very individualistic.

Migration and remittance transfers have been the result of individual optimising behaviour as a dominant mechanism, and are mostly uninfluenced by any social spillover returns they might generate. For example, it is indeed likely that positive probability of migration in a society induces human capital formation among the non-migrants when social return from such action accumulates over private returns. One needs to determine the flow of migrants and remittance receipts based on what is optimal for society. Given the huge stock of migrants, and yet a limited dependence on private actions to foster local economic growth, there is a strong cause for public intervention to take stock of the advantages and disadvantages and adopt corrective measures if required.

This calls for systematic information on the pattern of emigration and mode of transfers, which subsequently can help to design suitable tax-subsidy schemes for promoting technical education, language proficiency and necessary public goods. A greater provision of public goods, including schools, healthcare systems or publicly managed immigrant advice centres created with direct contributions from the emigrants themselves, can help to realise some of the positive externalities that individual decisions generate. It is established in the literature that probability of migration up to a certain level is welfare-enhancing for all non-migrants, both in terms of human capital formation and average income growth. This implies that a well-designed migration policy enforced by the government is always better than one that is fully influenced by private-market decisions alone.

The state's role in remittances and poverty reduction

The participation of the government in facilitating and managing remittance flows is important, as relevant information on various aspects that potentially influence migration and remittances are often external to individual agents and can be better acted upon from a macroeconomic national perspective. A central repository of information and resources might play a very important role in devising incentive schemes, either to stall or facilitate migration depending upon the social optimum. Thus, it is imperative on the part of the state to take constant account of the impact of migration and remittances and use the information to revise existing policies. While considerable information is available on Kerala, there are many other regions within India with a substantially large flow of emigrants that do not preserve any systematic account of either migration or remittance inflows. The concerned departments should prioritise the collection and dissemination of relevant information.

Seasonality of migration or remittance receipts can also be an important source of information for state budgetary provisions, to tide over periods of downturn. During the recent Gulf Wars, many migrants from Kerala had to leave their jobs and return home, facing an uncertain future. A state highly dependent on migrant income may consider making adjustments for various global shocks that migrants may face from time to time. In fact, government reports in Kerala state that various arrangements, including alternative occupational involvements, establishment of counselling and advisory cells and schooling for children on an emergency basis were made to ease the transition of returning migrants during the crisis. The Kerala model may act as a learning device for other states or even smaller countries that face similar situations.

The impact of remittances as commonly observed are rather localised in character, which again can potentially create pockets of affluence and high dependence on such external sources of income. The state could act more specifically to create buffers against any adverse income shocks (remembering that a significant share is generated from dependence on oil resources in the Middle East). The state could offer guidance towards alternative choices, among which fostering higher levels of human capital and access to public goods should be a priority. This is even more important in light of mode 4 (the movement of natural persons), as being negotiated under the GATS and now through various free trade agreements. The state can use migrant remittances to the advantage of both migrants and non-migrants by putting the funds towards building infrastructure that can generate high returns on each unit of capital invested. Some of these policies have been put to the test in Kerala, and the rest of the country needs to examine these features more seriously to explore a very potent source of development.

It must be re-emphasised that even conservative estimates of the impact of remittances on poverty are significant, and that migrant remittances may be considered a successful tool in favour of poverty reduction. However, it must also be noted that if migration is limited by the access to resources available to a limited number of households, its impact would be individualistic and would not spill over to the entire economy. In this regard, intervention from the government in devising appropriate tax-subsidy schemes to re-distribute the gains from migration and remittance receipts in the form of public goods may actually improve the conditions of the migrant household even more than what can be achieved on the basis of individual action.

Since migration is often the result of strategic decisions undertaken by an individual or by the family to which he/she belongs, interventions by the government may not be easy. However, keeping in mind that the state is often actively involved in managing the flow or representing the causes of non-residents, its policies aimed at improving the level of welfare would be acceptable to a large number of such households, and would be especially welcome by those who largely depend on public provisions and other forms of social capital.

In conclusion, this case study has highlighted three particular aspects regarding migrant labour and the impact of remittances: firstly, that there is a positive relation between remittances and poverty reduction in Kerala;

secondly, that inequality may increase as a result of a more individualised system of remittance flow; and thirdly, that some state intervention in the form of accurate statistical monitoring, tax incentives and direct policies are needed to develop public goods of benefit for the wider Kerala community, and indeed India as a whole. Future studies could consider these findings for more detailed analysis.

References

Adams, Jr., R. and Page, J. (2003), 'International Migration, Remittances and Poverty in Developing Countries', World Bank Policy Research Working Paper 3179: Washington, WA.

Aredo, D. (2004), 'Migrant Remittances, Shocks and Poverty in Urban Ethiopia: An Analysis of Micro Level Panel Data', research paper, Macroeconomic Policy Challenges of Low-Income Countries, GDN: Washington, WA.

Hodrick, R. J. and Prescott, E. C. (1980), 'Postwar US Business Cycles: An Empirical Investigation', Discussion Paper No. 451, Carnegie Mellon University: Pittsburgh, PA.

Kar, S. and Beladi, H. (2004), 'Skill Formation and Trade Reform – Welfare Perspective of Developing Countries', Japan and the World Economy 16(1): 35–54.

Kannan, K. and Hari, K. S. (2002), 'Kerala's Gulf Connection – Emigration, Remittances and their Macroeconomic Impact 1972–2000', CDS Working Paper No. 328: Thiruvananthapuram, Kerala.

Quartey, P. and Blankson, T. (2004), 'Do Migrant Remittances Minimize the Impact of Macro-volatility on the Poor in Ghana?' research paper, Macroeconomic Policy Challenges of Low-Income Countries, GDN: Washington, WA.

Stark, O., Taylor, J. E. and Yitzhaki, S. (1986), 'Remittances and Inequality', The Economic Journal 96(383): 722–40.

Stark, O. and Wang, Y. (2002), 'Inducing Human Capital Formation: Migration as a Substitute for Subsidies', Journal of Public Economics 86(1): 29–46.

Zachariah, K. C., Mathew, E. T. and Rajan, S. I. (1999), 'Impact of Migration on Kerala's Economy and Society', CDS Working Paper No. 297: Thiruvananthapuram, Kerala.

Zachariah, K. C., Prakash, B. A. and Rajan, S. I. (2002), 'Gulf Migration Study: Employment, Wages and Working Conditions of Kerala Emigrants in the United Arab Emirates', CDS Working Paper No. 326: Thiruvananthapuram, Kerala.

Appendix 4A

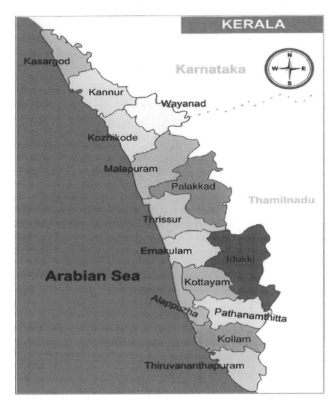

Figure 4T   District map of Kerala. *Source:* www.mapquest.com [last accessed 26 March 2009].

Migrant workers and the role of remittances in Indonesia

NUR HADI WIYONO AND DWINI HANDAYANI*

Background

In 2005, Indonesia was the fourth-largest populated country in the world, with a population of 218,868,791.[1] Such an abundance of human resources could be an asset or a burden to an economy, depending on the capability and productivity of the citizens.

After the financial crisis that struck Indonesia in 1997, the economy grew at a rate of 5.5 per cent in 2006.[2] However, this growth could not absorb all of the Indonesian labour force, and in 2006 it was estimated that 10 million people were looking for work. Some of those who were not absorbed in the local labour market chose to work abroad. Data from the Ministry of Manpower and Transmigration shows that the number of Indonesians temporarily working abroad (migrant workers) increased from 295,000 in 2001 to 1,680,000 in 2006.

Since the 1980s, four destinations have become the main 'receiving' countries for Indonesian migrant workers: Malaysia, Singapore, Hong Kong and Saudi Arabia. In these countries, the demand for low-skilled workers is high. Most Indonesian migrant workers are employed in '3D' (dirty, dangerous, difficult) jobs, as these are usually shunned by the local population in the receiving country. The types of 3D jobs include: agricultural work, construction, house cleaning, drivers and manufacturing work. In the four listed receiving countries, Indonesian men are likely to work in the agricultural field, whilst mainly women work in the personal services sector.

---

* Nur Hadi Wiyono and Dwini Handayani are researchers with the Demographic Institute Faculty of Economics at the University of Indonesia.
[1] Figure taken from www.datastatistik-indonesia.com/component/option,com_tabel/kat,1/idtabel,111/Itemid,165 [last accessed 6 March 2009].
[2] Figure taken from www.antara.co.id/en [last accessed 31 May 2008].

Indonesian migrant workers are generally unskilled as they have low levels of education. In the 1970s, the Indonesian Government implemented a nine-year compulsory education programme for its citizens. A study conducted by the Ministry of Manpower and Transmigration (1997) in four provinces (West Nusa Tenggara, East Java, Yogyakarta and Central Java) showed that more than half of Indonesian migrant workers had only elementary school education or did not complete their elementary schooling. Raharto (2002), who conducted interviews with 133 returned Indonesian female migrant workers in the Cianjur and Indramayu Districts, also had similar findings; that is, 93 per cent of the interviewees had either completed elementary schooling only, did not complete elementary school or had no schooling at all. Research undertaken by Sugiyarto *et al.* (2005) demonstrates that, regardless of the government's programme, 60% of Indonesian workers have no schooling or only finished primary school. Furthermore, only 3% have attained university qualifications.

The main reason for Indonesians choosing to work abroad is the ability to earn money (remittances) and send it home to their families. Remittances are also one of the key factors in local and regional development. Studies of remittances in Indonesia show that money sent by migrant workers to their village has created new jobs and improved the physical wellbeing of the families left behind. Remittances are also used by the migrant worker for house construction, daily consumption, paying debts, educational costs and buying consumer goods like radios, tape recorders and televisions (Mantra *et al.*, 1999; Raharto, 1999).

Trade policies and agreements relevant to Indonesian migrant workers

As a 'sending' country, Indonesia has actively exported migrant workers categorised as low-skilled workers since the 1970s. According to the Indonesian Government's policy, exportation of migrant workers is expected to earn foreign exchange of about US\$5.9 billion by the year 2009; therefore, such activities are an important part of the economy and foreign trade.

In relation to trade policy, governments face many sensitive issues surrounding the incorporation of low-skilled workers into a trade in services agreement regardless of it being an international, regional or bilateral treaty.

International commitments are found in the General Agreement on Trade in Services (GATS). The GATS mode 4 (movement of natural persons) is one of four modes of supply in trade in services, and refers to the provision of the service by an individual outside the country of his/her residence on a temporary basis. However, mode 4 generally only pertains to the transfer of professional and highly skilled workers linked to a commercial operation. The common application of mode 4 is done through the intra-corporate transfer of people consisting of professionals, technical and other workers usually affiliated with transnational corporations (TNCs) (Tullao and Cortez, 2006). Most of the temporary movement of labour from Indonesia, however, is not the result of capital movements and the transfer of professionals within TNCs, but is rather a response to economic and demographic asymmetries.

In relation to regional agreements, low-skilled labour issues are not seen as a priority. The 12th ASEAN Summit in Cebu, the Philippines, held on 13 January 2007, promulgated that 'the Leaders agreed to hasten the establishment of the ASEAN Economic Community by 2015 and to transform ASEAN into a region with free movement of goods, services, investment, *skilled labour*, and freer flow of capital'[3] (authors' italics).

In the absence of regional agreements, Indonesia uses bilateral agreements with receiving countries that are not part of a trade in services agreement. Agreements are needed to provide an understanding of, and transparency in, regulations so that migrant workers can enter a designated receiving country legally and with the appropriate skills and knowledge. Transparency and knowledge of regulations are key factors for protecting Indonesian migrant workers, especially because of their limited education and consequent poor communication skills. Interviewees accounted stories of legal Indonesian migrant workers who entered a receiving country and subsequently became illegal because they didn't know how to renew their work permit. Furthermore, allegations of human rights violations abound, in that migrant works have been beaten or, in extreme instances, sexually abused.

Malaysia and Korea are among the several receiving countries for the movement of temporary migrant workers from Indonesia. In 2004, the Governments of Indonesia and Malaysia signed a Memorandum of Understanding (MOU) on the placement of Indonesian workers in Malaysia. In 2006, Indonesia and Malaysia signed another MOU on the recruitment and placement of Indonesian domestic workers. Indonesia

---

[3] Available at www.wto.org/english/tratop_e/tpr_e/g184_e.doc [last accessed 6 March 2009].

has also signed an MOU with the Government of the Republic of Korea on the sending of Indonesian migrant workers. Both these bilateral agreements were developed to protect the wellbeing of Indonesian migrant workers.[4]

Government policies on migration and remittances

In 1983, the government introduced regulations for the sending of Indonesian migrant workers abroad. Private overseas labour agencies were given permission to send workers to Middle East countries (Ananta and Arifin, 2007). Since then, the government has actively promoted migration of workers abroad as one alternative to reduce unemployment.

In the 1990s, much of the migration of workers was directed to wealthier countries in Asia (Singapore, Malaysia, Hong Kong and Korea). However, such workers, especially women migrants, faced significant problems related to work, such as exploitation, abuse and underpayment. These problems have encouraged the Indonesian Government to make laws that protect migrant workers from the time of their departure until their return. In 2004, the government released a new regulation: Law No. 39/2004 on the Placement and Protection of Indonesian Overseas Workers. The new Law replaced the Ministry of Manpower and Transmigration's decree that regulates the placement of migrant workers abroad. The process of placement and the protection of migrant workers, as stated in the Law, can be divided into three stages: (i) pre-departure, (ii) the time overseas and (iii) upon return. Most of the articles in the Law apply only to the pre-departure and upon-return stages because Indonesian law does not, of course, have jurisdiction in the receiving countries.

In the departure stage, an important issue is ensuring that a prospective migrant worker has the skills that match the job requirements. The overseas labour agency should provide proper training to a prospective migrant worker, and at the end of the training, the individual must pass an examination and earn a competency certificate. Furthermore, a prospective migrant worker should be at least eighteen years old and have graduated from junior high school.

Upon arriving in a receiving country, a migrant worker should immediately report to the Indonesian Embassy or its representative so that the Embassy Officers can quickly locate the individual in an emergency

---

[4] These MOUs and other agreements/communications held with other countries are listed at www.deplu.go.id/download/treaties [last accessed 6 March 2009].

and the migrant worker has a direct point of contact if he/she should encounter difficulties. Upon returning to Indonesia, the government provides returned facilities and protection against blackmailing and cheating so that the individual can return home safely.

The Law states that the Ministry of Manpower and Transmigration is responsible for the making of regulations and laws regarding the placement and protection of migrant workers. Furthermore, the Law states that a National Board of Placement and Protection of Indonesian Migrant Workers (BNP2TKI) should be established. The BNP2TKI's task is to deal with day-to-day service operations and issues of placement and protection of migrant workers.

The Law further states that BNP2TKI has an obligation to improve the welfare of migrant workers and their families. BNP2TKI staff interviewed for this case study revealed that some activities had improved the welfare of migrant workers. For example, a one-week entrepreneurship training course for returned migrant workers is conducted. The training included how to develop a business, how to prepare credit proposals for a bank and advice on how to market products created by ex-migrant workers.

These interviews with BNP2TKI staff further revealed that the government does not have any regulations on migrant workers' remittances. Furthermore, during the pre-departure stage, there is an orientation seminar for prospective migrant workers in which they receive information on how to send money home and how to establish a bank account.

The Karawang district: research, results and findings

The setting

The Karawang district is located on the northern coastal plain of West Java. It is one of the richest agricultural areas in Java but is also strongly influenced by the size of Jakarta, which lies within commuting distance to the West. Karawang is known for its high-quality rice production and fertile soil. Most of the land in the Karawang district is used for agriculture. However, the contribution of agriculture to the regional gross domestic product (RGDP) is less significant compared to other sectors such as the manufacturing and services trade. In 2005, the manufacturing sector made the highest contribution to Karawang's RGDP (54%), followed by trade in the hotel and restaurant sector (20%) and the agriculture sector (10%). Other sectors contributed less than 5%. In 2005, Karawang's economy grew by 6.5% compared with 6% in 2004.

Table 4J *Population by sex and age group, Karawang district (2006)*

Age group	Male	Female	Total
0–14	282,666	259,840	542,506
15–64	683,250	712,383	1,395,633
65+	40,289	36,897	77,186
Total	**1,006,205**	**1,009,120**	**2,015,325**

Source: Karawang Statistics Office and Karawang District Manpower Agency (2006).

Table 4K *Distribution of labour force by sex, Karawang district (2006)*

	Male	%	Female	%	Total	%
Labour force	647,493	73.9	228,699	26.1	876,192	100
Employed	560,472	77.1	166,752	22.9	727,224	100
Unemployed	87,021	58.4	61,947	41.6	148,968	100
Not in the labour force	35,757	6.9	483,684	93.1	519,441	100

Source: Karawang Statistics Office and Karawang District Manpower Agency (2006).

The total Karawang population in 2006 was 2,015,325, 1,395,633 persons of which were of working age (fifteen to sixty-four years) (see Table 4J), 876,192 were in the labour force (employed or unemployed) and 519,441 were not in the labour force (students, housekeepers and retired workers). The number of unemployed person was 148,968, most of whom had low levels of education (see Table 4K).

With regard to education, in 2006, 38% of the population had no schooling or had some elementary school education, 34% graduated from elementary school, 14% attained junior high school education, 12% attained high school education and 2% had attained university-level education. The increasing job opportunities in the growing manufacturing industry could not be filled by those with lower education levels (elementary or under). On the other hand, job opportunities in the agricultural sector had decreased due to the land being converted to housing and factories. Hence, many Karawang district locals turned to migration work.

Migration and remittances

The interviews with returned migrant workers in the Karawang district conducted for this case study revealed that poverty and the lack of employment opportunities are the most important factors that drive people to leave their villages and work overseas. Typically, they sign on for a two-year contract in jobs such as domestic workers, drivers, shopkeepers and restaurant or factory workers in Saudi Arabia, South Korea, Malaysia and Brunei. Some earn Rp 1.2 to Rp 1.5 million (US$133 to US$166) a month as domestic workers, while those who work in South Korean factories can earn as much as Rp 12 million (US$1,333) a month. Compared to similar jobs in Indonesia, wages in the listed receiving countries are three to six times higher.

However, working overseas is not an easy process. One requires money to pay for administrative costs, training and medical check-ups. These costs range from Rp 3 million to Rp 20 million (US$333 to US$2,222) depending on the country of destination. This money is usually either borrowed from the 'sponsor' (recruiter/broker) or obtained by selling things (i.e. land, electronic goods and jewellery). The interest rate for borrowing from the sponsor is very high, and could be as high as 300 per cent. This means that if a prospective migrant borrows Rp 1 million (US$111) from the sponsor, they have to return Rp 3 million (US$333). This amount is deducted from their wages whilst working abroad. Usually, for migrant workers that borrow money from the sponsor, the repayment of the loan costs 2.3 months of their wage. Borrowing from the sponsor is needed because there is no borrowing system in the village that could accommodate a loan, as most migrant workers have no collateral.[5] On the one hand, this informal system seems like a helping hand, but on the other, the system can trap migrant workers into debt, especially those who bring home limited money because of work-related problems in the receiving country, or those who have to return home prematurely.

At the district level, remittances received by the migrant households were significantly higher than the total district revenue (*Pendapatan Asli Daerah* – PAD). In the Karawang district, the PAD that was collected from local tax, retribution tax and profits of district-owned corporations in 2005 was Rp 82.5 billion (US$9,166,666), compared with remittances in the same year received by households at Rp 306.6 billion (US$34,066,666) (see Table 4L).

---

[5] The Indonesian Government has provided credit for prospective migrant workers; however, citizens do not know that this is available.

Table 4L   *The number of household receiving remittances (Rp) from migrant workers, Karawang district, West Java (2006)*

Destination countries	Number of households receiving remittances			
	<Rp 2 million	Rp 2–5 million	>Rp 5 million	Total
Middle East	9,124	47,705	25,973	82,802
Malaysia/Brunei	1,557	698	–	2,255
Singapore/Hong Kong	–	213	–	213
Japan/Korea/Taiwan	–	–	814	814
Total	10,681	48,616	26,787	86,084

Source: Karawang Statistics Office and Karawang District Manpower Agency (2006).

The methods for remitting money that are mostly used by migrant workers are cheques, wired transfers through the banking system and hand-carrying money with them when they return home.

Migrant workers in Saudi Arabia found it convenient to send their money home by cheque, as domestic workers are not permitted to go alone to the bank – they are usually helped in this by their employers. However, sending money by cheque often took three to four weeks to reach the recipients, and the method was risky because some of the cheques received were forged or cheques were lost.

Furthermore, most migrant workers were reluctant to use bank accounts because their family members (as the recipients) were often une-ducated and bank illiterate. Dealing with the banking system in Indonesia is complicated. In many instances, the recipients were not familiar with banking-system procedures. The recipients of the remittances were hus-bands, wives, mothers, fathers and siblings.

The BNP2TKI officer interviewed emphasised that migrant workers should have a bank account to transfer their money home, since this system is the safest and fastest. In orientation seminars, they were told how to use a bank account to transfer remittances. The problem remains, however, that there is a fear of using the Indonesian banking system due to the low educational standards of many families.

Use of remittances

The uses to which remittances were put varied depending on the amount of remittances saved and sent. The first and most important thing was to repay the debt to the sponsor; this could be paid back in three or four instalments during the period of the contract.

Secondly, remittances were used to purchase consumer goods, including daily consumption (food). One of the returned migrant workers interviewed said:

> When I [twenty-five-year-old male, single] was working in Brunei, I still had to assume responsibility for the support of my family left behind, my grandmother and my siblings. The money I got mostly went on meeting the daily needs. I am like a mother bird leaving baby birds in the nest waiting to be fed.

In the daily consumption context, many families of migrant workers fail to fulfil these daily needs as they have to purchase their daily needs from the *warung* (small shops in the village). The purchasing is actually a borrowing with interest, which is repaid upon receipt of money from abroad. The system depresses these families. For example, if they borrow 1 kilogram of rice, they end up paying for 2 kilograms of rice. It is called the 'get one and pay for two' way. In the end, the family is often deeper in debt.

Thirdly, remittances were used to build or renovate houses, as having a good house is a dream of many migrant workers. Housing is a symbol of prestige and status in village society. As land and construction costs are expensive, it is common for migrant workers to construct a house stage by stage. Usually during the first contract period (two years), a migrant worker is only able to purchase a piece of land where the house would be built. In the second contract period, a simple house could be built. If a migrant worker is satisfied with the house, travelling aboard will cease. If not, another episode of migration will occur.

Using remittances for housing was widespread in the villages visited for this study. One of the returned migrants interviewed (forty-five-year-old woman, married) said that she built two houses, one for her mother and one for herself, during seven contract periods (a total of fourteen years).

Building and renovating houses also creates job opportunities for others in the village, such as material sellers and house builders. Workers in this sector, usually non-migrants, earn income, and this contributes to their wellbeing. In a small way, it creates a multiplier effect.

Fourthly, the remittances were used for various forms of investment, such as purchasing farm land, opening small shops, starting a recycling business and running a motorcycle taxi.

In a Karawang district village, investing in farm land is the most productive and profitable investment, as land is fertile and very suitable for cultivating a rice paddy – rice being a staple food for most Indonesians. However, the impact of remittance inflows into villages has inflated the price of fertile land.

One returned migrant worker (twenty-five-year-old male, married with one child) used his remittance to purchase three hectares of fertile land, which cost Rp 300 million. In addition, he continued his schooling by completing a university degree. He also married an ex-migrant worker (who has worked as a domestic worker in Saudi Arabia) and is now known as a successful person in his village because he owns a house and has a steady income from his rice paddy field. Furthermore, his education has led him to open a new business that is unusual in his village: a waste collection service that sells and buys waste.[6] This business is a joint venture with other returned migrant workers. The multiplier effect occurs because other villagers are involved.

The success of this migrant worker can be contrasted with that of another migrant worker (thirty-year-old female, divorced with one child, who worked in Hong Kong) who, with her friends, tried to make a difference by forming a savings group. Such enterprises are typically formed amongst people from the same region – they save an amount of money and then try to create a small business for their families back home. The individual and her friends attempted to breed cows. Unfortunately, they did not have the knowledge of how to manage such a business or of where to sell their cows. They went bankrupt, and she highlights that at that time, there was no one to ask for assistance.

Comparison with other regions of Indonesia

Although the contribution of remittances to the overall national economy is small, such contributions to a local economy (province and district level) are important. A World Bank study in 2006 (2006b) found that remittances (in Rp billion) that flow into the provinces of East Java and West Nusa Tenggara, two provinces that are major sources of migrant workers, exceed the total development revenue for the provinces. This is similar to findings in the Sukabumi district (West Java province), where the remittances received were much higher compared to development

---

[6] He collects waste such as used plasticware and home appliances from local villagers. The waste is then sold to a recycling factory.

revenue. It is important to note that the government only recorded remittances through formal channels (using wire transfers and the banking system), whereas remittances sent by migrant workers through informal channels were not recorded. If the remittances through informal channels were included, the amount of remittances received by the local economies would be substantially larger.

Research on remittance conducted at the household level in other regions in Indonesia confirms the findings of the Karawang district study. Based on a study in three provinces (East Flores (East Nusa Tenggara province), Central Lombok (West Nusa Tenggara province) and Bawean Island (East Java province)), Mantra *et al.* (1999) found that, besides being used to build and renovate houses, remittances were also used for daily consumption, paying debt, educational costs, buying radios, tape recorders and televisions. The remittances were also used to create productive jobs, such as buying a motorcycle for use as a motorcycle taxi.[7] Based on East Nusa Tenggara data, Hugo (2002) stated that a significant amount of remittance income is spent on building or substantially renovating houses.

In the Indramayu district (West Java province), Noveria (2001) found that some returned female migrant workers were able to purchase rice fields, open small shops and breed poultry. It was common for returned migrants to successfully transform their job status from agricultural labourers to land or business owners in their village.

In Sukasari Village of the Sukabumi district (West Java province), Adi (1996) found that 58 per cent of 189 migrant workers used their remittances to build/renovate their house, repay debts and purchase rice fields. The remittances they obtained created work opportunities for other villagers in Sukasari Village as a result of the multiplier effect from the construction or renovation of houses.

In the Tulungagung district (East Java province), returned female migrant workers from Saudi Arabia invested their money by financing their children's education, and some have even graduated from university. This is to be contrasted with the condition before large-scale migration of workers abroad, when many families could only send their children to elementary school (Kelana, 1999).

---

[7] Motorcycle taxis are becoming a popular mode of transportation in Indonesia, especially in villages where there is no transportation system.

Remittances, poverty issues and trade policy

Do remittances sent by migrant workers alleviate poverty? If alleviating poverty is indicated by the acquisition of land, brick houses, vehicles, jewellery or furniture, then most migrant workers have been successful and remittances do alleviate poverty.

Being a migrant worker is a trend among household members in the Karawang district, and it is seen as one avenue out of poverty. With little education, a person could earn SAR 600 (approximately Rp 1,200,000 or US$1,333.3) in Saudi Arabia, and this can enhance both their material wellbeing and their status at home. Many of the examples given above confirm the very important significance of remittances in the poverty reduction equation, especially where good advice and training has been put in place to assist women and men in using and investing their earnings wisely.

It is difficult to distinguish between investment and consumption in the context of remittance use. House construction, road construction, a social contribution for weddings, mosques and churches etc. can generate multiplier effects if the money received is spent on various goods, services and labourers within the village, or even neighbouring villages. Spending money on electronics and furniture, for example, also stimulates business opportunities for electronic shops, shopkeepers or for the furniture craft industry. In the short term, the indirect effects of remittances in villages are particularly important.

In connection with trade policy, the Indonesian Government is committed to further trade liberalisation to promote economic development and to alleviate poverty through social safety-net programmes including food safety, education, health and employment creation. The role envisaged for trade policy is to promote opportunity, community empowerment and capacity building, focusing on small and medium enterprises (SMEs) (WTO, 2007).

To some extent, remittances have stimulated the development of SMEs, especially in providing working capital to initiate the business. As there is a lack of credit provisions in villages, the remittance-funded capital has boosted many village economies.

Alternatively, 'remittances may ease credit constraint because a stable stream of remittance income may make households more creditworthy in the eyes of formal sector financial institutions. Remittance receipts that increase when the household receives an adverse shock may be more important in relaxing credit constraints, since they increase the lender's confidence that they will be repaid even if things turn badly for the household' (World Bank, 2006a).

With regard to capacity building for SMEs for returned migrant workers, the study found that the provision of entrepreneurship training conducted by the Ministry of Manpower and Transmigration was very limited. As the budget is limited, the Ministry is very selective in recruiting participants, and therefore not all migrants have access to such training.

The implications for policy makers in the future

Remittances received in Indonesia have not only benefited migrant workers and their families, but also have had a significant multiplier effect on other people within their village or even outside the village. Therefore, remittances are able to alleviate migrant workers and their families from poverty by directly increasing income. They also provide a safety net for a family, especially when facing adverse events such as crop failure. Indirectly, remittances are used by migrant families as working capital to initiate small businesses or as savings and investment vehicles, for example by purchasing land or jewellery (gold).

It is important to emphasise that not all returned migrant workers are successful in achieving their dreams. Unlucky returnees may come home empty handed or even with an injury because of bad treatment or an accident in the workplace.

Overall, however, this case study has put forward considerable evidence that remittances can play a vital role in both the direct and indirect reduction of poverty, particularly if those remittances are spent intelligently. The following recommendations therefore seek to ensure the safety and training needs of Indonesian migrant workers, along with incentives to ensure the best use of remittances for poverty alleviation.

Recommendations

Firstly, in the future, the Indonesian Government should consider improving the balance of unskilled workers (domestic workers, plantation labourers etc.) and semi-skilled or skilled ones (nurses, caregivers and engineers) sent overseas. This needs to be done by improving the education and training system, especially in vocational schools and through government training institutions. By sending more semi-skilled or skilled workers, the Indonesian Government not only will receive larger foreign exchange earnings, but it will also reduce exploitation and abuse in the workplace. However, this is a long-term goal as, at present, Indonesia is predominantly competing in the international labour market for unskilled workers.

Secondly, it is important that Indonesian migrant workers have the appropriate skills and are provided with information to ensure they can do the work well overseas, as well as be protected.

Thirdly, many prospective migrants heavily depend on the sponsor (middle man) to finance the pre-departure cost (medical check-ups, administration and training costs) and as a result often build up large debts. The Indonesian Government should encourage the establishment of a formal financial system that could help the migrant worker's financial needs, such as daily consumption and costs that occur during the pre-departure stage. Although the government has launched a credit programme for prospective migrants, this information needs to be accessible to all prospective migrants throughout Indonesia.

Fourthly, the Indonesian Government at district level should pay more attention to how remittances can most effectively boost village economic development. District governments could provide entrepreneurship training so that migrant workers and their families can operate their own business and generate employment in the village. The problem faced by returnees is that they do not know how to create business opportunities in the village, where the majority of people rely on agricultural work. District governments could also make the bureaucratic placement process of migrant workers simpler. This would reduce placement costs and in turn would reduce the migrant worker's burden. A final point is that Law No. 39/2004 should permit district governments to regulate the placement and protection of migrant workers abroad – such regulations should be implemented.

Finally, since it appears that it will take some time for negotiations to liberalise the movement of unskilled workers, either in the Doha Round or, for that matter, under the ASEAN Framework for Agreement and Services (AFAS), the Indonesian Government should strengthen bilateral agreements on labour mobility, emphasising the need of training and protection for migrant works. Indonesia could request that Malaysia, Korea and Japan, who have already signed MOUs, must do all that they can to enforce stringent measures on employers and intermediaries so that Indonesian workers will not be abused or underpaid in the workplace. The

Indonesian Government could also encourage other receiving countries, such as those in the Middle East, to sign comprehensive MOUs.

Bibliography

Adi, R. (1996), 'The Impact of International Labour Migration in Indonesia', unpublished PhD Dissertation for the University of Adelaide: Adelaide.

Ananta, A. and Arifin, E. N. (2007), 'National Agency of Placement and Protection of Indonesian Overseas Workers (BNP2TKI): Marketization of Public Service', paper presented at the Regional Symposium on Managing Labour Migration in East Asia: Policies and Outcomes Singapore, 16–18 May 2007.

Hugo, G. (2002), 'Effect of International Migration on the Family in Indonesia', *Asia and Pacific Migration Journal* 11(1): 13–46.

Karawang Statistics Office and Karawang District Manpower Agency (2006), *The 2006 District Labor Force Survey (Sakerda)*, Karawang Statistics Office: Karawang, West Java.

Kelana, Y. (1999), *Tulungagung Kabupaten TKI (Tulungagung District as Home for Overseas Migrant Workers)*, Pewarta Foundation: Jakarta.

Ministry of Manpower and Transmigration (1997), *Studi Kebijakan Perluasan Kesempatan Kerja bagi Tenaga Kerja Indonesia Purna Tugas (Policy Study on the Job Opportunities Extension for Indonesian Returned Migrant Workers)*, Ministry of Manpower and Transmigration: Jakarta.

Mantra, I. B., Kasto and Keban, Y. T. (1999), *Mobilitas Tenaga Kerja Indonesia ke Malaysia: Studi Kasus Flores Timur, Lombok Tengah, Pulau Bawean (Indonesian Migrant Workers Movement to Malaysia: Case Study in East Flores, Central Lombok, Bawean Island)*, PPK-UGM: Yogyakarta.

Noveria, M. (2001), 'Menjadi Pekerja Migran di Malaysia dan Arab Saudi: Pilihan di Tengah Keterbatasan Kesempatan Kerja di Dalam Negeri (Being Migrant Workers in Malaysia and Saudi Arabia: Choice Opportinities)', *Penduduk dan Pembangunan* 3 (December): 63–83.

Raharto, A. (2002), 'Indonesian Female Labor Migration: Experience Working Overseas (A Case Study among Returned Migration in West Java)', *Journal of Population* 8(1): 73–98.

Raharto, A. (ed.) (1999), *Migrasi dan Pembangunan di Kawasan Indonesia Timur: Isu Ketenagakerjaan (Migration and Development in Eastern Indonesia: Employment Issues*, PPT-LIPI: Jakarta.

Skeldon, R. (2002). 'Migration and Poverty', *Asia-Pacific Population Journal*, Vol. 17, No. 4.

Sugiyarto, G., Gardiner, M. O. and Triaswati, N. (2005), *Improving the Labor Market Condition in Indonesia*, Mimeograph: Jakarta.

Tullao, T. S. and Cortez, M. A. A. (2006), "Enhancing the Movement of Natural Persons in the ASEAN Region: Opportunities and Constraints', *Asia-Pacific Trade and Investment Review* 2(2): 71–91.

World Bank (2006a), *Global Economic Prospects: Economics Implications of Remittance and Migration*, World Bank: Washington, WA.

    (2006b), *Migration, Remittance and Female Migrant Workers*, available at http://siteresources.worldbank.org/INTINDONESIA/Resources/fact_sheet-migrant_workers_en_jan06.pdf [last accessed 6 March 2009].

WTO (2007), 'Trade Policy Review: Indonesia', WT/TPR/S/117, available at www.wto.org/english/tratop_e/tpr_e/s117-2_e.doc [last accessed 1 April 2009].

Labour mobility and poverty reduction in Tonga

SALOTE VAIMOANO TAUKOLO,[*] JIM REDDEN[**] AND
RAELYN ESAU[***]

Background

The Kingdom of Tonga has a population of 101,134 people inhabiting thirty-six of 170 islands, with a total land area of 700,000 square kilometres. It is clustered into three main groups: Tongatapu, Ha'apai and Vava'u. The island of Tongatapu is inhabited by more than 70 per cent of the population. The general household unit in Tonga is the extended family, which operates as a basic unit to fulfil socioeconomic obligations and therefore plays a vital role as the backbone of Tongan society.[1] Christianity plays a significant role in Tongan society, and it is the practice of families in Tonga to give a significant portion of remittance to their various churches.

The average age of the Tongan working population is very youthful at just under twenty-five years old, and the population of working-age inhabitants (fifteen to sixty five years old) is 63,085. A recent Labour Force Survey in Tonga indicated that the current income-receiving labour force was at 28,151. A large number work in subsistence agriculture with no formal income, and there are few opportunities for young people. Unemployment remains a problem, particularly for young people. The current youth unemployment rate (fifteen to twenty-four years old) is at

---

[*] Salote Vaimoana Taukolo is Deputy Director of Tonga Trade at the Ministry of Labour, Commerce and Industries for the Kingdom of Tonga.

[**] Jim Redden is Director of International Programmes for China and the Pacific and Senior Lecturer at the Institute for International Trade, the University of Adelaide.

[***] Raelyn Esau is Deputy Director of the Policy and Planning Division at the Ministry of Education, Tonga.

[1] B. D. Vaden (1998), 'Kainga: Tongan Families as Agents of Change', unpublished PhD Dissertation, A. Bell and Howell Company: Michigan, IL.

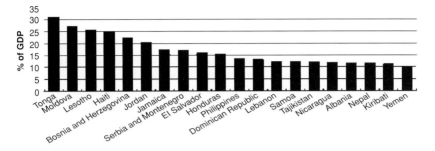

Figure 4U   Remittances as a percentage of GDP – top twenty countries. *Source:* IMF (2003), *World Economic Outlook Report.*

approximately 11.9 per cent, but this figure underestimates the real level of youth unemployment and under-employment.

All land in the country is the property of the Crown, with the provision that every Tongan male above the age of sixteen is entitled to a tax allotment of 3.3 hectares of farm land (*'api tukuhau*) and a town allotment of 700 square metres (*'api kolo*). This system of land tenure provides the basis for subsistence living and cash crop farming, which, in turn, is the major source of livelihood and security. However, the pressure generated by population increase has led to a decrease in the population being assigned an allotment. It is therefore one of the main factors either pushing people to the urban centre of Nuku'alofa in search of employment or pushing them to emigrate.

Given the lack of jobs and potential of higher wages overseas, many Tongan choose to emigrate. Evidence suggests that the number of Tongans working overseas is around 100,000, with the larger Tongan communities being in the US, Australia and New Zealand. This trend means that remittances are the single largest component of the Tongan economy, with Tongans displaying a strong commitment to their families and communities. In fact, if the level of remittances as a percentage of gross domestic product (GDP) is any measure, then Tonga ranks number one in the world (see Figure 4U).

Although remittances were predicted to decrease as Tongan families put down roots in their new countries, the trend is continuing towards sustaining the current high level of contributions, mainly because of close family and community ties, particularly if one takes account of both official figures and the transfer of in-kind goods. These official figures underestimate the real amount of remittances that enter Tonga, because significant amounts come through various unofficial channels[2] or are sent back as goods in kind.

Overall, the Tongan economy is characterised by large trade deficits, with a heavy reliance on external development assistance and private remittances from Tongan communities overseas. Tonga's export base is very narrow. Geographical isolation and a narrow land and resource base restrict the scope for export diversification and import substitution. That said, significant potential still exists to develop Tonga's export base, as will be discussed in the last section of this case study. Agriculture and services dominate the economy. Agricultural exports make up two thirds of total exports. Agriculture (including fisheries and forests) accounted for 28.3% of GDP in 2004 and consisted mainly of production of domestic food and a narrow range of cash crops (vanilla, squash, kava and watermelons) with declining tuna and fish exports. Services accounted for nearly 54.3% (50% in 2000) of GDP in 2004, of which about one quarter was government activity in one form or another. Tourism was the second largest source of hard currency earnings after remittances.

Tropical cyclones annually hitting Tonga are a major threat to the economy. Cyclones destroy vital infrastructure and disadvantage the country in competing for international trade market share. Hence, international migration is regarded not only as a safety valve[3] but as a buffer that could allow Tonga to develop its resilience and capacity to finance future economic development. By 2007, the Reserve Bank in Tonga estimated that the value of remittances had risen to almost 45 per cent of Tonga's GDP. Given the obvious value of overall remittances to Tonga as a small and vulnerable economy, the purpose of the rest of this case study is to:

- assess how significant labour mobility and remittances are for poverty reduction in Tonga
- give an initial evaluation of the Tonga–New Zealand labour mobility scheme as a useful model to progress labour mobility for unskilled, low-income earners

[2] R. P. C. Brown (1997), 'Estimating Remittance Functions for Pacific Island Migrants', *World Development* 25(4): 613–26; (1995), 'Hidden Foreign Exchange Flows: Estimating Unofficial Remittances to Tonga and Western Samoa', *Asian and Pacific Migration Journal* 4(1): 35–54; (1994), 'Migrants' Remittances, Savings and Investment in the South Pacific', *International Labour Review* 133(3): 347–67.

[3] J. Connell (1983), 'Migration, Employment and Development in the South Pacific'. Country Report No. 18, Tonga, Noumea, New Caledonia. South Pacific Commission and International Labour Organization.

Table 4M   *Private remittances per currency*

	AU$	NZ$	TOP	US$	Other
2001	14,741,762	10,255,658	6,917,233	89,632,997	3,570,273
2002	19,330,896	12,887,867	10,677,699	102,453,073	3,581,046
2003	20,432,193	17,464,282	10,103,799	111,715,154	5,279,877
2004	24,090,715	12,809,038	18,444,915	141,510,184	5,870,304
2005	18,538,847	17,415,778	58,883,017	98,472,767	9,359,869
2006	12,762,925	15,993,554	53,469,661	99,985,102	3,464,827

Source: National Reserve Bank of Tonga.

• examine the policy role of the Tongan Government, international trading partners and donor governments in the labour market mobility equation, particularly with regards to job creation back in the Tongan economy.

The case study involved interviews and meetings with government ministers and officials, the private sector, community representatives, workers and farmers in Tonga, New Zealand, Australia and Fiji, including meetings with members of the Tongan diaspora sending remittances and with Tongans receiving remittances.

Significance of labour mobility and remittances for poverty reduction in Tonga

During the last four decades, international migration has become a way of life for people in Tonga. To date, official statistics of Tongans abroad are recorded at 40,716 in New Zealand, 36,000 in the US and 14,000 in Australia. There has been a general increase in remittances per currency since 2001, with the greatest volume of remittances coming from the US, as Table 4M shows.

The total of private remittances is a combination of the remittances from households and non-profit organisations (NGOs) like churches, where remittances from the former make up a higher proportion of total private remittances. Table 4M shows that the sheer volume of remittances is significant.

There are two views about the ongoing level of remittances. Some believe the remittance decay-hypothesis, where there will be a tendency for migrant remittances to decrease over time,[4] while others argue that remittances will be unlikely to decline due to the strength of the extended family in certain communities.[5]

With respect to Tonga, this study takes the view that remittances are unlikely to decline significantly over time because of enduring family and community ties, which in Tonga's case tend to regenerate. Evidence for this is in the remittance data provided in Table 4M, showing an overall trend towards relative sustainability in the value of remittances, and indeed an overall increase from 2001 to 2006, notwithstanding two exceptional years in 2003 and 2004 when US remittances peaked. There has also been an increase in the number of Tongans working overseas and gaining dual passports so that they have the flexibility to return home and put their remittances to good use back in Tonga. According to Esau in her 2006 study on Tongans living in New Zealand, very few had taken out New Zealand citizenship as they wanted to be able to easily return home and therefore maintained their land ownership and close family ties.

Based on interviews and visits to various villages around the main island of Tongatapu, there is strong consensus about the value of remittances in reducing poverty, based on increases in material wealth, consumption and savings, particularly for lower-income families largely dependent on overseas remittances. This anecdotal evidence gained from Tongan communities is strongly supported by a number of more recent studies.

In the thematic paper for these case studies on labour mobility, Hugo points to a number of studies that show the positive impact of remittances on poverty reduction, including significant evidence that:

- each remittance dollar spent in consumption activity has multiplier effects that ripple through local and regional economies, having significant poverty reduction and developmental impacts.[6]
- remittances are effective in poverty reduction at a grass roots level because they are passed directly from the migrant and received by families and individuals in less developed countries (LDCs) so that

---

[4] S. T. Tongamoa (1987), 'Migration, Remittance and Development: A Tongan Perspective', unpublished MA Thesis, University of Sydney; Australia; M. L. A. Fuka (1984), 'The Auckland Tongan Community and Overseas Remittances, unpublished MA Thesis, University of Auckland: New Zealand; H. Lee (2003), *Tongans Overseas: Between Two Shores*, University of Hawaii Press. Honolulu.

[5] Brown, 'Estimating Remittance Functions for Pacific Island Migrants; R. P. C. Brown (1998), 'Do Migrants' Remittances Decline Over Time? Evidence from Tongans and Western Samoans in Australia', *The Contemporary Pacific* 10: 107–51.

[6] Taylor, J. E. and Wyatt, T. J. (1996), 'The Shadow Value of the Migrant Remittances', *Journal of Development Studies*.

they can be readily used to improve the situation of those people (as distinct from foreign direct investment (FDI) and official development assistance (ODA), which are mediated by an array of institutions that can dilute their impact at the level of individual communities and families)

- often it is in peripheral areas where remittances are the only source of foreign exchange and of capital inflow for development. With an increasing focus on regional and decentralised development in southern nations, there has been an enhanced realisation of the significance of remittances.

Hugo concludes that of all south–north financial flows, remittances are not only the largest for many smaller economies, but they also have the greatest impact upon improving the situation of ordinary people.

A World Bank report in 2006 entitled 'At Home and Away' notes that the Pacific in general has a youth population of almost 40 per cent, and that greater temporary labour mobility of lower-skilled workers would expand employment options available to younger Pacific Islanders.[7] The study undertook empirical analysis of data from remittance-recipient households in Fiji and Tonga, showing the poorest 40% of the population's share of cash income increased while the share of the richest 20% decreased in both countries. In fact, using a range of measures for deprivation, the study found remittances to have a direct and positive impact on poverty alleviation. These figures are for remittances in total, including from both permanent and temporary migration sources.

The report highlights the potential of temporary labour schemes and remittances to more specifically target the welfare of low-income households by offering employment opportunities to low-skilled and unskilled labourers. Temporary labour market schemes have the potential to make a unique contribution to poverty reduction for the following reasons:

- increased capacity to target low-income workers and unskilled labour and make an important contribution to reducing youth unemployment
- increased ability to have direct impact on income levels of lower-skilled workers' families with attendant multiplier effects in local villages and communities
- collective involvement of villages and communities in the planning and decision making of temporary labour schemes

---

[7] World Bank (2006), 'At Home and Away: Expanding Job Opportunities for Pacific Islanders through Labour Mobility', World Bank: Washington, WA, p. vii.

- the ability to design training programmes, before, during and after the temporary work programme, consistent with individual, village or broader economic needs of Tonga
- a boost to total GDP from a temporary increase in remittances over and above standing remittances from permanent migrants
- temporary labourers returning to their towns and villages with extra income and, ideally, additional skills, which address to some extent concerns about 'brain drain' issues.

There are, of course, concerns from both the Tongan point of view and from the recipient country with temporary schemes that target low-skilled workers. For example, some Tongans were concerned that low-skilled workers did not earn as much as high-skilled workers and so lessened the overall contribution to the economy. Others were concerned that remittances were not always used wisely to assist Tonga to achieve greater self-reliance, and were concerned about a tendency towards materialism, such as the noticeable increase in motor vehicles and four-wheel drives around Tonga. However, this is a general concern about use of remittances, not one specific to temporary labour.

Developed countries such as New Zealand, Australia and the US have expressed security concerns about illegal immigrants, about temporary workers overstaying, temporary labour being used to drive local wages down and that local labour will be replaced by cheaper labour from the supplier country. Future temporary labour market schemes will need to address these issues. However, while developed countries have expressed these concerns, the introduction of targeted, mutually beneficial and temporary employment schemes could be much more politically palatable in the future.

There is a growing shortage in many of these developed nations not only of agricultural labourers but of workers in the hospitality and service industries, manufacturing, construction and mining sectors, creating a clear demand for the supply of foreign labour. The World Bank report argues, for example, the benefit temporary labour schemes can have in significantly easing seasonal labour shortages in the horticultural or aged care industries of New Zealand and Australia.

With appropriate forethought and planning, there exists the potential for a 'win-win' situation, where the developed country fills specific labour shortages while the developing economy benefits from remittances, savings and the return, ideally, of more experienced and more highly skilled labour once the temporary contract is completed.

A recently devised scheme, negotiated between the Tongan and New Zealand Governments, has attempted to navigate the challenges of executing a 'win-win' seasonal scheme, endeavouring to learn from the failures of past schemes. It presents a useful model of particular relevance to this case study. It has particular implications on how future labour mobility schemes of a temporary nature might be designed to target low-skilled to unskilled workers in poverty-reducing schemes for the benefit of Tonga while assisting industry restructuring and labour market shortages in the developed country. The scheme is called the Registered Seasonal Employer (RSE) scheme, hereafter referred to simply as the RSE scheme.

The Registered Seasonal Employer scheme (RSE scheme)

The New Zealand Government recently negotiated a 'framework agreement' for the development of temporary seasonal worker schemes. Initially, at least, the RSE scheme would be open to five Pacific countries, those being Tonga, Samoa, Vanuatu, Tuvalu and Kiribati. The scheme allows Pacific workers to fill seasonal horticulture and viticulture jobs that cannot be filled by New Zealanders.

Tonga has been first off the mark to take up this offer and negotiate what is now the first labour market scheme the Tongan Government has managed. It is clearly treated as a business venture, with the New Zealand Immigration Minister describing it as part of an industry restructuring process involving employers and unions, while Tonga officials described it as an opportunity to develop and strengthen Tonga's reputation for the reliable provision of labour. The scheme has been branded as 'Tonga Works', and the benefits of the RSE scheme are being marketed to New Zealand employer organisations.

The Tongan Minister for Labour, Mr Lisiate 'Aloveita 'Akolo, has visited the farms of a number of New Zealand employers party to the scheme to hear their concerns while inspecting the accommodation and provisions made for prospective Tonga workers. Conversely, groups of New Zealand farmers have also visited specific villages in Tonga to gain a much better understanding of the environment and culture from which workers come. Before commenting on the scheme, which has only been in operation for approximately one year, it is important to outline some of the basic facts about it.

The RSE scheme commenced in April 2007 and is on target to provide temporary labour for approximately 300 workers in the first year of its operation. Seasonal work usually lasts between seven and nine months, and New Zealand employers must pay at least the minimum wage and guarantee at least thirty-hour work weeks. Trade unions have been involved in negotiating the RSE scheme from the start, and while, as stated, it is still early days, few complaints of exploitation or poor conditions have been received to date, although there have been concerns expressed about unrealistic expectations and a lack of pre-briefing information. Nevertheless, trade union involvement and the fact that employers must show that they can't fill these positions with local New Zealand labour has helped significantly in allaying any potential local fears about temporary low-waged labour undermining jobs for New Zealanders.

As noted earlier, the RSE scheme is seen not only as meeting a labour shortage in New Zealand and therefore supplying economic benefit to the New Zealand economy, but it is also part of an industry restructuring process. New Zealand employers must be registered and provide acceptable living conditions for the temporary workers. The New Zealand Government and industry bodies aim to 'upgrade' employer standards in the horticultural sector as part of this scheme. Employers must pay half of the airfare of the Tongan workers. This not only ensures employer commitment to the scheme but reduces the fixed cost borne by the Tongan worker and reduces his/her incentive to overstay.

The RSE scheme overall has involved detailed planning and negotiation. As the Minister for Immigration highlighted, for the scheme to be successful for both New Zealand producers and Tongan workers, there needed to be very significant investment in good design, consultation, negotiation, marketing and implementation. It required strong support from the New Zealand prime minister, from respective labour and immigration ministers in Tonga and from the Hon. Dr Fred Sevele, Prime Minister of Tonga.

In Tonga itself, a number of factors have so far contributed to the successful design of the RSE scheme.

Firstly, the RSE scheme involves electing local town officers and village communities in a cautious and selective process – local demand is high for a limited number of places. Tongan workers for the RSE scheme are selected at the village level by local leaders, elders and town officers keen to ensure that their respective village reaps practical gains. Selection is based on a person's income level and their suitability for the type of work required. Villages have a direct interest in ensuring that workers chosen will be responsible and will help promote the reputation of that village as a reliable source of productive workers who do not overstay. This obviously increases the chances of their village being selected again for the supply of temporary labour in the future.

It also acts as a strong disincentive for those chosen to overstay. Not only does the village community want the person chosen to return home and add valuable skills to the local economy, but they also want others to benefit or indeed the same person to be chosen again, to maintain or increase the flow of remittances to families in that village. The RSE scheme permits the rotation of the same workers.

The Tongan Government was keen that the RSE scheme be used to involve villagers in discussion about the wider implications of labour mobility schemes and use of remittances. Those consulted stated that, ideally, there would be some agreement before departure on how the individual remittance flows would be used – the aim being that remittances to villages would be used for a range of productive purposes. No doubt a significant proportion would be used for the direct benefit of the individual and his/her immediate family for basic consumption goods, housing and necessities. But there was also talk of the need to build in a personal savings component into the labourer's earnings, with a need to explore how compulsory superannuation payments from developed countries might be treated by the Tongan Government to encourage domestic savings. Town officers consulted also noted that a proportion of remittances already received had gone into village projects agreed by the local community, for example on school equipment, a fishing boat and a tractor. Further research and analysis of the expenditure patterns of remittances from low-skilled temporary labourers will be most useful in the future.

While incentives for the most effective use of remittances are still under discussion, there was no doubt about the initial positive impact of remittances for some of the first returned RSE scheme workers interviewed for the study. Paulo, for example, was using a significant proportion of his earnings to repair and build on to the one-room tin shack where a family of five lived together on a barren plot of land near the village of Kolovai. The rest, he told us, went on food, schooling and contributions to church-related activities, which are an essential part of community life in Tonga.

Tongan officials were keen for the RSE scheme to build the work ethic of Tongans, who would be exposed to how horticulture is managed in New Zealand and experience the work ethic of New Zealanders. Pre-departure briefings aim to provide each individual chosen for work in New Zealand with training and discussion on their future career objectives, how the temporary work scheme fits with those objectives, use of earnings and remittances while in New Zealand and on return, as well as discussion about training needs for adding value to the community on return and in the longer term. It was too early to assess how well this aspect had been integrated, but if such counselling and training can be well executed, requiring strong investment in pre-departure briefings, then the development objectives of the RSE scheme have a good chance of being realised.

The issue of reputation is an important one. It is not in the interest of any village or Tonga as a whole to end up with a poor reputation for their work standards or for overstaying. Tonga is competing with Vanuatu, Kiribati, Tuvalu and Samoa, not to mention in the broader picture the Philippines, Thailand and Indonesia, so it can't afford to have a bad reputation if it is to remain competitive in labour markets.

Concerns with the RSE scheme

In general, the planning and design of the RSE scheme is impressive, and the scheme deserves support and close monitoring as it proceeds. However, there are some initial concerns that will need to be either dealt with or closely monitored. There are two categories of concern. In the first category, concerns include:

(1) the scheme still being weighted to the benefit of New Zealand producers rather than for Tongan workers
(2) insufficient up-skilling of Tongan workers while in New Zealand
(3) insufficient pastoral care and contact with extended family/diaspora while in New Zealand
(4) the risk of employers swapping to cheaper Asian labour in the future
(5) unrealistic expectations by Tongan workers before they leave
(6) transaction costs of remittances
(7) lack of savings incentives such as superannuation schemes back in Tonga.

Point (1) is perhaps a bit cynical – there are benefits both ways, as Tongan workers who took part in the study were keen to point out, but at all points along this scheme's supply chain, there needs to be checks on how there will be both short-term and long-term benefits for Tongan workers – and one key to this is the emphasis that must be put on training, in terms of up-skilling and vocational training. Point (2) is therefore valid and can and should be addressed. Point (3) can be addressed with an agreed framework for liaison with family and the Tongan diaspora, and point (4) is about long-term demand and supply, which the scheme is trying to address by ensuring a good reputation for Tongan workers. A closer, less costly, reliable supply of Tongan workers can result in seasonal employers preferring Tongans in favour of Asian workers. However, many factors are at play here, and given future skill shortages in New Zealand throughout the wider economy, there should be room for both Pacific and Asian temporary labour market schemes.

The unrealistic expectations of workers before leaving requires urgent attention. Some of the returned workers had inflated ideas of the level of wages they were going to earn, while others found that the amount of wages being extracted for food and accommodation were exorbitant. On the one hand, there needs to be greater attention paid to the detail and quality of pre-departure briefings, while in New Zealand, close monitoring of wages and conditions are essential.

Transaction costs are a major bone of contention, with agents such as Western Union, the ANZ and various other financial intermediaries charging high transaction fees for each individual transaction. Various solutions are currently being negotiated to try and find alternatives with both New Zealand and Tongan Governments seeking meetings with the various financial institutions involved.

The treatment of superannuation and other non-wage benefit is also a matter requiring further discussion, but it would be ideal if New Zealand could work with the Tongan Government in developing consistent financial regulations to assist workers with superannuation, pension and leave-entitlement issues.

In addition to these concerns, there were also some more fundamental concerns expressed, which need to be carefully considered:

(1) Alongside insufficient training in New Zealand is the lack of training and jobs upon their return to Tonga. Job creation in Tonga is part of a longer-term issue that can't be immediately addressed through one RSE scheme, but it may be able to assist in a small way if remittances are used wisely for savings and for investment in agricultural production and trade in services. Job creation and productive investment in Tonga is the subject of the last section of this study.

(2) It was argued by some that a number of Tongan workers in the RSE scheme would see this scheme mainly as a ticket for eventual migration out of Tonga – either to New Zealand or to another developed country. They referred to past schemes of a similar nature where Tongans were granted temporary work visas, and most stayed or went

home only to return later permanently – some illegally. The test of this RSE scheme will be the measure of how many workers return long term to Tonga and contribute to their village and economy. Advocates of the RSE scheme argue that much is being done to address this issue through initial pre-departure planning and the involvement of village elders, town officers and the local community in the selection process, with strong penalties to the village and Tonga if workers overstay or 'go missing' in New Zealand. The Tongan Minister for Labour, Hon. Lisiate 'Aloveita 'Akolo, strongly reinforced this aspect, as did interviews with Tongans involved in the first RSE scheme. Time will tell, but there is no doubt that strong incentives and sanctions are in place to ensure both remittances and workers return home safely.

Notwithstanding these important concerns, initial anecdotal evidence would seem to suggest that the RSE scheme should lead to direct improvement in the standards of living not only for the Tongan workers themselves but through the multiplier effects of their remittances to extended families back home. If Tongans can improve and build on their reputation as good workers and use such schemes to start investing in their skills and projects back home, they should be given every opportunity to succeed. While it is far too early to be drawing conclusive lessons, the planning and consultation processes to date have been impressive.

Bringing them home – employment and sustainability

The case study has so far reflected on a number of specific benefits that greater labour-market liberalisation of low-skilled and unskilled workers can confer, whether that eventuates through trade agreements or through more general bilateral agreements. It has raised some important issues, including the significance of a 'bottom-up' selection process, continuous training, worker rights and safety, workers overstaying, the costs associated with sending remittances home and the wise use of remittances in Tonga. This final section focuses on that last point and further reflects on the importance of Tonga investing in its most valued resource – its people – and on how Tonga can best create investment and jobs for people back in Tonga so that in the future, temporary workers have further training and employment opportunities to come home to.

Working overseas and remitting are, after all, a means to an end – each worker wants to earn money for him or herself, their families and their community while developing skills and experience to secure their future. While for some, and particularly young people, there is a desire to experience the bright lights and opportunities of Sydney or Auckland, for most there is a real desire to return home to their own communities and land, so long as there are jobs and security to come home to. By providing greater opportunity for employment and training in Tonga, there is a mutually reinforcing three-fold effect:

(1) The tendency for workers to overstay is reduced, to the benefit of the village or community she/he will return to and to the relief of the migrant-receiving government.
(2) It increases the desire and the opportunities for returning migrants and temporary labour to use their labour and remittances to invest their time and money in industry and services back home.
(3) More jobs back home not only boosts economic growth in Tonga but assists in reducing over-dependence on remittances and aid in the future.

Achieving these outcomes will continue to be challenging, but there are a number of ways forward for Tonga to utilise labour mobility schemes and remittances alongside existing development strategies to increase jobs and economic growth at home.

Strengthen ongoing training and career guidance programmes

Throughout this case study there has been strong emphasis on the value of training and career counselling. The analysis of the Tonga–New Zealand RSE scheme points to the importance that must be placed on pre-departure counselling, of on-the-job training and follow-up debriefings once a temporary worker returns home if we are to ensure the up-skilling of workers and value-addition of such programmes.

Pre-departure counselling in the RSE scheme aimed to brief participants not only on what they should expect in New Zealand, but aimed to focus importantly on both the long-term career interests of the selected participant and the future needs of the local village community. It is not yet clear as to how well these pre-departure briefings and career counselling exercises are going in the RSE scheme. However, the ideal for this scheme and others that might follow is to match the participant's interests and ambitions with Tonga's development needs so that, ideally, a young labourer, for example, is being geared for a future in managing a sustainable SME in services or agriculture.

Using this example, the on-the-job training might then include, apart from performing the actual labour (such as fruit-picking), exposure to work ethics and practices in the developed country, a component of training or advice from the local employer/farmer in the developed economy on how to operate a successful business and manage farm finances and, if possible, some specifically designed vocational training in the developed country once the work is completed, for example a technical course on financial and business management. Finally, this training would be reinforced by vocational training to similar ends back in Tonga, with a strong focus on managing a small business with a clear understanding of Tongan conditions, problems and opportunities. There is significant room for cooperation and coordination between the two countries concerned across all levels of training.

This example extrapolates one stage in the temporary work/training cycle, but as many workers return to do further overseas contracts, there is the opportunity to coordinate and consolidate long-term work experience and training programmes for each individual.

Secondary and tertiary education in Tonga – improving qualifications at home

The previous example focused on the up-skilling of low-skilled labour during the course or life cycle of temporary work schemes in foreign countries. Tonga also needs to continue to increase the overall educational qualifications and skills of its people through its own secondary and tertiary teaching institutions in order to:

- build and consolidate its own skilled workforce, particularly for the future of its services industries
- take advantage of future increased demand overseas for more skilled workers, for example in health or tourist services.

Civil society representatives in Tonga emphasised the importance of improving educational standards across primary, secondary and tertiary institutions. They identified the problem of high student–teacher ratios, with as many as sixty students to one teacher in some primary classes. One of the key problems identified was that a number of teaching graduates pursue higher wages abroad, leaving a shortage of qualified teachers in Tonga – the same issue applied to nurses, doctors and medical staff pursing higher paid work abroad to the neglect of health services at home.

The Ministry of Employment in Tonga also highlighted the need for an increased focus on technical training and accreditation recognised not only in developed countries such as Australia but in other Pacific Island countries – an issue that could be addressed in Pacific Island Countries Trade Agreement (PICTA) negotiations.

Graeme Hugo discusses the possibility of the compensation of origin countries for the expenses incurred by the state, in this case the Government of Tonga, in the education of emigrants (see thematic paper). He suggests that this might take the form of extra, targeted development assistance. Options such as these need further research, but clearly there is significant room for increased cooperation between the Tongan Government and donor countries in prioritising the needs of the education sector in order to deal with the brain drain problem and resultant shortage of skilled labour at home.

Tonga might want to explore the Grenadian model of attracting private-sector investment in the tertiary off-shore education sector (see the case study in Chapter 5). This would require significant investment in services and accommodation for students, but some of this could be met through joint private-public sector partnerships. There is potentially a unique, niche market for tertiary educational institutions with a strong Christian ethos, which would be of appeal to markets in the US, Australia and New Zealand.

Remittances for development – tax incentives, savings and the private sector

The Government of Tonga should further explore how it can best utilise remittances for its development goals. To some extent, it is already doing this; for example, in the RSE scheme, selected participants are encouraged strongly, or in some cases told, to set aside a portion of their remittances for investment in village-based development projects. In addition to this, tax incentives such as concessions or tax credits can be directed to those who invest in particular industries in Tonga, such as in vital infrastructure or in the establishment of SMEs consistent with Tonga's development plans.

Hugo mentions a number of innovative programmes that have been introduced in Mexico with success. These include programmes where federal and state governments match remittances to undertake developmental activity in depressed regions. Given the small size of the islands that constitute the Kingdom of Tonga, along with the close-knit family and community networks across the islands, there is the potential to target those selected for work programmes and the use of subsequent remittances to areas or sectors of high need. The matching component could be on the basis of well-developed community/private sector-based business plans that can demonstrate adequate research, marketing advice and specified outcomes.

Compulsory savings schemes and incentives for future savings can be further developed through a government taxation policy and compulsory employer contributions to pension funds. Temporary labour market schemes should include foreign employers contributing a portion of overall wages paid to pension or superannuation funds that are transparent and transferable back to Tonga. The remittances of the Tongan diaspora should be targeted to encourage productive investment back in Tonga, with associated education and marketing campaigns directed to specific diaspora communities, for example in New Zealand or the US.

Tourism and services

The value of tourism to Tonga as the second-largest source of hard currency earnings has already been mentioned. Many of those consulted made it clear that Tonga did not seek to rival neighbouring Fiji in the luxury, multi-complex tourist industry, although it was hoped there would be room for a slice of that higher-end tourist market, given that Tonga already has its small share of up-market tourist accommodation venues.

Rather, the view was expressed that Tonga might attract a unique market for a mix of more eco-oriented tourists and for those seeking alternative, more spiritual and less materialistic escapes from the bustling cities of Beijing, Singapore, Sydney or Los Angeles. The small Christian communities spread around the islands of Tonga create a potentially very affordable and natural setting for Westerners and Asians seeking either respite, solitude or spiritual retreat. The challenge is to provide reasonable infrastructure and services consistent with these characteristics. However, given the enthusiasm for such an approach, considerable potential exists for job creation in:

- expansion of existing tourist services
- the development of physical and social infrastructure in support of an 'alternative boutique' tourist market
- indirect services, such as in transportation, cleaning, food, cultural and hospitality areas in support of an expanding tourist sector

- the expansion of financial services and credit services for both tourists and local entrepreneurs
- research followed by training for SMEs on the removal of business and trade barriers to the potential expansion of the tourist market (e.g. a number of clothing and craft shops in the capital Nuku'alofa don't have credit-card facilities).

Given that a high proportion of Tongan tourists are actually Tongans returning to visit families and friends, there exists the opportunity to more strongly tap into this market, through appropriate sports and health facilities, fishing facilities and services, financial services and bar/restaurant facilities.

Beyond tourism, Tonga is exploring the potential for the expansion of jobs in services in a range of sectors, not only those mentioned above in support of tourism but the potential for development of higher level education, health and off-shore financial services. Trade-related capacity building in support of market research, feasibility and training in services is a priority for Tonga and needs to be strongly supported.

Agriculture and niche markets

Increased tourism creates an expanded market for supply of fresh foods, and investment in home-grown products can meet the dual goal of greater agricultural self-sufficiency along with reduced dependence on food imports and drain on foreign reserves to finance these imports.

Meetings were held with various ministers in Tonga, where strong support was forthcoming for investment in the potential export of niche agricultural markets. Tonga has the potential to specialise in root crops and healthfood extracts, oils and fragrances, and specific crafts such as Tongan mats and textiles. The development of these markets not only harmonises well with the 'alternative tourism' image of Tonga, but exports of specific products could target segments of Organisation for Economic Cooperation Development (OECD) markets, for example the Tongan diaspora in New Zealand or the emerging healthfood/vitamin-conscious middle classes of the US and Australia. It would only take a very small share of one of these large market segments to secure an ongoing, viable export market.

Needless to say, all this is easier said than done, but both donor-funded and locally funded expenditure needs to continue to focus on the training and infrastructural needs of lower-skilled agricultural workers to increase productivity in farming and fishing, with a view not only to greater food security but to the potential of niche export markets.

Conclusion

The future for Tonga is bright. It has a strong culture with significant jobs and growth potential in a range of sectors, given appropriate training, education and capacity building. If the Tongan Government can adopt a strong holistic approach to trade-related development and economic reform, with clear messages about its future and its advantages, a number of the typical geographic disadvantages of a small and vulnerable economy can be turned into dynamic advantages. However, labour mobility and remittances will need to play a significant role, and in this respect, the case study brings home four clear messages.

Firstly, remittances from Tongan immigrants, both temporary and permanent, are not only vital for their direct impact on poverty reduction in Tonga, but they are also a significant part of the economy and will continue to be so for the foreseeable future. The good news here is that, provided the current volume of remittances is maintained or increased (and the case-study research says this is the most likely scenario), then they will provide an important safety net and transition mechanism for Tonga to finance its longer-term development goals.

Secondly, for this to be possible, there needs to be increased market access for low- and medium-skilled labour. With well-orchestrated schemes, for example, based on the principles of the RSE scheme, there are clear benefits for both sending and recipient countries. But none of these can be realised unless OECD countries, in particular the US, Australia and New Zealand, either through trade commitments or through general immigration framework agreements, liberalise segments of their labour markets.

Thirdly, the Tongan Government needs to undertake further policy reform to ensure the most productive use of labour sent abroad and in the use of remittances sent back. With respect to the former, this case study has highlighted the importance of a community-based selection process and continuous career-based training, while for the latter, it has emphasised the importance of policies on taxation, superannuation and matching government grants and investment incentives to direct remittances to their most efficient and effective use in terms of Tonga's development goals.

Finally, the study has emphasised the necessity of donor governments to work with the Tongan Government and Tongan diaspora to address supply-side constraints and employment-creating capacity. This requires not only reliable funding commitments, but also the transfer of technology and technical expertise. Tonga can only reduce its dependency on remittances in the future if it can build a more sustainable economy based on the expansion of services and increased agricultural productivity. In the meantime, greater market access for the temporary movement of labour will be vital for sustainable development and poverty reduction in Tonga.

V

Trade and poverty reduction in small and vulnerable economies

Trade strategies for poverty reduction in small and vulnerable economies

JIM REDDEN* AND RON DUNCAN**

Introduction

International trade and economic reform is driving rapid growth and poverty reduction, in absolute terms, across the Asia-Pacific region. Unfortunately, much of this growth has by-passed the small and vulnerable economies (SVEs) of the region, for a range of practical reasons such as their small economic size and geographical isolation. However, these small economies may now have a unique opportunity to harness the benefits of massive regional growth by undertaking reforms that will result in closer economic integration with the markets of Asia and Oceania. Rapid growth in the region, even in the face of global recessionary trends, creates opportunities for small and fragile states to achieve increased levels of trade and sustainable development opportunities that constitute the most viable path to economic and political self-reliance. However, navigating this path is challenging for all economies, let alone SVEs.

Developed nations, in particular those in the region, have a direct interest in providing technology and support to assist SVEs through this journey. The cost of failed states and political instability is significant in terms of economic welfare and strategic security issues. A robust and more prosperous region is not only good for developing nations in the region, but it's also good for developed ones as well. An overriding imperative, therefore, must be to ensure that no one in the region suffers unnecessarily from preventable poverty, for humanitarian reasons, but also as a means of reducing poverty-related instability and insecurity.

* Jim Redden is Director of International Programmes for China and the Pacific and Senior Lecturer with the Institute for International Trade at the University of Adelaide.
** Ron Duncan is Professor Emeritus at the Crawford School of Economics at the Australian National University.

This thematic paper provides an overview of a number of the major trade and development challenges facing small and vulnerable Asia-Pacific nations. It aims to suggest a number of ways forward whereby trade strategies can contribute to increased productivity and growth along with greater transparency, reform and the achievement of long-term poverty reduction objectives.

The paper begins with a discussion of some of the key characteristics and definitional issues relevant to SVEs and their trade implications, in particular the role of special and differential treatment. The authors then put forward the notion of 'strategic liberalisation'. This approach to trade reform acknowledges the reality of significant trade barriers in developed and large developing countries, which requires SVEs to adopt a context-specific approach to the timing and scope of trade reform. After a brief discussion of current trade negotiations and agreements of relevance to Asia-Pacific SVEs, the following section tackles a number of the 'hot issues' and 'ways forward' for SVEs in the key sectors of agriculture, fishing, textiles and clothing, services and labour mobility. This includes a discussion of important issues, including trade diversion, rules of origin and the implications of trade liberalisation for low-income communities.

The next section is devoted to the importance of domestic and regional trade reform, moving on to addressing global trade-reform and capacity-building commitments. Together, they reinforce the importance of cooperation and commitment from all trading partners concerned about the future economic and political stability of SVEs in the Asia-Pacific. The final section concludes with the main implications of this paper.

Definitional issues, characteristics and strategic liberalisation

Consistent with WTO, World Bank and Commonwealth Secretariat definitions, SVEs are defined as those having populations of less than 1.5 million and a share of global merchandise trade of less than 0.16 per cent. This paper focuses primarily on Pacific Islands countries (PICs) but includes examples from Timor-Leste and references to case studies from other regions such as the Caribbean and Africa. Papua New Guinea is included among the SVEs in the Asia-Pacific region, for while it has a population of around 6 million, its share of global merchandise trade is just 0.032 per cent.[1] Table 5A gives a statistical overview of the SVEs of primary interest to this study. Of note are the very small

---

[1] Figure taken from the UN Comtrade database.

Table 5A   *Population, GDP per capita, share of global merchandise trade and HDI of small and vulnerable Pacific Island states and Timor-Leste*

	Population	Population rank*	GDP per capita (US$)	% of global merchandise trade*****	HDI******
Cook Is.	21,750	5	9,100**	0.002	–
Timor-Leste	1,084,971	14	453	n/a	0.514
Fiji	918,675	13	4,100	0.014	0.762
Kiribati	107,817	7	745	0.002	–
Marshall Is.	61,815	6	2,696	n/a	–
FSM	107,862	8	2,254**	n/a	–
Nauru	13,538	3	4,468***	0.006	–
Niue	1,492	1	5,800**	0.000	–
Palau	20,842	4	7,705**	n/a	–
PNG	5,795,887	15	1,972	0.032	0.530
Samoa	214,265	11	3,072****	0.003	0.785
Solomon Is.	566,842	12	704	0.009	0.602
Tonga	116,921	9	2,138	0.001	0.819
Tuvalu	11,992	2	1,600	0.000	–
Vanuatu	211,971	10	1,842	0.004	0.674

* 1 = smallest.
** Classification according to 2005 GDP per capita, CIA, *World Fact Book* data.
*** Classification according to 2005 GDP per capita, Department of Foreign Affairs and Trade data.
**** Classification according to 2005 GDP per capita, Samoan Government statistics.
***** From UNCTAD export/import statistics for 2005 rounded to nearest third decimal place.
****** The HDI is the normalised measure of life expectancy, literacy, education, standard of living and GDP per capita for countries worldwide, 1.0 being the optimum.
Sources: IndexMundi, CIA, United Nations Development Programme, *The CIA World Factbook* and the Australian Department of Foreign Affairs and Trade 2007.

contributions to global merchandise trade and the Human Development Index (HDI) measures, which, while low, put most Pacific SVEs in the medium category of UN-HDI country rankings.

The term 'small and vulnerable economy' is regularly used in development literature and by the WTO. The authors believe that the word

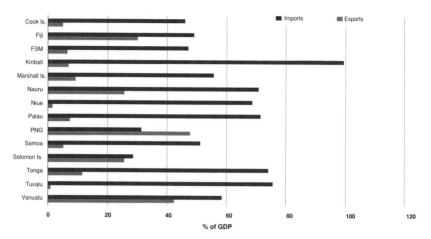

Figure 5A   Pacific Island nations are relatively open for their size.

'vulnerability' is questionable, as it implies that the problems facing small economies are prospective, and whilst this may be the case, there are many problems already present. Furthermore, the term can be interpreted to imply a sense of weakness or dependence, which we believe is contrary to the cultural and social strengths and potential of these small economies. However, we will use the expression 'small and vulnerable economies' as it has become a familiar term in distinguishing small, low-income per capita economies from small, high-income economies such as Singapore. It also has acceptance in the WTO, notwithstanding the debate about whether SVEs warrant a separate category deserving of special and differential treatment (Thomas, 2005).

Trade openness and SVEs

The starting point in this discussion of the relationship between trade and poverty reduction for SVEs is well accepted: that economic growth and increased trade, which implies openness to trade, are necessary but not sufficient conditions to ensure sustainable development and poverty reduction.

So how open are SVEs to international trade? While the contributions of SVEs in the Pacific to world trade may be very small, Pacific Island export and import flows are quite large relative to their gross domestic product (GDP) (see Figure 5A).

The relatively large trade flows, especially the import flows, lead many writers to classify the PICs as highly 'open' economies. However, this statement needs to be tempered by the fact that while most do have high levels of imports relative to their GDP, this does not necessarily mean that they should be thought of as open economies. Many protect various areas of manufacturing and services activity at significant levels and rely to some extent on revenue from customs duties.

With the exception of Papua New Guinea, the economies all run significant negative trade balances: export returns finance often quite small proportions of imports, although the extent of the deficit varies significantly across Pacific economies. The balance of export financing comes from fishing licence fees, remittances, overseas earnings on trust funds and foreign aid.

Economist Jeffrey Sachs asserts in relation to developing nations that:

> openness is not sufficient unto itself... much depends on the way a country opens up, the sequence that is followed, the speed and the internal capacity to manage the process. Improvements in productivity and competitiveness through trade liberalisation require a comprehensive policy for human resource and infrastructure development, education, technology, a policy that includes small and medium size enterprises, a strategy to raise the productivity of subsistence farmers and other measures.
>
> (Sachs, 2007)

Among the other measures, institutional factors such as secure property rights and impartial contract enforcement should be added, as well as openness to foreign investment and labour and an investor-friendly environment free of unnecessary bureaucratic control.

Special and differential treatment and a strategic liberalisation approach

This list of concerns above implies a broad and interactive trade-related development policy agenda. Yet, how this translates in the reality of trade negotiations is open to question. One hotly debated question is the degree to which SVEs warrant any kind of special treatment in global trade policy settings and, if so, what form(s) should this special treatment take to ensure it is not a disincentive to reform?

This question can be posed in another way: is it likely that, without intervention, the SVEs' growth rates will increase sufficiently to establish a trajectory toward the sustained reduction and eventual elimination of

Table 5B   *Summary of cost disadvantages for SVEs*

Cost inflation factors	Micro	Very small	Small
Industry			
Electronic assembly	36.5	14.3	2.7
Clothing	36.4	14.4	2.7
Hotels and Tourism	57.5	28.6	6.2

Source: Thomas (2005).

poverty? On balance, while there is no doubt that faster growth in the Pacific is possible (e.g. in mineral-rich Papua New Guinea and Timor-Leste[2]), it is reasonable to answer this question generally with a fairly assured 'no'. The disadvantages of size, lack of resources and capacity and geographic isolation alone are arguably sufficient to prevent SVEs from achieving the high rates of growth necessary for sustainable poverty reduction. It would appear, therefore, that some form of special consideration and strategic approach to trade liberalisation is required.

Clive Thomas (2005), in his summary of the concerns of small states in the global trading regime, argues persuasively that SVEs face irreducible and significant disadvantages that limit their capacity to reduce poverty even in the medium term. Thomas provides a table showing business cost disadvantages for micro, very small and small nations in three industries (see Table 5B). This data is highly suggestive that significant cost disadvantages are related to size. Although the cost disadvantages of small states are surmountable, the disadvantages for the very small and micro states would be very difficult to overcome. Note the particularly high cost barriers that are facing micro states, such as Tuvalu and Niue.

Adding to these disadvantages, SVEs face difficulties that derive from culture and history. It is only recently that these nations have attempted to integrate with the global economy. The necessary physical infrastructure and human capital, as well as the quality of institutions and political processes, impose significant limitations on their ability to move *rapidly* forward. These factors also suggest that SVEs require a degree of special treatment from developed and larger developing countries for them to be able to make sustained progress – so long as this is a two-way process where special treatment is matched by progressive trade-related, domestic reform.

[2] See AusAID (2008), p. xiv.

What form should any special treatment take? Notwithstanding the unpredictability of the outcomes of successive rounds of trade negotiations in the current Doha Round, it is clear that there is an ongoing trend towards trade liberalisation and global integration. All nations face pressure – to varying degrees – to reduce tariffs and subsidisation regimes. Proponents of open trading systems argue that any form of industry-based trade assistance, including tariffs and subsidies, only serves to detach these industries from the commercial signals of the global economy. This detachment tends to increase over time, creating competitively disadvantaged industries that exist only because of the preferences or special treatment and encourage rent-seeking behaviour.

The form of special and differential treatment therefore needs to strike a balance between flexible trade arrangements and well-targeted capacity-building for SVEs, along with firm commitments on their part to domestic trade reform. This paper is not concerned about a theoretical choice for SVEs between free trade and protectionism. That debate is largely over – and it is widely agreed that openness, or perhaps 'near-openness', is a precondition for growth and development. The paper instead focuses on the need for special and differential treatment, capacity building and a strategic approach that embraces the following aspects:

- the need to build fundamental economic capacity, competitiveness and skills through investments in education and training
- the appropriate rate of trade reform or liberalisation, taking into account adjustment costs and measures required to deal with these costs
- the need to relax any constraints on economically efficient activities responding to changes in relative prices due to the lowering of trade barriers
- strategies to embed dynamic efficiency and diversity into the foundations of SVEs – a domestically driven but internationally supported approach to building entrepreneurial capacity able to respond to unpredictable commercial opportunities over the long run.

In other words, SVEs need to develop policies that constitute what is called 'strategic liberalisation'. Strategic liberalisation policies acknowledge the benefits of liberalisation but seek to ease transition costs and inequalities that can result. Such policies recognise that liberalisation is very incomplete on a global basis, and so take a pragmatic view of the need to align domestic trade reform with domestic development objectives. The incomplete process of global liberalisation, where many markets (e.g. those in agriculture) remain distorted, leads to our view that strategic liberalisation for SVEs should:

- acknowledge the benefits of liberalisation but seek to ease transition costs and inequalities
- seek to build the fundamental drivers of economic competitiveness, including the development of institutions, education, political stability and infrastructure that can synchronise growth opportunities with domestic and global trade reform
- recognise that liberalisation is incomplete on a global basis and therefore take a pragmatic view of the need to align domestic trade reform with domestic development priorities
- eschew trade-based, industry-specific policies that encourage special preferences that only result in propping up inefficient industries and rent-seeking behaviour.

The remainder of this paper assumes that the best trade course for SVEs is one that embraces strategic liberalisation.

Current trade negotiations and agreements

There are several trade agreements and trade agreement negotiations currently impacting on SVEs in the Asia-Pacific region. In line with WTO principles, the recent emphasis of trade agreements between developed and developing countries, such as the Cotonou Agreement, is set to increase reciprocal trade liberalisation commitments, together with increased funding for trade-related capacity building and technical assistance. The risks for SVEs are two-fold: too rapid a transition schedule and reciprocity that does not allow sufficient time to develop competitive capacity. Conversely, failure to undertake sufficient reform to induce long-run investment and competitiveness would be equally detrimental. The key challenge is for both parties to balance the staging and pace of reform.

SVEs in the region are affected by a complex interplay of multilateral and regional trade agreements or systems of preferences (see Table 5C). Most of the PICs are signatories to several overlapping regional and international agreements, encompassing trade, aid and investment.

Regional relationships

For a long time, most of the southern PICs have been part of a special relationship with Australia and New Zealand in the form of the South Pacific

Table 5C   *Pacific SVE members of the WTO and selected preferential trade agreements*

	SPARTECA	US Compact	MSG	PICTA	Cotonou EPAs	PACER	WTO	LDC/EBA
Timor-Leste					×			×
Fiji	×		×	×	×	×	×	
Kiribati	×			×	×	×		×
Marshall Is.	×	×		×	×	×		
FSM	×	×		×	×	×		
Nauru	×			×	×	×		
Niue	×			×	×	×		
Palau	×	×		×	×	×		
PNG	×		×	×	×	×	×	
Samoa	×			×	×	×	*	×
Solomon Is.	×		×	×	×	×	×	×
Tonga	×			×	×	×	×	
Tuvalu	×			×	×	×		×
Vanuatu	×		×	×	×	×	*	×

* Currently considering accession.

Regional Trade and Economic Cooperation Agreement (SPARTECA). SPARTECA is a non-reciprocal arrangement between Australia and New Zealand on the one hand, and the Pacific Forum Island countries (FICs) on the other, which came into force on 1 January 1981. Of note, SPARTECA Rules of Origin (ROO) are such that to be eligible for preferential access, goods produced in PICs must have 50 per cent local content. At present, most exports from the PICs to Australia and New Zealand enter under SPARTECA.

For the western Melanesian countries, there is the Melanesian Spearhead Group (MSG) Trade Agreement. The MSG Preferential Trade Agreement is a trade treaty governing the four Melanesian states of Vanuatu, Papua New Guinea, Solomon Islands and Fiji. Signed in 1993, it is a subregional trade treaty established to foster economic development by ensuring that trade is undertaken on a Most Favoured Nation (MFN) basis.

Most PICs have now also signed and ratified a broad-based, inter-regional free trade agreement (FTA) among themselves: the Pacific Island Countries Trade Agreement (PICTA). Agreed in 2001, PICTA was formulated to encourage the expansion and diversification of trade in the region and to assist in building a single regional market among Pacific Island economies by eliminating trade-distorting tariffs and non-tariff barriers in a gradual and progressive manner.

A recent study on the impact of PICTA on the smaller SVEs (Institute for International Trade and Pacific Trade Consult, 2007) demonstrated that the near and medium-term impact on tariff revenues of implementing PICTA will be minor and should be offset by other revenue raising measures and the adoption of more cost-efficient implementation procedures that are either already in place or under consideration. The study argued that PICs should treat PICTA as a small stepping stone to a more open, integrated and transparent trading system where the potential benefits will outweigh the more immediate challenges, notwithstanding the need to address issues of trade diversion. That conclusion can be equally extended to the larger PICs. However, where tariff revenue losses will have a substantially higher impact will be in the formulation of future *reciprocal* trade agreements with the EU and with Australia and New Zealand.

The Pacific Agreement for Closer Economic Cooperation (PACER) between Australia, New Zealand and PICTA members was signed by most Pacific SVEs in Nauru in 2001, allowing for the creation of a single Pacific market with the two major developed countries of the Pacific region. Under PACER, PICs are required at some future date to enter into negotiations for free trade arrangements with Australia and New Zealand. If one or more of the PICs begins negotiations over free trade arrangements with another developed country partner, such as the EU, this would trigger a requirement for consultations with Australia and New Zealand, leading to negotiations over an FTA. If such negotiations are successful, they will create a formal FTA notifiable under Article XXIV of the General Agreement on Tariffs and Trade (GATT).

This brings us to the important renegotiation of the former Lomé Agreement with the EU, now known as the Cotonou Agreement, which was signed in 2003. At the top of the trade agenda for most PICs and East Timor officials at present are negotiations to establish Economic Partnership Agreements (EPAs) with the EU. While EPAs are generally about political cooperation and development assistance, they need to be comprehensive and reciprocal in trading arrangements so as to be WTO-consistent. As of January 2008, Fiji and Papua New Guinea had signed interim EPAs with the EU, reflecting the importance of preferences and the EU market for certain products. These interim agreements with the EU have triggered PACER trade negotiations towards what is being called a PACER-plus trade agreement.

There are a number of key issues emerging for SVEs in both the EPAs and the PACER-plus negotiations; here we highlight four. First is the treatment of ROO and the need for developed country negotiators to ensure that they are updated and sufficiently flexible to reflect the 'globalisation of the supply chain'. This point is dealt with later in the section on ROO.

A second key concern, especially in the triggering of PACER, is the current dominance of PIC imports by Australia and New Zealand and therefore the implications of a comprehensive and reciprocal trade agreement on lost tariff revenue as PICs reduce or eliminate tariff barriers. Studies have suggested that PICs will need to ensure that alternative revenue-raising measures are in place, along with industry restructuring in some cases, while developed nations should consider transitional compensatory mechanisms and flexibility in the timelines for tariff reductions, particularly for some of the most affected Pacific SVEs.

The third issue of high significance to most SVEs will be increased market access to Australia and New Zealand for the temporary movement of skilled and unskilled labour. This will have important implications not only in terms of the value of remittances but for the potential investment in training and education of Pacific workers that might accompany temporary labour market schemes.

The fourth key issue is the volume and quality of development assistance, compensatory or transition assistance and trade-related capacity building that will be seen as fair and reasonable on both sides.

None of these issues will be easily agreed, but, as stated earlier, the key challenge will be for both parties to balance commitments to serious trade reform with the staging and pace of reform.

Against the background of regional negotiations are the ongoing meetings and negotiations of small economies and SVEs globally within the multilateral system.

Multilateral

Several important issues are also on the agenda of the WTO Committee on Trade and Development, which has established a Work Programme on Small Economies, agreed to by the General Council of the WTO in March 2002.

The Work Programme on Small Economies has been an important platform for SVEs globally to raise concerns and discuss some of their key issues with the broader membership. Some of these issues have centred on definitional issues for what constitutes a 'vulnerable' SVE and, as mentioned earlier, the consequent eligibility for forms of special and differential treatment. Other issues have included the degree of technology transfer and firm financial commitments to technical assistance and capacity building from developed country members of the WTO, fishing subsidies, preference erosion, ROO and a range of specific concerns such as with the implementation of rules, sanitary and phytosanitary (SPS) requirements and technical barriers to trade (TBT) standards. Some useful suggestions on how trade rules, flexibility and assistance could be of most use to SVEs have been put forward.

However, the current WTO Doha Round is expected to fall well short of its original development expectations and, given the 'single undertaking', there is a distinct possibility that no comprehensive agreement will be reached in the foreseeable future. Therefore, an important threat looming for SVEs is that, in its efforts to strive for a fairer, multilateral, rules-based trading system, the WTO will be sidelined in favour of alternatives such as an OECD-only trade agreement or a Trans-Atlantic Agreement between developed countries with buy-in from the larger developing nations. Such an outcome would leave SVEs out of contemporary trade negotiations, with little prospect of gains from bilateral preferential trade agreements.

If this happens, SVEs could effectively lose:

- special attention as a separate working group within the WTO's Trade and Development Committee
- significant influence over relevant trade issues and policies of other countries
- some of the existing and potential special and differential treatment (SDT) and trade-related capacity-building funds
- access to a set of effective drivers of necessary reform.

The result would be an unbalanced process of liberalisation that SVEs cannot influence or control. Arguably, this could well be the number one issue for SVEs, overshadowing other vital issues discussed in the following sections. Can anything be done to avoid this situation or is it out of the hands of SVEs?

It is vital that SVEs do all that they can to prevent this course of events. If they have the necessary capacity and finances, SVEs that are not already WTO members should either seek to join the WTO, as Vanuatu and Samoa are doing, or obtain observer status. This would increase their representation on the multilateral playing field of negotiations. SVEs would also benefit from the experience in participating in the negotiations; they would be eligible for SDT and TRCB and, most importantly, they would be assisted and motivated to embark on the required trade reform that accession involves. If SVEs are too small and believe that joining would be of little value or too costly (Niue, with a population of less than 2,000, may fit in this category), they should still ensure strong and accountable representation in Geneva through regional alliances with other Pacific members, other SVEs or the Africa, Caribbean and Pacific (ACP) bloc of nations.

SVEs must be prepared to take on reasonable domestic reform measures and encourage other members to do so to in order to achieve a more comprehensive agreement and a successful multilateral round. Following the Hong Kong WTO Ministerial, least developed countries (LDCs) have, in principle, gained the Everything But Arms Agreement and so face fewer market access barriers, notwithstanding the exception for 3 per cent of products. A successful WTO round is needed to crystallise the implementation of in-principle agreements such as these.

If the Doha Round stalls indefinitely, SVEs will need to manage this risk as best they can. Firstly, this can be done by pursuing commitments from developed nations during the period that WTO negotiations remain in hiatus. Secondly, given that regional agreements will then take on increased significance, there will be a need for heightened commitment to negotiating mutually successful outcomes in agreements such as Cotonou and PACER-plus. As suggested in one of the case studies in this part of the book, East Timor would do well to join the Association of Southeast Asian Nations (ASEAN) and the ASEAN Free Trade Agreement. There is far more chance of a regionally integrated and united Pacific region being able to negotiate more favourable agreements with larger developing and developed nations.

SVEs could still realise a range of strategic liberalisation goals through regional trade agreements as they encourage, and in some cases enforce, the adoption of necessary democratic and institutional reform, market access, trade and economic reform, engagement and the prioritisation of capacity building. It will be advantageous for SVEs if they can gain more appropriate and flexible ROO, improve anti-dumping legislation, encourage further foreign direct investment (FDI), improve regulatory policy to protect consumers from anti-competitive behaviour and harmonise product standards in conformity with WTO requirements. There will be large administrative costs associated with these reforms, which could come from TRCB funds made available from donor bodies such as the EU and Australia, or through multilateral donors such as the UN Conference on Trade and Development (UNCTAD).

Regional and multilateral negotiations are complex and interrelated; close and patient cooperation will be required by all parties to these agreements. Much is at stake in all sectors, from agriculture and fishing to the future development of services and labour mobility. Preference erosion must be matched by capacity building, reform and diversification. The next section focuses on a number of the specific 'hot issues' for SVEs in key sectors, with suggestions of ways forward at the end of each subsection.

'Hot issues' and 'ways forward' for SVEs

Trade preferences

While preferences could help boost economic production in SVEs and contribute to short- to medium-term growth and poverty reduction, in general, preferences have had little positive impact on SVEs, or LDCs for that matter. The reasons are as follows:

- preferences can lead to the development of activities that are not viable when the preferences are removed and the activities have to compete on level terms with other producers
- many agricultural products produced by SVEs are already at zero or negligible tariffs in developed countries
- primary agricultural products and processed products with high tariffs are excluded from preferential agreements
- where preferences are substantial, they are often accompanied by strict quantitative and quarantine restrictions; moreover, the preferences are often targeted to a few countries
- there are often restrictive ROO on agricultural and NAMA (non-agricultural market access) goods
- preferences are often of a temporary nature: they are usually subject to the political whims of the day, and entrenched interests use various means to protect these economic rents.

Therefore, there is a limited role for trade preferences in assisting SVEs to gain sustainable market access. This is not to say that some SVEs have not benefited from preferences over recent years, for example Fiji. The main benefits for Fiji have been from preferential pricing for a fixed quantity of sugar exported to the EU, and for the development of the garment industry under the preferences provided through SPARTECA and the Multi-Fibre Agreement (MFA). But even in these cases the outcomes have been very mixed. In the case of sugar, the economic rents have been dissipated by the expansion of sugar cane farming into very marginal areas. Productivity in the sugar industry has been in long-term decline. While the productivity decline cannot be blamed totally on the provision of preferences, the preferences do not appear to have encouraged innovation, and there has been no incentive for diversification, with the result that Fiji's sugar industry has become one of the most inefficient in the world.

Similarly, the preferences provided to garment manufacturing and exports to Australia, New Zealand and the US have not resulted in the development of economically efficient firms. When the MFA expired at the beginning of 2006, Fijian firms exporting to the US closed down and moved their activities to China and elsewhere. Garment exports to Australia have only remained viable with reductions in the ROO requirements and adjustment assistance provided by Australia. There is no indication that the garment industry in Fiji will be able to continue when the SPARTECA preferences are removed. Prasad, Yenteshwar and Marr discuss some useful options for the Fijian garment industry in one of the case studies following this chapter.

For some SVEs in the Pacific region, revenues from preferences, while important, actually account for a relatively low proportion of GDP. For example, tariff revenue from Australian and New Zealand imports are less than 5% of total revenue for many of the fourteen Pacific Island Forum countries: exceptions are the Cook Islands, Kiribati, Samoa, Tonga and Vanuatu, whose shares range between 12% and 18% of overall revenue.[3] East Timor has an MFN low tariff rate of 5% with little dependence on preferential tariffs.

Whatever the relative benefits preferences have provided, the future erosion of preferences seems inevitable. The conclusion of the Uruguay Round in 1994, with its commitments to more liberalised trade, and especially to lower tariff rates for agricultural products, has contributed to the erosion of preferences. The lowering of MFN tariffs, the removal of non-tariff barriers by the EU on a multilateral basis and the extension of its preference beyond the ACP countries are factors that have accounted for this ACP erosion. Australia and New Zealand have lowered their MFN tariffs, and now products from Asia have replaced Pacific imports that were provided preferential access through SPARTECA. In Samoa, two coconut processing plants were closed because they lost their export market and, as discussed in a case study in Chapter 1, the Japanese manufacture of motor

---

[3] Based on statistics provided by the Pacific Islands Forum Secretariat (2007).

vehicle components is also struggling in the face of cheaper imports of parts into Australia from China.

Bilateral and regional agreements that have extended lower duty and duty-free arrangements to groups of countries also erode the benefits of preferences. With these arrangements increasing and successive rounds of MFN tariff reductions, even the limited value of current preferences is bound to decline, making it important for SVEs to carefully assess how much 'negotiating capital' should be invested to maintain levels of preferences that may not be helpful in the long run.

Attachment 2 of the current WTO Agreement on Agriculture Revised Draft of Modalities shows that the tariff reductions proposed by some developing countries (the G-20 group) could lead to the preference margins into the EU for sugar, bananas, strawberries, rum and other products being reduced by 10 per cent or more. These reductions would adversely affect countries such as Fiji, the Dominican Republic, Swaziland, Jamaica and Guyana, at least in the short run. In the longer run, more exposure to international competition may well be beneficial, for example through promoting innovation.

However, as the Food and Agricultural Organisation (FAO), UNCTAD, the World Bank and others have argued, SVEs themselves should strive to alleviate the domestic constraints that are proving to be obstacles to them achieving international competitiveness. For example, analysis often reveals that it is domestic constraints preventing the expansion of exports, not import barriers: constraints such as insecure access to land and the resulting difficulties in accessing credit, investment disincentives, pest and disease problems in agriculture and livestock industries and poor quality standards. Therefore, the catchwords have become 'market entry' rather than 'market access'. Donors and international organisations need to share responsibility in assisting SVEs with relevant analytical inputs, development of necessary research capacity, development of improved marketing chains and other long-term solutions, leading to less dependence on trade preferences.

There will no doubt be short-run costs of adjustment to the loss of preferences. In particular, as soon as a reduction in preferences is announced, or even anticipated, the value of the capital invested in those businesses will be reduced. As well, there will be the threat of job loss for employees. There is little that should be done for the owners of capital in these businesses, as they have benefited from the years of economic rent provided through the preferences. As regards the employees of affected industries, unless measures are in place to provide a good environment for growth of other industries, they will suffer. Hence, SVE governments should consider paying particular attention to creating an investor-friendly environment, while considering how compensation and transition costs could be met during a transition phase.[4]

There is a vexed question about whether it is better for the preferences to be removed immediately or gradually. Immediate removal means that the affected industries have to face the adjustment costs immediately. Gradual reduction of preferences would appear to make the adjustment costs easier to bear, and fits more closely with a strategic liberalisation approach. However, in some cases, immediate withdrawal of preferences may force firms to become more entrepreneurial in an effort to become internationally competitive. Gradual withdrawal may not provide this 'cold shower' effect, and firms may just wither away but in the meantime spend considerable resources on trying to maintain the preferences.

In summary, there will no doubt be pain associated with the loss of preferences in some Pacific SVEs, requiring a mix of adjustment assistance and technical assistance for establishing a more investor-friendly environment and trade facilitation. But SVEs will need to adjust to the inevitable, especially given that, for many, preferences have made little difference anyway, while distorting the allocation of resources within the economy. One issue associated with trade preferences is the resultant effects of trade diversion.

Trade diversion

Trade diversion arises as a result of preferential trade arrangements that lead to trade being diverted from lower-cost producers to higher-cost producers. Because of the preferential arrangements for members, lower-cost producers from outside the preferential arrangement lose trade to higher-cost producers within the group. As a result, economically inefficient activities are encouraged within the trading bloc; that is, industries that would not be internationally competitive in the absence of the preferences. The cost to the exporting country within the group is that the preferences allow resources to be bid away from other activities that would have been economically efficient.

---

[4] The principle of the Tariff Revenue Offset Fund for PICTA has been suggested as an offset to any initial shocks to FIC economies, and especially to the smaller economies, as a result of initial loss of tariff revenue from trade liberalisation commitments. See Institute for International Trade and Pacific Trade Consult (2007), p. 58.

The opposite effect to trade diversion is trade creation. This is the case when trade from lower-cost producers is encouraged through the lowering of trade barriers. If a preferential trade arrangement is agreed, the trade diversion effects can be minimised by keeping the trade barriers against third-party exporters as low as possible.

A major problem observed in preferential trade agreements among low-income countries is that the chances of trade diversion rather than trade creation are high. This is the case with PICTA and the MSG. In the absence of PICTA, trade between the Pacific FICs was very limited, because, for the most part, they produce the same exports. However, with the formation of PICTA, exporters within the trading bloc gain preferences over rest-of-the-world exporters. Hence, higher-cost exporters within the bloc gain preferences over lower-cost exporters. Thus, PICTA is likely to favour the more advanced economies within the bloc, for example Fiji and Papua New Guinea. But, as noted earlier, the implementation of PICTA has the potential for benefits in terms of regional integration and the implementation of trade liberalisation commitments. In order to address trade diversion, PICTA members should seek to keep trade barriers against third-party exporters as low as possible.

The next few sections deal with some of the most important trade issues for SVEs in the Pacific region in the key sectors of agriculture, manufacturing and services.

Agriculture issues for small economies

Agriculture contributes a significant part of the economic activity and employment of many small economies, even if, in most cases, the sector is much smaller than the services sector. In general, agriculture accounts for a greater share of employment than it does of GDP, which means labour productivity is lower than in the rest of the economy.

All the usual 'high costs of trade' challenges facing small economies are applicable to their agriculture sectors, particularly as agriculture production tends to be of bulk commodities (e.g. sugar or copra). Small-scale production, inefficient practices, high transport costs associated with small quantities and long distances from export markets as well as poor infrastructure all mean that it is difficult for many SVEs to be in a position to compete with lower-cost or more efficient producers in other countries.

In some SVEs, particularly the larger and relatively wealthier ones, such as Mauritius and Fiji, commercial farming does take place on a larger scale. In these cases, the main markets are usually developed countries, and production is usually focused on a narrow range of crops exported under preferential terms. As noted in the previous section, the adverse impact of the erosion of preferences, while often overstated, will affect the export of bulk commodities such as bananas and sugar, with a deleterious effect on their terms of trade. These exports are not subject to price fluctuations caused by the market, although they can be subject to sudden price changes that result from changes in European policies – such as the 36 per cent cut in the domestic price for sugar in the EU, which resulted from the reform by the EU of its sugar regime. For other agricultural commodities, producers in SVEs are, like producers in other countries, subject to the price fluctuations that characterise agriculture trade and, as they produce a small range of commodities, they are particularly vulnerable to these global-commodity price shocks.

It is difficult for small, geographically isolated producers to vertically integrate into global supply chains, given that most SVEs consist of small-scale farmers and one or two dominant exporting firms. At present, 80 to 90 per cent of global trade in the ten most important commodities is controlled by three to six transnational corporations,[5] and increasingly, supermarket chains are influencing both the price and quality of global food trade. Packaging and stringent SPS requirements, as well as changing patterns of demand, are making it increasingly difficult for SVEs to compete.

Much has been written about agricultural protectionism in OECD countries and suffice to say here that the net effect on their production (under-importing from foreign markets and then over-exporting at low prices because of subsidies) undermines the ability of small farmers in SVEs to compete globally. Thomas makes the point that many SVE farmers are vulnerable to global-commodity price volatility.[6] Given that SVE terms of trade are highly dependent on agricultural export prices, the prolonged regime of low commodity prices from which we are emerging has made it extremely difficult for SVEs to increase government revenue and thereby better manage other macroeconomic fundamentals such as interest rates and availability of credit, or the financing of vital services, including agricultural services. Perhaps there may be some relief from higher food prices of late; however, the benefits will be tempered pending an SVE's reliance on imported food products.

The problems and challenges facing SVEs in agriculture have been well documented. Perhaps the question now is: should SVEs largely abandon

---

[5] Thomas (2005), p. 35.   [6] Ibid., p. 34.

their agricultural sectors as a long-term goal in favour of services, or are there ways forward that would allow for improved subsistence farming, a higher degree of self-sufficiency and niche commodity market exports so as to afford SVEs a greater degree of self-reliance and export income?

As SVEs are unlikely to be competitive in global markets in exporting standardised, high-volume agricultural commodities, one answer is to develop niche markets through product differentiation. Consumers in other countries have to be convinced that it is in their interests to pay a higher price for a 'non-standard' product – a higher price that will cover the high international trade costs faced by SVEs. Outstanding examples of successful niche marketing in the Pacific are Fiji Water and Pure Fiji (cosmetics made from coconut oil). Other examples can be found in the marketing of organic products. For example, the Dominican Republic boasts that it is the world's leading exporter of organic bananas and organic cocoa. However, developing niche markets is not something that governments can or should try to do. This has to be left to those investors willing to risk their capital to try an idea. Governments can help by opening their economies to investment and trade, and thereby opening them to innovative ideas.

So while we argue in favour of SVEs continuing to target investment in services, we do not in any way see this as exclusive of developing a viable agricultural sector, given the current predominance of subsistence agriculture throughout. Rather, it is a matter of investing in the most strategic agricultural areas.

There are four areas deserving of particular attention:

(1) investment in agricultural human-resource productivity, including training, up-skilling, research and technical assistance to small-scale farmers to increase productivity for subsistence and for internal domestic trade
(2) investment in rural infrastructure, including telecommunications services, to lower trade transaction costs for domestic and international trade[7]
(3) assistance in the development of food marketing chains to supply regional and domestic tourist consumption
(4) trade facilitation to assist firms to export into segments of larger markets.

---

[7] See Chapter 3.5 on Vanuatu's successful approach to telecommunications reform and the implications for market access for low-income farmers.

With respect to the above points, it should be noted that international trade rules do not hinder support and protection in the areas of education, training, infrastructure and support services such as veterinary and plant health – a point elaborated on in the next section on the WTO and agriculture.

The WTO and agriculture

The most recent draft of modalities for agriculture, which sets out the formulae WTO members will use to calculate tariff and subsidy reductions, included specific and more flexible treatment for SVEs.[8] It is suggested that, in addition to the SDT available to all developing countries, SVEs would make lower tariff reductions and developed countries would be required to improve their market access for products from them. As noted at the beginning of this paper, the definition of an SVE in the WTO is any country that, in the period of 1999 to 2004, had an average share of: (i) world merchandise trade of 0.16% or less; (ii) world trade in non-agricultural products of no more than 0.1%; and (iii) world trade in agricultural products of no more than 0.4%. All Pacific SVEs fit this definition.

The suggested definition (which was based on a proposal made by the SVE Group[9] as part of the Committee on Trade and Development) would include those members listed in Annex C to the Revised Draft of Modalities, plus others that meet the criteria but for which data was not available. It should also be noted that LDCs, which would include some SVEs, would not be required to make any reductions in tariffs under the WTO agriculture negotiations.[10]

Under the Agreement on Agriculture, all members are entitled to provide unlimited support under the Green Box, which covers infrastructure, education, training and other government service programmes, as well as income support and insurance programmes for farmers. They may also provide unlimited support under the Blue Box, which covers direct payments to farmers under production-limiting programmes. Developing countries may also give investment subsidies and input subsidies

[8] Revised Draft Modalities for Agriculture, TN/AG/W/4 and Corr.1, 1 August 2007.
[9] Revised Consolidated Reference Paper on Modalities on Market Access – Contribution on the Treatment of Small Vulnerable Economies (SVES), Barbados, Bolivia, Cuba, Dominican Republic, El Salvador, Fiji, Guatemala, Honduras, Mauritius, Mongolia, Nicaragua, Papua New Guinea, Trinidad and Tobago, Job(06)/196, 19 June 2006.
[10] Annex A, paragraph 45, Doha Work Programme, Decision adopted by the General Council on 1 August 2004, WT/L/579, 2 August 2004.

targeted at resource-poor farmers without any limit to the amount that
can be provided. Developing countries may also give support of the most
trade-distorting kind, the Amber Box, of up to 10% of the value of
the product concerned or, for non produce-specific support, up to 10%
of the total value of agricultural production. In addition, export subsidies for transport and marketing may also be provided by developing
countries.

All WTO members have tariff bindings on all agricultural products,
with only a few exceptions. In most developing countries, including
SVEs, the tariffs applied are well below bound tariffs, and the tariff
reductions suggested in the Revised Draft Modalities would not affect
the applied tariffs. In addition, the Revised Draft Modalities suggest that
SVEs would apply lower reductions than the formula generally applicable to developing countries. For certain products they would also be
able to have even lower reductions if they qualify as special products or
sensitive products, and there will be a special safeguard mechanism that
could be applied when import surges occur or import prices fall. LDCs
would not have to reduce bound tariffs. Thus, it is probably safe to conclude that SVEs would be unlikely to have to reduce applied tariffs and,
for most products, would retain some degree of flexibility to increase
them even after the bound tariffs were reduced following a Doha Round
agreement.

Therefore, the key agricultural issue for many SVEs will not be so much
about agricultural concessions within the WTO, but more a question
of addressing production efficiency and supply-side concerns to ensure
food security. Their current lack of resources means that even allowable
government subsidies are not an option for many. Indeed, increasing
production through subsidies could lead to greater problems, as it would
create dependence on support; and greater production would require
higher subsidies, leading to a vicious cycle of higher support, higher
production and higher dependency.

Finding resources and solutions

For most SVEs to achieve investment in the four strategic areas suggested earlier, the restrictions on providing support do not arise from
international trade rules but from lack of resources. Production-related
agriculture subsidies are costly in terms of the distortion of resources;
and if agriculture is a large part of the economy, the burden on other
sectors is very high. Governments and international organisations have
a critical role in providing education and training services to farmers,

and in supporting them in other ways to improve their ability to produce and market their products. Such government or internationally provided services fall clearly under the Green Box, which also includes insurance programmes for farming in areas exposed to cyclones or other natural disasters – a concern most applicable to the Pacific.

It should be possible to find sufficient financial support for vital agricultural reforms. If local commitment to reform can be gained (in many cases this will require sensitive land reform and land-titling processes, the training of younger and middle-aged men and women in small- to medium-scale enterprise farm management and entrepreneurialism), then both private- and public-sector investment becomes more attractive.

The growth of tourism and the increasing populations of most SVEs mean domestic agricultural demand is increasing and new opportunities have arisen. Much of the tourism market is untapped, with major resorts still relying on food and beverage imports. In this case, many of the problems facing exports *from* SVEs also apply to those who would like to export *to* SVEs. In this case, the transport costs are often a greater problem for exporters to SVEs and would, to some extent at least, protect domestic production. In some cases, this would require reorientation of domestic production away from producing bulk commodities for export to preferential markets and towards meeting domestic demand for a wider variety of products, including for tourism and the expanding services market. It might also be noted that the production of fresh fruit and vegetables is labour-intensive, which would be a useful source of employment.

Insurance is a very important issue for SVEs. Pacific Islands and Caribbean countries are prone to tropical storms and climate change phenomena, which can have a potentially devastating effect on agriculture. In addition, agriculture prices fluctuate considerably. To encourage farmers to move from subsistence production and to provide some form of safety net for those already producing for sale, it might be worth considering how farmers could be protected from these market or weather-related impacts on their incomes. However, guaranteed prices or futures/options schemes would not protect them from production losses due to drought, flooding or tropical storms. Therefore, some form of income insurance scheme would be useful. It would have to be carefully regulated to ensure that it did not create incentives for unsustainable production, which could happen if the insurance payments are too high or are triggered too easily.

In summary, four strategic areas have been identified as ways forward for more sustainable agricultural production in SVEs: (i) improving the productivity of subsistence farming; (ii) investment in rural infrastructure; (iii) tapping into increased local and tourist demand; and (iv) trade facilitation. Consistent with our overall argument, reforms will be required at both local and international levels. Local reforms are necessary to ensure incentives and commitments to land reform, to rural education and training and to the accumulation of credit, savings, insurance and investment in rural reform. International action will be required in providing technology, training, customs reform and capacity to meet SPS requirements and TBT standards; as well as in reducing global distortions on trade in agricultural goods.

Non-agricultural market access or manufactured products

Fishing and fisheries

Perhaps no area better illustrates the challenges and potential of SVEs than the fisheries sector. Manufacturing industries, for example in clothing, textiles or crafts sectors of SVEs, can survive and even flourish through the identification of niche markets and productivity gains, as put forward by Biman Prasad, Yenteshwar Ram and Ariel Marr in the case study on textiles and clothing in Fiji and in the case study by Heather Baigent on the manufacturing and marketing of Lombok pots. However, one of the main areas of significant competitive advantage for Pacific SVEs is in the successful development of their fishing and fisheries sectors.

The revenue potential of fish and processed fish-product exports, along with the revenue from access license fees from foreign fishing countries, is obvious. Fishing also constitutes a basic way of life and subsistence income and nutrition for many in the region. So the challenge of competing globally needs to be carefully integrated with up-skilling, capacity building and ongoing sustainability of the fishing environment, especially for small-scale fishers.

Manleen Dugal in his case study notes that the small-scale artisanal fishing sector provides direct employment to tens of millions of people, and 'indirect employment to tens of millions more, many of them women involved in fish processing' (UNEP, 2005). The study points out that artisanal fishing accounts for 90 per cent of all fishing jobs worldwide and nearly a quarter of the world catch. While per capita consumption of fish is the highest in the Pacific region, artisanal fishers and their families in the Pacific region are amongst the poorest (World Fish Centre, 2005). Dugal concludes that fisheries development is the only way out of poverty and malnutrition for several economies in this region. Development of the domestic industry would mean a greater contribution to the economy, although this would take time and considerable investment in terms of infrastructure, processing facilities and trawlers.

There appear to be four main trade-related development issues here:

(1) the importance of revenue from license fees for access to Pacific fishing zones
(2) building the capacity of the Pacific region's own fleets to compete
(3) market access for Pacific and SVE exports, including the role of preferential treatment
(4) special consideration and capacity building for small artisanal fishers.

The outcome of the present WTO Doha Round negotiations on subsidy disciplines and market access negotiations on manufactured products (NAMA) will play a significant role in how SVEs balance the challenges of development in these four areas. While the debate about appropriate and flexible NAMA formulae for tariff reduction continues (and it is a debate that SVEs must monitor and influence), much attention has been focused on subsidies because of their relevance to the four issues mentioned above.

Several WTO members have been concerned about the ability of the Agreement on Subsidies and Countervailing Measures (ASCM) to cover some of the issues concerning the use of subsidies in the fisheries sector. There is concern that existing allowable subsidies are either directly or indirectly causing over-fishing and depleting stocks, as well as having trade-distorting effects.[11]

Fishing subsidy disciplines and access fees

For many years, there has been concern that subsidies of various kinds paid directly or indirectly to fishers are leading to over-capitalisation of fishing fleets, over-fishing of fish stocks and distortion of trade in fish. Subsidies may be in the form of subsidies on inputs of fishing fleets or subsidies of fish processing facilities (including through foreign aid) or preferential access for domestic or foreign fleets.

A key issue for SVEs is that any new rules on subsidies should not negatively affect the fees they obtain from licenses given to foreign fleets or their governments for market access to Pacific fishing zones. Fisheries Access Agreements are contractual arrangements whereby governments or private fishing fleets pay coastal states for access to fisheries resources

---

[11] This view is disputed by others who believe that over-fishing is more to do with poor management practices: a point we return to in the next subsection.

within the coastal states' exclusive economic zones (EEZs).[12] The main concern is with a second level of transactions relating to Fisheries Access Arrangements, which deal with a situation where the distant water fishing nation (DWFN) government transfers access rights to its private fishing fleets for less than the full cost of fishing, including the external costs associated with over-fishing.

According to a study commissioned by the International Centre for Trade and Sustainable Development (ICTSD),[13] more than 25% of total government revenue is obtained from access fees in several of the PICs,[14] while for Kiribati and Tuvalu it can be as high as 40 to 60% of GDP. Apart from direct impacts on revenue generation, any loss of access fees would have an adverse impact on employment generation and value-addition (growth of upstream and downstream activities).

The choice for WTO members is between allowing greater flexibility in the use of subsidies from DWFN governments to private fishing companies or to exempt such subsidies from any new disciplines for the time being, and to let another body such as the FAO deal with the problems of managing over-fishing and related environmental issues. Dugal argues for the latter solution. Whatever the final outcome, it needs to reflect the specific concerns of SVEs, either through allowable exemptions for SVEs or through sufficient transition periods to allow SVEs time to adjust and make new arrangements with DWFNs.

In an effort to address some of these complexities, in November 2007, the Chair of the Negotiating Group on Rules circulated a draft document on suggested amendments to the ASCM, including proposals for a legal text on new rules for fisheries subsidies in Annex VIII. The Chair adopted a 'bottom-up' approach that listed an ambitious number of subsidies that would be banned, instead of a 'top-down' approach that banned all subsidies and listed those that were permitted – a positive development for SVEs in the region that had promoted this approach (Campling, 2008).

The proposed prohibited list includes subsidies that are currently of commercial importance to DWFN partners of SVEs, with potential negative impacts on both parties. However, Pacific negotiators have sought to assess the list and the text generally in terms of its overall impact on the region's governments, domestic fishing and processing operations, including the impact on the artisanal, small-scale sector. They

---

[12] The EEZ is the area within 200 nautical miles from defined baselines (Article 57 of the 1982 United Nations Convention on the Law of the Sea).

[13] Mbithi (2006), p. 13.

[14] ACP communication on access fees, WTO Document TN/RL/W/209, 5 June 2007.

have focused on the extent and scope of coverage of SDT for developing countries.

Special and differential treatment: concerns for SVEs

On most issues, PICs and the broader group of SVEs were unanimous in their response to the Chair's text. The central issues in terms of SDT were as follows:

- Government-to-government fisheries access payments, and their further transfer is permitted where the agreement is to access a developing country's EEZ. This is an important outcome for Pacific SVEs as it provides legal security for subsidised access agreements.
- In terms of SDT for non-LDC fishing operations, subsidies for port infrastructure and other physical facilities, income support for fishers and price support for fishers' products (e.g. in the case of significant price declines) should all be permitted.
- The need for technical assistance is particularly important for SVEs to implement notification and surveillance requirements.

These issues will need to be closely monitored throughout the rest of the Doha Round negotiations.

Other problems cited in the text include concerns by non-LDC SVE fishing industries about prohibited subsidies for vessel construction, repairs, acquisition and subsidies for operating costs (e.g. fuel, bait and insurance).[15] This is highly problematic for Pacific SVEs, as one of the most important subsidies in the region for small-scale vessels are subsidies for day-to-day operating costs, which are relatively cheap and affordable to developing country governments.

This provision in the text at present represents a significant barrier to fisheries development. In terms of Pacific SVEs' existing (and potential) semi-industrial and industrial fleets, the only subsidies that are permitted under the Chair's text would be those for subsidised vessel construction, repairs and acquisition for vessels that are active only in the EEZ of the subsidising country.

These exemptions are of relatively limited benefit to most PIC governments because restrictions on the area of operation to the subsidising

---

[15] These subsidies are only allowed for decked vessels that are not greater than 10 metres in length.

states' EEZ exclude existing, mutually beneficial regional access arrangements and ignore the commercial reality of 'following the fish' when vessels are targeting highly migratory species such as tuna.

Aside from the exclusions for LDCs and for subsistence fisheries, all of the other SDT measures outlined above are contingent upon non-LDC members meeting a complex set of fisheries management requirements to ensure the conservation of fish stocks. Pacific SVEs supported an ACP statement that several developing countries have capacity constraints in meeting the demanding fisheries management requirements listed in the Chair's text. The Chair has been asked to simplify the language of this provision.

Ways forward

This paper has already suggested ways forward for WTO negotiations on subsidies, but it should be emphasised that any eventual agreement on fisheries subsidies is dependent upon the completion of the Doha Round, including negotiations over the Agreement on Agriculture and on industrial goods (i.e. non-agricultural market access, which includes fish products). Therefore, Pacific SVEs that are members of the WTO must be particularly diligent that horse-trading in other areas does not lead to negative outcomes for the Pacific in any future text on fisheries subsidies (Campling, 2008).

As mentioned earlier, there are four major concerns of SVEs with respect to fisheries, specifically:

(1) the importance of revenue from license fees for access to Pacific fishing zones
(2) building the capacity of the Pacific region's own fleets to compete
(3) market access for Pacific exports, including the role of preferential treatment
(4) special consideration and capacity building for small artisanal fishers.

With respect to point one, we believe there needs to be firm support in the WTO for the flexibility put forward in the Chair's text for government-to-government fisheries-access payments and their transfer where the agreement is to access a developing country's EEZ, as this provides legal security for subsidised access agreements. However, in the long run, it is highly desirable that the resource rents paid to SVEs for exploiting their fish stocks reflect the full social and private costs of exploitation. A transparent means of achieving this goal is through market pricing of sustainable quotas.

When provided by SVEs, subsidies often seek to integrate in-shore and artisanal fisheries with other sectors of the economy and to improve the benefits to be derived from offshore fishing for export. An inflexible disciplining of subsidies in this case is therefore contrary to the long-term strategic liberalisation goals of SVEs.

Therefore, it is important that allowable subsidies for capacity building of SVE fishery sectors and support for artisanal fishers, such as the current WTO member proposals for green-box subsidies,[16] deserve support from developed country members of the WTO.

In addition to these measures, there needs to be significant capacity-building support and national strategies put in place that promote domestic fisheries of SVEs. Of the strategies put forward, this paper highlights the importance of the following:

- incorporating small-scale fisheries into national poverty reduction strategies
- domestic incentives for private investment in small-scale fisheries
- support for small-scale aquaculture technologies with the objectives of improving the sustainability and profitability of the fishery resources of artisanal fishers and helping in lifting the poor out of poverty
- capacity-building support for transparency and notification procedures, given the importance of compliance and statistical analysis for future reform
- exclusion of inland fisheries in SVEs from any new subsidy disciplines
- national and regional efforts to foster effective fisheries management regimes in order to preserve fish stocks.

These strategies will require domestic, regional and international support and cooperation if SVEs are to successfully build more competitive fisheries industries and achieve increased productivity and wealth creation among poorer artisanal fishers, while maintaining significant revenue from access fees. There also needs to be progress in NAMA negotiations on the reduction of tariffs and expansion of quotas for fish and value-added fish product exports from SVEs.

The fisheries sector exemplifies much of what this paper is about. There is tremendous potential in the Pacific for sustainable competitive exports. There is also great potential to reduce the poverty levels of small-scale fishers. Yet, it will require strong political will by both developed and

---

[16] For a list of the green-box subsidies proposed, see Manleen Dugal's case study on fisheries in the central and western Pacific.

SVE partners to bring about the necessary capacity building, domestic reform, cooperation and flexible market-access arrangements for progress to be made. Ideally, the conclusion of the Doha Round will send the right political signals in this direction. However, even if a Doha Round agreement does not eventuate in the near future, there is good reason to expect domestic, regional and international cooperation from relevant developed countries in pursuit of enlightened self-interest: the protection of fish stocks, fewer trade barriers and regional wealth creation.

Rules of origin

Rules of Origin (ROO) are criteria used to define where a product was manufactured or otherwise produced. ROO are needed because, globally, trade is not free, and trade rules exist that discriminate between exporting countries through, for example, quotas, preferential tariffs, anti-dumping rules, safeguard measures and countervailing duties. ROO may be preferential or non-preferential. Non-preferential ROO should apply when all exporters, whether to an individual country or to bilateral or regional trade agreement partners, are treated the same. The WTO Agreement on Rules of Origin, an outcome of the Uruguay Round negotiations, was an attempt to establish harmonised ROO that were 'predictable, objective, and understandable'. However, there has been debate over the Agreement, and the WTO Committee on the Rules of Origin has been charged with looking for changes that will resolve the debate.

Non-preferential ROO are used within bilateral or regional trade agreements to establish whether a good or a defined percentage of the cost of manufacture of the good 'originates' within the exporting country(ies) and is eligible to receive the reduced rate of duty under the preferential arrangement. The ROO for exports from Pacific FICs to Australia and New Zealand (primarily with respect to garments from Fiji) have been the subject of considerable debate over the period that SPARTECA has been in operation. The original ROO was 50%, which meant that at least 50% of the substantial cost of manufacture of the good had to take place within Pacific countries or in Australia and New Zealand. Presently, there is pressure from Fiji to have the ROO lowered to 35%. Lowering the ROO percentage would allow Fijian garment manufacturers to source more inputs from cheaper overseas sources rather than domestically. The reason for this request is the pressure on their viability from the erosion of the value of the SPARTECA preference through the lowering of tariff levels in Australia and New Zealand. But this is a short-term measure to try to avoid the inevitable pressure to become internationally competitive. An undesirable effect of the ROO, which work in opposition to the need to become internationally competitive, is that they encourage firms to pad their manufacturing costs and avoid the need to become more productive or improve their quality and find new markets.

In the debate on improving preferential modalities, particular attention has been given to ROO. It is noted that in some export sectors, utilisation of trade preferences has been hampered by restrictive ROO. ROO are increasingly perceived as being founded on an obsolete vision of vertically integrated industries, while production has become internationally fragmented in the context of global interdependence and trade liberalisation, which has changed manufacturing processes dramatically. Finished goods are increasingly subject to multi-country and multi-industry interventions, with individual enterprises in different countries specialising in production stages, according to their comparative advantage. Accordingly, carrying out several processes to acquire originating status in a single country is no longer consistent with technological progress and global trends. Moreover, with lower MFN tariffs in all large markets, concerns about circumvention often appear outdated.

In the short to medium term, in the Cotonou EPA negotiations and the negotiation of PACER-plus as preferential agreements, it would be advisable for negotiating parties to reach an agreement, consistent with strategic liberalisation processes, that enables some flexibility around ROO.

Trade in services

The UNESCAP Economic and Social Survey for 2007 demonstrates the growing importance of services to SVEs. The report states that PICs showed positive economic growth in 2006, ranging from slightly less than 2% in Tonga to more than 6% in Vanuatu, and that this growth was led by the services sectors in most of them.

In 2002, the services sector in Kiribati accounted for 75% of GDP, while in Tonga it accounted for 56%.[17] However, in some cases, services comprises mainly government services. This is the case in Kiribati, where there is very little private-sector activity. The bulk of formal employment is in the public service. In other countries, such as the Cook Islands, Fiji, Samoa and Vanuatu, tourism has been growing vigorously in recent years, and this growth is showing up in the growth in the services sector.

---

[17] Commonwealth Secretariat (2006), p. 75.

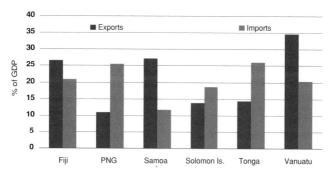

Figure 5B   Trade in services as a share of GDP. *Source:* CIE (2007).

According to UNCTAD statistics (UNCTAD, 2005a), from 2000 to 2004, exports from small developing countries in Oceania increased by 26.5 per cent. Figure 5B exemplifies the importance of trade in services for six Pacific SVEs, with trade in tourist services accounting for a significant component.

Many SVEs have developed their services sectors and are seeking to value-add and diversify further, seeing trade in services as vital for the future of economic growth, employment generation and poverty reduction. Four sets of issues are important for this expansion, and these are discussed briefly below.

Market access

A brief reflection on the mechanics of the WTO General Agreement on Trade in Services (GATS) is useful for an understanding of some of the market access issues facing SVEs. A unique feature of the GATS is that it allows WTO members to liberalise at their own pace by submitting offers to liberalise on a voluntary basis. While this feature allows flexibility for WTO members as to the timing and degree to which they liberalise services, it is a double-edged sword for SVEs as it also means that other developed and developing countries have no compulsion to open up their economies to services trade that might be of significant benefit to SVEs. Therefore, one key issue for SVEs is market access, particularly in the area of labour mobility.

GATS commitments are based on four modes of services delivery: mode 1 being cross-border supply (e.g. e-commerce, where neither the producer nor the consumer moves); mode 2 being consumption abroad (e.g. tourism, where the consumer moves to the producer); mode 3 being for commercial presence (e.g. a branch operation or joint venture); and

Table 5D   *Percentage of services liberalisation offers by mode of service delivery (2005)*

Mode	%
Mode 1	28
Mode 2	14
Mode 3	56
Mode 4	1.4

Source: Thomas (2005), p. 39.

mode 4 being for the temporary movement of natural persons (e.g. labour working abroad on a short-term contract). As shown in Table 5D, as of 2005, of all service liberalisation commitments offered to date, very few have been in the mode 4 area – an area of particular importance for SVEs.

So far, most of the running on services has been from developed countries acting in their own interests, and so it is critical in the future for SVEs to make up ground in this area.

Safeguards and review of the GATS

There have been calls from a number of developing countries, including some SVEs, for the introduction of disciplines around safeguard measures on trade in services to protect SVEs from sudden import surges. Given the small size of their markets, they fear being swamped by foreign-owned services in strategic industries. There is also concern that the WTO has been unable to develop a comprehensive assessment of the early impact of services liberalisation, which was originally scheduled in Article XIX of the GATS. In the section on ways forward, it is argued that it is in fact not only difficult to design effective safeguard measures on services but it may actually be undesirable for SVEs.

Recognition of standards and qualifications

As the case study on Grenada shows (Chapter 5.2), the importance of mutual recognition of qualifications and industry standards is vital for the increased flow of the benefits of liberalisation. For the Caribbean to successfully establish thirty-seven schools of medicine required onerous work on harmonising standards and qualifications for professors, students, medical staff, para-medicals, nursing staff and community health workers. For SVEs, any steps that facilitate the mutual recognition of standards and qualifications across the services sector will assist in their capacity not only to consolidate existing services but also to diversify into other services.

Supply-side issues, regulation and capacity building

This set of issues is arguably the most important. Apart from tourism, the case studies in this book illustrate success stories and existing potential for SVEs to diversify into areas of education and health services, ICT services, off-shore financing and call centres. For this strategy to be successfully pursued requires a mix of domestic reform, including regulatory reform, along with internationally and domestically funded capacity building.

Given that SVEs also import a wide range of services, and that non-traded services are a vital component of their economies, there is no doubt about the importance of services. The main issue is how best to move forward in the development of these sectors: how best to increase market access, diversify supply, appropriately regulate small economies and ensure that the benefits of development are captured by lower-income groups.

Ways forward

Market access   It is increasingly critical for SVEs – through the WTO for those who are members and through regional agreements for others – to increase the demand for trade liberalisation measures in areas of services of critical interest to their development. This may be particularly useful in those sectors of the economy where domestic suppliers need to be encouraged to engage in competition, such as in the utility services sector or in telecommunications services – areas essential to the efficient functioning of the rest of the economy. In EPA negotiations with the Europeans or in PACER-plus negotiations with Australia and New Zealand, SVEs should be seeking mutual reductions in barriers to trade in services, in particular for labour mobility and foreign investment in services. PACER-plus agreements should be a useful testing ground for Pacific neighbours to explore market access issues between smaller economies before negotiating agreements with the larger Asian and US economies.

To date, SVEs have been slow to place requests for services liberalisation and to respond to requests from other, mainly developed, countries. While no one doubts the need to further develop SVEs' capacity to realise the benefits of services liberalisation through prudential regulation, SVEs should be demandeurs in negotiations for the opening up of a range of services in other countries. Adopting a 'negative listing' approach is more transparent and easier for prospective investors, private or government, to negotiate. While ultimately SVEs must choose the most appropriate approach for their development needs, a 'negative listing' approach will allow for a necessary degree of exclusions while reaping the greater benefits of transparency and the inclusion of all four modes of services supply.

Safeguards and review of the GATS   As previously mentioned, there is some concern among SVEs that WTO members have found it difficult to carry out the comprehensive assessment of global trade in services envisaged and mandated in Article XIX, paragraph 3 of the GATS. While the Council for Trade in Services has met for this purpose, the key problems with undertaking a comprehensive review are the difficulty of measuring the impact, given the short period of time that has elapsed since the end of the Uruguay Round, and the serious gaps in relevant statistical data. In terms of a more comprehensive assessment of services trade by the Council, it may be more valuable for SVEs to request a specific assessment about how market access issues can best be addressed, given their specific needs, for example with a particular focus on how barriers to mode 4 liberalisation might be reduced.

Thomas (2005) among others, argues the need for progress on rules to govern safeguard measures for trade in services in order to protect SVEs from sudden import surges. Article X of the GATS mandated negotiations on safeguards for services and stipulated that the negotiations should produce a result not later than 1998. Ten years past the deadline, there is still no agreement on this issue because a large number of WTO members believe safeguard measures for trade in services are inappropriate, given the major differences in the way services are traded across borders as compared with trade in goods. Firstly, there is the serious problem of a lack of statistical data about the different modes of delivery to support an argument that there is a surge of 'imports'. Secondly, it would be very difficult to determine the nature of the safeguard measure itself and how governments would deal with the serious problem of acquired rights. Thirdly, most trade in commercial services to date has been conducted through mode 3, where the established commercial presence operations of foreign services suppliers normally employ far more local employees than they do expatriates. SVEs need to encourage this kind of investment rather than take on safeguard actions that could cost the jobs of their own citizens. For these and other reasons, introducing the notion of safeguards into trade in services is unlikely to progress or make much sense for the foreseeable future.

Recognition of standards and qualifications   SVEs should pursue reciprocity arrangements or, ideally, Mutual Recognition Agreements (MRAs) with their key trading partners of those regulated services sectors, whether bilaterally or through the various regional agreements, including PICTA, PACER-plus or the final Cotonou EPA. The GATS, under Article VII, allows WTO members to achieve MRAs with regard to 'education or experience obtained, requirements met, or licenses or certificates granted'. Recognition may be achieved through harmonisation or otherwise; that is, it may be 'based upon an agreement or arrangement with the country concerned or may be accorded autonomously'.[18] This guideline is based on the assumption that MRAs can potentially facilitate the movement of service suppliers, are instrumental to policy reform and represent a powerful tool for economic integration.[19]

MRAs are much more easily concluded in a regional or subregional arrangement than in a multilateral setting. For instance, the movement of natural persons (mode 4) may be easier to negotiate among a smaller group of countries because market opening may be perceived as being less of a threat. PACER Plus is in a good position as an FTA to 'test the waters' of the liberalisation of mode 4 services. However, the requirements of MRAs are many and complex. According to UNCTAD (2005b), a country that wishes to join the negotiation of an MRA must have in place a domestic system for regulating the profession at stake, an accreditation system, a national register of professionals and the capability to evaluate standards, compare education and training systems and formulate positions. All of these measures need considerable human and financial resources because the negotiations for MRAs may take several years. This raises the urgency of formulating harmonised standards, best practices and guidelines for specific professions. Therefore, the importance of capacity building cannot be overstated.

Supply-side issues, regulation and capacity building   For SVEs to confidently embrace services liberalisation and diversify their services sectors requires a detailed trade strategy that covers the timing and sequencing of trade reforms not only for the development of human resources but

---

[18] Article VII, No. 1 of the GATS.   [19] UNCTAD (2005b), p. 23.

also for the development of institutional capacity and legislative reform. International donors should commit to capacity-building support for reform of legislation, regulations, procedures, frameworks and institutions to ensure the development of competitive, prudentially regulated services.

In the case study on Grenada (Chapter 5.2), we see how a privately run medical school has been able to successfully meet a shortage in supply of medical training places for US and European students, reducing dependence on tourism and agriculture. Sacha Silva describes in some detail three of the key steps necessary for this success to become sustainable for Grenada in order to assist lower-income groups. These can be summarised as the 'expansion of vocational training', a 'reduction in the island's cost of living' and the 'diversification of educational services', for example to include agricultural services and tourist services. Each involves policy reform and capacity building and is instructive for other SVEs seeking diversification of services.

In general, the successful expansion and diversification of services and trade in services that would seem to be necessary for reform and poverty reduction are as follows:

- There is a need for a multi-pronged, whole-of-government approach to services reform.
- use of capacity-building support and technical advice on how best to stage reform in the services sector is needed so as to ensure that key economic backbone services such as utilities are prioritised as well as consumer protection policies.
- Social attitudes and behavioural patterns need to be reoriented towards appreciating the value of a services-driven economy – an obvious but often hard to achieve reorientation.
- Education and training are key, not only the vocational and technical education already mentioned but also a focus on increased literacy rates, computer skills and communication skills among lower-income communities.
- Attraction of local entrepreneurs seeking to start up small services businesses requires technical and financial assistance related to one or more of capital formation, equipment and technology management, market assessments and business development strategies. It would be desirable if international donors could work with SVE governments to establish one-stop resource centres for entrepreneurs, with seed funding available for SMEs.

- Given the importance of tourist services to many SVEs, it is important that they deal firmly with health risks, personal security concerns, insecure property rights for developers and diversification of tourist venues. As Chand (2006) points out, SVEs have a comparative advantage in providing security, given their size and community networks, and this needs to be strongly marketed to potential tourists.
- The case study on the successful development of ICT services in Uganda in the section of the book on services (see Chapter 3.1) points to the importance of governments partnering with private firms to develop innovative ways to cover high costs for services equipment and installation charges in rural areas. This applies as much to health and education services as it does to ICT services.
- The Ugandan case study also reflects the importance of strategic liberalisation. It began with the privatisation of the state monopoly, which opened up the market to new players. Competition improved the quality and range of ICT services on offer, and then an independent regulator reduced government interference in the telecommunications sector and provided the necessary regulatory framework to monitor the activities of all service providers. Uganda adopted a gradualist approach towards reform to protect the interests of the various stakeholders, especially low-income consumers.

Labour mobility

There is much in this book on the importance of labour mobility to developing countries, and most of the benefits apply especially to SVEs. Here, the particular challenges and benefits for Pacific SVEs are briefly summarised.

With a youth population of around 40 per cent, labour is one of the most significant resources available to many Pacific SVEs. Remittances from both the permanent and temporary movement of labour, if well channelled, can directly contribute to poverty reduction. The importance of labour mobility and remittances as a vital component of financial flows to many Pacific SVEs is illustrated in Table 5E.

A recent report from the World Bank (2006) confirms the importance of remittances for poverty reduction. The study undertook analysis of data from remittance-recipient households in Fiji and Tonga, which showed the poorest 40% of the population's share of cash income increased while the share of the richest 20% decreased in both countries. Using a range

Table 5E   *Trade, aid and remittances for Pacific Island countries (2003)*

	Imports (% of GDP)	Aid flows (% of GDP)	Remittances (% of GDP)	Exports (% of GDP)
Cook Is.	46.0	3.5	0.7	4.9
Fiji	49.2	2.3	7.0	30.1
Kiribati	99.4	31.5	12.0	6.9
Marshall Is.	55.8	53.9	0.6	9.3
FSM	47.3	49.7	1.0	6.5
Nauru	71.0	35.5	na	25.5
Niue	68.7	15.1	na	1.5
Palau	71.5	20.5	na	7.3
PNG	31.4	6.4	0.2	47.8
Samoa	51.3	10.4	14.2	5.2
Solomon Is.	28.6	25.7	0.0	25.2
Tonga	74.1	16.3	39.2	11.6
Tuvalu	75.6	38.6	35.9	0.9
Vanuatu	58.7	11.7	3.3	42.4

Note: the aid flow data for the Solomon Islands is probably a serious understatement, as national accounts and balance of payments data do not seem to be capturing the effects of the funding of the Regional Assistance Mission to the Solomon Islands. Recent estimates suggest that aid-funded development expenditure may now be closer to 75 per cent of measured GDP.
Source: ADB (2006), AusAID (2006).

of measures of deprivation, the study found remittances to have a direct and positive impact on poverty alleviation.[20]

Some of the key issues for Pacific SVEs are about access to the labour markets of developed countries, about building the capacity for the supply of labour through education and training programmes for low-income workers, which then also has vital dividends for when temporary labour returns home, and about improving the direct impact of remittances on wealth creation in their low-income communities. The following summarises the ways forward on these issues.

Market access

Market-access issues must primarily be addressed in OECD countries through a mix of complementary trade, development and immigration

[20] World Bank (2006), p. vii.

policies. Unfortunately, the attacks of 9/11, some consequent refugee and immigration concerns and the forestalled talks in the Doha Round appear to have closed down the possibility of further progress on the temporary mobility of natural persons, or 'mode 4' services negotiations at the multilateral level. It was noted earlier that mode 4 had generated only 1.4 per cent of total GATS offers by 2005. So for the immediate to medium-term future, trade-related labour mobility negotiations will need to progress either at the regional or bilateral level, placing particular interest on the Pacific negotiations on the EPA and PACER Plus.

Developed countries will need to deal with concerns around security, temporary labourers illegally over-staying their work permits and the often expressed fear of employers bringing in cheap labour to undermine local wages and conditions. Pacific SVEs and developed countries should cooperate closely in dealing with these issues.

It is possible, despite recent civil strife in East Timor, Fiji and the Solomon Islands, to promote Pacific SVE labour as non-threatening with respect to broader terrorist issues. The civil strife in these SVEs is mostly internally driven and is not associated with global terrorist movements. Arguably, Pacific Islanders may have a comparative advantage in that they are seen as relatively safe and easy-going people, New Zealand being testimony to a relatively harmonious multicultural community of indigenous Maori, whites and Pacific Island immigrants.

The problem of overstaying can most appropriately be addressed through careful selection processes and comprehensive pre-departure training programmes in the SVEs. The case study on labour mobility in Tonga (Chapter 4.4) points to a recently initiated temporary labour market scheme agreed between the governments of New Zealand and Tonga.

Supply of labour

SVEs already benefit from professionals and skilled labour (in education and health services, for example) working abroad. The challenge is to enable more lower-income and lower-skilled workers to benefit from working abroad. Firstly, there is a need for SVEs and donors to commit to literacy training and vocational education targeted at lower-income groups. Because of the ageing of their populations, OECD countries are experiencing labour shortages in agriculture, health services, security services, aged care services, mining, transportation and construction services. Skills in these sectors should be targeted. Secondly, the training needs to be well informed if not jointly sponsored by the OECD country so that qualifications and standards issues are dealt with.

Training should be a feature of the work undertaken in the developed country. Associated adult education relevant to the services sector they are in should be part of the negotiated package; for example, fruit pickers might undertake accredited courses in farm management, financial literacy or machinery repair to improve agricultural productivity at home. Such training could provide further incentives for workers to return home to use newly learned skills and work ethics to the benefit of their communities.

Use of remittances for wealth creation at home

Pre-departure and return training programmes need to be comprehensive and deal with career development, financial and social issues in the destination country and how best to use their newly earned income for the benefit of themselves, family and the broader community.

Temporary labour market schemes could include a compulsory savings component that is contributed to by both employer and employee. The repatriation of such savings could assist in the capital accumulation needed for investment in the local economy, whether that investment is for the education of other family members or for starting a small business. Obviously, remittances contribute directly to the purchase of consumer goods, including food and clothing, and as such are of direct benefit to lower-income communities. However, if direct consumption can be complemented through remittances contributing to a growing pool of savings available for investment, then so much the better.

In summary, temporary labour market schemes have the potential not only to employ a very significant pool of SVE labour but also the dual ability to satisfy labour skill shortages in developed countries while providing vital remittances to contribute directly to poverty reduction in the short term through expenditure on consumption goods, and in the long term through savings and investment.

Whether temporary labour market schemes will be pursued through trade agreements or other more general arrangements is still a matter of debate. However, the expansion of trade liberalisation agreements in mode 4 services, both regionally and multilaterally, would send strong messages about the seriousness with which developed nations are prepared to embrace the trade-related development agenda in the WTO and in the UN in pursuit of the MDGs.

Domestic and regional reform

Entrenched interests

To set the fundamental signals in place for attracting productive investments into their economies, Pacific SVEs will need to continue to strongly
pursue the path of domestic economic and trade reform. By joining the
WTO or a regional trade agreement, SVEs set in motion obligations that
require transparency and accountability, all of which work against the
entrenched interests of some established elites or protected firms. Resistance to such reform will be inevitable but needs to be dealt with if there
is to be serious progress in allowing trade to lead to growth and poverty
reduction.

Trade liberalisation is strongly resisted by a number of state-owned
enterprises (SOEs) (of which there are many in most SVEs) – the branches
of international companies that have been set up under import protection mechanisms – and many non-governmental organisations (NGOs),
which apparently do not see that in resisting trade liberalisation they are
supporting the use of very regressive taxes and punishing potential export
industries through raising the cost of their inputs.

The kinds of resistance to trade liberalisation can be illustrated by
the opposition to any inroads into protected markets made under the
umbrella of the MSG Trade Agreement. This agreement began with three
commodities being granted free entry (one for each country). Over the
years, the number of commodities included in the agreement has grown to
over 160. However, it appears that whenever a domestic industry believes
that its market share is being taken by imports, there is an appeal for
protection against the imports – an appeal that is usually granted. Hence,
recent years have seen the 'tinned beef war' between the Fiji Islands and
Papua New Guinea as well as the 'biscuit war' and the 'kava war' between
the Fiji Islands and Vanuatu. Some NGOs, trade unions and consumer
groups will then swing in behind the local business, arguing against the
liberalisation of trade. The unwillingness of these Pacific governments to
abide by the trade agreement illustrates not only the social tensions but
also the lack of will at the political level in the region to realise the benefits
of trade liberalisation.

Supply-side issues and engaging the private sector

The case studies on Timor-Leste and Papua New Guinea (Chapters 5.4 and
5.5 respectively) emphasise the challenges for SVEs of engaging the private

sector, both domestic and foreign, in the provision of entrepreneurialism, management expertise and the necessary investment capital for infrastructure development and economic growth. Given the concerns just expressed about entrenched interests, this engagement needs to be targeted to those domestic firms and individuals who are willing to embrace the opportunities provided through openness and competitive advantage.

A key issue is to improve the ability of the private sector to compete by reducing the cost of business and trade transactions. The following issues are highlighted as priorities for attention.

Prioritising the economic backbone fundamentals of transportation and communication infrastructure development

This includes dealing with poorly maintained infrastructure, such as roads and ports or cables for access to telecommunications. For some SVEs, these are huge challenges that will require much time and money to address. Integrating strategies for the development of key infrastructure in national plans is therefore essential. Attracting FDI is important for financing this process.

Lack of property rights and land titling

Communal rights do afford some degree of security and have performed this function well in the past, but through land titling and property rights for families, there is greater scope for raising collateral for future investment and borrowings. A mixed system of tenure may be appropriate in some SVEs, but land reform remains a priority to free up capital for investment. Too often, insecure land tenure is inhibiting production efficiency in agriculture and affecting the ability of SVEs to increase agricultural exports.[21]

Lack of an experienced and skilled workforce

This is an issue that can be addressed through a range of measures. Firstly, there needs to be a strong national emphasis on literacy and vocational and technical skills, as noted in the case studies on Grenada and Timor-Leste (Chapters 5.2 and 5.4 respectively). Secondly, as mentioned in the section on labour mobility, relevant practical training should be provided to those working overseas, before, during or at the end of their temporary work programme. Ideally, this training could be funded or at least jointly

---

[21] Ram *et al.* (2005), p. 17.

funded by the host country out of aid or trade-related capacity-building funds. Thirdly, private-sector businesses could also play a direct role in the provision of on-the-job training in SVEs. Finally, if SVEs are committed to opening up to trade in mode 3 services, there is increased opportunity for foreign expertise, managers and training providers to assist in the in-country up-skilling of the workforce.

Ensuring the development of an efficient and viable private sector

Promoting the private sector will also require SVE governments to reform and invest in sound regulatory institutions that can ensure not only fair competition but also clarify legal and dispute settlement mechanisms, insist on financial and investment transparency and assist companies in meeting important regulatory obligations, for example in meeting health and safety standards for agricultural exports. Transparent and well-regulated financial institutions are particularly important for the development of a comprehensive, private-sector banking system and the emergence of non-bank financial institutions. SVEs will need to ensure that regulatory bodies and processes are in place to ensure legal and financial contracts are strongly enforced. With this will come greater security and trust, which facilitates the flow of finances for imports and exports.

Tax reform and trade facilitation issues

Tax reform

Where tariff reductions will cause significant revenue loss to SVEs, for example in the case of Kiribati, governments will have to find alternative revenue sources if they wish to maintain expenditure and service levels. For this reason, a number of SVEs have already introduced or are preparing to introduce a broad-based consumption tax.

Grandcolas (2004) argues that a value-added tax (VAT) is preferred because it is non-distorting and because it has positive effects on the administration of tax in the public sector and on accounting practices in the private sector. As shown in the previous section, these are important factors in removing barriers to strengthening private-sector engagement. Table 5F provides information about SVE VAT taxation systems. Of particular interest is that, even in countries where the introduction of a VAT is relatively recent, VAT revenues make up a relatively large component of total tax revenue.

Table 5F   *International experience of VAT*

Country	Population (thousands)	Year of introduction	Rates	Threshold (US$ thousand)	% of VAT in total tax revenue	% of VAT in GDP
PNG	4,400	1999	10	30	19.0	4.5
Jamaica	2,550	1991	15/12.5	–	35.8	8.8
Trinidad	1,310	1990	15	25	23.6	4.3
Mauritius	1,160	1998	15 (10)	100	26.3	5.6
Fiji	810	1992	12.5 (10)	15/8	27.6	6.2
Cyprus	770	1992	8	–	18.9	5.0
Malta	380	1999	15	38	23.4	6.5
Iceland	270	1990	25/14	–	30.5	9.4
Barbados	260	1997	15/7.5	30	32.7	9.5
Vanuatu	180	1998	12.5	65/30	23.3	5.4
Samoa	170	1994	12.5	20	40.0	10.7
Tonga	100	2003	15	50	–	13.6*
Cook Is.	12	1997	12.5	15	49.0	13.0

* Tonga percentage of VAT approximated from 2006 figures.
Source: Grandcolas (2005).

Tonga exemplifies the change in attitude from dependence on trade taxes to revenue from consumption taxes. Tonga replaced all sales and indirect taxes with a 15 per cent consumption tax and introduced a new excise tax to apply to alcohol, tobacco, petroleum fuel and motor vehicles. The consumption tax has equity provisions and exemptions to assist low-income earners. In 2007, Tonga introduced a new personal income tax, business income tax and a yet-to-be developed system of road user charges to fund road maintenance. Tonga has also sought to completely overhaul the administration and management of customs in complying with new tariff schedules and taxation reform.

As with Tonga, other SVEs could consider raising import duties or excise taxes on luxury and non-essential items, at least until other revenue-raising measures have been implemented. Taxes could focus particularly on luxury items such as imported, high-priced spirits and wine.

Alternatively, in small states that are highly dependent upon imports, a small flat 'revenue' tariff at a modest level on all imports may be a less administratively costly and more effective form of taxation even than a VAT. In the case of several Pacific SVEs, most of their consumption and capital goods are imported. As most consumption, aside from subsistence consumption, and most capital goods are imported, there are no production and consumption distortions from such a tariff. As all imports come through a single port, and there are no differences in tariffs to encourage corruption through mis-specification of tariff items, leakage of customs revenue should be negligible.

Trade facilitation

The case study by Nolpi Kilwa (Chapter 5.5) serves as a useful summary of the importance of trade facilitation issues to development and poverty reduction in Papua New Guinea. Kilwa argues that, potentially, there are huge gains for Papua New Guinea out of international trade, but it will require, among other factors, domestic reforms to trade facilitation. He lists the key issues as standards and conformance, quarantine and customs clearance. The study recommends increasing human resource capacity and skills to adopt and comply with international standards bodies and with SPS requirements in developed nations such as in the EU and Australia.

These reforms will cost a great deal of money and therefore require not only national attention but also, as customs clearance issues are also in the interest of foreign exporters, the attention of regional and international trading partners. Reform of trade facilitation and customs procedures should form a key part of a country's trade-related capacity-building programme so as to attract funding from both regional and international sources.

Regional reform

Regional reform and integration of SVEs across the Pacific is an integral part of the domestic reform programme, as it will facilitate domestic reform and should allow for greater economies of scale. Across the Pacific there is a noticeable lack of horizontal integration and cooperation. Enhanced cooperation and coordination in the following areas will realise economies of scale, reduce duplication, increase transparency and greatly facilitate the implementation of regional trade agreements:

- Regionally harmonised customs-tax collection systems will help to deal with avoidance and corruption issues.
- The development of regional templates that can be adapted easily by SVEs will be useful in a number of regulatory reforms, for example in prudential regulation of the financial services sector. Regional templates will also assist in the drafting of legislation for trade law reform.

- Regionally coordinated customs training and reform, with a focus on training officials regionally in the development of efficient systems to deal with tariff classification and transparency of revenue collection, ROO, SPS measures and TBT issues and fast-track clearance systems will be particularly useful.
- A commitment to increased sharing and financing of regional infrastructure in some of the key areas for future exports is vital, for example regional investment in port facilities, maritime transport and air freight transport.
- A serious examination of the value of a common currency, for example the US or Australian dollar is needed. A common currency could make 'doing business' in the Pacific easier for domestic and foreign investors.

The 2005 report to the Pacific Islands Forum Secretariat entitled *Towards a New Pacific Regionalism* (ADB, 2005) supported a broader approach to regional integration that goes beyond the previous focus on cooperation and market integration to address some of the problems of governance confronted by Pacific SVEs. It argued that: 'A Pacific regionalism that speaks to Pacific needs must focus on easing capacity constraints for governments through increased regional provision of services, and on creating opportunities for Pacific citizens through increased regional market integration.'

Global integration and developed country issues

A clear theme of this paper is the importance of trade cooperation among SVEs and between SVEs and other countries, developed and developing, if all are to benefit from increased trade openness, poverty reduction and greater security. Given that significant parts of this paper have focused on the reforms and actions required by SVEs, the final section deals more with some of the reforms and 'ways ahead' for SVE trading partners to consider.

Lack of recognition and strategic issues

In the political debates at the multilateral level, it is easy for the interests of SVEs to be sidelined. The recent recognition of the special interests of small economies and the establishment of the work programme for SVEs have been useful developments. However, progress on many of the trade issues raised in this paper and by SVEs would be assisted by the success of the Doha Round. Should it end in a weak agreement, or if the Round is postponed indefinitely, there is a need to 'safeguard' key SVE interests for humanitarian, economic and security reasons.

It would be wise for key trading partners to support SVEs to overcome major trade barriers, particularly at a time when a number of SVEs are making efforts to adjust to the increasingly integrated and competitive global economy in which they must survive. In WTO terms, this means finding mutual agreement on definitional issues and market access issues and facilitating appropriate SDT and capacity building, which supports SVE efforts to reform and integrate. Regional agreements should ensure a balanced approach on such issues as ROO and temporary compensatory measures for loss of trade revenue. They should also seek to facilitate market access in goods and services of key concern to SVEs, and allow for increased trade-related capacity-building efforts to prepare SVEs for a more efficient and appropriately regulated regional trade environment. If the Doha Round fails, few developed nations will be seeking out SVEs for bilateral, preferential free-trade agreements and so, as noted earlier, the importance of regional trade agreements will escalate.

Because of their limited resources, both financial and human, small developing states are at a considerable disadvantage in negotiating regional agreements with larger developing and developed states and in negotiating accession to the WTO and being involved in subsequent WTO negotiations. The demands on small developing states for accession to the WTO are often completely unnecessary, for example insistence on comprehensive competition policy legislation when some have little need for such complexities. Larger, wealthier countries participate in trade negotiations with a number of well-trained staff. Small developing states are unable to match them in terms of the complexity of the issues involved. They often lack negotiating skills and the legal, research and statistical capacity to develop positions in their best long-term interests. Many SVEs find it difficult to keep abreast of developments in the WTO or within a regional trading arrangement.

The provision of training in trade policy and in negotiating skills can only go so far, as ultimately the lack of resources is their binding constraint. More effective arrangements need to be found to assist SVE participation and advocacy in these trade negotiating fora.

Market-access issues

It is up to OECD nations to take further steps to ensure market access for SVE goods, in particular in those areas where SVEs have comparative advantage in agricultural and tropical products and in labour market services. Even for SVEs that are LDCs, the Everything But Arms principle has a serious loophole in exempting 3 per cent of an LDC's exports and, until the successful completion of the Doha Round, the 'in principle agreement' is not binding.

Developing country trading partners of SVEs can also address trade and non-trade barriers to exports from SVEs. Papua New Guinea, for example, faces some of its highest export barriers in its trade with India (an average weighted tariff of 5.9%) and the Philippines (an average weighted tariff of 3.2%), while New Zealand and Australia have zero average tariffs. Both developed and larger developing nations alike should see how they can assist SVEs to export not only primary commodities but also, through capacity building and tariff reductions, how they can entertain more value-added and processed goods.

Special and differential treatment

We have seen throughout this paper, but particularly in the agricultural and fisheries sections, the need for special and differential measures for SVEs. SVEs must be allowed the policy space and time to build the necessary institutions, infrastructure and policy-reform processes – these measures are costly and time consuming. SDT should therefore allow SVEs time and flexibility to undertake serious trade-policy reform in the interest of the majority of their populations, with distributional programmes and regulation in place to address the needs of low-income consumers.

Trade-related capacity building and Aid for Trade

The two main issues to be addressed under this heading require close cooperation. One is the often perceived concern by developed country donors of trade-related capacity building that SVEs have not undertaken sufficient analysis to develop precise plans and priorities for the most effective spending of trade-related capacity building. The other is that developed countries, as is evident from recent Doha draft texts, are reluctant to make firm commitments to the amounts and timing of trade-related capacity building. In the final draft of the failed Cancun text, there were thirteen references to the importance of trade-related capacity building, yet there were no binding commitments had Cancun succeeded.

The first issue requires SVEs to more clearly identify personnel needs, training needs and the sequencing of trade policy reform. While some have done this, the case studies on Timor-Leste and Papua New Guinea

(Chapters 5.4 and 5.5 respectively) point out that much more work is required.

Nevertheless, as many of the case studies demonstrate, a number of priorities for trade-related capacity building or Aid for Trade (AFT) are evident and include:

- human resource development for trade negotiators and policy makers
- trade-related institutional capacity building, particularly in areas of regulatory capacity for financial, legal and economic reform
- technical assistance to the private sector
- compensation for loss of preference revenue and balance of payment considerations.

Development aid remains vital for a range of poverty reduction and sustainable development projects; however, while there will obviously be some blurring around the edges, the above four areas would appear as the domain of trade-related aid and capacity building and require specific commitments from aid donors.

A final point needs to be made about technology. While private investment can bring with it new technology, the transfer of technology can also be a very important element of trade-related capacity building. The World Bank's *Global Economic Report* (2008), which measures technological progress in its broadest sense (the spread of ideas, techniques and new forms of business organisation), found that the use of modern technology is coming on in leaps and bounds in emerging developing countries. The World Bank concluded that technology was fundamental to economic advancement in lower-income and emerging countries, and that the main channels through which technology was diffused can be directly attributed to foreign trade (buying equipment and new ideas directly), foreign investment (having foreign firms bring them to you) and emigrants or labour working abroad and bringing or sending ideas and technology back.[22]

In summary, across the donor community there is a growing consensus and commitment to the concept of AFT, to trade-related capacity building and to the MDGs in order to assist developing economies in their transition to a more open, fairer and competitive trading environment. It is vital for both SVEs and donor countries to work together more closely in the achievement of these aims. In practice, this means much hard work if the Doha Round, the Cotonou Agreement and PACER Plus are to deliver

[22] 'Technology in Emerging Countries', *The Economist*, 7 February 2008.

solid and sustainable outcomes. With heated debates over the Cotonou EPA with Pacific SVEs and the successful completion of the WTO Doha Round in doubt, there is a long way to go!

Conclusion

This paper began by reflecting on the importance of economic integration in the region, and with concerns over regional security. Should developed nations walk away from their role of supporting trade-related development in SVEs, there is increased risk of political instability and failed states in the Asia-Pacific region. On the other hand, SVEs that remain reluctant to tackle entrenched interests and political reform at home and who view AFT as another convenient form of dependence, will be as much to blame.

This paper has strongly argued the enlightened, mutual self-interest path for all parties to follow. Strategic liberalisation offers a clear path for SVEs, which involves balancing the pace and staging of liberalisation to ensure the trade and development goals are well aligned. Strategic liberalisation, it is argued, is about embedding the fundamentals of future competitiveness in SVEs while ensuring transition costs and safety nets are in place to allow people to adjust and to benefit from future trading arrangements.

For SVEs, the challenges are many. They are confronted with a multitude of demands, yet often have limited time, resources and capacity. This paper therefore emphasises two key messages. Firstly, while the challenges must at times seem daunting, there is an equal multitude of significant and practical opportunities for Pacific SVEs to benefit from trade and to implement more sustainable poverty reduction processes. By ambitiously locking in the necessary economic and trade reforms, the building blocks will be established for future investment in fishers and fisheries, in niche manufacturing, in agricultural diversification and in a range of services exports, including tourism, ICT industries, education and health services and off-shore financial services.

The second message is that developed and larger developing countries must also recognise the multitude of challenges facing SVEs and intensify their political efforts to ensure that sufficient market access, adequate time and policy space and capacity-building support is given to SVEs in order for them to adjust and consolidate reform.

It was noted, for example, that the opening of labour markets by OECD nations must be combined with mutual commitments to training, in both the host and sending countries. OECD nations can benefit from Pacific SVE labour filling labour shortages in their own countries, while SVEs can directly benefit from the use of remittances for savings and investment in capacity building. These are 'win-win' situations, but they will only come about if there exists the political will in both developed countries and SVEs to bring about the necessary trade rules and political reforms for this success.

The politics of reform imply that the process will require time and patience. Donor nations will need to allow time for trade reforms to take place, based on realistic and practical commitments by SVEs to these reforms. Trade negotiations, whether in Cotonou, PACER Plus or the WTO, must build on trust and the instilling of confidence in mutual partnership arrangements for both global and domestic reform.

There is no doubt that a number of SVEs have already undertaken some of the reforms necessary for greater diversification and competitiveness – as some of the case studies that follow so aptly demonstrate. However, much more needs to be done. The trade-reform process needs to be supported by short-term compensatory financing and transitional support as preferences erode, as well as by TRCB for SVEs to develop alternative trade strategies that contribute to economic growth and sustainable poverty reduction. This process can only be achieved if support for reform in SVEs is locked in internally and externally.

References

Asian Development Bank (ADB) (2005), *Toward a New Pacific Regionalism*, ADB: Manila.

(2006), *Outlook 2006: Routes for Asia Trade*, ADB: Manila.

AusAID (2006), 'Pacific 20', background paper, AusAID and the Commonwealth of Australia: Canberra.

(2008), Pacific Economic Survey, AusAID: Canberra.

Campling, L. (2008), *Fisheries Trade Briefing* 1(2).

Centre for International Economics (CIE) (2007), 'Pacific Island Economies: The Role of International Trade and Investment', paper prepared for the Institute of Policy Studies, Victoria University of Wellington: Wellington.

Chand, S. (2006), 'Economic Growth in Forum Island Countries: Lessons of the Past Decade and Opportunities Ahead', Crawford School of Economics and Government, Australian National University: Canberra.

Commonwealth Secretariat (2006), *Small States: Economic Review and Basic Statistics Volume 10*, Commonwealth Secretariat: London.

Grandcolas, C. (2004), 'VAT in the Pacific Islands', *Asia-Pacific Tax Bulletin* (January/February).
       (2005), 'The Occasional Failure in VAT Implementation: Lessons for the Pacific', *Asia-Pacific Tax Bulletin* (January/February).
Institute for International Trade and Pacific Trade Consult (2007), 'The Potential Impact of PICTA on Small Forum Island Nations', report produced for the Pacific Islands Forum Secretariat, Institute for International Trade and Pacific Trade Consult: Adelaide.
Mbithi, S. M. (2006), 'Fisheries Access Agreements – Trade and Development Issues', Issue Paper No. 2, International Centre for Trade and Sustainable Development: Geneva.
Pacific Islands Forum Secretariat (2007), *Trends and Developments: An e-Newsletter of the Economic Growth Work Programme*, available at www.forumsec.org/pages.cfm/newsroom/e-bulletins [last accessed 7 April 2009].
Ram, Y., Biman, P. and Duncan, R. (2005), 'Explaining the Supply-side Constraints to Export-led Growth in Selected Pacific Island Countries', Working Paper Series No. 2, Asia-Pacific Research and Training Network on Trade, p. 17.
Sachs, G. (2007), 'Breaking the Poverty Trap', *Scientific American*, September.
Thomas, C. Y. (2005), 'Making Global Trade Work for People: The Concerns of Small States in the Global Trade Regime', *United Nations Development Program* 6.
United Nations Conference on Trade and Development (UNCTAD) (2005a), 'Report on Shares of Total Exports and Imports of Services', in *Handbook of Statistics 2005*, UNCTAD: Geneva.
       (2005b), 'Training and Capacity Building Activity Report 2005', UNCTAD: Geneva.
United Nations Environment Programme (UNEP) (2005), 'Artisanal Fishing: Promoting Poverty Reduction and Community Development: An Issues and Options Paper', UNEP: Geneva.
World Bank (2006), At Home and Away: Expanding Job Opportunities for Pacific Islanders through Labour Mobility, World Bank: Washington, WA.
       (2008), *Global Economic Report: Technology Diffusion in the Developing World*, World Bank: Washington, WA.
World Fish Centre (2005), *Improving Livelihoods for Coastal Communities in the Pacific*, World Fish Centre: Penang.

5.1

Lombok pots

HEATHER BAIGENT[*]

Lombok, an island in the Indonesian archipelago, east of Bali

For centuries, the Sasak women of Lombok, in eastern Indonesia, have made beautifully designed and burnished clay pots for water, rice and ceremonial use, using traditional methods handed down from mother to daughter.

Local sales provided meagre cash income to supplement subsistence farming. By the 1980s, however, erosion of the domestic market was threatening the livelihoods of the poorest Sasak villagers and the survival of this unique art form. While tourist and export markets offered potentially lucrative returns, the pots were fragile and cumbersome, and accessing new markets was beyond the skills and resources of the illiterate women potters.

In contrast to neighbouring Bali, Lombok has limited resources and is one of Indonesia's poorest regions. The Sasak people comprise 85 per cent of the 2.6 million inhabitants of Lombok. Despite a history of invasion and famine, they have maintained an independent culture, based on strict Islamic values. In the 1980s, the Sasak people lived in crowded villages, eking out a precarious living on infertile land in the rain shadow of Mount Rinjani. These communities lacked healthcare and sanitation, and illiteracy rates were high.

> All available data confirms that this is one of the least developed areas in Indonesia...The people of eastern Lombok are mostly Sasaks who lost out in historical conflicts and were left with only unproductive, single-crop country and few opportunities for increasing or diversifying income...They do however produce crafts of unusually striking design and high quality and have taken advantage of abundant Kaolinite clay reserves to develop substantial village pottery production...Three

---

[*] Heather Baigent is an independent consultant in Auckland, New Zealand.

648

larger villages and many smaller ones are involved in this cottage industry. The larger ones are Banyumulek, Masbagik Timur and Penujak. (In Banyumulek alone some 500 families seem to be involved in pottery production.)[1]

A feasibility study in 1986 noted that the local market for Lombok pots yielded only limited returns compared with the potential of sales to the tourist market in neighbouring Bali. The producer price in Lombok was around Rp 500, compared with the tourist price in Bali of over Rp 20,000 and a large, untapped, global export market for superior-quality Lombok ceramics. The ability to access these more lucrative markets was, however, constrained by uneven quality resulting from traditional firing techniques, the difficulty of transporting the fragile, traditional storage containers and a lack of any management or marketing infrastructure.

A proposal from the New Zealand Government to assist in developing the industry received enthusiastic support from local and provincial authorities, who saw this as a means to bring real benefit to one of Indonesia's poorest regions. The Lombok Crafts Project was formally established in 1988, funded by the Government of New Zealand, with the Indonesian Department of Industry's Directorate of Small Industries as the counterpart agency.

The project's objectives were to improve the living and working conditions of the women potters and their families through helping them to develop high-quality products that could be sold at premium prices to the tourist and decorator markets in Bali and other parts of Indonesia and, potentially, in the global export market.

The project design envisaged two phases. Phase one involved the assignment of two women potters from New Zealand to work with the Lombok potters to extend the range and quality of products and establish village organisational structures. This first phase also had a strong training component, the focus being on training a group of potters who could then pass on new skills.[2] Technical support continued in phase two, but with a stronger commercial focus and the assignment of a New Zealand adviser with expertise in management and marketing.

The original intention was that after four years, New Zealand would withdraw from the project, having trained sufficient potters in improved

[1] New Zealand Embassy, Jakarta, file note, July 1985.
[2] New Zealand Ministry of Foreign Affairs and Trade (MFAT) funding submission, October 1987.

technologies and having introduced marketing and management structures that would enable the project to become self-sustaining. In fact,
New Zealand's assistance continued for ten years, with the project being
handed over to local management in 1997, finally ceasing in 2005 when
the project was established as a limited liability company.

Community development and poverty reduction

Lombok is one of the few places in the world where the ancient craft of
paddled pots, shaped with a stone and wooden paddle, has survived and
maintained its integrity and vitality. Once formed, the pots are burnished
by rubbing with smooth sticks and stones. Decoration may be added
before a final polish with a burnishing slip. Pots are then stacked to dry
thoroughly before being fired. Traditionally, firing was in shallow pits,
fuelled with coconut and rice husks, sticks, dry leaves, rice straw and
bamboo leaves.

Pottery was seen as women's work and an occupation of last resort. The
men provided support by collecting the clay, organising the firings and,
when decorating was completed, trudging many miles to market with
pots stacked in baskets swinging from poles. This could take up to three
days, and the fragile pots often did not survive the journey.

Traditional designs were associated with specific usage, with vessels for
various household storage functions or for use in rituals marking life mile-
stones or celebrating harvests. Innovation was limited since styles developed over generations were considered already perfect for their defined
purpose. Many of the ceremonial forms had their origins in an earlier,
animistic culture condemned by Islamic teachers as pagan, and this had
led potters to focus mainly on utilitarian, low-value household items.
Even this source of income was under threat, as the traditional domestic
market for household containers was eroded by unbreakable, 'modern'
plastic and enamel containers imported from Java.

In the 1980s, traditional Lombok crafts were promoted to increase
tourism, and this sparked a renaissance in the production of pottery
for both ceremonial and utilitarian use. The Indonesian Government
encouraged the pottery industry and sent people from the villages (usually
men) to train at ceramics institutes in Java. Attempts had been made
to introduce kiln-fired, glazed pottery, and small kilns had been built
in Penujak and Banyumulek. Unfortunately, no assistance was given to
enable villagers to meet the considerably higher costs of kiln firing or the

purchase of new glazes; nor was any assistance provided to encourage the village women to accept the new technology and methods.

Lombok Crafts Project

The Lombok Crafts Project sought to ensure that new techniques were introduced carefully in order to retain the intrinsic beauty of the traditional forms and designs while improving product quality and marketability.

The project began with a limited number of trainees. New glazes were experimented with, adding new decorative styles. The product range was extended to appeal to a wider market, with a focus on exports. Potters were taught to use more fuel and a longer firing time so that pots were more durable. The construction of simple, open-topped updraft kilns enabled the potters to increase firing temperatures and thus increase the strength of the products. Where traditional pit kilns were used, a major risk was largely removed through the construction of shelters: 'The firing shelters which have been built in Banyumulek and Masbagik Timur are a community resource paid for in part by the people. Potters no longer lose pots from sudden rain. Firings are shared by project and non-project potters, with the result that there is a noticeable improvement generally.'[3]

During the establishment period, trainees received an allowance of Rp 1,000 per day[4] to compensate for loss of earnings while being trained, although this was phased out as more potters were trained. A credit system was also introduced, enabling the women to obtain funds to pay for fuel and glazes prior to receiving payment for finished pots.

A project evaluation in 1990 noted that the objective of producing high-quality exportable pots had been achieved, although quality and consistency still needed improvement.[5] Training courses had been held in all three villages; seventy-five potters had received training in improved techniques of clay processing, design and firing, and a further eighty-five were being trained at the time. Interest in receiving training was high, largely due to the training incentives and the higher prices paid for the quality pots that resulted. Positive results were quickly apparent:

[3] Development Cooperation Division (1990), p. 6.
[4] A baseline study conducted in 1987 estimated the potters' average monthly cash income at Rp 15,909 (approximately US$16).
[5] Development Cooperation Division (1990), p. 11.

Benefits which have accrued to potters trained through the project have transformed their lives. In Penujak women no longer have debts or live from hand to mouth. They are able to store rice and buy clothes. As well as this, they have made home improvements and some have built new houses. Instead of working continually, women now take a day off when they need it to make them 'more fresh'.[6]

The need for a supply of potting materials and for packing and transport services created employment opportunities for others. Small businesses emerged as villagers sought to benefit from the increased prosperity. With the market coming to the villages, the men no longer needed to hawk pots over long distances, and many began working alongside the women, preparing clay or burnishing and firing pots to increase the family's production.

The empowerment of women has been a major feature of the project's success. This was evident within family units and in the wider community in both economic and social terms. Most of the women potters were illiterate and had relied on high school students to assist with reading and despatching orders. The project offered literacy and numeracy training. Participants were also trained to run meetings, to make decisions and to keep accounts, with the aim of equipping them eventually to manage village cooperatives: 'women talked about making decisions, having control over their finances, being strong, being able to support their families, being confident to face conflict and being independent . . . They showed high levels of interest in attending public meetings and making their opinions known.'[7]

Social benefits to a sector of Sasak society that had previously been seen as at the bottom of the social scale were also apparent:

Young men and women in Masbagik Timur remember going through their school years tagged with the nickname *kemeq* – the local word for rice pot. It was intended as an insult, aimed at children whose families survived by making clay wares, with the implied scorn for people who worked with dirt. The new markets, the elevation of pottery from common domestic utensil to art object, have begun to place potters in a new social category. They are earning money and their vocation has begun to be seen as attractive, even prestigious, in the eyes of other villagers.[8]

The project also helped to set up self-help and savings groups that evolved into effective, community-based organisations, including health support groups and village projects for education and sanitation. As

[6] Development Cooperation Division (1990).
[7] Nelson Polytechnic (1999), p. 81.   [8] McKinnon (1996), p. 140.

the project became self-supporting financially, a portion of profit was transferred to the project's community development division to finance community activities.

The appointment of a community participation coordinator and input from a social scientist resulted in an intensified community participation programme. Within potter groups, a range of leadership training and collective programmes helped to build personal confidence and to open up awareness of the outside world, and this was reflected in attitudes to quality:

> Application of technical innovations introduced by the project and necessary for continued success in the export market has shown a dramatic change as these programmes progress. As potters become more involved in and take control of their enterprise there has been a substantial improvement in the consistent application of the new methods and consequent high quality of the pots produced.[9]

The commercial success of the project encouraged a proliferation of other pottery enterprises, spreading technical skills to a wider group. According to one estimate, the incomes of the potters involved with the project had increased by between 300% and 500% and incomes for non-project potters by up to 300%. Another commentary noted that the project had had a substantial multiplier effect, as other potters outside the immediate project group had taken up ideas and techniques and also increased their incomes.

In 2000, the Indonesian Department of Trade and Industry estimated that the industry involved over 3,000 potters and had created jobs for other people in the villages in the finishing process – firing, burnishing, carving and painting – and associated activities such as freight-forwarding and supplies.[10]

Trade issues and challenges

Traditionally, pots were sold by family members or to vendors in each village, who then carried stacks of pots to sell in other villages or in the Mataram markets. As alternative markets emerged, local showrooms and art shops were established. These new markets demanded products suitable for tourist souvenirs and upmarket décor, and the potters themselves recognised the need to cater to a different type of customer. New products were developed, drawing on traditional designs and decorative

---

[9] McKinnon (2002), p. 7.   [10] MFAT file note, 1993.

motifs found on excavated wares held in museum collections, leading to a resurgence of interest in the rich heritage of Sasak decorative art.[11]

The project established promotional centres in each village to purchase quality pots produced by those who had completed the training course. The centres paid higher prices, providing an incentive to undertake training and to invest in the materials and time required to produce higher-quality products. Initial marketing focused on tourists, hotels, domestic traders and exporters. The first order was received in March 1989, and within a year the project had achieved sales worth over Rp 65 million (approx. US$60,000). In the first full year of operation, 68 per cent of sales were exports, with Australia alone accounting for almost half of total sales by value.

A factor in favour of exporting was that the local market was oversupplied with poorer quality, utilitarian pots and alternative containers, leaving the potters as price-takers rather than price-makers. As shown in Table 5G, the export market seemed to offer the best opportunities. Pricing structures for exports, however, were not advantageous, with all trade sales attracting a discount of 30 per cent, bringing profit margins to a barely sustainable level. Although the cost of the pot itself was a relatively insignificant element in the exporter's overall cost structure, the 1990 evaluation estimated that a pot purchased from the project for Rp 2,000 (AU$1) would have a wholesale value in Australia of around AU$20 and would retail at AU$39. As for the potters, their share barely covered costs.

The 1990 evaluation report identified other anomalies in pricing structures, including that the project was subsidising packaging and meeting the entire costs of transportation from the village to the main marketing outlet in Mataram. Nor was there any differentiation in return to the potters, irrespective of the time taken to make different types of pots. The report also noted a need for improvements in inventory management, rationalisation of product range and a greater focus on export opportunities: 'Promotion centre pot purchases are driven by customer demands. If marketing efforts cannot stimulate demand to provide potters with sufficient opportunities to sell their quality pots, the project will fail in its objective of lifting potters' incomes.'[12]

A producer-controlled and managed marketing organisation, the Lombok Pottery Centre (LPC), was established in Mataram in 1990, with support and guidance from New Zealand consultants. The LPC's role was to provide customer liaison officers, coordinate orders, maintain quality

[11] McKinnon (1996), p. 135.   [12] Development Cooperation Division (1990), p. 2.

Table 5G   *Trade purchases (March 1989 to February 1990)*

Destination		Value (Rp)	% of total
(a) Hotels			
Lombok		2,629,600	4
Bali		3,027,000	5
	Subtotal	5,656,600	9
(b) Trade – domestic			
Bali		9,610,400	15
Elsewhere in Indonesia		5,517,000	8
	Subtotal	15,127,400	23
(c) Trade – export			
UK		6,388,000	10
New Zealand		2,891,000	4
Australia		29,800,200	46
Europe		1,455,000	2
Southeast Asia		4,168,000	6
	Subtotal	44,702,200	68
	Total	**65,486,200**	**100**

Note: Value is pre-trade discount. All trade customers enjoyed a 30% price discount, hence actual revenue from trade sales was 30% less than the total shown, i.e. Rp 45,840,340.
Source: Development Cooperation Division (1990).

control, organise packing and shipping and undertake promotional work. It took over the functions of the promotional centres, as a centralised marketing arm, working with liaison officers in each village.

The LPC had a key advantage in that overseas buyers, lacking the language and cultural facility to deal direct at village level with potters or pottery brokers, were more likely to order through this central facility, which was also able to offer a one-stop service in terms of supply, packing and shipping.

By 1992, the LPC had held a very successful exhibition in Jakarta and two promotional exhibitions in New Zealand. Awareness among expatriates and wealthy Indonesians was high, and orders reached Rp 5 million, including a first order from a European importer for a monthly container. A hotel restaurant in Bali began using Lombok pottery for cooking and serving. Lombok pots were included in a UNIDO exhibition in Paris, resulting in exposure to the décor market and further sales to

European customers. The issue became not one of selling but of managing burgeoning demand.

Despite these successes, sales were largely reactive, with no cohesive sales plan. Export marketing efforts were hampered by a lack of basic data, such as quantities and value of pots sold, percentages of sales to each market segment and which pots were proving most popular. A more strategic approach to marketing was needed, with clear objectives, target markets, price lists and catalogues.

In mid 1992, a decision was made to contract professional marketing input through the services of an agency experienced in handicrafts marketing. Efforts were concentrated on off-island markets, with exporting continuing to be by far the most important in both volume and value. By early 1993, the Lombok Crafts Project was estimated to be contributing 20 per cent of Lombok's total export earnings.[13]

Development of the export trade was helped by the fact that Indonesia was a long-established member of the GATT (now WTO)[14] and operated under GATT rules. Lombok pots, being handmade in a traditional manner rather than produced on a potter's wheel, qualified as handicrafts and were eligible for zero tariff rates when entering the markets of other GATT members. The Indonesian Government also waived the export duties normally imposed on industrial goods.

The products did, however, face two technical market-access issues: (i) quarantine requirements for packaging and (ii) food safety requirements for ceramic tableware.

Transporting the fragile pots beyond Lombok had always been an issue. Large urns shipped to outlets in Bali and Jakarta were placed in crates made from local cane and packed with straw. Not surprisingly, however, this form of packaging was unacceptable for markets such as Australia and New Zealand, where quarantine requirements are strictly enforced. The project was faced with either finding an alternative to straw or paying for each shipment to be fumigated. The crates were also difficult to handle when loading and unloading, leading to a high number of breakages in transit to distant markets.

From the mid 1990s, stronger but more expensive imported packaging materials were introduced. Shipments for larger customers were packed on trays, loaded on to pallets and each pallet shrink-wrapped and

---

[13] Memorandum from New Zealand Embassy, 2000, Jakarta.
[14] The Generalised System of Tariffs and Trade (GATT) was replaced by the WTO on 1 January 1995.

strapped. This largely solved the immediate problem. By 2002, however, packaging was once more under review as buyers became more conscious of its environmental impact and sought packaging that was biodegradable or that could be recycled.

Early in the development of export markets, the safety of food and drink containers was queried, and tableware samples were sent for testing. The results reported that the samples complied with the New Zealand regulations at that time and were therefore safe for food contact use – at least in relation to the chemical characteristics of the materials used.

According to the project's website, samples have since been approved by the food safety authorities in other key markets: 'The clay used to produce Sasak pottery pots has been approved for food safety by the appropriate testing authorities in New Zealand and the United Kingdom, and is considered food safe by the US FDA. Certificate numbers available upon request. Earthenware products from the Lombok Pottery Center include food storage items as well as cooking vessels.'[15] The safety of the pots as food containers remains a concern in some key markets. Ceramics are porous and can harbour bacteria unless sealed with impermeable glazes. Glazes used on products in contact with food also need to be tested to ensure they do not contain lead or other toxic substances. Authorities in Europe have determined that Lombok pottery is too porous for food contact use and have banned the importation of items labelled as tableware. The only items now permitted on the European market must be clearly designed for decorative purposes only, for example garden pots and ornaments.

Expanding export markets enabled the project to become increasingly self-supporting. By 1997, earnings had reached a level where direct funding from New Zealand could be phased out. In the year 2000, sales through the Lombok Pottery Centre reached Rp 2.5 billion, with a net profit of Rp 1.7 billion. Exports were valued at approximately US$1.2 million in 1999 and US$1.5 million in 2000 (Indonesian Department of Industry data).[16]

The project has also benefited from increasing interest in environmental sustainability and social responsibility and has received support from the Indonesian Government to obtain fair trade and environmental certification for its products.

Lombok pots are now marketed worldwide. An internet search throws up dozens of outlets, from Fair Trading and Oxfam to eBay. While the

---

[15] The Lombok Pottery Project website: www.sasak.com [last accessed 9 March 2009].
[16] MFAT file note.

LPC remains a key outlet, and export orders still account for a large percentage of sales, tour operators, craft outlets and décor retailers are also promoting this beautiful traditional pottery.

Lessons and ways forward

From a development perspective, and in terms of meeting the objective of raising the incomes and thereby the standards of living of women potters, the Lombok Crafts Project has been a notable success. The 1999 review team was enthusiastic about the outcomes, while acknowledging that the project had a number of shortcomings in some management and planning aspects:

> It is clear that thousands of people have benefited from this project since its inception in 1988; far more than the 258 or so [Lambok Crafts Project] women potters and their families. Community development programmes and Project facilities have been open to the wider community. Skills have been transferred to many village potters between villagers through exposure to new techniques and information. The status of the project and the villages has been enhanced as tourists nationally and internationally negotiate with these villages for pottery business. The [Lambok Crafts Project] is considered a market leader and is watched locally, regionally, nationally and internationally for innovations in both the commercial and social aspects of its activities.[17]

Table 5H illustrates the four-fold increase in the average monthly income of the women potters over the ten years, from 1988 to 1998.

The final phase was to establish a new legal structure. Following discussions with potters and project staff, a decision was made to form village cooperatives with potters and staff as shareholders in a centralised pottery marketing company.

In November 2005, the Lombok Crafts Project ceased to operate as a bilateral project of the Indonesian and New Zealand Governments and became a limited liability company. The new entity, PT Lombok Putri Cenderamata (LPC) is owned jointly by women potters' cooperatives from the three project villages (around 30% shareholding for each village) and a staff cooperative (10% shareholding).

The New Zealand Government is justifiably proud of the project's achievements and has highlighted the very real benefits to the three pottery villages: 'NZAID's marketing advice and technical improvements turned

---

[17] Nelson Polytechnic (1999), p. 8.

Table 5H   *Monthly income in Rp of Lombok Crafts Project potters (1988, 1993, 1997 and 1998)*

Year	Banyumulek (82 potters)	Penunjak (94 potters)	Masbagik Timur (82 potters)	Daily income	Average total (258 potters)
1988	12,976	18,003	16,642	1,587	15,874
1993	80,000	77,199	72,100	2,547	76,433
1997	83,435	81,454	145,379	3,447	103,423
1998	85,389	77,529	219,899	4,254	127,606

Source: LCP potters income obtained from LCP financial records (Nelson Polytechnic (1999).

a traditional village craft in Lombok into a successful export industry valued at US$1.5 million, and employing 3,000 people. The money stays in the village to build and maintain bridges, sewerage, community services and helps with scholarships for children.'[18]

Contacts in the Indonesian Ministry of Trade confirm that the project is recognised as having had a positive impact on local incomes and in improving village life.

This tells only part of the story. The project has certainly achieved remarkable improvements in the economic wellbeing of women potters, and there is no doubt that, without this project, the lives of these women, and their children, would have been poorer in every sense. In hindsight, however, the project would almost certainly have benefited from a longer-term vision and strategy.

The original concept was to improve the marketability of Lombok pottery, and therefore the cash income of the potters. A baseline survey and feasibility study both confirmed the development benefits, but planning did not go beyond the four years of technical support originally proposed. Looking back, there is a lack of coherence, of assistance provided to address specific, identified problems rather than programmed inputs to a strategic project plan, and insufficient attention to developing local capacity in management and marketing. An integrated long-term plan and a more strategic approach might have enabled issues to be identified

---

[18] 'Trade Can Reduce Poverty' leaflet, available from the NZAID website, at www.nzaid.govt.nz [last accessed 1 April 2009].

and addressed earlier, leading to greater assurance of sustainability beyond donor involvement.

One specific area is export marketing. The first New Zealand project advisers were ceramic artists, well-qualified to work with the women potters of Lombok on technical improvements and quality control. But they were not marketers and, although successful in establishing promotional centres and, later, the centralised LPC in Mataram, they had neither the time nor the skills to address issues such as market access, pricing, packaging and exporter liaison.

It had been assumed that Lombok pots would appeal to an international market, and this proved to be the case, but the essential links between the product and the market were not adequately addressed. If there is a lesson to be learned, it is that in order for trade to assist in reducing poverty, there needs to be a coherent development strategy that ensures a globally competitive product or service, an export infrastructure to ensure delivery and a willing foreign buyer. All three are essential, and require planning and nurturing, if the venture is to be sustainable.

The project also faced cultural and social challenges. According to the first director, the original approach was wholly technical, an approach she now considers paid insufficient attention to social components. In retrospect, had the project adopted a culturally informed and participatory approach, technical innovations would have been more readily accepted and higher quality standards maintained. As it was, project management failed to appreciate fully the social dynamics within Sasak communities, the attitudes to government and to outsiders and the low cultural self-esteem of the Sasak villagers. Project advisers also failed to recognise that cooperative work and community support in Sasak society is limited to clan lines and patron–client relationships.[19]

This improved in the latter stages of New Zealand's involvement, when the purely technical approach was modified:

> This approach should have been part of the design and implementation strategy from the start of the project...The participatory approach requires a longer period of adviser input because of the range of skills that must be developed with the potters and staff, and the process of social change involved...In a society accustomed as this one is to not having enough, to taking every advantage possible to get ahead of or on top of one's neighbours, where those on the bottom expect to be taken advantage of and cheated and abused by those with a bit more (power or property

[19] McKinnon (2002), pp. 5–6.

or money), the time required to bring about such changes is very long indeed.[20]

The project was also affected by the reluctance of some potters to accept and maintain technical improvements to their normal working methods. On reflection, according to the first director, this may have been due to the way new skills and knowledge were transferred:

> The innovations that were easily and consistently adopted independent of adviser or staff supervision had all been transferred through a participatory programme in which potters were involved with advisers at every stage: experimentation and discussion, identification of the solution, evaluation of results . . . The innovations that were unsuccessful had been taught by staff, after experiments by advisers and staff identified them as 'desirable' techniques, or after they had been trialed and found workable in other villages. From the point of view of the potters all of the preliminary work had been done without them, and then presented to them as instruction. They had not been part of the process and therefore did not have a sense of ownership of the new ideas.[21]

Cultural issues also impacted. Project staff members, although local, were educated and therefore seen as of higher social status. Initially, they were selected by village leaders and were invariably male. Their efforts to introduce new ideas were viewed as just another example of the women potters being told what to do by 'bosses'. Unsupervised, potters often reverted to previous practices, and improvements in quality were difficult to sustain.

It also became apparent early on that a factor working against greater participation by the women potters was the paternalistic attitude of some Indonesian officials and senior project staff. Traditional hierarchies placed subsistence farmers at the bottom of the social scale and assumed a level of ignorance and a lack of ability, particularly where women were concerned. These hierarchies were reinforced when the commercial success of the project became evident and the (mostly male) personnel in management roles or other positions of influence sought to impose control over what was becoming a valuable resource.

Another issue was the desirable, but inherently impractical, objective of the women potters themselves eventually owning and managing the enterprise. As the project developed into a large export business, it became apparent that self-management by the potters was unlikely to be successful. As the 1999 review noted:

---

[20] McKinnon (2002), p. 7.   [21] Ibid., p. 5.

The project attempted to use a community-based strategy to bring approximately 258, primarily older, illiterate, poorer village women to effectively
control and sustain an export industry... There has been a fundamental incompatibility between the establishment of an international export
business (a viable commercial venture) and the community development
objective that it be 'under the ownership of women potters'... In hindsight the goal of developing village based women potters, with limited
literacy and management experience to manage a large centralised business enterprise, seemed visionary but unrealistic.[22]

A further threat to sustainability is the now rapidly depleting supply
of good-quality clay. As early as 2003, concern was being expressed at the
effect on quality of the trend to buy clay processed by huller (mechanical
extraction and sifting) rather than potters collecting and processing their
own raw material. The clay supply was also dwindling, with evidence of
environmental damage in areas now over-mined.

A perhaps more serious outcome has been the impact of competition
and financial return on traditional art forms. Lombok pottery is attractive
to the premium end of the market largely because of its aesthetic appeal
and as a 'primitive' art form. Among the potters themselves, however,
there was little of the sense of vocation associated with makers of ceramic
art in the developed world. The driver for the Lombok potters was sales:

Their primary goal is to secure a good future for their children and perhaps manage the Holy Pilgrimage to Mecca before they die... Although
the returns for their work have improved, with the exception of those who
benefit from the fair pricing policy of the project, most potters still find
their income insufficient to greatly improve their situation. Within the
network of artisans, traders and middlemen, it is the artisans who invariably fare least well. In such an environment questions of style and form
and artistic merit apply only to economic viability.[23]

Whether the potters of Lombok can maintain the aesthetic value of their
traditional craft or become yet another mass producer of earthenware
souvenirs for undiscerning tourists remains to be seen. Nevertheless,
it is trade that has lifted the women potters from hopeless poverty and
provided the resources for a better life, and it may be trade that guarantees
the survival of their greatest asset: their art. As the first director puts it:

Fortunately much export trade is conducted by people whose interest in
Sasak pottery goes deeper than mere profitability and whose clients easily
discriminate between the crass inventions of a faddish market and the quiet

[22] Nelson Polytechnic (1999), pp. 8 and 34.   [23] McKinnon (1996), p. 143.

integrity of timeless utilitarian forms. This is the other, more enduring face
of export trade . . . We seek out these vessels precisely because they resonate
with the imprint of skilled human hands. It is this aspect that gives cause
for optimism that the vocation of Sasak potters will continue to thrive and
that the heritage of their grandmothers will not be lost.[24]

The new company is based on a cooperative model. This followed
legal advice on an appropriate structure and consultations with potters'
representatives and project staff. Cooperatives were chosen because 'they
provide for participation by the potters and collective ownership, as well
as independence, transparency and accountability'.[25]

Unconfirmed reports suggest that the new structure is not working
as well as hoped, partly due to insufficient management training and
experience in managing cooperative structures, and partly due to internal
politics and rivalries both within villages and within the overall management structure. Marketing has also suffered through a lack of business
planning and marketing expertise.

Nevertheless, the women potters of Lombok have acquired new technical skills and have been exposed to the basics of business management
and marketing. Perhaps even more important has been the empowerment of a generation of women, confident of their ability to participate
in decision-making and of their role as economic contributors. While
incomes are still low, and the pottery villages lack many services taken
for granted in more developed communities, the hopelessness of abject
poverty has given way to aspiration.

Earthenware pottery from Lombok is now exported widely, sought
after by connoisseurs of traditional crafts and available through Fair Trade
outlets and upmarket design stores, but challenges remain. The potters
themselves do not have the skills to manage what is now a major export
industry.

The future rests with the coming generation, the children of the original
beneficiaries. These young people are educated and have been exposed
to a wider range of opportunities, and many may choose alternative
careers. Whether Lombok pottery can continue as a tradeable product,
contributing to local prosperity, and as a unique art form is now in their
hands.

International recognition of its value, both artistically and commercially, does, however, provide hope for the future of the unique and

---

[24] McKinnon, p. 144.   [25] MFAT file note, 2003.

beautiful traditional pottery of Lombok. The website of the LPC remains upbeat:

> Our pottery is the finest export quality in Lombok, produced with care and tight quality control. Since 1998, we have been complying with ISO 9002 and safety purpose. We have more than 600 designs ranging from traditional and modern. Classified in five major categories, interior, exterior, table ware, kitchen ware and bathroom accessories. We also ready to work together with you to develop your own designs for your market. As trends are changing fast, we have a design update regularly and it would be great if we could keep introducing you to our development. Should this interest you please kindly contact us for further information or your feed back and input, which is enabling us to tailor our product closer to your market requirements.[26]

References

Development Cooperation Division (1990), 'Lombok Crafts Project: A Mid-term Evaluation Report for the Crafts Project at Lombok, Indonesia', Ministry of External Relations and Trade: New Zealand.

McKinnon, J. (1996) *Vessels of Life: Lombok Earthenware*, Saritaksu: Bali.

(2002), 'Participation and Technology Transfer: A Case Study from the Lombok Crafts Project', paper presented at Development That Works! Lessons from the Asia-Pacific Conference, Massey University, New Zealand.

Nelson Polytechnic (1999), 'Lombok Craft Project: Review of Community Development', report prepared for New Zealand Overseas Development Assistance, Ministry of Foreign Affairs and Trade: New Zealand.

[26] LPC website: www.lombokpottery.com [last accessed 9 March 2009].

Plantations to professors in Grenada

SACHA SILVA[*]

Introduction

This case study explores the poverty implications of Grenada's shift from agriculture to services as the island's main employer and source of hard currency. It assesses the extent to which expanding offshore services sectors (tourism and education) were able to absorb low-skilled labour from declining agricultural sectors, and the role of Grenada's public and private sector in encouraging this shift. The analysis has particular relevance for small states as they face the multiple challenges of preference erosion, new trading opportunities in services and the need to achieve adequate poverty-reducing growth in a highly competitive global trading environment.

At the outset, it is important to note the absence of reliable labour- and poverty-related time-series data for Grenada. This paucity is especially acute for the agricultural sector, and in particular for bananas, as it has been a relatively marginal crop in Grenada for nearly two decades. While some labour and production statistics are available post-1995, analysis of trade- and poverty-related phenomena in Grenada is mainly speculative in nature. As such, this case study, while utilising the limited data available, relies heavily on a series of interviews conducted in May 2007. The interviewees included government officials, civil society, private-sector firms and representatives of the rural communities in Grenada. Responses have been quantified wherever possible.

* Sacha Silva is a Consultant with Caribbean Regional Negotiating Machinery, commissioned by the Institute for International Trade, the University of Adelaide. The author wishes to thank the UNDP offices in Barbados and Grenada for assistance in preparing this case study.

Background and key trends

The case study focuses on the Grenadian labour force formerly employed within the banana industry from the 1950s until the present day. This section provides a general background on Grenada and its economy, followed by an outline of three key trade and poverty trends shaping the employment incentives of this community: the decline of both the agricultural and manufacturing sectors and the rise of the services sector.

Background

Grenada is an island of 103,000 citizens located among the Windward Islands, a chain of islands in the Caribbean stretching between the South American continent and the larger islands to the north, such as the Dominican Republic and Cuba. While the island is relatively small (133 square miles – the island is the second-smallest independent country in the Western Hemisphere, after St Kitts and Nevis) the largely English-speaking population is concentrated in the southern tip of the island close to the capital of St George's. Grenada includes two smaller islands to the north (Petit Martinique and Carriacou). Until its independence in 1967, Grenada was a UK colony. Grenada became internationally known in 1983 after a US-led invasion of the island, following a hard-line coup within the socialist revolutionary government of the time. The gross national income per capita was recently (in 2006) estimated by the World Bank at nearly US$4,000 per capita, slightly below the average of its island neighbours in the English-speaking Caribbean.

The population of Grenada is largely employed in construction (male workers) and services (female workers), although informal labour is prevalent in many rural districts. The economy is heavily weighted towards domestic services, particularly government services, which saw the largest increase in its percentage share of gross domestic product (GDP) between 2000 and 2004 (see Tables 5I and 5J).

The decline of the banana industry

The banana industry, once a primary export crop and a key source of hard currency for the government, has experienced a steep decline since the early 1980s. The amount of labour shed by the banana industry is difficult to gauge given that the industry began to decline as early as 1976 (see Figure 5C below), preceding most labour-force datasets.

Officials from the Ministry of Agriculture and the Windward Islands Banana Development and Exporting Company (WIBDECO) estimated

Table 5I *Percentage distribution of employed population in Grenada (2005)*

Activity	%
Agriculture	8.5
Fishing	1.4
Manufacturing	2.8
Construction	22.6
Wholesale/retail	9.2
Hotel and restaurant	5.0
Transportation	2.8
Services	21.1
Administration/social security	4.0
Education/health/social work	7.4
Other	15.3

Source: Government of Grenada (2005).

Table 5J *GDP by economic activity at current factor cost (2000–04 – % shares of GDP)*

	2000	2004
Primary sector	8.6	9.0
Agriculture	7.7	8.5
Mining and quarrying	0.8	0.6
Secondary sector	23.4	22.5
Manufacturing	7.6	5.5
Construction	10.7	10.7
Electricity and water	5.1	6.3
Services	75.8	78.6
Wholesale and retail trade	10.7	10.9
Hotels and restaurants	9.0	7.9
Transportation	15.1	14.5
Communications	8.7	7.5
Banking and insurance	9.9	12.6
Real estate and housing	3.3	3.2
Government services	15.9	19.3
Other services	3.2	2.7

Source: IMF (2005).

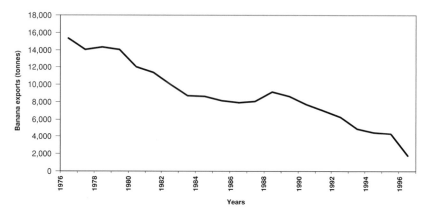

Figure 5C   Grenadian banana exports (1976–96).

that, at the peak of the industry in the mid 1970s, the number of farmers actively engaged in banana cultivation was estimated at nearly 3,000. As the industry declined, the number of active growers fell to 600 in 1990 and then to 60 in 2003. However, to reach an estimate of the *total* labour force engaged in banana cultivation, one must also include the farm labourers hired on a seasonal basis by the banana estates, which on average equalled twice the number of growers.[1] Additionally, the banana industry in Grenada relied on a small number of transportation workers, packers and dockworkers as well as some thirty employees of the local Banana Growers Association. As a result, one could estimate the total number of workers released from the Grenadian banana industry in the last three decades at slightly over 6,000 workers. While this amount is relatively low compared to other larger islands such as St Lucia, which registered nearly 14,000 banana-related jobs in 1998, the figure is substantial given that Grenada's total labour force has not exceeded 43,000 workers in the last two decades.[2]

The factors behind the decline of the banana industry can be classified into two categories,[3] which will now be discussed.

[1] The Grenadian labour force engaged in banana farming can be divided into two main groups: (i) banana growers, whose average age tended to be between fifty-five and sixty-five and who often owned their own plots of land and thus were more reluctant to leave their north and central parishes in search of work in the southern parishes near the capital; and (ii) banana estate workers, whose average age tended to be between thirty and thirty-five and who often did not own their own plots of land, apart from small tracts used for subsistence agriculture. Estimates are based on Sandiford (2000).
[2] Statistics taken from Central Statistics Office (2005).
[3] These factors are drawn from Sandiford (2000).

The impact of the WTO 'banana wars'

The creation of the European Single Market in 1993 and 1994 led to pressures within the EU to reconcile differential arrangements within Europe for the importation of bananas. Significant difficulties arose from competing interests within the EU: protection of the EU's own high-cost banana producers in the Caribbean (Martinique and Guadeloupe); the demand from EU consumers for low-cost bananas; the desire of Germany and the Benelux countries for a free-trade regime; the commercial interests of European banana marketers; the EU's commitments under the WTO; and its treaty obligations to the African, Caribbean and Pacific (ACP) states. After months of negotiations, a single banana regime came into place that established quotas discriminating between, on one hand, banana suppliers in the ACP states and, on the other hand, those produced in Latin America (especially Honduras, Costa Rica and Ecuador) and marketed by American multinationals such as Dole and Chiquita (so-called 'dollar bananas'). The European Community's (EC) proposed regime was deemed unsatisfactory by the 'dollar banana' suppliers and was immediately challenged in the WTO. What followed was a series of WTO Panel rulings against the EC's successive attempts to craft a regime that would satisfy all of the global banana stakeholders. The impact of the WTO Banana Wars in the Windward Islands and Grenada in particular was to create a growing disincentive towards the continued cultivation of bananas. Producers faced falling prices in the EU market as the volume of 'dollar bananas' grew. While Windward Island bananas maintained a price advantage provided by their duty-free quota, the reduction in prices put pressure on already-thin profit margins, driving many small-island Caribbean producers to seek alternative employment. A number of initiatives aimed at restructuring the industry were not able to address the inherently high-cost nature of banana production in the Windward Islands (notably Grenada, which never developed large-scale estates), nor bring production costs in line with larger Caribbean and Latin American producers.

Crop disease

According to many experts interviewed for this study, the inability of Grenada's banana farmers to prevent infestation and disease was the primary cause of the industry's demise, far in advance of the first WTO Panel ruling. The poor quality of Grenadian bananas – often at levels one third below the minimum industry standard – led to the suspension of shipping by WIBDECO in 1995 after widespread infestation. The causes behind the quality problems in Grenada were manifold, ranging from financial difficulties within the national Banana Grower's Association, low levels of government support, lack of timely inputs provided to farmers and a lack of proper training within the farming community to apply pesticides to prevent infestation.

Both as a cause and effect of these two factors, Grenada's agricultural sector has always been marked by diversity. Unlike other Windward Islands, even at the height of the banana industry in Grenada, other cash crops (mostly nutmeg and cocoa) were grown on the same land as banana crops. Banana farmers also grew a significant amount of subsistence crops alongside their banana plants. Banana farming in Grenada never reached the same level of development as other Caribbean producers, who had large estates and infrastructure dedicated to the banana industry. The Grenadian banana industry has always retained an informal 'backyard' character, which, on the one hand, mitigated the negative impact as the industry slowly declined and, on the other hand, prevented the Grenadian banana industry from reaching the necessary scale to meet rising quality standards.

The rise of the services-export sector

Partly in response to the decline of both agricultural and manufacturing sectors in Grenada, the island has developed several successful offshore services industries, despite several obstacles, such as high transportation costs, competition from neighbouring islands and other non-Caribbean countries and the small size of both the local market and the local labour force.

The sector's fortunes have survived political turmoil (including the overthrow of the government in 1979 by a Marxist coup and the subsequent invasion of the island by US-led forces in 1983) and a number of natural disasters, including the passage of Hurricanes Ivan and Emily in 2005. There is no indication that the development of the sector, particularly in offshore medical services, was part of a deliberate policy effort of the Grenadian Government, but was rather the initiative of private individuals who secured cooperation from successive governments to carry out their expansion. This underlies the important role the private sector can play in future economic development and trade for Grenada.

The rest of this section will examine in turn the three major services-export industries that have developed in Grenada: (i) offshore education, (ii) tourism and (iii) offshore financial services. (Offshore call centres were established but failed to develop following the impact of Hurricane Ivan.)

Offshore education[4]

In the Caribbean, there are some thirty-seven medical schools offering programmes leading to a medical degree. Of these thirty-seven schools, Grenada's St George's University School of Medicine (USG) is the oldest (established in 1977) and largest, with a student body of 2,400 students, nearly 10 per cent of the total for the entire Caribbean. The school's main offering is the medical degree, but it also offers programmes leading to a bachelor degree, masters and PhD programmes and a veterinary programme. While the university has partnered with the Government of Grenada in a number of education- and health-related initiatives, the university remains a wholly private enterprise.

USG, along with other offshore schools in the Caribbean, have exploited an unfulfilled demand in the market for American (and increasingly European) medical students. As the offshore schools eschew the more costly research activities undertaken by traditional 'on-shore' medical schools, they are able to offer accreditation at nearly half the price of their traditional competitors (although the cost of living on the smaller islands is often higher than on US campuses). Moreover, the time required to complete an offshore degree is often two years less, and the more established offshore schools in the Caribbean (including USG) are accredited by the US National Committee of Foreign Medical Education and Accreditation (NCFMEA), allowing students to draw on US federal student loans for their offshore degree.

USG is the largest private-sector employer in Grenada and the largest single source of hard currency. At present, the university employs some 500 support staff, of which 280 are classified as non-clerical, i.e. in ground maintenance (100), security (75) and housekeeping (91). The university also employs 300 faculty members who hire local staff for housecleaning and grounds-keeping. In addition, the 2,400-plus student body are resident for at least ten months per year. It is estimated they inject on average US$12,000 annually per student into the local economy. Total

---

[4] This section draws from Swedish Development Advisors (2004) and interviews with officials from St George's University, Grenada.

estimated spending by students and faculty is estimated at nearly US$23 million, or 5.5 per cent of GDP. The university is currently constructing a new hotel on its grounds, in addition to several new dormitories, which are expected to further increase student numbers and local staff requirements.

Tourism[5]

This industry has emerged as a lead sector-driving economic activity in the Grenadian economy in terms of foreign exchange earnings and employment. According to data provided by the Central Statistics Office, tourism accounts for one third of GDP, and spending by tourists pre-Hurricane Ivan totalled some US$220 million per year. The majority of visitors arrive from the US, the UK and other Caribbean countries, totalling some 130,000 visitors annually. Until recently, the Grenadian tourism sector – unusual for the Caribbean – has been nearly 100 per cent Grenadian-owned (although officials interviewed indicated that senior-level management tended to be brought in from the UK or US).

Tourism growth in Grenada has increased despite both minimal marketing efforts and the perception of Grenada as a high-cost destination without the variety of beaches and natural attractions to be found in other nearby islands. The number of hotels doubled from fifteen in 1987 to thirty in 2000, falling slightly after the September 2001 attacks and falling sharply after Hurricane Ivan. The sector, after extensive rebuilding, has recently approached pre-Ivan levels for numbers of hotel rooms, although tourist numbers remain at half their pre-Ivan levels.

On the employment side, the World Bank estimates that 30 to 40 per cent of the Grenadian workforce is employed either directly or indirectly in the tourism sector, with at least 4,000 Grenadians registered as being directly employed in the sector (World Bank, 2004). Direct/formal employment in the hotel sector is largely female, with the greatest proportion employed as cleaners and restaurant staff, while male employment is largely confined to security, grounds-keeping and maintenance. Apart from formal employment within the hotels, the industry supports significant numbers of restaurant workers, taxi drivers, guides and craft makers. Ministry of Agriculture officials estimate that a large share of local agricultural production is absorbed by the tourism sector.

---

[5] This section draws on interviews with and statistics provided by the Grenada Hotel and Tourism Association.

Offshore financial services[6]

The development of the offshore financial services sector in Grenada dates back to the 1980s. The sector grew throughout the 1990s, with an estimated contribution to government revenue of EC$8.9 million in 1998 and EC$14.5 million in 1999. Its expansion, however, was halted by Grenada's 'blacklisting' by the Organisation for Economic Cooperation and Development (OECD) Harmful Tax Initiative from 2000 to 2003. Currently, the jurisdiction, comprising some forty banks and two trusts, offers services in the area of insurance, banking, trusts, international betting and economic citizenship. The employment impact, however, is quite limited, as prevailing legislation requires that offshore banks employ only two staff members in Grenada.

Offshore call centres

Until recently, Grenada housed a fledgling offshore information and communications technology (ICT) sector, which included a small number of offshore call centres, including a UK-based firm employing some 300 people and a public-private partnership between the Government of Grenada and Cable & Wireless, a UK-based telecommunications company with a significant presence in the Caribbean. Inquiries with private-sector associations in Grenada, however, indicated that the call centres closed down soon after the passage of Hurricane Ivan, and there were no immediate government plans to re-start the initiative.

So far, this study has outlined Grenada's unique economic reality: declining agricultural and manufacturing sectors followed by the growth of two thriving services industries. The growth in services and trade in services has been positive for the economic growth of Grenada, but what has been the actual impact on poverty reduction, particularly for those previously employed in the banana-production industry? The next section explores this issue.

Where did all the banana workers go?

This section addresses three key questions:

(1) Faced with these shifting patterns of growth, where did the 7,000-strong labour force released from the banana industry find new employment?

---

[6] This section draws from Lazare *et al.* (2001).

(2) Did labour move in large numbers from the agricultural sector into
    the growing services sectors, and if not, why not?
(3) How has this labour movement impacted poverty levels in Grenada?

Movement of labour out of agriculture

According to the interviews carried out in Grenada, the agricultural workers found work in the following industries: construction (46%), other
agricultural products (22%), informal labour (15%), small business (8%),
the services-export sector (7%) and other areas (2%).

Construction (46 per cent)

According to stakeholders interviewed in Grenada, the vast majority of
young unskilled labourers from the banana industry (the former estate
workers) found employment in construction. The construction industry
in Grenada is largely linked to major public projects rather than private-
sector initiatives. During 1986 to 1989, following the initial exodus of
workers from the banana-production industry, there were a number of
large public-sector investment projects (largely in road construction),
and the 1995 to 1998 period, immediately following the suspension of
WIBDECO shipping of Grenadian bananas, saw another public sector-led
construction boom (e.g. a Ministerial complex and a national stadium)
(Lazare et al., 2001). The reconstruction effort following Hurricane Ivan
has provided another boom in construction; 2005 post-Ivan labour-force
statistics indicate that 37.5 per cent of Grenadian employed males worked
in the construction sector.

Other agricultural products (22 per cent)

The majority of older banana growers, given their status as small land-
holders and their age, stayed in agriculture. As prospects for the banana-
production industry diminished, many growers cut down their banana
plants and diversified into non-tradable crops (e.g. root crops and tomatoes) for the local market; several farmers maintained their banana production solely for the local market. A smaller number of growers diversified into cash crops such as nutmeg and cocoa (or simply increased their
existing cultivation); however, the long planting and harvest time required
for these products (eight years for nutmeg) diminished the appeal of these
crops, despite rising world prices in the past decade. The passage of Hurricane Ivan had a devastating effect on the industry, destroying nearly
all nutmeg trees on the island, although exports were able to continue
through 2006 thanks to inventories of past harvests.

Informal labour (15 per cent)

Grenada, like other Caribbean countries, has experienced a significant rise in informal labour – estimated by labour-force surveys to have increased from 19% of total employment in 1991 to 23% in 1998 (World Bank, 2004). Interviews with officials from the Ministry of Labour and civil society indicated that unskilled banana workers, when not able to find construction work, often found short-term, low value-added employment within the informal sector as street vendors, petty traders, taxi drivers or domestic workers. Other informal sector activities exist in the form of small-scale agriculture, fishing, vending and animal husbandry (Caribbean Development Bank, 1999).

Small business (8 per cent)

A number of former banana workers, especially growers with access to land as collateral, benefited from a soft-lending programme carried out by the Small Enterprise Development Unit within the Grenada Development Bank, as a joint venture with the government-owned Grenada Industrial Development Corporation. Recent funding post-Ivan has also been provided by the European Investment Bank, through a lending window at the Grenada Development Bank. While precise data on loan portfolios is not available, Ministry of Labour officials indicated that most recipients of these loans went into small-scale trading operations for the domestic market and a small number of crafts-making operations for the tourist market.

The service-export sector (7 per cent)

The consensus among representatives from the public, private and civil-society sectors is that 'a very small number' of former banana workers found employment within the four services-export industries in Grenada (i.e. offshore education, tourism, offshore banking and call centres), despite the first two industries doubling in size during the decline of the banana industry (1987 to 1998). The following section explores this issue in further detail.

Other areas (2 per cent)

Stakeholders interviewed highlighted two other residual areas where former banana workers would also have found employment after the decline of the industry:

(1) Migration: migration rates for Grenada are high – estimated at 30 per cent of the total labour force (World Bank, 2004) – and it is likely that

a number of former banana workers, especially young males, found
work in the oil-fields of Trinidad or small service and agricultural
industries in the UK or North America.

(2) Security: although Grenada has one of the lowest crime rates in the
Caribbean (United Nations Office on Drugs and Crime and the World
Bank, 2007), incidences of theft and small-scale narcotics trafficking
have increased (notably in the wake of Hurricane Ivan), and while
precise statistics are unavailable, the security industry has grown as
an employer of unskilled males.

Why more workers didn't move into offshore services sectors

Stakeholders interviewed for this case study highlighted four principal reasons why former banana workers did not find their primary
source of employment within Grenada's growing services-export industries. Once again, responses are classified according to percentage shares.
Policy responses to these obstacles will be proposed in the following
section.

Skills/training mismatch (83 per cent)

To quote former economic advisor to the Grenada Banana Growers Association, 'the services sector demands a certain level of skills that banana
farmers and growers just didn't have'. As the banana industry began
to shed labour, many workers found that they did not have the necessary skills needed for the services sector, even for lower-end jobs such
as landscaping, maintenance and security. While perhaps inevitable at
the outset, the agriculture/services skills mismatch in Grenada has persisted largely through a lack of concerted effort by either the public or
private sector to address the problem through adequate training. The
burden of training workers has largely fallen on individual companies;
however, these efforts are limited to those workers who have entered the
industry and who already possess a required skill level. The initiatives
highlighted were training courses at the island's sole community college,
which focused on hospitality, and the IMANI Project, a public-private
partnership spearheaded by the Department of Youth Development and
funded by donors and private-sector associations, which provides one-
year training stipends to young graduates with Grenadian firms. These
initiatives, however, tended to focus on 'high-end' students – mostly urban
youth from the St George's region – who had already passed through the
formal education system.

Inadequate number of jobs (65 per cent)

Another factor that was highlighted by a majority of respondents was the simple lack of jobs within the services industries. While the hotel industry and USG have boomed in relative terms, in actual terms the number of jobs available has been insufficient to offer steady employment for labour released from agriculture, even at the lower end of the skill spectrum. USG, for example, as the single largest source of jobs outside the government, provides 280 non-clerical positions. The tourism sector as a whole provides a significantly larger number of jobs – some 2,000 directly employed and an equal number indirectly employed; however, the bulk of direct employment by hotels and restaurants is focused on housekeeping and catering, for which employers generally prefer female applicants, who were less likely to come from a banana-farming background. For unskilled males, services sector-related employment is more likely to emerge from related construction projects, although these are most often one-off contracts rather than steady salaried employment. Turnover in the services sector is low, compounding the difficulties for new applicants, notably those without prior experience. The paucity of jobs has been exacerbated by what was characterised by some stakeholders as a 'deliberate policy' on behalf of the major hotels to hire only within a restricted geographic area, since worker benefits often include free transportation to and from the workplace. Thus, recruitment efforts have remained concentrated in the south of the island, far from the rural farming communities in the north.

High reservation wage (28 per cent)

The 'reservation wage' is a concept in labour economics that suggests that there is a specific wage rate at which each worker can be induced to perform paid market work; wages offered below the reservation wage can be considered to keep workers from participating in the labour force. In the case of Grenada, the inability and/or unwillingness of workers outside the labour force to fill vacant services positions was highlighted by Grenadian stakeholders as a major obstacle. A recent survey (Government of Grenada, 2005) found that nearly half of those unemployed indicated 'own choice' as the reason for unemployment, far more than the 27 per cent who indicated 'no work available'.

The root of the problem is perceived to be salaries that, compared to the high cost of living in Grenada, discourage unemployed workers from seeking work. For example, most rural communities lie to the north of the island. While the island's total landmass is some 344 square kilometres, its topography, poorly developed road system and high cost of fuel means that a journey from the northern parishes to the services industries in the south takes approximately 1.5 hours each way at a cost of EC$8 (US$3). Monthly salaries for non-clerical workers within the hotel industry rarely exceed EC$1,000 (US$370), falling as low as EC$650 (US$240) for cleaners, cooks and security guards. For women, although they are generally in higher demand, salaries are nearly one third lower than men for equivalent positions.[7] This implies, based on a five-day working week, that nearly half of a low-skilled worker's salary is taken by transportation alone – a significant disincentive to labour mobility. If the prospective worker elects instead to move to the capital region to benefit from employer-provided transportation, he or she faces an average monthly rent bill of EC$500 (US$185) for a small rented room – more than half the average monthly salary.

Another important contributor to the Grenadian reservation wage (with respect to services industries at least) is the impact of out-migration. Nearly every Grenadian family has at least one, if not several, relatives living abroad. The impact of remittances – both in cash and in kind – adds another disincentive to take up low-paying work. For example, members of rural communities in Grenada indicated that a single barrel of clothing and foodstuffs from a relative living in the US or the UK could, in combination with small-scale subsistence farming, sustain a family for an entire year. Combined with significant inflows of cash remittances (recently estimated by the World Bank at some US$25 million per year, some 6 per cent of GDP) the close-knit families and support networks on the island act both to support depressed rural communities and to limit migration to the urban areas.

Politicisation of hiring process (8 per cent)

The last factor highlighted by stakeholders interviewed for this paper is the political nature of hiring in Grenadian firms. Like many small, tightly-knit societies facing high unemployment, public- and private-sector hiring processes in Grenada, even for unskilled jobs, can be subject to political influence. Respondents suggested that politically connected families are often guaranteed first pick at even the most menial jobs in lucrative sectors. As a result, job candidates from rural areas often stand at a disadvantage vis-à-vis their urban peers, who are more likely to belong

---

[7] Data provided by the Central Statistics Office, based on Grenada National Insurance registrations.

to families and/or a social network of political influence. The problem has even been highlighted in the IMANI youth programme, which has been accused of channelling traineeships for political purposes.[8]

Impact on poverty in Grenada

Given the paucity of historical economic data for Grenada, it is diffi-cult to establish the precise impact of this economic transformation on poverty rates. However, one statistic clearly stands out: the poverty rate, across more than a decade and multiple studies, has remained at nearly 30% of the Grenadian population (Caribbean Development Bank, 1999; World Bank, 2004; Government of Grenada, 2005). The unemployment rate, while fluctuating significantly since 1991, has averaged some 17% according to government data, despite a near-doubling of Grenada's GDP per capita over the same time period. The last measure (Caribbean Devel-opment Bank, 1999) of the Gini coefficient in Grenada (measuring the inequality in the distribution of income in the population) was con-ducted in 1998; the result of 0.45 suggested a medium level of inequality. However, the poverty gap of 15% measured in the same study (repre-senting the amount needed to raise the expenditure of all poor indi-viduals to the level of the poverty line, as a proportion of the poverty line) and the incidence of extreme poverty recently estimated at 5%[9] suggests that the severity of poverty in Grenada remains a concern.

The fact that poverty rates have remained high yet constant suggests that the movement of labour from agriculture to services has not necessarily increased poverty; however, neither has it reduced poverty. In many cases, the labour force formerly employed in agriculture found alternative work in construction and other areas, or supplemented their income with subsistence farming and remittances. The fluctuating unemployment rate, from a high of 26.7% in 1994 to a low of 10% in 2001, returning to nearly 20% in the wake of Hurricane Ivan in 2005 (Central Statistics Office, 2005), suggests that job insecurity has been a staple feature of Grenada's labour market, although it is impossible to ascertain whether the agriculture-to-services movement has provided less or more security, especially for lower-wage labour.

---

[8] 'Flush Them Out!!!, Grenada Today editorial, 23 September 2006, available at http://www.belgrafix.com/gtoday/2006news/Sept/Sept23/Flush-them-out.htm [last accessed 2 April 2009].

[9] See Grenada Country Profile, United Nations Development Programme, available at www.bb.undp.org/index.php?page=grenada [last accessed October 2007].

The prospect that Grenada's economic transformation has left poverty rates untouched suggests that insufficient effort has been made to integrate low-skill labour into emerging industries. Grenada faces the classic hurdles of a small state: high transaction costs, a small skill base and domestic market and a 'price-taking' relationship with the external economic environment requiring profound and constant economic adaptation. Unlike many other small states, however, Grenada has not only transitioned out of primary agricultural production but has now managed to build two thriving offshore services industries. Yet the impact on poverty in Grenada of this transformation has been mixed. Despite booming tourism and offshore education sectors, which promise an alternative, market-oriented path to employment and development, unemployment and poverty remain stubbornly high at historical levels.

What is to be done?

The growth and future prospects of Grenada's services industries, and of the economy as a whole, depend on a set of urgent reforms. While Grenada has managed to overcome the so-called 'tyranny of distance' imposed by its small size and distance from large markets to create world-class services-export industries, insufficient efforts are being undertaken at the policy level to address the inclusion of all skill levels in the emerging growth opportunities. This concluding section outlines a number of policy areas in which action is needed to address the movement of labour into services in order to assist in overall poverty reduction. Three policy areas in particular merit attention:

(1) tackling the high cost of living
(2) increasing the level of vocational and technical training
(3) diversifying into new services industries.

Tackling the high cost of living

In the interviews carried out for this case study, the high ratio of living costs to wages was cited on numerous occasions as a chief obstacle in moving labour – especially poor, unskilled labour – into new, offshore services industries, chiefly citing the 'reservation wage' problem outlined in the previous section. The major challenge for Grenadian stakeholders is how to manage externally determined costs while maintaining competitiveness. On the one hand, Grenada faces high costs of transportation, largely ascribed to rising fuel import prices; high costs of basic consumer items; and high cost of housing, constrained by land availability in urban areas and the slow reconstruction effort and low insurance rates post-Ivan. On the other hand, Grenada must compete with its larger neighbours for investment, skills and tourists. However, a number of key measures can be taken to address the problem, including several regionally based solutions with other neighbouring islands facing similar obstacles.

Price controls

The Grenadian Government has been reluctant to increase subsidies on transportation, housing or wages due to budget constraints. The International Monetary Fund (IMF) estimates that total public-sector debt as a percentage of GDP rose from 56% in 2000 to 129% in 2004, and the subsequent passage of Hurricane Ivan and the resulting reconstruction efforts have proved an additional burden (IMF, 2005). For example, on the transportation cost issue, the government traditionally maintained a fiscal buffer in the form of a gasoline tax, which it raised and lowered to reflect fluctuations in the price of oil, with the view of maintaining a more or less constant nominal price. However, this price adjustment mechanism was recently abandoned – as it was across many neighbouring states such as St Lucia – as the constantly rising price of imported oil led to the Grenadian Government levying a negative fuel tax (a subsidy), which quickly exacerbated the already fragile finances of the central government.

The Grenadian Government has attempted to use price controls for key staples, although, like many small states, the absence of local production and the resulting high share of imported goods mitigates the impact of these measures. The government's price control efforts have thus been limited to negotiations with large importing firms to reduce margins on imported items. These efforts have not been successful due to: (i) the importers' insistence that they are subject to the same high costs as the rest of the economy, and that their profit margins have already been reduced as much as possible; and (ii) the economic and political power of the importing firms, which limits the negotiating leverage of the state. The government, in concert with its smaller island neighbours facing similar hurdles, may wish to consider a bulk-purchasing scheme for major staples such as fuel (similar to the one already in operation in the subregion for medicines) to reduce the cost of inflation on imported goods and to check the economic power of the importing firms.

Tariff policy

Another important factor in cost-of-living considerations for Grenada is the current tariff regime, which reflects the common external tariff (CET) of the Caribbean Community. Although intra-Community trade is largely conducted on a duty-free basis, the CET prescribes rates as high as 40 per cent for imports of many agricultural staples, including nearly all fruits and vegetables, both in their fresh and prepared forms, from third parties. These measures are in place to protect the regional market for Community producers; however, smaller states such as Grenada, with minimal production, may wish to consider reducing tariffs on these items for third-party imports to source from more competitive producers outside the region (especially from North American and Latin American sources). While it is often argued that high tariffs provide small states with essential government revenue, the Grenadian tariffs on agricultural staples are prohibitive as to currently prevent nearly any non-Caribbean Common Market (CARICOM) imports of these goods. Thus, the effect of market openings for these goods will be to displace more inefficient intra-regional imports rather than to deprive the government of duty revenue.

Non-traded agriculture

Although sourcing cheaper imports may relieve some cost-of-living concerns, due to balance-of-payments considerations, a key goal for the Grenadian Government should be the revival of the domestic agricultural sector. Many stakeholders voiced the opinion that Grenada's transition out of agriculture has eliminated those particular fruits and vegetables that could be produced locally. The agricultural industry, however, faces a number of obstacles: (i) the decline of the banana industry; (ii) the repair bill from Hurricanes Ivan and Emily; (iii) shortages of manpower, capital and infrastructure extending from the farm-gate to the dock; and (iv) a weak marketing system for Grenada's agricultural produce. Although high world-market prices exist for nutmeg, the long planting times required will most likely dissuade most farmers. There is, however, a strong potential for growth within the non-traded agricultural sector as Grenada's growing tourism sector generates higher demand for locally grown produce. Donor efforts and government adjustment efforts for the agricultural sector have traditionally focused on either produce for export (e.g. bananas, nutmeg) or traditional crops (e.g. root crops). With the growth of the tourist market, however, the Grenadian Government may wish to focus funds on the domestic agricultural market, and in particular on vegetables in demand in the resorts, such as fresh lettuce and cucumbers, which are currently being imported.

Trade facilitation and labour costs

Another important area for action is the port in Grenada, one of the most costly ports in the Caribbean. The above-average cost for container clearances puts direct upward pressure on prices for nearly every intermediate and finished product that arrives in Grenada, and in nearly every case the clearance and handling costs are passed on to the consumer. The port, like many in the region, is unionised, and the government has been unable to finalise an agreement with the unions on their demand for a 70 per cent pay increase.

This case highlights the particular dilemma facing Grenada. On the one hand, it is a small country facing a competitive marketplace for its goods. On the other hand, it faces high input costs in nearly every phase of production. In the absence of local production, the only input whose costs can be adjusted downwards is labour; however, the 'floor' on wages (e.g. the reservation wage) is set at a high level by the high (and often fixed) costs of the other inputs to production, all of which, in turn, act as a brake on economic adjustment. Addressing this 'vicious circle', common to so many small states, will be perhaps the greatest challenge Grenada faces in adjusting to its new economic environment. Only by a multi-pronged approach – reducing the cost of imported items through regional action, increasing local production of essential staples, tailoring targeted lending programmes to revive domestic firms and market opening for goods that cannot be produced locally – can the problem be effectively addressed.

Increase the level of vocational and technical training

Another key to moving more ex-agricultural labour into services, nearly all agreed, was greater focus on vocation and technical training. In the words of a Grenadian economist, the economic base of the island has 'seen a paradigm shift and only now is the Grenadian government waking up to the inadequacies of the voc-tech system'. Although Grenada, like many OECD countries, has near-universal primary enrolment rates and a high (88 per cent) enrolment rate for secondary school, the Grenadian education system appears not to provide skills needed by the private sector, in particular by services-sector employers. The resulting skills shortage has proved to be a major obstacle to the growth of services industries as

well as to national poverty and unemployment reduction efforts. While
job-training efforts have increased, they overwhelmingly benefit medium-
and high-skilled workers, while training for workers at the lower end of
the skill spectrum is often perceived by employers as costly and ineffective.

Fortunately, recent government awareness of the problem has led to
efforts to establish Grenada's first comprehensive vocational-technical
training programme (Grenada Broadcast, 2007). This effort, led by donors
under the aegis of the Agency for Reconstruction and Development, is a
public-private initiative that includes several line ministries and private
firms and will develop several public and private training centres. The
curriculum is expected initially to focus on key areas such as construction,
hospitality and marine/yachting repair and servicing before expanding
into other sectors.

The St George's University offshore medical school has begun a public-
private partnership with the local T. A. Marryshow Community College
to re-orientate its curriculum in a number of areas, and more importantly has led a push to use secondary schools in the north of the island
to deliver distance learning at the tertiary level to rural communities. The
key challenge for these new programmes and institutions is to ensure that
access is focused on unskilled Grenadian labour, which currently lacks
viable employment opportunities, rather than on the more educated college graduates who are more easily absorbed into the labour market. In
order for this change to occur, greater public-private-sector collaboration is required in the creation of training curricula in order for skills
teaching to be as job-oriented as possible. Another potential option is to
build on existing regional educational networks, in particular the University of the West Indies, an autonomous regional institution supported by
and serving the sixteen English-speaking Caribbean countries, with three
major campuses (Barbados, Trinidad and Jamaica) and several satellite
'university centres' in the smaller islands (including Grenada). The university infrastructure can be easily harnessed to provide more targeted,
job-oriented training (beyond standard degree offerings) to increase the
ability of Grenadians to fill services-sector labour demand.

Diversifying into new services industries

The final policy consideration is the need to diversify into other services industries. As noted earlier, Grenada is unique among many small
developing states in that it enjoys two world-class offshore services industries. While offshore education and tourism have grown, however, the

collective staffing requirements, even when projected into the future, may not alone be sufficient to alleviate chronic poverty and unemployment within Grenada. Increased public-private efforts are needed to develop value addition and new services industries with a strong focus on an appropriately trained local labour force. Given the high (and rising) incentives for immigration from Grenada, only the net creation of jobs on the island, at a sufficient level of remuneration given the high cost of living, can both attract and retain the labour force needed to assure growth and poverty reduction in Grenada.

Develop offshore medical services

The outlook for this sector in Grenada holds significant promise. The number of medical schools in North America has remained stable for the past twenty years, while the demand for physicians has grown due to a number of factors such as population aging and increasing difficulties post-9/11 for foreign physicians to enter North America (Swedish Development Advisors, 2004). This has created a shortage in the market in which Caribbean countries, and in particular a well-established institution such as St George's University, stand to benefit in the longer term. Interviews with university officials indicate that these market trends are leading to an expansion of the university's facilities, including several new student dormitories and a concomitant increase in faculty numbers. University human-resources officials expect a 10 to 15 per cent increase in staffing requirements – mostly non-clerical – within the next five years. The increase in dormitory requirements and related infrastructure needs for the larger student body is also projected to feed the current boom in construction, although industry representatives were not able to specify what the impact on unskilled labour employment may be.

The first challenge for the university and the Grenadian Government will be not only to harness the increase in demand for medical education, but also to diversify the range of educational services provided by the university beyond medicine. At present, the university offers bachelor's degrees in business, international business, life sciences and management information systems and a masters in business administration. While these programmes are smaller relative to the more established medical curriculum, the university is well-placed to fill unmet demand in these areas (especially the masters in business administration offering) in the North American market.

The second challenge will be to use the university and its provision of offshore services as a platform for other growing services industries. A promising initiative has emerged between the government and USG in the planned provision of offshore medical services in Grenada in order to capitalise on the growing cross-border delivery of health services worldwide. It has been estimated that, currently, the value of the global health-services sector amounts to US$4 trillion, and that the value of exported (traded) health services comprises approximately 5% of the global market ($140 billion). Growth in exported health services is expected to be around 6% annually, but given the growth in ICT and the greater openness of health systems, it may grow at much higher rates (World Bank, 2004). Mimicking the establishment of many other health centres in the Caribbean, the university administration, in conjunction with the Ministry of Health, plans to renovate the existing General Hospital in St George's to provide medical services for both local citizens and 'health tourists', with a pilot project already established for offshore dental work. The programme aims to train and employ local physicians to provide 'front-line' treatment and employ university graduates as consultative physicians. The initiative has already generated several meetings between major tourism developers and the university administration to coordinate a marketing campaign, aimed at the US and EU market, to attract 'health tourists' to Grenada.

Diversify tourism products

The tourism sector is similarly expected to enjoy a boom in the near future. The most significant change in the Grenadian tourism industry is the emergence, for the first time, of large foreign-owned hotels. According to officials from the Grenada Hotel and Tourism Association, tourism capacity is projected to double within the next five years.

While nearly all stakeholders in Grenada see potential employment growth within the hotel industry, several concerns remain, in particular the potential impact on poverty reduction. The Grenadian tourism sector remains focused on the south of the island, suggesting that rural communities to the north may remain excluded from new job opportunities. However, tourist resorts, especially high-end foreign-owned resorts, have begun to emerge further away from the St George's area, attracted by their relative seclusion and lower land prices. A key priority for the Grenadian Government should be the geographic diversification of resorts and hotels away from the south of the island, both through financial incentives (e.g. tax concessions for land purchases) and infrastructural improvements. There is concern that Grenada, like neighbouring islands such as the Grenadines, Tobago and Antigua, is attracting primarily higher-end, affluent tourist developments. While these resorts tend to be high-yield investments, upscale resorts tend to be smaller than the larger 'package' tourism developments and thus require higher levels of staff training to cater to more affluent and discriminating clients. This development puts increasing pressure on the Grenadian Government to increase hospitality training for its local labour force. Broadening the marketing efforts of the unique Grenadian tourist product beyond the higher end of the tourist scale (e.g. following the successful exploitation of backpacker-type eco-tourism by Dominica, Belize and other small Caribbean states) could successfully diversify the Grenadian tourism sector and increase its positive impact on local hiring across the skill spectrum.

Another concern relates to competition from other Caribbean islands and destinations outside the region. During the 1990s, the expansion of lower cost 'sun, sea and sand' offerings combined with mass-marketing techniques by emerging destinations (mainly the Dominican Republic, the Cancun/Cozumel region in Mexico and more recently Cuba) resulted in increased market share for these destinations at the expense of traditional Caribbean destinations, including Grenada. In addition, with the decline in transportation costs worldwide, long-haul destinations have become increasingly attractive, as evidenced by the rising share of tourists worldwide travelling to Africa, Asia and the Middle East (World Bank, 2004). As tourism is highly price-elastic, unless Grenada tackles its high cost of labour, utilities and local transportation (especially for tourists) and the relatively low quality of accommodation, the island may not reap the potential benefits of the boom in global tourism.

Conclusion

In Grenada, many small states can see a mirror of their own concerns: on the one hand, a small island facing the decline of its principal agricultural and manufacturing industries and a growing disconnection of their goods trade with the global economy; on the other hand, a rise of services-export industries where strong evidence suggests that these new economic engines are delivering employment and revenue benefits, albeit insufficient alone to tackle chronic unemployment and poverty. This study suggests that while Grenada has managed to carve out an alternate path for development with the growth of not one but two services-export industries, the impact on poverty and unemployment levels, especially for the unskilled workers formerly employed in agriculture, remains mixed, and that more will need to be done to address pro-poor growth in the future.

There is, however, room for optimism, providing that there is a concerted effort from the Grenadian Government, the member states of the Caribbean Community and the external donors to make Grenada's services growth 'poor-friendly'. The primary lesson of the Grenadian agriculture-to-services story is that sustainable poverty reduction cannot be achieved without coherence between domestic policy measures and changes in the external trading environment. Unless both the private and public sectors are both fully seized of new challenges and opportunities, and actively involved in the process of economic transformation, historically high poverty rates will remain a feature of Grenadian life for the foreseeable future. A number of measures outlined in this paper, if adopted thoroughly and without delay, could allow growing, high value-added services-export industries to absorb employment across all skill levels, the average skill level of the Grenadian labour force being upgraded through training. A number of measures already in Grenada suggest that these positive trends can be harnessed for poverty reduction while tackling the classic challenges of a small economy. It is imperative that all stakeholders – government officials, private-sector firms, donors and civil society – avail themselves of what may prove to be a relatively short window of opportunity to address these important challenges.

References

Caribbean Development Bank (1999), 'Poverty Assessment Report – Grenada', Caribbean Development Bank: Barbados.

Central Statistics Office (2005), *Grenada Labour Force Survey 2005*, National Statistics Office, Ministry of Finance: St George's.

Government of Grenada (2005). *Grenada Core Welfare Indicators Survey 2005*, National Statistical Office, Government of Grenada: Grenada.

Grenada Broadcast (2007), 'Grenada is One Step Closer to Establishing its Own Technical Vocational Education Programme', broadcast by *Grenada Broadcast* on 21 May 2007 (website: www.grenadabroadcast.com – last accessed 11 March 2009).

International Monetary Fund (IMF) (2005). *Statistical Appendix: Grenada*, International Monetary Fund: Washington, WA.

Lazare, A., Antoine, P. and Samuel, W. (2001), *RNM/OECS Country Studies to Inform Trade Negotiations: Grenada*, Caribbean Regional Negotiating Machinery: Barbados.

Sandiford, W. (2000), *On the Brink of Decline: Bananas in the Windward Islands*, Feddon Books: St George's.

Swedish Development Advisors (2004), 'Offshore Education in the OECS', paper prepared for the World Bank: Washington, WA.

United Nations Office on Drugs and Crime and the World Bank (2007), *Crime, Violence and Development: Trends, Costs and Policy Options in the Caribbean*, World Bank.

World Bank (2004), *A Time to Choose: Caribbean Development in the 21st Century*, World Bank: Washington, WA.

Fisheries subsidies and the western and central Pacific

MANLEEN DUGAL[*]

Introduction

Disciplines on fisheries subsidies have been identified as a global priority for addressing sustainability concerns associated with the state of global fisheries resources.[1] Fisheries subsidies are believed to contribute significantly to the creation and perpetuation of excess fishing capacity[2] and are understood to have the potential to encourage over-fishing and to distort trade patterns (WWF, 2001).

The international legal and policy framework that relates to fisheries trade and sustainable development is spread over a number of agreements, instruments, management schemes and economic policies that operate at the national, regional and international level (ICTSD, 2006a, p. 1). The rules currently being formulated at the WTO are recognised as a key multilateral initiative to ban capacity-enhancing fishing subsidies (such as subsidies to vessel construction, modification, engine and gear improvement) that lead to fleet over-capacity, and effort-enhancing subsidies (such as subsidies for fuel and other variable cost and price supports) that potentially contribute to over-fishing. The central economic arguments underlying the demand for improved disciplines on fisheries subsidies by proponents at the WTO are that:

---

[*] Manleen Dugal is Technical Advisor (Trade Policy) and Permanent Representative for the Pacific Island Delegation to the WTO. The author would like to thank Liam Campling, Fisheries Trade Consultant at the Forum Fisheries Agency, for his substantive inputs to this paper.
[1] The World Summit for Sustainable Development in Johannesburg held in September 2002 agreed to replenish fish stocks to sustainable levels by 2015, 'where possible'.
[2] This position was based upon research by, amongst others, the Food and Agriculture Organisation (FAO) and the Organisation of Economic Cooperation and Development (OECD) in the early 1990s.

- fisheries subsidies have *production*-distorting effects, in that they cause over-capacity and over-fishing resulting in over-exploitation of fisheries resources and subsequent depletion of fish stocks as a consequence[3]
- fisheries subsidies have *trade*-distorting effects through production and export-market distortions.

The objective of disciplining fisheries subsidies, however, poses a serious threat to the legitimate promotion of developing country fishing industries and communities. Restricting policy space for the strategic use of subsidies to attract domestic and foreign investors and to support fishers in times of need is a serious limitation on developing countries, especially those that have not yet had the opportunity to develop the sector. The fisheries sector is of significant economic and trade importance to the small island states of the Western and Central and Pacific Ocean (WCPO), and is a key factor in the maintenance of basic livelihoods, especially in the case of small-scale and artisanal fishing. To sketch briefly the central importance of the fisheries sector in this region, it is conservatively estimated that the tuna industry alone accounts for between 8 and 11 per cent of total formal employment to Pacific Island countries (PICs) (Gillett *et al.*, 2001). In addition, access payments by distant water fleets (DWFs) to gain fishing rights within PIC exclusive economic zones (EEZs) constitute a significant amount of direct revenue for the governments of several of these economies. Thus, to the extent that they may impact on fishing activities in the region or the access payments that are made, any new fisheries subsidy disciplines at the WTO would have significant implications for fisheries development, trade and livelihoods in PICs.

The inherent conflict between the objectives of preserving environmental sustainability and developing fishing industries in PICs and other small island developing states presents a major challenge to the crafting of new rules on fisheries subsidies at the WTO. The rules not only seek to prevent the use of subsidies that cause over-fishing and over-capacity but also seek to place conditions and limits on the use of other types of fisheries subsidies that would fall outside an eventual ban. This chapter discusses certain key issues in the WTO negotiations on fisheries subsidies that may have significant implications for economic development and poverty reduction in PICs, due to their heavy economic dependence

---

[3] Fisheries subsidies cause resource-depleting production distortions through a reduction in both the fixed costs of productive capital and variable costs of fish production (WWF, The Best of Texts, the Worst of Texts).

on the fisheries sector. The case study is divided into sections, as outlined below:

- the fisheries subsidies debate at the WTO
  - fisheries subsidies in the Doha Round: the rationale
  - can the WTO become a fisheries management organisation?
  - Hong Kong Ministerial Conference as a turning point
- implications of fisheries subsidies disciplines for small and vulnerable economies in the Pacific
  - fisheries access fees
  - artisanal and small-scale fisheries
  - policy space for (semi)industrial development
- special and differential treatment in the fisheries subsidies debate
  - Argentina's proposal
  - Norway's proposal
  - Brazil's proposal
  - small and vulnerable economies
- conclusion and policy recommendations
  - efforts at a multilateral level
  - efforts at the national/regional level

The fisheries subsidies debate at the WTO

Fisheries subsidies in the Doha Round: the rationale

At the Fourth Ministerial Conference of the WTO in Doha in 2001, members agreed to 'clarify and improve WTO disciplines on fisheries subsidies, taking into account the importance of this sector to developing countries'.[4] The key reason behind the call for enhanced fisheries subsidies disciplines was the inadequacy of the existing disciplines under the Agreement on Subsidies and Countervailing Measures (ASCM) to address all fisheries-related concerns. Proponents of new disciplines for fisheries subsidies have claimed that 'there are significant practical problems' in applying the current ASCM disciplines to fisheries subsidies as they 'are not designed to address the exceptional and distinctive market distortions that subsidies in the fisheries sector can generate'.[5] Some of the arguments

---

[4] Paragraph 28 of the Doha Ministerial Declaration, WT/MIN(01)/DEC/1, 20 November 2001.

[5] Communication from Australia, Chile, Ecuador, Iceland, New Zealand, Peru, the Philippines and the US, The Doha Mandate to Address Fisheries Subsidies: Issues, TN/RL/W/3, 24 April 2002, paragraph 16.

in support of the limited applicability of the ASCM to address the specific fisheries context have been: firstly, the ASCM provides a limited definition of a subsidy; secondly, the existing notifications for subsidies are at a level of aggregation that prevents precise determination of which species of fish are being targeted; and thirdly, it is difficult to calculate the effects of subsidies, as they are first and foremost a production – not a trade – distortion.

On the flip side of these approaches, two important conclusions arise from the paper by Chang (2003):

(1) A review of the current ASCM suggests that most problems originate from the inherent imperfections of the current rules that apply to all sectors across the board, rather than from the allegedly unique features of the fisheries sector.
(2) The current ASCM can resolve fisheries subsidies issues to a considerable extent through dispute settlement.

Can the WTO become a fisheries management organisation?

A major initial argument against the formation of new rules at the WTO is the unclear economic linkages between subsidies and over-fishing. There are many drivers of over-capacity and over-fishing, such as technological innovation, the expansion of fish processing, the expansion of the global market for fish, environmental stresses affecting fisheries resources and, most importantly, the lack of responsible fisheries management.

Concerns have also been expressed about the systemic implications of the current negotiations on fisheries subsidies and the need to avoid or minimise the institutional risk for the WTO in its move towards sustainability (Chang, 2003). According to this approach, the WTO is not an appropriate forum for, and should not be engaged in, the elaboration of environmental policy or making judgments about environmental goals and priorities. Issues that do arise would typically come in the form of a dispute as to whether or not subsidies existed and caused over-capacity and over-fishing. Technical issues might well arise in such a dispute. There could be a need to determine, for example, the specific fish species that face stock depletion, the specific causes of over-fishing and over-capacity (management failure or subsidies) and the sustainable and hence permissible levels of fish stocks and national fishing capacities. These issues, however, would best be dealt with on an ad hoc basis by panels who can consult appropriate experts as necessary.

The Small and Vulnerable Economies group (including PIC members of the WTO) initially argued firmly that the approach of extending the application of subsidies beyond trade effects to include over-capacity and over-fishing went 'beyond the technical and administrative competence of the WTO'.[6] The economic rationale behind this position is that fish-stock depletion is largely a result of bad fisheries management, and the causal link between fisheries subsidies and over-capacity and over-fishing is not obvious and is also difficult to ascertain. In addition, over-capacity and subsequent over-fishing can be a result of various other economic factors ranging from high market prices for fish to oceanographic dynamics.

Whether over-capacity and over-fishing actually create trade-distorting effects at the expense of unsubsidised exporters is also open to question, necessitating a case-by-case analysis. According to Grynberg and Rochester (2005), it is widely recognised, as a result of decades of research on the question of fish-stock depletion in open-access fisheries, that fish-stock depletion will occur in open-access fisheries in the absence of good fisheries management irrespective of whether subsidies exist or not. Subsidies, at most, may accelerate the rate of depletion of fisheries resources (Grynberg and Rochester, 2005). According to Arnason (1998), in cases where an effective and sustainable management regime exists, or where a system of tradable quotas is created, then subsidies simply become rents that are transferred to either producers or consumers depending upon the particular market situation. Therefore, Grynberg and Rochester (2005) conclude that: 'This raises the key policy question of whether the current negotiations at the WTO on enhanced fisheries subsidies disciplines constitute a "second best" approach to fisheries management.'

Hong Kong Ministerial Conference as a turning point

These debates became null and void in practice at the WTO Ministerial Conference held in Hong Kong in December 2005. Not only did this meeting produce a text that recalled and reaffirmed the Doha mandate on rules negotiations (including fisheries subsidies),[7] but ministers also articulated a commitment to strengthening the disciplines on fisheries subsidies in a separate annex of the Hong Kong Declaration (paragraph 9, Annex D). This Ministerial Declaration recognised the existence of a broad

[6] See Small Vulnerable Economies proposal, WTO document TN/RL/GEN57/Rev/1, 13 September 2005.
[7] WT/MIN (05)/DEC, 22 December 2005.

agreement that disciplines on subsidies in the fisheries sector should be strengthened, including through the prohibition of certain forms of fisheries subsidies that contribute to over-capacity and over-fishing. It also recognised that appropriate and effective special and differential treatment (SDT) for developing and least developed countries should be an integral part of the fisheries subsidies negotiations, taking account of the significance of the fishing sector to 'development priorities, poverty reduction, and livelihood and food security concerns' (paragraph 9, Annex D). Therefore, by 2006, the focus of the debate had shifted from whether there is a need for any specific disciplines of fisheries subsidies to the question of what the nature and extent of such disciplines should be.

Implications of fisheries subsidies disciplines for small and vulnerable economies in the Pacific

In the spirit of the Doha Round, SDT for developing countries has been at the centre of the fisheries subsidies debate from the outset. Given that PICs do not have the political and economic clout to substantially influence the framing of the debate, they have instead focused on carving out effective SDT. They have sought to ensure that, whatever disciplines emerge, the core interests of Pacific fishers should be maintained. The demandeurs of disciplines, however, are targeting not just the subsidies granted by OECD countries to their fishing industries but also those provided by large developing countries. The broad scope of the disciplines that could emerge from these negotiations means that PICs, which are minnows on the world stage (they are small vulnerable economies (SVEs) and have had almost no impact on the sustainability of global fish stocks), nevertheless risk being caught in the net of disciplines crafted for much bigger fish.[8]

Fisheries access fees

Fisheries access agreements are contractual arrangements wherein governments or private fishing fleets pay a coastal state for access to fisheries resources within the coastal state's EEZ.[9] There are generally two types of fisheries access agreements: (i) government-to-government, whereby the government of a Distant Water Fishing Nation (DWFN) purchases

[8] For detailed analysis of the issues touched on here, see Campling *et al.* (2007), especially Chapters 11, 12 and 13 by Elizabeth Havice.
[9] The breadth of the EEZ is an area not exceeding 200 nautical miles from defined baselines: Article 57 of the 1982 United Nations Convention on the Law of the Sea (UNCLOS).

fisheries access rights from coastal state governments and then sells
those rights to its private-sector fishers; and (ii) private-to-government,
whereby the private sector or industry associations of the DWFN purchase fisheries access rights directly from coastal state governments.[10] It
is the former type of access arrangements, government-to-government,
that fall within the ambit of WTO fisheries subsidies negotiations, due to
the fact that private DWFN fleets are often not charged the full amount
of the payments that have been made by their DWFN governments to
coastal and island states in exchange for fisheries access rights.[11]

As regards these government-to-government fisheries access arrangements, the mere existence of government-to-government transfers of
funds has not been viewed as problematic. Indeed, there seems to be
a general consensus amongst the WTO membership that such payments
alone do not constitute a subsidy within the meaning of the ASCM. They
have therefore been excluded from the general prohibition on certain
types of subsidies in new disciplines.[12] As stated in an African, Caribbean
and Pacific (ACP) Group communication on access fees,[13] government-
to-government transfers of funds clearly constitute state-to-state payments for the legitimate trading of a natural resource that is consistent with UNCLOS. It is, rather, the second-level transactions relating to
government-to-government fisheries access arrangements that have been
the subject of much debate. Of issue are situations where the DWFN
government transfers access rights to its private fishing fleet for less than
the full amount of the access fees that it paid to the coastal government.
Some WTO members consider that these transactions are, or should be,
challengeable under WTO disciplines.

This is of huge concern to PICs. In several of these states, significant government revenue has been generated from fees paid in exchange for fisheries access to the PIC's EEZs. According to a study commissioned by the
International Centre for Trade and Sustainable Development (ICTSD),[14]
in several PICs more than 25% of total government revenue is obtained

[10] ICTSD (2006b). For more focused coverage of access agreements in the WCPO, see Havice (2007).
[11] See 'Access Fees in Fisheries Subsidies Negotiations – Communication from the ACP Group', WTO Document, TN/RL/W/209, 5 June 2007.
[12] See Argentina's proposal, WTO document TN/RL/GEN/138/Rev.1, 26 January 2007; US proposal, WTO document TN/RL/GEN/145, 22 March 2007.
[13] 'Access Fees in Fisheries Subsidies Negotiations – Communication from the ACP Group', WTO document TN/RL/W/209, 5 June 2007.
[14] Mbithi (2006), p. 13.

from such access fees.[15] The cases of Kiribati and Tuvalu are particularly striking. For those islands, nearly 42% of gross domestic product (GDP) comes from access payments, and the threat to their economic development if those payments were to be cut is significant. In addition to the direct impact on government revenues that access fees have for PICs, the payments also have indirect and positive impacts on employment generation, value-addition (growth of upstream and downstream activities) and stimulating effects on fisheries development efforts in PICs. The main point though is that subsidised access agreements tend to have a far higher rate of return and are generally more beneficial than non-subsidised ones. From the perspective of the PICs, the fees paid by nations that do not pass on the full amount to their private sector tend to be larger, both in absolute and in relative terms, than the fees paid by other nations where the subsidy element is less obvious or does not exist.

Making subsidised access payments subject to challenge may well mean that governments paying the access fees will focus their efforts on reducing the level of the access fees instead of raising the amount in the fees required from the private sector. Or, if the full amount charged is passed on, then some private-sector fisheries may opt out of the region due to higher costs, which may also lead to a decrease in payments. Either scenario puts PICs that depend so heavily on these fees at risk, and so the issue needs to be dealt with carefully.

Of course, in practical terms, challenging alleged subsidies from a government's onward transfer of access rights to a private fleet would be difficult, even under the existing disciplines of the ASCM. For example, as reflected in the ACP Group communication, "it is not always easy to segregate whether the amount paid in "access fees" by a DWFN government to the coastal state represents only the commercial rate for access to those fisheries or also includes a component of development assistance".[16] A DWFN government's subsidisation of the onward transfer of access rights to its private fleet will only constitute a prohibited subsidy under Article 3 of the ASCM if the transfer is either contingent upon export of the catch or contingent upon the use of domestic rather than imported goods, for example in downstream processing. As to whether the onward transfer of access rights by DWFN governments to private fleets might be considered actionable subsidies under the disciplines of Part III of the

---

[15] 'Access Fees in Fisheries Subsidies Negotiations – Communication from the ACP Group', WTO document TN/RL/W/209, 5 June 2007.
[16] Ibid.

ASCM, there are complicating factors in the fisheries sector that make the existing requirements and standard of proof even more onerous. It is generally difficult to prove 'adverse effects', within the meaning of Article 5 of the ASCM, on the interests of other WTO members, and it may be particularly difficult to do so in the fisheries sector. Effects such as altering competitive conditions in markets, either by undercutting or suppressing prices or displacing or impeding imports, do occur in the fisheries sector, but, as has been observed, 'they are particularly difficult to demonstrate'.[17] The unique nature of fisheries products, a lack of reliable unsubsidised reference prices, along with the potential for cross-subsidisation, all make it difficult to establish the effects of subsidies on prices and market share. Various problems also arise in the definition of domestic industry and in seeking to establish injury to that industry for purposes of taking action under Part III of the ACSM, or imposing countervailing duties.

In addition to the above arguments, many developing countries and their DWFN partners argue that access fees should not be subject to challenge as long as they are not environmentally damaging. As reflected in the Hong Kong mandate, and as already discussed, the historical premise of ongoing fisheries subsidies negotiations at the WTO has been that the ASCM needs to be clarified and improved in order to address only those subsidies that directly contribute to over-capacity and production distortions in the fisheries sector.

Artisanal and small-scale fisheries

On a global scale, the artisanal/small-scale fishing sector provides direct employment to tens of millions of people, and 'indirect employment to tens of millions more, many of them women involved in fish processing' (UNEP, 2005). Some striking statistics published by the World Fish Centre point out that more than 95% of the 200 million people involved in fishing are small-scale fishers, processors and traders. In addition, more than 90% of people working in small-scale fisheries are in developing countries. It is also interesting to note that of the 70% share of world fish produced and consumed by developing countries, small-scale fishers account for 70% of that production (Hall, 2007). Small-scale fishers' share of the fish produced and consumed by developing countries is expected to increase to 80% (from 70%) in 2020.

---

[17] Proposal from New Zealand, 'Fisheries Subsidies: Limitations of Existing Subsidy Disciplines', WTO document TN/RL/W/12, 4 July 2002.

Table 5K   *Estimates of per capita fishery product consumption in PICs (kg/year) and WTO membership*

PIC	WTO membership	Range of estimates of per capita consumption (kg/year)
Cook Is.	Non-member	47.0–71.0
Fiji	Member	44.0–62.0
FSM	Non-member	72.0–114.0
Kiribati	Non-member	72.0–207.0
Marshall Is.	Non-member	38.9–59.0
Nauru	Non-member	46.7
Niue	Non-member	49.0–118.9
Palau	Non-member	84.0–135.0
PNG	Member	18.2–24.9
Samoa	Acceding	46.3–71.0
Solomon Is.	Member	32.2–32.7
Tonga	Member	25.2–30.0
Tuvalu	Non-member	85.0–146.0
Vanuatu	Acceding	15.9–25.7

Source: Gillett and Lightfoot (2001), using various studies.

As is the case elsewhere in the world, artisanal and small-scale fishers in PICs are among the poorest of the poor. Despite this, artisanal fisheries are an essential aspect in the livelihood and food security strategies of Pacific Islanders throughout the region. Worldwide per capita consumption of fish is highest in the Pacific Region (World Fish Centre, 2005), and much of that fish is supplied on a local level by artisanal fishers. Table 5K provides data on annual average per capita fish consumption for each PIC, which, when compared with the FAO's 2007 estimate of a global average of around 16 kg per capita, demonstrates the deep importance of artisanal/small-scale fishing to the basic survival of Pacific Islanders.

The small-scale fisheries sector plays two important roles in PICs: that of a social safety-net and that of an economic driver. In its social safety-net function, it has already been noted that the small-scale fishing sector contributes heavily to food and nutrition security. Additionally, it contributes a significant part of diversified livelihood strategies where the sector and its people are often marginalised and are without access to basic services and amenities. Many artisanal fishers' activities are part time, and they only enter the sector when times are hard, for example when crops fail or in particular seasons. In its role as an economic driver, the small-scale fishing sector is an important cash generator, has strong multiplier effects and is sometimes export-focused.

In light of the above, the development of artisanal/small-scale fisheries is a rational undertaking for governments and other organisations in the region. These fisheries are a key entry point for investing in poverty reduction and human development. A central objective for many national governments and regional agencies, along with scientific and research-based non-governmental organisations (NGOs), therefore, is to preserve and enhance the productivity of the inshore and freshwater fisheries (mostly carried out by artisanal fisheries) on a sustainable basis, in order to improve food security and increase income obtained from these activities. Proposed new disciplines at the WTO should not complicate these efforts through increased red tape or unnecessary conditionalities. In short, PICs need to receive deep, wide-ranging and effective SDT in any rules on subsidies to artisanal/small-scale fisheries.

Special and differential treatment in the fisheries subsidies debate

SDT principles and provisions have been an integral part of the WTO negotiations on fisheries subsidies disciplines since the outset. However, in order to provide safeguards for the sustainability of fisheries resources, various proposals have called for conditionalities to SDT with the aim of providing parameters to determine 'objective' situations where subsidies should be granted or maintained.[18] The following summarises the most important recent proposals on SDT.

Argentina's proposal

According to Argentina's proposal,[19] the specified subsidies could be granted or maintained only on the condition that the existing fishing capacity is substantially lower than that needed to: (i) cover the total allowable catch of a given species or a group of species in its maritime domain; and (ii) fill fishing quotas agreed within the framework of a regional fisheries management organisation or other international

---

[18] Argentina's proposal, WTO document TN/RL/GEN/138/Rev.1, 26 January 2007.
[19] Ibid.

agreement. To operationalise these conditions, Argentina suggests a quantitative threshold in order to define when national fishing capacity will be deemed 'substantially lower' than that needed for the sustainable fishing of a species or group of species. According to its proposal: 'Developing country members would be able to resort to subsidies only when the existing fishing capacity does not exceed (50 per cent) of that needed to cover the total allowable catch of a species or group of species.'

Norway's proposal

Norway[20] suggests that: (i) for developing countries, subsidies subject to the general prohibition may be granted to fishing vessels up to 20 metres in overall length whose main area of operation is within that member's area of fisheries jurisdiction extending up to 12 nautical miles from the baselines; (ii) developing countries may grant such subsidies to fishing vessels up to 28 metres in overall length for the purpose of exploiting under-utilised fish stocks within their area of fisheries jurisdiction, in accordance with a comprehensive resource management plan that has been approved by an independent international authority and notified to the WTO.

Brazil's proposal

Brazil's proposal[21] calls for SDT for subsistence and livelihood (for fishers and their families); fuel, bait and/or ice (for fishing activities); construction, repair, modernisation of vessels and gear acquisition or improvement under conditions that refer to exploiting fisheries resources in their own EEZ/maritime zones or exploiting high seas quotas and other rights established by regional fisheries management organisations (RFMOs).

Small vulnerable economies

Central to the negotiating position of the SVE Group of the WTO[22] is the belief that SDT provisions are fundamental to all WTO agreements and should be attached without conditions. This is based on the premise that SVEs, least developed countries (LDCs) and some smaller developing countries have a minimum impact on over-fishing and over-capacity.

[20] Norway's proposal, WTO document TN/RL/GEN/144, 26 January 2007.
[21] Brazil's proposal, WTO document TN/RL/W/212, 29 June 2007.
[22] SVEs' proposal, WTO document TN/RL/W/210, 6 June 2007.

Hence, according to the SVEs, the limitations should not be unduly punitive. Doing so would hamper the legitimate and much-needed growth of their fisheries industry. In addition, SVEs have strongly contended that SDT conditionality relating to fisheries management regimes should take into account capacity constraints of SVEs and LDCs. According to the SVEs' proposal, not all developing countries, especially the SVEs and the LDCs, have the capacity to enact a management regime that can produce statistics, analyse data or secure its waters from illegal, unreported and unregulated fishing to the extent that major fishing nations do.

Conclusion and policy recommendations

To ensure that fisheries trade policy contributes to poverty reduction and human development in PICs, effective policy interventions have to be made both at the domestic and multilateral levels to better inform the WTO negotiating process of the specific trade and development concerns of PIC members. The following are some recommendations to contribute to a positive way forward for the small island developing states of the WCPO.

Efforts at the multilateral level

Core elements of a development-conducive multilateral trade negotiating strategy with respect to the fisheries sector are as follows:

- It is crucial to ensure that multilateral rules designed to discipline fisheries subsidies fully take into account the importance of artisanal and small-scale fisheries to the small island developing states of the Pacific region. These remain the core of PIC development priorities for poverty reduction. The maintenance of livelihood and food security and seeking adequate SDT for this sector should remain central to the Pacific's goals on the multilateral policy front.
- Central among the PIC multilateral priorities is also the maintenance of adequate policy flexibility for domestic, commercial fisheries development. This has to be done through negotiating appropriate carve-outs, fundamentally in the form of SDT, in any new treaty on fisheries subsidies. It is to be noted here that, on 30 November 2007, the Chair of the Negotiating Group on Rules released the first draft text agreement[23]

---

[23] Chair's Consolidated Rules text, WTO document TN/RL/W/213, 30 November 2007.

on fisheries subsidies, which adopted a bottom-up approach (through the provision of a list of 'red-box' subsidies) and which has been structured in the form of an annex to the ASCM. This legal text proposed by the Chair was being used as a negotiating document at the time of writing (early 2008) and as a base to move forward in the discussions with a view to reaching a consensus among members on new rules. PICs, allied with the SVE and the ACP groups, are currently seeking greater exemptions and policy flexibility for their existing and emerging small-scale and industrial fleets. Some of the negotiating tools currently being used, in the context of the existing text, include the expansion of the definition and coverage of small-scale fleets (currently defined using the size of fishing vessel as the variable) and exemption from the disciplines on subsidies given for operating costs. Operating costs are a major form of government intervention in the fisheries sector in the PICs, and are perceived as affordable, targeted and easy to withdraw by the governments concerned (unlike capital subsidies for boat building, for example).

- As mentioned before, sustainability-related conditionality remains a central component of the proponents demand for new disciplines and the textual proposals on the table. While PIC negotiators support the design of appropriate sustainability criteria to meet the objectives of conservation and management of fisheries, it is important that members strive to ensure that these conditions are simple, streamlined, non-intrusive and not administratively burdensome for already overstretched fisheries and trade departments in PICs.

- PICs must also emphasise the importance of the exclusion of fisheries access arrangements from the scope of new disciplines on fisheries subsidies, based on the significant role of revenues from access payments in their economic development.

Efforts at the national/regional level

National-level fisheries and trade policies must be designed in a way that serves to complement each other, and negotiating strategies at the multilateral level must take account of these policies and interactions. At the same time, so as to ensure the effective reflection of PIC interests at the WTO in fisheries subsidies negotiations, the following recommendations could be taken into account by national governments:

- Identification of the specific characteristics of small-scale and artisanal fishing and of their social safety-net function and economic driver role in PIC economies is of utmost importance for the purpose of better informing the WTO negotiations on fisheries subsidies.[24] In addition, highlighting national policy objectives and the benefits to be obtained from securing much-needed investment in small-scale fisheries, and emphasising ways in which WTO rules could enhance such investments, would help to strengthen negotiating positions at the multilateral level. The type of information that would be typically required to better inform the multilateral process includes information on the level and type of subsidies and fiscal incentives deployed in the national fisheries sector. Putting together such information could be facilitated through the development of a nexus of information flows among RFMOs and their scientific and biological bodies, national trade and fisheries authorities and Geneva trade representatives. This will also enhance PICs' negotiating positions on such issues as 'sustainability indicators'.

- Increasing the flow of information is key to the role played by national policy in fisheries development and the representation of concerns at the WTO. Development of a comprehensive, reflective negotiating strategy in international policy-making necessitates coherence with the objectives of national policy makers, incorporating the concerns of the private sector and the rigour of evidence-based research. Information exchange between national authorities and international trade negotiators could have complementary benefits for both parties (such as the formulation of negotiating strategies in Geneva and implementation of WTO commitments by national authorities). This requires effective communication channels across relevant institutions, national authorities and Geneva-based representatives.

- Ideas for developing a system for the flow of information include the designation of representatives in relevant authorities/agencies in the Pacific who would liaise with staff members of the Pacific Islands Mission in Geneva on a regular basis, in order to provide timely information on request-based enquiries (the idea of informal 'enquiry points'). These would preferably include two representatives from the national fisheries authorities of each of the WTO member countries in the Pacific, at least one representative from the Western and Central Pacific Fisheries Commission, one or two representatives from the Secretariat of the Pacific Community and at least two representatives from the Forum Fisheries

---

[24] While an initial study has already been undertaken on this, additional evidence-based analysis is required. See Gillett (2005).

Agency (FFA). Steps have already been taken to advance an approach like this, particularly with the FFA, but the institutionalisation of these relationships would help to ensure that PIC interests are maximised at the WTO.

References

Arnason, R. (1998), 'Fisheries Subsidies, Overcapitalization and Economic Losses', in *Overcapacity, Overcapitalisation, and Subsidies in European Fisheries, Proceedings of the First Workshop of the EU Concerted Action and the Common Fisheries Policy*, eds. A. Hatcher and C. Robinson, University of Portsmouth: Portsmouth.

Campling, L., Havice, E. and Ram-Bidesi, V. (2007), *Pacific Island Countries, the Global Tuna Industry and the International Trade Regime*, Forum Fisheries Agency: Honiara.

Chang, S. W. (2003), 'WTO Disciplines on Fisheries Subsidies: A Historic Step towards Sustainability', *Journal of International Economic Law*.

Gillett, R. (2005), 'Artisanal Fisheries in the Pacific Islands: Some Terminology Considerations for Discussions on Fisheries Subsidies within the Framework of the World Trade Organization', report prepared for the Commonwealth Secretariat: London.

Gillett, R. and Lightfoot, C. (2001), 'The Contribution of Fisheries to the Economies of Pacific Island Countries', a report prepared for the Asian Development Bank, the Forum Fisheries Agency and the World Bank: Manila.

Gillett, R., McCoy, M., Rodwell, L. and Tamate, J. (2001), *Tuna: A Key Economic Resource in the Pacific*, Asian Development Bank: Manila.

Grynberg, R. and Rochester, N. (2005), 'The Emerging Architecture of a World Trade Organization Fisheries Subsidies Agreement and the Interests of Developing Coastal States', *Journal of World Trade* 39(3): 503–26.

Hall, S. (2007), 'Towards a Diagnosis of Small-scale Fisheries in Developing Countries', paper for the UNEP-WWF Workshop on Disciplining Fisheries Subsidies: Incorporating Sustainability at the WTO and Beyond: Geneva, 1 to 2 March 2007.

Havice, E. (2007), 'The State of Play of Access Agreements with Distant Water Fishing Partners: Implications and Options for Pacific Island Countries' FFA Briefing Paper: Honiara.

International Centre for Trade and Sustainable Development (ICTSD) (2006a), 'Fisheries, International Trade and Sustainable Development: Policy Discussion Paper', ICTSD Natural Resources, ICTSD: Geneva.

(2006b), *Natural Resources, International Trade and Sustainable Development: Fisheries Access Agreements*, ICTSD: Geneva.

Mbithi, S. M. (2006), 'Fisheries Access Agreements – Trade and Development Issues', Issue Paper No. 2, ICTSD: Geneva.

United Nations Environment Programme (UNEP) (2005), 'Artisanal Fishing: Promoting Poverty Reduction and Community Development: An Issues and Options Paper', UNEP: Geneva.

World Fish Centre (2005), *Improving Livelihoods for Coastal Communities in the Pacific*, World Fish Centre: Penang.

World Wide Fund for Nature (WWF) (2001), *Hard Facts, Hidden Problems: A Review of Current Data on Fishing Subsidies*, WWF: Washington, WA.

5.4

Trade and youth unemployment in Timor-Leste

JOAO SALDANHA* AND JIM REDDEN**

Background

Timor-Leste (or East Timor) is a small economy of just under 1 million people, with a gross domestic product (GDP) per capita of US$341, making it one of the most economically deprived countries in the Asia-Pacific region. The newly born nation has faced enormous challenges since it gained full independence as a country in 2002. Following the unrest and civil disturbance of 1999, the UN Security Council established a UN Transitional Administration in East Timor (UNTAET) to oversee the elections. Although East Timorese voted for independence, widespread violence led by pro-Indonesian militias resulted. As a result of this violence, the civil service collapsed, professionals left the country, the economy contracted by more than 35 per cent and almost 300,000 people were displaced. Timor-Leste had to rebuild from the ground level up under the UN's tutelage, and since 2002, the country has embarked on a long-term process of recovery and nation building. One of the major challenges for Timor-Leste is how best to deal with an unemployment rate of more than 50 per cent, at a time when the economy is experiencing negative economic growth and while political unrest continues.

More than 40 per cent of Timor-Leste's population live on less than US 50 cents a day. Furthermore, poverty has risen since 2001 as economic growth has been slow and unemployment high, especially in rural areas. Youth unemployment continues to fuel post-election political divisions, and presently there are limited prospects for job creation for young people. Consequently, the need to identify potential sectors to promote

---

* Joao Saldanha is the lead negotiator on the Millenium Challenge Account for the Ministry of Finance, Timor-Leste.
** Jim Redden is Director of International Programmes for China and the Pacific and Senior Lecturer at the Institute for International Trade, The University of Adelaide.

economic growth, poverty reduction and employment creation is a matter of urgency.

As a 'half-island' country, Timor-Leste has the potential for trade activities that, if appropriately developed, can contribute significantly to economic growth, poverty reduction and employment creation. At present, however, Timor-Leste suffers from chronic trade deficits as the country exports less and imports most of its capital and consumption goods. The main export commodity for Timor-Leste is coffee, earning approximately US$10 million a year. Therefore, the challenge for Timor-Leste is how to promote and diversify trade activities that provide incentives for market-oriented production thereby contributing to job creation in a country where more than half of the labour force is either engaged in subsistence agriculture or is unemployed.

It is against this background that the case study was conducted. The case study aims to examine the potential for trade policy and trade capacity-building strategies to assist in the reduction of youth unemployment through sustainable employment creation in Timor-Leste.

To this end, the authors firstly reviewed existing documentation and reviews of trade and trade-related activities in Timor-Leste, and secondly, conducted interviews with key stakeholders, especially unemployed youth, policy makers, the private sector and aid donors.

The results of the research and consultations are organised as follows. The next section overviews the characteristics and state of the economy of Timor-Leste. A discussion on the current trade environment and possible trade agreements of use to Timor-Leste follows. The next section examines trade policy and unemployment issues based on a summary of the primary interviews, with the following section suggesting useful ways forward for policy makers to assist in the reduction of youth unemployment.

Overview of the economy

Economic growth

Since 1999, the economy of Timor-Leste has been characterised by dependency and lack of sustainable economic growth. At the start of the reconstruction period, the engine for economic growth was international aid. For two consecutive years, economic growth was more than 15 per cent. However, the growth levels were not sustainable and turned negative following the decline of international aid (see Figure 5D).

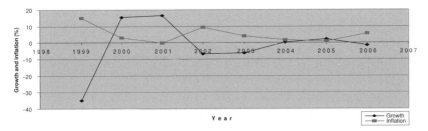

Figure 5D   Timor-Leste: GDP growth and inflation. *Source:* IMF (2007).

Economic growth was boosted by the increase of oil and gas revenues from the Timor Sea in 2004 and 2005. However, the increase was dashed by the political crisis of 2006,[1] which reset the growth rate to negative levels.

When disaggregating growth by sector, the agriculture, forestry and fisheries sectors suffered less than the manufacturing industry, services and public sectors (see Table 5L). Agriculture, forestry and fisheries only suffered negative growth in 2003 due to a long dry season and the decrease of global market prices for coffee. Overall, the growth of the agricultural sector was detached from international aid, and received less than 10 per cent of funding during the reconstruction period.

The growth of the industry and services sectors has fluctuated more than the agricultural and public sectors. Manufacturing, transportation and communications recorded high growth during the reconstruction period before reverting to negative growth after the downsizing of international presence during 2002 and 2003. These subsectors nevertheless have the potential for economic growth when reform measures are adopted, including improvement to infrastructure (such as the upgrading of rural roads and the provision of reliable electricity supplies).

Mining and quarrying, private construction and the financial subsectors remain sensitive to political instability and international presence. These subsectors were negative in 2002 and 2003 following the downsizing of the international presence, and again in 2006 following the civil unrest.

---

[1] In 2006, a political crisis emerged as a result of the government firing almost 600 soldiers who complained about discrimination in promotion. As a result, more than 150,000 people were displaced, police authority disintegrated and burning and looting occurred, especially in Dili (the capital of Timor-Leste). Stability was restored when international forces – led by Australia, with New Zealand, Portugal and Malaysia – sent troops and police to the country.

Table 5L   *Timor-Leste: Economic growth by sector (2001–06 – %)*

Sectors	2001	2002	2003	2004	2005	2006
Agriculture, forestry and fishery	8.7	6.0	−0.4	6.0	6.3	0.0
Food sector	10.9	−2.8	−7.0	6.6	6.6	3.8
Commercial agriculture, forestry and fishery	−2.2	54.8	22.5	4.3	5.2	−10.3
Industry and services	9.9	−0.4	−1.2	1.7	2.3	−16.6
Mining and quarrying (non-oil)	0.0	−15.8	−21.9	4.0	3.8	−33.3
Manufacturing	25.3	0.9	0.0	0.9	0.9	−25.0
Private construction	2.5	−6.8	−8.6	0.7	2.2	−26.8
Transport and communications	10.9	8.3	6.2	4.5	4.9	−16.3
Wholesale and retail trade	4.1	−6.6	−2.5	0.4	0.9	−8.9
Financial and other services	16.1	3.1	−1.5	0.4	1.1	−13.1
Public sector	25.8	−17.1	−13.8	−5.1	−1.1	11.3
Government services	123.1	12.9	14.2	7.4	7.6	−2.5
Public utilities	−48.1	92.9	25.9	14.7	20.5	−4.3
Public construction	1.1	−21.9	−31.2	−7.3	25.2	−2.9
UN	9.7	−34.1	−36.0	−27.5	−39.3	91.2
Total	**16.5**	**−6.7**	**−6.2**	**0.3**	**2.3**	**−1.6**

Source: Processed from IMF (2007).

The public sector suffered from the decrease in international aid and experienced negative growth from 2002 through to 2005. This was mainly determined by UN growth rates, which were linked very closely to international deployments so that growth rates were high during the period of deployment and negative after downsizing. These factors are responsible for this subsector recording positive growth rates in the early 2000s and again in 2006. However, government services and public utilities enjoyed positive growth rates from 2002 through to 2005.

To date, Timor-Leste's economic growth has been largely influenced by external factors; however, two sectors would appear as particularly significant for future growth and sustainability. Services (including exploration and mining) along with agriculture, forestry and fishing all appear to have the best growth potential to become the backbone of the national economy in years to come. If Timor-Leste can create sustainable growth

Table 5M   *Estimated oil and gas revenues from the*
Timor Sea (2007–10)

	2007	2008	2009	2010
Oil and gas (in US$ million)	683	983	1.08	1.05

Source: IMF (2007).

in these areas, there is significant potential for the employment of young people not only in the direct provision of services or in farm labour, but also in building the infrastructure required in support of improved services and agricultural productivity.

It is expected that oil and gas revenues from the Timor Sea will continue to rise in the future, particularly given the increase in world prices.

Table 5M shows the projected revenues from the Bayu-Undan fields in the Timor Sea; however, they will likely double and possibly triple when the Greater Sunrise area, which has larger deposits of oil and gas, is developed. Therefore, over the next thirty years, Timor-Leste will have a substantial amount of revenue, which, if properly managed, will have a significant impact on economic growth and poverty reduction in Timor-Leste.

To this end, a carefully constituted petroleum fund has been established in close cooperation with the Government of Norway. The investment management of the fund has been outsourced to the US Central Bank, and the Government of Timor-Leste has established an independent advisory board to guide and assist in the prudent management of the fund. By the end of September 2007, the petroleum funds deposited in the Federal Reserve Bank of New York accumulated to US$1.8 billion. According to the Petroleum Fund Law, the Government of Timor-Leste can withdraw a significant but limited amount of that fund to finance the national budget annually. The challenge then is to direct the flow of these funds wisely into economic activity and employment generation that grows the economy and reduces poverty – while avoiding the pitfalls of corruption and vested interest that have been the downfall of some oil-rich developing countries in the past.

Labour force

According to the Timor-Leste government census, about 60.2% of the population of Timor-Leste were in the labour force, with more than

Table 5N   *Labour force in Timor-Leste (2004)*

	Men	Women	Total
Population	469,919	453,279	923,198
Labour force (%)	68.7	51.5	60.2
Paid labour force (%)	16.0	10.8	13.4
Working in subsistence (%)	51.3	40.1	45.7
Unemployment (%)	8.3	5.4	7.2

Source: Census 2004, Government of Timor-Leste.

Table 5O   *Balance of payments (US$ million)*

Indicators	2000	2001	2002	2003	2004	2005	2006
Current account	−275	−301	−244	−208	−15	193	329
Trade balance	−237	−257	−211	−186	−154	−127	−133
Exports	5	4	6	8	8	9	8
Imports	242	−262	−211	−186	−154	−127	−133
Capital and financial account	−29	−40	148	103	18	49	71
Overall balance	16	8	20	18	121	341	482

Source: IMF country reports.

45.0% engaged in subsistence agriculture and only 13.0% engaged in the paid labour force (see Table 5N). It is expected that the labour force will increase by more than 15,000 persons annually.

Although the official statistics show that the unemployment rate was only 7.2% in 2004, the number was actually far higher (above 50.0%) if those in subsistence agriculture and the informal sector were included. Of particular note, only a total of 13.4% were regarded as being part of the paid labour force.

Balance of payments

Timor-Leste has suffered from chronic trade deficits (see Table 5O). This is due to the fact that Timor-Leste imports most of its capital and consumer goods, while exports have been limited to coffee and crafts. However, the overall balance of payments has been able to remain positive because of international aid, especially from 2000 through to 2003. From 2004 onwards, it was driven by the increased flow of oil and gas revenues from the Timor Sea.

Foreign direct investment

In relation to foreign direct investment (FDI), as of June 2007, the foreign investment arm of the government, TradeInvest Timor-Leste, had certified fifty-seven companies. Some of these companies have been operating in Timor-Leste since 2000 but only recently were given official authority to do so because TradeInvest has only recently been established.

The amount of certified investment as of June 2007 was US$200.8 million, with major investments in the hotel, agriculture (coffee, fishery and other) transportation and communications industries. If these investments were all realised, they should have created about 30,600 jobs. However, only 36.0 per cent of these licensed investments were implemented due to inadequate services provisions affecting investors, for example delays with customs, working visas, land and property issues and infrastructure problems, especially in relation to accessing power and water.

Some projects relating to power, water and sanitation, communications, wholesale and retail trade, financial services and security services were implemented, whilst projects affecting hotels, fisheries, construction, property development and manufacturing were only partially implemented. Most of these projects are financed by the foreign private sector.

Remittances

Statistics on remittances from abroad are still not available, although there are a significant number of East Timorese currently living abroad, especially in Australia, Portugal, Indonesia and Macau. Since 2000, the number of East Timorese going to the UK and Ireland looking for jobs also increased. This last group entered the UK and Ireland using Portuguese passports. Therefore, remittances to Timor-Leste can come from four different sources.

The first source is the East Timorese who left Timor-Leste in the mid 1970s and 1980s who have not returned to Timor-Leste but instead chose to settle in Portugal. Although no data is available, this group comprises approximately 1,000 people who send money back to Timor-Leste regularly, which amounts to approximately US$500,000 per year.

The second source is those living in Australia, estimated to be around 15,000 persons, who have established themselves and are enjoying relatively good salaries. In addition, there are a number of East Timorese workers working in the Timor Sea. Although not sizable, they can send money back to their families in Timor-Leste. Therefore, it is likely that, annually, the Australian diaspora sends approximately US$1 million back to Timor-Leste.

The third source is the East Timorese living in Indonesia who were relocated after 1999 (approximately 100,000 to 120,000 people) and are predominately based in West Timor. Many of this group still live in refugee camps in Atambua and Kupang and so obviously cannot send money to relatives in Timor-Leste. However, approximately 5,000 to 10,000 other East Timorese have joined the Indonesian middle class as civil servants, teachers and nurses who earn medium to high incomes. A number of them are now based in Jakarta or other major cities in Indonesia. This group can afford to send money to their relatives in Timor-Leste and is likely to remit US$300,000 annually.

The final source comes from a group of East Timorese who have recently migrated to the UK and Ireland looking for employment. This group migrated directly to the UK or Ireland from Timor-Leste, whilst the group mentioned earlier first joined through Portugal. Annually, it is likely that this group remits to Timor-Leste approximately US$1.2 million. Therefore, it is possible that remittances to Timor-Leste are close to around US$3 million a year, excluding those East Timorese living in Macau, Mozambique and other parts of Europe outside Portugal, Ireland and the UK.

This revenue is significant, as most remittances are channelled privately from one family to another in order to provide for the purchase of consumption goods and vital services such as health and education. If these funds can be harnessed for investment and savings as well, they could provide important stimulus for future growth from a relatively sustainable source. A former emigrant who lived in Portugal and the UK and who is now a businessman in Dili believes it is possible to increase the number of East Timorese working abroad, especially in Europe. However, to achieve this, the Timor-Leste Government must facilitate an increase in opportunities for labour market access to these countries, as well as to neighbouring Australia and New Zealand. This can be done through both trade and/or bilateral immigration arrangements. To provide incentives for those who are already working abroad, the government can encourage increased remittances through special savings incentives, for example through targeted higher interest rates for remittances hypothecated for savings, so that migrant workers are motivated to save their money back in Timor-Leste.[2] The government will therefore need to develop appropriate policies to facilitate labour mobility, increase remittances and try to encourage savings and investment into public goods, such as in schools and other public infrastructure.

Current trade environment

Agreements and challenges for Timor-Leste

The flow of labour and remitting of capital is but one part of the international trade system, which, if properly harnessed, can, together with oil and gas revenues, act as a safety valve while Timor-Leste develops its competitive advantage and grows the economy.

This section of the case study, mindful of the economic structure and challenges just presented, looks in more detail into some of the trade policy decisions Timor-Leste faces with respect to current global and regional trade negotiations and the potential implications for the employment needs of young people.

Timor-Leste is and will continue to be confronted by decisions about involvement in three key trade-policy forums: (i) membership in the WTO and participation in multilateral trade negotiations; (ii) decisions regarding regional trade agreements such as the Cotonou Agreement; and (iii) the desirability of negotiating specific bilateral free-trade agreements with important trading partners.

The WTO

There is no urgency about the decision of whether Timor-Leste should join the WTO or not. Presently, Timor-Leste enjoys observer status, and it should take its time in decisions relating to accession. Timor-Leste has an average applied import Most Favoured Nation (MFN) tariff rate of 6 per cent, which reflects its present and future reliance on cheaper consumer goods and imports for its people.

There are, however, some positive reasons for Timor-Leste to eventually join the WTO. It is useful to be a player in global trade negotiations

---

[2] Phone interview with Rogerio Pereira (6 November 2007) who recently returned from the UK and is now running his own business as well as providing transaction services to different agencies in Timor-Leste.

both as an individual economy and as a partner in strategic alliances with other least developed countries (LDCs), small island states and with similar small and vulnerable economies (SVEs) in the Pacific region. This requires a level of skilled personnel within the Timor-Leste Government able to monitor and influence the trade decision-making process.

Therefore, there are two matters that are vital to Timor-Leste in the context of the WTO. Firstly, it must develop a skilled cadre of informed trade negotiators, trade lawyers and trade economists who can advise in favour of Timor-Leste's best long-term interests. This will require the development of an accurate database of key trade and economic statistics accompanied by adequate research capacity both in government and universities. Secondly, Timor-Leste must ensure that this cadre of advisors remains on board after the accession negotiations. To achieve such a goal, this will require that wage or other incentives be in place for a core of public officials so that they remain in their roles post-accession, when many of the implications of accession must be addressed in the local economy.

One other benefit of joining the WTO is the impending institutional reform, accountability and transparency that is required for accession. Implementing and administering a range of trade policies that are WTO consistent, whether in agriculture, anti-dumping policy, sanitary and phytosanitary standards, investment policy or intellectual property, demands effective and transparent institutions that are able to enforce and monitor these policies. This can lead to a positive flow on effect whereby greater transparency and accountability is required across various arms of government, reducing any tendency that may arise towards poor governance or corruption. Of course, these transition arrangements come with a number of adjustment costs that will need to be anticipated.

As an LDC, Timor-Leste will benefit from special and differential treatment in the application of trade rules and obligations. Given its low average applied tariff rate of 6 per cent, it is highly unlikely that the current Doha Round negotiations in manufactured (NAMA) goods or in agriculture will have any impact at all on Timor-Leste's tariff rates. Timor has no agricultural subsidies and so won't be affected by either proposed disciplines or reductions in agricultural subsidies. Timor-Leste's bigger problem in this regard is rising agricultural prices generally as a result of growing global demand and related factors, thus increasing the cost of basic food imports for consumers.

Membership of the WTO should facilitate access to a range of trade-related capacity-building and technical assistance funds that may not otherwise be available, and these funds should be targeted to assist not only in the training of personnel but in the development of institutional reform, research capacity and infrastructure development. Furthermore, membership of the WTO increases a nation's global trade profile and helps to acquaint other members with key markets or potential markets in Timor-Leste. The International Monetary Fund (IMF) and the World Bank look favourably on the accountability required by WTO membership, which can also free up further funds for trade and economic capacity-building projects.

The principal downside of joining the WTO is the cost of implementing reform. The WTO itself needs to become more flexible with accession arrangements for SVEs and ease the demands on countries like Timor-Leste for accession. Lessons from other states would be useful in this regard, and in particular how states such as Mauritius or Fiji are managing the cost of reform.

The point of accession and ensuing legislative reform and capacity building is to ensure appropriate regulation is in place to encourage productive business investment, fair competition policy and consumer protection as necessary. The benefits poorer communities should derive are a responsible and accountable government pursuing practical and more open trade policies that are able to attract productive investment, resulting in jobs. Therefore, the authors of this case study have less concern about the domination by foreign suppliers in the market place, and exploitation of Timor-Leste's resources as 'liberalisation' does not mean the same as 'deregulation'. On balance, the authors believe there are more positives to Timor-Leste joining than not, although a decision on WTO accession is not urgent.

Regional trade agreements

The two regional trade agreements of interest to Timor-Leste are currently the Cotonou Agreement and, in the medium term, the possibility of joining the Association of Southeast Asian Nations (ASEAN) and acceding to the ASEAN Free Trade Area (AFTA).

The key issues for Timor-Leste in the Cotonou economic partnership agreements are similar to Pacific Island nations. Timor-Leste, as the section on remittances suggests, should pursue more generous labour-market access from the EU, using as leverage its special historical relationship with Portugal. Timor-Leste can offer reciprocal access to EU goods based on its import needs while maintaining its low-level tariffs of

6 per cent for some of its sensitive agricultural exports, such as coffee and vanilla. Obviously, it will be important for Timor-Leste to secure a significant package of trade-related capacity-building finances targeting infrastructure and construction activities that can increase the employment of young people. Services liberalisation should be unilaterally embraced to encourage commercial investment and commercial presence, again in exchange for labour-market access commitments from the EU.

Timor-Leste might also like to consider the benefits of joining the ASEAN grouping in the next few years and the signing of the ASEAN AFTA. Apart from similar benefits of increased technical assistance and capacity-building support as with WTO membership, regional integration into ASEAN locks Timor-Leste into the fastest growing region in the world. This gives Timor-Leste the potential to become a subsupplier to ASEAN regional industries, including manufacturing industries where both low- and high-skilled jobs may become available to the Timorese. Some reports have suggested that if Timor can develop its fishing and fisheries potential, then ASEAN represents a huge market for raw and value-added fish exports.[3]

The most obvious bilateral trade arrangements for Timor-Leste to consider would be with its close neighbours, Indonesia and Australia. Both countries have strong historical and economic ties with Timor-Leste, and closer integration through either free trade agreements or 'closer economic relations' agreements will assist Timor-Leste in its trade-related capacity-building requirements and in integrating into neighbouring markets. Labour-market access should be considered as a priority in negotiations with both countries.

Given the future revenue supply from oil and gas operations mainly from Australian-based companies in the Timor Sea, there is significant potential for job creation for younger Timorese in construction and mining-related services. Close integration with operations in Australia's Northern Territory will assist in developing business and investment relations. Australia has also been keen to offer vocational training in a range of practical trades such as mechanics, electrical engineering, hospitality and construction, which should be thoroughly exploited by young people in Timor-Leste.

Finally, Timor-Leste might also want to consider the maintenance of close relations with SVEs in the Pacific. Tonga has just joined the WTO, and Vanuatu and Samoa are likely to follow. Together, they face many similar trade challenges, including institution building and

---

[3] See, for example, IBM Consulting (2006).

infrastructure development. There is therefore considerable scope for the sharing of information and ideas for successful trade reform and for close cooperation on global and regional trade negotiations. It would be useful for Timor-Leste to monitor the progress of the closer economic relations agreement to be negotiated between the Pacific Islands, New Zealand and Australia over the next few years (PACER) for any implications it may have for its own trade and regional integration considerations.

Interviews and consultations

Trade policy and reducing unemployment: what the people say

What has been discussed so far is that, with political stability, strategic involvement in trade agreements and regional interaction, along with the prudent use of oil and gas funds and remittances, there is a strong base for Timor-Leste to grow and diversify its economy in order to address the problem of unemployment generally and, in particular, youth unemployment. The potential challenges and benefits were put to policy makers and to young people themselves in Timor-Leste to reveal their views and priorities.

Policy makers (government)

The authors interviewed policy makers about the government's position on economic and trade priorities, the role of the private sector on tariff policy, the potential benefits of international economic agreements and the capacity-building needs of Timor-Leste.

Some key challenges that were identified included:

- the lack of a legal framework for implementing reform
- the lack of human resources capacity and training in trade policy
- the need for a more comprehensive trade strategy
- the lack of services (transportation/government/communication) supporting the private sector.

The government intends to review the legal framework for private-sector development in Timor-Leste because this area did not get appropriate attention in the past. A sound legal framework would help instil confidence in investors, as well as provide mechanisms for dispute settlement.

According to those consulted, Timor-Leste has limited human resources capacity and experience in trade policy and trade negotiation issues, which needs to be addressed through training in Timor-Leste, studies abroad and provisions for obtaining degrees in trade policy overseas.

Capacity building, they argued, should include understanding how to engage the private sector to encourage investment and jobs.[4] Procedures for business registration were identified as unclear, and often investors were being told to wait without certainty. In addition, technical assistance and capacity building needed to include linguistic training, especially in English, because most trade negotiations, investment and business forums are conducted in English.

Another challenge for Timor-Leste is that it does not have a comprehensive trade strategy to guide policy makers and the private sector alike. Most of the policies are conducted on an ad hoc basis. Some suggested the formation of a centralised government or semi-state body to research, develop and coordinate trade policy in the future in a holistic manner so that all arms of government are synchronised to achieve trade-related development goals.

It was argued that the formulation of trade policy needed to be in close partnership with the private sector. This is being pursued and there have already been a number of business dialogues between the government and the private sector, with the support of donors. The last one was held in June 2007, where participants identified four major impediments to private-sector development.[5] These impediments were:

(1) land and property issues
(2) the procurement process
(3) streamlining of business approvals
(4) licensing and national taxation.

Land and property issues are a major challenge for the expansion of trade and investment because of the multiple claims against land ownership. The lack of dispute settlement mechanisms make it difficult for change of ownership and for the rental market. This, of course, affects investment decisions given that land is one of the primary factors of production.

The procurement process at the Ministry of Public Works was cited in the forum as one of the main impediments to private-sector development because major government projects are processed and tendered out

---

[4] Interview with José Guterres, SEP II, Ministry of Economy and Development, 30 October 2007.

[5] 'Breakthrough in Private Sector-Government Talks', Forum dos Empresarios de Timor-Leste press release, 8 June 2007.

through the Procurement Division of the Ministry, often with cumbersome processes and bureaucratic time delays. Public procurement can be an important source of employment creation, and there were suggestions that decentralising the tendering process to district level would benefit small businesses and assist in employment creation.

Donor organisations

As for the donor bodies that were consulted as part of this study, the International Finance Corperation (IFC), the private-sector arm of the World Bank, believed that it could help create jobs indirectly by improving access to micro-financing and by assisting in lowering the costs of doing business, for example through recommending lower tax rates, better provision of utility services and less bureaucracy in business registration: 'When more companies have access to micro-finance, more investment will happen and therefore it will help to create jobs in the economy.'[6] Timor-Leste ranked 168 out of 178 selected countries in the world for ease of doing business (World Bank, 2007). These business indicators did not include political instability. If this variable is included, then Timor-Leste's ranking would slip further to the bottom.

Other donors stated they would be assisting in the provision of jobs through their development assistance projects, such as the Asian Development Bank (ADB) with funding for the construction of roads, ports and bridge projects. The World Bank, with its Fundamental School Quality projects, has already built more than 100 primary schools nationwide, and the International Labor Organization (ILO) with Cash for Work programmes is targeting work programmes for the rural population. Bilateral assistance from the Australian aid agency AusAID is also active in rural water and sanitation projects that have helped to create jobs, and the United States Agency for International Development (USAID) projects have been focusing on coffee and private-sector development with potential job-creation effects.

Private sector

From the perspective of those interviewed from the private sector, employment creation in Timor-Leste needs to come from the re-structuring of

---

[6] Interview with Rainer Vanghaussen of the IFC, Dili, 25 October 2007.

the public procurement process, as noted earlier. Of interest, they admitted that many Timor-Leste companies only focused on winning contracts but then had difficulties in project management and implementation.[7] This resulted in penalties and even the loss of contracts. Therefore, they argued for technical assistance and training for the private sector in private management (organisation, administration and finance) and project implementation.

Young and unemployed people

A number of young and unemployed people in Dili were consulted, especially those in Comoro (the western part) and Becora (the eastern part) to get their perspectives on how they were using their spare time, their prime career interests and training needs.

Many of the youths consulted used their time searching for jobs: 'I use my spare time to find jobs, any kinds of job to feed myself.'[8] Others said they helped parents at home or assisted in the running of small businesses, such as small kiosks: 'I use my spare time to run a small recycling business.'[9] But some young people were losing hope of finding jobs because they knew that it was very difficult to find one. Other young people interviewed used their spare time to help relatives and friends at home. Of those employed young people we spoke to, some worked as labourers in construction projects either in full-time or part-time positions in the public sector.

Nearly all those consulted were interested in working abroad on a temporary basis because of the limited opportunities within the country: 'I want to work overseas, especially in big companies. The most important thing is to get some experiences.'[10] However, a few were not interested in working overseas, probably because of family and community ties and the difficulties in adapting to new situations and the language of another country.

All of those consulted would like to participate in training to improve their skills and knowledge for gaining jobs in Timor-Leste or in preparation for work abroad. There was a consensus for training in construction and services sectors, but some also mentioned agricultural management, with a number keen to acquire tertiary education qualifications and skills.

[7] Telephone interview with Alberto Belo, Modena Co., 25 October 2007.
[8] Interview with Krisanto Colo, Comoro, Dili, September 2007.
[9] Interview with Senhorinha Oliveira de Jesus, Becora, Dili, 30 September 2007.
[10] Interview with Domingos Soares, Comoro, Dili, 25 September 2007.

However, most hoped that the training, especially courses conducted by the government, could be free of charge since they have little or no money to pay for such training: 'What I need to help me get a job is to increase my capacity through training or short courses. However, only if these trainings are available but not costly.'[11]

In light of these comments from the authors' consultations in Timor-Leste, and based on the trade and economic information discussed earlier, there are a number of trade strategies that can be identified to assist in reducing youth unemployment.

Ways forward to reduce unemployment

Targeted sectors and trade strategies

The trade-related sectors that have the most potential to promote economic growth and employment creation are, as previously stated, construction and infrastructure development, the services sector, especially in the oil and gas- and mining-related services but also in tourism and labour-market mobility, and in the niche marketing of agricultural products (such as coffee, vanilla and water buffalo) and in the development of the fisheries sector.

Construction

There was a consensus that, because of the limited role at present of the private sector in the economy, public procurement should become a major source of economic growth and employment creation. Previous analysis showed that around 10 per cent of GDP came from construction (public and private), which employed a significant number of people both on a permanent and temporary basis. It is expected that this sector will continue to grow given increases in government revenues from oil and gas over the next two decades. Construction projects should be developed as a priority and should include schools, health centres, office buildings, roads, bridges, dams and irrigation – all of which can create employment for young East Timorese if accompanied by adequate preparatory or on-the-job training. Private-public partnerships and joint ventures with foreign investors would assist in financing and managing the construction of these and other infrastructure projects.

One important element that needs to be addressed is how best to create conditions to decentralise economic activities to districts and rural

---

[11] Interview with Agapito do Rego, Becora, Dili, 30 September 2007.

areas. There is a need to ensure that job creation is spread across regions and rural districts evenly, and this requires the careful planning and distribution of projects. Ideally, projects tendered should require labour-intensive components targeting low- to semi-skilled workers.

The tendering process needs to be administered in a more transparent and user-friendly way; for example, the Fundamental School Quality Project (FSQP) of the World Bank followed an open bidding process with intensive monitoring from World Bank personnel hired for this purpose. Major roads, bridges, ports and irrigation will attract foreign skilled workers and, if well administered, the skilled workers should be required to help train local young, unemployed workers.

Construction also has a number of forward and backward linkages throughout the economy. Backward linkages include demand for products such as cement, concrete blocks, batubara, iron, wood and so on. These pose many opportunities for growth of support industries to the construction sector, so that these industries can also contribute substantially to employment creation. A successful construction industry can then achieve forward linkages by stimulating growth in sectors such as communication and transportation, again with valuable job-creation implications.

Mining and gas sector

An oil and gas pipeline to Timor-Leste will benefit the economy. This capital-intensive sector may not absorb many workers in Timor-Leste because of the lack of technicians for this area. However, with training and technical assistance, there are a number of mining services and related positions that could develop. Bringing the main pipeline from the Timor Sea direct to Timor-Leste will be beneficial to the economy in two other aspects. Firstly, it might well create confidence in the Timor-Leste economy, which in turn will attract more investors. Secondly, the pipeline industry in Timor-Leste will create derived demands from other sectors of the economy, especially agriculture and infrastructure (roads, energy and markets) to support the oil and gas project. These derived demands can in turn stimulate trade, economic growth and employment creation.

Services

Timor-Leste has the potential to develop a unique tourism industry, in particular in eco-tourism. Its pristine coastline and relatively unscathed forests and tropical settings can attract a niche tourist market in trekking and mountaineering, bird watching, whale or dolphin watching, scuba diving and snorkelling, given Timor's aqua biodiversity. There is also fishing as a sport in itself, and educational tourism that highlights Timor-Leste's involvement in World War II and its historic struggle towards independence.

The liberalising of Timor-Leste's services sector and attracting foreign investment and management skills to this sector can be utilised to first build the industry and then to assure skills development and training for local Timorese. A strong tourist sector will in turn have multiplier employment effects in agriculture, fishing and the crafts industry supplying the tourist market. Unfortunately, an initial prerequisite for building the tourist market is ongoing political stability, which hopefully will become easier with time and increased employment.

Labour mobility

Timor-Leste does not have an overall employment-creation strategy, and one is urgently needed. Statistics on labour mobility in Timor-Leste are not available, making it difficult to assess the current situation, although we can estimate that up to 150,000 East Timorese are working overseas at present. What we do know is that there are 6 million[12] temporary workers in Southeast Asia and Australia (mainly skilled and semi-skilled) and as such there is significant potential for Timor-Leste to tap into the increasing regional demand for labour.

Over the last two years, the government was able to send seventeen people to work in Korea, but with proper planning, Timor-Leste could place between 3,000 to 4,000 people in this market. However, a number of important steps have to be taken.

Firstly, Timor needs to approach the governments of the region, whether Korea or Australia, to understand the potential import of skills needed. Secondly, Timor needs to prioritise relevant training programmes for potential temporary workers according to those needs. Thirdly, there is also a need for training in language and cross-cultural communication that enables potential workers to adapt to different cultures and languages. These measures obviously cannot be done by the government alone, so a partnership with the private sector and international donors is required. As mentioned previously, labour-market access for low-skilled to unskilled workers should be a priority in all trade negotiations for Timor-Leste.

---

[12] Interview with José Assalino, ILO, Dili, 24 October 2007.

The Australian and New Zealand markets may present strong potential for temporary workers of all sorts – low-, semi- and skilled workers. However, labour-market access is still a complex issue – New Zealand has recently introduced a special, seasonal labour-market scheme with Pacific Island neighbours, and the new Rudd Government in Australia is considering similar approaches.

The importance of an overall labour market and employment strategy is to find that difficult balance between training and up-skilling workers required to build the local economy while allowing a degree of that up-skilling and training to happen overseas. Temporary labour-market schemes offer the advantage of ensuring most return to use their skills (and their remittances) to develop the local economy.

Niche markets in agriculture: coffee, vanilla and water buffalo exports

Commodities in the agriculture sector that have the potential for increased trade and investment are coffee, vanilla and water buffalo. Timor-Leste's coffee is known as one of the best in the world and it is Timor-Leste's major export commodity, excluding oil and gas exports. However, most of the coffee exported is not processed and, as such, does not create value addition to the economy. Therefore, it is vital to encourage coffee investors to undertake coffee processing before it is exported. That way, it will generate additional income and employment in Timor-Leste. The Cash for Work programme of the ILO actually attracted many young people to participate in some agricultural projects across the country. There is the potential for young people to become interested in working in coffee and vanilla businesses in the future. In this regard, the rejuvenation of coffee plantations across Timor-Leste is important, and a strategy is needed for coffee rejuvenation that again helps create employment.

Vanilla has been discussed as one of the potential export commodities for Timor-Leste. However, more research needs to be done on plantation and production capacity and on potential export markets. Water buffalo is another potential source of export with attendant job-creation effects. There are already trans-island shipments of water buffalo to West Timor to reach the richer and larger market of Java in Indonesia. With the support of USAID, Cooperative Café Timor (CCT) is working together with farmers in Suai to breed buffaloes along the border, with the specific purpose of exporting to West Timor.

Fishing and fisheries

Timor-Leste can develop its potential to produce fish and fish products both for self-sufficiency and for export. The report by IBM Consulting (2006) on Timor-Leste suggested that a fisheries management plan be developed and implemented in partnership with the Australia Timor-Leste Fishery Management Capacity Building project. Such a plan will work to develop and diversify fisheries' products towards niche markets while ensuring health and quality standards are appropriate for meeting export demand. IBM Consulting also recommends the development of an environmentally friendly aquaculture industry capable of attracting foreign investment and jobs for Timorese.

Removing overall barriers to trade

Other areas that need attention to promote trade in Timor-Leste include tax incentives, the streamlining of bureaucracy and regulations and land and property issues.

For example, while Timor-Leste has a low, applied average tariff of only 6%, undermining that relatively low tariff rate are excise taxes of between 12 to 36% and a 5% sales tax, which means a total tax of up to 50% on some tariff lines.

The new government is preparing a package for tax reform, which will include the removal of these barriers. President José Ramos-Horta in March 2007 issued an official statement that Timor-Leste will embrace free trade and tax cuts to promote business and investment and lessen the tax burden on consumers: 'Timor-Leste does not receive much revenue from tariffs levied on imports, but these taxes are an administrative burden and discourage trade. In my view Timor-Leste should become a "Free Trade State" by eliminating tariffs on all imports.'[13] He argued that there should be an exception for 'undesirable' imports such as on tobacco and alcohol, and on those goods that are damaging to the environment or to the health of the people of Timor-Leste. These undesirable goods should be transparently listed and made subject to a high fixed tariff. He noted that, as tariffs were reduced, no Timorese producers should be disadvantaged by the lower costs of imports, and some local producers may need to be compensated.

These are all welcome moves by the President and should improve Timor-Leste's ability to attract investment while enabling consumers'

[13] President José Ramos-Horta, Statement to the Parliament of Timor-Leste, March 2007.

access to cheaper imports, which in turn increases their disposable income, but these moves will need to be firmly and clearly implemented. It is suggested that in order to attract more domestic and foreign investors, it is important to streamline the bureaucracy by bringing IADE and Trade-Invest (the two government departments responsible for trade and investment in Timor-Leste) under one roof, with both reporting directly to the Prime Minister.

Conclusions

Timor-Leste may be a small, vulnerable and low-income country at present, but this case study has endeavoured to highlight its strong potential. It has been that, with certain conditions and strategies in place, Timor-Leste should be able to successfully embrace economic growth and job creation.

Firstly, there needs to be a sustained period of political stability and domestic reform within Timor-Leste. This would assist the development of a whole-of-government approach to employment and labour-market strategies, for economic reform that addresses barriers to trade and business investment and for the development of an international trade strategy that pursues regional integration while maximising the advantages for Timor-Leste of various trade and economic arrangements both globally and with its neighbours.

Secondly, Timor-Leste can utilise current oil and gas revenue, remittances and foreign aid to buy time and anchor reforms that will be necessary to build a sustainable future.

Thirdly, based on this reliable revenue base, Timor-Leste should invest in key job-creating sectors, in particular in infrastructure development, services and increased agricultural productivity. Investment in training and education will be fundamental to these developments and should also be strongly supported by donor bodies.

With these fundamentals and related strategies in place, Timor-Leste can gradually grow its economy and absorb the current large pool of unemployed young people. However, there should be no illusion about the time, patience and the need for support both internally and externally for these policies. A number of officials consulted in Timor-Leste put forward the suggestions offered in this case study, but the ability to implement these strategies requires skilled personnel, functional institutions and stability.

So, can trade and related economic policy contribute to job creation for young people in Timor-Leste? The research and interviews undertaken suggest a qualified but positive correlation between well-crafted trade policies and their potential to create an appropriate environment for direct and indirect job creation targeting young people.

President Ramos-Horta's advocacy for the removal of trade and investment barriers in order to create a business-friendly economy as well as one that reduces the burden on the poor augurs well for sending the right signals to investors and consumers alike. What is needed desperately is the political stability to allow these economic reforms and developments to unfold. The recent attempts on the lives of President Ramos-Horta and Prime Minister Xanana Gusmao are extremely unfortunate and undermine this potential.

The acceleration of trade-related employment programmes and job creation for young people will hopefully assist in addressing the instability that so often confronts new and emerging democracies.

Bibliography

Atkinson, K. (2007), 'Timor-Leste: Special Economic Zone', presentation, Dili, Timor-Leste.

Bordia Das, M. and O'Keefe, P. (2007), *Enterprises, Workers and Skills in Urban Timor-Leste*, World Bank: Dili.

Hill, H. (2001), 'Trade and Commercial Policy', in H. Hill and J. M. Saldanha (eds), *East Timor: Development Challenges for the World's Newest Nation*. ISEAS: Singapore.

IBM Consulting (2006), 'Assessment Report on the Trade Related Needs of Timor-Leste', IBM: Belgium.

International Monetary Fund (IMF) (2007), 'Staff Report for the 2006 Article IV Consultation', IMF: Washington, WA.

Ministry of Labour and Community Reinsertion and International Labour Organization (ILO) (2007), *YES, Youth Employment Survey – Timor-Leste 2007*, Dili.

Saldanha, J. M. *et al.* (2002), *Trade and Economic Growth in East Timor*, Timor institute of Development Studies: Dili.

Saldanha, J. M. and da Silva, H. (2003), *Competitiveness of Industries in East Timor: The Story of the SMEs*, Timor Institute of Development Studies: Dili.

Soesastro, H. (2007), 'East Timor's Economic Relations with Indonesia', in H. Hill and J. M. Saldanha (eds), *East Timor: Development Challenges for the World's Newest Nation*, ISEAS: Singapore.

World Bank (2004), *The Labor Market Impact of Minimum Wage Policy: The Case of Timor-Leste in Comparative Perspective*, World Bank: Dili.

(2005), *World Bank Country Assistance Strategy for Timor-Leste FY 06–07 – Creating the Conditions for Sustainable Growth and Poverty reduction*, World Bank: Dili.

(2007), *Doing Business 2008*, World Bank: Washington, WA.

Trade reform and poverty reduction in Papua New Guinea

NOLPI KILWA[*]

Introduction

Given the small-scale manufacturing base and a perceived need to protect local small to medium infant industries, Papua New Guinea's trade
policy has tended to be inward-looking. As a result of a World Bank and
International Monetary Fund (IMF) initiated Structural Adjustment Programme, however, Papua New Guinea has become, since 1996, one of the
more open economies in the Pacific. The highest tariff rate on restrictive
goods is bound at 40% and is due to be reduced over the next few years,
while tariffs on most basic goods have been reduced to zero.

Yet, Papua New Guinea still lacks clear vision and a coherent trade
policy that would enable it to make full use of international trade as
an instrument for national economic growth. A lack of microeconomic
reforms, poor-quality public services and law and order problems have
also undermined the potential gains from trade.

Sound trade-policy analysis, formulation and implementation are lacking, as are links between policy makers and industry initiatives that could
drive an export-led growth strategy. The Papua New Guinea Ministry of
Trade and Industry (MTI) would seem the natural candidate to take the
lead in coordinating efforts in this area, but at present there is no clear
leader in policy development and coordination, and communication with
and amongst stakeholders is poor.

Policies affecting trade and investment are currently being reviewed
including negotiations on market access and trade facilitation measures
within the WTO and the Asia-Pacific Economic Cooperation (APEC).
Negotiations are also currently underway on an economic partnership

---

[*] Nolpi Kilwa is Principal Research Analyst for the Policy Planning, Research and Information
Division at the Department of Commerce and Industry, Papua New Guinea.

agreement (EPA) with the EU. Papua New Guinea is playing a central role in market-access negotiations, in particular at the regional (Pacific ACP, or PACP) level, and the EPA is vital for Papua New Guinea to maintain its EU preferences for many products. Yet Papua New Guinea lacks the institutional, human and financial capacity to adequately represent and articulate its national interests.

This case study consists as follows. The following section briefly outlines the main characteristics of the Papua New Guinea economy, including a discussion of poverty in the country. The next section identifies some of the areas that hold the most potential for trade-led development, as well as some of the principal factors that constrain such growth. This is followed by a section that looks specifically at the ongoing EPA negotiations and priorities for Papua New Guinea and other PACP countries in those negotiations, including discussion of some of the supporting policies that will be required to ensure that the EPA assists Papua New Guinea in realising its growth and development potential. Finally, the case study concludes with a summary of the state of play in the Cotonou Agreement negotiations and some final thoughts on strategies that Papua New Guinea could pursue to develop trade as an instrument to reduce poverty.

The Papua New Guinea economy and poverty issues

The Papua New Guinea economy

The agriculture, forestry and fisheries sectors are the mainstays of the economy, employing over 85% of the population and accounting for 27% of gross domestic product (GDP). Services account for 17% of GDP, while manufacturing contributes 8% of GDP. The mining and petroleum sector is also an important component of the economy.

Agriculture

The significant percentage of Papua New Guinea's population involved in agriculture consists of subsistence farmers who raise livestock and poultry and grow food and cash crops on traditional land holdings. Smallholder agriculture is based on a low-input/low-output mode of production, and productivity is well below potential. The major staple crops are sweet potato, banana, yam, taro and cassava, and the most important cash crops are cocoa, palm oil, coffee, tea, copra, rubber and fresh fruit and vegetables. High-value spices and vanilla are becoming increasingly important cash crops and are contributing to a more diversified export base.

Notwithstanding extensive production in rural areas, surpluses often do not reach the market due to the high costs of transportation, which are in turn due to poor infrastructure. Poor practices and a lack of standards from harvesting to packaging and warehousing are also major constraints on the sale of agricultural production. Yet the sector has high growth potential, which, if realised, could significantly improve the living standards of the rural population.

Manufacturing

The manufacturing sector contributes only 8 per cent of the country's GDP, and investment in this sector has been minimal. Although there are specific incentives, including a ten-year tax holiday and tax exemption on capital goods for investment, in this sector, these have rarely been utilised. The Papua New Guinea Institute of National Affairs (PNGINA) found that the limited investment in downstream processing activities was due to various impediments, including: corruption at almost all levels of government; poor transportation and utilities infrastructure; lengthy, cumbersome processes in visa, work permit and business registration issuances; and unnecessary delays in customs clearance.

Services

Papua New Guinea is a net importer of services. The sector contributes around 17 per cent of GDP and employs up to 200,000 people. There remain many state-run monopoly service providers in Papua New Guinea in services such as electricity, telecommunications and air transportation. More liberalised services are tourism, health, construction and education, although these remain subject to limitations.

Services subsectors currently undergoing significant growth are those that support the mining and petroleum industry, including catering, consultancy and construction. Like agriculture, the services sector – especially tourism – has huge potential. However, the high costs of electricity, telecommunications and transportation have also limited investment in services to date. In addition, many technical experts in mining and construction have left Papua New Guinea in favour of overseas employment in places like Australia, the US and Africa.

Poverty issues

According to an income per capita report released by the World Bank in 2006, nearly 60 per cent of the population lives under the poverty line.

However, in the Papua New Guinea context, this does not mean absolute poverty.

Indeed, in comparison to many developing nations, poverty levels are not as critical in Papua New Guinea. This is because the rural population generally has shelter, as well as access to food (especially garden produce), protein and clean water. Some produce from rural farmers is sold in urban markets for cash to obtain basic necessities, although this does not occur on a large scale.

Signs of poverty are more evident in urban settlements. The most disadvantaged of the population are those found in urban settlements. Many of them have migrated to urban areas from rural settings in search of employment and a better livelihood that is not readily available. They often live illegally on state land in unapproved buildings that they have erected. Basic amenities, including paved roads, water supply, electricity and telecommunications, do not exist, but unemployment is rife and there is often a strong criminal element within these communities.

Overall, the population of Papua New Guinea is not involved in the cash economy. Most people are unable to earn sufficient cash to obtain many basic necessities. A lack of basic healthcare, education services and road infrastructure also contribute to the low social indicators.

Strategic trade issues

For Papua New Guinea to take full advantage of global opportunities, it needs to focus on its areas of competitive strength, embrace international best practices and develop its manpower skills. At this stage, its competitive strengths lie in agriculture, forestry, fisheries, mining and petroleum. The emerging strengths are in manufacturing, value-adding downstream processing, tourism and natural gas.

In agriculture, encouraging export-related activities or import-substitution activities has the potential to generate employment and entrepreneurship and reduce poverty by bringing cash into rural areas. For instance, crops such as carrots, tomatoes and lettuce are grown organically in Papua New Guinea, and farmers have the capacity to supply the domestic market as well as overseas markets. At the same time, while agriculture will remain the mainstay of the economy for decades to come, a foundation for emerging industries needs to be put in place.

In order for Papua New Guinea to realise its huge trade potential, however, it must first address many priority trade-facilitation issues. Key among these are issues relating to standards and conformity assessment, quarantine and customs clearance. Effective poverty reduction and development will also depend on the elaboration of socioeconomic policies to underpin and support the development of trade.

Standards and conformity assessment

The National Institute of Standards and Industrial Technology (NISIT), the state body responsible for standards, lacks the skills and technology to implement standards and conformity assessment programmes. While appropriate norms and standards have been adopted from Standards Australia and other international standards bodies, NISIT still lacks the skills and the technology to fully implement them and give the necessary attention to quality-control issues in manufacturing and agricultural production.

Quarantine

Stringent quarantine measures imposed by export destinations such as New Zealand, Australia, Japan and EU markets have a huge impact on potential exports of produce such as taro, cassava, bananas, vegetables and fruit. The Papua New Guinea National Agriculture Quarantine Inspection Authority (NAQIA), the state agency responsible for quarantine issues like its counterpart NISIT, lacks the technical capacity to conduct training and fully implement its mandate. This means that although Australia and New Zealand offer preferential market accesses for many agricultural exports from Papua New Guinea, it does not fully utilise this preferential market access because Papua New Guinea does not have the capacity to meet the stringent quarantine requirements and standards imposed by these countries.

Customs clearance

Papua New Guinea has adopted the ASYQUDA system at all its ports to facilitate the flow of goods. However, because the ASYQUDA system has been introduced recently, and customs officials have not undergone appropriate training on the use of the system, unnecessary delays still occur in customs clearance processes. Other factors such as customs officials not working on weekends or after normal business hours contribute towards the delays in clearing goods. Moreover, there is a need to overhaul visa issuance, work permit and business registration processes to make them transparent, simple, speedier and more customer-friendly.

Complementary policies

Poverty reduction and trade strategies must be part of a wider development strategy. Some issues that will require particular attention in Papua New Guinea's socioeconomic development plans are as follows:

- The population is growing faster then the GDP or the general economic growth rate. If the current trend continues, the economy cannot cater to a large population.
- HIV/AIDS is becoming a concern. The active/productive population is at risk of infection, and the threat is increasing to such an extent that a generation could be wiped out, leaving the country with an unproductive population.
- Substantial amounts of semi-processed or unprocessed agricultural products, including bananas, onions, Irish potatoes, carrots, pineapples, oranges and apples are imported, even though Papua New Guinea is capable of producing them locally. These products often come with high import bills. There is the need to cut down on costly imported products, particularly when domestic production could satisfy all domestic demand and still be exported.
- Papua New Guinea is generally an open economy, with all tariffs for basic goods at zero and the highest being 25 per cent. This poses the danger of dumping, which is already occurring, as Papua New Guinea does not have an anti-dumping policy. Anti-dumping legislation complementing an export-led economic-growth strategy is needed for the country.

These are a few trade issues that Papua New Guinea is faced with in trying to diversify its exports and participate in the global market. Other issues include supply-side constraints such as road infrastructure. These issues must be addressed for Papua New Guinea to participate in the global trading system on a level playing field. Least developed countries (LDCs) and developing countries such as Papua New Guinea must be assisted in efforts to address these issues in multilateral fora (such as the WTO Doha Development Agenda) and in arenas (such as the EPA with the EU). At present, the WTO negotiations are stalled. The EPA negotiations, however, are expected to be completed by the end of this year, and thus warrant a closer look.

The economic partnership agreement with the European Union

The Cotonou Agreement, between the EU and African, Caribbean and Pacific (ACP) states, contemplates the negotiation of a series of reciprocal trade agreements between the EU and the various ACP states, to take effect in 2008. Following the first phase of the EPA negotiations at the all-ACP level that started in September 2002, the regional negotiations between the PACP countries and the EU were launched in September 2004. At that time, all PACP member states, including Papua New Guinea, agreed to negotiate the EPA with the EU. At the first ministerial-level session, both sides agreed on a joint road map fixing the main goals and principles of the negotiations as well as the structure and an indicative schedule for their completion.

The EPA negotiations are crucial for Papua New Guinea. Firstly, the EU represents 15% of Papua New Guinea's total exports, of which the majority are agricultural goods, while imports from the EU accounted for 2% of total imports in 2005. Secondly, even if the overall aggregate effect of the EPA on Papua New Guinea is minimal, the flow-on effects will be much greater. This is because Papua New Guinea is also a signatory to the Pacific Agreement on Closer Economic Relations (PACER). Under Article 6 of that treaty, if any PACP member state enters into a free trade agreement (FTA) with any developed country other than Australia and New Zealand, consultations will take place with the latter countries with a view to negotiating a similar FTA. Hence, as soon as the EPA is concluded, it will trigger negotiations of a similar FTA among Australia, New Zealand and the PACP states.

The remainder of this section examines specific issues in the EPA negotiations with the EU and identifies some of Papua New Guinea's main objectives for the agreement, along with some of the areas in which these have been resisted by the EU.

Development

In late 2007, the initial deadline for the conclusion of EPA negotiations was fast approaching, and the Pacific region was yet to come to some form of consensus on a range of key issues, one of them being the development aspects of the EPA. The central objectives of the Cotonou Agreement are the reduction and eventual eradication of poverty, these being consistent with the goals of sustainable development and gradual integration of the ACP countries into the global economy. These objectives are to be tackled through an integrated approach taking into account the political, social, cultural and environmental aspects of development in the ACP states. Consistent with these objectives, Papua New Guinea and the PACP member states wish to see the development component delivered through the EPA. It is their position that the EPA will achieve the Cotonou Agreement objectives only if the development component is at the heart of the negotiations.

Papua New Guinea simply cannot benefit from full market access and special and differential treatment (SDT), or develop its export potential, without additional trade-related assistance. Duty-free or expanded quotas will not increase exports if domestic enterprises cannot produce enough or cannot properly promote their goods through effective marketing efforts. Even if the trade rules are flexible in favour of developing countries such as Papua New Guinea, it will continue to lose out on the potential benefits of global trade and lack the means to alleviate poverty if it does not have the capacity to participate effectively in global trade.

This means that the EPA must address supply-side and export capacity constraints. For Papua New Guinea, there must be a clear commitment from the EU on the development component and financing instruments. The development component of the EPA must be demand-driven, free of economic conditions and must be predictable and complementary to – rather than a substitute for – better and fairer trade rules. It must aim to help Papua New Guinea and the rest of the PACPs to adapt to the global trading system The development component is not about training trade negotiators or the capacity building of trade negotiation institutions. It is about enhancing worker's skills, modernising customs systems, building roads and ports and improving agricultural productivity and export diversification.

At the same time, the PACP's capacity to absorb and implement the development component must be enhanced. For example, Papua New Guinea lacks coordination, and the linkages between the sectoral agencies are very weak. These linkages must be strengthened and the capacity to absorb funding under the development component must be enhanced. Papua New Guinea is currently implementing a project funded by the EU under the 9th EDF (Enterprise Development Fund) for the strengthening of the linkages between the sectoral agencies and to build the capacities of its implementing agencies. This project will enhance the coordination and linkages among the agencies.

Without these types of meaningful commitments to development, the flow-on effects call into question the utility of signing an EPA. Papua New

Guinea is looking for a good EPA with the EU that will set a precedent when other FTAs are negotiated, such as with PACER.

Trade in goods

Although trade in goods is not central to the majority of PACP member states, it is crucial to Papua New Guinea, considering its huge tuna exports to the EU, as well as exports of products such as coffee, copra, cocoa, palm oil and tea. As mentioned before, Papua New Guinea's exports to the EU represent 15 per cent of its total exports, and that represents a significant proportion to a small and vulnerable developing nation. Papua New Guinea is, accordingly, keen to improve its market access and share of the EU market.

Together with the other PACP member states, Papua New Guinea is requesting full duty-free and quota-free market access for PACP products entering the EU market, with flexible rules of origin (ROO). Many issues relating to trade in goods have been discussed in the negotiations, including market access, tariffs, asymmetric commitments, trade facilitation and trade promotion, ROO, transitional periods and adjustment costs. The following are some of Papua New Guinea's principal objectives in the negotiations:

- maintaining and improving current market access
- duty-free access to the EU market for all Papua New Guinea products
- flexible ROO on all exports to the EU
- the agreement to cover 100% of all EU imports from the PACP and at least 60% of PACP imports from the EU
- the EU to renounce recourse to safeguard and anti-dumping actions against Papua New Guinea exports
- SDT to be extended to all PACP members
- the transitional period to be over twenty years for the PACP, but EU tariffs to be eliminated immediately
- permanent or temporary exclusion of sensitive products from tariff reductions, provided that these sensitive products have the potential to make an impact in the long run on the socioeconomic development of the country
- the agreement to include flexible, efficient and accessible dispute settlement procedures, including a process for prompt action for financial and technical assistance

- assistance to be provided to address the potential impact of the trade in goods agreement, for example the loss of tariff-revenue income for some countries.

At the time of writing, the EU had not accepted all of these PACP proposals, especially with respect to the proposal to provide assistance to deal with the impact of the agreement. The EU maintains that the impact of changes to trade in goods will be as a result of other trading arrangements and not the EPA, and does not wish to pay for costs that are not directly related to the EPA. Generally speaking, the EU also wishes to see uniform, ACP-wide rules for issues like origin and other trade in goods issues. The EU has been reluctant to acknowledge the diversity and the individual needs of different regions, or to accept arguments by the PACP countries that they require distinct EPA provisions. Yet the circumstances of African countries are totally different from those in the Pacific and from those in the Caribbean. Papua New Guinea maintains that each of these groups therefore requires a different approach that specifically addresses the needs of each regional configuration.

Agriculture

The agriculture sector is the backbone of the Papua New Guinea economy as it involves over 80 per cent of the population. Much can be done in this sector to increase output, improve productivity and sustainability and thereby improve the living standards of the rural people and alleviate poverty. It is vital to Papua New Guinea that this sector be treated well in the EPA negotiations.

To this end, Papua New Guinea's focus in the negotiations is on measures to address supply-side constraints affecting competitiveness, including the promotion of downstream processing, the development of marketing, distribution and transportation of agricultural commodities and an improved ability to comply with sanitary and phytosanitary (SPS) standards.

In addition to seeking improved market access for its agriculture commodities, Papua New Guinea will concentrate on issues relating to supply-side constraints' defined as:

- low labour productivity (due to poor education and health systems)
- limited management know-how and innovation technology

- scarce integration of upstream and downstream activities, with the consequence of non-maximisation of employment opportunities and knowledge spillovers
- poor or non-existent infrastructure
- high transportation costs
- high costs for utilities such as electricity and telecommunications
- unstable macroeconomic policies.

Papua New Guinea therefore needs more on the development component of the EPA to develop its agricultural sector and make it more competitive in the international market. Other significant trade issues affecting trade in agricultural goods, notably SPS and technical barriers to trade (TBT) measures, will need to be addressed separately.

Fisheries

The fisheries sector is essential to Papua New Guinea and, because it is a shared resource, to other PACP member states as well. Papua New Guinea currently exports around K 350 million (US$125 million) of tuna a year to the EU market, and it is estimated that this will increase by 2 to 5 per cent annually. Thus, the fisheries sector includes one of the major products that are currently exported to the EU in large quantities and therefore creates employment and income-generating opportunities in rural-Papua New Guinea coastal areas.

Papua New Guinea has been pushing for a Multilateral Fisheries Partnership Agreement as a subsidiary agreement, but that now looks unlikely to happen. Instead, fisheries products will be covered by the general trade in goods provisions, while development aspects will be covered by the development provisions of the EPA.

Given the importance of this sector to the Papua New Guinea economy, it must attract investment in the sector and secure markets for fisheries products. EU ROO are quite stringent and need to be relaxed for Papua New Guinea to compete well with other countries such as the Philippines, Korea and Malaysia. In addition, the high costs of fuel, transportation and poor landing and handling facilities are hindering the growth of the industry.

Papua New Guinea is the only country among the PACP, apart from Fiji, that processes fish in large quantities. Papua New Guinea has six downstream processing plants and needs to build another four. For Papua New Guinea to derive maximum benefits from the fisheries sector and assist the other PACP members, it intends to offer shares in these processing plants to PACP member states and come up with some arrangements for labour in the factories. For example, Papua New Guinea can offer a 30 per cent share to Federated States of Micronesia, along with a quota on labour (employment). This is to ensure that fish caught within the PACP are landed and processed within the PACP.

According to the fisheries officials, Papua New Guinea needs a trade in goods agreement by the end of 2007, when the WTO waiver expires, in order to maintain current market access. If there is no trade in goods agreement, at the end of this year, it may be costly to Papua New Guinea, as occurred when the current waiver was negotiated and the quota was extended to Thailand and the Philippines. In the face of uncertainty as to what will happen if there is no agreement before the waiver expires, it is critical that Papua New Guinea preserve EU market access for its tuna.

Rules of origin

The ROO issue is fundamental to Papua New Guinea as it is currently one of the technical barriers that hinders the country from utilising available market access. Papua New Guinea supports the PACP proposal to have ROO based on changes in tariff subheadings. This is a very simple criterion that will assist the PACPs to meet their economic and social development objectives. The main reasons for this proposal are:

- The private sector in the PACP is largely import-based. In some cases there are no economies of scale or raw materials to produce locally intermediate goods; in other cases, local suppliers are able to produce at a cost and quality that is uncompetitive.
- Cumulation provisions are of little use, as exporters are too distant from the EU (bilateral), from each other (regional) or have no recognised 'neighbouring country' (developing country diagonal).
- The alternative, value-added ROO would bias exporters in favour of local inputs, making the products less competitive or uncompetitive in the EU market.

The EU, however, wishes to see value-added criteria for ROO across all ACP countries. The EU does not recognise the individual needs of each region. This is unfortunate because the unique geography of these Pacific Island states means that transportation between the member countries is very poor and many imports need to be brought in from other sources.

ROO that might be acceptable for other ACP countries do not make sense for the PACP.

Trade in services

The services sector in Papua New Guinea already contributes 17 per cent of GDP. It is one of the most significant sources of formal employment in the region, and will likely play an important role in determining the quality and speed of economic development. The main services sectors of interest to Papua New Guinea, and those that are considered good candidates for liberalisation, are air transportation services, shipping services, financial services, telecommunications services, health services, education and tourism.

In its efforts to liberalise and expand trade in services, Papua New Guinea has agreed to a positive list approach in the negotiations, with SDT and safeguard provisions.

Liberalisation commitments

Papua New Guinea is committed to liberalisation in air and sea transportation, telecommunications and health services. The first two of these services sectors are monopolies. All of them involve high costs, are uncompetitive and have become a hindrance to economic growth. It is an appropriate time to liberalise them and bring in competition.

Despite some negative media portrayals, Papua New Guinea has huge potential in the tourism sector, with over 800 languages, diverse cultures and colourful flora and fauna. The country is currently focusing on promoting eco-tourism and intends to soon move into leisure-connected tourism. In the negotiations, Papua New Guinea is focusing on the development and investment aspects of tourism. Nonetheless, a draft services offer, including the tourism sector, has been prepared. In drafting the offer, Papua New Guinea has made a number of reservations, including that certain tourism activities may only be pursued by nationals, for example the running of small guest houses and lodges in rural areas and tour-guide operations.

Of course, services liberalisation can also have adverse effects, as firm closures for uncompetitive services suppliers, unemployment and skills becoming redundant. Given the small size of the economy, there is also the likelihood that domestic monopolies will become foreign monopolies. Since services liberalisation is also very complex and requires regulatory

and policy reform, financial and technical assistance must be channelled
to this sector to address the constraints affecting liberalisation.

Mode 4: labour mobility

The PACP is proposing to establish a mode 4 quota for PACP nationals.
This quota would be a regional one covering skills where EU member states are experiencing shortages. The PACP recognises that the EU
encounters shortages in labour for workers whose qualifications are below
the tertiary level, and the PACP is able to supply people with certificates
and diplomas to fill the shortages.

Papua New Guinea aims to enable its nationals, especially nurses, car-
penters, plumbers, electricians and other technical people, to work in EU
member states for specific periods. This will assist them to get wide exposure and experience and return to the country once their terms of service
are up. In addition, Papua New Guinea anticipates that this scheme will
help bring in foreign currency.

Although certain EU members, such as the UK, Germany and France,
are supportive of the PACP proposal, the official EU response has been
that this may not be possible. The EU has requested that PACP negotiate
this issue at the bilateral level, although these negotiations have yet to take
place.

In pursuing the PACP proposal, Papua New Guinea is nevertheless conscious of the risk of 'brain drain'. Even if the proposed liberalisation relates
to qualifications below the tertiary level, there is still a risk that skilled
nationals will leave the country for better pay and working conditions in
developed countries where their skills are in demand. Another potential
hurdle is the standardisation of the qualifications. The EU requires high
standards of education and experience in all fields. This will require the
EU to build up the capacity of training institutions in the PACP member
states to meet EU minimum requirements.

Investment

Although the issue of investment does not form part of the WTO negotiations in the Doha Round, the PACP and the EU have agreed to include it
in the EPA. Papua New Guinea wishes to have an Investment Protection
and Promotion Agreement Plus. This means an agreement with general
investment provisions, along with additional provisions on issues such
as market access and financial and technical assistance. The additional

provisions will help Papua New Guinea in terms of putting in place a more appropriate regulatory and policy framework that is transparent for all investors. Creating an investment environment that will attract both domestic and foreign direct investment is a priority for Papua New Guinea, but the current regulatory framework needs to be overhauled to make it more user-friendly.

Conclusion

Although the role of trade policy in economic development has been subject to much debate, it is widely accepted that liberal trade policies enable countries to produce and allocate resources more efficiently, facilitate access to new ideas and technologies, increase access to cheap foreign goods and realise export-led growth through the exploitation of new markets. In recognition of this, Papua New Guinea has participated in multilateral trade negotiations within the Doha Round and, more recently, in the EPA negotiations with the EU. Papua New Guinea has sought, in those negotiations, to preserve and improve access to the EU market for its goods and services exports, especially for agricultural and fisheries products. Papua New Guinea has also made a number of commitments to liberalise services, and has sought market openings for its nationals who are capable of providing needed services in the EU.

However, trade alone cannot produce sustainable economic development. There are other factors that come into play, such as macroeconomic policy and a country's capacity to trade. Papua New Guinea currently lacks sufficient capacity to allow it to benefit fully from trade opportunities.

Papua New Guinea will need to put in place a coherent trade policy together with other policies that will enhance its ability to participate meaningfully in and benefit from international trade. However, this cannot be achieved without assistance, in particular from its trading partners. This means that both the DDA and the EPA need to deliver a robust development component in order to enable developing countries like Papua New Guinea to participate in international trade on a level playing field.

The central objective of the Contonou Agreement is to reduce poverty in line with the Millennium Development Goals. Therefore, the EPA has to be negotiated to achieve this objective, and development needs to be at the heart of the negotiations. It is important, in this connection, that the EPA includes provisions that will assist Papua New Guinea to overcome supply-side constraints and enhance its ability to comply with SPS and TBT requirements as an exporter. Also needed are provisions that recognise that the Pacific is different from the Caribbean and African regions, notably with respect to ROO. Overall, the agreement must be sufficiently beneficial to Papua New Guinea to make it worth signing, given that the provisions of the PACER will require Papua New Guinea to enter into similar negotiations with Australia and New Zealand once the EPA is signed.

Pressure was brought to bear for PACPs to conclude EPA negotiations by December 2007. As far as Papua New Guinea negotiators were concerned, consensus on some key issues – including the development component – had still not been reached, and it was unlikely to be reached by that end-of-year deadline. However, it was agreed that the trade in goods component of the agreement be signed and the negotiations of the remaining components of the agreement be completed over the following two years. On this basis, given the importance of preferential market access for Papua New Guinea goods exports, Papua New Guinea signed a seperate trade in goods agreement with the EU. This will now trigger PACER negotiations with Australia and New Zealand.

Papua New Guinea looks forward to a beneficial and development-friendly EPA that will help it to addresses its major constraints to trade and to become competitive in the global trading arena. This, in turn, will ultimately assist Papua New Guinea in working through other trade agreements and in achieving the millennium objectives of poverty reduction.

Bibliography

Bank of Papua New Guinea (2006), *Quarterly Economic Bulletin* 34(4).

Campling, L. (2008), 'Fisheries Aspects of ACP-EU Interim EPAs: Trade and Sustainable Development Implications', *IETSD* 6.

Delegation of the European Commission in Papua New Guinea (2006), 'Trade Related Assistance to PNG', Financing Procedures and Financing Agreements\Fed\001-05(9).

Department of Agriculture and Livestock (2006), *National Agriculture Development Plan 2007–2012*, Department of Agriculture and Livestock: Port Moresby.

Department of National Planning and Monitoring (2002), *Poverty Reduction Strategy*, Department of National Planning and Monitoring.

(2004), *Medium Term Development Strategy 2002–2007*, Department of National Planning and Monitoring.

Department of Trade and Industry (2001), *Draft Industrial Development Master Plan*, Department of Trade and Industry.

(2004), *Papua New Guinea EPA Negotiating Strategy*, Department of Trade and Industry: Port Moresby.

(2006), *Statistical Digest*, Department of Trade and Industry.

Development Component of Possible Trade and Goods and Services Agreement, PIFS (2006), PACP TWG-GAF 1.6.

Draft Fisheries Legal Text, PIFS (2006), TWG-F/TWG-LICB/PACPNG.0207.

PACP Draft Legal Text, PIFS (2006), TWG-F/TWG-LICB/PACPNG.0206.

United Nations Center for Trade and Development and Department of Trade and Industry (2006), *Draft Trade Policy for Papua New Guinea.*

The future of the Fijian garment industry

BIMAN CHAND PRASAD,* YENTESHWAR RAM** AND
ARIEL MARR***

Introduction

The Fijian garment industry has had a short and often turbulent history.
A product of the post-1987 crisis strategy of export-led economic
development, coupled with key preferential trading arrangements, it
experienced a dramatic early growth. The industry rapidly became a
critical part of the economic structure of Fiji, often surpassing sugar
as the number-one export sector. It was also recognised as the largest
employer of urban low-income earners in the country in the late 1980s
and throughout the 1990s. Despite the industry's rapid and impressive
growth, there has always been a concern over the sustainability of the
industry and the benefits of garment factory employment for employees,
especially women. While the garment sector has proved to be a critical
source of livelihood for low-income earners, it has also come under
sustained criticism over the years regarding poor labour conditions, low
wages and exploitation of female labour.

Arguably, these conditions have been accentuated by regional and
global trade agreements, which essentially consign the garment sector in
Fiji to a low-wage and low-skill role, thus perpetuating industry dependence and its workforce to 'working poverty'. The industry's economic
base has remained fragile and dependent on markets and buyers over
which it has little control. Consequently, the sector has continued to
struggle to grow into an efficient and sustainable industry. Reliance on

* Biman Chand Prasad is Professor of Trade and Development and Dean of Faculty of
  Business and Economics at the University of the South Pacific, Suva, Fiji Islands.
** Yenteshwar Ram is a tutor at the School of Economics, University of the South Pacific,
  Suva, Fiji Islands.
*** Ariel Marr is a postgraduate student at the University of the South Pacific, Suva, Fiji
  Islands.

preferential trade agreements, which gave rise to its rapid growth, has masked the garment sector's inability to add value to products and develop key markets outside the region. Some of these vulnerabilities have been exposed by the loss of quota access to the US as a result of the expiration of the Multi-Fibre Arrangement (MFA) (Agreement on Textiles and Clothing –ATC) on 1 January 2005. Both government and garment-factory owners appear to be indifferent to the sustainability of the industry, considering garments to be a 'stagnating' or even 'dying' sector. Despite this predicament, the garment industry can still provide a very significant contribution to employment generation and in national poverty reduction. However, for this to happen, the industry will have to rely on continued access to preferential markets in Australia and New Zealand. The rules of origin (ROO) will have to be made more favourable for the continued production of garments in Fiji, preferential access to markets maintained until the garment industry is able to adjust to changing global trade regimes and until such time when Fiji could develop other export alternatives.

Given this background, the aim of this case study was to analyse the relationship that exists between trade polices and poverty within the garment industry in Fiji. The rest of the chapter is structured as follows. The next section presents an overview of the textiles and clothing industry in Fiji. This is followed by a section that describes the impact of changes in the global and domestic economy on the textiles and clothing sector, with particular reference to changes in the global trading environment. The next section discusses the results from the primary interviews, while the penultimate section of this chapter offers some policy recommendations on the complex relation between trade policy and poverty reduction. The chapter ends with conclusions.

An overview of Fiji's textiles and clothing industry

The clothing and textile industry in Fiji was born in the wake of the political instability created by the military coups in Fiji in 1987.[1] Out of the export-oriented initiatives adopted by the government to revive the economy after the political crisis, the clothing and textile industry was actively supported by the then interim government. The Fijian Government's tax-free status offered to export companies, preferential trade agreements with

---

[1] See Narayan and Prasad (2003) for an analysis of the contribution of the garment industry in Fiji.

Australia and New Zealand under the South Pacific Regional Trade and Economic Cooperation Agreement (SPARTECA) and guaranteed access to the US market via the MFA provided the initial boost to the industry, and significant investment by garment entrepreneurs, both foreign and local, was achieved.

Trade agreements and domestic incentives

Several trade agreements and domestic incentives in the last two decades have shaped the initiation and development of the garment sector in Fiji.

The first and probably most influential for the Fiji garments industry was SPARTECA, which was signed in 1981, granting producers in the South Pacific Forum Island countries preferential and non-reciprocal, unrestricted duty-free access of their goods into the Australian and New Zealand markets. Garments were also included in the agreement on the condition that they met a 50 per cent local-content requirement.

In 1987, the newly appointed Interim Government of Fiji sought to rebuild the economy through the adoption of export-oriented policies. One scheme that came out of this new policy direction was the Tax Free Factories (TFF) scheme, which granted a thirteen-year tax holiday and other benefits to companies that would export 70 per cent or more of their output.

A further agreement signed between Australia and Fiji in 1991 was the Import Credit Scheme (ICS), which allowed Australian fabrics to be shipped to Fiji at competitive prices for the production of garments that would be re-exported back to Australia. Support also came from the MFA, under which Fiji enjoyed quotas from the US, resulting in certain Asian manufacturers establishing garment factories in Fiji, as the quotas in their home countries were reduced. Furthermore, a few manufacturers managed to gain access to the EU under the rules of derogation granted in Protocol 1 of the Lomé Convention.

Production and exports

The trade agreements and domestic incentives that were established in the late 1980s and early 1990s fuelled the growth of a new industry. In the first five years of its establishment, the industry grew rapidly as the number of new manufacturers increased. In 1988, there were twenty-seven clothing and textile factories in Fiji, but the number grew to eighty-eight by 1991, representing a threefold increase in just three years (Adhikari and Yamamoto, 2006).

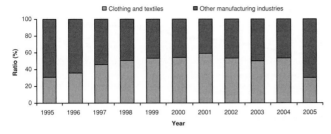

Figure 5E   Fiji's ratio of the clothing and textiles industry in the manufacturing sector. *Source:* Fiji Islands Bureau of Statistics (2006b).

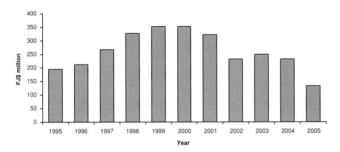

Figure 5F   Fiji's clothing and textiles exports. *Source:* Fiji Islands Bureau of Statistics (2006a).

Given the influx of foreign and local investors in this industry, the value of production of garments rose from FJ$2.5 million to an estimated peak of around FJ$188 million in 2001. In fact, by 2001, clothing and textiles accounted for about 60% of all production in the manufacturing sector (see Figure 5E) and close to 6% of gross domestic product (GDP). The significance of this sector's economic contribution to the Fiji economy had indeed grown since the late 1980s.

A favourable and interesting development also occurred a few years after the first garment manufacturers established operations in Fiji. The growth in the number of garment manufacturers in Fiji also led to an emergence of support and 'backward linkage' industries such as weaving and knitting, as well as textiles and button manufacturing. These new activities helped reduce production costs, shortened lead time and in a small way contributed to a more diversified industry.

In terms of exports, the peak was recorded in 2000, when clothing and textile exports reached FJ$353 million (see Figure 5F). This represented about 31 per cent of all merchandise exports, placing it in the top three

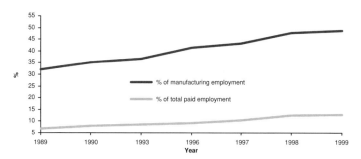

Figure 5G Employment in Fiji's clothing and textiles industry. *Source:* Fiji Islands Bureau of Statistics (2000).

categories of Fiji's exports. (Refer to Appendix 5A (Table 5Q) for a category versus placement list of Fiji's merchandise exports for the year 2006.)

Employment and wage conditions

Since the introduction of the TTF scheme, the clothing and textile industry has proven to be a major source of employment for Fiji's growing labour force. The contribution of the clothing and textiles industry to employment in the manufacturing sector rose from about 32% in 1988 to 49% in 1999. The contribution to total paid employment also records a similar trend of 6.8% in 1988 to 12.8% in 1999 (see Figure 5G).

However, cut, make and trim (CMT)[2] operations are at the low-value end of the apparels commodity chain, and the skill level required for employment is not very high. Hence, such operations are able to effectively employ first-time job seekers who lack specialised technical training and put them through quick training before engaging them in productive work. Apart from packers and machinists, there are several other positions in this segment that require skilled and experienced workers for jobs, but the proportion is small.

With regards to remuneration, industry-level data shows that wages and salary conditions for those employed by garment producers have been progressive and stable. In comparing the mean hourly wage rate of those employed in garment production to the mean hourly rate of the

---

[2] In CMT production, manufacturers in the producing countries merely receive all the components for the apparel from their country of export, then assemble the components in the producing country and export the finished apparel back to the country from which inputs came. In Fiji, entrepreneurs who are engaged in CMT operations account for 92 per cent of the domestic production.

entire Fijian manufacturing industry, it appears that, from 1988 to 1999,[3] the wage rates of garment employees grew faster relative to the mean wage rate of the entire manufacturing sector (see Table 5P).[4] While the same cannot be said for the annual salary of the salaried personnel in the industry, one must keep in mind that salaried individuals make up a small percentage of those employed by garment producers in Fiji.

Overall, the clothing and textiles industry is one of the major contributors to the income of much of the peri-urban population in the Central and Western Divisions of Viti Levu, most of whom are women.[5] This indicates that the livelihood of many low-income households in these areas is dependant on the clothing and textiles industry.

Twenty years on from 1987, with increased global competition, the erosion of preferential trade agreements and the end of domestic tax holidays, the future of the clothing and textile sector's viability hangs in the balance.

Impact of changes in the global and domestic economy on Fiji's garments and textiles trade

The gradual erosion of preferential access of garments to developed countries has caused the production and export of garments from small island states such as Fiji to decline. The first set of arrangements to affect Fiji were the end of the ICS with Australia and the end of the first TFF thirteen-year tax holiday. Both of these occurred simultaneously in 2000 during the political crisis.[6]

---

[3] The Fiji Islands Bureau of Statistics latest report is the '1999 Annual Employment Survey Report' (Fiji Islands Bureau of Statistics, 2000).

[4] A salary is a periodic payment made by an employer to his/her employees as specified in their employment contract. With regards to a salary, no reference is generally made to a specified number of hours that a worker should work for. Wages, however, are paid in cash for a specified quantity of labour, normally measured in units of time (such as hours worked). Wages are also paid at a certain wage rate. With regards to the garment industry, office workers normally receive salaries, while factory workers get wages.

[5] Fiji is officially divided into four geographic subdivisions, which are named the Central, Western, Northern and Eastern Divisions. Peri-urban areas are those areas that lie on the peripheral of the urban areas – not necessarily rural but falling outside of the boundaries of the major urban municipalities.

[6] Fiji had another coup and experienced continued political instability until 2001, when a general election led to a democractically elected government. After the 2006 general election, the military again overthrew the elected government – a total of four coups in twenty years.

Table 5P *Mean earnings in the clothing and textile and manufacturing industries*

| | Normal mean hourly wage rate of wage earners | | | | Mean annual salary of salaried personnel | | | |
| | Clothing and textiles | | Manufacturing | | Clothing and textiles | | Manufacturing | |
Year	FJ cents	Growth (%)	FJ cents	Growth (%)	FJ$	Growth (%)	FJ$	Growth (%)
1988	78	–	157	–	–	–	–	–
1989	79	1.3	142	–9.6	9,509	–	9,728	–
1990	92	16.5	143	0.7	11,045	16.2	10,668	9.7
1993	109	18.5	174	21.7	9,401	–14.9	13,448	26.1
1996	127	16.5	204	17.2	10,298	9.5	12,679	–5.7
1997	124	–2.4	189	–7.4	11,186	8.6	13,603	7.3
1998	126	1.6	181	–4.2	9,935	–11.2	14,210	4.5
1999	136	7.9	189	4.4	11,979	20.6	15,750	10.8

Note: most of the data for 1988 are missing, as these data were not collected/compiled for this year. Since these 1988 figures are missing, some of the growth rates for 1989 also cannot be calculated. *Source:* Fiji Islands Bureau of Statistics (2000).

The industry was directly affected by the 2000 crisis through power shortages and the lack of regular and safe travel for workers. However, the indirect effect of international buyers and investors losing confidence in Fiji as a viable producer of garments had a greater impact. The combination of this and the end of the tax holidays for some producers and the cessation of the ICS caused a significant decline in production and exports. Approximately fourteen garment factories closed or transferred out of Fiji, and exports to Australia were reduced by about 50 per cent in the eight months following the May 2000 coup (ADB, 2006a). As a result, an estimated 2,600 garment workers had lost employment by the end of 2001. Some commentators have noted that Fiji has not recovered since then.[7] Indeed, that may be true considering that the production levels and export proceeds from garments (as plotted in Figures 5E and 5F) reveal a downward trend since 2001.

The next arrangement that drew to a close was the Multi-Fibre ATC in 2005. This provided access for Fiji garments into the US market, under a quota system that distorted prices to the advantage of Fiji producers. The effect on the local garment industry was swift and brutal. Within a month of the cessation of the Multi-Fibre ATC quotas, the major manufacturer engaged with the US market closed operations and relocated out of Fiji to countries with lower-cost labour. This closure also saw the closure of all other smaller factories to which this major manufacturer once outsourced part of its operations. According to the Asian Development Bank's South Pacific subregional office, an estimated 6,000 people lost employment.

Much of the competition for Fiji garment producers came from China's entry into the WTO and its increasing dominance in the Australian garment market. In the first half of 2004, China's share of the Australian market exceeded 80 per cent for many of the segments of the clothing and textiles market. This dominance is on the increase as Australia continues to liberalise its garment market to meet WTO commitments. The liberalisation of the Australian market is thus eroding the preferential position afforded under SPARTECA to Fiji's garment producers, forcing them, and indeed Australia's textile, clothing and footwear industry, to compete against much cheaper garments from China and India. The erosion of Fiji's preferential position will continue into the next nine years as Australia's general tariffs on garments are scheduled to fall from 17.5% to 15% in 2010, and then to 5% in 2015 (ADB, 2006a).

[7] ADB (2006b).

Prospects for the future

In spite of the losses experienced by the clothing and textiles industry in terms of production, exports and employment, it still remains a significant contributor to the Fijian economy. In 2005, the industry accounted for 2% of GDP, 30% of production in the manufacturing sector and 11% of merchandise exports.

This means that what is left of the industry in Fiji is still able to effectively produce and export to the preferential markets in Australia, in spite of the reduction in Australia's general tariffs last year from 25% to 17.5%. However, it also means that the domestic industry will have to work more strategically at improving competitiveness and productivity in order to survive the next reduction of general tariffs, which is scheduled for 2010.

Furthermore, the local garment manufacturers have been lobbying for more concessions similar to the ICS in order to artificially maintain their competitiveness. Lobbying has been undertaken at the industry level, Foreign Minister to Foreign Minister level and even Prime Minister to Prime Minister level during trade talks between Australia and Fiji. Notwithstanding this, it is becoming increasingly clear that a concession similar to the ICS will not be entertained. Officially, Australia will not move on this issue, as such a concession would be considered inconsistent with its liberalisation strategies as well as with WTO rules. Regardless of the real reason, the fact remains that Fiji will most probably never broker an ICS-similar arrangement with Australia.

Interview results

For the purpose of this study, thirty current garment-factory workers and ten former garment-factory workers who are now unemployed were interviewed. All forty of them were females. Moreover, twenty garment-factory owners were interviewed to obtain their views on the state of the garment industry in Fiji. Of the thirty current garment-factory workers, fifteen were based in the Central Division, while the other fifteen were based in the Western Division of Fiji. As far as the former garment-factory workers were concerned, five of them were based in the Central Division, while the other five were based in the Western Division. With regards to the garment-factory owners that were interviewed, ten of them were based in the Central Division, while the other ten were based in the Western Division. These two divisions account for over 95 per cent of all the garment factories in Fiji. The following paragraphs will discuss the findings that were obtained through the interview process.

Upon interviewing the workers, it was discovered that all interviewees had worked within the garment industry for an average of about five years. When asked about their families' financial backgrounds (before they started working), it was found out that all of them had a total family income of less than or equal to F$90 per week. This is well below the basic-needs poverty line income of about F$95 per week for Fiji reported by Narsey in his 2006 study on just wages for Fiji (Narsey, 2006).

However, when they started working, it was discovered that the well-being of the families of these workers had improved markedly. Almost all of these families had experienced a doubling of their income and, therefore, had moved beyond national basic-needs poverty line income. With regards to training, all the interviewees stated that they were given training for their jobs when they started working. In this regard, 20 per cent of the participants mentioned that they received training without pay from their superiors for an average of three months. Once they had learnt what they had to do and had started doing it satisfactorily, they then started receiving their normal pay. On the other hand, the remaining 80 per cent of the participants mentioned that they received on-the-job training with normal pay for an average of about three months.

As machinists (70% of the participants), cutters (10%), fitters (10%), packers (5%) and quality checkers (5%), all the current and former garment-factory workers mentioned that they were getting wages in the range of F$50 to F$100 per week (which consisted of forty hours). However, all of them mentioned that they were still content with what they were getting, as they knew that garment-factory workers in all developing and least developed countries generally received lower, if not similar, wages to what they were receiving. With regards to annual increments, 80 per cent of the participants mentioned that they received annual increments ranging from a marginal two cents to five cents per hour. As expected, these increments depend on the performance/productivity of individual workers. Another positive finding was that all the participants mentioned that they were receiving other benefits normally provided by employers, such as overtime pay, meal allowances and transportation home after over-time work.

Furthermore, all the participants mentioned that they were satisfied with the working conditions that they were exposed to. According to workers from the relatively bigger garment factories, some overseas buyers

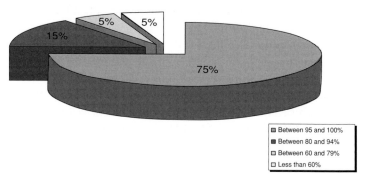

▣	Between 95 and 100%
▪	Between 80 and 94%
▢	Between 60 and 79%
▢	Less than 60%

Figure 5H   Share of females in the participants' workforce.

visited Fiji regularly and examined the machines that were being used, as well as the general environment where work was carried out. These examinations ensure that employers maintain good-quality machines and a clean and safe working environment. Another positive finding was that all the workers who were employed stated that they never came across a situation where they felt that they were exploited/abused by their superiors.

One of the notable contributions of the garment industry has been its ability to increase the participation of women into the labour force. In this regard, the garment-factory owners were asked about the gender composition of the workers in their companies. Figure 5H summarises the responses that were received on this issue.

The results shown in Figure 5H look very promising: 75% of the participants mentioned that the share of females in their workforce was between 95 to 100%, while 15% highlighted that the share was between 80 to 94%. Half of the remaining 10% mentioned that females comprised between 60 to 79% of their workforce and the other half reported that they comprised less than 60% of their workforce.

However, on a sad note, all the participants responded that they were not paid fairly; that is, the pay that they were getting did not match up with the amount of effort they were putting into their work. Moreover, it was discovered that during the period 2000 to 2006, their wages had increased by an average of only 0.3% per year. On the other hand, consumer prices had increased by an average of 2.6% every year during the same period.[8] These figures clearly imply that these workers have experienced a fall in

---

[8] Data taken from the Fiji Islands Bureau of Statistics Website, at www.statsfiji.gov.fj/ Economic/prices.htm [last accessed 6 April 2009].

their real wages by an average of 2.3% every year during the 2000 to 2006 period.

When asked about the changes that they had experienced at their workplace over the years, the relatively older participants (with ten or more years of experience) mentioned that their garments factories were performing really well in the 1990s, as export orders from their buyers were continuously increasing. Consistent with increasing export orders, their companies continued to employ more workers on an annual basis. They also received better annual increments. However, since the May 2000 political crisis, the performance of their companies has taken a nose dive as a result of declining overseas demand for their products. In line with their poor performance, nearly all the companies have reduced their workforce by an average of about 30%. Annual increments for those who have retained their jobs are also not as good as before.

With regards to the political disturbance of 2000, 90% of the participants mentioned that they suffered reduced working hours, while the remaining 10% were unaffected. Moreover, the military coup of December 2006 has had no effect on their employment so far, but the majority expect it to become worse.

Given the current upheaval the garment industry in Fiji is facing, when the workers and former workers were asked about their job security in the industry, all of them mentioned that they were very insecure about their jobs and did not see a bright future for themselves in the industry:

> Even with this job, I am facing a lot of problems in meeting the needs of my family, as I'm the only person working in my family. My husband passed away about three years ago and I have three children (two boys and a girl) to look after. My older boy is in class 8 and the younger one is in class 6. My girl is in class 3. I really don't know what will happen to me and my kids if I don't have my job. My kids will be out of school, we will become homeless and it will become very hard for me to even put food on the table for my kids and me.

These were the words of a very emotional participant from the Western Division whilst discussing the possibility of losing her job as a result of the erosion of preferential treatment that her garment factory is receiving at present.

During the interview process, the unemployed participants were asked to highlight the reasons for losing their jobs. Figure 5I shows the reasons given by the participants.

As shown in Figure 5I, 60% of the unemployed participants lost their jobs due to the closure of the factories in which they were employed. It is

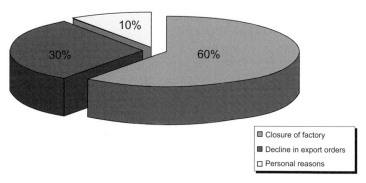

Figure 51   Reasons for becoming unemployed.

interesting to note that 80% of the participants who are unemployed due to the closure of factories were formerly employed by Ghim Li Limited (based on the western side of Fiji). This factory closed down in early 2005 due to the loss of quota access to the US market as a result of the expiry of the Multi-Fibre ATC on 1 January 2005. Moreover, 30% of the participants lost their jobs as a result of their employers facing a decline in export orders, while the remaining 10% lost their jobs due to personal reasons, which they did not wish to disclose.

When asked if they had tried to secure another job, all the participants mentioned that they tried very hard to find another job but were simply unsuccessful, as they didn't have the relevant education and skills to secure a decent job in any other industry. Therefore, about 20% resorted to doing tailoring work from their homes to supplement their families' income, whilst the remaining 80% opted to stay at home and undertake their household chores.

Finally, the unemployed workers were asked to discuss their families' standard of living now as opposed to what it was like when they were employed. As expected, all of them mentioned that their families' standard of living is much worse now than what it was when they were employed. With regards to the 80 per cent who stay home, their family's total income has fallen well below the basic-needs poverty line income of F$95. They are really struggling to make ends meet:

> When I was working as a machinist, my kids used to go to school and come back from school by taxi.[9] We had good food to eat every day and we had also managed to buy a refrigerator on hire purchase. However, since I lost my

[9] For a person working as a machinist in a garment factory, using a taxi to send children to school and bring them back home is considered a luxury exercise.

job, everything has changed in a big way. My kids now have to go to school by bus. Sometimes, they don't have the bus fare and so I have to borrow money from my neighbours just to send them to school. Now, we also cannot afford to eat good food every day. Usually, Saturday is the only day when we get to eat good food. My husband and kids also have to take noodles for lunch for three days in a week. Also, since we couldn't afford to pay instalments for our fridge, the company from where we bought it had to come and repossess it.

These were the sentiments expressed by a participant who was trying to describe the extent to which her family's standard of living had reduced since she lost her job.

The garment-factory owners also shared extensive useful information about the garment industry in Fiji.

As expected, all the garment factories started in the late 1980s to take advantage of the government's TFF/zone scheme, which was a product of its post-1987 crisis strategy of export-led economic development. Moreover, a number of textiles, clothing and footwear-related preferential trade agreements on offer at that time also made it even more tempting to establish a garment factory.

According to all the garment-factory owners, their businesses were doing very well in the late 1980s and the 1990s. However, their businesses started to spiral downwards after the political events of 2000, when orders started to decline. Moreover, increasing pressure by the WTO on developed countries such the US, Australia and New Zealand, with whom Fiji have or had a number of preferential trading arrangements, to liberalise their trade regimes has meant a decline in demand for locally produced garments, textiles and footwear.

The garment-factory owners also mentioned that the emergence of China onto the global trade scene, after its entry into the WTO, has made things 'even tougher for them'. According to them, their products will never be able to compete with similar products from China, as China produces its own raw materials, while the owners have to import theirs at a relatively higher cost. Moreover, China's labour costs are significantly lower than Fiji's. To be able to survive in the future, these garment-factory owners mentioned that they require the continuation of the current preferential treatment they are receiving: 'There's just no other way out', one of the participants stated.

Whilst the advent of the garment industry in Fiji has significantly increased the participation of women in the labour force and, therefore, has enabled these women to make a notable contribution towards increasing the wellbeing of their families, the garment-factory owners warned that the opposite could be true if their factories closed in the near future as a result of the loss of preferential treatment. This scenario has the potential of dragging many families into poverty and the other social problems associated with it.

Policy considerations

In light of recent macroeconomic concerns of Fiji's balance of trade position as well as emphasis lent to the major reforms undertaken in the sugar industry, it is not easy to ignore the current predicament of the clothing and textiles industry. To do so would be to the social and economic detriment of the economy in the next four to five years.

The industry will struggle to survive in its current form given the next few waves of trade liberalisation measures (e.g. in agreements with the EC on Cotonou), which in turn will trigger a new PACER-plus agreement with Australia and New Zealand.

Orderly exit of uncompetitive firms

One of the first considerations to be made by policy makers is that there still exist in the domestic clothing and textiles industry a significant number of inherently uncompetitive firms. These firms are mainly those involved in CMT operations, which realistically cannot compete against the bigger volume and lower-cost countries like India and China.

Preferential trade access and domestic concessions cannot continue to prop these firms up indefinitely. These firms effectively remove resources from more productive activities that could be engaged in earning greater returns. Since these firms are the most labour intensive in the industry and are involved in low value-added production, it is very important that their exit is properly planned.

There are a few CMT firms that have already branched out and diversified into niche market production. These firms would be the ones that could easily reorganise their operations and effectively expand their niche market supply.

Retraining

In conjunction with the orderly exit of CMT operations, an industry-level retraining programme should be coordinated to effectively train displaced workers with new skills so that they can find employment in other competitive garment factories or even in other sectors. This initiative cannot be overemphasised because it is the sustainable way of providing support to the displaced workers.

The new training will give them opportunities for employment and will ultimately save the government from having to deal with more complex and costly matters that could result (such as poverty alleviation schemes, squatter settlement issues and unemployment) if a proper transition of garment-industry workers is not facilitated.

Trade facilitation

Adhikari and Yamamoto (2006) define trade facilitation as: the simplification and harmonisation of international trade procedures, with such procedures encompassing the activities, practices and formalities involved in collecting, presenting, communicating and processing data required for the movement of goods and international trade.

Certainly, Fiji has much scope for improvement in these areas. In fact, if a concerted effort and focus could be given to the modernisation and automation of trade facilitation procedures, exporters and importers alike would make significant savings on trade transaction costs. Likewise, studies on other clothing and textile producing countries have highlighted the importance of efficient port infrastructure, reliable and competitive modes of transport and efficient customs procedures for maintaining 'an edge'. Furthermore, apart from the benefits to the tradables sector, the government will also benefit through revenue increases from the gains from trade reaped by the tradables sector. In addition, more efficient and transparent customs and licensing procedures increase good governance, better regulation, due process and public-private sector relationships (Adhikari and Yamamoto, 2006).

The improved facilitation will make the possible transition of existing CMT firms into more original equipment manufacturing (OEM) and original brand name manufacturing (OBM) operations much easier. It will also significantly improve the attractiveness of Fiji to other firms in Australia and New Zealand to relocate part of their operations to Fiji and to access the buyer-driven commodity chains in Australia and other possible markets. Lastly, it will raise the competitiveness of the existing but small-scale OEM and OMB producers in Fiji, which may be able to improve their market penetration and share.

Political stability

Political instabilities (such as coups) generally lead to a fall in investor confidence, which then translates into a decline in both domestic and foreign investment in a country. With the occurrence of four coups in Fiji over the last twenty years, the country is all too familiar with such a scenario. Before the first coup in 1987, Fiji's investment-to-GDP ratio was well above 20%. However, since 1987, it has fallen below 15% and has remained at that level up until now. More depressing, however, is the level of private-sector investment, which amounts to only 5% of GDP. Therefore, if Fiji wants to attract more local and foreign investment within the garment and textiles sector, as well as other sectors of the economy, it is imperative that the nation takes strong steps to address the coup culture.

The potential role for the Pacific Agreement on Closer Economic Relations, Pacific Island Countries Trade Agreement and the economic partnership agreement

The PACER and PICTA[10] can also play a major role in assisting the garment industry in Fiji through their focus on trade facilitation. Article 9 of PACER and Article 18 of PICTA address the issues regarding trade facilitation.

The EPA[11] can also contribute in assisting Fiji's ailing garment industry. One of the principles guiding the Pacific/African, Caribbean and Pacific (PACP) EU negotiations on EPA is that this agreement should be an instrument of development for the ACP countries. In this regard, the EPA should promote the development objectives of the countries of the region and should be consistent with their development strategies. In doing so, it will take into account the specific economic, social, environmental and structural constraints of the PACP states, as well as their capacity to adapt their economies to the EPA process.

The role of the services sector

With the agricultural and manufacturing sectors (particularly the garments and textiles subsector within the manufacturing sector) not performing at their potential levels at the moment, the services sector can

[10] Information on the PACER and PICTA was taken from the actual PACER and PICTA texts sourced from the Pacific Islands Forum Secretariat website, www.forumsec.org.fj [last accessed 6 April 2009].
[11] Information on the EPA was sourced from the materials that were distributed at the UN Market Access Workshop for the Pacific Region held in Suva, Fiji, from 8 to 12 May 2006.

improve its performance to offset or even more than offset the dismal performances recorded by the other two sectors. In this regard, there is a genuine need to support industries like audio-visual and information and communications technology (ICT), which are showing signs of promise and potential. In addition, the tourism industry would need all the support (from all its stakeholders) to reach its full potential. On a positive note, the interim Minister of Finance, while presenting the revised 2007 Budget earlier this year, did highlight that tourism, audio-visual and ICT were all priority sectors for the interim government and, therefore, would be given all the consideration they need.[12]

The need to review the wage structure within the garment industry

In order to attract foreign direct investment into the garment industry and to maintain a reasonable standard of living for those working in the industry, the wage structure needs to be seriously reviewed. In this regard, all the relevant stakeholders should come together and work out a structure that is more productivity based and therefore fair to both the employers and employees. However, in order to introduce a more fair and productivity based wage structure, the skill level of the workers should also be improved markedly. For this to happen, it is strongly recommended that the government, with the help of donor countries and all other relevant stakeholders, should expose garment-industry workers to more meaningful education and training.

Conclusions

The garment industry is not a viable exporting sector in its current form. Trade liberalisation policies on the international front and cessation of tax concessions on the domestic front will wipe out the industry if policy makers and industry stakeholders do not recognise the need for a reorganisation of the industry.

An orderly transition of the industry is needed. If it is ignored, the social and economic impact on Fiji's labour market, government and ultimately the overall economy will be significant.

However, there are steps that can be taken to mitigate the global effects on the industry. The uncompetitive CMT operations can be given an orderly exit in conjunction with the training and transition of displaced

---

[12] '2007 Revised Budget Address', available at www.fiji.gov.fj/publish/page_10350.shtml [last accessed 6 April 2009].

workers to new areas of employment. Furthermore, there is much room for improvements in trade facilitation in Fiji, which has the potential to improve the competitiveness of the remaining players in the clothing and textile industry.

The other steps that can be taken to revive the industry include the need for political stability in Fiji, the use of trade agreements of importance to Fiji and the need to review and change the current wage structure within the industry.

Given ample support, the services sector could also rise to the occasion and help to offset or even more than offset the slackness experienced in the agricultural and manufacturing sectors.

The contribution of Fiji's garment industry to employment and poverty reduction has been significant since 1987. It continues to be a significant employer of unskilled workers, but its sustainability is not guaranteed in the future. It is already in a difficult situation as a result of the political crisis of 5 December 2006, and this could act as a further disincentive for the growth of a local and internationally competitive manufacturing sector. While Fiji pursues alternative exports and strives to achieve a competitive edge to its garment production, it will need continued access to preferential markets in Australia and New Zealand. In the transition period, which may be over the next ten years, the ROO will have to be made more favourable so that Fiji's garment manufacturers can have time and space for adjustment.

References

Adhikari, R. and Yamamoto, Y. (2006), 'Sewing Thoughts: How to Realise Human Development Gains in the Post-Quota World', Tracking Report, Asia-Pacific Trade and Investment Initiative, UNDP Regional Centre: Colombo.

Asian Development Bank (ADB) (2006a), *Laying the Foundations for Growth, Policies for Prosperity in Fiji Islands*, ADB: Manila.

(2006b), *Asian Development Outlook – Routes for Asia's Trade*, ADB: Hong Kong.

Fiji Islands Bureau of Statistics (2000), *1999 Annual Employment Survey*, Government Printing Press: Suva.

(2006a), *Overseas Merchandise Trade Statistics 2006*, Quality Print Limited: Suva.

(2006b), *Statistical News: Gross Domestic Product at Constant Price, 2006*, Government Printing Press: Suva.

Narayan, P. K. and Prasad, B. C. (2003), 'Fiji's Sugar, Tourism and Garment Industries: A Survey of Performance, Problems and Potentials', *The Fijian: Journal of Contemporary Studies* 4(1): 3–28.

Narsey, W. (2006), *Just Wages for Fiji: Lifting Workers Out of Poverty*, Ecumenical Centre for Research and Advocacy and Vanuavou Publications: Suva.

Appendix 5A

Table 5Q   *Category versus placement list of Fiji's major domestic exports*

Export item	2006 (FJ$ m)	Rank/placement
Sugar	215.09	1
Fish	97.95	2
Garments	94.92	3
Mineral water	86.88	4
Gold	43.11	5
Lumber	37.59	6
Fruits and vegetables	32.77	7
Molasses	19.16	8
Sweet biscuits	17.84	9
Flour	11.07	10
Folding cartons, boxes and cases	10.89	11
Uncooked pasta	9.88	12
Textiles, yarn and fabrics	9.81	13
Coral and similar materials	9.30	14
Corned meat of bovine animals	6.97	15
Ginger	5.68	16
Footwear and headgear	4.15	17
Yaqona	3.68	18
Coconut oil	2.14	19
Copra	0.04	20

Source: Fiji Islands Bureau of Statistics (2006a).

INDEX

Abrenica, Joy 11–12
Acemoglu, D. 32, 351
Acer 177
Adams, Richard 489, 525, 541
adaptability of economies 30–2
Addison, T. 50
Adelman, I. 490
Adhikari, R. 763
Adi, Rianto 566
Adidas 77, 86, 149, 161–3, 168, 170
Afsar, R. 526
agriculture
  See also specific countries
  Agriculture Agreement. See
      Agriculture Agreement
  biotechnology 214–15
  changing consumer preferences
      212
  climate change 215–16
  commodity price volatility 613
  country specificity 223
  current state 196–207
  duties 202–3, 263, 638–40
  education 219
  food prices and biofuels 213
  hot issues 211–18
  infrastructure 199, 200
  institutional reform 221–2
  niche markets 614
  population share 198
  price distortions 202
  productivity constraints 214–15
  public and private partnerships
      220–1
  public goods 219–20
  public policies 218–22
  retail expansion 217–18

safety nets and sequencing 222
significance 195–6
SPS issues 203–7, 211, 213–14,
    220
standards 216–17, 221
subsidies 7
sustainable growth 219–20
SVEs 612–15
  strategic areas 614–15, 617
  WTO 615–16
trade liberalisation 196
trade-poverty linkages 10–11,
    207–11
  public policies 218–22
traditional practices 209
water 216
WTO issues 204, 615–16
Agriculture Agreement
  food aid and 236, 241
  SVEs and 615–16
  tariff reductions 610
Ahmad, Sufi Khurshid 164
Ahmed, S.A. 353, 354
Aid for Trade
  supply-side constraints 427
  SVEs 644
  Tanzania 445–7
Airbus 83
'Akolo, Lisiate 'Aloveita 579, 584
Anderson, K. 53
anti-globalisation movement 69–70,
    86
APTECH 178
Aredo, Djene 542
Argentina 700–1
Armason, R. 694
Arnold, Jens 348

ASEAN
    ASEAN-China FTA 133, 331
    ASEAN-India Regional Trade and
        Investment Area 134
    customs procedures 102
    East Timor and 607, 718
    Food Security Reserve 234
    free movement and 558
    intra-regional exports 75
    migration and 498–500
    negotiations 110
Asia Trust Fund 254
Asian Development Bank 188–9, 282,
    755
Athukorala, Prema-Chandra 74–5,
    90–1
Atlanta Charter 164, 165, 168
Australia
    Button Plan 117
    China FTA 331
    development aid
        East Timor 721
        Pacific Islands 456–7
        Samoa 275, 281–2
        telecommunications 455
        Vanuatu 459–60
    East Timor and 718, 727
    food aid 237, 245
    free trade with LDCs 277
    immigrants
        East Timorese 713, 714,
          725–6
        Filipinos 485
        occupations 479
        Pacific Islanders 605
        skilled workers 468
        temporary labour schemes
          505–7, 578
        temporary visas 479
        Tongans 573, 575
        Vietnamese 485
    Malaysian FDI in 81
    PACER 129, 279, 280
    regional trade dominance 605
    Samoan trade 129, 274
    tariffs 609, 643
    trade preferences 609
        Fiji 749, 750

Import Credit Scheme 750, 755,
    756
    rules of origin 624–5
    SPARTECA 8, 95, 112–13,
        116–17, 279, 280, 603, 750
avian influenza 207, 214

Bahadur, Lal 257
Baigent, Heather 16, 618
Balasubramanyam, V.N. and A. 408
Baldwin, Robert 91
Bali
    eco-tourism 209
    fishing cooperation 220
    Minibakti Soansari fishing group
        294–7
        initial condition 294–6
        transformation of fishery 296–7
        use of cyanide 295–6
        women 297
    ornamental fish farming 11, 287–9
        domestic measures 298–300
        exports 289
banana wars 669
Bangladesh
    bird flu 214
    development aid to 517–18
    emigration
        access to information 533
        costs 530–1
        destinations 517, 521–2
        economic significance 517–20
        facilitation 514, 533
        GATS negotiations 535–6
        human rights 535
        increase 520
        labour supply 514
        legal prohibitions 531–2
        manpower agencies 534–5
        markets 520–3
        policy recommendations 532–6
        profile 517
        skill levels 466, 522
        support for returnees 535
        women 531–2, 534
    female clothing workers 87–8
    flood (2004) 528
    human trafficking 499, 532

Bangladesh (*cont.*)
  NGOs 516, 528
  remittances
    access to education and health
      527–8
    adjustment to natural disasters
      494, 528
    community development 529
    efficiency improvements 533–4
    employment 526–7
    Hundi system 533–4
    income improvement 526
    income inequality 494, 529–30
    inflation 530
    maximising use 534
    negative impact 529–32
    positive impact 525–9
    poverty reduction 489, 490–1,
      524–32
    savings and investments 527
    significance 14–15, 354, 485,
      486–8
    statistics 520
    women 493, 528
  remittances case study 515
    methodology 515–16
    objectives 515
    study area 516–17
  rice 222, 307
  trade openness 518
banking. *See* financial sector
Barbados 684
Barber, C. 355, 356
Barrett, Craig 182
Barro, R.J. 45
Belize 687
Benin 214, 374
Benjamin, D. 50
Berdegué, J.A. 346
Beschorner, Natasha 456
'Better Factories Cambodia' 102, 104,
  106, 107–8, 109
Bhagwati, J. 43, 44–5
Bigsten, A. 31
BIMST-EC 253
biofuels 213, 229
biotechnology 214–15
bird flu 207, 214

Birthal, Pratap Sing 195
Black, R. 355, 356
Blankson, T. 542
Boeing 83
Borensztein, E. De Gregorio 46
Bowman, Chakriya 13
BRAC 528
brain drain 466–8, 501–2, 505, 578,
  744
Brazil 466, 701
Brunei 562
BSE 214
Bui Van Quyen 179
Bulgaria 345

Cable & Wireless 458, 459, 460, 673
CAFRA 35
call centres, Grenada 673
Cambodia
  agriculture 98
  'Better Factories Cambodia' 102,
    104, 106, 107–8, 109
  customs procedures 102, 109
  economy 98–100
  FDI diversification 110
  GDP growth by sector 99
  human trafficking 499
  regional integration 110
  textile industry 97–110
    competition issues 103–4
    competition with China 8, 94
    competition with Vietnam 103,
      108
    EU market 102
    FDI 103–4
    global value chain 107–8
    growth 98–100
    labour costs 108
    labour standards 107–8
    Multi-Fibre Arrangement 102
    productivity options 109–10
    remittances 105–6
    rural women 97–8, 104–6, 110
    trade-policy options 109–10
    trade reforms 100–8
    US and EU preferences 7, 97,
      104
    US market 102, 103–4

TRADE 101
WTO membership 100–2, 110
Cameroon 31
Canada
  Cambodian textile imports 101, 102
  Filipino immigrants 485
  food aid 237, 245
  Vietnamese immigrants 485
CEDAW Committee 119
Chand, Satish 450, 632
Chang, Seung Wha 693
Charumilind, C. 49
Chaudhuri, S. 356
Chile 2, 448
China
  agriculture
    development 325–7
    duties 202, 203
    employment share 197
    grain production 328, 329
    horticulture 11, 335
    imports 326
    intensive farming 328–9
    international trade negotiations 330–1
    new policy initiatives 329–31
    NRD 326, 328, 329–30, 331–2, 334, 336
    outcomes 328–9
    poverty alleviation 331–2
    pre-reform era 327
    reform 327–8
    soybean imports 199
  Beijing Olympics 335, 336
  bird flu 214
  competition in textiles
    Cambodia 8, 97
    Fiji 755, 761
    Indonesia 95, 143–86
  competitive advantage 448
  effect of trade on Latin America 39
  emigration of skilled workers 466
  export quotas 82
  FDI
    Intel 183
    levels 78, 93

    TNC risks 76–7
  food aid 228
  football stitching industry 165
  footwear industry 147
  horticulture 11, 332–5
    characteristics 332–3
    Mentougou 335
    pesticides 333
    recommendations 335–6
    Shandong 333–4
  Household Responsibility System 328
  Hukau system 76
  human trafficking 499
  immigrants 481
  increasing food consumption 213, 229
  Indonesian textile imports 132
  inequality and growth 50
  internal migration 477
  labour costs 76–7, 108
  life expectancy 80
  logistics 346
  poverty alleviation
    agricultural reforms 331–2
    FDI 72–3, 336
    immiserising growth 70
    poverty levels 2, 325
  regional integration 331
    ASEAN-China FTA 133, 331
    Australia FTA 331
    exports 75
    imports 75
  rice exports 307
  road network 199
  Shanghai World Expo 336
  SOEs 330
  textile industry 325
  transnational companies in 76–7
  UN embargo 327
  wages 76–7
  WTO membership 53, 328, 346
    anti-dumping investigations 331
Chiquita 669
CITES 291, 293, 300
climate change 215–16

Cline, W.R.   42, 43
Clinton, Bill   86
Coca-Cola   86
Collyer, M.   355
comparative advantage principle   33–5
competition
  CSR as tool of competition   169
  developing countries   93
  gains   35–7
  long-term effects   47–8
Consultative Committee on Surplus
    Disposal (CSSD)   239–40, 246,
    248
consumers, changing preferences and
    agriculture   212
contracts, enforceability   93
Convention on Migrant Workers
    (1990)   496
Cook Islands   116, 609, 625
Corden, W.M.   30
Cornia, G.A.   50
corporate social responsibility   169,
    170–1
corruption
  Central America   84
  distribution channel   27
  Indonesia   142, 302, 320
  Vietnam   176, 184
Costa Rica   177, 183, 669
Côte d'Ivoire   36
Cotonou Agreement
  East Timor   715, 717–18
  EPAs and   737
  objectives   737–8, 745
  rules of origin   625
  SVEs   602, 604, 625, 644
  WTO waiver   278
crafts, GATT   656
Crowby, Patrick   460
Cuba   687
customs procedures
  ASEAN   102
  Cambodia   102, 109
  efficiency   25
  Papua New Guinea   735–6
CUTS   40
cyanide   288–90, 295–6
Czech Republic   348

Davidson, C.   30
De, Prabir   13
De Bruyun, T.   494
De Soto, H.   32, 52
Dee, P.   344
Delgado, C.   27–8
Deng Xiaoping   325
Denmark   245
Dev, M.   411
development aid
  Aid for Trade   427, 445–7, 644
  LDC status and
  OECD targets   249
  Pacific Islands   605
  Samoa   275
  tied aid   501
Diagnostic Trade Integration Studies
    (DTIS)   101, 109, 435
diasporas   472–3
Digicel   450, 460
Dihel, Nora   345
Dimzon, C.S.   484
distribution channel
  completeness of markets   27
  efficiency of customs procedures
    25
  infrastructure quality   26
  intermediate organisations   26–7
  nature of trade liberation   26
  non-trade taxation and policies   26
  trade/poverty reduction and   23,
    24–8
Doan Hong Quang   189–90
Doha Round
  agriculture   10
  capacity building   643
  developing countries and   53, 427
  direction   601
  failure   642
  fishing subsidies   692–3
  food aid and   230–1, 243
  Indian services commitments   407
  NAMA subsidies   619
  rice   308
  SVEs and   606–7
Dole   669
Dollar, D.   44
Dominican Republic   610, 687

DSC Communication 177
Dubai 531
Dugal, Manleen 16–17, 618, 620
Duncan, Ron 16
Duong Minh Tam 182
Dutch disease 488

East African Community 428–9
East Timor
  ASEAN and 607, 718
  Australia and 718
  balance of payments 712–13
  capacity building 643
  civil conflict 634–41, 707, 709
  coffee 726
  construction sector 723–4
  eco-tourism 724–5
  economy 708–15
  employment strategies 723–8
    targeted sectors 723–5
  EU trade 717–18
  FDI 713
  fisheries 727
  growth 708–11
  labour force 711
  labour mobility 725–6
  LDC status 716
  niche markets 726
  occupational sectors 709–11
  oil and gas 711, 724
  poverty 707–8
  private sector 636, 721–2
  regional integration 717–19
  remittances 713–15
  services 724–5
  skill gap 637
  special and differential treatment
    600
  tariffs 609, 716
  tax reform 727
  telecommunications 457
  trade 708, 715–19
  trade barriers 727–8
  unemployment
    case study 719–23
    donors' opinions 721
    policy makers on 719–21
    rate 712

  reduction strategies 723–8
  views of private sector 721–2
  youth unemployment 17, 722–3
  vanilla production 726
  water buffaloes 726
  WTO and 715–17
Easterly, W. 45
Ebrill, L. 41
eco-tourism 687, 724–5
Ecuador 669
education
  agriculture 219
  Costa Rica 177
  Grenada 16, 587
  human capital 30
  India 408, 409, 420
  Indonesia 557, 561, 568–9
  overriding strategy 18
  remittances and 492–3
    Bangladesh 527–8
  SVEs 637–8
  Tonga 586–7
  Uganda 376
  Vietnam 177–8, 189
Edwards, S. 44
Egypt 30, 214, 354–5
Ellerman, D. 466
emergencies 232
enterprise channel 28
'Esau, Raelyn 15, 576
Eschenbach, F. 351
Ethiopia 350, 542
European Union
  See also Cotonou Agreement
  biofuels policy 213
  development aid
    Samoa 275
    Tanzania 440
  East Timor and 717–18
  EBA programme 278
  EPAs
    Pacific Islands 604
    Papua New Guinea 737–45
    Samoa 278–9
    Tanzania 428
  food aid 237, 245
  Indonesian textile imports 132
  migrant workers 499

European Union (*cont.*)
non-tariff barriers, removal 609
preferences
Cambodia 97, 102
Indonesia 148
rules of origin 741
safeguard measures, footwear
147–8
sugar prices 613
WTO banana wars 669
Euysung, K. 48
exclusive economic zones 620, 621–2,
691, 695
export processing zones 93
external factors 53

failed states 595
Fair Labour Association 166, 167
Falconer, Crawford 308
FAO 212, 238–40, 248
FDI. *See* foreign direct investment
Fernandes, A.M. 48
Fiji
agriculture 610, 612, 614
clothing industry 17–18, 748–62
Chinese competition 755, 761
employment 752
end of MFA 609, 749, 750, 755
exit from uncompetitive
firms 762
exports 751–2
global changes 753–6
history 748, 749–50, 761
insecurity 759–61
interview results 756–62
overview 749–53
production 750–1
prospects 756
recommendations 762–5
sustainability 748–9
taxation 749, 750, 761
trade facilitation 763
training 757, 762–3
wages 752–3, 757, 758–9, 765
women 758, 761–2
working conditions 757–8
exports 767
niche markets 614, 618

political instability 634–41, 749,
759, 764
protectionism 636
remittances 577, 632
services sector 764–5
strikes 117
telecoms 450
tourism 588, 625
trade agreements 750, 764
MSG PTA 603
PICTA 612, 764
trade preferences and
Australia and New Zealand 749,
750
Australian Import Credit Scheme
750, 755, 756
SPARTECA 116, 608–9, 624–5
financial sector
Grenada 673
impact of liberalisation 345
liberalisation 350, 357–8
Findlay, Christopher 11–12, 346,
359
Finn, John 10
fisheries
East Timor 727
Papua New Guinea 741–2
subsidies 690–2
Doha Round 692–3
Hong Kong Ministerial 694–5
SVEs 619–21, 695–700
WTO 690–5, 703
SVEs 618–19
access fees 619–20, 695–8
artisanal fisheries 698–700
national measures 703–5
recommendations 622–4, 702–5
special treatment 621–2, 700–2
subsidies 619–21, 695–700
WTO negotiations 703
western and central Pacific 16–17,
691
Flextronics 76, 77
food
changing preferences 212
food prices and biofuels 213,
229
increasing prices 228–30

food aid
  commercial displacement and
    additionality 234
  coordination 10, 223
  development alternative 230
  efficiency 244–6, 247
  emergencies 232
  humanitarian aid 231–2
  impacts 231
  in-kind aid 233–4, 245
  international comparisons 241
  international organisations 237–44
    CSSD 239–40, 246, 248
    Food Aid Convention 240, 246,
      247, 248
    OECD DAC 236–7, 244–5, 246
    World Food Programme 238,
      246
  issues 227–8
  local purchases 233–4, 245–6
  need 228–31
  policy considerations 246–9
  programme aid 232
  project aid 232
  tied aid 236–7, 247–8
  triangular transactions 233–4,
    245
  types 231–6
  wheat 235–6
  WTO and 10, 230–1, 236, 241–3,
    246, 248
    Marrakesh Decision 242–3
Food Aid Convention 240, 246, 247,
  248
footwear industry
  China 147
  Indonesia. See Indonesia
  subcontracting pattern 149–50
  Vietnam 147–8
Ford 92
foreign direct investment
  motivations 80–3
  poverty reduction and 77–80
  trade liberalisation and 46–7
Forum Island countries 116
France 485, 744
France Telecom 458, 459, 460
free trade. See trade liberalisation

GAP 86, 99
Gap 87
Gardner, K. 528
GATS
  flexibility 626
  Mode 4. See GATS Mode 4
  modes of supply 342, 626–7
  negative listing 629
  safeguards and 627, 629–30
GATS Mode 4
  Bangladesh and 514, 523, 535–6
  EU-NPG EPA 744
  FTA agreements 499
  Indian services 407, 408–9
  Indonesia and 558
  Malaysian health services 390
  meaning 342
  scope 352, 356, 476–7
Gavian, S. 28
gender. See women
General Electric 79
Germany 214, 245, 255, 485, 669,
  744
Ghana 31, 41, 526, 542
Global Alliance 87
Global Commission on International
  Migration 476
Global Compact 86
global supply chain 8–10, 90–2, 160,
  162
Gomba Enterprises 445
good governance 92–4
Gordon, J. 406
governments
  See also specific countries
  border prices and 29–30
  corruption 27, 84, 142, 176, 184,
    302, 320
  effect of trade liberalisation on
    41–2
  government channel 23, 29–30
  taxation. See taxation
  trade/poverty reduction interaction
    and 55
Grandcolas, Christophe 638
Grange Resources 82
Green Revolution 28, 195, 199
Greenpeace 84–5

Grenada
  background 666
  decline of banana industry 666–70
    crop disease 669–70
    labour shift 673–80
    WTO banana wars 669
  economy 673
  education 16, 587
  labour shift 665, 673–80
    construction sector 674
    emigration 675–6
    IMANI project 676, 679
    informal labour 675
    other farm production 674
    out of agriculture 674–6
    poverty 679–80
    recommendations 680–7
    security industry 676
    services sector 675, 676–9
    small businesses 675
  lack of data 665
  non-traded agriculture 682–3
  occupational sectors 667
  openness to trade 5
  port 683
  price controls 681
  recommendations 680–7
    high cost of living 680–3
    new services 684–7
    tourism diversification 686–7
    training 683–4
  remittances 678
  services exports
    call centres 673
    financial services 673
    high reservation wages 677–8,
      680
    medical school 631, 671–2, 677,
      684
    medical services 670, 685
    new services 684–7
    paucity of jobs 675, 676–7, 679
    politicisation of hiring 678–9
    rise 670–3
    skills and training 676
    tourism 672, 677, 682, 686–7
  skill gap 637
  tariff policy 682

  trade facilitation 683
  tyranny of distance 680
  US invasion 666, 670
Grossman, G.M. 45
growth
  healthcare services 385
  human capital and 49
  inequality and 49–51, 56
  infrastructure and 49
  pro-poor 48–9
  services liberalisation and 350–1
  sustainable agricultural growth
    219–20
  technological differences 45–7,
    55–6
  trade liberalisation and 43–5
  volatility and 51–3, 56
Grynberg, Roman 693–4
GTZ 254
Guadeloupe 669
Guatemala 84
Gulf wars 540, 552
Gupta, P. 406
Gusmao, Xanana
Guyana 610

Haiti 246
handicrafts, GATT 656
Hanson, G.H. 36
Hari, K.S. 548
Harrison, A.E. 36
Harrod, K. 493
healthcare services
  growth 385
  health tourism 385
  Malaysia. See Malaysia
  public health insurance 389
  remittances and 493
    Bangladesh 527–8
Heckster-Ohlin trade model 33, 37
Helpman, E. 45
Hernández, R. 346
Hewlett Packard 77
Hildegunn, N. 32
HIV/AIDS 736
Hnatkovska, V. 52
Hodrick-Prescott filter 547
Hoekman, Bernard 53, 341, 351

Holden 122
Holmes, T.J. 48
Honduras 84, 669
Hong Kong 477, 481, 556
Howarth, Rick 182–3
Hugo, Graeme 14, 566, 576–7, 587
human capital 30, 31, 46, 49
Hundi 533–4

IBM 178
ICT sector
    Cambodia. *See* Cambodia
    India. *See* India
    poverty reduction 364
    Uganda. *See* Uganda
IMAC 167, 168, 172
IMANI project 676, 679
IMF 282, 525, 681, 731
India
    agricultural employment 197
    ASEAN-India Regional Trade and
        Investment Area 134
    bird flu 214
    competition effects 36
    emigration
        diaspora 486
        Kerala 540–1
        skilled workers 466
        structural changes 546
    employment rates 414
    FDI in 79
    foreign currency conditions 543–4
    GDP 79
    import barriers 643
    increasing food consumption 213,
        229
    India-Nepal FTA 252
    IT-BPO 359, 407
        capacity building 421
        employment 417
        exports statistics 416–18
        gender 412–15
        growth 415–16
        inequalities 417–19
        participation of states 422
        planning 421–2
    labour costs 108
    life expectancy 80

poverty levels 2
reform process 406
remittances 544–50
    externalities 550–2
    forms 545
    income cycles 546–7
    informal channels 545
    Kerala 15, 542–3, 545–50
    official amounts 542
    poverty reduction 547–50
    significance 354–5, 408–9, 486
    state facilitation 552–3
    structural changes in emigration
        546
rice exports 307
rural-urban disparities 417–19
services sector 13
    capacity building 421
    comparative advantage 406–7
    Doha Round 407
    education 420
    growth 405–6
    higher education 408, 409
    liberalisation 406
    Mode 1 407–8
    Mode 4 407, 408–9
    outsourcing 406–7
    policy recommendations 419–22
    poverty reduction and 409–19
    skill shortages 420–1
    trade 406–9
    training 420
social security 420
sports goods industry 161
textile industry 755
Indira Gandhi National Open
        University 408
Indonesia
    agriculture
        duties 202, 203
        food security 209
        irrigation and water supply 208
        policies 306
        share of employment 197
    bird flu 214
    Bulog 309–11, 321
    corruption 142, 302, 320
    crafts. *See* Lombok pots

Indonesia (*cont.*)
  decentralisation 292
  East Timorese immigrants 713, 714
  education 557, 561, 568–9
  emigration
    3D jobs 556
    competition with Pacific Islanders
      582
    costs 562, 569
    destinations 556
    education levels 557
    numbers 556
    public policy 559–60
    skilled workers 466
  EU preferences 148
  fair trade 657
  FDI in 77
  financial crisis (1997) 291, 310
  fish exports 302
  food security 309–10, 320–22
    direct feeding programmes 320
    income-transfer programmes
      321–2
  footwear industry 9, 95–6, 148–50
    contribution to poverty reduction
      150–4
    dependence on imported leather
      155, 156
    designs 155, 158
    employment status 152
    external barriers 155–6
    growth 146–7, 148
    hindering factors 154–6
    internal barriers 154–5
    labour costs 156
    labour intensity 148–9
    markets 146
    policy recommendations 156–8
    productivity 154–5
    subcontracting 149–50
    survey methodology 158–9
    transport costs 155
    wages 151, 152–3
    working hours 152
  GDP 79
  growth 556
  human trafficking 499
  industrial relations 143

Karawang case study
  agriculture 560
  education 561
  migration costs 562
  population 561
  remittances 562–5
  setting 560–1
  unemployment 561
life expectancy 80
Lombok potters. *See* Lombok pots
manufacturing sector 146
minimum wage 151
natural resources, access 292
ornamental fish farming 287–90
  destruction of reefs 290
  international standards 293–4,
    300–1
  market expansion 292
  Minibakti Soansari fishing group
    294–7
  national measures 291–3,
    298–300
  use of cyanide 289–90, 295–6
population 556
poverty 131
poverty reduction 5
regional integration 133–4
  Iran CTEP 134
  Japan EPA 133
  Japan MOU on migration
    569
  Korea FTA 134
  Korea MOU on migration 559,
    569
  Malaysia MOU on migration
    558, 569
  migration 558–9, 569
  Pakistan CEP 134
remittances
  banking 563
  development and 504
  efficient use 569
  estimates 481–2
  footwear industry 153
  impact 557
  individual experience 15
  investment 503
  Karawang case study 562–5

land investment 565
  policy recommendations 568–70
  poverty reduction 490, 491–3, 567
  public advice 560
  regional comparisons 565–6
  textile industry 140
  trade policy and 567–8
  use 563–5
rice
  food security 309–10, 320–2
  government program dependency 316
  imports 306–7, 310–11, 316
  irrigation 316
  Karawang, West Java 11, 311–17
  land tenure 312
  lower prices 309
  market structure 314
  opportunity creation 319–20
  policy recommendations 317–22
  policy reforms 308–11
  poverty and 306, 311
  price transmission 223, 319–20
  trade liberalisation 315, 316–17
  types of farmers 314
textile industry 131–3
  competition issues 143–86
  employment status 136
  future 142–3
  gender 135
  health and safety 138
  hindering factors 141–2
  holidays 139
  markets 132–3
  policy recommendations 143–4
  rights at work 137–8
  social dialogue 139–40
  social protection 139
  socioeconomic background 134–5
  trade unions 139–40
  wages 136
  workers' evaluation of conditions 140–1
  working conditions 9, 95, 134–41
  working hours 136–7

trade
  growth 2
  negotiations 569–70
  policies 557–9
  unemployment 156
  wages 76, 88–9
inequality
  growth and 49–51, 56
  institutions 51
  remittances and 494
Information Technology Agreement 179
infrastructure
  agriculture 199, 200
  growth and 49
  quality 26, 31
  SVEs 637
Institute for International Trade 49
institutions
  agriculture and 221–2
  definition 31
  growth and 49
  inequality and 51
  poverty reduction and 23, 32
  volatility and 52
insurance
  cyclone areas 617
  output and price insurance 52
  public health insurance 389
  Samoan crops 223, 284
Integrated Framework process 100–2, 254, 280, 282–3, 285
Intel 9, 77, 96, 177, 182–5, 187
intellectual property rights 46, 364
INTERFAIS 238
intermediate organisations 26–7
International Centre for Trade and Sustainable Development 620
International Development Association 275
International Finance Corporation 721
International Food Policy Research Institute 238

International Labour Organisation
Better Factories Cambodia 102, 104,
  106, 107–8, 109
core labour standards and Pakistan
  173–4
East Timor 721, 726
International Trade Centre 282
Iran 134, 214
Ireland 713, 714
Irhamni, Milda 11
island paradox 283
Israel 214
Italy 245
ITS-Global 84–5

Jackson, Lee Ann 10, 11
Jamaica 35, 610, 684
Jansen, M. 32
Japan
  development aid to Samoa 275
  food aid 228, 237
  immigrants 485, 569
  Indonesia-Japan EPA 133
  labour costs 156
Javorcik, B. 348
Johnson, S. 351
Joseph, Michael 452
JVC 187

Kabeer, Naila 88
Kaldor, Nicholas 49–50
Kalinova, Blanka 345
Kannan, K. 548
Kapur, D. 473
Kar, Saibal 15
Karsenty, G. 342
Keban, Yeremias 566
Keith, Minor 84
Keller, W. 45, 46
Kenya 31, 41, 428
Khalid, S. 32
Khatun, Fahmida 14–15, 489, 490
Kilwa, Nolpi 17, 640
Kim, S.-J. and Y.J. 31
Kiribati
  emigration 579, 581–2
  fisheries, access fees 620, 697
  PICTA and 42

services sector 625
SPARTECA 116
  tariff revenue 609, 638
Kiyota, K. 350
knowledge economy 364
Konan, Denise Eby 345, 352
Kose, Ayhan 52, 350
Krishna, P. 48
Kuddus, U. 494
Kumar, Praduman 195

labour markets
  efficiency 30–2
  Lewis model 40
  Stolper-Samuelson model 37–40
labour mobility. *See* migration
labour standards
  Cambodian textile industry 107–8
  Indonesian textile workers 134–41
  Pakistan 165, 173–4
  TNCs 84–7
Laksono, Beta Gitaharie 9, 95–6
Lam, Amanda Sunasse 13
land tenure
  Nepal 258–9
  rice production and 312
  SVEs 637
  Tonga 573
Laos 79, 80, 484–5, 499
Laursen, T. 51
LDC status
  advantages of status 277
  development finance and
  Samoa 276–83
  technical assistance 282–3
  trade and 277–80, 426
  Uganda 365
Lesotho 354
Levi Strauss 86
Levine, R. 45
Lewis, W.A. 40
Lim, Aik Hoe 11–13
Lin, Justin Yifu 329
Lini, Walter 453, 458
Lipsey, Robert 88–9
Litvin, Daniel 84, 86, 88
Loayza, N. 52
Lodge, George 70–1, 92

logistics 346
Lombok island 648–50
Lombok pots
background 648–50
clay supply 662
community development 651–3
community participation 653
craftsmanship 650
cultural and social challenges
660–1
empowerment of women 652, 663
export earnings 656, 657
export marketing 660
food safety 657
GATT rules 656
job creation 653
legal structures 658, 663
lessons 658
maintenance of traditional art
662–3
management 661–2
monthly incomes 659
New Zealand contribution 649–50,
658–9
niche market 618
paternalism 661
project 649–50
social benefits 652–3
success 16, 658
technical skills 653, 661
tourism promotion 650–1
trade issues 653–8
use 650
women's work 650
Lomé Convention 750
Lopez, J.H. 48–9
Lucas, R.E.B. 472
Lucent Technologies 177
Luo, W. 346
Lynas Corporation 82

Macau 713, 714
Macedonia 345
Macmillan, Euan 4–7
McMillan, M. 27
Mahajan, S. 51
Mahathir Mohamad 81
Mahmood, R.A. 527

Malawi 41, 246
Malaysia
Asian financial crisis (1997) 387,
390
FDI 77, 81–2, 183
GDP 79
health services 359, 385–6
costs 386–7
funding 404
GATS commitments 387–90
Mode 1 388–9
Mode 2 389
Mode 3 389–90
Mode 4 390
privatisations 387
public and private sector 386,
397–8, 402–3
teleconsulting 388
wages 402
health tourism 12–13, 390–404
distributional issues 393
employment 397–9
equity 399–401
FDI and growth 394–7
opportunities and risks 393–401
packages 391–2
policy 390–3
recommendations 401–4
regulatory environment 392,
403–4
standards 392
target groups 391
immigrants 485, 491–2, 556, 558,
562, 569
income inequality 400–1
life expectancy 80
Master Plans 388, 398, 404
poverty alleviation 399–400
rice imports 307
tourism 391
Mali 374
Malua, Margaret 8, 94–5
Manasse, P. 38
Mantra, Ida Bagoes 566
Maori 634
Marine Aquarium Council 293
market access 19, 626–7, 628–9, 642–3
Markusen, J.R. 45, 348, 349

Marr, Ariel 17–18
Marshall Islands 116
Marston, Neil 82
Martinique 669
Maskus, Keith 345, 352
Mattoo, Aaditya 348, 351, 356
Matusz, S.J. 30, 42
Mauritania 246
Mauritius 2, 448, 612
MCC 85–6
meat 212
Melanesian Spearhead Group PTA
    603, 636
Mellor, J.W. 28
Mexico 36, 490, 503, 541
micro-credit 272
Micronesia 116, 742
Microsoft 177, 178
migration
    See also specific countries
    Asia-Pacific, trends 477
    benefits 513–14
    brain drain 466–8
        international comparisons 467
        Papua New Guinea 744
        policy 501–2, 505
        temporary migration 578
    circular migration 473–7, 505–6
    diaspora 472–3
    EU/PNG EPA 744
    GATS Mode 4 342, 352, 356, 407,
        408–9, 476–7, 514, 523, 535–6
    global discourse 465, 466–8
    hyper-connectivity 465
    illegal migrants 578
    increase 465, 479, 513
    management 497–500
    market access 633–4
    NGOs 496–7
    poverty reduction and 13–15,
        352–6
    remittances. *See* remittances
    south-north 465, 479
    SVEs 632–5
    temporary labour schemes 451,
        505–7, 577–8
Millennium Development Goals 249,
    364

Minibakti Soansari fishing group
    294–7
Mishkin, F.S. 350
Mitra, D. 48
Mitsubishi 122
MNCs. *See* transnational companies
mobile phones 372, 452, 453, 457
mobility. *See* migration
monopoly importers 27
monopsonies 26, 28, 36, 171
Morocco 354–5
Morris, Matthew 456
Motorola 177
Mozambique 27, 374, 714
Multi-Fibre Agreement, termination
    Cambodia 102, 103
    China 325
    countries outside agreement 54
    Fiji 609, 749, 750, 755
    increased competition 26
    Nepal 262
Museveni, Yoweri 365
Myanmar 214

NAFTA 499
Napitupulu, Lydia 11
Narciso, Gaia 348
Natapei, Edward 459
Natawidjaja, R. 346
Nauru 116
Neak, S. 104
neoclassical economics 426
Nepal
    agriculture 199
        duties 202, 203, 263
        NGO support 268
        trade barriers 263
        value-added exports 264
    Byas Municipality 255–8
        access to services 258
        business community 267
        capacity building 262–3
        farm products 256, 259, 260–1,
            263
        farming transition 10–11
        hilly lands 208, 209
        irrigation 263
        Lal Bahadur 257

land holding 258–9
land use 259
new vs indigenous communities
259–60
remittances 260
survey 256–8
capacity building 254–5
crafts 264
decentralised development 267–8
democratic government 252
economy 252–4
energy crisis 267
government role 267
human trafficking 499
India-Nepal FTA 252
infrastructure 253, 261
migration 256, 264–5
participatory policy making 221,
267–8
regional integration 253
remittances 260, 486
road network 199, 261, 265
trade in services 264–5
trade/poverty reduction strategies
266
trade reform 252, 253–4, 261–2
transport 253, 265–6
WTO accession 252–3
nepotism 142
Nestlé 86
New Guinea 450
New Zealand
immigrants
East Timorese 726
Pacific Islanders 605
temporary labour schemes 578
Tongans 573, 575, 576
indigenous population 634
Lombok project 649–50, 658–9
minimum wage 580
PACER 129, 279, 280
Recognised Seasonal Employer
scheme 451
concerns 582–4
non-wage benefits 583
overstayers 580–1, 583–4
overview 579–84
selection of workers 580–1

standards 580
trade unions 580
training 585
transaction costs 583
work ethic 581–2
regional trade dominance 605
Samoa and
development aid 275, 280, 281–2
trade 274
tariffs 609, 643
trade preferences 609
Fiji 749, 750
LDCs 277
rules of origin 624–5
SPARTECA 116–17, 279, 280,
603, 750
Newberry, D.M.G. 52
Nguyen Thi Bich Van 190
Nicaragua 530
niche markets
East Timor 726
Fiji 614, 618
Lombok pots 618
SVE agriculture 614
Nike
anti-globalisation protesters 86
Hong Kong 77
Indonesia 9, 95
labour standards 86–7
Pakistan. See Pakistan
Sialkot Initiative 172–3
subcontracting 90, 149
Nissanke,M. 51
Niue 116, 607
North, D. 31
Norway 277, 701, 711–12
Noveria, Mita 566
Nuryakin, Chaikal 11

OECD
DAC 236–7, 244–5, 246
Harmful Tax Initiative 673
Policy Framework for Investment
190
OECD countries
agricultural protectionism 613
brain drain from developing
countries 501–2

international trade reform 6–7
market access to SVEs 642–3
migration fears 474, 633–4
temporary emigrants 480–1
offshoring. *See* outsourcing
openness to trade
    precondition 5, 601
    SVEs 598–9, 636
ornamental fish farming
    destruction of reefs 290
    Indonesia 287–90
    Indonesian policies 291–3,
        298–300
    international standards 293–4,
        300–1
    prices 299
    SPS measures 302
    tariffs 302
    use of cyanide 289–90
Orozco, M. 503, 504–5
outsourcing 73–6, 83, 160, 173–4,
    406–7
Oxfam-IDS 36

PACER 129, 279, 280, 285, 604, 719,
    764
PACER-plus 604–5, 625, 628, 630
Pacific Data Solutions 458–9, 460
Pacific Islands
    connectivity 449–57, 460–1
    openness to trade 598–9, 636
    regional trade agreements 602–5
    remittances 451
    SVEs. *See* SVEs
    teledensity 453
Pacific Islands Forum 129, 603
Pacific Regional Digital Strategy 453
Page, John 525, 541
Pakistan
    core ILO standards and 173–4
    human trafficking 499
    Indonesia-Pakistan CEP 134
    Nike-Saga partnership 9, 96, 161–3
        audit 166
        cancellation 9, 96, 160
        child labour 168, 169–70
        ethical partnership 164–6
        growth 165–6

impact of cancellation 171–2
indigenisation of CSR 170–1
ineffective remediation 167
informal labour market 169
labour standards 165
lessons 172–4
management weaknesses 168–9
monitoring deficiencies 168
trade unions 170–1
unravelling 166–71
wages 166
remittances 485, 486–8
rice exports 307
Sialkot Initiative 172–3
soccer ball industry 161–6
    child labour 171–2
    impact of brands 163–4
    production 161
    Sialkot 161, 162, 163
    social profile of stitchers 163
    supply chain 162
    wages 162, 164
    way forward 172–4
Pallage, Stephane 51
Panasonic 187
Papua New Guinea
    access to Indian market 643
    agriculture 732–3, 734, 740–1
    brain drain 744
    capacity building 643
    customs procedures 735–6
    dumping 736
    economy 732–3
    EU EPA 737–45
        agriculture 740–1
        development 737–9
        fisheries 741–2
        investment 744–5
        liberalisation commitments
            743–4
        Mode 4 labour mobility
        rules of origin 742–3
        services 743
        trade in goods 739–40
    HIV/AIDS 736
    manufacturing 733
    MCC in 85–6
    monopolies 453

MSG PTA 603
PICTA 612
political unrest 117
population control 736
poverty 733–4
private sector 636
protectionism 636
quarantine 735
Rimbunan Hijau in 84–5
services 733
small and vulnerable economy
      596
SPARTECA 116
special and differential treatment
      600
standards 735
structural adjustment programme
      731
tariffs 731, 736
telecoms 450, 457, 461
tourism 733, 743
trade facilitation 640
trade strategy 17, 734–6
Parsons, C. 353, 354
Peitsch, Barbara 350
pesticides 211, 333
Pham, M.H. 493
Pham Chanh Truc 181
Phan Hien Minh 179–80
Phan Van Sam 9, 96
Philippines
    emigration 468, 582
    human trafficking 499
    import barriers 643
    Intel investment 183
    ornamental fish farming
        288
    remittances
        extent 482–3
        impact 488
        income inequality 494
        origins 484
        poverty reduction 489
    rice imports 307
    trade growth 2
    wages 76
PICTA 42, 115, 129, 603–4,
      764

Pierre-Guillaume, M. 32
Poland, bird flu 214
policy reform 5–6
political will 7
Portugal 713
poverty
    meaning 1
    reduction. See trade/poverty
        reduction links
    rural Asia-Pacific 196–7
Prakash, Siddhartha 12
Prasad, Biman 17–18, 618
Prasad, Eswar 350
preferences. See trade preferences
preferential trade agreements
    See also specific countries
    commitment device 29
    non-discrimination clauses 81
    poverty reduction and 29
    rules of origin 624
    trade diversion 611–12
prices
    agriculture 202, 218
    commodity price volatility
        613
    Grenadian controls 681
    impact of remittances, Bangladesh
        530
    ornamental fish farming 299
    regulations 26
    services liberalisation and 344–5
    trade liberalisation and 38
    Ugandan telecoms 371
private sector
    East Timor 636, 721–2
    farming public/private partnerships
        220–1
    Malaysian health services 386,
        397–8, 402–3
    Papua New Guinea 636
    precondition 6
    SVEs 637, 638
    Tanzanian transport 440–1
    Ugandan telecoms 367, 379
production sharing agreements 72–6
property rights, SVEs 637
Puma 149, 171
Purushottam, Ojiha 10–11

Qihe Green Foodstuff Company 334, 336
Qu Guoqiang 333
Quartey, P. 542

Ram, Yenteshwar 17–18
Ramey, G. and V.A. 52
Ramos-Horta, José 17, 727, 729
Rathindran, R. 351
Ravi, C. 411
Raychaudhuri, Ajitava 13
Reardon, R. 346
Recognised Seasonal Employer scheme 451, 579–84
Redden, Jim 15, 16, 17
Reebok 9, 95, 149, 170
regional integration. *See* preferential trade agreements
remittances
    adjustment to natural disasters 494
    balance of payments 486–9
    Bangladesh. *See* Bangladesh
    development 481–501, 503–4
    Dutch disease 488
    East Timor 713–15
    education 492–3
    estimates 482
    Fiji 577, 632
    Grenada 678
    healthcare access 493
    impact 469–71
    income inequality and 494–5
    increase 482, 495
    India. *See* India
    Indonesia. *See* Indonesia
    Laos 484–5
    Mexico 490
    Nepal 260, 486
    Pacific Islands 451
    Pakistan 485, 486–8
    Philippines 482–3, 484, 488, 489, 494
    policy recommendations 500–1, 502
    poverty reduction 471, 489–95
    protection 496–7
    role 354, 469–71
    Samoa 274–5

scale 469
scholarship 541–2
Sri Lanka 486, 493, 494, 503
SVEs 632–3
    use 635
taxation 503
Tonga. *See* Tonga
transaction costs 502–3
Vietnam 485
women. *See* women
research and development 47
return migration 473–7
Ricardo, David 33
rice
    Asian diet 212
    export subsidies 307, 308
    global market 307–8
    Indonesia. *See* Indonesia
    subsidies 310
Rimbunan Hijau 84–5
RMIT 178
Robbins, D. 39
Robe, Michel 51
Rochester, Natallie 693–4
Rodriguez, Francisco 44
Rodrik, Dani
Rogoff, Kenneth 350
Romania 345
Rudd, Kevin 122, 726
rule of law 93
rules of origin
    EU/PNG EPA 742–3
    European Union 741
    PTAs 624
    SPARTECA 116, 121–2, 126, 603, 624–5
    SVEs and 624–5
    trade preferences and 608
    WTO Agreement 624
Rural Urban Partnership Programme (RUPP) 257
Russia 214, 352, 485
Rutherford, T.F. 348, 349, 352

Sachs, Jeffrey 6, 44, 599
Safaricom Kenya 452
safeguard measures 53, 103–4, 627
SAFTA 253

Saga Sports 160, 164–72
Saggi, K. 46
St Lucia 681
Sala-i-martin, X. 45
Saldanha, Joao 17
Samoa
    agriculture 271–2
        case study 113, 197, 199
        crop insurance 223, 284
        development 283–5
        LDC status and 11
        micro-credit 272
    coconut processing 609
    development finance
    EC EPA 278–9
    economy 113–16, 270–5
        challenges 113–14
        sectors 271, 273
    emigration
        competition with other islands
            582
        RSE scheme with New Zealand
            579
    foreign aid 275
    geography 270
    infrastructure 118, 125, 284–5
    investment policy 115–16
    island paradox 283
    LDC status 113, 270, 276–83
    manufactures 272–3
    minimum wage 125
    national strategies 114–15
    natural disasters 210, 219, 271–2,
        277
    PACER 279, 280, 285
    political stability 118
    population 113
    regional integration 115–16
    remittances 274–5
    SPARTECA 112–13, 116–17, 279,
        280
    taxation 115, 609
    technical assistance to 282–3
    telecommunications 450
    tourism 275, 285, 625
    trade
        Australia 129
        exports 274

        external trade 273
        imports 274
        LDC status and 277–80
        liberalisation 456
        main trading partners 275
        workforce 113–14, 118
        WTO accession 115, 129, 279–80,
            606, 718
Yasaki company 8, 94–5, 112–13,
    130
    community assistance 124
    competitive pressures 125–6
    contribution to GDP 123
    employment 118–19
    female workers 118
    future 126–9
    government assistance 121
    market 120–1
    output 273
    poverty reduction 122–4
    reasons for investment 117–18
    SPARTECA rules of origin
        121–2, 126
    threats 124–6
    up-skilling workforce 124
    wages 119, 125
Samosir, Omas Bulan 9, 95
Samsung 79, 187
Sasak people 648–9, 660–1
Saudi Arabia 522, 531, 556, 562, 563,
    567
Sawtek 177
Schmitz, J.A. 48
Schultz, Theodore 236
second-round effects 27–8,
        347–8
Self, R. 356
Senegal 41
services
    See also specific countries
    impact of liberalisation 352
        destruction and creation of
            systems 346–7
        elasticity of labour 349
        growth 350–1
        investment risk 350
        issues 341–2
        localised effects 351–2

services (*cont.*)
  poverty reduction 11–13
  prices 344–5
  public revenue 349
  second-round effects 347–8
  unemployment in poor
    households 352
  international trade 342–3
  liberalisation
    design 357–8
    gains 356–9
    impact 352
    packaging 358–9
  migration and poverty reduction
    352–6
  modes of supply 626–7
    Mode 1 342
    Mode 2 342
    Mode 3 342
    Mode 4 342, 352, 356, 407,
      408–9, 476–7, 514, 523, 535–6
    relative importance 343
  SVEs 625–32
    market access 626–7, 628–9
    recognition of standards 627–8,
      630
    safeguards and GATS 627,
      629–30
    supply-side issues 628,
      630
Sevele, Fred 580
Shepotylo, O. 352
Shrestra, Omkar 189
Sialkot Initiative 172–3
Siddiqui, T. 493, 528
Sidorenko, A. 344
Silva, Sacha 16, 631
Singapore 477, 481, 498, 501,
  556
Sjöholm, Fredrik 88–9
Skeldon, R. 354
Slaughter, M. 39
small and vulnerable economies. *See*
  SVEs
small companies, support 6
Smith, Adam 21
Smith, Hamish 11
Soares, Eduardo Belo 452

soccer balls industry 96, 161–6
Sohail, Safdar 9, 96
Solomon Islands 116, 117, 451, 457,
  603, 634
Somare, Michael 453
Sony 187
South Korea
  competitive advantage 448
  food aid 228
  immigrants 485, 559, 562, 569, 725
  Indonesia-Korea FTA 134
  trade growth 2
SPARTECA
  Fiji and 609, 624–5, 750
  members 116–17, 603
  provisions 279
  rules of origin 603
  Samoa and 280
  Yasaki in Samoa and 8, 95, 112–13,
    117, 121–2
specialisation 32–42
SPS measures
  agriculture 203–7, 211, 213–14,
    220
  ornamental fish farming 302
  standards 216
Sri Lanka 486, 493, 494, 499, 503
Srinivasan, T.N. 43, 44–5
standards
  See also labour standards
  agriculture 216–17, 221
  ornamental fish farming 293–4,
    300–1
  services, SVEs 627–8, 630
  SPS measures 216
Stark, Oded 494, 541
state-owned enterprises 330, 636
Stern, R. 350
Stiglitz, Joseph 37, 52
Stokes, Bruce 83
Stoler, Andrew 9, 96
Stolper-Samuelson theory 37–40
strategic liberalisation 19, 601–2
Su Jianchang 334, 336
Subramanian, A. 351
subsidies
  agriculture 7
  FDI 81, 93

fishing. *See* fisheries
rice exports 307, 308, 310
WTO, NAMA 619
supermarkets 217, 346, 613
supply-side issues 18–19, 427, 628,
        630, 636–8
Surono, S. 308
SVEs
    agriculture
        insurance 617
        issues 612–15
        niche markets 614
        resources and solutions 616–18
        strategic areas 614–15, 617
        WTO 615–16
    Australia and New Zealand
            dominance 605
    cost disadvantages 600, 612
    definition 596–8
    development aid 605
    fisheries 618–19
        access fees 619–20, 695–8
        artisanal fisheries 698–700
        national efforts 703–5
        recommendations 622–4,
            702–5
        special treatment 621–2, 700–2
        subsidies 619–21, 695–700
        WTO negotiations 703
    global integration
        Aid for Trade 644
        capacity building 643–4
        lack of recognition 641–2
        market access 642–3
        special and differential treatment
            643
        transfer of technology 644
        WTO negotiations 605–8
    hot issues 608–35
    labour mobility 632–5
        Australia and New Zealand
            605
        labour supply 634–5
        market access 633–4
    land tenure 637
    market entry 610
    negative trade balances 599
    openness to trade 598–9, 636

overview 16–18
    property rights 637
    regional integration 602–5
        Cotonou Agreement 604
        EU EPAs 604
        MSG PTA 603, 636
        PACER 604
        PACER-plus 604–5
        PICTA 603–4
        recommendations 640
        SPARTECA 603
    remittances 632–3
        use 635
    rules of origin 624–5
    services 625–32
        market access 626–7, 628–9
        recognition of standards 627–8,
            630
        safeguards and GATS 627,
            629–30
        supply-side issues 628,
            630
    special and differential treatment
        599–601, 621–2, 643
    state-owned enterprises
        636
    strategic liberalisation 601–2, 611,
        632
    technical assistance 595
    tourism 617, 632
    trade integration 602–8
        global integration 641–5
        regional agreements 602–5
        risks 602
        trade diversion 611–12
        WTO negotiations 605–8
    trade liberalisation 636–41
        duties 638–40
        education and skills 637–8
        entrenched interests 636
        infrastructure 637
        private sector 637, 638
        supply-side issues 636–8
        trade facilitation 638–41
    trade preferences 608–11
    training 637–8
    Work Programme on Small
        Economies 605–6

Swaziland 610
Switzerland 245, 277

Taiwan 485
Tanzania
  agriculture 431, 433, 447
  Aid for Trade 445–7
  BEST 428
  economy 430–4
    growth 430
    sectors 431
  export processing zones 428
  exports
    growth 434
    poverty reduction and
      434
  infrastructure 436–7
  LDC status 429
  MKURABITA 428
  poverty 430, 433
  privatisations 440, 441
  regional integration 428–9
  services 13, 359
    GDP share 430, 432
    growth 432
    liberalisation 427–30, 442–5
  small enterprises 446–7
  supply-side constraints 434–9
    categorisation 437
  telecenter 374
  tourism 429, 430, 432, 442
  trade liberalisation 427–9
  transport 439–41
    EU funding 440
    privatisations 441
    public-private partnerships
      440–1
    shipping 440, 443
    World Bank funding 441
  WTO commitments 429–30
tariffs
  agriculture 202–3
  effects 24
  ornamental fish farming 302
  revenues and trade liberalisation
    41–2
Tarr, D. 30, 42, 348, 349, 352
Taukolo, Vaimoana 15

taxation
  Fijian clothing industry 749, 750,
    761
  policies 19
  remittances 503
  Samoa 115
  services liberalisation and tax
    revenue 349
  TNCs 81, 82, 93
  Vietnamese IT sector 179–80
Taylor, Edward 490, 494, 541
technical assistance
  LDC status and 282–3
  SVEs 595
  transfer of technology 644
technological differences 45–7,
    55–6
telecoms
  Africa 449, 452, 453
  impact of liberalisation on prices
    345
  mobile phones 372, 452, 453, 457
  Pacific Islands 449–57, 460–1
  regulation 93
  Uganda. See Uganda
  Vanuatu. See Vanuatu
Tenaglia, P. 355, 356
Tendler, Judith 174
Terry, D.F. 503
Tevi, Odo 458
textiles
  See also Multi-Fibre Agreement
  Cambodia. See Cambodia
  China 8, 95, 97, 143–86, 755, 761
  Fiji. See Fiji
  India 755
  Indonesia. See Indonesia
  Vietnam 103, 108
Thailand
  emigration 582
  FDI in 91–2
  GDP 79
  health tourism 391
  human trafficking 499
  life expectancy 80
  rice exports 307
  wages 76
Thomas, Clive 600, 613, 629

Thorbecke, E. 49, 51
Tibu, David 85
Tiglao, R. 488
Timmer, P. 27, 316, 318, 319
Timor-Leste. *See* East Timor
Titu Eki, A. 491–2
TNCs. *See* transnational companies
Tokarick, S. 53
Tonga
  Christianity 572
  cyclones 574
  economy 574
  emigration 573, 575
  employment 584–90
    agriculture 589–90
    education 586–7
    labour force 572–3
    services 589
    tourism 574, 588–9
    training 585–6, 587
  extended families 572
  future 590–1
  infrastructure 117
  land holding 573
  population 572
  poverty reduction 5
  reforms 456
  remittances 15, 632
    best use 587–8
    future 590
    poverty reduction 575–9
    RSE scheme 581, 587
    savings 588
    significance 573–4
    use 581
    volume 575
  RSE scheme with New Zealand 451
    concerns 582–4
    non-wage benefits 583
    overstayers 580–1, 583–4
    overview 579–84
    selection of workers 580–1, 634
    standards 580
    trade unions 580
    training 585
    transaction costs 583
    unrealistic expectations 583
    use of remittances 581, 587

  work ethic 581–2
  services sector 625
  SPARTECA 116
  tariff revenue 609, 639
  telecoms 450, 457
  WTO accession 718
Torero, M. 346
Toshiba 187
tourism 358
Toyota 120, 122
trade
  facilitation, definition 763
  free trade. *See* trade liberalisation
  openness to 5, 598–9, 601, 636
  poverty reduction. *See*
    trade/poverty reduction links
  preferences. *See* trade preferences
  services. *See* services
  trade diversion, SVEs 611–12
trade liberalisation
  competition gains 35–7
  dynamic effects 22, 42–54
  effect of increased competition
    47–8
  effect on governments 41–2
  effect on wages 37–40
  growth effect 43–5
  increasing returns 47
  inequality and 49–51
  institutions and 23
  LDC dismal performance 426
  long-term effects 43–53
  medium-term effects 43
  nature 26
  price changes 38
  second-round effects 27–8, 347–8
  specialisation gains 32–42
  static effects 22, 32–42
  strategic liberalisation 19, 601–2,
    611, 632
  supply-side constraints 427
  SVEs 636–41
trade/poverty reduction links
  adaptability of economies 30–2
  agriculture 10–11, 207–11
    policies 218–22
  context specificity 21, 58
  distribution channel 23, 24–8

trade/poverty reduction links (*cont.*)
  dynamic effects 22, 42–54
  enterprise channel 23, 28
  external factors 53
  factors 54–8
  FDI and 77–80
  government channel 23, 29–30, 55
  growth and 48–9
  ICT sector 364
  Indian services 409–19
  Indonesian footwear industry 150–4
  labour mobility 13–15
  Nepal 266
  outsourcing and 173–4
  preconditions 5–7
  regional integration and 29
  Samoa and Yasaki 122–4
  static effects 22, 32–42
  theoretical shift 426
  TNCs. *See* transnational companies
  Tonga 5
  trade in services 11–13, 352–6
  transmission mechanisms 22–32, 426
  Vietnam electronics 188–90
trade preferences
  Australia. *See* Australia
  European Union 97, 102, 148
  LDC status and 277–8
  New Zealand. *See* New Zealand
  rules of origin 608
  SVEs 608–11
  United States 7, 97, 104, 609
  WTO 609
trade unions 139–40, 170–1
training
  Fiji 757, 762–3
  Grenada 676, 683–4
  Indian services 420
  overriding strategy 18
  SVEs 637–8
  Tonga 585–6, 587
  Vietnam 177–8, 189
transfer of technology 644
transnational companies

  See also specific companies and countries
  agents of change 70–2
  critique 69–70
  debate 83–90
  efficiency 69
  FDI. *See* foreign direct investment
  gender issues 87–8
  global supply chain 8–10, 90–2, 160
  good governance and 92–4
  labour standards 84–7
  motivation for investment 80–3
  numbers 69
  poverty reduction and 8–10, 77–80
  production sharing agreements 72–6
  regulatory environment 6
  taxation 81, 82, 93
  trade policies and corporate strategies 76–83
  wage rates 88–90
Transparency International 184
Treffer, D. 38
Trinidad 676, 684
Tunisia 345
Turkey 36, 99, 214
Turrini, A. 38
Tuvalu 116, 579, 582, 620, 697
Tybout, J.R. 48
typhoons 210

Uganda
  debt relief 366
  economic reforms 365–6, 369
  infrastructure 377
  internet 378
  mobile phones 372
  Nakaseke Telecentre 374–7
    benefit of reforms 375
    constraints 377
    education and health services 376
    empowering the poor 375–6
    farming information 376
    lessons 378–9
    policy lessons 378–9
    women 376–7
  openness to trade 5

poverty 365
regional integration 428
remittances 526
telecom reforms 12, 359, 366–9
  better services 371–2
  exports 372
  FDI 369–70, 381
  GATS commitments 369–70
  global markets for local talent
    372–3
  ICT policy 368–9
  impact 370–4
  independent regulation 366–7
  jobs for the poor 373
  lessons 632
  lower prices 371
  policy recommendations 379–80
  privatisation 367, 379
  rural areas 367–8, 373–4, 379
Ukraine 214
UNCLOS 696
UNCTAD 77–9, 81, 282, 347, 607, 626
UNDP 254, 257, 282, 364
UNEP 293
UNESCAP 625
UNIDO 255, 655
Unilever 86, 92
United Fruit Company 83–4
United Kingdom
  bird flu 214
  food aid 237, 245
  immigrants
    Bangladeshis 527, 529
    East Timorese 713, 714
    Grenadians 676
  Indian services trade 408
  mobility schemes 355
  Papua New Guinea and 744
United Nations
  Convention on Migrant Workers
    (1990) 496
  ECOSOC 270, 276–7
  embargo on China 327
  food aid 237, 245
  migration and 477, 499
  World Food Programme 238, 246
United States
  Cambodian policy 102, 103–4

Chinese policy 327
development aid 445–6
ethanol production 213
Fiji textile market 749, 750
fish imports 293, 302
food aid 228, 235, 237, 245,
    247
immigrants
  Bangladeshis 527, 529
  Filipinos 468, 482
  Grenadians 676
  Mexicans 474
  temporary migration 479
  Tongans 573, 575
  Vietnamese 485
Indian services trade 408
Indonesian textile imports 132
invasion of Grenada 666, 670
preferences 7, 97, 104, 609
rice exports 307
sanctions on India 544
SPARTECA and 116
Vietnamese policy 178
WTO banana wars 669
Uyen Ho 186

value-added tax 638
Van Diermen, Peter 8, 94
Vanuatu
  emigration 579, 581–2
  growth 457
  monopolies 453
  MSG PTA 603
  political stability 458
  protectionism 636
  reforms 457–60
  SPARTECA membership 116
  telecoms 13, 450, 457, 458–60
  tourism 457, 625
  WTO accession 606, 718
VAT 638
Vertovec, S. 475–6
Vietnam
  bird flu 214
  competition with Cambodian
    textiles 103, 108
  competitive advantage 448
  corruption 176, 184

Vietnam (*cont.*)
  economic liberalisation 176–7
  education and training 177–8, 189
  electronics 9, 96
    export growth 188
    firms 187–8
    Intel investment 182–7
    poverty reduction 188–90
    public policy 179–82
    taxation regime 179–80
  FDI in 77
  footwear industry 147–8
  high-tech park 181–2, 184
  human trafficking 499
  Information Technology Agreement
    179
  Intel investment 182–7
    employment 186–7
    global supply chain 185
    new assembly and test facility
      184
    positive factors 183–4
    wages 186–7
  path to high-tech economy 176–9
  policy change 175–6
  post-war 176
  regional integration 178–9
  remittances 485
  rice exports 307
  trade growth 2
  wages 76
  WTO accession 103, 178–9
volatility, growth and 49, 51–3, 56
Von Braun, Joachim 346

wages
  See also specific countries
  effects of trade liberalisation 37–40
  Lewis model 40
  Stolper-Samuelson theory 37–40
  TNCs in developing countries
    88–90
Walmsley, T. 353, 354
Warner, A.M. 44
Warr, P. 311
Washington Consensus 426
water, agriculture and 216
Wei, Shang-Jin 350
Wellington Declaration 453

Westbrook, M.D. 48
wheat 212, 235–6
Wheat Aid Convention 240
WIBDECO 666, 670, 674
Wilson, Craig 70–1, 92
Wilson, J.S. 25
Wilson, S.R. 503, 504–5
Windward Islands 666, 669
Winter, Alan 513
Winters, A 22, 28, 29, 36, 40, 51, 341,
  353, 354
Wiyono, Nur Hadi 15
Wolf, Martin 71–2, 87–8, 92
women
  Bangladeshi migrants 531–2, 534
  Cambodian textile industry 97–8,
    104–6, 110
  Fijian clothing industry 758,
    761–2
  ICT access 377
  Indian services 412–15
  Indonesia
    Lombok potters 16, 650, 652,
      663
    Sasak women 648–9
    textile workers 135
  Minibakti Soansari fishing group
    297
  Nakaseke Telecentre 376–7
  remittances and 493
    Bangladesh 528
    Cambodia 105–6
  Samoan workers in Yazaki 118
  TNCs and gender 87–8
Women's Edge Coalition 35
Wood, A. 37, 39
World Bank
  Cambodian poverty reduction 98
  Chinese poverty reduction 72
  on Dar es Salaam 440
  DTIS 101, 109, 435
  East Timor 721
  Egyptian labour markets 30
  finance to Samoa 282
  Ghana capital market 31
  on Grenada 666, 672, 678
  on India 2
  Indonesian cyanide fishing
    290

Integrated Framework process 282
labour mobility in Pacific Islands
577–8
Mozambique cashew nuts and 27
Papua New Guinea 731, 733
poverty in East Asia 196–7
poverty reduction and growth 48
on remittances 469, 489, 502, 565,
632–3
rice prices 311
Tanzanian funding 441
Ugandan ICT finance 373–4
on Vanuatu 458
Vanuatu funding 459–60
Vietnamese electronics 189–90
World Fish Centre 698
World Food Programme 238, 246
Wougnet 369, 376–7
WTO
See also Agriculture Agreement
agriculture 204, 615–16
banana wars 669
Doha Round. See Doha Round
erosion of preferences 609
farming issues 204
fisheries 619, 620–1, 622–4
subsidies 690–5
SVEs 703
food aid and 10, 230–1, 236, 241–3,
246, 248
Marrakesh Decision 242–3
GATS. See GATS
GATT and handicrafts 656

Integrated Framework process
100–2, 254, 280, 282–3,
285
intellectual property rights 364
membership 90
NAMA subsidies 619
negotiations on rice 308
rules of origin 624
simplification of customs procedures
25
SPARTECA and 116
SPS standards 216
SVEs and 605–8, 641–2
Work Programme on Small
Economies 605–6

Xu, B. 46

Yamamoto, Y. 763
Yao, Shunli 11
Yasaki 8, 94–5, 112–13, 273
Yem, S. 104
Yitzhaki, Shlomo 494, 541
Yue Yuen 77

Zachariah, K.C. 543, 548
Zambia 31, 36, 246
Zemurray, Samuel 84
Zhao, J. 47
Zhong Funing 332–3, 336
Zhu, S.C. 38
Zimbabwe 31, 36
Zoellick, Robert 175